GERMAN DIALECTS

GERMAN DIALECTS

PHONOLOGY AND MORPHOLOGY

WITH SELECTED TEXTS

by

R. E. KELLER

Henry Simon Professor of German Language and Medieval German Literature
in the University of Manchester

MANCHESTER UNIVERSITY PRESS

© MANCHESTER UNIVERSITY PRESS 1961

Published by
Manchester University Press
Oxford Road, Manchester M13 9PL

ISBN 0 7190 0762-3

reprinted in a paper edition with
minor corrections 1979

Printed in Great Britain by
J. W. Arrowsmith Ltd, Bristol

CONTENTS

ACKNOWLEDGEMENTS

I wish to express my indebtedness and gratitude to the scholars and informants who willingly made tape-recordings of the dialect texts and without whose help and contributions this book could not have been written: M. Ernest Beyer of the Institut des Hautes Etudes Alsaciennes, Strasbourg; Herr Wilm Böckenholt, Münster, Westphalia; Professor Robert Bruch, Luxemburg; Herr W. Buhrke, Hamburg; Professor William Foerste of the University of Münster; Herr Karl Gattermeyer, Linz, Austria; Mlle Michèle Keller, Strasbourg; Herren E. Luckow, R. Stromberger, Walter Kugler, Herr Sperling and Frau Baumann of Darmstadt; Dr R. Möller, of the *Westfälisches Wörterbuch*, Münster; Professor Walther Niekerken, of the University of Hamburg; M. Roger H. Reinbold and Mlle A. Specht, Barr, Bas-Rhin; Fräulein Inge Stoschek, Gmünden, Austria; Frau S. Suter, Aarau, Switzerland; Nordwestdeutscher Rundfunk, Cologne; Studio Radio Bern.

Further, I am deeply grateful for the help and advice I have received from my friends and colleagues: Professor R. Peacock, Mr. William Haas and Dr. F. W. Ratcliffe of the University of Manchester; Professor K. C. King of the University of Nottingham; Mr. D. Barker of the University of Liverpool. I wish also to express my thanks to the Manchester University Staff Travel Fund for the grants which enabled me to travel in Germany and Austria.

For kind permission to reprint dialect texts included in this book I am indebted to the authors, publishers and literary executors: Herr Traugott Vogel, Zürich, and the editor of *Schwyzerlüt* for permission to reprint 'De truurig Umwääg'; Francke Verlag, Berne, for the extract from Rudolf von Tavel's novel *Ring i der Chetti*; Mme Engel-Bastian, Strasbourg, for the extract from her father's play, *D'r Hans im Schnokeloch*; Eduard Roether Verlag, Darmstadt, for Robert Schneider's 'Wie de ,,Datterich" in de Himmel kumme is'; Frau Hilde Muck, Buchhandlung und Verlag, Linz, Austria, for the extract from Karl Mayer-Freinberg's *De wåhre Liab*; Librairie du Centre, Luxemburg, for the extract from Michel Rodange's *Renert*; Hermann Heckmann Verlag, Münster, Westphalia, for the extract from Augustin Wibbelt's *Dat veerte Gebott*; Herr Ernst Wisser, Göttingen, and Verlag der Fehrs-Gilde, Hamburg-Wellingsbüttel, for the fairy-tale 'De Prinzessin mit de lange Nääs' ' by Wilhelm Wisser.

My manuscript was typed in the most expert manner by Miss Janet Briggs to whom I would also record my sincere gratitude, as well as to Miss E. A. Lowcock of the Geography Department of Manchester University, who drew the dialect map. Last but not least, I am most thankful to my wife for her unfailing support and patience.

R. E. K.

Manchester,
  October, 1960.

ABBREVIATIONS

Abbreviations of book titles are found in the Bibliography.

Alem.	Alemannic
Als.	Alsatian
Annuaire	*Annuaires Jahrbücher.* Publications de la Section de Linguistique . . . de l'Institut grand-ducal, Luxembourg, 1925 ff.
Bav.	Bavarian
Bd.	Bärndütsch, Bernese
Beitr.	*Beiträge zur Geschichte der deutschen Sprache und Literatur*
BSG	*Beiträge zur schweizerdeutschen Grammatik,* ed. A. Bachmann, vols. 1–20, Frauenfeld, 1910–41
BSMaf.	*Beiträge zur schweizerdeutschen Mundartforschung,* ed. R. Hotzenköcherle, Frauenfeld, 1950 ff.
Bull. ling. et éth.	*Bulletin linguistique et éthnologique.* Publications de la Section de Linguistique . . . de l'Institut grand-ducal, Luxembourg, 1953 ff.
DDG	*Deutsche Dialektgeographie,* ed. F. Wrede, W. Mitzka, Marburg, 1908 ff.
DPhA	*Deutsche Philologie im Aufriss,* ed. W. Stammler, vols. 1–3, Berlin, 1952–7.
Dst.	Darmstadt
EG	*Etudes Germaniques*
E.Mos.Franc.	East Moselle Franconian
Fr.	French
Franc.	Franconian
Gmc.	Germanic
GR	*Germanic Review*
GRM	*Germanisch-Romanische Monatsschrift*
H.Alem.	High Alemannic
H.Dst.	Hesse-Darmstadt
HG	High German
JEGP	*Journal of English and Germanic Philology*
L.Alem.	Low Alemannic
LG	Low German
Lux.	Luxemburgish
Lux.Jb.	see *Annuaire*
Lux.Vjbl.	see *Revue Trim.*
MHG	Middle High German
MLG	Middle Low German
MLQ	*Modern Language Quarterly*
NHG	New High German (standard language)
NdJb.	*Jahrbuch des Vereins für niederdeutsche Sprachforschung*

NdKbl.	*Korrespondenzblatt des Vereins für niederdeutsche Sprachforschung*
Nd.Mitt.	*Niederdeutsche Mitteilungen*
NS	North Saxon
obs.	obsolete
OHG	Old High German
OS	Old Saxon
PGmc.	Primitive Germanic
PLMA	*Publications of the Modern Language Association of America*
Revue Trim.	*Revue trimestrielle/Vierteljahrsblätter*. Publications de la Section de Linguistique . . . de l'Institut grand-ducal, fasc. 1–36, Lux., 1935–50.
Rh.Franc.	Rhenish Franconian
Rip.	Ripuarian
SGm.	Swiss German
Teuth.	*Teuthonista*, i–xi, 1924–34
Westphal.	Westphalian
WGmc.	West Germanic
W.Mos.Franc.	West Moselle Franconian
ZfdA	*Zeitschrift für deutsches Altertum und deutsche Literatur*
ZfdB	*Zeitschrift für deutsche Bildung*
ZfDk.	*Zeitschrift für Deutschkunde*
ZfdMaa.	*Zeitschrift für deutsche Mundarten*, 1906–24
ZfdPh.	*Zeitschrift für deutsche Philologie*
ZfdU	*Zeitschrift für deutschen Unterricht*
ZfhdMaa.	*Zeitschrift für hochdeutsche Mundarten*, i–vi, 1900–5
ZfMaf.	*Zeitschrift für Mundartforschung*
Zt.	Züritüütsch, Zürich dialect

The abbreviations of grammatical terms, e.g. adv., inf., dat., etc., are conventional.

PHONETIC SYMBOLS

Three ways of rendering sounds are employed. Wherever possible, e.g. where historical references are made, the letters of the ordinary alphabet are used. Phonetic transcriptions are given in the alphabet of the International Phonetic Association[1] and are enclosed in square brackets [ ]; phonemic notations are given between slant lines / /.

Vowels

	Front unr.	Front rounded	Central	Back rounded
High . . .	i	y		u
Lower-high . .	ɪ	ʏ		ɷ
Higher-mid . .	e	ø		o
Lower-mid . .	ɛ	œ	ɜ	ɔ
Higher-low . .	æ		ə	
Low . . .	a		ɑ	ɒ

Consonants

	Labial vl. v.	Labio-dental vl. v.	Dent.-alv. vl. v.	Palato-alv. vl. v.	Palato-velar vl. v. vl. v.	Glottal
Stops . .	p b		t d		k g	ʔ
Fricatives .	w	f v	s z	š ž	ç ɟ x γ	h
Nasals . .	m		n		ŋ	
Laterals .			l		ɫ	
Trills . .			r		R	
Semi-vowels	w				j	

Other Symbols

: and ⁻ signify length; : also denotes opposition.
ᴗ = short vowel.
~ = nasalized vowel.
ͺ signifies a more open degree of the vowel than the sign normally indicates, e.g. ẹ.
> = 'becomes' or 'has become'.
< = 'derived from'.
₀ indicates voiceless lenes, e.g. ḅ.
- indicates the position in the word, e.g. k- (initial), -k- (medial), -k (final).

KEY TO DIALECT MAP

TOWNS

1. Flensburg	37. Warendorf	73. Sarreguemines	108. Aarau
2. Kiel	38. Rheda	74. Wissembourg	109. Olten
3. Neumünster	39. Beckum	75. Speyer	110. Biel
4. Itzehoe	40. Hamm	76. Heidelberg	111. Murten
5. Glückstadt	41. Paderborn	77. Mannheim	112. Fribourg
6. Lübeck	42. Dortmund	78. Mainz	113. Thun
7. Hamburg	43. Essen	79. Wiesbaden	114. Bern
8. Wismar	44. Düsseldorf	80. Frankfurt am	115. Burgdorf
9. Brandenburg	45. Wesel	Main	116. Luzern
10. Stade	46. Recklinghausen	81. Aschaffenburg	117. Brig
11. Bremerhaven	47. Bocholt	82. Darmstadt	118. Zürich
12. Harburg	48. Köln	83. Bamberg	119. Winterthur
13. Bremen	49. Bonn	84. Nürnberg	120. Schaffhausen
14. Verden	50. Siegen	85. Regensburg	121. St. Gallen
15. Lüneburg	51. Marburg	86. Ingolstadt	122. Bregenz
16. Lauenburg	52. Kassel	87. Ulm	123. Chur
17. Oldenburg	53. Fulda	88. Tübingen	124. Innsbruck
18. Emden	54. Giessen	89. Stuttgart	125. Augsburg
19. Nienburg	55. Koblenz	90. Karlsruhe	126. München
20. Osnabrück	56. Gerolstein	91. Baden-Baden	127. Langnau
21. Minden	57. Malmédy	92. Haguenau	128. Salzburg
22. Herford	58. St. Vith	93. Niederbronn	129. Passau
23. Detmold	59. Clervaux	94. Worms	130. Neumarkt
24. Hannover	60. Bastogne	95. Würzburg	131. Ried
25. Braunschweig	61. Wiltz	96. Saverne	132. Grieskirchen
26. Magdeburg	62. Neuerburg	97. Phalsbourg	133. Vöcklabruck
27. Münden	63. Bitburg	98. Sarrebourg	134. Gmünden
28. Göttingen	64. Wittlich	99. Strasbourg	135. Wels
29. Halle	65. Ettelbrück	100. Offenburg	136. Linz
30. Weissenfels	66. Arlon	101. Barr	137. Enns
31. Rheine	67. Luxemburg	102. Séléstat	138. Steyr
32. Enschede	68. Esch	103. Colmar	139. Weyer
33. Ahaus	69. Thionville	104. Freiburg	140. Krems
34. Coesfeld	70. Metz	105. Mulhouse	141. Wien
35. Dülmen	71. Merzig	106. Altkirch	
36. Münster	72. Saarbrücken	107. Basel	

ISOGLOSSES

Where two forms are contrasted, e.g. p/pf, the former is found north and/or west of the isogloss, the latter south and/or east.

A p/pf   'Pfund'   (*DSA*, 62)
B k/ch   'machen' (*DSA*, 3)
C p/f   in 'auf' (*DSA*, 3)
D t/s   in 'das' (*DSA*, 3)
E k/ch   'Kind' (*DSA*, 17)
F p/f   'Dorf' (*DSA*, 17); ū/au 'Haus' (*DSA*, 24);
    i/ei   'Eis' (*DSA*, 74)
G au/ū, ü 'Haus' (*DSA*, 24); ei/ī 'Eis' (*DSA*, 74)
H -en/-et (west) and -et/-en (east) '3rd pers. pl. pres.' (*DSA*, 7)
I ü, i/üe, ie (diphth.) 'müde' (*DSA*, 96)
J 2 - form pl. of verbs/1 form pl. of verbs (Bangerter)
K ei, ou/ī, ū in hiatus 'speien, bauen' (Bohnenberger)
L long vowel/short vowel in 'Wagen' (Bohnenberger) Leichtinnendehnung
M gehn/geh (inf.) (Stœckicht 5)
N ä, ei/ā in 'heiss'   (*DSA*, 16)
O Bavarian *enk* 'euch' (*DSA*, 21)
P ā/ō 'Hasen, Gassen' (Kranzmayer)
Q Middle Bavarian l - vocalization (Kranzmayer)
R̃ -a (inf.) after nasal and after *ch* but not after *f* 'machen, verkaufen' (*DSA*, 32,
    Kranzmayer)
S a/e, o, ö (MHG i) 'Kind' (*DSA*, 17)
T a/o 'gebrochen' in Lux.; ua, uo/o in Westphal. (*DSA*, 29)
U Westphal. *Wisk, Wiesch* 'Wiese'   (*DSA*, 41)
V Westphal. *geis* 'Gänse'   (*DSA*, 45)
W di/dik 'dich'   (*DSA*, 5)
X North Saxon *fleg-* 'fliegen'   (*DSA*, 122)

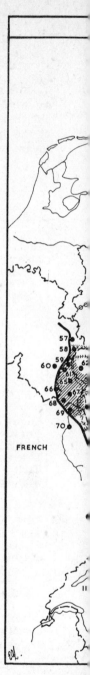

FRENCH

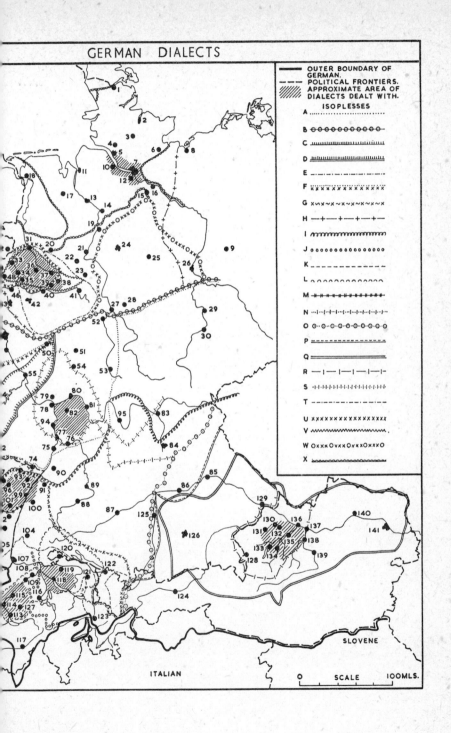

GERMAN DIALECTS

OUTER BOUNDARY OF GERMAN.
POLITICAL FRONTIERS.
APPROXIMATE AREA OF DIALECTS DEALT WITH.

ISOPLESSES

A ....
B ⊙⊙⊙⊙⊙⊙⊙⊙⊙⊙⊙
C ⊓⊓⊓⊓⊓⊓⊓⊓⊓⊓⊓⊓⊓⊓
D ⊓⊓⊓⊓⊓⊓⊓⊓⊓⊓⊓⊓⊓⊓
E ._._._._._._._._.
F ×××××××××××××××××
G ×∾∼×∾×∼×∼×∼×∾×
H —+—+—+—+—
I ∿∿∿∿∿∿∿∿∿∿∿∿∿
J ○○○○○○○○○○○○○○○○○
K _ _ _ _ _ _ _ _ _ _
L ∩∩∩∩∩∩∩∩∩∩∩∩∩
M ─#─#─#─#─#─#─#─
N ··|··|··|··|··|··|··|·
O ○·─○·─○·─○·─○·─○
P ─ ─ ─ ─ ─ ─ ─ ─ ─
Q ════════════
R —|—|—|—|—|—|—
S ·|·|·|·|·|·|·|·|·|·|·|·|
T _. _. _. _. _. _. _.
U ×××××××××××××××××
V ∿∿∿∿∿∿∿∿∿∿∿∿∿.
W ○×××○×××○×××○×××○
X ∼∼∼∼∼∼∼∼∼∼∼∼∼∼∼

SLOVENE

ITALIAN

O   SCALE   100 MLS.

CHAPTER I

INTRODUCTION

The aim of this book is practical. It is to afford the student of German a descriptive phonological and grammatical survey of certain dialects and to enable him to acquaint himself more closely with those dialects by studying a fairly long text. The number of dialects has naturally to be rather small if the treatment of each is to be more than superficial and if the texts are to be more than just specimens. In the choice of dialects I have again been guided by practical considerations. I have chosen such dialects as are spoken by a considerable number of speakers of somewhat higher level than the least educated classes. It is only such dialects that have produced any dialect literature worth considering. The description of the dialects chosen is synchronic.[1] The dialects are examined as contemporary forms of speech and not primarily as a stage of development from MHG, OHG or PGmc. As this is an *introduction* to dialects attention is naturally focused on phonology and morphology, but points of word-formation and syntax are discussed in the notes to the texts. The texts themselves offer lexical material, which is frequently lacking in other types of dialect studies. Intonation, though an essential and characteristic element of all forms of speech, is complex and difficult to render on paper.[2] It has regrettably had to be left out of account. Tape recordings, which speakers are often willing to make, and gramophone records[3] with recitals in dialect, which can be purchased, may help to fill this gap in a satisfactory way.

If non-German countries such as Switzerland, Luxemburg and Alsace are numerically over-represented it is because in these countries dialects are more alive than in Germany and Austria. I have nevertheless attempted to include the main dialect areas and thus deal with the main characteristic types, e.g. Austro-Bavarian, High

[1] I am indebted to the synchronic studies of Carroll E. Reed, *The Pennsylvania German Dialect Spoken in the Counties of Lehigh and Berks. Phonology and Morphology*, Washington U.P., 1949; 'A Survey of Pennsylvania German Phonology', *MLQ*, viii, 1947, 267–89; 'Survey of Pennsylvania German Morphology', *MLQ*, ix, 1948, 322–42; H. Kratz and H. Milnes, 'Kitchener German: A Pennsylvania German Dialect', *MLQ*, xiv, 1953, 184–98, 274–83.

[2] An attempt is made by B. J. Koekkoek, *Zur Phonologie der Wiener Mundart*, Beitr. z. dt. Philologie, vi, Giessen, 1955.

[3] Such records are available, for instance, at the *Phonogramm-Archive* in Vienna and Zürich, while the *Lautbibliothek der deutschen Mundarten*, Göttingen, Vandenhoeck und Ruprecht, issues tape recordings with its *Hefte* containing transcriptions (see the publisher's prospectus).

and Low Alemannic, Rhenish and Moselle Franconian, South and
North Low Saxon. Central and East Germany (e.g. Thuringia,
Saxony) are not represented for various reasons. But it is hoped that
an approach to the dialects of those regions is nevertheless facilitated
by a study of the dialects included in this book, dialects which are
the most widely spoken, linguistically the most diversified, and which
have produced the most significant dialect literature.

The texts chosen to illustrate the dialects discussed are intended
to show, above all, genuine dialect of the present day. I have, with
one exception, excluded the dialect classics of the nineteenth century,
but have chosen various *genres* of twentieth-century writing. Lyric
poetry is not represented, for its syntax and choice of words is mostly
ill-suited to the illustration of a dialect. Among the texts chosen are
a serious and a comical, satirical short story, a fairy-tale and extracts
from a verse epic of the nineteenth century, from an epic ballad of
to-day, from a play, from a serious religious novel and from an
historical novel.

It is hoped that the texts, together with the grammatical studies,
will give the student an impression primarily of the linguistic significance of present-day German dialects. For a literary anthology a
different choice would have had to be made, although the texts are
nevertheless representative dialect literature, including the chief
genres.

§ 1. HISTORICAL GRAMMAR AND MODERN DIALECTS

Most philologists are of the opinion that the study of older stages
of a given language benefits the serious study of that particular
modern language. University courses in German thus usually devote
some time to Old High German or Gothic and even more to Middle
High German. No proper understanding of present-day German
phonology, morphology, syntax or vocabulary is possible without
the study of the historical development of the language. A language
evolves in history and its present character is to a large extent understandable only against its historical background. Different forms in
etymological groups, recognized as such even by the layman, as e.g.
hoch—Höhe; *singen—sang—gesungen*; *Hand—Hände—abhanden—
behende*, or words now etymologically obscure such as *heute, Nest,
Messer* are elucidated by historical research. The facts of linguistic
life, such as phonological and grammatical changes which we may
observe in contemporary language, receive new light from an historical consideration. The student of German who hears pronunciations
of *Tag* such as [thak, ta:g, tha:k, thax] in what is known as the New
High German standard language will find the explanation of this
variety, based on the regional provenance of the speakers, in histori-

cal grammar. But history is not the only source which provides
answers. To derive one's insight into German solely from a study of
its history would imply a neglect of a most abundant source of information: *the modern dialects.*

In historical grammar we are confined to paper and parchment.
It is from the written letter that we have to reconstruct linguistic
reality. The modern dialects allow us to *hear* phonological phenomena
such as lenition, assimilation, various degrees of mutation, unrounding and labialization. Here lies a rich source of material which has
the advantage of being alive.[1] Thus in Westphalian, for instance, one
is witness of the change of $d > r$ in certain conditions. In most
Austrian dialects one can study the labializing effect of l on a preceding front vowel. A phenomenon such as polymorphism,[2] well known
to the student of OHG but comparatively rare in NHG, is exemplified
in modern dialects. Thus one may find within the same dialect the
plural of 'day' as *Tag* or *Täg*, the subjunctive present of 'to be' as
sei, seig, seigi, sig, sigi (cf. chap. ii, § 47); for 'we go' *mir gaa, gange,
göö, gönge* (cf. chap. iii, § 31).

This book intends to tap some of these sources. It attempts to
place beside the historical, diachronic study of German the synchronic study of contemporary dialects. Instead of looking down the
long corridor of history we focus our attention on some spots on the
broad canvas of contemporary linguistic life.

§ 2. German Dialectology

The study of dialects is almost as old as modern comparative
Germanic philology. Its founder, Johann Andreas Schmeller, was a
contemporary of Jakob Grimm. The last quarter of the nineteenth
century saw the birth of dialect geography. Dialectology has become
an important branch of Germanic philology[3] as well as of Romance
philology. From writing dialect grammars on historical principles
scholarship has proceeded to the interpretation of linguistic distribution in a given geographical area. The dialect boundaries, isoglosses
or isophones, are interpreted in the light of political, economic and
cultural history as well as with regard to the physical features of the

---

[1] See E. Kranzmayer, 'Lautwandlungen und Lautverschiebungen im
gegenwärtigen Wienerischen', *ZfMaf.*, xxi, 1952, 197–239.

[2] See M. Szadrowsky, 'Fortleben althochdeutscher Mehrstämmigkeit',
Beitr., lii, 1928, 398–423; A. Saxer, *Das Vordringen der umlautenden Plurale
bei den Kurzverben in der Nordostschweiz*, Zürich, 1952.

[3] See Sever Pop, *La Dialectologie*, Louvain, 1951, vol. ii; K. Helm, 'Von
deutscher Dialektforschung', *Hess. Blätter f. Volkskunde*, xxvi, 1927, 142–56;
L. Jutz, 'Grundzüge der deutschen Mundartforschung', *ZfDk.*, 1932, 465–88;
K. C. King, 'The Study of Dialect in Germany', *Journal of the Lancashire
Dialect Society*, iv, 1954, 2–15; id., 'The Study of German Dialect in Switzer-
land', *ib.*, v, 1955, 11–22; Bach; Mitzka, *Hdb.*, *Maa.*, *DPhA.*

country concerned. *Kulturmorphologie*, brilliantly launched by Theodor Frings[1] and the Rhenish School, has secured for itself a firm place in Germanistic studies while the recording and presentation of the enormous mass of dialect material collected has continued and borne fruit such as the *Deutscher Sprachatlas*, ed. F. Wrede, later W. Mitzka and B. Martin, 1926–56, and W. Mitzka's *Deutscher Wortatlas*, Giessen, 1951 ff.; and the numerous dialect dictionaries such as *Schweizerisches Idiotikon*; *Schwäbisches Wörterbuch*, ed. Hermann Fischer, Tübingen, 1904–36 (7 vols.); *Rheinisches Wörterbuch*, ed. Josef Müller, Bonn, 1928 ff.; Otto Mensing, *Schleswig-Holsteinisches Wörterbuch*, Neumünster, 1927–35 (5 vols.); *Wörterbuch der elsässischen Mundarten*, ed. E. Martin and H. Lienhard, Strassburg, 1899–1907 (2 vols.); *Niedersächsisches Wörterbuch*, ed. W. Jungandreas, Neumünster, 1953 ff.; *Luxemburger Wörterbuch*, 1950 ff., to mention but a few. The study of the grammar of individual dialects has been further advanced and become ever more refined. Recent outstanding grammars include A. Bertrang, *Grammatik der Areler Mundart*, Brussels, 1921; R. Hotzenköcherle, *Die Mundart von Mutten*, BSG, xix, Frauenfeld, 1934, and on a smaller scale Ursula Feyer, *Die Mundart des Dorfes Baden, Kreis Verden* (= Arbeiten aus dem Institut für Lautforschung an der Universität Berlin, No. 7), Leipzig, 1941. What these works do not do is provide a practical introduction to these dialects as living forms of speech. They are all scholarly analyses of the historical evolution which the particular dialect has undergone since WGmc., OHG or MHG times.[2] The foreign (and nowadays even many a native) student of German in approaching these works is frequently aware of a painful lack of practical acquaintance with one or more German dialects. The whole field of dialectology must remain rather nebulous to the undergraduate student without some first-hand knowledge of dialects. If this book facilitates access to the great works of German dialectology it will have achieved one of its aims.

§ 3. DIALECT AND STANDARD

It is illusory to think that the notions of standard and dialect can

---

[1] e.g. *Rheinische Sprachgeschichte*, Essen, 1924; *id.* with H. Aubin, J. Müller, *Kulturströmungen und Kulturprovinzen in den Rheinlanden*, Bonn, 1926; *id.*, 'Sprachgeographie und Kulturgeographie', *ZfDk.*, xliv, 1930, 546–62; *id.*, *Sprache und Geschichte I.*, Halle, 1956 (incl. a reprint of *Rheinische Sprachgeschichte*).

[2] Criticizing the exclusively historical approach Jean Fourquet says, 'La dialectologie ne pourrait que gagner, si la traditionelle *Laut- und Formenlehre der Mundart von*... évoluait vers l'établissement méthodique du système phonologique et du système grammatical du dialect étudié.' 'Linguistique structurale et dialectologie', *Fragen u. Forschungen*, Festgabe T. Frings, p. 193, 1956.

be defined exactly. They are largely abstractions and do not exist uncontaminated and neatly distinct. The considerable body of critical literature on the topic, with its divergent views and shifting terminology, shows this clearly.[1] Most German commentators have given up Jakob Grimm's distinction between *Dialekt* and *Mundart* (a subdivision of dialect),[2] though a recent suggestion has been to use *Mundart* for the psychological and sociological aspect, for what others call *Volkssprache*, and *Dialekt* for a geographical-linguistic unit of relative uniformity.[3] Another recent article uses *Volkssprache* for both these aspects.[4] It seems useful to continue using *Volkssprache* in F. Maurer's sense for the psychological aspects of the language of the lower social strata,[5] irrespective of whether their language is in fact 'dialect' or approaches 'standard'. *Volkssprache* is thus concerned with extra-linguistic phenomena in language, e.g. vulgarity, illogicality, primitivity, etc.

There is no single completely satisfactory expression in German for the notion of standard language. *Schriftsprache* puts the stress one-sidedly on writing but is the current popular term for the NHG standard language. *Hochsprache* has definite cultural, literary and social connotations, while *Gemeinsprache* would appear to need further definition, since forms which are definitely not standard are nevertheless *Gemeinsprache*. The English word *standard*, in contrast to these German terms, places the stress exactly on the most essential feature, namely on *norm*. The standard language is what the foreigner learns, what is codified in prescriptive grammars and what is found in its purest written form in the everyday prose of the most educated, and in its purest spoken form in the *Bühnenaussprache*.[6] Its characteristic is general validity which is not subjected to regional restriction and is relatively unlimited by time. Expression in standard

---

[1] See Henzen, pp. 9–42 with bibl.; further H. Brinkmann, 'Hochsprache und Mundart', *Wirkendes Wort*, vi, 1955/6, 2, 65–76; E. Geissler, 'Schriftsprache, Hochsprache, Hochlautung und Gemeinsprache', *Muttersprache*, xviii, 1933, 316–18; F. Maurer, 'Schriftsprache und Mundarten', *Deutschunterricht*, viii, 1956, 2, 5–14; E. Mudrak, 'Schriftsprache und Mundart', *Muttersprache*, 1953, 3, 111–15; A. Schmitt, 'Volksmundart, Gemeinsprache und Schriftsprache', *GRM*, xix, 1931, 434–48; L. Weisgerber, *Die Leistung der Mundart im Sprachganzen*, Münster, 1956.
[2] A. Socin, *Schriftsprache und Dialekte im Deutschen nach Zeugnissen alter und neuer Zeit*, Heilbronn, 1888, 467–72.
[3] Kurt Wagner, 'Hochsprache und Mundart in ahd. Zeit', *Deutschunterricht*, viii, 1956, 2, p. 20.
[4] H. Moser, 'Mundart und Hochsprache im neuzeitlichen Deutsch', *ib.*, p. 36.
[5] *Volkssprache*, Erlangen, 1933, see bibl. in Bach, § 247, and chap. vi, 'Die Mundart als geistige Gestaltung'; Henzen, p. 36 f.
[6] Norm fixed by Theodor Siebs in 1898: *Deutsche Bühnenaussprache*. Now *Deutsche Hochsprache*. Bühnenaussprache, 16 ed. by H. de Boor and P. Diels, Berlin, 1957.

B

aims at achieving the norm set by others and by former generations; it aims at correct, even if creative, imitation. Its written form has a fixed orthography, a change of which is only arrived at after official and usually protracted discussions which compare with the process of legislation. The standard bridges the mutual unintelligibility of widely separated dialects and is available to speakers of practically all dialects as a second language.[1]

Dialects have no fixed norm, no rules which command respect and which are deliberately applied by the speakers. Dialect is a free-and-easy, expressionistic form of speech without censure from desk or pulpit and without attempt at correct imitation on the part of the speakers. Naturally there is linguistic tradition of right and wrong, but it is natural and makes no demands on the speakers. Dialect lacks what Henzen calls 'die Absicht auf Überbrückung verschiedener horizontaler oder vertikaler Sprachschichten' (p. 18). This does not mean that dialects are static. The opposite is true, because there is no fixed norm, the floodgates are wide open and innovations are constant. Dialect borrows as easily as standard or perhaps even more easily but it does not digest so easily. Every word borrowed by standard is an enrichment of the standard, for it aims at universality. Every word borrowed by dialect is a blow at its basic principle of regional autarchy, at its own self-sufficiency. If borrowing means the loss of a native word, dialect is impoverished because it loses one of its pillars, part of its *raison d'être*. Innovations born of its own resources testify to the vitality of a dialect. They are also responsible for the stylistic stratification which occurs within dialects as much as within standard languages. Slang or *argot* is thus found also in dialects. Schoolchildren use their speech playfully whether they speak a dialect or the standard. Slang and dialect are fundamentally different.[2] Slang is always only a second possibility of expression and the speaker is usually aware of its special character. Dialect is complete in itself; it can be a person's only language. Slang is confined to certain semantic features; it has no phonology or morphology of its own.

Certain misconceptions obscure the character of dialect. Thus the statement is frequently met with that dialects are debased, corrupt forms of standard. This is, of course, not so. Rather, it is standard which has risen from the dialects to its level of social and cultural

---

[1] German dialects not covered by the NHG standard are Pennsylvania German (Pennsilfaanisch), certain German enclaves in Eastern Europe, and to a lesser degree Alsatian. Knowledge of standard German is, however, hardly ever totally lacking in such speech communities.

[2] See e.g. A. Dauzat, *Les argots*, Paris, 1929; H. Lipps, 'Sprache, Mundart und Jargon', *Blätter f. d. dt. Philosophie*, ix, 1935/6, pp. 388 ff.; W. von Wartburg, 'Vom Ursprung und Wesen des Argot', *GRM*, xviii, 1930, 376–91.

prestige. Whether the German dialects all go back to one *uniform* language, e.g. Proto-German or Proto-Germanic, is not ascertainable as there is no historical evidence. Romance scholars see in the French dialects, for instance, the result of geographical segmentation, of the split-up of a language, Latin.[1] Whether the development of the German dialects has in fact been divergent or convergent is a moot point. It seems certain, however, that in modern times the development has definitely been convergent.

In the romantic view German dialects are frequently seen as the repositories of genuine old, untainted German. This view is, of course, just as erroneous as the above opposite opinion. The dialects are no older and no younger than the standard. They preserve many features which NHG has shed. On the other hand they are in many ways more modern, e.g. by being more analytic in their grammatical structure or by having done away with certain features of the MHG phoneme inventory (e.g. the rounded front vowels) which NHG preserves. What makes their study so interesting and so rewarding, however, is that they mingle old and new in a way unlike that of NHG. In them we may find as a living reality what we otherwise can only reconstruct from the documents which have come down to us from the Middle Ages, or they can give us a glimpse of what NHG might be like in future should the reins of strict norm ever be relaxed.

A frequent prejudice heard accuses dialect of coarseness and vulgarity.[2] This arises mainly from a confusion which allows extra-linguistic factors to colour the judgement. Dialect is, of course, also *Volkssprache* in the definition given above, but dialect can and should be studied as a linguistic phenomenon first and foremost. *Volkssprache* exists independent of dialects and the attributes of coarseness and vulgarity, the lack of detachment and the excess of exaggeration have nothing to do with dialect as a linguistic phenomenon.

Lastly, it is frequently asserted that dialects should not be allowed to wither away since the standard needs them as a blood-donor, as a source of constant enrichment, without which the standard would suffer from desiccation.[3] The dialects are naturally valuable as the sources for the terminology of regional activities and features. Low German has given NHG its terminology of seafaring and the Alpine dialects of Bavaria and Switzerland have contributed the terms for mountain topography. There is no doubt, however, that a language can always create the terminology it needs and develop along lines

[1] See A. Dauzat, *Les patois. Evolution, classifications, étude*, Paris, 1927.
[2] See on this also W. Meyer-Seedorf, 'Die Bedeutung der Mundart für die heutige Sprache', *Muttersprache*, 1949, 314–19.
[3] 'Verjüngungsquelle für die erstarrende Schriftsprache', K. Bergmann, 'Streifzüge durch die bayrischen Mundarten', *ZfdU*, xxxiii, 1919, 424–7; Mudrak, *op. cit.*, p. 113 f.; Dauzat, *Les patois*, p. 87 f.

which the speakers desire, even if there are no dialects to draw upon
or if these are not made use of.

Wherever the ideal of the standard has led to the abandonment
of the native dialect a third form arises between the two: the *Umgangssprache*.[1] The speech of few people will qualify for the title
standard, the majority will adopt a half-way house between the ideal
and the abandoned dialect. This distinguishes itself from dialect,
which is self-sufficient, by wanting to be considered standard. *Umgangssprache* naturally varies according to the tributaries. The Austrian *Umgangssprache* is noticeably different from the Swabian or
Rhenish *Umgangssprachen*. It is the regional *Umgangssprache* which
first benefits from the abandonment of local dialect. In Darmstadt, for
instance, the dialect form [dɒ:g] 'day' makes way not for standard
[tha:k] but for Rhenish colloquial [da:x]. The *Umgangssprache* may
still be near dialect, in which case Bach (p. 2) speaks of *Halbmundart*,
or it may approach standard very closely. By its very nature it is
difficult to investigate and has been least studied, although more
attention to *Umgangssprache* has been demanded recently.[2]

In Germany and Austria *Umgangssprache* takes precedence over
the dialects.[3] In the centre and south, where the distance between
standard and dialect is smaller, *Umgangssprache* reaches higher in the
social scale than in the north where the Low German dialects are
considerably removed from the High German standard. Dialect can
be said to be confined to the peasant and artisan class.

In the German linguistic areas to the west and south outside Germany, i.e. in Switzerland, Alsace, Lorraine, and Luxemburg, there is
no *Umgangssprache*. There is no attempt to approach the NHG standard by deliberately abandoning native dialect. If in Alsace and
Lorraine dialect is given up it is French which replaces it. NHG
standard is there a reading language and to some extent a written
language, especially among the older generations. In Luxemburg a

[1] Bach, pp. 2 ff., pp. 230–44; Henzen, pp. 20 ff., 196 ff.; Mitzka, *Maa.*,
pp. 94–101; P. Kretschmer, *Wortgeographie der hochdeutschen Umgangssprache*,
Göttingen, 1918; H. Küpper, *Wörterbuch der deutschen Umgangssprache*,
Hamburg, 1955.

[2] A. Schirmer, 'Die deutsche Umgangssprache. Stand und Ziele ihrer Erforschung', *GRM*, ix, 1921, 42–53; *id.*, 'Die deutsche Umgangssprache',
ZfdU, xxxiii, 428–30; A. Simon, 'Hoch- und Umgangssprache', *ZfdB*, xvi,
1940, 2 ff.; F. Beranek, 'Die Umgangssprache und ihre Erforschung', *Muttersprache*, 1950, 65–71; Hugo Moser, 'Mundart und Hochsprache im neuzeitlichen Deutsch', *Deutschunterricht*, viii, 1956, 2, 36–61. See also U. Engel,
Mundart und Umgangssprache in Württemberg. Beiträge zur Sprachsoziologie
der Gegenwart, typescript diss. Tübingen, 1954.

[3] See Henzen, p. 19: '... so muss man feststellen, dass für gewöhnlich von
den hundert und mehr Millionen Deutschen kaum ein Drittel Mundart,
sozusagen niemand die Schrift- oder Hochsprache und alle übrigen diese
Zwischenstufe sprechen', i.e. *Umgangssprache*.

kind of a Luxemburg *Umgangssprache*, a *koinè*, is taking shape as the result of levelling and amalgamation of the regional dialects. But this is not the result of an attempt to adopt the NHG standard and the word *Umgangssprache* in the above definition would therefore be a misnomer. In the same way it is quite wrong to refer to *Schwyzer-tütsch* or Swiss *Grossratsdeutsch* as the regional *Umgangssprache*.[1] Local dialects, summarily called *Schwyzertütsch*, are the everyday language of all classes in German-speaking Switzerland and there is no deliberate attempt to bridge the gap either between the dialects and to create a *koinè* or between them and the NHG standard which would lead to an *Umgangssprache*. It is likely that the levelling tendencies of the present age will eventually bring about a *Schwyzer-tütsch koinè*[2] but of an *Umgangssprache* in the German sense there is no question.[3] *Grossratsdeutsch* is not an *Umgangssprache*—it is NHG used in an imperfect way. It is the sub-standard of the bilingual speaker and more on a par with a foreign language spoken with an accent. It is heard only on the occasions when NHG standard is demanded and in no way encroaches on the use of the *Schwyzer-tütsch* dialects.[4] By no means all cantonal parliaments or municipal councils use NHG or *Grossratsdeutsch* for their deliberations, as Zinsli (p. 67) has pointed out.

The question arises whether dialects which are current in a whole society for all activities except a few, e.g. most writing, sermons, school teaching, scholarly lectures, certain types of formal public speeches, should not be regarded as 'languages' rather than 'dialects'. H. Kloss[5] examines this question with regard to three German dialects: *Sassisch* (Low German), *Letzeburgisch*, and *Schwyzertütsch*, apart from *Pennsilfaanisch* and *Zimbrisch*. In order to qualify for the title 'language' such a dialect must be sufficiently removed linguistically from its cognate, NHG, and be generally used. The latter condition is specified to the extent that there must be a specialist prose (*Fachprosa*). *Sassisch* and *Lallans* (Lowland Scots) benefit, in Kloss's view, much from the fact that in the Middle Ages they were written languages, though it is difficult to see what this can have to do with

---

[1] Thus Bach, p. 291, 'Andere umgangssprachliche Typen im alem. Raum sind das Grossratsdeutsch in der Schweiz . . .'; Schwarz, p. 19, calls *Schwyzer-tütsch* a 'mundartliche Umgangssprache'; Wagner, *Sprachlandschaften*, p. 78; Moser, *Deutschunterricht*, viii, 1956, 2, pp. 51, 53; E. Öhmann, 'Hochsprache und Mundarten im Mittelhochdeutschen', *ib.*, p. 32: 'Sogar noch heute klafft zwischen der schweizerischen Umgangssprache (Verkehrssprache und Kantons-ratsdeutsch) und der neuhochdeutschen Hochsprache auch in lautlichen Dingen eine gewaltige Kluft . . .'
[2] See P. Zinsli, *Deutschunterricht*, 1956, 2, p. 72.
[3] On the position of NHG in Switzerland, see chap. ii, § 1.
[4] See P. Zinsli, *op. cit.*, p. 67.
[5] *Die Entstehung neuer germanischer Kultursprachen von 1800 bis 1950*, Munich, 1952.

their present status. It seems that much too much importance is attached to former literary status and present-day *Fachprosa*. This leads to the fantastic exaggeration of the importance of Lallans—supported by a few dozen romantic enthusiasts and spoken in various local forms by the peasantry only. *Sassisch* is also placed high on the ladder to the status of a language in spite of its social inferiority. *Letzeburgisch* might be considered with some hesitation as a *Halbsprache* but *Schwyzertütsch* is for Kloss beyond the pale and he merely concedes that certain circumstances make it difficult to decide whether it might not after all qualify for the status of a *Halbsprache* (p. 36). Close contact with the Luxemburg and Swiss scenes would have shown the existence of a spoken *Fachprosa* far superior to and more widespread than anything *Sassisch* or Lallans have to offer. In Luxemburg, for instance, the meetings of the committee of philologists preparing the *Luxemburger Wörterbuch* (1950 ff.) are conducted in dialect just like all other discussions of professional or trade groups. The Swiss radio broadcasts in *Schwyzertütsch* such specialist subjects as a discussion of three University professors on how far Siebs' *Bühnenaussprache* ought to be accepted in Switzerland (August 1955). The solemn occasion of the funeral of a well-liked Federal Councillor (i.e. a minister) was reported on the wireless (August 1955) in dialect. Such examples can be adduced *ad lib*. Literary production in both countries is sizeable.[1] In addition to this there is the important fact that these two dialects—or languages—are the daily medium of *all classes* of 300,000 people in the case of Luxemburgish and of over three million people in the case of *Schwyzertütsch*. The question is merely one of terminology and insignificant in itself, but if it is answered the statement must be substantiated and all relevant factors must be taken into consideration.

§ 4. DIALECT BOUNDARIES

Speaking of a certain dialect, e.g. Swabian, implies that such a

---

[1] See H. R. Schmid, 'Schwyzertütsch' in T. Vogel, *Schwizer Schnabelweid*, Aarau, 1938, p. 345: 'Wenn Zahlen die Lebensfähigkeit und kulturelle Bildungsfähigkeit der deutschschweizerischen Volkssprache belegen können, dann die folgenden: In den 18 Jahren von 1916–1933 sind 851 Bücher und Broschüren in schweizerdeutscher Sprache erschienen. Das macht nahezu 50 Publikationen im Jahr. Obenan steht die populäre Dramatik mit ungefähr 450 Bänden und Stücken, einige Festspiele und Tendenzdramen inbegriffen. Gedichtbände wurden im genannten Zeitraum etwa 70 herausgegeben, Liederbücher ebenfalls 70, dazu an die 140 Prosa-Erzählungen, darunter viele Werke von bedeutendem literarischem Wert.' In the six years between 1953 and 1958 the dialect publications in Switzerland totalled 331. Of these 162 were plays, 74 novels or volumes of short stories, 35 volumes of poetry, 10 anthologies and 50 children's books.—In Lux. dialect there appeared in the ten years from 1948 to 1957 92 publications (mainly plays and volumes of poetry), excluding calenders and periodicals.

dialect has an identity which distinguishes it more or less clearly from other dialects. When dealing with languages, French or German, for instance, it is easy to point to this identity and to state without difficulty the geographical location and boundaries of such a language. If the languages are genetically closely related, as for instance Swedish and Danish or Dutch and German, the fixing of a boundary tends to become more problematical. In dialectology the problem of boundaries is crucial but extremely difficult. It is found that one form of speech shades off almost imperceptibly into another form. In the German linguistic area there is probably not a village or even a hamlet which is not in some way linguistically differentiated from its neighbours. It has been shown that even within a small isolated village[1] there is no linguistic uniformity. There are differences between the generations, the sexes and individual families in the smallest isolated speech community. Absolute homogeneity is, in fact, an impossible demand not only in the case of dialects but also in the case of standard languages.

Dialect geography has shown that there are areas where dialect differences, isophones and isoglosses, accumulate and others where they are relatively scarce, though never absent. Furthermore it can be shown that the former are usually the areas where the most salient, the most noticeable, differences occur. Thus an isophone separating two qualities of $\bar{a}$ will not be felt so distinctly as for instance one separating p- from pf-. Equally if after some distance the student hears $\bar{o}$ instead of an a- sound he cannot fail to realize that he is in a different dialect area. The factor of intelligibility or the degree of strangeness is very important for the fixation of dialect areas and dialect boundaries, though it is rather neglected in German dialectology. Within Swiss German there are at least three clearly marked reflexes of MHG $\check{a}$: [a ɑ ɒ] roughly associated with east (St. Gallen), west (Berne) and centre (Zürich). These differences do not affect intelligibility in the same degree, as for instance the differences in the reflexes for MHG $\hat{\imath}$, e.g. between Bavarian ai and Alemannic $\bar{\imath}$, or the differences in the reflexes for MHG ei, e.g. between Bavarian oa, Alemannic ei or $\ddot{a}i$, and Rhenish Franconian $\bar{a}$.

The problem is even more complicated by linguistic stratification according to social classes. This is practically always neglected in the presentation of dialect material.[2] All German dialect maps based on the *DSA* take no account of stratification and the boundaries they show refer to peasant dialects only.

---

[1] E.g. see Hotzenköcherle, *BSG*, xix, p. 28.
[2] It is considered by J. Brøndum-Nielsen, *Dialekter og Dialektforskning*, Copenhagen, 1927, p. 24, and K. Schulte Kemminghausen, *Mundart und Hochsprache in Norddeutschland*, Neumünster, 1939, 86–101.

Since the beginning of this century the question of dialect boundaries has been eagerly discussed.[1] It is now accepted that in spite of the linguistic fragmentation mentioned above one is nevertheless entitled to speak of dialects. The boundaries, however, are never sharply defined lines but rather wide zones or bundles (fascicles) of isoglosses and isophones. *Saumzonen* with their *Übergangsmundarten* and *Kernlandschaften* with their *Vollmundarten* (Frings, Wagner, Bohnenberger and others) are now accepted both by the scholars who see the present-day dialects mainly as the results of settlements (tribal and later) and by those who see them as the linguistic survivals of the late medieval German principalities.[2] In this way the traditional names of the German dialects taken from the German tribes of the time of the *Völkerwanderung* can be used without implying that these modern dialects are necessarily the tribal dialects of early medieval times, and in spite of the fact that present-day dialects, in the west of the German linguistic area at least, are largely the result of the political and economic map of late medieval and more recent times. Thus when descriptions of the general characteristics of certain dialects are given here, e.g. of Low Alemannic or Middle Bavarian, the factors of fragmentation and of extra-linguistic elements (e.g. tribal settlement) operative in the identification of dialects (*Kernlandschaften*) and dialect boundaries are not overlooked. Where an historical and political boundary, e.g. between Frankish and Alemannic tribal areas, and the isophone of *p-/pf-* (*pund—pfund*) and other isophones (e.g. monophthong in *gut* against diphthong) run more or less together in a broad belt the extra-linguistic tribal names Franconian and Alemannic may serve as names for the present-day dialects with some justification.[3]

[1] See L. Gauchat, 'Gibt es Mundartgrenzen?' *Archiv f. d. Stud. d. neuern Sprachen u. Lit.*, lvii (iii), 1903, pp. 365 ff.; K. Haag, '7 Sätze über Sprachbewegung', *ZfhdMaa.*, i, 1900, 138–41; *id.*, 'Sprachwandel im Lichte der Mundartgrenzen', *Teuth.*, vi, 1929/30, 1–35; K. Bohnenberger, 'Sprachgeschichte u. politische Geschichte', *ZfhdMaa.*, iii, 1902, 321–6; *id.*, 'Über die Ostgrenze des Alemannischen. Tatsächliches und Grundsätzliches', *Beitr.*, lii, 1928, 217–91 (273–84, 'Über Mundartabgrenzung'); Mitzka, *Hdb.*, 93; 98–103; 129–78; Henzen, pp. 174 ff. with bibl.; Bach, §§ 51–4; 70 ff. with bibl.; the most recent statements are: Bohnenberger, *Alem. Ma.*, 245 ff.; Hugo Moser, 'Sprachgrenzen und ihre Ursachen', *ZfMaf.*, xxii, 1954, 87–111; Kurt Wagner, *Die Gliederung der deutschen Mundarten. Begriffe und Grundsätze*, Akad. d. Wiss. u. d. Lit. Abh., 1954, No. 12, Wiesbaden, 1955; T. Frings, 'Zur Grundlegung einer Geschichte der deutschen Sprache. I. Territorium u. Sprache, Stamm u. Sprache', *Beitr.*, lxxvi, 1955, 401–534.
[2] See H. Moser, 'Stamm und Mundart', *ZfMaf.*, xx, 1952, 129–45; Frings is the chief advocate of the importance of the late-medieval territory (see fn. 1, p. 4, and *Beitr.*, lxxvi, 1955, 401–534.); R. Bruch, 'Sprache und Geschichte', *ZfMaf.*, xxiv, 1956, 129–50, and pp. 185–7, demands the consideration of earlier (Roman, tribal, etc.) political configurations.
[3] See Bohnenberger, *Alem. Ma.*, p. 293: 'Kurze Kennzeichnung heutiger deutscher Mundarten durch bedeutsame Merkmale hat sich immer mehr als

§ 5. DIALECT LITERATURE

Literature written in dialect is generally regarded with suspicion. Objections are of two kinds, on the one hand against the writer and on the other hand against dialect as the medium.[1] It has frequently been stated that many dialect writers are incapable of escaping from standard German in which all were educated. They think in standard and merely translate into dialect by giving their language dialect phonology and grammar. Their vocabulary is to a large extent influenced by standard as are their style, their locutions and idioms. Thus E. Schwarz says (p. 15): 'Die wenigsten Mundartdichter verstehen es, wirklich in der Mundart zu denken und aus ihr heraus zu dichten. Sie denken gewöhnlich hochdeutsch und setzen dann in die Mundart um, gebrauchen dabei oft unbewusst Wendungen, die das Volk nicht kennt, unmundartlichen Satzbau, mundartfremde Wörter'; and Henzen (p. 187): 'Die Mundartdichtung, auch die ernst zu nehmende, ist jedenfalls immer noch zu sehr Übersetzung der schriftsprachlichen.'

There is no doubt that much that is written in dialect has a false ring. This is especially true of literature which has not grown out of a dialect with wide social currency. If a dialect is confined to the near-illiterate social classes it cannot possibly fulfil literary functions. Dialect literature of some merit will therefore only be found in areas where the dialect enjoys a certain prestige and is spoken habitually also by the educated classes. Such a dialect is capable of expressing the feelings and thought of people with literary taste and can therefore be a vehicle of literature. In most areas of Germany this condition is not, or rather, is no longer fulfilled, for genuine dialect is spoken only by people incapable of writing literature, and a dialect literature is therefore impossible for want of dialect writers. Imitations attempted by the social outsider—the non-dialect speaker—either lead to this false dialect literature or aim at comic effects. Nothing has discredited dialect writing more—and even dialect itself—than the use made of it by the comedian. The impression is created that dialect is something ludicrous and the suitable medium for soppy or bawdy stories. But where dialect is still the everyday language of a whole society, where it is spoken by all, or almost all classes, in

schwierig erwiesen, selbst wenn man die Grenzstreifen mit ihrer Formenfülle ausser Betracht lässt . . . Auch entheben die Schwierigkeiten nicht von der Verpflichtung, selbst wenn es auf einen Notbehelf oder eine umständliche Fassung herauskommen sollte. Eine Kennzeichnung ist unentbehrlich.'—In the short general descriptions offered in this book a few salient features from among infinite numbers are selected. Where possible the same features are mentioned of each dialect to facilitate comparison.

[1] Bach, p. 311; Henzen, pp. 185–91, with bibl.; O. Behaghel, *Geschichte der deutschen Sprache*, 5th ed., Berlin, 1928, pp. 214–20.

all or almost all of their activities, it can be the equal of any standard language as a literary medium and will be used skilfully and effectively by a talented writer. It is true, the writer lacks the training in writing traditionally afforded in the case of a standard language by the schools. The effort needed to write dialect well is greater than that needed to write a standard language well. Too many dialect writers write in dialect because they think it is easier than to write standard. That is another reason for the low literary level of much dialect literature, which has discredited—undeservedly—dialect literature as a whole. The dialect writers represented in this book have all the backing of relatively solid dialect areas although dialect is not in all cases spoken by all classes. It is hoped that the extracts will show that dialect writers are able—in favourable circumstances—to produce works of some standing and value.

The second objection to dialect literature is to the attempted writing of dialect. It is maintained that dialect cannot be written, or as Henzen (p. 37) says, 'Auch die Mundart kann zwar geschrieben werden, aber es läuft dies eben doch mehr oder weniger ihrem Wesen zuwider.' It would appear that German critics in particular have often been misled by the term *Mundart*.[1] *Mundart*, so the argument runs, is spoken language *par excellence*. There always is a gulf between spoken language and written language. The standard language possesses a polished, well-proven instrument: the written language (in German *Schriftsprache* is synonymous with standard language), and any attempt at reducing the *Mundart* to writing, the objection continues, is bound to lead to an undialectal, spurious kind of mixture between written standard and spoken dialect. It is true the difference between spoken language and written language is considerable, but it is as great in any standard language as in a dialect. To write exactly as one speaks would not so much be impossible as unpleasant and aesthetically objectionable.[2] What the ear tolerates at first hearing it already finds difficult to tolerate on second hearing if it is repeated on a tape recorder. The eye would find it unacceptable in any circumstance. A tape recording made at random of a conversation reveals tedious repetition, numerous sentences begun but left unfinished, much humming and hawing, frequent illogical con-

---

[1] See H. Brinkmann, 'Hochsprache und Mundart', *Wirkendes Wort*, vi, 1955/6, 65–75: 'Mundart ist, wie schon der Name sagt, *mündliche Rede*. Sie tritt immer nur als gesprochene Sprache auf, und zwar in einer bestimmten Lebenslage, in der Begegnung von Menschen derselben räumlichen Gemeinschaft. Zu ihrem Wesen gehört es, dass sie nicht geschrieben wird (man kann nur versuchen, sie aufzuzeichnen), dass sie nicht in derselben Weise wie die Hochsprache objektiviert werden kann' (p. 65).

[2] A. H. Smith and R. Quirk give an interesting specimen of actually recorded English speech in 'Some Problems of Verbal Communication', *Transactions of the Yorkshire Dialect Society*, part liv, vol. ix, 1954, 10–20.

structions such as *zeugma*, and a speed which on the whole is painfully slow and laborious. Much that would seem redundant on paper is necessary for oral communication. The written language cannot, and indeed must not, attempt to be a faithful mirror of speech. It must shed all abortive utterances which abound in speech, and it streamlines thought. It is a much more economical and efficient means of expression than speech. Written dialect shares, and indeed *must* share, these qualities with written standard. But written dialect can nevertheless be just as genuine a reflection of dialect as written standard is of standard. A dialect writer must be allowed to handle his dialect and fashion his work with this tool just as must any writer in the standard.[1] The criterion by which we must judge his work is not whether a certain expression or sentence is in fact used in the dialect but whether it can be used. Henzen (p. 190) puts it: 'Denn nicht darauf kommt es schliesslich an, ob für gewöhnlich das gedacht oder gesprochen werde, was der Mundartdichter schreibt, sondern ob so gedacht oder gesprochen werden kann, ohne dass der Ton echter Mundart gröblich verletzt wird. . . . Worum es aber geht, ist, dass ein Dichter sich keinesfalls gegen den Sprachgeist versündigen darf.' To give an example. German dialect speech in general makes sparing use of attributive adjectives. The dialect writer will use them more liberally. There can be no objection as long as the adjectives and the attributive combinations are in fact native in his dialect. A certain amount of hypotaxis is also permissible, as the dialects do not by any means make use of paratactical constructions alone. Especially the 'higher' dialects, i.e. those which are spoken by all classes of a society, have developed a syntax which permits hypotaxis to a limited degree. Constructions which are, however, alien to the dialect must be avoided, e.g. the non-periphrastic genitive of standard German, or conjunctions and prepositions which have obviously originated on the desk of the bureaucrats (*nichts destoweniger*, *anlässlich*, *in Anbetracht*, etc.).

The question of what is alien to a dialect is not always easy to answer. This raises the whole problem of the so-called 'purity of dialects'.[2] There are, of course, no pure dialects—any more than there

[1] Alfred Schlagdenhauffen, *La Langue des poètes Strasbourgeois Albert et Adolphe Matthis, Publ. de la Fac. des Lettres de l'Université de Strasbourg*, fasc. 65, Paris, 1934, 1–154, shows how the dialect writers Matthis do not write as Strasbourg people talk but that their dialect is nevertheless genuine because it catches the true spirit of Strasbourg dialect. Poetry demands more than everyday language, but this does not mean that the character of any given dialect is automatically falsified. Similarly Käthe Scheel, *Untersuchungen über den Satzbau der niederdeutschen Volkssprache und Kunstprosa*, Hamburg, 1939, p. 3 f. and W. Niekerken, 'Von den Grenzen der niederdeutschen Sprache', *Festschrift Boeck*, pp. 214–22 (written in LG).

[2] See the pertinent points made by Angus McIntosh, *An Introduction to a Survey of Scottish Dialects*, Edinburgh, 1952, p. 38 f.

are pure standard languages. They are as much exposed to the interference[1] by other dialects and languages through social intercourse
as any written language. Some are geographically and socially more
isolated than others and have been thrown back on their own resources for a longer period than others. But all language serves
communication and is exposed to the effects of contact.

The Walser dialect on the southern, Italian, side of the Alps has
been isolated for a long time and the influence of other German dialects and the German standard has been severely limited. But although we do find many ancient features and words which have died
out over most of the German-speaking linguistic area, e.g. *chneie* 'to
know', OHG *knawen*; *schiech* 'sick', for usual *krank*, MHG *siech*; *der
ischt fascht schieche*[2] 'he is very ill', with *fascht* in the MHG sense of
fast = 'very', we also meet innovations such as *steisch woul?* 'are
you well?'; *wi mängs Johr hesch?* 'how old are you?'; or the use of the
verb for 'to go' in the passive. Can one speak of a 'pure' dialect in
view of such loan-constructions? (from Italian *stai bene?*; *quanti anni
hai?*). E. Kranzmayer[3] has shown how the native Austrian form
Hirz 'stag' has almost everywhere been replaced by Central German
Hirsch and has pointed to many forms in present-day Austrian dialect which infiltrated in the past from earlier standard language. The
spoken standard of Hanseatic Middle Low German is responsible
according to K. Bischoff[4] for the form *uns* 'us' in Mecklenburg and
other Low German dialects. Many of the words which the first Basle
editor of Luther's Bible translation thought necessary to explain in
his appended glossary for Alemannic readers are now in common use
in Swiss German dialects, e.g. *Lippe, Narbe, deutlich*.[5] The Slav word
Grenze 'frontier' has ousted German *Mark* even in the dialects
farthest removed from the Slavs.

'Purity' and 'mixture' have only historical application. Comparing
successive stages in the evolution of a dialect we note whether the
difference from its neighbours increases or decreases. If one cannot

---

[1] U. Weinreich's term (*Languages in Contact*, New York, 1953).
[2] Emil Balmer, *Die Walser im Piemont*, Bern, 1949, p. 219.
[3] *Sprachschichten und Sprachbewegungen in den Ostalpen I* (= Arbeiten zur
Bayr.-Österr. Dialektgeographie, 2. Heft), Vienna, Munich, 1931, p. 49;
'Hochsprache und Mundarten in den österreichischen Landschaften', *Wirkendes
Wort*, vi, 1955/6, 262–9; see also K. Zwierzina, *Schriftsprache als Mundart*,
(Rektoratsrede), Graz, 1930.
[4] 'Hochsprache und Mundarten im mittelalterlichen Niederdeutschen', *Der
Deutschunterricht*, viii, 2, 1956, p. 83.
[5] Adam Petri's glossary, 1523, is discussed in detail by A. Socin, *op. cit.*,
pp. 236–45. See also Schütt, *Über Adam Petris Bibelglossar*, Freiburg, 1908;
Bachmann, *Der Einfluss von Luthers Wortschatz auf die schweizerische Literatur
des 16. und 17. Jahrhunderts im Anschluss an Adam Petris Bibelglossar*, Freiburg,
1909; F. Kluge, *Von Luther bis Lessing*, 4th ed., Strassburg, 1904, where the
glossary is reprinted, pp. 94–100.

speak of *pure* dialect one can however speak of *genuine* dialect.
Genuine dialect is what is accepted as correct by the majority and
especially the culturally most alive and leading members of a community.[1] After all, good standard German is what the best writers of
German accept. With regard to the dialects the situation is analogous. Many people in Zürich will use words such as *Schlagrahm*
'whipped cream', *Kleinkindergärtneri* 'nursery school teacher', *Butter*;
tailors' assistants talk about *de Rock* 'man's jacket', *d Hose* (sg.)
'trousers'. But these words are not genuine dialect and nearly every-
body would admit it when challenged. It is laziness or mistaken
correctness (the printed price-lists use such words) which leads people
to make use of these words in preference to what would still generally
be regarded as *genuine dialect*: *gschwungne Nidel* (Schlagrahm),
Anke (Butter), *Tschooppe* (Rock), *d Hose* (pl.). In the case of *Kleinkindergärtneri* for *Gfätterlischuelleereri* it is mistaken politeness which
leads to the neglect of the established word (from *gfätterle* 'playing
of children', literally playing at being fathers and mothers).

Good dialect writers can be relied upon to have a feeling for what
is genuine. Attempts are sometimes made to reintroduce obsolete
words. It is usually a mistake. Such writers only estrange their
readers. They render their dialects the greatest service if they faithfully write what is current and thereby strengthen the sense of
genuineness in the readers, rather than try to reform them. Naturally
they would always protect what is still alive and keep away alien
intruders (e.g. the words mentioned above).

The dialects from which texts in this book are chosen are capable
of literary expression. In fact all of them have a considerable tradition of successful epic, lyric and dramatic writing. The authors
chosen fulfil our condition of genuineness. Some slips and lapses do
occur—just as they do in spoken dialect—but no more, and they can
therefore be taken as faithful, representative literary products of
their dialects.

§ 6. DIALECT SPELLING

One of the great difficulties with which dialect writers have to
wrestle is spelling. Most laymen resignedly state that dialects cannot
be written or spelt because they have too many sounds which are too
complicated and too varied for our alphabet, while most dialectologists take refuge from this dilemma in some forbidding-looking
phonetic script. The laymen are wrong, for this difficulty exists when-
ever human speech is translated into alphabetical writing. In Europe

---

[1] Rob. B. Christ, 'U- und Non-U in Basel', *Der Monat*, Heft 104, 1957,
80–8, equates U-dialect with genuine dialect and finds corrupt dialect above
all in Non-U speech.

we have to manage with an alphabet of 26 letters plus any modifications we choose to invent, e.g. ö, ä, ü, å, ø, š, ð, þ which are found in German, Swedish, Czech, or Icelandic. Few standard languages manage well, for the ideal is one sign for each phoneme. Most languages or dialects have about three or four dozen phonemes. But spelling tradition has created the impression that standard languages can be spelt but dialects not. It is, of course, entirely a matter of practice and tradition. In the case of our standard languages we merely follow the example of others, teachers or grammarians, whilst in the case of dialects we lack almost all practice and experience. Spelling in dialect thus means a creative act on the part of the writer, for which few are trained, and a considerable effort on the part of the reader. The absence of a tradition not only entails lack of practice and experience but also the necessity to be more exact. Tradition and schooling help to tolerate inexactitude and unphonetic spelling in a standard or school language. Dialect spelling must be more phonetic because it has no tradition to back it up. The dialect writer has in fact a very difficult task indeed if he attempts to spell his dialect phonetically satisfactorily and at the same time to reach a public used to the spelling conventions of the standard language and unwilling to adjust itself to anything else.

This Gordian knot is neatly severed by the dialectologist who adopts a phonetic script. He rids himself of the shackles of an obtrusive spelling tradition and gains a system of symbols which affords as many as he chooses to use. Views differ as to whether a phonetic transcription of a dialect ought to be narrow and impressionistic or broad and systematic (phonemic). Most Romance dialectologists tend to favour the former method, whilst Scandinavian scholars distinguish clearly between the aims of a phonetician and those of a dialectologist.[1] Zetterholm argues that when studying a modern language the student occupies himself with phonetic texts and exercises only at the beginning, and that the study of dialects should also proceed from phonetics to other fields of grammar where exaggerated phonetic exactness is only harmful and an impediment. D. Abercrombie[2] is also of the opinion that dialect material should always be presented in a systematic transcription, and that it should above all be readable. It should, in fact, never be forgotten that as S. Pop (*op. cit.*, ii, 1163) says, 'Toute notation phonétique n'est qu'un faible reflet du langage vivant.' [3] If we take into consideration that some

---

[1] M. Eriksson, 'Dialektüppteckningens metoder', *Svenska Landsmål*, lix, 1946, 32–57; D. O. Zetterholm, 'Über die Aufzeichnung von Dialekttexten', *Studia Linguistica*, vi, 1952, 2, 65–78.

[2] 'The Recording of Dialect Material', *Orbis*, iii, 1954, 1, 231–5.

[3] In a similar sense Mitzka, *Hdb.*, p. 42.

phoneticians themselves view the so-called impressionistic method with suspicion[1] a broad phonemic transcription appears much more desirable for the study of a dialect in any but its narrowest phonetic aspect.

The phonetic script most often met with in German dialectology, but with many individual deviations, is the system of *Böhmer-Ascoli*.[2] It is characterized by the use of diacritic marks for different degrees of openness or closeness of the vowels, starting from a cardinal vowel. In its unamended form it is always narrow. It is used in *BSG*, *Beiträge zur schweizerdeutschen Mundartforschung*, in the *Sprachatlas Italiens und der Südschweiz*, *Vox Romanica*, the forthcoming *Sprachatlas der deutschen Schweiz* and the *Atlas linguistique de l'Alsace, Schweizer Dialekte in Text und Ton. I. Schweizerdeutsche Mundarten*, Frauenfeld, 1951 ff. The *Lautschrift des Teuthonista*,[3] though deriving from Böhmer's system, is a broad and simple system, using diacritic marks sparingly, among the vowels only for openness but not for closeness. Thus, while for instance H. U. Rübel[4] in Böhmer's system distinguishes nine different *e*-sounds, the *Lautschrift des Teuthonista* provides only three: *e, ẹ, æ*.

The phonetic script of the *Association phonétique internationale* (API)[5] is used by the *Arbeiten aus dem Institut für Lautforschung an der Universität Berlin*, ed. D. Westermann, e.g. vol. vii, U. Feyer, *Die Mundart des Dorfes Baden*, 1941; vol. x, B. Martin, *Waldeckisch-Westfälisch*, 1941; and, among others, in the excellent *Grammatik der Areler Mundart*, by A. Bertrang.

The *DSA* uses ordinary alphabetic writing, as the material upon which it is based was provided by laymen, i.e. the schoolteachers of all the communes to whom Wenker's forty sentences were sent for translation into the local dialect.

It is clear from what has been stated above that, the aims of the phonetician and of the dialectologist not being the same, the dialectologist has to choose a phonetic system which is most practical and

---

[1] See W. F. Twaddell in the Foreword to R. M. S. Heffner, *General Phonetics*, Madison, 1952, 'impressionistic description of a sound and of its production is unreliable'.

[2] See E. Dieth, *Vademecum der Phonetik*, Berne, 1950, 45–50. Also M. Heepe (ed.), *Lautzeichen und ihre Verwendung in verschiedenen Sprachgebieten*, Berlin, 1928, 'Deutsche Mundarten', pp. 31–49.

[3] *Teuth.*, i, 1924/5, p. 5; *ZfMaf.* adopted the same system, likewise the *Lautbibliothek der deutschen Mundarten*, see Heft 1: E. Zwirner, W. Bethge, *Erläuterungen zu den Texten*, Göttingen, 1958, p. 31 f. The phonetic alphabet of A. Götze, *Proben hoch- und niederdeutscher Mundarten*, Bonn, 1922, is a forerunner, and the *Lautschrift der Wiener Wörterbuchkanzlei* follows largely the same tradition.

[4] *Viehzucht im Oberwallis*, BSMaf., ii, Frauenfeld, 1950, p. xxix.

[5] See *The Principles of the International Phonetic Association*, Dep. of Phonetics, University College, London, 1941; E. Dieth, *op. cit.*, appendix.

convenient for his task. This is, by and large, to give a broad but systematic and phonemic transcription.[1] Here he is almost on common ground with the dialect writer whose aim it is also, or should be, to give a practical but faithful rendering of his dialect. This would be achieved by a phonemic transcription. The dialectologist, however, can neglect the NHG orthography and proceed freely. The dialect writer must never forget that his reader comes to him with the NHG orthography in his mind. The NHG orthography has, in fact, willy-nilly to be his starting-point. His first difficulty then is that the application of many spelling conventions of NHG is impossible. The NHG use of *ie* for long *i*, for instance, is impossible or confusing in a dialect which has a diphthong [iə]. If the dialect has a diphthong [ei], how is the writer to express it in view of the circumstance that *ei* in NHG stands for [ae]? The use of double consonants to indicate the shortness of the preceding vowel (e.g. *kommen, Mutter*) is possible in NHG where all consonants are short, but in dialects where there are both short and long consonants this method would be confusing and has to be abandoned. The difference between *p, t, k* and *b, d, g* is basically one of voice in NHG, but in many dialects *b, d, g* are voiceless lenes. Many sound values cannot be expressed within the limitations of NHG orthography. For the very advanced *a* of Alsatian and the rounded back *a* of Austro-Bavarian NHG provides only the letter *a*, so that a word spelt *Rachen* would in an Alsatian text be [raxə] 'rake' (*Rechen*) and in a Bavarian text be [rɔxɒ] 'throat' (*Rachen*). It is therefore understandable that E. Dieth in his *Schwyzertütschi Dialäktschrift*, Zürich, 1938, should state: 'Müssig ist es darum, Dialekte mit den Bildern und Schreibregeln der Hochsprache wiedergeben zu wollen' (p. 41). Arising from this feeling of insufficiency certain regional spelling conventions have developed, e.g. *å* in Austria, *ao* in Low German for the rounded back *a* approaching *o*. Swiss-German writers commonly use *y* for long *i*, so that *ie* is free to express the diphthong [iə].[2] Where the NHG rules of pronunciation are not commonly followed, e.g. with regard to *st, sp, g, w, ch, k*, the dialect writers see no need to depart from the NHG orthography. In North Low Saxon *st* and *sp* are pronounced *s + t* or *s + p* even in NHG where the pronunciation is [št] and [šp], and in Switzerland and Swabia, at least the older generation say [št] and [šp] in all positions and are unaware of the NHG arrangement. In the Low German pronunciation of NHG *sagt* or *Tag* the *g* is a fricative. In consequence *g* is used in **Low German** dialect writing for a fricative. Many Swiss

---

[1] See Martin, *op. cit., Schweizer Dialekte in Text und Ton*, and *Lautbibliothek der deutschen Mundarten* where phonemic transcriptions are given alongside phonetic ones.
[2] See Mitzka, *Hdb.*, pp. 42–7.

speakers will pronounce NHG *w* as a bilabial, NHG *ch* always as a velar fricative and NHG *k* always as an affricate [kx]. The dialect writer sees therefore no need to indicate this local dialect feature in spelling. Sounds which are notoriously troublesome in dialect writing are *r* and *l* with their frequent vocalizations and front and back varieties. All these difficulties are immaterial so long as a particular piece of dialect writing is not supposed to be read by any but the speakers of that dialect. Max Dingler[1] is a representative of the view that it is not the task of the dialect writer to instruct the reader who is unfamiliar with the dialect about the correct pronunciation. In contrast to this negative attitude we find frequently the wish expressed that the orthography of a dialect should bring out as far as possible the phonetic peculiarities. Part of the attraction of dialect writing is, of course, the sound of the dialect, which ought not to be lost. Thus E. Dieth in his Swiss anthology *Soo reded s dihäi*, Zürich, 1939, gives the texts in an orthography so that 'Der Leser sollte aus der Umschrift den besonderen Dialekt gleichsam heraushören . . .'. The *Hamburger Richtlinien* of C. Borchling and W. Niekerken are also meant to give the non-North Low German reader guidance with regard to the correct pronunciation of North Low German dialect texts. (See p. 24.)

There are broadly speaking three different approaches to the problem of dialect spelling: (*a*) the resigned attitude which makes no attempt to render the dialect sounds in a manner instructive to the outsider, and which retains the NHG orthography with fewest possible deviations; (*b*) the compromising attitude which wants to have a script which conveys the sounds of the dialect to the non-dialect speaker but nevertheless follows NHG orthography wherever possible; and (*c*) the radical attitude which wants to get completely away from NHG orthography either for reasons of spelling reform or for other reasons.

The first attitude is that of M. Dingler who says (*op. cit.*, p. 12): 'Der Mundartschriftsteller soll (im Gegensatz zum Sprachgelehrten) nicht vom Schriftdeutsch, von der allgemein gültigen hochdeutschen Rechtschreibung loszukommen, sondern umgekehrt sich an sie anzulehnen trachten.' His *Richtlinien für die bairische Mundartschreibung* (pp. 97–103) include the following rules: nasalization of vowels need not be expressed; the apostrophe is to be used where in the dialect, in comparison with NHG, sounds or syllables are dropped, thus the dat. and acc. of certain pronouns, indistinguishable in dialect, use the apostrophe because the distinction is made in NHG; the

---

[1] *Geschriebene Mundart, d. i. wohlerwogene und beherzigenswerte Regeln für die einheitliche und gemeinverständliche Schreibung der bayrischen Redeweise in Vers und Prosa*, Erfurt, 1941.

C

dialectal unrounding of *ö, ü, eu, äu* is not to be indicated; lengthened *i* is to be spelt *ie*, but for the diphthong the spelling *ia* is traditional and to be retained; assimilations and the vocalization of *r* and *l* are not to be expressed. He does, however, provide for the distinction of front *a* from the rounded back *a* [ɔ], by spelling *aa* for the former and *a* for the latter. The spelling with *o* is rejected.

Max Dingler's attitude is the attitude of most dialect writers inside Germany[1] and Austria, although many of them would not so willingly and deliberately abandon all attempts at rendering their dialect so that its phonetic character would be indicated or at least hinted at. The criticism[2] which has been raised against this mixture of the NHG orthography with arbitrary and unsystematic attempts at phonetic rendering of a dialect has had little success. Mostly it demanded a phonetic spelling system which was plainly impossible for the purposes of the dialect writers.[3] However, the second approach, the compromising attitude, is rarely more than a pious wish. The basic factor of these two approaches is, however, the retention of NHG orthography. This has an enormous practical advantage. The writer has at once a public ready to read his works. The readers are used to the NHG orthography—misleading and inconsistent as its principles are. They recognize the dialect words easily and are not confused. Any departure from NHG orthography erects a barrier between the dialect writer and his ordinary reader. It takes a great deal of effort for most people to read an unfamiliar spelling system. Few will be prepared to make it. For this reason a group of the most successful Swiss dialect writers, e.g. Rudolf von Tavel, Simon Gfeller, and Josef Reinhart, agreed not to depart from the NHG orthography except where it is absolutely necessary.[4] The spelling *ie* for long *i* is obviously impossible for Swiss German as *ie* must render the diphthong [iə]. On the other hand long vowels are left in the inconsistent NHG orthography, e.g. *Moos, Sohn, rot*. Double spelling of long vowels in open syllables is, however, necessary as there are also short vowels in that position. The NHG consonants are retained, e.g. *kenne* or *känne* not *kchäne* or *kchänne* 'to know'.

---

[1] See e.g. *Ons Muselland*, ed. J. Feiten and H. Spoo, Trier, 1950, p. 5: 'Hier ist ein Mittelweg gewählt, der sich soviel wie nur möglich an das vom Hochdeutschen her gewohnte Wortbild hält.'

[2] See K. Haag, 'Über Mundartenschreibung', *ZfhdMaa.*, ii, 1901, 289–96, and his rev. of R. Wintermantel, *Von des Schwarzwalds Höhen, ib.*, i, 1900, 185–7.

[3] E.g. F. Lüers, 'Die bayerischen Mundarten und ihre Wiedergabe im Schriftbild', *Bayerische Wochenschrift für Pflege von Heimat und Volkstum*, ix, 81–7, 97–101, 113–18, with his detailed phonetic system of over four dozen signs. His attitude is: 'Oberster Grundsatz muss jedoch immer bleiben: Schreibe, wie du sprichst, ohne Rücksicht auf die Regeln schriftdeutscher Rechtschreibung.'

[4] See G. Küffer, *Heimatglüt*, Berne, 1921.

Gotthold Schmid, the editor of *Schwyzerlüt*,[1] the only periodical entirely in Swiss German, follows their policy. For him the main thing is that his language is written and read by as many as possible even if the spelling system is defective and does not satisfy every philologist, phonetician or spelling reformer. He has success on his side, for any reform inclined to make the step from NHG orthography to dialect spelling more difficult has failed and is bound to fail as long as dialect orthography is not taught at school.

In Luxemburg, for instance, it is not the excellent phonemic spelling system of the *Lezebuurjer Ortografi* of 1946 which has had some measure of success but the Engelmann-Welter spelling system which follows the NHG orthography.[2] In the nineteenth century the Luxemburg dialect had been spelt mainly in the method of Dicks (Edmund de la Fontaine)[3] with its French-inspired diacritic marks (*e, é, è, ê*). R. Engelmann published his 'Vorschläge zur Regelung der luxemburgischen Rechtschreibung' in 1916[4] and subsequently agreed with Nikolaus Welter on an orthography which is based on the NHG spelling system.[5] Their rules include: long consonants are not usually indicated but shortness of vowel is expressed by doubling of the subsequent consonant (therefore NHG *Katze*: Lux. *Kaz* but NHG *Tal*: Lux. *Dall*, NHG *dumm*: Lux. *domm*); the long vowel before consonantal clusters is indicated by circumflex (*mâchen*: NHG *machen*); [ɛ] is spelt either *e* or *ä* as in NHG; [ə] in stressed syllables is spelt *e*, or *ē* in cases where confusion might arise, or *ö* according to the etymology; the diphthongs [ou] and [ei] are rendered by *o'* and *e'* (*gro'ss*: NHG *gross*; *schwe'er*: NHG *schwer*); the hardening of final consonants is expressed except where the NHG counterpart is spelt with what represents a voiced consonant (*en ass*: NHG *er ist* but *Hand, Lidd*: NHG *Lied*); *v* and *f* are used as in NHG.

Michel Rodange, the author of Luxemburg's national epic *De Renert*, 1872, created his own orthography, which, in contrast to nineteenth-century practice, was largely based on the NHG orthography.[6] The modern editions since J. Tockert's *Jubiläumsausgabe* follow the Engelmann-Welter orthography. It is highly significant that the excellent *Luxemburger Wörterbuch*, 1950 ff., did not adopt the radical solution of 1946 but returned to the attitude of compromise, along the lines of Engelmann-Welter with NHG orthography as the basis.

---

[1] Fribourg, Schwyzerlüt-Verlag, 1938 ff.
[2] See *Luxemburger Wörterbuch*, 1950, vol. i. *Einleitung*, pp. xlv-li.
[3] *Versuch über die Orthographie der Luxemburger deutschen Mundart*, 1855.
[4] In *Auf heimatlichen Pfaden*, Diekirch, pp. 64–98.
[5] See N. Welter, *Mundartliche und hochdeutsche Dichtung in Luxemburg*, Luxemburg, 1923, pp. 381–7.
[6] See J. Tockert, *Jubiläumsausgabe von Rodanges Werken in Luxemburger Mundart*, Luxemburg, 1927, chapter on 'Sprache und Rechtschreibung des Renert'. Rodange's rules are reprinted also in the 1939 edition, p. 17 f.

In no region has the problem of dialect spelling been discussed so much as in North Germany. Since Klaus Groth's *Quickborn*, 1851, and the subsequent Low German renaissance there have been many attempts to draw up rules for a Low German orthography which would not be so dependent on NHG as to make an adequate rendering of Low German phonology impossible, but which would be close enough to NHG to enable the North German man in the street to read Low German, and which would help to bridge the gap between the numerous local dialects.[1] Reuter wanted to re-create a Low German written language. The ghost of Middle Low German has played a very great part in the Low German discussion. The alleged former unity, alas now lost, was a dream which inspired many a reformer, e.g. Garbe. However, most Low German experts favour etymological spelling rather than phonetic spelling and most also acknowledge the supremacy of NHG, the orthography of which must, by and large, be accepted. Few, however, go as far as Bremer, who, like Dingler, was of the opinion that the spelling should not be expected to instruct the non-dialect speaker as to correct pronunciation. By contrast, the *Lübecker Richtlinien* and C. Borchling do not want to create a common Low German written language, but to set up an orthography based on a few simple rules which can be easily followed by the dialect writers while retaining the characteristics of their own particular dialects. Where the etymological and phonetic principles clash the former is to give way. Nevertheless any phonetically unnecessary departure from NHG, even where it would lead to greater consistency, is ruled out. The *Hamburger Richtlinien* by W. Niekerken, in agreement with C. Borchling, deviate very little from Borchling's earlier suggestions, and it is claimed that 'wer aber die niederdeutsche Sprache nicht beherrscht, kann sich durch die vorliegende Schreibweise sicher führen lassen'. As *ee* and *öö* denote diphthongs (cf.

---

[1] F. Reuter, preface to *Läuschen un Riemels*, 4th ed., 1859; K. Groth, *Quickborn*, preface to 1st ed. and 3rd ed., 1854, with introduction by Müllenhoff; A. Stuhlmann, *To'r nederdüütsche rechtschriwung*, 1901; Robert Garbe, *Upkwalm*, pref., 1921; O. Bremer, *Regeln für die plattdeutsche Rechtschreibung*, 1914; *Lübecker Richtlinien*, 1919, by a committee; Franz Fromme, 'Was wollen wir mit den Lübecker Richtlinien?', *Niederdeutsche Monatshefte*, viii, 1933, 17–22; against the Lübecker Richtlinien: Wilhelm Wisser, 'Zur plattdeutschen Orthographie', *Niedersachsen*, xxxiii, 1928, 281–6; and: H. Stolte, *Wie schreibe ich die Mundart meiner Heimat? Ein Beitrag zur niederdeutschen Rechtschreibung und Mundartforschung auf der Grundlage der Ravensberger Mundart in Brockhagen und Steinhagen*, Leipzig, 1925 (primitive); C. Borchling, *Regeln für die Mundarten des Nordniedersächsischen Raumes*, Neumünster, 1935; J. Sass, *Plattdeutsches Wörterverzeichnis mit den Regeln für die plattdeutsche Rechtschreibung*, Hamburg, 1935; *Hamburger Richtlinien*: W. Niekerken, *Niederdeutsche Lehr- u. Lesehefte, Niklaas von J. H. Fehrs*, Neumünster, 1949, pp. 5–11; *Fehrs-Gilde: Regeln für die plattdeutsche Rechtschreibung*, Hamburg—Wellingsbüttel, 1956; J. Sass, 'Möglichkeiten, Voraussetzungen und Grenzen einer plattdeutschen Rechtschreibung', *Festschrift Boeck*, pp. 232–40.

English name; Gm. *öi*) the long monophthongs are expressed by the new signs *ę* and *ǫ*. Hardening in final position is indicated by the letters *-f, -s, -t, -ch* while the final lenis sounds with overlong preceding vowel are spelt *-v, -ſ, -d, -g*. Sass rejects letters which do not occur in NHG and spells the final sounds as in NHG. His spelling system is thus closer to NHG orthography but less phonetic than the Borchling-Niekerken system. Under the auspices of the Fehrs-Gilde representative specialists (Prof. Braak, Flensburg; H. Ehrke, Kiel; H. Diers, Oldenburg; Prof. Niekerken and Joh. Sass, Hamburg) met in February 1956 and settled their differences. The new compromise makes, for instance, the following provisions:[1] only NHG letters are used; *h* as a mark of length is used as in NHG; vowel length is expressed by doubling except where NHG uses other means, e.g. *h, ie*; shortness of a vowel is indicated by doubling the following consonant; the NHG spelling of *d, t, g, ch* in final position is retained; overlength of a vowel can be indicated by an apostrophe, *de Lüüd'* 'people'; with regard to the diphthongal and monophthongal varieties of *e* and *ö* the diphthongal form is spelt *ee* and *öö*, the monophthongal is either not distinguished from it or is spelt *ä, ę, oe* or *ǫ*. In this latter respect no agreement was therefore achieved and the new rule amounts to little more than an agreement to disagree.

In many ways the Low German discussion, adopting an attitude of compromise, has led to a solution which is very close to that of the Engelmann-Welter orthography for Luxemburg.

The radical attitude with regard to dialect spelling of those who want to cut free from the NHG system is found mainly outside Germany and Austria. It is primarily inspired by national interest. Such is the case of the *Šwizer Folchšrift* of E. Baer and A. Baur[2] and of the *Lezebuurjer Ortografi*, 1946. E. Dieth's *Schwyzertütschi Dialäktschrift*[3] departs from the NHG orthography mainly for phonetic reasons, but was naturally aided by the political circumstances of the times, which were favourable to such a departure.

The fundamental difference between the Baer-Baur system and that of Dieth is that the former aims at a uniform spelling system for the whole of German-speaking Switzerland. It minimizes dialectal differences and hides them wherever possible. It is in effect a skeleton orthography which achieves its aim merely by sacrificing nearly all phonetic considerations. It pretends as little as English orthography to be a guide to pronunciation for the outsider. It was intended to

---

[1] The Fehrs-Gilde rules are reprinted and applied in Joh. Sass, *Kleines plattdeutsches Wörterbuch*, Hamburg, Fehrs-Gilde, 1957.

[2] *Schribed wien er reded! Ifüerig id Schwizer Folchschrift*, Zürich, 1937; A. Baur, *Praktische Sprachlehre des Schweizerdeutschen*, Zürich, 1939, 2nd ed., 1941.

[3] *Schwyzertütschi Dialäktschrift*, Zürich, 1938.

pave the way in Switzerland for a national Alemannic *Schriftsprache*.
Some of its recommendations are: vowel length is not to be indicated
(the dialect words corresponding to NHG *lehren, gesehen, Zeit, Zahl,
Seele, Klee* take the form of *lere, gse, zit, zal, sel, chle*); *ei* represents
[ai], [æi] [ei], e.g. Zt. *frei* [ei] and *weis* [æi] = Bd [ei]; there are only
single consonants even where the dialects have a geminate or a long
consonant; *ou* stands for [ou] and [æu]; *z* for [ts], *f* for [f], e.g. *nazion,
fom fater*: NHG *Nation, vom Vater*; *q* for [k] as *k* represents [kx], e.g.
eqe, qä: NHG *Ecke, gegeben*; for NHG *sch š* is suggested and for *ch*
and *ng* there are non-compulsory alternative new signs; no capitals
for nouns. The following extract illustrates not only the orthography
but also the spirit which guided the venture:

Iez wil der ferzele, wie mer uf die šribwis sind cho. S eršt, wo
mer is gseit händ, iš gsi: Wän mer öusi eige šproch in iren eigene
gseze wänd gšpüren und erläbe, so müend mer eren es šriftgwändli
gä, won ere past. Iri gštalt und iri šöni mues durešine dur d šrift
wie d forme fomene šöne lib dur s chleid. S hochtütš gwand past
ere numemol nöd. Das wüsed mer. Drum heist s: Frei wärde fom
hochtütše šriftgsez! Wie men im tütšen es wort šribt, got öus i der
šwizeršproch nüt me a (p. 7).[1]

The *Folchšrift* has been an abortive attempt largely because it took
on too much. The NHG standard language is entrenched so firmly in
Switzerland that not even the Nazis succeeded in seriously shaking
it. It is true, its position has changed. It is regarded more as a foreign
though closely related tongue, which one has to learn. The dialects
have acquired a patriotic halo which will sustain them for some time
to come in their difficult struggle against the ever-increasing pressure
of the standard language. The second line of attack was even more
foolhardy. The dialects are local dialects. People take pride in and
love their local speech first—the *Bärndütsch, Züritüütsch* or *Baaselditsch*—and only in the second place the vaguer notion of *Schwyzertütsch*. Dialect writers will want to bring out the characteristic features
of their dialects, not to hide them. In short, in view of the present-day

---

[1] Cf. with NHG: 'Jetzt will ich Dir erzählen, wie wir auf diese Schreibweise
gekommen sind. Das erste, das wir uns sagten, war: Wenn wir unsere eigene
Sprache in ihren eigenen Gesetzen spüren und erleben wollen, so müssen wir
ihr ein Schriftkleid geben, das ihr passt. Ihre Gestalt und ihre Schönheit muss
durch die Schrift hindurchscheinen wie die Formen eines schönen Körpers
durch das Kleid. Das hochdeutsche Kleid passt ihr nun einfach einmal nicht.
Das wissen wir. Darum heisst es: Frei werden vom hochdeutschen Schrift-
gesetz! Wie man im Deutschen ein Wort schreibt, geht uns in der Schweizer-
sprache nichts mehr an.'—Much of this is, incidentally, the sort of spurious
dialect written by people who think in NHG and translate into dialect phonology and morphology. (See p. 13.)

linguistic situation of Switzerland, Baer's attempt was bound to fail.

It is precisely on this point that Dieth's *Schwyzertütschi Dialäktschrift* is realistic. It does not set up one uniform spelling system for all Swiss dialects, but lays down rules which allow the individual features to be expressed. Dieth's idea was 'Während wir bis jetzt neben der Buntheit der Ortsdialekte noch die Buntheit der verschiedenen Schreibmethoden gehabt haben, so haben wir von nun an nur noch *eine* Methode, und diese gestattet, den wirklichen Laut hinter dem Buchstaben zu hören.' Some of his recommendations are: everyone writes as he hears; long consonants and geminates are spelt with double consonants (*lauffe, macche, Sune*: NHG *laufen, machen, Sonne*); *sch* is replaced by ʃ; vowel length is expressed by doubling (*Baad, Beder*: NHG *Bad, Bäder*) except for [i:] for which *y* is traditional in Switzerland since MHG times; *ei* = [ei], *äi* = [æi], *ē* = [ɛ], *ä* = [æ]; the open, lax vowel variant is indicated by the *grave* (*o, ò*); apostrophes and hyphens are to be avoided; capitals are used only at the beginning of a sentence, for proper names and polite forms.

Dieth's proposals envisage a less radical solution for the 'transition period' which preserves a number of spelling devices of NHG, e.g. doubling of consonants in words like *Bett, Stimm*; use of capitals; and abandons the innovations ʃ, *cch, ò, ù,* etc. In its radical form the *Dialäktschrift* is found in *Soo reded s dihäi*, Zürich, 1939. Its great drawback is that it expects every writer and reader to be a minor phonetician, to observe himself constantly and to decide whether a consonant is long (or fortis) or short (lenis) and whether a vowel is open or close, long or short. As these quantities are frequently dependent on sentence stress the decision is by no means easy. Few writers will make this effort, which is troublesome and directs their attention too much to the technical detail of spelling and makes a major operation out of it. The moderate version is, however, excellently suited. It retains much of the phonemic character of the radical solution without making the departure from NHG orthography too big. Compared with the traditional, unsystematic spelling of the text by R. von Tavel (pp. 105 ff.) the modified *Schwyzertütschi Dialäktschrift* of T. Vogel's short story (pp. 73 ff.) is a definite improvement.

The following passage is a transcription of the Baer text in Dieth's *Schwyzertütschi Dialäktschrift*:

'Iez wil der verzele, wie mer uf die ʃrybwys sind choo. S eerʃt, wo mer is gsäit händ, iʃ gsy: Wän mer öisi äige ʃpraach in iren äigene gsetze wänd gʃpüüren und erläbe, so müend mer eren es ʃriftgwändli gëë, won ere passt. Iri gʃtalt und iri ʃööni mues dureʃyne dur d ʃrift wie d forme vomene ʃööne lyb dur s chläid. S hoochtüütʃ gwand passt ere numemaal nöd. Daas wüssed mer. Drum häissts: Frei wëërde vom hoochtüütſe ſriftgsetz! Wie men im tüütſen es woort ſrybt, gaat öis i der ſwyzerſpraach nüt me aa.'

Another radical solution is the *Lezebuurjer Ortografi* of 1946.[1] It is a bold and ingenious attempt to break loose from the NHG orthographic traditions and to base the spelling on modern phonemic methods. It is successful in every respect but one: it has not won the popularity it deserves. It is an excellent reflection of Luxemburg phonology, observes the principles of phonetic spelling, yet is graphically and visually satisfactory. Its first principle is reminiscent of Baer's attitude: 'Et get net derno gekukt, vou e vuurt hiirkennt ooder vei et an ènger aanerer shprooch geschrive get. Et get nemen derno gekukt, vei et am lezebuurjeshe geshwaat get.' [2]

Some of the rules are: vowel length is indicated by doubling; the e- sounds are spelt as in French é, è—e indicates both the unstressed neutral vowel and the stressed central vowel [ə]; nasalized vowels in French loan-words have a circumflex (*shâber*: Fr. *chambre*); the voiced consonants *b, d, g, v, jh, j, gh* are replaced in final position by *p, t, k, f, sh, ch* (*Auslautsverhärtung*) even where sandhi prevents this hardening; *l, n, m, ng* occur both long and short and this is expressed in spelling, otherwise there are only single consonants; *f* is the voiceless labiodental, *v* the voiced, *w* the bilabial fricative in certain positions (*kwafeur*: Fr. *coiffeur*); *s* is voiced, the voiceless [s] is doubled (*ss*) but only where voiced *s* also occurs, *z* stands for [ts]; for NHG *sch* the English *sh* or, if voiced, *jh* is used; *ch* is as in NHG a palatal and a velar fricative, if voiced *gh* is used; the foreign spellings *th, ph* are replaced by *t, f*; capitals only for proper names and the beginning of a sentence.

This spelling system is used in at least one schoolbook: *Lezebuurjer Gedichter a Proosashteker fiir ons Shoulen*, Luxemburg, 1951.

The following passage gives the first two strophes of the extract from Rodange's *De Renert* (p. 281) in the *Lezebuurjer Ortografi*:

> Am shlas hieft fuus de shwènzchen
> sou riicht aals vi e poul,
> géét mazen duurch seng fainden
> éériicht zum kineksshtul.

---

[1] Arreté ministériel du 5 juin 1946 portant fixation d'un système officiel d'orthographe luxembourgeoise. Extrait du « Mémorial » No. 40, du 7 septembre 1946.

[2] Cf. NHG: 'Es wird nicht darnach geschaut, wo ein Wort herkommt, oder wie es in einer anderen Sprache geschrieben wird. Es wird nur mehr darauf geschaut, wie es im Luxemburgischen ausgesprochen wird.'

E sèzt sech duur op t kneien,
de kinek kukt ewèch.
De fuus fèngt un ze leien,
an aal aablèk mei frèch.

What this survey has shown is that if a dialect spelling system is to give the reader any idea of the dialect phonology it must be phonemic and systematic. Dialect spelling should, however, not be confused with the spelling reform of NHG. Dialect spelling should be alphabetic and, if it is to appeal to a wider public, it must avoid all unnecessary departures from the NHG orthographic system. All dialect texts given in this book fulfil this latter condition. It has, however, been necessary occasionally to alter the spelling of the author where it obliterated certain important phonemic differences. This is clearly indicated wherever it has been done.

CHAPTER II

SCHWYZERTÜTSCH: ZÜRITÜÜTSCH

§ 1. AREA AND STATUS

Schwyzertütsch is a somewhat artificial name for a great variety of dialects spoken in Switzerland north of the Romance–Germanic linguistic boundary. Some of the most salient features of these dialects are also found in adjacent dialects beyond the political frontiers of Switzerland, e.g. in the Austrian province of Vorarlberg, in Liechtenstein, in the frontier regions north of the Rhine in Baden-Württemberg and in the southernmost part of Alsace. A few isolated villages south of the Alps in Italy belong linguistically also to the same Alemannic area. Most dialects spoken in this fairly extensive region are grouped together as *High Alemannic*, while some, nevertheless known as *Schwyzertütsch*, notably the dialect of the City of Basle, belong to *Low Alemannic*.[1]

The justification for the use of *Schwyzertütsch* for a multiplicity of dialects lies in the social attitude of the Germanic speakers of Switzerland towards their dialects and in the fact that the linguistic divergences are not such as to make intercourse in dialect impossible or even difficult. All Germanic-speaking Swiss use their dialect habitually amongst themselves irrespective of social rank or position or regional provenance. Standard German is employed only for writing and as the language of public lectures, sermons and tuition.[2] This

---

[1] On these two terms, see § 2 and chap. IV, § 1.2, and for internal divisions: A. Bachmann in *Geographisches Lexikon der Schweiz*, v, 58 ff.; E. Steiner, *ZfdMaa.*, xix, 1924, 241.

[2] Professor Hotzenköcherle, with an eye on the future development, has well characterized the situation: 'Comme langue de tous les jours, nous parlons tous notre dialecte local au sens le plus strict du terme « local ». Mais à côté de ce dialecte local, ou lui étant superposés, il y a un certain nombre de dialectes régionaux—« le » bernois, « le » zurichois, « le » saint-gallois, etc.; il y a en plus, nous venons de le voir, certaines tendances à une koinê suisse-alémanique; et il y a enfin, la « Schriftsprache », le « Hochdeutsch », que nous ne parlons qu'avec les étrangers et comme « Vortragssprache », mais que nous écrivons et lisons—et que nous écoutons à la radio', p. 130 in 'L'Atlas linguistique et éthnographique de la Suisse alémanique', 115–32, *Essais de Philologie Moderne* (1951), Bibl. de la Fac. de Phil. et Lettres de l'Univ. de Liège, Paris, 1953. On the problem of the linguistic dualism of standard German and *Schwyzertütsch*, see: J. C. Mörikofer, *Die schweizerische Mundart im Verhältnis zur hochdeutschen Schriftsprache*, 1838; W. Wiget, 'Sprachen und Mundarten in der Schweiz', *Språkvetenskapliga Sällskapets i Uppsala Förhandlingar*, 1913–15, 121–34; Otto von Greyerz, 'Vom Wert und Wesen unserer Mundart', pp. 226–47, in *Sprache, Dichtung, Heimat*, Berne, 1933; A. Senn, 'Verhältnis von Mundart und Schriftsprache in der deutschen Schweiz',

universal attitude of at least implied respect for the Swiss dialects distinguishes these dialects from all other German dialects with the exception of that of Luxemburg. *Schwyzertütsch* has a geographical, political, and social existence even if its linguistic homogeneity is rather nebulous. Although the great majority of the *Schwyzertütsch* speakers have no difficulty in understanding each other there is a good deal of mocking and ridiculing of each other's dialectal idiosyncrasies. But with the political significance of *Schwyzertütsch* very much in the foreground after 1933, there is probably less of it among the present generation than ever before. The most archaic dialects of the highest Alpine valleys (*Höchstalemannisch*) spoken by less than 100,000 people are not so easily understood by the rest of the other three million *Schwyzertütsch* speakers. But the difficulties are never so great that recourse must be had to another language, e.g. standard German.

GENERAL CHARACTERISTICS OF HIGH ALEMANNIC

§ 2. THE AREA

The feature which is traditionally singled out to mark off High Alemannic from the rest of the Alemannic dialects (Low Alemannic, Swabian)[1] and from other German dialects is the *ch-* reflex of MHG/NHG initial *k-*. This is Bohnenberger's, Maurer's, Mitzka's *Kind/Chind* isogloss. It runs[2] through the southernmost part of Alsace towards the Rhine (leaves Basle a L. Alem. enclave in H. Alem. territory), follows the river to south of Freiburg and thence crosses the Black Forest in the direction of the Lake of Constance. The upper end of the southern shore, much of the Upper Rhine Valley and Vorarlberg are left north of the isogloss. Keeping these exceptions in mind it is permissible to state that High Alemannic and *Schwyzertütsch* are more or less the same. The former term is based on the

JEGP, xxxiv, 1935, 42–58; Adolf Guggenbühl, *Warum nicht Schweizerdeutsch? Gegen die Missachtung unserer Muttersprache*, Zürich, 1937; L. Forster, 'The Language in German Switzerland', *German Life and Letters*, iv, 1939, 65–73; G. Thürer, *Wesen und Würde der Mundart*, Zürich, 1944; R. E. Keller, 'Schweizerdeutsch', *Archivum Linguisticum*, iv, 1952; P. Zinsli, 'Hochsprache und Mundarten in der deutschen Schweiz', *Der Deutschunterricht*, 1956, Heft 2, 61–72.
  [1] See also E. Ochs, 'Die Gliederung des Alemannischen', *GRM*, ix, 1921, 56–8, reprinted in *Beiträge zur Sprachwissenschaft und Volkskunde, Festschr. f. E. Ochs*, Lahr, 1951, 11–15, with its division into *Nordalem.* (Low Alem. and Swabian), *Mittelalem., Südalem.* (High and Highest Alem.). Different nomenclature: Mitzka, *DPhA*, i, 675–90; Jutz, *Alem. Maa.*, pp. 18–23, Maurer, *Oberrheiner*, etc.
  [2] See the maps in Bohnenberger, *Alem. Ma.*, or Mitzka, *DMaa.*, p. 40; *DPhA*, i. 663–4. L. Jutz, 'Die Grenze k/x < anl. germ. k und die Gliederung des Alemannischen', *Teuth.*, vi, 1929/30, 39–49, attaches more importance to the stop/affricate, fricative contrast before consonants (kxl, khl, xl: kl, gl).

tribal settlement of early medieval times, the latter on the present-day political reality. The dialects of the Alpine valleys show a number of particularly archaic features which place them somewhat apart from the usual High Alemannic. For them the term *Höchstalemannisch* has been used. Occasionally reference is made in the following general description to these peculiarities.

§ 3. Phonological Features[1]

3.1 The Vowels

(1) The MHG long vowels *î, û, iu* are generally preserved. In hiatus position they are diphthongized to *ei, ou, öi,*[2] though not in Highest Alem.

(2) The MHG diphthongs *ie, uo, üe* are generally preserved.

(3) The MHG diphthongs *ei* and *ou* are preserved in the west (Bernese) but lowered in Zürich. Monophthongization occurs both in the west and the east.

(4) Of the three different MHG short *e*- sounds (*e, ẹ, ä*), the primary umlaut occurs as a comparatively close vowel (ε in Berne, *e* in Zürich), *ẹ* and the secondary umlaut coincide in a very open *æ*- sound. Zürich restores however a series of three by calling into being an ε. (See § 8.3.)

(5) MHG *a* is generally preserved, but MHG *â* is in a wide area in the west and east rounded to *ō*, leaving out the Alpine south, Berne and Zürich (cf. § 9.9). Before *sch* (< Gmc. *sk*) *a* is generally palatalized > *ä*.

(6) MHG *ê* and *ô* are generally preserved.

(7) MHG *i* and *u* are also generally preserved, especially before nasals, e.g. *Sunne* 'sun'.

(8) The Lowland dialects do not participate in the unrounding (of *ü, ö, öi*) which is widespread in Alpine dialects. Rounding of MHG *i* and *e* in the surroundings of labials is frequent, e.g. *wüsse* 'to know'.

(9) Nasalization is unknown in the majority of the Alem. dialects, notably Zürich and Bernese, but occurs sporadically.

(10) Initial vowels have a smooth onset. Glottal stop is unknown and *liaison* is general.

3.2 Vowel Quantity

(1) The MHG short vowels in open syllables are on the whole preserved as short vowels, e.g. *zele* 'count', although lengthening in

---

[1] The synchronic description of the eight selected dialects is preceded by an outline survey or an historical identification parade, so to speak, of the larger dialect regions to facilitate a comparison of the various dialects (see fn. 3, p. 12).

[2] For the phonetic value of these letters see § 7.

certain surroundings is met with (§§ 5, 12) and is more general in the north-west of the area (Bohnenberger's *Leichtinnendehnung*).

(2) In monosyllabic words ending in a lenis consonant lengthening is the rule, e.g. *waas?* 'what'; *Spiil* 'play' (Bohnenberger's *Leichtschlussdehnung*, see p. 43).

(3) The MHG long vowels before consonantal clusters are usually preserved, e.g. *praacht* 'brought'. In the west (Bernese) the MHG long vowels *î*, *û*, *iu* are frequently shortened before certain consonants, e.g. *t*, e.g. *Zÿt* 'time'.

(4) *r* has generally a lengthening effect on the preceding vowel.

3.3 Vowels in Unstressed Syllables

(1) The NHG prefixes *ge-* and *be-* generally lose their vowel.

(2) The OHG abstract ending *-î* and the MHG adjectival ending *-iu* are preserved as *-i*.

(3) MHG *-e* has generally dropped, e.g. *Reed* 'speech'.

3.4 The Consonants

(1) The consonantal system is based on an opposition of fortis and voiceless lenis sounds.

(2) Gmc. initial *k-* is shifted to *ch-*.

(3) The cluster *-nk-* occurs as *-nkch-*,[1] except in Highest Alemannic where the nasal is vocalized and *k > ch*.

(4) The velar fricative *ch* has generally no palatal counterpart (no *ich-* sound).

(5) *st* and *sp* are, within one morpheme, always *scht* and *schp*.

(6) MHG medial *-b-* and *-g-* are preserved.

(7) The MHG liquids *r* and *l* are usually preserved, although *l* is frequently 'thick' and in some parts (most Bernese country districts) realized as *u*.

(8) MHG or NHG final *-n* is generally dropped but reintroduced if the next word begins with a vowel, cf. *guete Taag*: *gueten Aabig* 'good day, good evening'. In Highest Alem. this unstressed *-n* is frequently preserved.

(9) Before *s*, *f* plus consonant *n* is usually dropped, the resultant vowel is either long or a diphthong, e.g. *föif*//*füüf* 'five'.

§ 4. Morphological Features

4.1 Noun and Article

(1) The noun has an ending for only one case, the dative plural, in certain dialects, e.g. Zürich. Other dialects do not indicate any cases. The genitive survives only in stereotyped formulas and is otherwise expressed by means of a preposition or a possessive dative

[1] Consonants given in the usual alphabet have the German sound values.

paraphrase (§ 21). No distinction is made between subjective case and direct object.

(2) The general diminutive ending is *-li* usually with umlaut. Without umlaut the dim. (*-eli*) is more intimate. Other suffixes occur in the Alpine dialects.

4.2 *The Adjective*

(1) In the strong declension the plural common case (nom./acc.) and the fem. sg. common case end in *-i*.

4.3 *The Pronouns*

(1) Most personal pronouns distinguish dative and accusative.

(2) The personal pronoun for NHG *uns* goes back to a mutated form (*üns*).

(3) The possessive pronouns NHG *unser, euer* have forms without *-r*.

(4) The attributive possessive pronoun is inflected in the common case neuter sg., e.g. *mys Huus* 'my house'.

(5) The reflexive *sich* is only acc. in genuine dialect.

(6) The relative pronoun is *wo*.

4.4 *The Verbs*

(1) The tense system consists of a present, a perfect and a pluperfect. There is a pres. subj.

(2) The subjunctive preterite serves as a conditional; strong verbs have either strong forms or an analogical weak form in *-ti*.

(3) Eastern dialects (incl. Zürich) have a uniform plural ending in *-ed* (*-id* for subjunctive), while western dialects (incl. Bernese) have two forms: *-e, -ed* (second pers.). Archaic Alpine dialects of the Valais have three forms.

(4) *Rückumlaut* is unknown.

(5) The verb NHG *haben* has mutated forms in 2nd, 3rd pers. sg. and pl.

(6) Mutation occurs only where the root vowel of a strong verb is *-ä-* (*-ē-*). It goes through the whole sg.

(7) For NHG *gewesen* High Alemannic has *gsy*.

(8) The NHG verbs *gehen, stehen* are represented by forms which go back to MHG *gān, stān*.

§ 5. ZÜRITÜÜTSCH

The two fairly homogeneous SGm. dialects which are spoken by the greatest numbers of people are *Züritüütsch* and *Bärndütsch*.[1]

[1] The different ways of spelling *-tütsch* 'German' are accounted for by the different dialectal pronunciations. Thus *Züritüütsch* with long vowel and

Züritüütsch[1] is spoken with only comparatively slight phonological differences by nearly the whole population of the Canton of Zürich, i.e. by about 700,000 people. Adding adjacent areas in the south and west, where the speech differs relatively little from that of Zürich, it can be said that Zt. and the linguistic type it represents is the daily language of nearly a million people. The great importance which the number of speakers, the political and economic weight of the area give it is, however, not matched by any specific linguistic merit. Owing to the cosmopolitan and urban melting-pot character of its centre, Zürich, this dialect is to-day more threatened by linguistic erosion through dialect mixture and the influence of NHG than most other dialects.[2] But Traugott Vogel's short story, chosen to illustrate this dialect, testifies to its vitality and character. Although his language is free from recent and undigested excrescences it is not in the least archaic. It is what would be recognized as good and genuine *Züritüütsch*.

The detailed description of the phonology and the phonetic transcription of part of the text is based on my own dialect, that of Winterthur. It differs from the speech of the rural uplands to the east (Zürcher Oberland) by not sharing the latter's *ō* for MHG/NHG *â*, e.g. Winterthur and Zürich *Haarnaadle*, Oberland *Hoornoodle* 'hair-pin'. There are a number of less striking features which are hardly noticed by the speakers. Winterthur speech is further distinguished from that of the rest of the Canton by its close and tense short *i*, *u*, *ü*, *ö* (= MHG corresponding short vowels), which are lax and open elsewhere. Where lengthening has occurred, these lengthened close vowels coincide with the old close long vowels, while in the rest of the Canton they are kept apart, cf. Winterthur *Züüg* 'stuff' and 'trains', Zürich *Züüg* 'stuff' (*ü* close as in NHG *Hüte*) and *Züüg* 'trains' with open lax *ü* (= a lengthened form of the *ü* in NHG *Hütte*). The number of vowel phonemes in Zürich speech is therefore larger than in Winterthur speech. This is, however, not noticed by the linguistically untrained person. The differences which he regards as characteristic concern different phonemes in certain words, e.g. Winterthur *nid* 'not', Zürich *nüd* (open *ü*), or Winterthur *Bese* initial fortis, *Bärndütsch* with short vowel and initial lenis. Cf. also *Baaselditsch* with unrounded vowel.

[1] On the geographical location, see the maps in E. Steiner, *Geschichtlicher und geographischer Abriss der Schweizerdeutschen Mundart*, Basle, 1937; Weber, *BSG*; *id.*, *ZGr.*; and the article by R. Hotzenköcherle, 'Zur sprachgeographischen Stellung und Struktur des Kantons Zürich', in *Atlas zur Geschichte des Kantons Zürich*, ed. P. Kläui and E. Imhof, Zürich, 1951.

[2] The tendency of regional forms to be eliminated in favour of the form of the capital and the largest number of speakers is well illustrated in an article by R. Hotzenköcherle, 'L'Atlas linguistique et ethnographique de la Suisse alémanique', in *Essais de Philologie moderne* (1951), Paris, 1953, p. 131. The same argument with the map is also found in Henzen, p. 232.

'broom'—Zürich *Bääse*,[1] or certain differences in quantity, e.g. W'thur *zale* 'to pay', Zch. *zaale*.[2]

PHONOLOGY
THE VOWELS
§ 6. The Vowel Phonemes[3]

The vowel system of Zt. in its Winterthur form is very simple. There are nine close or tense vowels which occur both short and long, and one short vowel which occurs only in unstressed position (it can be regarded as an allophone of one of the vowels of the *e-* type). In the case of one vowel (*u*) there is a slight qualitative difference between long (close) and short (tends to be open), but there is a definite tendency for the short vowel to fall into line with all the others and to become close. It is quite clearly quantity which is phonemically distinctive. The tenth vowel /œ:/ occurs only long. It is probably a relic of the former system in which the reflex of MHG *â* was rounded (*ō*).[4] /œ:/ is always the product of mutation of former ɔ̄ (now /ɒ:/).

Front, unrounded	Front, rounded	Back, rounded
i(:)[5]	y(:)	u(:)
e(:)	ø(:)	o(:)
ɛ(:)	œ :	
æ(:)		ɒ(:)

There are nine falling diphthongs: [6]

	Front		Back
high	iə	yə	uə
mid	eɪ	øɪ	oꭥ
low	æɪ	œɪ	æꭥ

[1] For the phonetic value of the letters, see § 7.

[2] On quantity, see § 12; Weber, *ZGr.*, p. 72 and fn. 1.

[3] To include the full phonemic analysis is impossible for reasons of space. The criteria for establishing the phonemes (the types of minimum distinctive sounds) are those of contrasting with other phonemes, of complementary distribution or free variation of the realizations (allophones) of one phoneme, and of phonetic similarity of the allophones constituting a phoneme. Where more than one interpretation is possible (e.g. often in the case of diphthongs and long vowels) I have been guided less by the principle that the smallest number of phonemes affords the best solution than by the consideration of what constitutes the simplest, practical statement of the whole phonological structure of a given dialect. For summary statements of phonological analysis, see B. Bloch and G. L. Trager, *Outline of Linguistic Analysis*, Baltimore, 1942; A. Martinet, *Phonology as Functional Phonetics*, Oxford, 1955.

[4] See B. Boesch, *Untersuchungen zur alemannischen Urkundensprache des 13. Jahrhunderts*, Berne, 1946, p. 74; Weber, *BSG*, pp. 200–2.

[5] The bracket indicates that the vowel occurs both short and long.

[6] A different interpretation of Swiss-German diphthongs is given by A. S. Schultz, 'Segmental Phonemes of Brienzerdeutsch', *Studies in Linguistics*, ix, 1951, 34–65, with remarks by George L. Trager.—The same analysis in principle as mine is given of the dialect of Baselland by W. G. Moulton, *Language*, xxxii, 1956, 751–60.

In Zürich and the rest of the Canton this ten-vowels system based on quantity distinction is slightly complicated by a difference in quality among the high-tongue vowels. Instead of three high-tongue vowels (short and long) there are six (both short and long): i(:) ɪ(:) y(:) ʏ(:) u(:) ɷ(:).[1] The high-tongue elements of the diphthongs are open and lax in this case.

§ 7. SPELLING

The author of our specimen text, Traugott Vogel, uses the simplified *Schwyzertütschi Dialäktschrift* of E. Dieth. (See chap. i, § 6.) It is largely phonemic and therefore on the whole satisfactory. The letters have the following sound values:

Phoneme	Letter	Phoneme	Letter	Phoneme	Letter	Phoneme	Letter
i	i	y	ü	yə	üe	iə	ie
e/ə	e	ø	ö	øɪ	öi	eɪ	ei
ɛ	ë	œ	œ	œɪ	œi		
æ	ä	o	o	oɷ	ou	æɪ	äi
ɒ	a	u	u	uə	ue	æɷ	au

Length is expressed by double letter, e.g. [y:] *üü*. In the case of the high-tongue vowels of which T. Vogel's dialect has six he only distinguishes [i:] = *y* and [ɪ:] = *ii*. The letter *y* for [i:] is traditional and goes back to medieval spelling conventions. The simplified *Schwyzertütschi Dialäktschrift* departs from strictly phonemic principles also in rendering the open and close varieties of the rounded mid-tongue vowel uniformly by *ö*. Dieth's suggestion was to use the grave accent for the open variety. I have preferred the symbol *œ*.

§ 8. STRESSED SHORT VOWELS

8.1 [i] this is a close, high-front vowel which represents:

(i) MHG *i* in positions unaffected by lengthening (see § 12): *isch* 'is', *Chind* 'child'. Only in Winterthur is this *i* close, elsewhere it is open.

(ii) MHG *ĭ* in a few cases where it has been shortened. This shortened *i* is close everywhere: *Side* 'silk'. In unstressed position it is open and lax.

8.2 [e] this is a close, tense, mid-front vowel representing:

(i) MHG *e* (the so-called primary umlaut[2] including Gmc. *e* not

---

[1] Most SGm. dialects have six high-tongue vowels (both short and long), see chap. iii, § 2. Winterthur goes in this respect with its northern neighbour dialect of Schaffhausen, cf. H. Wanner, *BSG*, xx, p. 7.

[2] On the occurrence of the primary umlaut, see W. Braune—W. Mitzka, *Althochdeutsche Grammatik*, 8th ed., 1953, §§ 26, 27, 51; H. Paul—W. Mitzka, *Mittelhochdeutsche Grammatik*, 18th ed., 1959, § 41.

D

raised $> i$ before i- sounds) in positions unaffected by conditional changes (see §§ 8.3; 8.4; 8.8; 9.2): *Gsell* 'journeyman', *setze* 'put'.

This primary umlaut e ($<$ Gmc. a or in rare cases $<$ Gmc. e before i) was in MHG and is to-day in most Alem. dialects carefully kept apart from the reflex of Gmc. e before sounds other than i- sounds.[1] This is all the more remarkable as phonetically speaking the two sounds must have crossed each other at one stage: Gmc. $a > æ > ε > e$/Gmc. $e > ε > æ$. Recent studies have shown how this phenomenon, inexplicable in phonetic terms, can be explained from a structural, phonemic point of view.[2]

8.3 [ε] is an open, mid-front vowel, approximating to NHG e in *Bett*. It derives from:

(i) MHG e before r- clusters, before ch and in a few isolated cases if the quantity remains unchanged; *mërke* 'to notice', *hërt* 'hard', *schwëcher* 'weaker'.

(ii) MHG $ë$ in *Wërchstatt* 'workshop'.

(iii) It occurs in loan-words: *Fërie* 'holidays'.

This vowel cannot just be regarded as a positional variant of [e] before r- clusters because we also find [ε:] and [e:] and because both [e] and [æ] can occur before r- clusters (*Erle* 'alder', *Kärli* 'chap'). It appears, however, that [ε] was first a positional variant before r-clusters. It is rare.

8.4 [æ] is a very open, low-front vowel which derives from the following sources:

(i) MHG $ë$ where it is unaffected by the context (see [ε:] and [æ:]): *Wält* 'world', *Fäld* 'field'.

(ii) MHG $ä$ (the so-called secondary umlaut[3]) where it is unaffected

---

[1] See H. Paul, 'Zur Geschichte des germanischen Vokalismus', *Beitr.*, vi, 1879, 85; *id.*, 'Nachträgliches zum germanischen Vokalismus', *ib.*, xii, 1887, 548–54; K. Luick, 'Die Qualität des mhd. e nach den lebenden Dialekten', *Beitr.*, xi, 1886, 492–517; Fr. Kauffmann, 'Geschlossenes e aus ë vor i', *Beitr.*, xiii, 1888, 393 f.; A. Heusler, 'Zur Lautform des Alemannischen', *Germania*, 1889, 112–30; K. Zwierzina, 'Mittelhochdeutsche Studien. Die e- Laute in den Reimen der mhd. Dichter', *ZfdA*, xliv, 1900, 249–316; J. W. Nagl, 'Zur Aussprache des ahd. mhd. ë in den oberdeutschen Mundarten', *Beitr.*, xviii, 1894, 262–9; K. von Bahder, *Grundlagen des nhd. Lautsystems*, Strassburg, 1890, 104–54; W. Streitberg, V. Michels, M. J. Jellinek, *Die Erforschung der indogermanischen Sprachen. Germanisch*, Berlin, 1936, 381–95; L. Jutz, *Alem. Maa.*, 37–9, 49–55.

[2] W. F. Twaddell, 'A Note on OHG Umlaut', *Monatshefte f. dt. Unterricht*, xxx, 1938, 177–81; *id.*, 'The Prehistoric Germanic Short Syllabics', *Language*, xxiv, 1948, 139–51; H. Penzl, 'Umlaut and Secondary Umlaut in OHG', *ib.*, xxv, 1949, 223–40; J. Kuryłowicz, 'The Germanic Vowel System', *Bulletin of the Polish Academy*, 1952, 51–4; J. Fourquet, 'The two e's of MHG: a diachronic phonemic approach', *Word*, viii, 1952, 122–35; J. W. Marchand, 'The Phonemic Status of OHG E', *Word*, xii, 1956, 82–90.

[3] See fn. 2, p. 37.

by lengthening (see § 9.4): *Gschlächt* 'family', *Bäch* 'streams', and the analogical umlaut:[1] *Wälder* 'woods', *Händ* 'hands'.

(iii) MHG *a* before *sch* (< *sk*): *Täsche* 'bag'.

(iv) MHG *e* (primary umlaut) before nasal clusters: *Mäntsch* 'human being', *tänke* 'think'.

(v) It occurs frequently in loan-words: *Adrässe* 'address', *Chäler* 'Keller' < Lat. *cellarius*, or 'cellar'. It is altogether the most frequent of the *e*- sounds.

8.5 [ɒ] is a low-back, slightly rounded vowel, about like Northern English *a* in *all*. Pronunciation varies a good deal and the slight rounding (*o*- colouring) may be absent altogether. It is, however, always a definite back vowel. It represents:

(i) MHG *a* where lengthening has not interfered and no conditional changes have occurred (see § 8.4 (iii)): *Vatter* 'father', *fascht* 'almost'.

8.6 [o] is a close, rounded, mid-tongue back vowel. It represents:

(i) MHG *o* where lengthening has not occurred, except in a few cases where a shift to *u* has taken place: *Hose* 'trousers', *Wonig* 'flat'.

8.7 [u] is a rounded, high-tongue, back vowel which in Zürich is open [ɷ] if not the product of recent shortening, in Winterthur only slightly more close. It represents:

(i) MHG *u* in cases where lengthening has not interfered: *Kunscht* 'art', *bsunders* 'especially'.

(ii) MHG *o* in certain words especially before nasals and liquids: *gschwume* 'swum', *Wule* 'wool', *Wuche* 'week'.

(iii) MHG *û* in certain frequently unstressed words: *usse* 'outside'.

(iv) MHG dialectal *u* where umlaut had not taken place particularly before a fortis velar:[2] *Rugge* 'back', *Chuchi* 'kitchen'.

In Zürich a distinction is made between open *u* (the large majority of cases) and close *u* (onomatopoeic words and in cases of recent shortening of *û*. Such cases of shortening are rare in Winterthur).

8.8 [ø] is like [o] a close, rounded, mid-tongue vowel, but of the front series. It stands for:

(i) MHG *ö* except where lengthening has occurred: *chöne* 'to be able', *Chöpf* 'heads'.

(ii) MHG *e* in labial surroundings: *schmöcke* 'smell', *chlöpfe* 'bang'.

(iii) MHG *ē* in the words *öpper* 'somebody', *öppis* 'something', *öppe* 'about' adv.

Outside the Winterthur district this vowel tends to be open [œ] before *ch* and *r*, at least among the older generation.

---

[1] By analogical umlaut is meant an umlaut which was not brought about by a phonetic process (palatalization) but which was introduced for morphological reasons.

[2] See W. Wiget, *ZfdMaa.*, 1924, pp. 250–69.

8.9 [y] is a close, high-tongue, front vowel and represents:
(i) MHG *ü* except where it is lengthened: *Züri* 'Zürich', *übel* 'evil'.
(ii) MHG *i* in labial surroundings: *schwüme* 'swim'.
(iii) MHG *iu* in *hüt* 'to-day'.

As in the case of the other high-tongue vowels *i* and *u*, this vowel is open [Y] outside the Winterthur area except where it occurs in onomatopoeic words or where it has been shortened from MHG *iu* after the lowering of *ü* > [Y].

§ 9. LONG VOWELS

9.1 [i:] is a tense, close, high-front vowel. It derives from:
(i) MHG *î* except where shortening occurred (see [i]) or in hiatus position where it was diphthongized (see § 10.7) or in some isolated cases of 'breaking' before *ch*: *blybe* 'remain', *Zyt* 'time'.
(ii) MHG *i* in monosyllabic words ending in a lenis: *Spiil* 'game', but cf. *spile* 'to play'. T. Vogel spells this long vowel *ii* since it is lax and open and distinguished from the old long *i* outside the district of Winterthur. This also holds good for:
(iii) MHG *i* before *r*- clusters: *stiirbt* 'dies', *Wiirt* 'innkeeper'.
(iv) MHG *î* where this is the result of contraction of OHG *-igi*: *lyt* 3rd p. sg. of *lige* 'lie'.

9.2 [e:] is a tense, close, mid-front vowel. It represents:
(i) MHG *ê*: *Leer* 'apprenticeship', *eebig* 'eternal'.
(ii) MHG *e* (primary umlaut) before *r*- clusters in many cases: *Eermel* 'sleeve'.
(iii) MHG *ë* in cases of contraction: *gsee* 'see', *gschee* 'happen'.

9.3 [ɛ:] is an open, mid-front vowel. It occurs for:
(i) MHG *æ*, the umlaut of OHG *â*, in words which have no unmutated cognates in [ɒ:] (see § 9.9): *Chëës* 'cheese', *Strëël* 'comb'.
(ii) MHG *ë* before *r*- clusters: *Hëërz* 'heart,' also *ëër* 'he' stressed. Altogether this is the most frequent e-sound before *r*- clusters.
(iii) in *wëërmer* 'warmer', *gëë* 'give', *nëë* 'take'.

9.4 [æ:] is a very wide, open, low-front vowel. It is exclusively the product of lengthening of MHG short vowels. It represents:
(i) MHG *ë* and MHG *ä* lengthened in monosyllabic words ending in a lenis: *Wääg* 'way'.
(ii) Analogical umlaut of [ɒ:]: *Stääb* 'sticks', *Zää* 'teeth'.

9.5 [ɒ:] corresponds to the short *a*- vowel (see § 8.5). It derives from:
(i) MHG *â*: *Jaar* 'year', *Haar* 'hair'.
(ii) MHG *a* in monosyllabic words ending in a lenis: *waas* 'what'.
(iii) MHG *a* before *r*- clusters: *Gaarte* 'garden'.

9.6 [o:] is a close, tense, rounded, mid-tongue back vowel. It derives from:

(i) MHG *ô*: *grooss* 'big', *schoone* 'clearing up of the weather'.

(ii) MHG *o* in monosyllabic words ending in a lenis: *Hoof* 'courtyard'.

(iii) MHG *o* before *r*- clusters: *oordeli* 'rather'.

(iv) MHG *u* in *Soon* 'son' (NHG influence).

9.7 [u:] is a close, rounded, high-tongue back vowel. It derives from:

(i) MHG *û* except in hiatus position and in a few isolated cases where shortening has occurred (see § 8.7 (iii)): *truurig* 'sad', *uuf* 'on' stressed.

(ii) MHG *u* in monosyllabic words ending in a lenis: *Zuug* 'train'.

(iii) MHG *u* before *r*- clusters in many words: *Puurscht* 'lad'.

The long *u* which is the result of lengthening is outside Winterthur carefully distinguished from the old long *u*, the former being open and lax.

9.8 [ø:] is a close, rounded, mid-tongue front vowel. It derives from:

(i) MHG *œ*: *grööscht* 'biggest', *böös* 'bad'.

(ii) MHG *ö* in monosyllabic words ending in a lenis: *Hööf* 'courtyards'.

(iii) MHG *ö* before *r*- clusters: *Wöörtli* 'word' dim.

9.9 [œ:] is a lax, open, rounded, mid-tongue front vowel. It is comparatively rare and derives exclusively from the analogical umlaut of [ɒ:]:

(i) MHG *â*: *spœœter* 'later', *frœœge* 'ask'. Weber, *BSG*, pp. 200–2 and Boesch, *op. cit.*, p. 74, have made it clear that this umlaut may serve as evidence that Zürich had formerly *ô* < MHG *â* in common with the adjacent dialects.[1]

9.10 [y:] is a close, rounded, high-tongue front vowel. It represents:

(i) MHG *iu* (both *iu* < Gmc. *eu* and the umlaut of *û*) except in the position of hiatus and in a few isolated cases where it has been shortened: *tüütsch* 'German', *Lüüt* 'people'; also specifically Upper German *iu* (see Braune-Mitzka, § 47): *tüüff* 'deep', *Flüüge* 'fly'.

(ii) MHG *ü* in monosyllabic words ending in a lenis: *Züüg* 'trains'.

(iii) MHG *ü* before *r*- clusters: *wüürge* 'swallow with difficulty'.

(iv) It occurs by analogical extension from MHG *iu*- forms in the paradigm: *schüüsse* 'to shoot', *flüüge* 'to fly'. Outside the district of Winterthur the lengthened *ü* is open and lax and kept distinct from the old, close, long *ü*.

---

[1] See also the dialect geographical implications in F. Maurer, *Oberrheiner, etc.*, pp. 304–8, and maps 39 and 80; and the refutation of his thesis by R. Hotzenköcherle in *Vox Romanica*, vii, 1943/4, p. 298.

§ 10. Diphthongs

Seen historically the nine diphthongs can be grouped into six 'old' ones and three 'new' ones. All diphthongs are stressed on the first element, which in quality is more or less identical with the corresponding single vowel. The second element is less distinct and usually lax. For the description see the relevant paragraphs on the single vowels.

10.1 [æɪ] derives from:

(i) MHG *ei* except in labial surroundings (see 10.3): *Stäi* 'stone', *räise* 'travel'.

(ii) MHG *en* + fricative: *Fäischter* 'window'.

(iii) MHG *egi*, frequently already contracted in MHG: *Mäitli* 'girl'.

10.2 [æɷ] derives from:

(i) MHG *ou*: *Aug* 'eye', *au* 'also'.

10.3 [œɪ] derives from:

(i) MHG *öü*: *Frœid* 'joy', *Hœi* 'hay', *Bœim* 'trees'.

(ii) MHG *ei* in labial surroundings: *Sœipfe* 'soap'.

10.4 [iə] derives from:

(i) MHG *ie*: *Brief* 'letter', *lieb* 'dear'.

(ii) MHG *î* before *ch*: *liecht* 'easy'.

10.5 [uə] derives from:

(i) MHG *uo*: *Bluet* 'blood', *Bueb* 'boy'.

10.6 [yə] derives from:

(i) MHG *üe*: *Füess* 'feet', *früener* 'earlier'.

(ii) MHG *iu* before *ch*: *füecht* 'damp'.

10.7 [eɪ] derives from:

(i) MHG *î* in hiatus position: *frei* 'free', *Schüüsserei* 'shooting'.

(ii) MHG *in-* before fricative, *s, sch, f*: *feischter* 'dark'.

10.8 [oɷ] derives from:

(i) MHG *û* in hiatus position: *troue* 'trust'.

10.9 [øɪ] derives from:

(i) MHG *iu* in hiatus position: *nöi* 'new', *öi* 'you' acc. pl.

(ii) MHG *ün* + fricative: *föif* 'five'.

If the vocalization of *n* or *m* before fricatives is not mentioned in the cases of all vowels this is because examples are very rare or concern only obsolete words.

§ 11. Unstressed Vowels

Except in foreign words and compounds only *i* and the neutral central [ə] occur in unstressed positions.

11.1 [I] is lax and open. It derives from the following sources:

(i) MHG prefix *be-* before stops and some fricatives and especially in words recently borrowed from NHG: *bidüüte* 'mean'.

(ii) MHG *i* in the following suffixes: *-lih, tüütli* 'clearly'; *-ig, fërtig*; *-isch, änglisch* 'English'; *-inne, Schwyzeri* 'Swiss woman'; *-e* (< OHG *-î*) *Güeti* 'goodness'; *-ing/-ung, Wonig* 'flat'; *-lin, Güferli* 'suit-case' dim.

(iii) MHG *i, ie, iu, e* in certain inflexional endings: adj. and pron. *e chranki Muetter* 'a sick mother', *iri Aart* 'her manner'; past subj. of weak verbs, *läbti* of 'to live'; 2nd pers. sg. of certain verbs, *wuurdischt* of 'to become'; pres. subj. of all verbs, *öb er na läbi* 'if he was still alive'; and in unstressed particles, *di* (pl. or fem. article), *si* 'she, they'.

(iii) unstressed elements of a compound: *Läbtig* 'life', *öppis* (MHG *etewaz*) 'something'.

11.2 [ə] is best regarded as an unstressed weak central variant of [æ]. It occurs in the following instances:

(i) in the prefixes corresponding to NHG *vor-, ver-, verusse* 'outside', *verzele* 'tell', *ge-* only a few cases: *Gedanke* 'thought'.

(ii) in the suffix *-er, Läder* 'leather'.

(iii) in inflexional endings corresponding to MHG *-en*, e.g. in the infinitive, the conjugation, here also in the case of MHG *-et*, the adjectival and nominal declensions.

(iv) in the unstressed elements of compounds, e.g. *-hin/-her:use* (< MHG *ûz-hin*) 'out'; *Häimet* 'homeland', *Waret* 'truth'.

§ 12. VOWEL QUANTITY

In the course of the description of the vowels and their origins reference is repeatedly made to changes in quantity. These changes in vowel quantity since MHG times can be summarized as follows:

12.1 Short MHG vowels are lengthened in monosyllabic words ending in a lenis consonant (*l, r, m, n* count as lenis consonants). Bohnenberger, *Alem. Ma.*, p. 155, calls this *Leichtschlussdehnung*. Where the monosyllabic form is part of a paradigm the short vowel is sometimes preserved, and always in the case of the imperative, e.g. *Taag* 'day', *waas* 'what', *Reed*[1] 'speech' but *rede* 'speak' and *red!* imperative. A number of nouns have a long vowel in the sg. and a short vowel in the pl.: *Glaas— Gleser* 'glass'.

---

[1] MHG *rede* occurs thus with a long vowel in NHG and SGm. for quite different reasons. In NHG the long vowel is the result of lengthening of a short vowel in an open syllable, in SGm. the result of lengthening in a monosyllabic word (after apocope of *-e*) ending in a lenis.

12.2 MHG short vowels are almost always lengthened before *r* + consonant, e.g. *Doorff* 'village', *Chaarte* 'map'.

12.3 Winterthur has not participated in the lengthening of short *a*, *ä* (MHG *ë*) in open syllables of which there are instances in the rest of the Canton.

12.4 Shortening of a long vowel occurs usually in compounds, e.g. *Waret* 'truth', *hüraate* 'marry'.

§ 13. COMPARISON WITH THE NHG VOWELS

The most typical differences between the vowels of *Züritüütsch* and indeed of most SGm. dialects and those of NHG are:

(1) The MHG short vowels in open syllables are generally preserved in SGm. while these are lengthened in NHG. SGm. vowel lengthening in monosyllabic words ending in a lenis consonant produces occasional differences.

(2) SGm. lengthening before *r* + consonant.

(3) SGm. preservation of MHG diphthongs *ie*, *uo*, *üe* for which NHG has long monophthongs *i* (spelt ie), *u*, *ü*.

(4) The so-called SGm. hiatus-diphthongs: *ei*, *ou*, *öi* where NHG has the diphthongs [ae], [ao], [ɔø] spelt *ei*, *au*, *eu/äu* developed from MHG *î*, *û*, *iu*.

(5) SGm. preservation of the MHG long vowels *î*, *û*, *iu* except in hiatus position where NHG has the diphthongs *ei/ai*, *au*, *eu/äu*.

(6) The *e*- series. NHG has [ɛ] for the short and [eː] for the long vowel irrespective of origin. The distinction between [eː] < *e* and [ɛː] < *a* is not obligatory and not phonemically relevant (*Ehre*: *Ähre*). *Züritüütsch*, on the other hand, keeps MHG *ë* distinct from MHG *e* but lets the former coincide with MHG *ä*. It introduces [ɛ, ɛː] mainly before *r* as a third *e*- vowel.

(7) The NHG rule: short vowel lax—long vowel tense, does not apply. There are short tense, close vowels in SGm.

(8) The umlaut of OHG *â* is, if analogical, [œː] in Zt. not [ɛː] or [eː] as in NHG.

(9) SGm. rounding of *i* and *e* in labial surroundings.

(10) The umlaut of *u* is restricted in Zt. It generally does not occur before a fortis velar consonant, cf. *zrugg*—*zurück* 'back' adv.

(11) The unstressed NHG *e* disappears in SGm. in the prefixes *ge*- and generally *be*- and in final position (Upper German apocope). NHG *-el* in fem. nouns is usually *-le* in SGm. Characteristic of SGm. is further the extensive occurrence of unstressed *-i*.

Chief Vowel Correspondences

Zt.[1]	e ë ä[2]	y	uu	üü	ăi au	ei öi ou	ie ue üe
MHG	e ë ä	î	û	iu	ei ou	-î/ -iu/ -û/	ie uo üe
NHG	e, ä [ɛ]	ei	au	eu/äu	ei au	ei eu au	ie [i:] u ü

NHG	e, ä [ɛ]	ei		au		eu/äu		ie u ü
MHG	e, ë, ä	î -î/	ei	û -û/ ou		iu -iu/ öu		ie,i uo üe
Zt.	e, ë, ä	y	ei äi	uu ou au		üü öi œi		ie,i ue üe

[1] For the phonetic value of the letters, see § 7. MHG and NHG sounds are given in their respective orthography.
[2] Zt. e < MHG e; Zt. ä < MHG ë, ä.

THE CONSONANTS

§ 14. THE CONSONANTAL SYSTEM

Stops		Fricatives		Affricates	Sonants		
fortis	lenis	fortis	lenis		nasals	liquids	semi-vowels
p	b	f	v	(pf)	m		w
t	d	s	š z	(ts tš)	n	l, r	(j)
k	g	x		(kx)	ŋ		h

14.1 The consonantal system falls into three groups of which one, the affricates, are not, strictly speaking, phonemes but clusters of homorganic phonemes. Only nasals, liquids and semi-vowels are voiced (sonants). Voicing thus plays no phonemically distinctive part. The stops and fricatives (but not /š/ and /x/) form an opposition of intensity and duration (fortis and lenis). Certain sonants /m, n, ŋ, l/ also show the difference between lenis and fortis, but it is non-phonemic as in the case of the fricatives /š/ and /x/.

14.2 The lenis sounds are short and weak in intensity, but without a noticeable or relevant amount of voice.[1] Initially they predominate; only the stops occur as fortes /p, t, k/. For the fricatives /f—v/ and /s—z/ the opposition lenis/fortis is neutralized in initial position. Phonetically they are lenes like the other fricatives (/š/ and /x/) and the sonants /m, n, ŋ, l/. In clusters of stops and fricatives the

[1] K. Ketterer, *Experimentelle Dialektgeographie des Alemannischen in Baden*. Teil I: *Die Konsonanten*, Berlin, 1942, calls them voiced because voice is not entirely absent but this blurs the differences between these lenes and NHG, French or English b, d, g.

opposition is also neutralized, the result being somewhat weaker fortis sounds or so-called semi-fortes,[1] cf. [žri:bə] 'to write': [ɛr žri:pt] 'he writes': [kšribə] 'written'.

14.3 The opposition of fortis/lenis is phonemically relevant in the following cases:[2]

(i) Initially before vowels or sonants, medially and finally after vowels or sonants in the case of stops, e.g. *Paar* 'couple': *baar(zale)* 'to pay cash'; *tœœrff* 'may': *Doorff*[3] 'village'; *Wätter* 'weather': *weder* 'than'; *halte* 'to hold': *Halde* 'slope'.

Initially the opposition is somewhat tenuous and rare and probably comparatively recent. The dental stop is practically always fortis. Exceptions which are widespread over a large geographical area are the forms of the demonstrative pronoun *dëë*, etc., the personal pronoun *du*, *drei* 'three', *Doorff* 'village', *Dräck* 'dirt', *Dienscht* 'service', *verdiene* 'to earn'. The labial and velar stops are mostly lenis except in the prefixes MHG *be-* and *ge-*. Cases of sandhi-assimilation further increase the occurrence of initial fortis labial and velar stops. See on this also R. Hotzenköcherle, *Mutten*, BSG, xix, pp. 43, 288, 300–5, and K. Stucki, *Jaun*, BSG, x, § 117; W. Henzen, *Freiburg*, BSG, xvi, § 125; and §§ 16.1, 16.3, 16.5.

(ii) Medially and finally after vowels or sonants in the case of the fricatives /f—v/ and /s—z/, e.g. *offe* 'open': *Ofe* 'stove'; *nass* 'wet': *Graas* 'grass'; *hilff* 'help' imp.: *Wolf* 'wolf'.

14.4 The fortis sounds vary in character according to position:[4]

(i) Initially in the case of /p, t, k/ and finally in the case of /p, t, k, f, s/ the fortis sound is about twice as long as the lenis.

(ii) Between vowels or sonants the fortis is about three times as long as a lenis. Especially after a short vowel this fortis tends to have the character of a geminate. In Zt. this tendency is slight, but there are many SGm. dialects with clear geminates. (See Dieth-

---

[1] This rule is known as Heusler's Law, formulated first for the dialect of Basle by A. Heusler, *Der alemannische Consonantismus in der Mundart von Baselstadt*, Strassburg, 1888, p. 24.

[2] The SGm. dialects vary in the distribution of lenis/fortis as well as in the phonemic relevance of the opposition. The North-west, for instance, has only lenes in initial position. See R. Schläpfer, *Die Mundart des Kantons Baselland*, Frauenfeld, 1956 (= BSM, v), 30–8 and Baumgartner, BSG, xiv, 100, 105, 108, 117. A. S. Schultz, *op. cit.*, 56, interprets the fortes of the dialect of Brienz, Bernese Oberland, as geminate clusters.

[3] Where minimal pairs are difficult to find analogous environment is considered sufficient for establishing a phonemic opposition.

[4] See E. Dieth, R. Brunner, 'Die Konsonanten und Geminaten des Schweizerdeutschen experimentell untersucht', *Sache, Ort und Wort, Festschrift Jakob Jud*, Zürich, 1943 (= Romanica Helvetica, xx), 737–62; and Weber, BSG, xv, 20–3. R. Hotzenköcherle, BSG, xix, 47–9; BSG, x, §§ 7, 15; BSG, xvi, § 14; BSG, xiii, § 18, state that geminates are non-existent or hardly perceptible in their respective dialects.

Brunner, *op. cit.*, p. 745; Heusler, *op. cit.*, pp. 32–3.) Assimilation produces the same long fortis also at the beginning of a word (so-called 'Potenzierte Fortis', see Jost Winteler, *Die Kerenzer Mundart des Kantons Glarus*, Leipzig, 1876). The affricates, fortis in character, differentiate in the same way according to the position. Examples: [ɛr tæŋkxt] 'he thinks': [ɛr hæ ttæŋkxt] 'he has thought'; [puːr] 'peasant': [toppəl] 'double'; [is] imp, 'eat': [kæssə] 'eaten'; [tsiːt] 'time': [ɣɑttsə] 'cats'; (the 'geminate' fortis is spelt with double letters, the 'normal' fortis with a single).

14.5 Fortis and lenis occur in complementary, i.e. mutually exclusive, positions in the case of the fricatives /š/ and /x/ and the sonants /m, n, ŋ, l/. The difference is therefore not phonemically relevant.

(i) /m, n, ŋ, l/ are normally weakly articulated, but they occur as fortis sounds after a stressed short vowel in the same syllable, in final position only if the following word does not begin with a vowel. /n, m/ are also fortis after short vowel + *r*. Examples: [briŋə] 'to bring': [ɛr briŋːt] (this fortis character is indicated by:); [ɣumː] 'come' imp.: [ɣum inə] 'come in'.[1]

(ii) Fortis [š] is medially and finally, except in some loan-words, the allophone of initial lenis [ž], e.g. [žyːli] 'terribly': [tæššə] 'bag': [tiš] 'table', exception in a loan-word: [guˈrɒːži] 'courage'. The verbal morphemes *-sch*, *-isch*, *-tisch* (§§ 42, 43, 46, 47) have the lenis allophone.

(iii) Medially and finally after short vowels fortis [x] is the allophone of lenis [ɣ] which occurs initially, medially and finally after long vowels or *r*, *l*, e.g. [ɣuxxi] 'kitchen', [gliːɣ] 'same', [krux] 'smell'.[2]

14.6 The distribution of the chief allophones can be summarized as follows:

---

[1] This phenomenon, named Winteler's *Silbenakzentgesetz* after its discoverer (Jost Winteler, *op. cit.*, p. 142), is connected with the quantity rule that the vowel in monosyllabic words before a lenis consonant is long. A short, stressed vowel does not tolerate a lenis after it in the same syllable. MHG introduced a fortis consonant in final position (cf. *tac-tages*), SGm. lengthened the vowel (*Taag-Tage* (dat. pl.) or has a fortis (*vill* 'much'—*vili* (pl.)). But it appears that this consonantal readjustment is only possible where is does not involve a change from one phoneme to another. Thus it occurs among the sonants where it is phonemically not relevant. In the case of stops no change takes place inside a paradigm, e.g. *red*! 'speak' imp.: *rede* inf., but *Reed* 'speech'. Both vocalic and consonantal adjustment are seen in *überaal* 'everywhere': *all* 'all': *ali* (pl.). See also Heusler, *op. cit.*, pp. 13–24.

[2] There seem to be two exceptions in *gsäch, gschäch* (with lenis), pres. subj. of *gsee*, 'to see', *gschee* 'to happen'; the younger generation appears to prefer the lenis also in *mache* 'to make' (as a free variant).

Allophones in following positions:

Phoneme	Init. bef.	Med. betw. vowels or sonants	Fin. after	Cluster of stop + fric.	Med. or fin. after stressed short vowel in same syll.
fortis p	p-	-pp-	-p	} p³	
lenis b	b-	-b-	-b		
fortis t	t-	-tt-	-t	} t	
lenis d	d-	-d-	-d		
fortis k	k-	-kk-	-k	} k	
lenis g	g-	-g-	-g		
fortis f	v-	-ff-	-f	} f	
lenis v		-v-	-v		
fortis s	z-	-ss-	-s	} s	
lenis z		-z-	-z		
š-ž	ž	-šš-	-š	š	
x-ɣ	ɣ-	-xx-¹	-x¹	x	
		-ɣ-²	-ɣ²		
m		m		m: } also fin.	
n		n		n: } after short	
ŋ		ŋ		ŋ: } vowel + r.	
l		l		l:	

¹ After short vowel.　　　² After long vowel.
³ Means that the contrast is neutralized. Only one of the two phonemes occurs.

§ 15. SPELLING

The simplified *Schwyzertütschi Dialäktschrift* as applied by Traugott Vogel is much less satisfactory in its treatment of the consonants than of the vowels. Its two main principles of a) rendering long consonants by doubling, short ones by single letters; and b) following the NHG orthography wherever possible, lead to a number of inconsistencies. The result, however, recommends itself by its easy legibility.

The following correspondences generally hold good:

Phoneme	Letter	Phoneme	Letter	Phoneme	Letter
p	p, pp (1)	f	ff(2)	m, n, ŋ, l, r	m, n, ng, l, r (4)
t	t,tt, (1)dt	v	f/v(2)	w, j, h	w, j, h
k	gg(6)	s	ss	pf	pf
b	b	z	s	ts	z, tz(5)
d	d	š	sch(3)	kx	k, ck, gch(5)
g	g	x	ch		

Notes

(1) The geminate fortis is indicated by doubling in words or forms unknown in NHG, e.g. *gfätterle* 'to play'; otherwise the NHG orthography is followed: *Vater* 'father', *Muetter* 'mother'.

(2) Vogel's spelling gives no guidance as to the occurrence of fortis [f] and lenis [v]. I have introduced *ff* for the fortis in medial and final positions, but otherwise use *f* and *v* as in NHG.

(3) In the case of initial *št-* and *šp-* the NHG spelling is retained.

(4) It is in the case of the nasals and liquids that the rule 'short consonant is indicated by single letter' is mainly applied. In the case of the fortis allophone there is much inconsistency, e.g. *sell* 'shall' but *Gfel* 'luck'.

(5) The letters *z/tz* and *k/ck* are used as in NHG. *K/ck* always represent the affricate. This is why /k/ has to be expressed by *gg*.

(6) In the case of clusters where the opposition lenis/fortis is neutralized NHG spelling rules prevail, e.g. *gschlage* 'beaten' phonetically [kšlɒgə].

§ 16. THE CONSONANT PHONEMES

16.1 [p] is a non-aspirated, bilabial fortis stop and derives from:
(i) MHG *p* in loan-words: *Paar* 'pair'.
(ii) MHG *b* in a few words: *Puurscht* 'lad'.
(iii) MHG *b* in cases where assimilation[1] occurred: *Puur* (< *gebûre*) 'peasant'.
(iv) Assimilation: *öpper* (< *etewer*) 'somebody'. It is introduced between *m + f*: *Zuekumpft* 'future'.
(v) MHG prefix *be-* where the vowel is dropped: *plange* 'to long for', *peelände* 'to make sb. feel miserable'.
As to the chief allophones, see § 14.6. Aspiration which is to be interpreted as a cluster of /p/ + /h/ occurs in recent loans from NHG. See § 16.19 on *h*.

16.2 [b] the bilabial lenis stop derives from:
(i) MHG *b*: *Bueb* 'boy', *Bluet* 'blood' except in a few cases (see § 16.1 (ii)). There is a good deal of wavering in the articulation of the labial stop in initial position. Many speakers make hardly any distinction between lenis and fortis except where it is meaningful, e.g. *bache* 'to bake', *pache* 'baked' p.p., *Päärli* 'couple' dim., *Bäärli* 'bear' dim.
(ii) MHG *w* after *r* and *l* and occasionally between vowels, *eebig* 'eternal', *gĕrbe* 'to tan'.

16.3 [t] is a non-aspirated, alveolar fortis stop which derives from:
(i) MHG *t*: *trätte* 'to step', *gläitig* 'quickly'.

---

[1] Cases of assimilation at the juncture of words are treated in § 17.

(ii) MHG *d* (< Gmc. *d* and Gmc. *þ*) in initial position except in few cases: *tänke* 'think', *tüütli* 'clearly'.

(iii) MHG *d* before the adjectival suffix *-li*: *früüntli* 'friendly'.

(iv) MHG *d* in the def. article, NHG *die*, *d Lüüt* 'people', *d Aart* 'the manner'.

(v) It is introduced in the consonant groups [n + š]: *Mäntsch* 'human being'; [l + š]: *faltsch* 'wrong'; and at the end of a word after [š] in *suscht* (< MHG *sús*) 'otherwise', *anderscht* 'other', and in *näbet* 'beside', *zwüschet* 'between'. Aspiration occurs in a few loan-words: *Schuelertheek* 'school satchel'. On the chief allophones, see § 14.6, and on assimilation § 17.

16.4 [d] is an alveolar lenis stop. It hardly occurs at the beginning of a word except in frequently unstressed words such as pronouns. It represents:

(i) MHG *d* (< Gmc. *þ*) in initial position in a few words, e.g. *Ding* 'thing', *du* 'thou' and the dem. pron.

(ii) MHG *d* in medial and final position where MHG hardening in final position has generally disappeared: *Läder* 'leather', *schaad* 'a pity'.

(iii) OHG *t* after *n* and in the plural ending MHG-Alemannic dialect *-nt*: *hinder* 'behind', *si säged* 'they say'.

(iv) MHG *t* in a few isolated cases, *tood* 'dead', *gschyd* 'clever', *nüd* 'not'.

16.5 [k] is an unaspirated velar stop. It derives from:

(i) MHG dialectal *gg* (= NHG *ck*): *Rugge* 'back'.

(ii) MHG prefix *ge-*: *ghaa* 'had' p.p., *ggëë* 'given', *ggeerbt* 'inherited'.

(iii) Medially and finally foreign *k*: *Lagg* 'lacquer'. [k] as the result of assimilation is dealt with in § 17.

16.6 [g] is the lenis corresponding to [k]. It derives from:

(i) MHG *g* except in the cases mentioned under 16.5: *gëë* 'give', *äige* 'own' adj.

(ii) Foreign *k* initially in loan-words:[1] *Güferli* 'small suit-case', *Guraaschi* 'courage'.

(iii) MHG *j* in the past subjunctive of the verbs *tue* 'do', *sy* 'be', *haa* 'have': *tüeg*, *seig*, *heig*.

16.7 [f] this labio-dental fortis fricative never occurs in initial position. It derives from:

(i) MHG *f* (< Gmc. *p*): *Prueff* 'profession', *Doorff* 'village', but lenis in *uf*, *ufe* 'on' prep. and adv. where lenition is caused by lack of stress in the sentence. As to the chief allophones, see § 14.6.

---

[1] This is an interesting case of sound-substitution. [k] initially is felt to derive from and represent the prefix *ge-* or to be the result of assimilation, hence it is not available for French [k]. Aspirated *k-* of NHG or English is rendered either by [kx]- or, more rarely, by *g-*.

16.8 [v] this labio-dental lenis fricative occurring in all positions (except before stops and fricatives) derives from:

(i) MHG *f*, *v* (< Gmc. *f*): *fræœge* 'ask', *Yfer* 'eagerness'.

(ii) *f* in foreign words: *Brief* 'letter'.

(iii) Gmc. *p* in some frequently unstressed words, e.g. *uf*, *ufe*, 'on, up'.

16.9 [s] is an alveolar fortis fricative never occurring in initial position or before *t*, *k* of the same morpheme.[1] It derives from:

(i) MHG *z* (< Gmc. *t*): *häisse* 'be called', *Gass* 'street'.

(ii) MHG *s* (< Gmc. *ss*) in *Ross* 'horse'.

As to the chief allophones, see § 14.6.

16.10 [z] is an alveolar lenis fricative which occurs in all positions except before stops (before *p*, *t* > [š]) and fricatives and before *l*, *m*, *n*, *w* (MHG *s* has become [š]). It derives from:

(i) MHG *s* (< Gmc. *s*): *Huus* 'house', *läse* 'read', *säb* 'this'.

(ii) Foreign *s*: *quaasi* 'as if', *kurioos* 'strange'.

(iii) Gmc. *t* in some frequently unstressed words, e.g. *use* 'out'.

16.11 [š] is a post-alveolar grooved fricative which has the two chief allophones [š] and [ž]. As to their occurrence, see §§ 14.5 (ii), 14.6. It derives from:

(i) MHG *s* initially before the consonants *p*, *t*, *l*, *m*, *n*, *w*: *Stuude* 'bushes', *schlüüffe* 'to slip in'.

(ii) MHG *s* medially and finally before *p*, *t*: *suscht* 'otherwise', *feischter* 'gloomy'.

(iii) MHG *sc*: *schüüsse* 'shoot'.

16.12 [x] is a velar fricative articulated rather far back. The place of articulation is not influenced by the surrounding sounds. About the distribution of the lenis and fortis variants, see § 14.5 (iii). It represents:

(i) MHG *k* in initial position: *chlöpfe*' to bang', *Chaschte* 'wardrobe'.

(ii) MHG *ch* medially and finally: *Gruch* 'smell', *tuuch* 'depressed'.

(iii) MHG *k* after *l* and *r* where the 2nd Sound Shift had not taken place: *Wulche* 'cloud', *starch* 'strong'.

16.13 The affricates [pf] and [ts] derive from the same sources as the corresponding NHG affricates. There are a few cases where SGm. differs from NHG, e.g. *Sœipfe* 'soap', *grüeze* 'to greet', cf. NHG *Seife*, *grüssen*.

16.14 [tš] occurs where [d, t] and [š] have come together, and in onomatopoeic words and loan-words: *tüütsch* 'German', *Mäntsch* 'human being'.

16.15 [kx] this velar affricate is a typically Swiss-German or High

---

[1] But *glööst* 'loosened', *rysst* 'pulls'.

Alemannic sound or rather cluster, although it occurs also in South
Bavarian dialects. It derives from the following sources:

(i) MHG *k* after *n* [ŋ]: *tänke* 'think'.

(ii) MHG *ck* (< Gmc. *kk*): *Dräck* 'dirt', *tick* 'thick'.

(iii) MHG *k* initially only if the prefix *g-* (MHG *ge-*) has become
assimilated, *käne* 'to know' (< *gekennen*). For cases of assimilation
which are recognized as such by the speakers, see § 17.

(iv) NHG *k* initially or in other positions in loan-words from NHG:
Kärli 'chap', *tuberkulöös* 'tubercular', *kremiere* 'cremate'.

16.16 The nasals [m, n, ŋ] and the liquids [l] and [r] occur as in
NHG and derive from the same sources. Concerning the chief
allophones of [*m, n, ŋ, l*], see § 14.5 (i). It is characteristic of Zt.
among the SGm. dialects that these sonants are never long (fortis)
between vowels, e.g. *stele* 'stand'. [ŋ] never occurs in initial position.
[l] is an alveolar lateral and [r] is a short tongue-tip trilled sound.
The younger generation in the town of Zürich tend to go over to a
back, uvular [R]. In the transition from MHG to SGm. the consonant
n has suffered greater losses than any other. In a number of cases it
has become vocalized and been dropped, in others it has become
'mobile' (see § 18).

(i) *n* is vocalized before a fricative, e.g. *föif* 'five', *Fäischter*
'window', *feischter* 'gloomy', *öis* 'us', cf. NHG *fünf, Fenster, finster,
uns*. This loss of a nasal before a fricative in Alemannic, paralleled
as it is in Anglo-Frisian and Low German, has played a considerable
part in Wrede's *Ingvaeonentheorie*.[1] It has however been shown[2] that
the Alemannic phenomenon occurred at least several centuries later
than the 'Ingvaeonic' loss of the nasal.

(ii) It has disappeared in the pl. ending of the pres. of the regular
verbs: *-ed* (< MHG *-ent*).

(iii) The MHG/NHG prefix *an-* is always *aa-*. The NHG prepositions *an, von, in* are also without nasal in SGm.: *a, vo, i*.

(iv) For loss after stressed and unstressed syllables, see § 18.

16.17 [w] is a voiced bilabial semi-vowel without lip-rounding
and friction, occurring mainly in initial position; in compounds
(e.g. *gwont* 'dwelled', *Häiwee* 'homesickness'), onomatopoeic words
or loan-words it is also found medially. It derives from:

[1] F. Wrede, 'Ingwäonisch und Westgermanisch', *ZfdMaa.*, 1924, pp. 270 ff.;
for bibl. see T. Frings, *Grundlegung einer Geschichte der deutschen Sprache*, 2nd
ed., Halle, 1950, pp. 33–43, and Bach, p. 201 f.; *DSA*, map 39 *uns-*.
[2] F. Maurer, 'Zur Geschichte der Nasalierungen vor Reibelaut' in *Volks-
kundliche Ernte*, Hepding-Festschr., 1938, pp. 164–73; see also B. Boesch, *op. cit.*,
176–9; K. Bohnenberger, 'Zur Auflösung des n vor Reibelaut im Alem.',
ZfdMaa., ix, 1914, 377–82; O. Behaghel, 'Wann ist im Südalem. der Nasal vor
Reibelaut geschwunden?', *Beitr.*, lviii, 1934, 294–6; F. Maurer, *Nordgermanen
und Alemannen*, 3rd ed., 1952, pp. 75–7.

(i) MHG *w* in initial position: *wüsse* 'to know', *Wääg* 'way'.

(ii) MHG *w* in initial clusters [šw, tw, tsw]: *schwèèr* 'heavy', *zwo* 'two' fem., *detwèris* 'across'.

(iii) *qu* or *v* in loan-words: *kwitt* 'quits', *wisewii* 'vis-à-vis'.

16.18 [j] is a voiced palatal semi-vowel without friction. It occurs only before stressed vowels, that is, in positions in which *i* does not occur. It can therefore be regarded as an allophone of the *i*- phoneme. But for practical reasons, because no other vowel phoneme has such a semi-consonantal allophone, it is here treated separately from the *i*-phoneme. It derives from MHG *j*-: *Juged* 'youth'.

16.19 [h] is a slightly voiced, weakly produced aspiration which occurs only initially except in a few loan-words where it follows an initial *p* or *t*:

(i) MHG initial *h*: *Hose* 'trousers', *ghöörig* 'thoroughly'.

(ii) in loan-words from NHG: *Schuelertheek* 'satchel'.

§ 17. ASSIMILATION

Two types of assimilation can be distinguished. First, historical assimilation in words which are now felt to be simple words. Here the assimilation is no longer felt by the speaker, e.g. in former compounds *öpper* (< MHG *etewer*) 'somebody', also *öppis* 'something', *öppe* 'about', *goppel* 'I hope' (< *got welle*); in simple words: *frönd* (< *vremede*) 'foreign', *chunt* 'comes'.

Secondly, assimilative changes in compounds and sentence units (in sandhi). They take place regularly in the following cases in normal speech, but are not obligatory in slow and deliberate speech, except where the prefix *g-* or the article *d* are involved:

(i) Identical consonants form a so-called 'potenzierte Fortis' or geminate fortis: *hät tänkt* 'has thought' > [hæt'tæŋkxt], *abbysse* 'to bite off' > ['ɒppi:ssə].

(ii) first consonant is absorbed in the second:

d, t + b, p	> pp	: *d Bruut* [pru:t] 'fiancée'.
d, t + g	> gg [k]	: *häd ghürated* 'has married' [kkh].
s + š	> š	: *es schrybt* 'she (dim.) writes'.

(iii) first element is made homorganic with the second:

nd, nt + b, p	> mpp	*findt mer* 'one finds'.
d, t + m	> pm	*d Muetter* 'the mother'.
nd, nt + m	> mpm	*chund mer* 'one comes'.
d, t + f	> pf	*d Frau* 'the woman'.
nd, nt + f, pf	> mpf	*sind d Fraue* 'the women are'.
nd, nt + g	> ngg	*händ ggèè* 'have given'.
d, t + ch, k	> kch	*d Chind* 'the children'.
nd, nt + ch, k	> ngkch	*sind choo* 'have come'.

E

All dentals are thus assimilated to labials and velars.

(iv) The SGm. prefix g- (MHG ge-) is also regularly assimilated to the stops b-, p-, pf-, d-, t-, ts-: *punde* (< *gebunden*) 'bound', *pfiffe* (< *gepfiffen*) 'whistled', *zoge* (< *gezogen*) 'pulled'.

§ 18. The Mobile -*n*

In prevocalic position in a given speech unit *n* is introduced—or preserved, if seen historically—in the following cases. In any other position these words end in a vowel.

(i) In the root of many words ending in a stressed vowel which in MHG and NHG end in -*n*: *Stäi* 'stone': *Stäine* dat. pl.; *Maa* 'man': *Mane* pl. Here the *n* reappears only before an inflexional ending.

(ii) In unstressed syllables which end in -*n* in MHG/NHG: inf. *lache* 'to laugh': *lachen und brüele* 'to laugh and to cry'; pp. *gstande* 'stood': *gstanden isch* 'has stood'; pl. of nouns *Fraue* 'women': *Frauen und Chind*. The mobile -*n* occurs also in adjectival and pronominal endings. This mobile -*n* is rather felt to be part of the following word. The syllabic boundary lies before the consonant *n*, hence the hyphenated spellings preferred by many dialect writers: *gstande-n-isch*.

(iii) To break the hiatus an *n* is frequently introduced in analogy to the above cases where it is historically not justified: *wo-n-er* 'when he', *wie-n-er* 'as he'.

§ 19. Comparison with the NHG Consonants

The most salient differences are:

(1) The consonantal system of *Züritüütsch*, and in fact of SGm. as a whole, rests on an opposition between lenis and fortis. Intensity and duration in SGm. play the part of voice in NHG.

(2) SGm. preserves the MHG consonants more faithfully than NHG in so far as it continues the old opposition lenis/fortis and still distinguishes Gmc. *f*, *s* from HG *ff*, *ss* (even in final position) and Gmc. *gg* from Gmc. *kk*.

(3) *Züritüütsch* makes no difference between *d* (Gmc. *þ*) and *t* (Gmc. *d*) in initial position.

(4) Zt. does not distinguish the *ich*- sound from the *ach*- sound.

(5) Initial NHG *k*- is *ch*- in Zt.

(6) Among the consonants alien to NHG the most characteristic of SGm. is the velar affricate *kch*.

(7) The loss of final *n* in Zt.

(8) Hardening in final position is unknown in SGm.

(9) The fortis stops are unaspirated in SGm.

(10) The clusters [šp, št] in medial and final position in SGm.

(11) The widespread assimilations of SGm.

(12) The absence of the glottal stop before stressed initial vowels in SGm. and the linking of words in sequence.

(13) The preservation of the cluster *chs* which is [ks] in NHG.

THE MORPHOLOGY OF ZÜRITÜÜTSCH

NOUNS AND ARTICLES

§ 20. FORMATION OF THE PLURAL

The nouns[1] of Zt. may be classified according to the way in which their plurals are formed. There are two chief endings which serve to express plurality: *-e* and *-er*. In comparing the formation of the plural in SGm. with that of NHG it has to be remembered that where NHG has a final *-e* or *-n* SGm. has dropped them. Mutation of the root-vowel of the singular may combine with the addition of an ending or be used alone to indicate the plural. There are four main types of plural formation:

Type A: without a special ending in the plural or mutation;
Type B: without a special ending in the plural but with mutation;
Type C: adding *-e* in the plural;
Type D: adding *-er* in the plural and with mutation where possible.

Note: Mutation of the root-vowel is an important morphological factor in SGm. (e.g. plural formation of the nouns, comparison of the adjectives, diminutives). All back vowels are capable of mutating. The correspondences are:[2]

Back vowel:	a	aa	o	oo	u	uu	au	ou	ue
Mutated vowel:	ä	ää	ö	öö	ü	üü	œi	öi	üe

Of *a, aa* the analogical, morphologically active mutation is *ä, ää*. But there are a number of historical mutations, e.g. *a, aa > e* (primary umlaut, see § 8.2); *a, aa > ĕ, ëë* (primary umlaut before *r* and *ch* and secondary umlaut, see §§ 8.3; 9.3); *aa > œœ*. (See § 9.9.)

Type A: To this type belong:
(i) Most neuter nouns, including those diminutives with a front root-vowel: *Jaar* 'year', *Mäitli* 'girl'.
(ii) Most masculine nouns with a front root-vowel: *Brief* 'letter', *Wääg* 'way', *Stäcke(n)*[3] 'stick'.
(iii) Those feminine nouns ending in *-e(n)* in the sg.: *Chappe(n)* 'cap'.

---

[1] Cf. W. Friedrich, 'Die Flexion des Hauptworts in den deutschen Mundarten', *ZfdPh.*, xxxii, 1900, 484–501; xxxiii, 1901, 45–84.
[2] For the sound values of the letters, see § 7.
[3] Mobile *-n* (see § 18) is throughout the morphology section indicated by brackets. But it must be realized that in absolute position, i.e. in the position given here, *-n* is *not* found.

Type B: To this type belong:

(i) Most masculine nouns with a back root-vowel: *Prueff—Prüeff* 'profession', *Haagge(n)—Hœœgge(n)* 'hook'.

(ii) Those monosyllabic feminine nouns which mutate in NHG: *Hand—Händ* 'hand', *Stadt—Stedt* 'town'.

This type of plural formation is more frequent in SGm. than in NHG.

Type C: -e. To this type belong:

(i) The majority of feminine nouns: *Waar—Waare(n)* 'goods', *Spraach—Spraache(n)* 'language', *Chuchi—Chuchene(n)* 'kitchen'. (Feminine nouns ending in *-i* reintroduce *-n* (< MHG *in*) before the plural ending *-e(n)*. See § 18.)

(ii) The majority of masculine nouns denoting animate beings: *Bueb—Buebe(n)* 'boy', *Goof—Goofe(n)* 'child', a few other masc. nouns: *Schmëërz—Schmëërze* 'pain'.

(iii) A few words denoting members of the family show also umlaut: *Tochter—Töchtere(n)* 'daughter', *Vater—Vätere(n)* 'father'.

(iv) The neuters *Hëërz* 'heart', *Aug* 'eye', *Oor* 'ear'.

Type D: -er. To this type belong, mutating in the case of a back root-vowel:

(i) A number of neuter nouns: *Muul—Müüler* 'mouth', *Mitgliid-Mitglider*[1] 'member'.

(ii) A few masculine nouns: *Wald—Wälder* 'wood'.

§ 21. CASE FORMS

In contradistinction to many other SGm. dialects Zt. has one special case form, a dative plural, which is formed of all nouns except those with the plural ending *-e* (Type C) and those nouns of Types A and B which end in *-e* in the sg. The dative pl. ending is *-e(n)*, e.g.

Type A: *Schirm* sg. and pl. 'umbrella'—dat. pl. *Schirme.*

Type B: *Hand—Händ* 'hand'—dat. pl. *Hände.*

Type D: *Buech—Büecher* 'book'—dat. pl. *Büechere.*

Some nouns ending in a stressed vowel, e.g. *Stäi* 'stone', Type A, form their dat. pl. in *-ne*: *Stäine*, where the *n* is historically justified (see § 18). But there are also analogical forms, e.g. *Chue-Chüe* (pl.) —*Chüene* (dat. pl.) 'cow'; *Chnüü* (sg. and pl.)—*Chnüüne* 'knee'; *Schue* (sg. and pl.)—*Schuene* 'shoe'. Nouns ending in *-i* or *-li* have *-ene*, *-lene*: *Fingerli* (sg. and pl.) 'finger' dim., (< MHG *vingerlin*) dat. pl. *Fingerlene.* Unstressed final *-el* in the sg. is changed to *-le* in the dat. pl.: *Schlüssel—Schlüssle* 'key'.

Relics of former genitive case forms occur in a few fixed formulas,

---

[1] On vowel quantity, see § 12.1.

e.g. *s Tüüfels Dank* 'base ingratitude'. Possession and personal relation is expressed by a dative paraphrase, e.g. *em Horscht syn Vater* 'Horst's father', *em Mäischter sys Huus* 'the master's house', or by the preposition *vo*: *d Tochter vom Mäischter* 'the master's daughter'. The latter construction is the only possible one if no possessive meaning is implied, e.g. *e schmaali Gass vo der Altstadt* 'a narrow street of the old city'; *Zaalmäischter vo irem Veräin* 'treasurer of their club'.

§ 22. GENDER

The majority of nouns have the same gender as in NHG but about a hundred vary (Weber, *ZGr.*, p. 119), e.g. *Ferse* m. 'heel' (NHG f.), *Egge* m. (NHG f.) 'corner', *Faane* m. (NHG f.) 'flag', *Gufere* f. (NHG m.) 'suitcase', *Bank* m. (NHG f.) 'bench'.

§ 23. THE DECLENSION OF THE DEFINITE ARTICLE

Only two case forms are preserved, a common case and a dative. No distinction is thus made between subject and direct object. Historically speaking the common case derives from the nominative. The forms are:

	m.sg.	f.sg.	n.sg.	pl.
Common Case	de(r)	d (3)	s	d (3)
Dative	em	der	em	de(n)

Notes

(1) *e* always means [ə] and *d* (f. sg. and pl.) is fortis and assimilated according to § 17. *s* is lenis.

(2) Bracketed endings apply in prevocalic positions (see also below).

(3) Before adjectives *di*.

(4) There are relics of genitive forms such as *nid der Zyt haa* 'to have no time'.

§ 24. THE DECLENSION OF THE INDEFINITE ARTICLE

	m.	f.	n.
Common Case	en	e(n)	es
Dative	eme(n)	ere(n)	eme(n)
	emene(n)	enere(n)	emene(n)

Notes

(1) *e* is [ə], also in the extended dative forms ['əmənə, 'ənərə]. The shorter dative forms are used after prepositions, otherwise mainly the extended ones.

(2) Before adjectives *es* (n.) can be replaced by *e(n)*, e.g. *s Elsi isch*

e groosses blonds Mäitli gsy 'Elsi was a tall blonde girl'; *in en uusspränts Doorff* 'into a burnt-out village'.

§ 25. AGGLUTINATIONS

In addition to those known in NHG (e.g. *im < in dem, vom < von dem*, etc.) Zt. has the following fusions:

(i) The prepositions *a* 'at', *i* 'in,' *vo* 'from', *bi* 'at, with', *zue* 'to', with the def. article m. and pl. in cases where they take the accusative in NHG: *an (an Hals:* NHG *an den Hals), in (in Veräine:* NHG *in den Vereinen),* also *von, bin, zun.*

(ii) Prepositions ending in a vowel and the dative forms of the indefinite article: *ame* or *amene* (NHG *an einem), ime* or *imene* (NHG *in einem), bime, bimene, binere* (NHG *bei einem, bei einer*).

ADJECTIVES

Zt. belongs to those SGm. dialects where the adjectives are inflected for gender, number and case only when they precede the noun or are used as nouns. There are only two case forms, a common case and a dative case. The weak and strong declensions are used on the whole as in NHG.[1]

§ 26. THE STRONG DECLENSION

	m.	f.	n.	pl.
Common Case . .	junge(n)	jungi	jungs(1)	jungi(2)
Dative . . .	jungem	junger	jungem	junge(n)

Notes

(1) If the adjective ends in a sibilant the ending is *-es*. The *s* is lenis.

(2) The uniform plural *-i* is a comparatively recent development. The older forms, often retained in rural areas, are *jung* for m. and f. and *jungi* for n. See Vogel, p. 79, *nu kä fuul Umwääg mee mache.*

§ 27. THE WEAK DECLENSION

No distinction is made for gender.

	sg.	pl.
Common Case . .	jung(1)	junge(n)
Dative . . .	junge(n)	junge(n)

[1] Strong Declension: adjective stands alone or is preceded, in the common case only, by the indefinite article or the m. poss. pron. Weak Declension: adjective is preceded by the definite article or a demonstrative pronoun or the dative of the indefinite article or the possessive pronoun.—Cf. K. Rühl, *Unflektierte (nominale) und starke Form im Singular des attributiven Adjektivs in den hochdeutschen Mundarten,* Giessen, 1909.

Note

(1) There is a tendency among the younger generation to add *-i* in the sg. common case. (See Weber, *ZGr.*, p. 121.)

§ 28. SOME SPECIAL FORMS

(i) Some adjectives, ending in a vowel, reintroduce an original *-n* before vocalic endings, e.g. *chly* 'little': *chlyne, chlyni*, etc., but *chlys* (n) or *chlyses* (with double ending); *offe* 'open': *offne, offni* but *offes*; and by analogy also *frei* 'free', *früe* 'early' where *n* is historically not justified: *freine, freini* but *freis, früene, früeni* but *frües*.

(ii) Adjectives ending in *-el* (*tunkel*) drop the *e* in the same cases, i.e. before vocalic endings (*tunkli*).

(iii) Adjectives ending in *-li* (= NHG *-lich*) have *ch* before vocalic endings, e.g. *nützli* 'useful'—*nützlichi*.

§ 29. COMPARISON

The endings of the second and third degrees are: *-er, -scht*. After sibilants and frequently after *t* the superlative ending is *-ischt*, e.g. *jung-jünger-jüngscht—häiss-häisser-häissischt*. The consonants *n* and *ch*, introduced before vocalic endings as is shown in § 28, are also found in the comparative and hence the superlative: *chly-chlyner-chlynscht*, also *eener* 'sooner' and *früener* 'earlier'.

Umlaut is much more frequent in SGm. and is the rule in monosyllabic words with a back root-vowel. *A* mutates to *e* (primary umlaut), with *ē* and *ēē* before *r* or *ch* and in the case of positional lengthening (see § 12), *aa* (< MHG *â*) > *œœ*. e.g. *chalt: chelter*; *schwach: schwēcher*; *aarm: ēērmer*; *spaat: spœœter* (cf. Note, § 20).

The comparative particle is *weder* or *als*, the latter an importation from NHG.

NUMERALS

§ 30

The indefinite article is the reduced unstressed form of *äin*, which declines like the possessive pronoun *myn* and can also be used both as a noun or an indefinite pronoun ('somebody' = NHG *jemand*) and as an adjective. For the forms see § 33 *myn*. The fem. adjectival common case form is *äi* which is also the neuter form before adjectives. The numerals *zwäi* '2' and *drüü* '3' distinguish three genders and two cases, a common case and a dative, when used as nouns.

	m.		f.		n.	
Common Case	zwee;	drei;	zwoo;	drei;	zwäi;	drüü
Dative	zweene(n);	dreine(n);	zwoone(n);	dreine(n);	zwäine(n);	drüüne(n)

In the speech of the younger generation there is a good deal of confusion between the genders.

PRONOUNS

§ 31. PERSONAL PRONOUNS

The forms of the personal pronouns vary according to whether
they are stressed or not. Stress usually produces a lengthened vowel,
lack of stress causes a reduction of the vowel. It is possible to distinguish a stressed, a semi-stressed and an unstressed form. The
stressed form is used for contrasting, e.g. *iich, nid duu* 'I, not you',
the unstressed form mostly before other pronouns, in final position
and between stressed words, in other words enclitically. The personal
pronoun is the only word-class which distinguishes subject and direct
object, i.e. has a nom. and an acc.

	1st Person	*2nd Person*
Nom. sg.	iich, ich, i, e, -	duu, du, de, d, -
Acc. sg.	miich, mich, mi	diich, dich, di
Dat. sg.	miir, mir, mer	diir, dir, der
Nom. pl.	miir, mir, mer	iir, ir, er
Acc. pl.	öis, is	öi, i
Dat. pl.	öis, is	öi, i

	3rd Person			
	m.	*f.*	*n.*	*pl.*
Nom.	ëër, ër, er	sy, si, s	ëës, ës, es, s	sy, si, s
Acc.	inn, in, en, e	sy, si, si	ins, s	sy, si, s
Dat.	imm, im, em	ire, ere, re	imm, im, em	ine, ene, ne

Notes

(1) *e* is always [ə]; *d* (2nd pers.) is fortis; *s* is lenis; *inn, imm* with
fortis nasal, see § 14.5.

(2) The form of polite address *sy* is never reduced to *s*.

(3) The enclitic *i* of the 1st pers. is omitted before a further pronoun beginning with a vowel; and after verbs the pers. pron. of the
2nd pers. sg. is omitted.

(4) It must be realized that usage is infinitely varied as factors of
rhythm and emphasis and the character of the surrounding sounds
all play their part, cf. Weber, *ZGr.*, pp. 153–62; Baur, pp. 54–8 and
the following examples: 'Alte, mach was *d* wottscht, aber *miich*
tunkts, *es* ghöör *si* nüd, und *i* wett, *du* wuurdischt *öis* ychauffe,
zmindescht *miich*' (Old man, do what you want, but to my mind

it is not right, and I should like you to get us naturalized, at least me). 'Wän *er* nu gwüsst het, was *ēēs* von *em* tänkt, öb*s* öppis uf *em* heig und öb*s en* überhaupt gwaari!' (If he had only known, what she[1] thought of him, whether she liked him and whether she took notice of him at all). 'Wie*s es* amig*s*, wo*s* na Chind gsy sind, gmacht händ?' (As they used to do it when they were children).

The enclitic *s* for 'they, them, it, she, her' and the preceding word are usually spelt as one word.

The indefinite personal pronoun is *me*, in prevocalic position *men* or *mer*, dat. *äim*, acc. *äin*.

§ 32. REFLEXIVE PRONOUNS

As in NHG there is only one special form *si(ch)* for the third pers. sg. and pl., which in genuine dialect is only used for the acc. Otherwise the personal pronouns function as reflexive. E.g. 'er hät *si* wele wyterbilde' (He wanted to improve his knowledge); 'si truckt s Gööfli a *sich* ane' (she presses the child to herself); 's Elsi[2] nimt en mit *em*' (Elsie takes him to herself).

§ 33. POSSESSIVE PRONOUNS

They are *myn, dyn, syn, öise, öie, ire.*

(i) *myn, dyn, syn*

	m.	f.	n.	pl.
Common Case . .	myn(2)	myni(1)	mys	myni(1)
Dative . . .	mym	mynere(n)	mym	myne(n)

Notes

(1) The older form is *my*, cf. Vogel: *sy Stell* 'his job'.

(2) When used as a noun or anaphorically the poss. pron. referring to a masc. noun has, in the common case, a special form: *myne(n)*. Otherwise the same forms are used but they are not preceded by the definite article (cf. NHG *der meinige*).

(3) When unstressed the vowel *y* is shortened to *i*.

(4) Relics of genitive (pl.) forms are *syner Läbtig* 'all his life'; *synerzyt* 'long ago'.

(ii) *öise, öie, ire* (f. sg. and 3rd pers. pl.)

	m.	f.	n.	pl.
Common Case . .	öise(n)	öisi	öises	öisi
Dative . . .	öisem	öisere(n)	öisem	öise(n)(2)

---

[1] SGm. uses the neuter for females as a form of endearment.

[2] *Elsi*, like all other feminine Christian names ending in the diminutive *-i* or *-li*, is neuter, as this gender is felt to be more polite and endearing.

Notes

(1) *öise* and *öie* have extended forms: *öisere, öiseri, öisers*, etc., which are used indiscriminately with the shorter forms, e.g. Vogel, *öiserem Verliebte* 'our lover' dat.

(2) Besides this form there is also *öisne, öine*.

§ 34. DEMONSTRATIVE PRONOUNS[1]

For 'this' and 'that' Zt. has *dëë* and *desäb*.

34.1

	m.	f.	n.	pl.
Common Case . .	dëë	die	daas	die(3)
Dative . . .	dëm(2)	dëre	dëm(2)	dëne

Notes

(1) All these forms are spoken with strong emphasis. When used anaphorically the length of the vowel is reduced: *dë, das*. The unstressed forms, *de, d, s* are the definite articles (see § 23).

(2) *m* is fortis, *d* is everywhere lenis, so is *s*.

(3) There is an alternative form *diene*.

34.2

	m.	f.	n.	pl.
Common Case .	desäb	disäb	säb	disäbe(n)
Dative(1) {	säbem	säbere(n)	säbem	säbe(n)(2)
{	emsäbe(n)	dersäbe(n)	emsäbe(n)	desäbe(n)

Notes

(1) The compound dative forms are used when special emphasis is given.

(2) In the dat. pl. there is an alternative form *säbne, desäbne*.

34.3 In the sense of 'the other one' Zt. uses *dise(n)*, which is declined according to the strong declension of the adjectives.

For 'such' the dialect possesses a bewildering number of alternative forms, e.g. *settig, esettig, sonig, esonig, e soo, ase* (see Glossary.)

§ 35. INTERROGATIVE PRONOUNS

Common Case	Dative
who? wëër, wër	wëm
what? waas, was	—
which? sg. wele(n) (m.), weli (f.),	welem (m., n.), welere(n) (f.)
weles (n.)	
pl. weli	wele(n)

---

[1] E. Schwyzer, 'Die Demonstrativpronomina des Schweizerdeutschen', *Indogermanische Forschungen*, xxvi, 1909, 283–91.

§ 36. INDEFINITE PRONOUNS

äine-, -i, äis; dat. *äim, äinere* (§§ 30, 33)	} somebody
öpper, dat. *öpperem* (or *öppertem*)	
niemer(t), dat. *niemer(t)em*	nobody
öppis, dat. *öppisem*	something
echli (before nouns)	some, a little
nüüt	nothing
vil(i) adj.—as a noun *vili, vilne(n)*	many, much
männge(n), -i, -s, dat. *männgem, -ere(n)* (only sg.)	many a
epaar adj.—as a noun: *epaari*, dat. *epaarne(n)*	a few
etli(chi), dat. *etliche(n)*	several
iede(n) -i, -es; dat. *iedem, -ere*	each
all or *ali*, dat. *ale* or *alne* (pl.)	all
alls or *ales*, dat. *alem, alere* (sg.)	all
kän(2) -käin or *ekän—ekäin*	no, none

Notes

(1) *l* in *vil, vilne* is fortis, but lenis in *vili* (see § 14.5).

(2) When emphasized the vowel is usually *äi*. The form with prefixed article is used indiscriminately with the shorter form. *Kän* is declined as follows:

	m.	f.	n.		pl.
Common Case	kän	kä(n)	käs	kä(n)	käni
Dative	käm	känere(n)	käm	kä(n)	käne(n)

When used as a noun the forms are in the common case *käne* (m.), *käni* (f.). Before adjectives the neuter form, c.c., is *kä(n)* rather than *käs*, see indefinite article § 24. The short form *kä* is used before nouns of all genders which denote goods or ideas. The following examples illustrate the usage: '*Kän* Mäntsch het tänkt, das er *kän* Hiessige wëër' (nobody would have thought that he was not a native of the town); 'Gfel häd . . . er ä gaar *e käs*' (he had no luck at all); 'en rächte Yfer für de Prueff häd er äifach *e käne* mee uufpraacht' (he simply could not gather any more enthusiasm for his job); *kä Läder* (no leather); '*e käs* Stëërbeswöörtli' (not a word); 'nu *kä* fuul Umwääg' (no more silly detours); 'En Huet zum Abnëë häd er *e känen* aa' (he had no hat to take off).

§ 37. RELATIVE PRONOUNS[1]

In all cases and genders Zt. uses *wo(n)*, e.g. 'äine, *wo* bätet' (one who prays); 'de Mäischter, *won* es Lädergschäft . . . ghaa häd' (the master who had a shop for leather-goods). *Wo* functions also as a conjunction of time (NHG *als*): '*wo* de Horscht us der Schuel choo ischt' (when H. left school).

[1] Cf. O. Weise, 'Die Relativpronomina in den deutschen Mundarten', *ZfdMaa.*, 1917, pp. 64–71.

VERBS

§ 38. Forms and Classification

The SGm. verb has the following form classes: infinitive, impera-tive, past participle, present indicative and present subjunctive, past subjunctive (= conditional), and the compound tenses perfect, pluperfect, and a passive.

The *infinitive* ends in *-e(n)*, except in the case of the monosyllabic verbs enumerated in § 47. The infinitive particle is *z*, e.g. de Horscht häds chuum gwaaget, em Elsi *z mĕrke z gĕĕ* 'H. hardly dared to let E. know'.

The *imperative* is in the sg. identical with the sg. of the present but endingless and in the plural it corresponds to the pl. of the present indicative.

According to the formation of the past participle the verbs can be classified as follows:

Type A: p.p. ending in *-e(n)*;
Type B: p.p. ending in *-t*;
Type C: p.p. ending in *-et*.

The *past participle* is characterized by the prefix *g-*. Exceptions: *choo* 'to come', *woorde* 'become', and all modal auxiliaries, see § 46, but including the verbs with the suffix *-iere*. Verbs with prefixes are excepted as in NHG.

This prefix is assimilated under the conditions outlined in § 17, e.g. *bäte* 'pray': *pätet*; *gĕĕ* 'give': *ggĕĕ*; *tänke* 'think': *tänkt*.

§ 39. Verbs of Type A

(p.p. ending in *-e*)

The distinguishing mark of the majority of verbs of Type A is the difference in the root vowel between the present and the past parti-ciple, though there is one sub-group with identical vowel. The so-called strong verbs of MHG and NHG belong to Type A. Com-paratively few verbs which were strong in MHG have become weak in SGm. Owing to the loss of the simple preterite the vowel-alterna-tion classes are much fewer than in NHG.[1]

If we classify the verbs[2] according to the stem alternants we can distinguish the following classes, leaving out of account the mono-syllabic verbs (see § 47):

I. The vowel of the infinitive and present is the same as that of the past participle:

---

[1] Bjarne Ulvestad, 'The Strong Verb Conjugation System in German', *Word*, xii, 1956, 91–105, distinguishes 48 different classes covering 165 strong verbs according to the root-vowels. The OHG ablaut classes are of course an in-adequate system of classification for modern dialects including NHG.

[2] They are listed in alphabetical order in Weber, *ZGr.*, pp. 372–5.

(i) [ɒ:] *faare* 'go by vehicle', *blaase* 'blow', *schlaaffe* 'sleep', *braate* 'roast', *raate* 'advise';

(ii) [ɒ] *fale* 'fall', *halte* 'hold', *wachse* 'grow'—*wäsche* 'wash' and the isolated verbs *haue* 'hit', *lauffe* 'go' but p.p. now usually *gloffe*; *häisse* 'to be called', *wöische* 'wish', *schäide* 'to turn (of milk)', *stoosse* 'push', *boue* 'build'. This class, including about 24 verbs, corresponds mainly to the OHG classes VI and VII.

II. Vowel alternation [i:/i]: *schrybe*, 22[1] verbs and *lyde* 'suffer', *schnyde* 'cut' with change of the consonant $d > t$ (Grammatical Change). This is the OHG class I.

III. Vowel alternation [y:/o]: *flüüsse* 'flow', about 17 verbs and *süüde* with consonantal change $d > t$. This is largely the OHG class II.

IV. Vowel alternation [i, y/u] before nasal: *finde* 'find', *schwüme* 'swim', about 24 verbs, corresponding to the OHG class III a.

In most cases where the root-vowel of the infinitive is [æ], or [ɛ:] before *r*, all persons of the sg. present indicative have the root-vowel [i].[2] Three classes belong to this category:

V. Vowel alternation [æ/u] before *l*: *hälffe* 'help', 4 verbs, but not *stäle* 'steal', which belongs to the following class. This corresponds to part of the OHG class III b.

VI. Vowel alternation [æ/o]: *bräche* 'break', about 12 verbs. This class corresponds to part of the OHG class III b and class IV. Here also belong the 4 verbs with [e] in the inf.: *verdeerbe* 'spoil', *schmelze* 'melt', *verschrecke* 'be frightened', *befele* 'order'; and *schwööre* 'swear'. The stem vowel *e* results mainly from confusion with the causative verb or is due to NHG influence.

VII. Identical vowels *ä*: *ässe* 'eat', about 10 verbs. This class derives from the OHG class V.

VIII. Vowel alternation [i/æ]: *ligge* 'lie', *sitze* 'sit', *bitte* 'beg' (OHG class V).

IX. Vowel alternation [u:/o]: *suuffe* 'drink' and *suuge* 'suck' (OHG class II).

X. Vowel alternation [iə/o]: *zie*—*zoge* 'pull', *schiebe* 'shove' (OHG class II).

XI. The verbs *röie*—*groue* 'regret', *schreie*—*gschroue* 'cry'.

§ 40. VERBS OF TYPE B

(p.p. ending in -*t*)

This type continues essentially the OHG weak -*jan* class. Thus especially verbs with root-vowels which are the result of mutation

---

[1] The complete lists are found in Baur, pp. 89–93.
[2] Exceptions: *fächte* 'fight', *flächte* 'weave (basketry)', *wäbe* 'weave', *wäge* 'weigh', *mälche* 'milk'.

[*e, ü, ö, ä, ē*], e.g. causative verbs, belong to this type; so do the verbs with the suffix *-iere* and most of those ending in a vowel. There has, however, been a good deal of confusion between the original classes and many verbs which one would expect to be of Type C are found to have changed to Type B. Examples: *setze-gsetzt* 'to set'; *läbe-gläbt* 'to live'; *wëërme-gwëërmt* 'to warm'; *blüe-plüet* 'to flower'; *spaziere-gspaziert* 'to walk'. Irregular verbs, which according to the formation of the p.p. belong to this type are: *wüsse-gwüsst* 'to know', pres. sg. *wäiss, wäisch*, pres. pl. *wüssed; bringe-praacht* 'to bring', cond. *brëëcht*.

§ 41. VERBS OF TYPE C
(p.p. ending in *-et*)

By and large, this type continues the OHG weak *-ēn* and *-ōn* classes, i.e. mainly verbs derived from adjectives and nouns with inchoative meaning. Further, all verbs in *-le, -ere, -ne, -me* belong to Type C.
Examples: *lose-gloset* 'listen'; *waarme-gwaarmet* 'become warm'.

§ 42. THE PRESENT

The endings are:

		Indicative	Subjunctive
	1	-e(n)(1)	-i
sg.	2	-sch(2)/-isch(3)	-isch
	3	-t /-et(4)	-i
pl.		-ed	-id

Notes

(1) *n* in prevocalic position, but not before the pers. pron. *i* in inversion. In the latter case the inflexional ending is dropped: *i mache(n)—machi.*

(2) The second pers. ind. has no pers. pron. in inversion, e.g. *machsch?*

(3) The ending *-isch* occurs in all verbs ending in a sibilant [s, š, ts] and in all verbs of Type C. Occasionally before a vowel *-t* is added (*-ischt*). See § 14.5.

(4) Verbs of Type C and verbs of Type A ending in *-t* add *-et* in the third pers. sg. ind.

(5) There is a uniform plural for all persons.

§ 43. THE CONDITIONAL

43.1 Zt. has not preserved many old subjunctive forms in the case of the verbs of Type A (strong verbs). Only the following are still current:

Type A *-ie-*: *fange-fieng* 'to catch'; *gfale-gfiel* 'to like'; *verraate-verriet* 'to betray'.
-uu-: *wëërde-wuurd* or *wüür* 'to become'.

Monosyllabic verbs: *-ëë-* or *-ie-*, *gëë-gëëb* 'to give'; *nëë-nëëm* 'to give'; *choo-chëëm* or *chiem* or *chëëmti* 'to come'; *sy-wëër* 'to be'; *tue-tëët* 'to do'; *gaa-gieng* 'to go'. (See § 47.) As an irregularity the weak verb *mache-miech* 'to make'. The endings are: first and third pers. sg. endingless, 2nd *-isch*, pl. *-id*.

43.2 The majority of verbs form the conditional by means of the ending *-ti*:

sg.	1, 3	*-ti*	*er frœœgti*	*flüügti*
	2	*-tisch*	*du frœœgtisch*	*flüügtisch*
pl.		*-tid*	*mer frœœgtid*	*flüügtid*

43.3 These synthetic conditional forms receive strong competition from the periphrastic conditional with the auxiliary verb *wuurd* or *wüür* and *tëët*, e.g. instead of *ich frœœgti*: *ich wüür frœœge, ich tëët frœœge*; *er flüügti*: *er wüür flüüge, er tëët flüüge*. In fact *wüür* is preferred except in the case of the most frequently recurring verbs where the synthetic form is still firmly entrenched.

§ 44. The Compound Tenses

To express that an action took place or a state existed in the past, SGm. uses two compound tenses consisting of one of the two auxiliaries *haa* and *sy* plus the past participle. Most verbs of motion form these tenses only with *sy*; otherwise conditions do not vary substantially from those prevailing in NHG. The pluperfect is formed by means of the perfect of those two auxiliaries.

> Perfect: *er isch ggange; er häd ggëë*
> Pluperfect: *er isch ggange gsy; er häd ggëë gha.*

Future time is more often than not indicated by a particle (e.g. *bald* 'soon') or an adverbial of time with the verb in the present. The auxiliary *wëërde* expresses an assumption or supposition.

§ 45. The Passive

The passive is formed with *wëërde* as in NHG, e.g. Vogel *da wiirt mer gleert* 'there one is taught'; *won er zum tüütsche Heeresdienscht yzoge woorden ischt* 'when he was called up for service with the German army'.

§ 46. The Modal Auxiliaries

These verbs share a number of characteristics. Infinitive and past participle are identical. A following infinitive is linked without the particle *z*. The conditional ends in *-t* in the first and third persons sg. and is otherwise conjugated in the regular manner in *-tisch* (2 sg.),

-tid (pl.). The present subjunctive has also the regular rendings *-isch* (2 sg.), *-id* (pl.). The following forms must therefore be distinguished.

	Inf.— p.p.	1st, 3rd Pers. Sg. Pres. Ind.	2nd Pers. Pres. Ind.	Pl. Pres. Ind.	Pres. Subj.	Condit.
'to be able' 'should like'	chöne	cha	chasch	chönd	chönn(2)	chönt(3)
or 'be able'	möge	mag	magsch	möged	mög	möcht
'must'	müese	mues, muen	muesch	müend	mües	müesst
'to want'	wele	wott, will(1)	wotsch	wänd	well	wett
'shall, should'	söle	söll(1)	sölisch	söled	söll	sött
'to be 　allowed'	tœœrffe	tœœrff	tœœrfsch	tœœrffed	tœœrffi	tœœrft

Notes

(1) On fortis or lenis *l*, see § 14.5.

(2) For the forms listed here one also hears *chöni*, etc.

(3) There are alternative forms with the regular *-ti* formation, e.g. *chönti*, etc.

§ 47. Monosyllabic Verbs

About a dozen monosyllabic verbs have forms which are substantially different from those of the corresponding verbs in NHG. As they are among the most frequent verbs the student is advised to take note of them. These monosyllabic verbs and the modal auxiliaries contribute much to the strangeness of SGm. for the student who approaches it from NHG.

Notes

(1) Before unstressed pronouns the shorter forms are usual. The longer ones derive from the inversion *tueni* > *tuene* like *schrybi*: *schrybe*.

(2) Like *gsee* goes *gschee* 'happen'.

(3) In inversion there are fusions such as *gömer* < *gönd mer*; *hämer* < *händ mer*, etc., with *mer* 'me' dat. *gimer* < *gib mer*.

(4) Present subjunctive and conditional take the regular endings set out in §§ 42 and 43, with the *-i* also occasionally in the first person of both the pres. subj. and the conditional.

(5) Beside the regular *heig, seig* there are also the forms *hei, häig, heb* and the extended forms *häigi, heigi, hebi* and *sei, seigi*. (See Weber, *ZGr.*, p. 186.)

(6) When used as an auxiliary.

(7) But with p.p. in *-t*: *trüet, plüet, gglüet*.

	Inf.	*Imp.*	*Sg. Pres. Ind.*	*Pl. Pres. Ind.*	*Pres. Subj.* (4)	*Condit.*(4)	*P.P.*
'to have'	haa	heb!	ha(n) häsch hät*	händ	heig (5)	het	ghaa
'to be'	syt	bis!	bi(n) bisch isch	sind	seig(5)	wëër	gsy
'to do'	tue	tue!	tue(nen)(1) tuesch tuet	tüend	tüeg	tëët	taa
'to give'	gëë	gib!	gibe(n) gisch git	gänd	gäb	gëëb	gëë
'to take'	nëë	nimm!	nime(n) nimsch nimt	nämed	nämm	nëëm	gnaa
'to come'	choo	chumm!	chume(n) chunsch chunt	chömed	chömm	chëëm or chiem	choo
'to see'	gsee(2)	lueg!	gsee(nen)(1) gseesch gseet	gseend	gsäch	gsëëch	gsee
'to go'	gaa	gang!	gaa(nen)(1) gaasch gaat	gönd	göng	gieng	ggange
'to stand'	staa	stand!	staa(nen)(1) staasch staat	stönd	stönd	stiend	gstande
'to let'	laa	las!	laa(nen)(1) laasch laat	lönd	lös	liess	glaa laa(6)
'to pull'	zie	zie!	zie(nen)(1) ziesch ziet	ziend	ziei	zieti	zoge

and like *zie*: *trüe* 'to grow fatter', *blüe* 'to flower', *glüe* 'to glow' (7)

* Our text has usually *häd* and sometimes *-ed* in p.p. and third pers. sg. ind., but fortis is more usual.

† Cf. Th. Schachner, *Das Zeitwort 'sein' in den hochdeutschen Mundarten*, Darmstadt, 1908.

PARTICLES

§ 48

One group of particles are particularly frequent and characteristic of SGm.: the particles of place and direction. In the case of the adverbs of place implying motion SGm., unlike NHG, does not distinguish between movement towards the speaker and movement away from the speaker (cf. NHG *hinein—herein*). The particles of direction go back to a compound of the type of preposition plus

F

particle *her/hin*, cf. MHG *ûf hin* > SGm. *ufe*, NHG *hinauf, herauf.* These particles are practically always used to reinforce the prepositions, cf. NHG *er geht in die Stadt*—SGm. *er gaat i d Stadt ie.*

The adverbs of place implying rest have a form beginning with *d-*, which is used when no further definition by an adverbial of place is given, and a form without initial *d-*, which is used when the place is further defined, e.g. *er isch dobe* 'he is upstairs', *er isch i der Wonig obe* 'he is upstairs in the flat'.

In the case of an impersonal pronominal object the prepositions and the corresponding adverbs take a prefixed *dr-*, e.g. *us der Trucken use nëë* 'to take something out of the box', *drus use nëë* 'take something out of it'. Thus also: *drin ie* (motion), *drin ine* (rest); *druf ufe, druf obe; drunder undere, drunder une.*

The most frequent particles are:

	Preposition	Movement	Adverb of Place (a) defined Rest	(b) undefined
'in, into'	i(ı) (drin)	ie, ine	ine	dine
'out'	us (drus)	use	usse	dusse
'on, on to'	uf (druf)	ue, ufe	obe	dobe
'down'	ab (drab)	abe	une	dune
'under'	under (drunder)	undere	une	dune
'over'	über (drüber)	übere	äne	däne
'through'	dur (derduur)	dure	äne	däne
'before'	vor (dervoor)	füre	vorne	divorne
'behind'	hinder (derhinder)	hindere	hine	dihine
'roundabout'	um (drum)	ume	ume	drumume
'to'	{ z (dezue)	zue	—	—
	{ a (dran)	ane	—	—

Notes

(ı) Some adverbs corresponding to these prepositions have long vowels, e.g. *y, uus, uuf, aab, duur, voor, aa,* and *dry, druus, druuf,* etc. E.g. *er git uuf* 'he gives up', *er lueget druuf* 'he sees to it'.

PHONETIC TRANSCRIPTION[1]

The following transcription is on the whole phonemic but indicates the chief allophones. The so-called geminate fortis (see § 14) is marked by doubling of the symbol. The semi-fortis in voiceless clusters is not distinguished from the normal fortis. The fortis of the voiced consonants is shown by (·). The assimilations are given as they occur in reading this text carefully at a normal speed. A description of the individual vowels and consonants is given in §§ 8, 9, 10, 11, 16. [b, d, g, v, z, ž, γ] are voiceless lenes.

Words of two or more syllables have the main stress on the first syllable, except where marked otherwise.

[1] A transcription of the Winterthur dialect of Zt. is also found in A. Götze, *Proben hoch- und niederdeutscher Mundarten*, Bonn, 1922, pp. 15–17.

əm hoːršt mɛːrts‿im vɒttər išt i juŋə jɒːrə vo ænət əm riː i
tšwiːts iə ɣoː: . ɛr hætsi i zim pruəf welə wiːtərbil·də un tnæbət‿iə
twæl·t əɣlɪ kšæɷ. ɛr išt‿ən žyːlɪ ɛːrnštə, vɒšt veištərə zɒttlərksel-
ksiː und hæts vər'štɒn·də mit‿ɒlər gɒttɪg lædər, æɷ kxunštlædər,
um·tskɒː . ts'tsyrɪ iž‿ər bimənə mæištər, wo væɪnɪ lædərwɒːrə
væɪlkhɒː hæt, ɒlz eːrštə werxštɒtɒːrbæɪtər iːtrættə, hæt‿tæŋ gliː ə
kšɒffɪgɪ žwiːtsərɪ kleːr‿kxænə, hæk‿khyrɒːtət und išt ziːnərlæptɪg
uvəm plɒts plibə.

ən žwiːtsər iž‿ər tswɒːr niə woːrdə, də vɒttər mɛːrts, wedər‿ən
pɒ'piːrigə nɒ æɪnə im hɛːrts‿inə; und eːbiks hæpmər ziːnər šprɒːɣ
ɒːkmɛrkxt, dɒz‿ər nit‿tɒː uːfkwɒxsə‿niš. nitnu zmuːl hæt‿tə uss-
læn·dər və'rɒːtə, æɷ zinɪ møːdəlɪ. ɛr hæt liəbər mit‿sinə tyːtšə
lɒn·tslyːtə wedər mit‿tə iːhæɪmišə vər'ɣeːrt, iš‿pmikliːd un tsɒː l-
mæištər von‿irəm və'ræɪŋ ksiː , iš mit ə pɒːr vryn·də vliːsɪg uf
t jɒk‿kɒŋə und hæt‿tussə ɒ tyːtšə žytsəvæštə mikmɒxt, unt‿sin
æɪntsigə buəb hæt‿ər ebə horst odər hoːršt tæɷfə lɒː .

də hoːršp‿mɛːrts išt‿ən vreɪnə pyːrštəl ksiː, gɒːr‿ə kxæɪm‿vər'
trukxtə, und ər hæt eːnər dər muətər nɒ·kšlɒgə wedər‿əm vɒttər.
kxæɪm‿mæn·tš het‿tæŋ·kxt, dɒz‿ər ə kxæn hiəsigə wɛːr. ɒbər
pfrœɪd ɒm pruəf und ɒm žyːsə hæt‿ər vom vɒttər keːrpt. wo də
hoːršt us‿tər žuəl ɣoː išt, hæt‿ən də vɒttər tsu ziːɣ i t leːr knɒː ,
ebə tsu zæbəm mæištər, wo‿nəz lædərkšæft mit‿ərə‿næɪgənə
wɛrxštɒk‿kfyərt hæt. zæp kšæft hæn·ts inərə žmɒːlə gɒs vo dər
ɒl·tštɒk‿khɒː ; unəninə iš‿tə lɒdə unt s mɒgə'tsiːn ksiː , woz
porpmənə: , hɒn·tæššə, briəftæššə, žuələrtheːkx, gyvərli um‿p‿
mɒppə vər'ɣæɷft hænd, und im hin·dərhoːv t wɛrxštɒt. də mæištər
hæt tspɛːrg khæɪsə und hæ‿p‿mit sinərə vɒ'miliə im eːrštə štokx
obə kwon·t, grɒd obənəm lɒdə. ybər dər gɒs ænə, grɒd wizə'wiː,
æɷ im eːrštə štokx, zin ts mɛːrtsə tshuːz ksiː . un teːt iš‿tə hoːršt
uːfkwɒxsə. tsum xuxxivæɪštər uːz hæt‿ər grɒd i twonig vom hɛr
tspɛːrk‿kse: , und ər hæk‿keːrn ump‿fil ybərəkluəgət, wæg‿əm
el·zɪ, dər toxtər vom mæištər.

zel·zɪ tspɛːrg iž ə groːsəz, blon·ts mæɪtlɪ ksiː, ə'ɣli ə veshts, ɒbər
ksun·d und uːrɣig, und wilz ə ɣrɒŋkxɪ muətər khɒː hæt, ižəz žo
bitsiːtə ə gurɒžiərts woːrdə und hæt ə'ɣli ə mæištərɣɒts ɒpkɛː .

TRAUGOTT VOGEL[1]: DE TRUURIG UMWÄÄG[1]

(En ëërnschti Gschicht)

Em Horscht Mëërz syn Vater ischt i junge Jaare vo änet em Rhy i d Schwyz ie choo. Er häd si i sym Prueff wele wyterbilde [2] und näbetie d Wält echli gschaue [3]. Er ischt en schüüli ëërnschte, fascht feischtere Sattlergsell gsy und häds verstande, mit aler Gattig Läder, au Kunschtläder, umzgaa. Z Züri [4] isch er bimene Mäischter, wo fäini Läderwaare fäilghaa [5] häd, als eerschte Wërchstatt-Aarbäiter yträtte, hät dän gly e gschaffigi Schwyzeri gleert käne, häd ghüraated und ischt synerläbtig uf em Platz plibe.

En Schwyzer isch er zwaar nie woorde, de Vater Mëërz, weder en papiirige na äine im Hëërz ine; und eebigs häd mer syner Spraach aagmërkt, das er nüd daa uufgwachsen ischt. Nüd nu s Muul häd de Ussländer verraate, au syni Möödeli. Er häd lieber mit syne tüütsche Landslüüte weder mit de Yhäimische vercheert, ischt Mitgliid und Zaalmäischter von irem Veräin gsy, isch mit e paar Fründe flyssig uf d Jagt ggange und häd dusse a tüütsche Schützefäschte mit-gmacht, und syn äinzige Bueb häd er ebe Horst [6] oder Horscht tauffe laa.

De Horscht Mëërz ischt en freine Pürschtel gsy, gaar e kän Ver-truckte, und er häd eener der Muetter naagschlage weder em Vater. Kän Mäntsch het tänkt, das er e kän Hiessige wëër. Aber d Frœid am Prueff und am Schüüsse häd er vom Vater geerbt. Wo de Horscht us der Schuel choo ischt, häd en de Vater zu sich i d Leer gnaa, ebe zu säbem Mäischter, won es Lädergschäft mit ere äigene Wërchstatt gfüert häd. Säb Gschäft händs in ere schmaale Gass vo der Altstadt ghaa; unen ine ischt de Lade und s Mageziin gsy, wos Portmenee, Handtäsche, Brieftäsche, Schuelertheek, Güferli und Mappe ver-chauft händ, und im Hinderhoof d Wërchstatt. De Mäischter häd Zbërg ghäisse und häd mit synere Familie im eerschte Stock obe gwont, grad oben am Lade. Über der Gass äne, grad wisewii, au im eerschte Stock, sind s Mëërze zhuus gsy [7], und deet ischt de Horscht uufgwachse. Zum Chuchifäischter uus häd er grad i d Wonig vom Hërr Zbërg gsee, und er häd gëërn und vil übereglueget, wägem Elsi, der Tochter vom Mäischter.

S Elsi Zbërg isch e groosses, blonds Mäitli gsy, echli e feschts, aber gsund und urchig, und wils e chranki Muetter ghaa häd, isch es scho bizyte e guraschierts woorde und häd echli e Mäischterchatz abggëë.

---

[1] See *Notes* on pp. 80 ff. For spelling, see §§ 7 and 15. The few alterations of Vogel's spelling are indicated there. I have also made his spelling of the names Meerz and Zberg more phonetic. In the few cases where Vogel's dialect forms (*nüd, Tüür, achzääni, chuurz, Chaart, schwaarz, häd, taage*) differ from my Winterthur dialect (*nid, Türe, achzäni, churz, Chaarte, schwarz, hät, tage*) I have retained his forms. See also §§ 6 and 9.1 on *ii*.

Iri uschiniert Aart häd em Horscht nüd schlächt gfale; vilicht häds
en tunkt, es ghöör si, das e rächti Huusfrau dihäimen öppenemaal
d Hose aaheig, wils syni Muetter au echli esoo ghaa häd und s em
Vater Mëërz ämel nie ygfale wëër, ire dryzrede.

Daas ales wëër rächt und guet gsy, wän nu äis nüd gsy wëër; näi,
äigetli ischt zwäierläi dezwüsched choo: de Horscht häds chuum
gwaaget, em Elsi z mërke z gëë, das ers eso guet mög. Bigryffli, es isch
ebe zu alem ane d Mäischterstochter gsy. S het dän na gly chöne
uusgsee, er hebs s Gschäft wele hüraate. Und de ander Haagge ischt
dëë gsy: im Tüütschen [8] usse isch es doozmaal echli gaar luut zue-
ggange, und s häd äin fascht tunkt, em Horscht sym Vater seig daas
gaar nüd bsunders läid. Ämel häd er in Veräine yfrig mitgmacht und
und häd ä wele haa, das syn Horscht deby seig. Bsunders s Schüüsse
häd em Horscht oordeli Frœid gmacht; jä nu, s Chlöpfe lyt [9] ja au
öis Schwyzere im Bluet. Er häd scho gwüsst, wie de Mäischter und
s Elsi zu säbem tüütsche Läbtig ygstelt gsy sind, und er wëër paraat
gsy, em Elsi zlieb nüd mitzmache und em Vater d Chappe z wäsche
und, wäns het müese sy, de Sack vor d Tüüre z gheie: ,,Alte, mach
was d wottscht, aber miich tunkts, es ghöör si nüd, und i wett, du
wuurdischt öis ychauffe, zmindescht miich!"

Näi, er häd nüd gnueg Rassen uufpraacht, derewääg vor de Vater
anezstaa! Er häd em halt nüd wele wee tue. Aber es wëër öppedie
gschyder, wämer äim en äinzigs Maal ghöörig wee tëët, weder das
mer en schoonet und em defüür syner Läbtig häimli öppis naaträit.

De Horscht Mëërz ischt doo öppen achzääni [10] gsy und häd
wääger nüd gwüsst, wo y und uus und öb er em Hëërz oder der
Stim vom Vater sell folge [11]. Zu alem ane stiirbt em na d Muetter,
und er häd quaasi mit ire s Muetterland, d Schwyz, verloore. Und
vo doo aa ischt de Vater chuum mee amenen Aabig dihäime plibe
und häd si ganz syne tüütsche Landslüüt überlaa.

Wo de Horscht emaale nach em Fyraabig eläige dihäimen ischt
und d Wonig uufruumet, wien ers vo der Muetter sälig gleert häd,
doo gseet er zum Chuchifäischter uus über der Gass äne s Elsi am
Stubefäischter staa und en Brief läse. Äigetli häd er nu de Schatte
von em am Umhang gsee, aber ganz tüütli. Gläitig häd er s Liecht
i der Chuchi glöscht, ischt am Fäischter staa pliben und häd gguenet
und gsüüfzget. So nëëch ischt das Mäitli gsy, biräits [12] zum Aalange,
und glych e soo wyt ewëgg. Wän er nu gwüsst het, was ëës von em
tänkt, öbs öppis uf em heig und öbs en überhaupt gwaari! Zum
Aarede manglet em s Guraaschi. Aber me cha ja schrybe; wäge waas
nöd schrybe? Grad iez bigoscht! Und ere s Briefli [13] über d Gass ie
gëë; amene lange Stäcke oder emänd imene Schwäbipäändli über-
eschicke, wies es amigs, wos na Chind gsy sind, gmacht händ?!

Uf äimaale isch em en chuurze Spruch dur de Chopf gfaare; äine

vo früener: „Horst Merz schenkt dir sein Herz!" — Häts Gugger,
daas wëër tüütli gnueg und verriet goppel ales!

Also öppis häd müese gschee! Und zwaar grad iez bigoscht, und
solang s Elsi deet äne am Fäischter gstanden ischt. Es Lœifterli von
irem Fäischter ischt offe gsy. Mer het sele e Brieftuube haa und ere
sys Gständnis uf eme Papiir-Röleli und mit eme Bändeli an Hals oder
an es Bäindli binde! Aber wohëër es Tüübli nëë?

Iez falt öiserem Verliebten öppis y; er isch halt de Soon vo sym
Vater, wo gëërn schüüsst. Es chund em in Sii, er heig ja emaal als
Bueb vom Vater e Pischtolen überchoo, mit dëre cha mer en hölzene
Zapfe furtschüüsse [14], ämel sicher so wyt, das er deet äne durs
Lœifterli ieflüügti. Me chönt ja dëë Zapfe uushööle und s Zädeli mit
em Vëërs drinie schoppe. Näi, das gieng z lang. Me schrybt de Vëërs
am ringschte grad ussen uf de Mantel vom Zapfen ane!

De Horscht häd si nüme lang bsune. D Pischtole ischt im Chaschte
bim alte Spiilzüüg ggläge, e paar Zäpfe denäbet. Er rybt äine devoo
hantli ab und schrybt mit Tinte rings drum ume: „Horst Merz
schenkt dir sein Herz!" Er ziilet lang — und zitteret deby, wien er
suscht nie uf em Schüüss-Stand tuet. Er truckt ab. Däne schëër-
belets [15]. Er häd dernäbet troffe, nüd is offe Lœifterli ie. Am Umhang verschwindt d Gstalt, s Fäischter wiirt tunkel. Schëërbe liged
uf der Gass une, grad vor em hele Schaufäischter vom Lade.

Es rägelet i d Gass abe. D Lüüt gönd mit offene Schirme verby.
Choge Züüg! Was häd er ä Äifeltigs aagstelt! Wän nu dëë blööd Zapfe
in nüd verraate tuet! [16] — De Horscht schlycht vors Huus aben
und suecht. Er findt nüüt. Er list gläitig di grööschte Schëërben uuf
und truckt si mit nasse Haare truurig wider i d Wonig ue. Er ischt
über en sälber taub.

S Elsi Zbërg häd si nüüt la aamërke, weder mit eme Woort, na mit
eme Blick. Vilicht wäiss si ä gaar nüd, was das Schëërbele z bedüüte
ghaa häd. Näi, Gfel häd öisere Horscht i der Liebi aber ä gaar e käs,
und d Schëërbe bringed em nüüt weniger weder Glück! [17]

Er häd syni Leer bim Mäischter Zbërg fërtig gmacht; aber en
rächte Yfer für de Prueff häd er äifach e käne mee uufpraacht. Dëë
chreftig, häimelig Gruch vo nöiem Läder, Lagg, Bäizi und Gërbsüüri
häd en alewyl as Elsi gmaanet und a die Tumhäit, won er mit em
Zapfe gmacht häd. Es isch em voorchoo, sider lueg si an em verby
oder gsëch en gaar nüme.

Wo doo im Nüünedryssgi de Chrieg aazettlet woorden ischt, häd
si de Horscht ä müese go mälde [18] und stele. Es isch em zimli
wuurscht gsy; ämel het er s Guri nüd ghaa, em Vater z widerspräche
und dihäime z blybe. Chuum öpper hets zwäg praacht, im de Chopf
und s Hëërz i d Oornig z mache, niemer weder d Muetter oder s Elsi.
Aber ebe, d Muetter ischt nüme daa gsy, und s Elsi häd schynts

anders z tue ghaa, und wäns öppis vo dem junge Maa sym Chumer gwüsst het, so hets goppel tänkt, s mües äine sälber wüsse, wo ane das er ghööri.

Säb häd er scho gwüsst, de Horscht Meerz; aber d Häimet, das sind schliessli d Mäntsche. Und i synere tüütsche Häimet häd de Vater gsäit wo dure; und i der Häimet vo der Muetter isch niemert gsy, won en a der Hand gnaa und em is Hëërz gredt häd. Soo isch es dërewääg truurig use choo, wien i iez prichte muen.

Er häd sy Stell bim Mäischter Zbërg uufggëë; er häd überhaupt de Prueff an Nagel ghänkt und ischt für e frönds Gschäft go räise. Er häd efäng e kä Läder mee möge gschmöcke [19]; vilicht häd er si vor em Elsi gschämt. Ëër, en Schütz, trifft nüd besser weder e soo, wäns emaal gilt! Won er zum tüütsche Heeresdienscht yzoge woorden ischt, häd er si nüd gweert und ischt ggange, ooni adie z säge. Er ischt i dere schüülige Hackmaschine äifach verschwunden und häd em Vater nie Pricht ggëë.

Syn Vater, de alt Mëërz, won em äntli d Augen uufggange sind und er naadisnaa mërkt, wohii die truurig Gugelfuer deet usse gaat, ischt tuuch und na feischterer woorde, häd si vo syne Landslüüte zruggzogen und faat aa drüber naatänke [20], was für es Ziil die Veräins-Schüüsserei häd. Da wiirt mer gleert, zeerscht es Aug zue z trucke. Wäge waas? Für waas? Hë, das mers Ziil besser gseet. Jää, erchänt mer d Wält und d Wored besser, wämer si nu mit äim Aug aalueget? Stëërneföifi, da mues öppis lätz sy und cha nüd stime! — De Vater Mëërz ischt i chuurzer Zyt en alte Maa woorde. Es häd uusgsee, er waarti nu na ufs Änd vom Chrieg, dän gäb er au uuf. Wies usechunt und choo mues, säb häd er guet gnueg gmërkt; aber wän syn Horscht glych umechunt und em Voorwürf macht und em ali Schand säit, säb wet er ooni en Mux uf si nëë, . . . wän er nu chiem!

Emaale zmitts im Chrieg ischt s Elsi Zbërg zum Vater Mëërz durechoo; si sitzt zuenem an Chuchitisch ane und faat aa, vom Horscht rede und de Vater Mëërz über en uusfrœœge; aber dëë häd taatsächli de ganz Chrieg dure e käs Stëërbeswöörtli vo sym Bueb vernaa ghaa und ischt druuf gfasst gsy, das er em als gfale oder suscht umchoo oder vermisst gmäldet wëërdi. Er häd em Elsi daas zueggëë. Doo wicklets useme Sidepapiirli öppis use und läits vor en ane. Es ischt de säb Zapfe gsy. De Vater Mëërz erchänt en grad und säid ä, es seig ooni Zwyfel em Horscht syni Schrift druff. Er holt d Pischtole füre und zäiget em Elsi, wie mer demit schüüsst. S Elsi laat de Zapfe nüd lige, es packt en wider is Papiir ie und nimt en mit em, und suscht säits nüüt, weder es seig eebig schaad, eebig schaad. Der alt Mëërz verstaat scho, was si demit wott säge: schaad, das es esoo häd müese choo! schaad, das s Hëërz dërewääg e Fuer macht!

Nüd lang drüberabe häd s Elsi Zbërg Hoochsig ghaa und als Frau

en Name überchoo, wo si nüd uf Hëërz rymt; und de säb Zapfe, wo
d Fäischterschybe verheit häd, versoorget si in es Schubläädli und
zäiged en e käm Mäntsch mee.

De Horscht Mëërz ischt underdessen en Weermaa, en Soldaat, en
Chrieger und sogaar en Möörder woorde, fryli ales nüd mit Flyss.
Syni Kameraade und Voorgsetzte händ im nu de „Schwoizer" gsäit,
und naso gëërn wëër er iez äine gsy. Epaarmaal isch er verwundet
und wider gflickt woorde und zletscht bimenen Aagriff uf en Bunker
is Maschinegweerfüür von äigene Truppe iegstürmt. Er isch lige
plibe, is Laazerett choo und dän mit eme styffe Chnüü als „Hilfs-
Chraft ooni Waffen" ygsetzt woorde. Oo, es isch em wien es Gschänk
vo der Muetter voorchoo, won er als Hülpi [21] nüme häd müesen a
d Front. Er häd bis oben ue vom Chlöpfe gnueg ghaa! S Häiwee isch
em zäntume naagschlichen und häd en alewyl ëërger aafëë plaage.
Nüd nach em Vater, säb nüd, aber na der stile Aarbet i der Buude
vom Mäischter Zbërg deet im Hinderhoof. Wän er emaale nöis Läder-
züüg gschmöckt häd, sind em biräits Trëëne choo. Mit em Gruch
isch wie hinder ere Wulchen es Bild füre choo: d Gass dihäime z Züri
i der Altstadt, de Lade und drin s Elsi, won er äifach nüd häd chöne
vergässe. Er ischt im ene Mageziin vo der Weermacht verwändet
woorde, und emaal, won ires Laager vo änglische Bombe troffe
woorden ischt und pränt häd, isch er mit eme Kameraad uus und
druus, äifach furt, ooni Ziil. Spœœter häd er mängsmaale verzelt,
wän er doozmaal gwüsst het, waas ales underwägs für en peraat gsy
ischt, so het ers alwääg nüd risgiert. Ämel dise [22] häd underwägs
müesen uufgëë; de säb ischt zwaar vil besser uf de Füesse gsy weder
ëër, aber er häds uf der Lunge ghaa und häd Bluet ghueschtet;
Theebee seigs, also tubërkulöös. Er heig die uhäimli Chranket uf em
russische Winter-Fäldzuug uufgläse; und nach de Hueschtechrämpf
häd er amigs gschumpfe, wän er draa zgrund göng, so müesed aber
die Dräckfiicher, ebe d Tubërkle, ä grad hiigaa. — Und er häd würkli
defüür gsoorget! Ämel won er chuum mee häd wyter mögen und s ime
Hœeigaden underegschloffe sind, doo verwached de Horscht zmitts
im häiterhele Taag. De Gade häd pränt. Er häd schier nu na sys
blutt Läbe chöne rette, und de Chrank ischt verbränt, samt de
Tubërkle. De Horscht häd sich nüd chöne uusrede, das dëë aarm
Kärli sich also quasi sälber kremiert häd.

Er isch eläi wyter gwalzet; am Taag isch er mäischtes amene ver-
steckte Plätzli underekroche, defüür znacht gloffe. Emaal isch er
wider in en uuspränts Doorff choo; er häd under de vercholete
Trämel gnüelet und öppis z Ässe gsuecht und ä alerhand z Bysse und
zum Aalege gfunde. Under em Grümpel ziet er ä en aaprœiseleti
Wandchaart a zwee runde Stääbe füre. Waarschyndli ischt dëë Stäi-
huuffe vorhëër es Schuelhuus gsy. Uf dere Chaart häd er gsee, won

er äigetli ischt; ganz am Rand une ischt na de Bodensee druff und
es Stuck vo der Schwyz. De Horscht ischt aneghockt und häd di
lengscht Zyt i die Landchaart iegstuunet und deet übere glueget,
won er emaale dihäime gsy ischt. Am liebschte het er die Chaart mit
em gnaa; aber si häd em doch echli zvil Gstelaasch gmacht. Ëër nüd
fuul und schnyt mit em Hegel en Rieme drus use, so bräit wien e
Hand und mee weder anderthalb Meeter lang. Druff ischt syn Wääg
gsy über Bëërg und Taal, dur Bäch und a Oortschafte verby bis zum
Rhy abe: häi zue! Er häd dëë Rieme zämegrugelet; es häd en ticke
Rugel ggëë, und er häd em Soorg ghebt, wie eme Kompass.

Won er äntli an Rhy chunt, abgschunde, halbe verhungeret,
ghetzt, aber glych gottefroo, so isch es für en hööchschti Zyt gsy.
Vom Schwaarzwald äne dure händ si di uufglööste tüütsche Verbänd
zruggzoge, und di Allierte händs mit Panzere und Fluugzüüg vor
si ane tribe. D Straasse, d Wälder und d Döörffer sind vole Flüchtling
gsy. Und dëë Durenand vo Uniforme und Spraache! Däne uf der
Schwyzersyte vom Rhy blüend d Schleedörn, schynt d Sune und
chäreled grad es Isepaanzügli wie zum Gfätterle so hëërzig i den
Ächere und Wisen umenand. Es häd de Horscht tunkt, nu deet seigs
Früelig und heigs rächte Suneschy, da äne seig ales zhinderfüür. Er
häd s Häiwee chuum mee chöne uushalte; na ebs rächt timbered häd,
isch er is Wasser gstige und schwümt under Liecht [23] übere. Niemer
häd en erlickt, kän Poschte häd gschosse. Ase blutt isch er däne s
gëëch Poort ue kläderet, mit em Gwand amene Bündeli uf em Rugge.
I de Stuude häd er si wider aagläit. Und was häd er doo gmacht?
Am liebschte het er di eerschte beschte Bœim umaarmet. Ämel isch
er aneghuuret und häd d Händ zämegläit und häd vor si ane gsäit:
Gottloobundtank, Gottloobundtank.

Er häd nüd gwüsst, öb syn Vater na läbi; föif Jaar isch er ja furt
gsy, de Horscht Mëërz; föif Jaar häd er verlooren und verbutzt. Wie
das Band chömeds em voor, won er us der aapränte Wandchaart use
gschnitte häd: ganz schmaal und mager, wien en truurigen Umwääg;
nüd nu über Bëërg und dur d Tääler: dur d Höll vo dem Chrieg dure,
dur Sumpf, Dräck, Bluet und Äiter dure. — Oo, ir aarme föif Jaar,
wie truurig, gschämig hani öi traktiert! Du aarms, liebs Land, diir
bini devoo gloffe, wie de verloore Soon. Nüd de Vater hani verraate,
nüd s Vaterland, defüür s Muetterland.

Er ischt ghuuret und häd d Händ zäme ghebt wien äine wo
bätet.

De ganz Chrieg dure häd er es Goldstückli, es Vreeneli [24], amene
Läderriemli und imene Läderseckli um de Hals träit. Das Vreeneli
häd er am nëëchschte Taag, won er e paar Stunde dur d Nacht i sys
Muetterland ie gloffe gsy ischt, uf eme Baanhoof anegläit und es
Bileet glööst: Züri äifach. Dän isch er im Doorff zum ene Haar-

schnyder ggange, und dëë häd e käs bitzeli uufgmüpft, hë wil dëë
Maa ja züritüütsch gredt häd wien öiseräin.

Won er doo i der Stadt inen aachunt, gaat er zeerschte in e groossi
Würtschaft, bstellt es Bier und frœœged nach em Adrässbuech. Was
er deet drin suecht, staat fascht z hinderscht under em Zëtt: Zbërg.
Ja, der alt Mäischter ischt drin aaggëë; aber s Elsi findt er nüd. D
Muetter Zbërg ä nüd. Die ischt alem Aaschy naa gstoorbe. Jeeger
Gott, es wiirt doch nüd sy! Waas dän? Hë, das au s Elsi nüme daa
ischt! Mol, daa staat si ja, aber mit emen andere Gschlächtsname.
Er isch uf e soo öppis gfasst gsy; het si öppe sele uf en waarte? Aber
es schwynt em iez glych fascht vor den Auge. Er trinkt syn Bächer
uus, und iez wäiss er ämel, wäge waas es em trümlig ischt. Derig
starchs Bier häd er halt scho lang nüme ghaa.

Dän suecht er de Vater Mëërz im Buech ine und findt en na im
glychen alte Huus wisewii vom Lade. De Horscht wäiss iez, was er
z mache häd. Nänäi, nüd zeerscht zum Vater gaa, bhüetis, nu kä fuul
Umwääg mee mache! Anestaa, und nüd ufs Muul hocke, rede! Nüd
wider go Zäpfe verschüüsse und d Lüüt demit go vergelschtere! Aber
wän s Elsi alewyl na nüüt wott wüsse von em, iez eerscht rächt nüd,
won er dërewääg abbrännt und als en halbe Chrüppel umechunt? Jä
nu, dän häd er äntli de Bschäid und füert si dernaa uuf! Wän er nu
wider en Poschte findt und syner Aarbet cha naagaa, frisch Läder
tœœrff schmöcke und wäiss, won er dihäimen ischt.

Sys Gwand, won er underwägs gfunde und zämepättlet häd, macht
na ganz en oordeligi Fale, es ischt nu e chly z wyt. Aber er macht e
rächti Gattig drin. Und wän er si Müe git und fescht uf d Zää bysst,
so falt äim sys Hülpe sicher gaar nüd so schüüli uuf. Im Fäld sett er
bigoscht gleert [25] haa, wie mer mues uufträte, das mer de Lüüte
Ydruck macht. Nu so dän, loos!

D Ladeglogg schäled wie amigs, so lang hinderem d Tüür offen
ischt. Es ischt scho feischter im Lade, und niemer ischt daa. Iezt
gaat s Liecht aa, und e Frau chund hinder de Gstell und Chäschte
hinefüre; es ischt s Elsi. Er känt si grad. Si träit es Chindli uf em
Aarm.

„Grüezi," säit de Horscht.

Si lueged en aa und känt en nüd, vilicht wil er gäge s Schaufäischter
staat und si d Heli [26] tuet blände. Aber syni Stim chunt ere goppel
bikannt voor.

„Grüezi, Elsi," säit er und hebt ere d Hand über de Ladetisch ane.
En Huet zum Abnëë häd er e känen aa.

Iez taagets inere. Si säit lysli: „Du myni Güeti, duu bisch es?"

„Ja," säit ëër. „I ha der wele cho grüezi säge, und ha wele frœœge
. . ." Er cha nüd wyter rede, es wëër en Luug, wän er säiti, er heb
wele frœœge, öb em de Mäischter Aarbed heig. Er hielts ja nüd uus

amene Platz, won er al Taag ire verchëëmti und sich voorhebe
müessti, er heig si mit syner äifeltige Schüüsserei das Mäitli vertumet.

S Elsi häd s Chindli uf de Ladetisch abgstelt, bhaltets aber im
Aarm und laats stämpfele; si nimt em Horscht syni Hand und säit:
„Du myn Trooscht [27], Horscht. I ha gmäint . . ." Si schwiget und
lueget en mit groosse, füechten Augen aa.

Er frœœget nüd, was si gmäint und erwaartet heig; er chas verraate. Si häd gwüss tänkt, er heig si eebigslang verloffen und seig
zgrund ggange. — Äigetli häd si rächt. Es ischt en andere, wo
umechoo ischt.

Er hebt alewyl na iri Hand, und si laat em si [28]. Was ischt daas
für e waarmi, wäichi Hand! Wie hërt und chnochig und chalt lyt syni
drinine! „Ischt das dys Chind?" frœœged er, wil er gschpüürt, das
er äifach öppis mues säge. „Bisch goppel ghüraate?"

Si laat syni Hand loos und läit si em Chind as Rüggli. „Ja," säit
si, „aber i bin eläige. S ischt nüd ggange; s ischt alerläi dezwüsched
choo. I bi gschide." Si truckt s Gööfli a si ane.

De Horscht häd nüd chöne truurig sy bi dem Pricht. Er häd em
eener Muet gmacht. „Du stuunischt, gäl," säit er, „das i daa bin.
Iich stuune sälber. Kurioos, hë? Eerscht iez gaats mer uuf, warum
i dëë wyt Wääg ha möge, mym Bäi ztrotz."

Er lupft sys Bäi und rybt s Chnüü. Si chund hinderem Korpus
füre. Und er verzelt ere vo säbene Chugle, won en nüd tööt händ
und im Gägetäil vor em Alerëërgschte bhüeted händ. Und iez mërkt
si sälber, wäge waas er choo ischt. „Horscht," säit si, „los, i wott de
Vater go hole. Er häd vil z tue, und si möged fascht nüd naa mit der
Aarbed. Duu, dëë frœit si ää! Mer händ mängsmaal vo der gredt. —
Së daa."

Si häd em s Chind zum Hebe ggëë und ischt ggange. Er häds uf
der Aarm gnaa und em i d Œigli glueget, und ëës häd em mit de
Fingerlene im Gsicht umetœœpelet.

Es sind grad beed us der Budig hinefüre choo, de Vater Mëërz und
de Mäischter. De säb Aabig sinds [29] nüme a d Aarbed, und i der
Wonig obe nach em Znacht häd de Horscht syn Landchaarte-Rieme
hinefüre gnaa, häd an uufgrolet und ene zäiget, uf was für böösen
Umwäägen ëër zletschtemänd de Häiwääg gfunde häd. Und ganz
spaat, wo di beeden Alte scho undere sind, macht s Elsi s ghäim
Schublädli uuf und holt de säb Zapfe füre, und si läsed mitenand,
was druff staat.

NOTES

It is assumed that the reader will have acquired some idea of the
grammar of the dialect before tackling this text. Thus points dis-

cussed in the phonology and morphology sections are not commented upon in these notes, which touch mainly upon questions of syntax and word-formation.

[1] *Traugott Vogel*. Born 27 February 1894 near Zürich, schoolteacher and author in dialect and NHG. His publications in dialect are: *De Baschti bin Soldate*. *Bletter ab em Gschichtebaum*, Büchergilde Gutenberg, Zürich, 1941; *De Läbesbaum, Gschichten us em Züripiet*, Büchergilde Gutenberg, Zürich, 1952 (contains *De truurig Umwääg*); *Züri-Fible* (*für Eerschtklässler*), Sauerländer, Aarau, 1947. Anthologies ed. by him: *Schwyzer Schnabelweid, E churzwiligi Häimetkund i Gschichte und Prichte us allne Kantön*, Sauerländer, Aarau, 1938; *Es Blüemli rot und wyss*, Schweizerdeutsche Liebes- und Heimatlieder, Auswahl und Geleit, *Der Bogen*, Heft 19, Tschudy, St. Gallen, 1951. A special number of *Schwyzerlüt* (xii, 7–9, 1950) is devoted to his work. Dialect plays: *De Schnydertraum*, Zwingli-Verlag, Zürich, 1939; *De Tittitolgg*, Sauerländer, Aarau, 1939; *Tokter Schlimmfürguet*, Märchenspiel, Orell Füssli, Zürich; *D Sunestraale*, Schweizer Schulbühne Heft 18; *De Chaschper i der Schuel*; *S Glöggli vo Bethlehem*, the last three by Sauerländer, Aarau.

De truurig Umwääg with its sentimentality and touch of smugness catches the atmosphere of Swiss petit-bourgeois mentality very well.

[2] In the sequence past participle plus infinitive SGm. lets the p.p. of the modal auxiliary precede the infinitive while NHG places the p.p. last, cf. *er häd si . . . wele wyterbilde* (p. 73): *er hat sich weiterbilden wollen*. See also: *s het dän na gly chöne uusgsee, er heb s Gschäft wele hüraate* (p. 74); *mer het sele e Brieftuube haa* (p. 75); and with *laa*: *s Elsi häd si nüüt la aamërke* (p. 75). But: *er hät e Schwyzeri gleert käne* (p. 73).

[3] The semantic field of verbs denoting vision is differently arranged from the corresponding NHG field: *luege* is 'to look', *gsee* 'to see', *aaluege* 'to look at', *gschaue* is 'looking at intently'.

[4] The preposition corresponding to NHG *in* + place name is *z* (< MHG *ze*), e.g. *z Züri, z Bëërn, z Basel*, etc.; for direction *uf* is used, e.g. *uf Züri* 'to Zürich'.

[5] For NHG *halten* (*feilhalten*) SGm. uses *hebe* or *haa* except in the sense of *to stop*. Cf. *d Händ zämehebe* (p. 78), *voorhebe* (p. 80), *s Chind zum Hebe gëë* (p. 80).

[6] Horst is a Christian name which is not used in Switzerland. It strikes the Swiss as typically German. Christian names and names denoting members of the family are always preceded by the definite article; in the case of female Christian names the neuter gender is usual (p. 61, fn. 2).

[7] *zhuus sy* is 'to rent a flat', NHG *zu Hause sein* is *dihäime sy*.

[8] As names of countries or regions SGm. can, in some cases, use adjectives elliptically, e.g. *im Tüütsche* lit. 'in the German (lands)', *im Wältsche ine* 'in French-speaking Switzerland', *im Fryburgische* 'in the Canton of Fribourg'.

SGm. has a vivid sense of direction which expresses itself in the luxurious growth of adverbs of place. Thus it is not enough to say 'to Zürich' but the speaker will always say 'out to Z.' or 'into Z.' or 'up to Z.' or 'down to Z.' according to the place where he finds himself. In Winterthur one says, e.g. *uf Züri ie*; *uf Bëërn ue*; *uf Gämf abe*; *uf Schaffuuse use*, *is Tessin abe* 'down to the Canton of Ticino', although the Alps have first to be crossed; *ie* (into) is used for places in the interior of Switzerland but strangely enough also for Paris: *uf Parys ie*. Basle, which lies on the way there, is *abe*, *uf Basel abe*. German towns are *use*, e.g. *uf Münche use*, except those down the Rhine which are *abe*. Italy and places south of the Alps or on rivers which flow down from Switzerland are also used with *abe*. London and England are *äne*, e.g. *z London äne*. Naturally when place is meant rather than direction the corresponding particles replace those of direction. They are set out in § 48.

[9] The MHG contracted forms *lît* (< *ligit*), *leit* (< *legit*), *seit* (< *segit*), *treit* (< *tregit*) are preserved as *lyt*, *läit*, *säit*, *träit*; Bd. *leit*, *seit*, *treit*.

[10] When substantivized the numerals end in *-i* (< OHG neuter *-iu*), e.g. *si isch föifi* 'she is five'; *es isch föifi* 'it is five (o'clock)'; *im Nüünedryssgi* (p. 75) 'in 1939'.

[11] In the subordinate clause the modal auxiliary precedes the infinitive, cf. also *wän er nu wider syner Aarbet cha naagaa, frisch Läder tœœrff schmöcke* (p. 79); *wie mer mues uufträte*.

[12] *biräits* 'almost', not NHG *bereits*.

[13] The diminutive of the noun ends in *-li*, which usually produces umlaut. It is very frequently used. Nursery language has also a diminutive in *-eli* without umlaut of a back root-vowel, e.g. *Händli—Handeli* 'hand'. Cf. Weber, *ZGr.*, 327–31; Stalder, 251–5; H. Stickelberger, 'Die Diminutiva in der Berner Mundart', *Philol. Studien für Ed. Sievers*, Halle, 1896, pp. 319 ff.; H. Gubler, *Die Liquid- u. Nasalsuffixe in der schwzd. Substantivbildung*, Basle, 1920.

[14] Note here the parataxis in preference to hypotaxis. This is frequent in all dialects.

[15] The formation of diminutives of verbs by means of the suffixes *-le*, *-ele* is quite frequent in SGm., e.g. *rägele* 'to drizzle', *stämpfele* (p. 80) 'to stamp with the foot (of a child)'. See Weber, *ZGr.*, pp. 363–5; Stalder, pp. 251–5. The suffix *-ele* expresses also something connected with the basic word, e.g. *schëërbele* 'to sound like broken glass or crockery'; *chärele* (p. 78) with iterative meaning 'to drive to and

fro'; *gfätterle* (p. 78) 'to play' (< *Gevatter*, i.e. 'play at fathers and mothers').

[16] The periphrastic use of the auxiliary *tue* in the present is frequent, especially in spoken dialect. (See Weber, *ZGr.*, p. 249 f.)

[17] It is a popular superstition that broken crockery presages luck.

[18] The verbs *gaa*, *choo* and *laa* combine very closely with a dependent infinitive and hence appear in a shortened form (*go, cho, la*), *er häd si müese go mälde* 'he had to report' (lit. 'go and report') and are divested of meaning. Thus they also appear with verbs of motion, e.g. *er gaat si go mälde* 'he goes and reports', and can even be doubled, *er gaat si goge mälde*. Cf. Weber, *ZGr.*, pp. 245–7.

[19] After *möge* the infinitive takes the prefix *g-* which has in this case perfective meaning. Cf. *er cha choo* 'he can come'; *er mag scho gchoo* 'he can get there/here (in time)'. Here: 'he could not stand the smell of leather any longer'.

[20] The infinitive follows without *z* also after *aafaa* 'to begin' and *uufhöre* 'to stop', cf. *si faat aa vom H. rede* (p. 76). Hence the word-order discussed in Note [2] applies here as well: *s Häiwee . . . häd en alewyl ëërger aafëë plaage* (p. 77).

[21] *Hülpi*. Nomina agentis in *-i* formed from verbs (*hülpe* 'to limp') have the connotation of irony or slight mockery at something that is disagreeable. (See Weber, *ZGr.*, pp. 335–6; M. Szadrowsky, *Nomina agentis des Schweizerdeutschen in ihrer Bedeutungsentfaltung*, BSG, xii, 1918, 87–99.)

[22] *dise* 'the other'—*de säb* 'this one', see § 34.

[23] *under Liecht* 'at dusk'.

[24] *es Vreeneli*: 20-franc gold coin.

[25] SGm. does not distinguish between 'to teach' and 'to learn' (NHG *lehren* and *lernen*). *Leere* serves both purposes.

[26] Of almost all adjectives an abstract noun can be formed in *-i* (with umlaut where possible), e.g. *d Heli* (NHG *Helligkeit*), *Tröchni* (NHG *Trockenheit*), *Güeti* (NHG *Güte*). See H. Wissler, *Das Suffix -i in der Berner, resp. Schweizer Mundart*, Frauenfeld, 1891; Stalder, p. 207 f.; M. Szadrowsky, *Abstrakta des Schweizerdeutschen in ihrer Sinnentfaltung*, BSG, xviii, 1933, 6–8, 22–40.

[27] Excl. 'my goodness'.

[28] If the dative of the personal pronoun is unstressed it precedes the accusative of the personal pronoun; if it is stressed the sequence is the same as in NHG.

[29] After the modal auxiliaries and *sy* 'to be' the verb of motion may be omitted, e.g. *si sind a d Aarbet* (*ggange*) 'they went to work', *er wott as Fäscht* 'he wants to go to the fair'.

GLOSSARY

Only words without a NHG equivalent which can be arrived at by application of the sound-correspondences set out in the phonology section (especially § 13) or words with a different meaning are listed below. For points concerning etymology, word-formation or usage the reader is referred to the *Idiotikon*. Stress is indicated by the symbol ['] before the stressed syllable only where a syllable other than the first is stressed. In the case of nouns, spelt with an initial capital, the letters A, B, C, D refer to the types of plural formation (see § 20), in the case of verbs these letters refer to the conjugations (see § 38).

Aabig, B. evening.
aabrœisele, C. scorch slightly.
aafaa, A. p.p. *aagfange*, start.
aafēē, unstressed inf. of above vb.
aalange, C. touch.
aalege, C. p.p. *aagläit*, put on (clothes).
Aarbed, C. work.
Acher, B. field.
adie, good-bye.
ä or *au*, also.
ämel, at any rate; at least.
äne, see § 48, adv. yonder.
änet, prep. dat. on the other side.
alewyl, always.
alwääg, probably.
amigs, formerly; usually.
anehuure, C. crouch down.
ase, so; cf. *esoo*.

Bäizi, f. C.(i) staining-matter.
beed, both.
bhüetis, excl. good Lord!
bi'goscht, excl. good heavens!
Bi'leet, n. A. ticket.
bi'zyte, early.
blööd, stupid.
blutt, naked; bare.
Bodesee, Lake Constance.
Budig, f. C. workshop.
Buude, f. C. workshop.

chärele, C. clatter to and fro.
chlöpfe, B. bang.
choge Züüg, excl. damned thing.

däne, see § 48, adv. yonder.
deet, there.
de'näbet or *der-*, beside.
děrewääg, so, in this way.
děrig, such.
de'zwüsched, in between.
doo, then.
doozmaal, at that time.
Dräckviich, n. D. vermin (term of abuse).
drüber'abe, afterwards.
dur, prep. through.
Durenand, m. sg. confusion.

ebs, conj. before.
e'chli, also *e chly*, a little.
eener, rather.
e'fäng, *e'fangs*, meanwhile, for the present.
e'läige, alone.
e'maale, once.
e'mänd, perhaps.
er'licke, B. catch sight; catch on.
e'so, *e'soo*, so; the same; such.
e'wěgg, away.

Fale, f. sg. appearance. *e F. mache*, it looks.
fescht, stout; firm.
Flyss, *mit F.* purposely.
frönd, strange, foreign.
frœœge, C. ask.
Fuer, f. B. mess.

84

gäl, sg. pl. *gäled*, polite form: *gäletsi*, cf. NHG *gell, gelt*.
Gattig, e G. mache, it looks . . .
gëëch, steep.
gfätterle, play (of children).
Gfel, n. sg. luck.
gheie, B. throw; fall.
gläitig, quickly.
gly, soon.
glych, adv. in spite of it all; *und glych*, and yet.
glych, adj. same.
Gööfli, dim. of *Goof*, m. C.(ii), little one.
goppel, surely; indeed.
gottefroo, very glad.
Grüezi, the most frequent and general formula of greeting.
Grümpel, m. sg. rubbish.
gschämig, disgraceful.
gschaffig, hardworking.
Gste'laasch, n. sg. bulk; *G. mache*, be bulky.
Güferli, n. A. suitcase.
guene, C. gaze, look at something wonderful.
Gugelfuer, f. mad behaviour or journey.
Gu'raaschi, n. sg. courage; *Guri*, short for above.
guraschiert, brave.

häimelig, homely.
häts Gugger, excl. of annoyed surprise.
hantli(-ch-), deft.
Hegel, m. A. pocket-knife.
hine'füre, see § 48, from behind.
Hœigade, m. B. hay-barn.
Hoochsig, f. B. wedding.
hüraate, C. marry.

iez, now.
Isepaanzügli, dim. A. railway train.

jää, emphatic, querying form of *ja* 'yes'.
jä nu, well, after all.
Jeeger Gott, excl. good God!

kläderet, p.p. < *chlädere*, C. climb.
Korpus, m. A. shop-counter.
kuri'oos, strange, odd.

G

Läbtig, m. sg. way of life; *synerläbtig*, all his life.
lätz, wrong.
Lagg, m. B. lacquer.
Lœifterli, n. A. small sliding window.
lose, C. listen.
lupfe, B. lift.
Luug, m. B. lie.
lysli, quietly, softly.

Mäischterchatz, C. domineering woman.
mee, more.
Möödeli, n. A. manners.
mol, yes (= NHG *doch*).
Mux, m. sg. movement; *ooni en M.*, without batting an eyelid.

na, = NHG *noch*.
naa-, after; *naagaa*, go after.
naadisnaa, gradually.
näbetie, besides.
nä'näi, no (emphatic).
nanig, not yet.
naso, the more so.
nëëch, near.
nüd, nöd, not.
nüele, C. rummage.
nüme, no longer.
nüüt, nothing.

obe, prep. dat. above.
öb, if.
öppe (see § 36) perhaps, about.
öppedie, occasionally.
öppenemaal, sometimes.
öppis, something.

par'aat, per'aad, ready.
Pürschtel, m. A. lad.

quaasi, so to speak.

rägele, C. drizzle.
ring, easy.
Rugel, m. B. roll (paper).
rugele, C. roll.

säge, B. p.p. *gsäit*, say.
schoppe, C. push right in.
Schuelertheek, m. A. school-satchel.
schüüli(-g-), terrible.

Schwäbipäändli, dim. A. cable-railway.

schwyne, B. vanish; *es schw. em*, he faints.

sĕ daa! here, take it.

sider, since.

Sii, m. sg. memory, mind.

Soorg hebe, look after (things).

spaat-spœcœter, late(r).

stĕĕrnefôifi, excl. damned.

suscht, otherwise.

taub, angry.

timbere, get dark.

Trämel, m. A. beam.

trümlig, giddy.

tunke, B. seem.

tuuch, depressed.

überchoo, vb. § 47, receive.

umechoo, vb. § 47, return.

umenand, about

umetœcœpele, C. dab.

Umhang, m. B. curtain.

urchig, genuine, natural, homely.

uschiniert, unrepressed.

uufmüpfe, B. take notice, stop to wonder.

uus und druus, up and off.

ver'butze, B. waste.

ver'chĕĕmti, cond. < *verchoo*, meet.

ver'gelschtere, C. frighten, anger.

ver'heie, B. smash, go to pieces.

ver'truckt, sneaky.

ver'tume, C. loose through stupid behaviour.

wääger, really.

wämer < *wän mer*, if one.

wise'wii, vis-à-vis, opposite.

Wored, f. sg. truth.

ychauffe, B. naturalize.

Zää, pl. < *Zaa*, B. tooth.

Zädeli, dim. A. slip of paper.

zäme, together.

zäntume, everywhere.

zhinderfüür, topsy-turvy.

zletschtemänd, at last.

Znacht, m. B. evening meal.

zwääg, healthy; *z. bringe*, bring about.

CHAPTER III
SCHWYZERTÜTSCH: BÄRNDÜTSCH

§ 1. BÄRNDÜTSCH[1]

This is the name popularly given to all German dialects spoken in the Canton of Berne. Topographically this Canton, by far the largest of the German-speaking Cantons, is extremely diversified, embracing the flat country at the foot of the Jura, the hilly districts south-west and east of Berne and the grandiose Alpine peaks and steep valleys of the Bernese Oberland. The dialects show, correspondingly, a greater diversity than those spoken in the Canton of Zürich. Nevertheless many features give them a unity to the ear of the outsider at least. Beyond the cantonal boundaries the Bernese type of High Alem. stretches into the adjoining Cantons of Fribourg, Solothurn, Aargau and Lucerne, so that it can be said that 'Bernese' is spoken between the Alps and the Jura from the French linguistic border in the west to a line running more or less south from Olten on the Aare to the Alps (say Brünigpass).[2] Taken in this wide sense the dialect is spoken by over three-quarters of a million people.

The variety of *Bärndütsch* described in the following paragraphs is that spoken by the middle and professional classes in the city of Berne and also in most other Bernese country towns. Owing to its proud and long history as a republican city state governed by a wealthy patriciate of landed gentry, Berne seems to have preserved differences in speech between town and country and between upper and lower classes more distinctly than Zürich.[3] The author of our specimen text, Rudolf von Tavel, was himself a member of the formerly ruling patriciate, and wrote in the urban upper-class language of his background, while the farmers in his novels speak the appropriate rural dialects.

A number of the peculiarities of Bd. are set out in the paragraphs dealing with the *General Characteristics of High Alemannic*. The urban variety of Bd. is distinguished from the speech of the surrounding rural district by the following features: *l* before consonants, in final position and when doubled between vowels is

---

[1] See E. Friedli, *Bärndütsch als Spiegel bernischen Volkstums*: i, Lützelflüh, 1905; ii, Grindelwald, 1908; iii, Guggisberg, 1911; iv, Ins, 1914; v, Twann, 1922; vi, Aarwangen, 1925; vii, Saanen, 1927.

[2] See the maps in Baumgartner and A. Bangerter, *Die Grenze der verbalen Pluralendungen im Schweizerdeutschen*, BSMaf., iv, Frauenfeld, 1951.

[3] Baumgartner deals with the social structure of Bernese society and its dialect stratification.

preserved but vocalized to *u* in rural speech;[1] *nd* is preserved but velarized to *ng* in the country;[2] *-ie-* against rural *-öi-* in words like *tieff* 'deep', *Fliege* 'fly' (cf. Zt. *tüüff*, *Flüüge*); preservation of the MHG diphthongs *ei, ou, öi (öü)*, while much of the countryside to the south of Berne (except the eastern and western Oberland) has monophthongs (*ē, ō, ȫ*);[3] Berne has *füüf* 'five', *fyschter* 'dark' against rural *föif* and *feischter*;[4] the northern half of the Canton has *ō* for MHG *â*, the southern including Berne has *ā*; those verbs which are generally monosyllabic in SGm. have long forms in urban speech as against short forms in the country:[5] *mer näme/nää* 'we take', *gäbe/gää* 'we give', *chönne/chöi* 'we can', *gange/gaa* or *göö* 'we go'; the city favours the ending *-ung* (*Zÿtung* 'newspaper') while rural speech has *-ig*; the city uses *abe, ufe, ine* 'down, up, in' (adv.), the country *ache, uche, iche*. Further marked regional features are: the north-west at the foot of the Jura has only lenis stops initially and partakes of the lengthening of MHG short vowels in open syllables (*Leichtinnendehnung*) much more widely than the rest of the Canton. The Oberland and western districts (incl. the German-speaking part of the Canton of Fribourg) belong to Highest Alem. which has very strongly marked differences from the rest of *Bärndütsch*, e.g. MHG *î, û, iu* are not diphthongized in hiatus (*frī/frei* 'free'); dissolution of the nasal even before velar fricative (*treiche* 'to drink'); widespread diphthongization of MHG *ê, æ, ô, œ*; unrounding of *ö, ü, öi*; preservation of unstressed vowels other than *ə* and *i*; frequent preservation of final unstressed *-n*; the strong declension of the predicative adjective (*si isch roəti* 'she is red', Henzen, *BSG*, xvi, 191).

THE PHONOLOGY OF BÄRNDÜTSCH

THE VOWELS

§ 2. THE VOWEL PHONEMES

The number of the vowel phonemes is increased compared with MHG owing to the fact that the lengthened, formerly short, high-tongue vowels do not coincide with the old, long, high-tongue vowels nor the shortened MHG long vowels with the old short ones. These products of shortening /i, u, y/ and of lengthening /ɪ:, ɔ:, ʏ:/ are, however, relatively infrequent. The mid-tongue vowels are all marked by a considerable degree of openness and laxness. /ɑ:, ɑ/ are central vowels without any lip-rounding.

---

[1] See Baumgartner, pp. 73–7. [2] *id.*, pp. 77–81.
[3] *id.*, pp. 91–4. [4] *id.*, pp. 82–6. [5] *id.*, pp. 46 f., 95–9.

	Front	*Front, rounded*	*Central*	*Back*
	i(:)	y(:)		u(:)
	ɪ(:)	ʏ(:)		ɷ(:)
	ɛ(:)	œ(:)		ɔ(:)
	æ(:)		ɑ(:)	

There is also the unstressed short central ə. There are six falling diphthongs:[1]

ɪə	ʏə	ɷə
ɛɪ	œɪ	ɔɷ

Before the semivowels *j* and *w* homorganic vocalic glides produce non-phonemic diphthongs, e.g. [blɑːṷ—blɑːuwa] 'blue'. Country dialects in which *l* is vocalized in certain positions have a much larger number of apparent diphthongs which are, however, better interpreted as single vowel plus vocalic allophone of *l*.

§ 3. SPELLING

Rudolf von Tavel, the author of our specimen text, follows the spelling conventions of NHG as closely as possible. He retains, for instance, the inconsistencies in the expression of vowel length. Thus in *rot, gross* length is not indicated, but in *wohl, froh* the NHG length sign *h* is retained. To facilitate the reading of the text I have indicated vowel length by doubling (thus *root, grooss*) in all cases where it is not already expressed in Tavel's spelling, e.g. by *h*. All vowels not so marked are short. The only difficulty is the distinction between the close and open varieties of the high-tongue vowels. The short close /i, u, y/ are spelt thus: ŷ, ŭ, ŭ̈. The long close /u:/ and /y:/ are doubled: *uu, üü*, but long /i:/ is rendered by the traditional Swiss *y*. The letters *i, u, ü* therefore stand for the short, open, lax varieties, which when lengthened are spelt *ii, uu, üü*. The two phonemes left without clear marking are /ʏ:/ and /ɷ:/. They are rare. The latter does not occur in our text, the former is found in the words *gspüürt, wüürde, derfüür, düür*. The letters and vowel phonemes correspond as follows:

Phoneme	*Letter*[2]	*Phoneme*	*Letter*	*Phoneme*	*Letter*
i i:	ŷ y	y y:	ŭ̈ ⎱ üü	ʏə	üe
ɪ ɪ:	i ii	ʏ ʏ:	ü ⎰ üü	ɪə	ie
ɛ/ə ɛ:	e ee	u u:	ŭ ⎱ uu	ɷə	ue
æ æ:	ä ää	ɷ ɷ:	u ⎰ (uu)	ɛɪ	ei
ɑ ɑ:	a aa	œ œ:	ö öö	œɪ	öi, eu
		ɔ ɔ:	o oo	ɔɷ	ou

[1] See the different interpretation for the dialect of Brienz, Bernese Oberland, in Schultz, *Studies in Linguistics*, ix, 1951, 34–65.

[2] As stated, where v. Tavel indicates length by *h* this is left unaltered.

§ 4. STRESSED SHORT VOWELS

4.1 [i] this short, close, high-front vowel occurs only as the product of shortening of MHG *î*: *Zÿt* 'time' (see § 8), *si sÿge* subj., 'they are'.

4.2 [ɪ] this open, high-front vowel is the regular correspondence of MHG *i* in positions unaffected by lengthening: *Fride* 'peace', *hinder* 'behind'; also *sid* 'since', *wil* 'because' (= MHG *î*) where the shortening preceded the shift i > ī.

4.3 [ɛ] is an open, lax, mid-front vowel representing:

(i) MHG *e* (the so-called primary umlaut) in positions unaffected by conditional changes (see §§ 4.9, 5.3). As distinct from Zt. the primary umlaut is [ɛ] also before some nasal clusters,[1] especially nasal geminates. E.g. *rede* 'to talk', *erchenne* 'to acknowledge', *geng* 'always', but see § 4.4 (iv).

(ii) Certain MHG words with *ë* must have exchanged this *ë* with *e* in medieval Alem., for these words, e.g. *geschter* 'yesterday', *Schwöster* (with rounding) 'sister' (for the others, see Jutz, p. 54) have generally the *e-* sound which corresponds to that continuing the primary umlaut.

4.4 [æ] is a very open, low-front vowel deriving from:

(i) MHG *ë*: *Gäld* 'money', *Wärchstatt* 'workshop'.

(ii) MHG *ä* (the so-called secondary umlaut):[2] *nächti* 'last night' and the analogical umlaut (see chap. ii, § 8.4) *hässig* 'spiteful'.

(iii) MHG *a* before *sch* (< *sk*): *wäsche* 'to wash'.

(iv) MHG *e* (primary umlaut) before certain nasal clusters: *dänke* 'to think', *aawände* 'to spend on clothing'.

(v) *e* in loan-words: *Fänschter* 'window', *Regimänt* 'regime, regiment'.

4.5 [ɑ] is a central, low-tongue vowel about like short *a* in NHG. It derives from:

(i) MHG *a* where no conditional changes have occurred: *Gass* 'road', *si gange* 'they go'.

(ii) MHG *â* shortened before a consonantal cluster: *fragt* 'asks'.

4.6 [ɔ] is an open, lax, mid-back vowel. It represents MHG *o* where lengthening has not interfered: *hocke* 'to sit', *gloffe* p.p. 'run'. In *fromm* 'pious' we have borrowing from NHG.

4.7 [ɷ] is an open, lax, rounded, high-back vowel. It derives from:

(i) MHG *u*: *Zunft* 'guild', *Chlumpe* 'lump, crowd'.

(ii) MHG *o* in certain words especially before nasals and liquids: *ghulfe* p.p. 'helped', *Wuche* 'week'.

---

[1] Berne lies in the transition zone between a northern area with MHG *e* > *ä* before nasal clusters and a southern zone where MHG *e* does not coincide with MHG *ë* before nasal clusters. See Baumgartner, p. 31 f., and the map *geng* (p. 31).

[2] See Braune-Mitzka, *Althochdeutsche Grammatik*, §§ 26, 27, 51; Paul-Mitzka, *Mittelhochdeutsche Grammatik*, § 41.

4.8 [u] this short, close, rounded, high-back vowel occurs only as a product of shortening of MHG *û*: *Hŭt* 'skin', *ŭfe*, adv., 'up'. But in the unstressed prep. *us*, *uf* 'out, up' the open variety is due to early shortening.

4.9 [œ] is an open, lax, rounded, mid-front vowel. It stands for:

(i) MHG *ö*: *Loubeböge* 'arcades'.

(ii) MHG *e* in labial surroundings: *frömd* 'strange', *brönne* 'to burn'.

(iii) MHG *ē* in the words *öppis* 'something', *öpper* 'somebody', *öppe* 'about' adv.

(iv) MHG *ü* in: *möge*, *sölle*, *chönne* (see § 30), *gönne* 'to grant'.

(v) MHG *œ*, shortened before consonantal clusters: *böscht* sup. 'most wicked'.

4.10 [Y] is an open, lax, rounded, high-front vowel and represents:

(i) MHG *ü*: *Chünig* 'king', *Usrüschtung* 'outfit', *Bschüsi* 'cobbled pavement', *lüpfe* 'to lift', *Rügge* 'back',[1] *schlücke* 'to swallow'.

(ii) MHG *i* in labial surroundings: *zwüsche* 'between', *Schümel* 'white horse', *wüsse* 'to know'.

(iii) MHG *iu* in a few words with early shortening, e.g. *hütt* 'to-day', *Fründ* 'friend'.

4.11 [y] this short, close, rounded, high-front vowel occurs only as the product of shortening of:

(i) MHG *iu*: *Lŭt* 'people', *Hŭser* 'houses', *bäärndŭtsch* 'Bernese dialect'.

(ii) the product of the dissolution of *n* before *s* with later shortening: poss. pron., *ŭse* 'our'.

§ 5. LONG VOWELS

5.1 [iː] is a tense, close, high-front vowel and derives from:

(i) MHG *î*: *sy* 'to be', *wyss* 'white'. In hiatus position MHG *î* has become diphthongized (see § 6.1) and in some positions it has become shortened. (See § 8.)

(ii) MHG *i* where *n* before a fricative has been dissolved: *fyschter* 'dark'.

5.2 [ɪː] is the corresponding lax, open, high-front vowel and occurs solely as the result of lengthening (see § 8) of MHG *i*: *miich*, *diich*, strongly emphasized 'we, you', *Spiil* 'game', *Wiirtshuus* 'inn'.

5.3 [ɛː] is an open, lax, mid-front vowel. It corresponds to:

(i) MHG *ê*: *meh* 'more'.

(ii) MHG *e* when lengthened: *Schleeg* 'blows', *Reed* 'speech'.

5.4 [æː] is a very open, low-front vowel and more frequent than the preceding vowel. It corresponds to:

(i) MHG *æ* (umlaut of OHG *â*): *dir nähmtet* cond., 'you would take',

---

[1] Umlaut has not been hindered by following fortis velar stop. Cf. chap. ii, § 8.7.

späät 'late', *Chääs* 'cheese' and analogical umlaut of *â*: *Räät* 'councillors'.

(ii) MHG *ē* when lengthened: *nää* 'to take', *gää* 'to give', *Schmäär* 'fat, grease'.

(iii) MHG *ä* when lengthened: *fäärbe* 'to colour'.

5.5 [ɑ:] corresponds to the short vowel (§ 4.5). It derives from:

(i) MHG *â*: *Raat* 'council', *Chraam* 'small wares'.

(ii) MHG *a* lengthened (§ 8): *graad* 'straight', *fahre* 'to ride', *aa-* NHG *an-* (prefix).

5.6 [ɔ:] corresponds in quality to the short vowel (§ 4.6). It derives from:

(i) MHG *ô*: *root* 'red', *Ooschtere* 'Easter'.

(ii) MHG *o* lengthened: *antwoorte* 'to answer', *Troog* 'trough'.

5.7 [ɷ:] is an open, rounded, high-back vowel and occurs exclusively as the product of lengthening of MHG *u*: *Luug* 'lie', *wuurd* condit. of *wäärde* 'to become'.

5.8 [u:] is the corresponding close vowel and continues MHG *û* where shortening has not occurred and except in hiatus position: *Huus* 'house', *verbruuche* 'to spend'.

5.9 [œ:] is a lax, open, rounded, mid-front vowel. It represents:

(i) MHG *œ* where length is preserved: *böös* 'wicked'.

(ii) MHG *ö* where lengthening has occurred (§ 8): *Wöörtli* dim., 'word'. From MHG *ü* in *döörffe* 'to be allowed'.

5.10 [Y:] is an open, rounded, high-front vowel and occurs exclusively as the product of lengthening of MHG *ü*: *wüürde* 'would', *gspüürt* p.p. 'felt'.

5.11 [y:] is the corresponding close vowel and continues

(i) MHG *iu* except in hiatus position and where shortening has occurred: *grüüslech* 'very', *nüüt* 'nothing' (< OHG *niwiht*), *süüfze* 'to sigh'.

(ii) MHG *ü* where *n* before a fricative has been dissolved: *füüf* 'five', *üüs* dat. pl. 'us'.

§ 6. Diphthongs

All diphthongs are stressed on the first element which corresponds to the short vowels described in § 4. Where the second element is not [ə] it also corresponds to the respective short vowels. The 'new' diphthongs, developed in hiatus position from MHG *î*, *û*, *iu*, have coincided with the 'old' diphthongs.

6.1 [ɛɪ] derives from:

(i) MHG *ei*: *Meinung* 'opinion', *reise* 'to lead, travel'.

(ii) MHG *î* in hiatus position: *frei* 'free', *parteiisch* 'partisan'.

(iii) MHG *-egi-*: *treit* 3rd pers. sg. pres. 'to carry', *seit* 'says'.

(iv) OHG -âi- in geit 'goes', steit 'stand', mer hei 'we have' (see § 31).

6.2 [ɔʊ] derives from:

(i) MHG ou: Ouge 'eyes', chouffe 'to buy'.

(ii) MHG û in hiatus position: boue 'to build'.

6.3 [œɪ] derives from:

(i) MHG öü: Töubi 'anger'.

(ii) MHG ei in labial surroundings: höische 'to demand'.

(iii) MHG iu in hiatus position: reue 'to regret', euereine 'one of you', zwöierlei 'two different things', Chnöi 'knees' (< MHG iuw).

6.4 [ɪə] derives from:

(i) MHG ie: schier 'almost', bschliesse 'to decide', präsidiert 'presides'.

(ii) MHG i before ch: giechtig 'malicious'.

(iii) Specifically Upper German iu (see Braune-Mitzka § 47): tieff[1] 'deep'.

6.5 [ʊə] derives from:

(i) MHG uo: Buesse 'fines', luege 'to look'.

6.6 [ʏə] derives from:

(i) MHG üe: füehre 'to lead', müesse 'must'.

(ii) MHG iu before ch: füecht 'damp'.

(iii) after dissolution of nasal in -ünch-: düecht 3rd p. sg. of dünken 'to seem' (but this is a rural form).

§ 7. UNSTRESSED VOWELS

See chap. ii, § 11. As the conditions are largely the same as in Zt. no separate treatment is necessary. Special Bernese features are the suffix -ung in urban speech (cf. Meinung), and the development of the MHG ending -inne after -er to -e, cf. Lehrere 'woman teacher', Zt. Lehreri.

§ 8. VOWEL QUANTITY

The changes in vowel quantity which have occurred since MHG are not developments without exceptions, but rather tendencies which are interfered with by morphological factors and by influences from neighbouring dialects with different developments.

8.1 The Leichtschlussdehnung is common High Alem. (see chap. ii, § 12.1).

8.2 MHG short vowels are usually lengthened before r- clusters, e.g. Bäärner 'Bernese', Wiirt 'landlord', döörffe 'be allowed', but short in hert 'hard', hurti 'quickly', surre 'to hum'.

---

[1] See Baumgartner, p. 81 f.

8.3 A specifically Bernese (and generally West High Alem. and Low Alem.) development is the shortening of MHG *î, û, iu*:

(i) before fortis stops in monosyllabic as well as polysyllabic words: *Zÿt* 'time', *lüt* 'loud', *Lüt* 'people'.

(ii) before intervocalic lenis sounds, especially *d, g, b, s, f, l*: *Hüser* 'houses', *schrÿbe* 'to write', *gschÿder* 'cleverer'.

8.4 Shortening in compounds occurs frequently as in other SGm. dialects.

8.5 In particles, auxiliaries and pronouns vowel quantity is dependent on sentence stress, cf. *nid—niid* 'not'.

§ 9. COMPARISON WITH THE NHG VOWELS

Much of what is stated in chap. ii, § 13, holds good for Bd. and a repetition is therefore superfluous. But the following phenomena are noteworthy:

ad (1) and (2): The lengthening of MHG short vowels before lenis in monosyllabic words has its counterpart in the shortening of long vowels (*î, û, iu*) before fortis stops. The preservation of the short vowels in open syllables is paralleled by the shortening of long vowels (again only MHG *î, û, iu*) before fortis and lenis stops and also fricatives in intervocalic position. These developments are only tendencies and have not led to a clear-cut new distribution of short and long vowels.

ad (6): Of the MHG *e-* sounds Bd. has, in contrast to NHG, preserved the distinction between *e* and *ë* (which has absorbed *ä*). MHG *e* before nasal clusters, especially nasal geminates, is not fused with the reflex of MHG *ë* as in Zt.

ad (8): The umlaut of OHG *â* is [æː] in Bd.

ad (10): Bd. stands nearer NHG in its adoption of umlaut *ü* before fortis velar consonants, where the umlaut was prevented in Zt.

Chief Vowel Correspondences

Bd.*	e ä	y uu üü	ei	ou	öi	ie	ue üe
MHG	e ë, ä	î û iu	ei, -î/	ou,-û/	öü, -iu/	ie	uo üe
NHG	e /ä[ɛ]	ei au eu/äu	ei/ai	au	eu/äu	ie[iː]	u ü

NHG	e, ä[ɛ]	ei/ai	au	eu/äu	ie[iː] u ü
MHG	e ë, ä	î -î/ei	û -û/ou	iu -iu/öu	ie uo üe
Bd.	e[ɛ] ä [æ]	y ei ei	uu ou ou	üü öi öi	ie ue üe

* For the phonetic value of the letters, see § 3. MHG and NHG sounds are given in their respective orthography.

THE CONSONANTS

§ 10. THE CONSONANTAL SYSTEM

Stops		Fricatives		Affricates	Sonants				
fortis	lenis	fortis	lenis		lenis	fortis	lenis	fortis	semi vowels
p	b	f	v	(pf)	m	mm		r	w
t	d	s	š	z	(ts tš)	n	nn	l	ll	j
k	g	x	γ	(kx)		ŋ			h

What has been stated in chap. ii, § 14, is valid for Bd. as well. The differences can be summarized as follows:

10.1 The opposition /x:γ/ is confined to the medial position after short vowel. In this position most words have fortis geminate, and but for the few isolated words with lenis in this position (e.g. *nache* 'after', *Spÿcher* 'barn'), lenis and fortis could be regarded as allophonic realizations of one phoneme as in Zt. In all other positions only the lenis occurs.

10.2 What has been said about the allophones of the nasals and liquids in Zt. holds good also in Bd. But here the fortis of *n, m, l* occurs also in opposition to the lenis in medial position after short vowels.[1] Finally and medially before vowels [ŋ] appears as fortis or geminate, e.g. [zɪŋŋə] 'to sing'.[2]

10.3 [j] and [w] have geminate allophones in intervocalic position, in which case the first element is a vocalic glide: [blɑ:uwɪ] pl. 'blue', [dræ:ijə] 'to turn'. In initial position they are more consonantal and in final position more vocalic [blɑ:u̯].

§ 11. SPELLING

Rudolf von Tavel retains on the whole for his consonants the spelling system of NHG, but expresses the geminate fortis, e.g. *Vatter* 'father', *Huuffe* 'heap'. Owing to the fact that the NHG spelling system is fairly conservative it is not ill-suited to rendering the conservative consonantism of SGm., cf. *weiss—Haus*, NHG [s] in both cases SGm. [s] and [z] respectively.

Letters and consonant phonemes generally correspond in the following way:

---

[1] There is much to be said for regarding these fortes as clusters, as Schultz, *op. cit.*, does, and the statement would then be that in Bd. *n, m, l* occur intervocalically in geminate clusters (double) but not in Zt.

[2] In many rural Bernese dialects [ŋŋ] is also a reflex of former (and urban) *nd*, e.g. *binge* 'to bind', *Hung* 'dog'.

Phoneme	Letter	Phoneme	Letter	Phoneme	Letter
p	p, pp	f	ff	m/mm	m/mm(5)
t	t, tt, dt	v	f, v(1)	n/nn/ŋ	n/nn(5)/ng
k	gg(3)	s	ss	l/ll/r	l/ll(5)/r, rr
b	b	z	s	w, j, h	w, j, h
d	d	š	sch(2)	pf; ts	pf; tz/z
g	g	x	ch(4)	kx	k, ck, gch

Notes

(1) The letters *f* and *v* for /v/ are used as in NHG (see chap. ii, § 15).

(2) Initial *št-* and *šp-* are spelt *st-*, *sp-*. As to the allophonic distribution, see chap. ii, § 14.

(3) The prefix *g-* is always fortis, though the spelling *gg-* is only adopted if the verb begins with *g-*.

(4) Medially after a short vowel *ch* represents the fortis geminate except in the words *nache* and *Spýcher*.

(5) Note that the spelling *-nn-*, *-mm-*, *-ll-* (*chönne, fromme, billig*) represents fortis geminates, but that *-rr-* (*Herre*) is merely conventional.

§ 12. The Consonant Phonemes

As they derive from the same sources as in Zt. no separate treatment is necessary. Therefore see chap. ii, § 16.

The few differences are:

ad 16.4: [d] in initial position is much more frequent in Bd. than in Zt. as a reflex of Gmc. *þ*. In our text: *dänke* 'to think', *dunke* 'to seem', *döörffe* 'may', *dick* 'fat, thick', *dŭtsch* 'German', which have [t] in Zt.

ad 16.16: *mm, nn, ll* in Bd. derive from the following sources:

(i) OHG *mm, nn, ll* after short vowels: *gränne* 'to cry', *stelle* 'to stand'.

(ii) assimilation, *nümme* 'no longer'.

(iii) doubling before the ending *-er*, *Hammer*. When geminate, in final position or before consonant *l* is 'thick', i.e. [ł]. Aristocratic circles, to whom von Tavel belonged, articulate a uvular *r*, but von Tavel himself had a front *r* according to Baumgartner, p. 36.

ad 16.17–18: [j] and [w] occur also medially after *ää, ei, öi, üe* and *aa, ou* respectively but only before [ə, i], e.g. *drääje* 'to turn', *tüeje* 'they do' subj., *grauwi* 'grey' pl.

The remarks on *Assimilation* and *Mobile -n* in chap. ii, §§ 17, 18, apply also to Bd.

THE MORPHOLOGY OF BÄRNDÜTSCH

NOUNS AND ARTICLES

§ 13. FORMATION OF THE PLURAL

Bd. has the same four types of plural formation as Zt. (see chap. ii, § 20). The only major difference is found in the case of those masculine nouns which were strong in MHG and have a non-mutatable root-vowel. These are endingless in the plural in Zt. (Type A(ii)) but retain a plural mark -*e* in Bd. These belong therefore to Type C(ii) and go like old weak masculines denoting animate beings, e.g. *Bueb—Buebe* 'boys'. Among them are: *Bäärg(e)* 'mountain', *Wääg(e)* 'way', *Tisch(e)* 'table', *Chrieg(e)* 'war', *Chünig(e)* 'king', *Brief(e)* 'letter', *Wiirt(e)* 'inn-keeper', *Fründ(e)* 'friend', *Taag—Tage* 'day'.

Vowel mutation shows the same results as in Zt. with the exception that the historical umlaut *aa* > *œœ* does not exist in Bd.

§ 14. CASE FORMS

Bd. has no special case forms except as relics in fixed formulas, e.g. gen. *der Gotts Wille, Tüüfels Dank,* dat. pl. of *Lüt: de Handwärchslüte.* On the expression of possession and personal relation see chap. ii, § 21.

§ 15. THE DECLENSION OF THE DEFINITE ARTICLE

There are only two cases. The forms are:

	m.	*f.*	*n.*	*pl.*
Common Case	der(1)	d(2)	ds	d(2)
Dative	dem/em(3)	der	dem/em(3)	de(n)

Notes

(1) *e* has always the value [ə]. After prep. the masc. form is *e* (< former acc.), e.g. *für e Fridesbruch, über e Trog, uf e Schümel,* before a vowel *en: für en Übermuet.*

(2) Before adjectives *di; d* is always fortis.

(3) The form *em* is used after prep.

§ 16. THE DECLENSION OF THE INDEFINITE ARTICLE

	m.	*f.*	*n.*
Common Case	e(n)(1)	e(n)(1)	es(1)
Dative	(e)mene	ere	(e)mene

Notes

(1) *e* is [ə] throughout.—After prep. the indef. article is *(e)ne* (m.f.) and *(e)nes* (n.), e.g. *um nes Bündnis.*

§ 17. AGGLUTINATIONS

(i) After prep. ending in -*n* in NHG there is no masc. def. art. in the common case: *i Chrieg* (cf. NHG *in den*).

(ii) The agglutinated forms *imene, inere, binere, amene, zumene, vomene* are regularly spelt *i mene, i nere*, etc., by von Tavel while Vogel and the *Dialäktschrift* prefer *im ene, in ere*.

(iii) In addition to the usual forms *im, vom*, etc., Bd. has *nam* (cf. *nach dem*).

ADJECTIVES

§ 18

While the dialects of the Bernese Oberland decline the adj. also in predicative position those of the lowlands have declensions only for attributive position. There are only two case forms and the weak and strong declensions are used on the whole as in NHG.

The only difference from Zt. (see chap. ii, §§ 26 ff.) is in the weak declension where the fem. common case ends in -*i* (*di groossi Raatsstube*, Zt. *di grooss R.*) and the neuter common case in -*e*.

NUMERALS

§ 19

The full forms for one, two, three are the same as in Zt. with the regular sound correspondences, i.e. Zt. *äi* = Bd. *ei*, except in the case of *zwöi* 'two' (neuter) where the diphthong is labialized. See chap. ii, § 30. The indef. art., i.e. the unstressed forms of the numeral 'one' are given in § 16.

PRONOUNS

§ 20. PERSONAL PRONOUNS

The quantity of the vowels varies substantially, as in Zt. (§ 31), according to stress and position.

	1st Person	*2nd Person*
Nom. sg.	iig, ii, i, -	duu, du, de, d, -
Acc. sg.	mii, mi	dii, di
Dat. sg.	miir, mir, mer	diir, dir, der
Nom. pl.	miir, mir, mer	diir, dir, der
Acc. pl.	üüs, üs, is	öich, ech
Dat. pl.	üüs, üs, is	öich, ech

	3rd Person			
	m.	*f.*	*n.*	*pl.*
Nom.	äär, är, er	sii, si	ääs, äs, es, s	sii, si, se
Acc.	iin, in, ne(n)	sii, se	iins, ins, s	sii, se
Dat.	iim, im, em	iire, ire (e)re	iim, im, em	iine(n), ine(n) ne(n)

Notes

(1) *e* is always [ə]; *d* is lenis.

(2) The form of polite address is the 2nd pers. pl. *diir*.

(3) For further comment, see *Notes* in chap. ii, § 31.

§ 21. REFLEXIVE PRONOUNS

The usual form for the 3rd pers. sg. and pl. is *sech*, occasionally shortened to *si*. This has become general in dat. as well, whereas in conservative dialect the dat. forms of the personal pronouns are still used.

§ 22. POSSESSIVE PRONOUNS

They are *mỹ, dỹ, sỹ, ŭse, öije, ire*. The forms are the same as in Zt. (§ 33) except that the monophthongal root-vowels are shortened in open syllables and that the adjectival common case forms *mỹ, dỹ, sỹ*, have dropped the final *n* (cf. Zt. *myn, dyn, syn*).

§ 23. DEMONSTRATIVE PRONOUNS

The only dem. pron. in Bd. is *dää, dämm; die, dere; daas, dämm;* pl. *die, dene. Desäb* and *dise* of Zt. are unknown.

§ 24. INTERROGATIVE PRONOUNS

They are identical with those of Zt., but with Bd. *-ä-* corresponding to Zt. *-ĕ-*, cf. *wĕĕr—wäär* 'who?'.

§ 25. INDEFINITE PRONOUNS AND RELATIVE PRONOUNS

As in Zt. See chap. ii, §§ 36, 37. Zt. *kän* corresponds to Bd. *kei(n)*.

VERBS[1]
§ 26. FORMS AND CLASSIFICATION

Bd. has the same form classes as Zt. (chap. ii, § 38) and the verbs can be grouped according to the formation of the past participle into the same three types.

[1] See S. Singer (and others), 'Beiträge zur Kenntnis des berndeutschen Verbums', *ZfhdMaa.*, ii, 1901, 13–25, 226–36; E. Fankhauser, *Die Flexion des Berner Dialekts nach Jeremias Gotthelf*, Lausanne, 1898.

Type A (p.p. ending in *-e*)

The same classes can be distinguished as in Zt. but there is a slightly different distribution.

1. Class II [i:]/[ɪ] is much smaller and has a sub-class [i]/[ɪ]: *rўte—gritte* 'to ride' (see § 8.3).

2. Class III *üü/o* with its sub-class *ŭ/o* is much smaller, the majority of the Zt. verbs belonging here are in Class X in Bd.

Types B and *C* contain almost the same verbs as in Zt. (See §§ 40, 41.)

§ 27. THE PRESENT

The endings are:

		Indicative	Subjunctive
sg.	1	-e(n) (1)	-(i) (4)
	2	-sch/-isch (2)(3)	-isch
	3	-t, -et (3)	-(i) (4)
pl.	1	-e(n)	-e(n)
	2	-et	-et
	3	-e(n)	-e(n)

Notes

(1) *n* in prevocalic position, also before *i* (*schickeni* inverted 'I send').

(2) The 2nd pers. sg. is without pron. in interrogative form, e.g. *schicksch?*

(3) See *Notes* (3) and (4) in chap. ii, § 42.

(4) Can be endingless or have *-i*.

§ 28. THE CONDITIONAL[1]

28.1 Bd. has many more old past subjunctive forms of verbs of Type A (old strong verbs) than Zt., the rural dialects even more than the urban.

Class I: (i) *-ie- blaase—blies* 'to blow', *raate—riet* 'to advise', *schlaaffe—schlieff* 'to sleep'.

(ii) *falle—fiel* 'to fall', *hange—hieng* 'to hang', *halte—hielt* 'to hold', *louffe—lieff* 'to run'; and in analogy to this class: *blўbe—blieb* 'to remain', *mache—miech* 'to make', *säge—sieg* 'to say'. Also the mono-syllabic verbs: *faa—fieng* 'to catch', *laa—liess* 'to let', *gaa—gieng* 'to go'.

Class II: *-i- bysse—biss* 'to bite', *gryffe—griffi* 'to seize', *pfyffe—pfiff* 'to whistle', *rysse—riss* 'to pull', *rўte—riti* 'to ride', *schlyche—schlich* 'to creep', *schlyffe—schliff* 'to sharpen (knives)', *schnўde—schnitt* 'to cut'.

Class III: *-öö- flüüge—flöög* 'to fly', *früüre—frööri* 'to be cold'.

Class IV: *-ä- singe—sängi* 'to sing', *springe—sprängi* 'to leap',

---

[1] Cf. H. Zimmermann, *Der Konjunktiv in der alem., Mundart des Emmentals*, Giessen, 1925.

zwinge—zwängi 'to force', *finde—fändi* 'to find', and the monosyllabic verb *staa—ständ* 'to stand'.

Classes VI, VII and VIII: *-ää- bräche—bräächi* 'to break', *läse— lääs* 'to read', *stäche—stääch* 'to prick', *träffe—trääff* 'to meet', *ässe— äässi* 'to eat', *mässe—määss* 'to measure', and the monosyllabic verbs: *gschee—gschääch* 'to happen', *choo—chääm* 'to come', *nää— nääm* 'to take', *gsee—gsääch* 'to see', *ligge—lääg* 'to lie', *sitze—sääss* 'to sit'. But *stäärbe* 'to die' has *stüürb*, *wäärde—wuurd* 'to become', *wäärffe—wuurff* 'to throw'.

Class X. *-ö- schiesse—schöss* 'to shoot'.

There is also an *-üe-* class, made up of the Type A verb: *fahre— füeri* 'to ride', the monosyllabic verb *schlaa—schlüeg*, and the Type B verbs *traage—trüeg* 'to carry', *fraage—früeg* 'to ask'.

The endings are: 1st and 3rd pers. sg. endingless, but the ending *-i* in analogy to conditional in *-ti* (of Types B and C verbs) is spreading; 2nd pers. sg. *-isch*; 1st and 3rd pers. pl. *-e*, 2nd pers. pl. *-et*.

28.2 The majority of verbs form the conditional by means of the ending *-ti* (including verbs of Types B and C and a growing number of Type A).

The endings are:

1	*i choufti*	*mer choufte*
2	*du chouftisch*	*dir chouftet*
3	*er choufti*	*si choufti*

28.3 The periphrastic conditional with *wuurd* is popular in the towns while the country prefers *täät*.

§ 29

The compound tenses and the passive are formed as in Zt. See chap. ii, §§ 44, 45.

§ 30. THE MODAL AUXILIARIES

The characteristics are the same as of the modal auxiliaries in Zt. (chap. ii, § 46), but the forms differ in some instances.

Inf. P.P.	1st, 3rd Pers. Sg. Pres. Ind.	2nd Pers. Sg. Pres. Ind.	1st, 3rd/2nd Pers. Pl. Pres. Ind.	Pres. Subj.	Condit.
chönne	chaa	chasch	chönne/-t (1)	chönn (1)	chönt(-i)
möge	maa	maasch	möge/-t (1)	mög (1)	möcht(-i)
müesse	mues	muesch	müesse/-t	mües	müesst(-i)
welle	wott, witt	wotscht	wei/-t	wel	wett(-i)
sölle	söl	sölsch	sölle/-t	söl	sött(-i)
döörffe	daarff	daarfsch	döörffe/-t	döörff	döörfti

H

Notes

(1) The rural forms are *chöi/-t*, *chöi* and *möi/-t, möi*.

(2) *nn, ss, ll* are geminate fortes.

§ 31. MONOSYLLABIC VERBS

There are often characteristic differences between the Zt. and the Bd. forms so that they have to be listed separately. For comparison, see chap. ii, § 47.

	Inf.	*Imp.*	*Sg. Pres. Ind.*	*Pl. Pres. Ind.*	*Pres. Subj.* (6)	*Condit.*(6)	*P.P.*
'to have'	haa	häb!	haa hesch het	hei heit hei	heig	hätt(i)	ghaa
'to be'	sy	bis!	bi bisch isch	sy syt sy	sy̆g	wäär	gsii
'to do'	tue ztüe (1)	tue!	tue tuesch tuet	tüe tüet tüe	tüeg	täät	taa
'to catch'	faa	fa!	fange (2) faasch faat	fange (2) fanget fange	fangi	fieng	gfange
'to give'	gää	gib!	gibe gisch git	gäbe (3) gäbt gäbe	gäb	gäbti	ggää
'to take'	nää	nimm!	nime nimsch nimt	näme (3) nämet näme	näm	nääm	gnoo
'to come'	choo	chumm!	chume chunsch chunt	chöme chömet chöme	chömm	chääm	choo
'to see'	gsee (4)	lueg!	gsee gseesch gseet	gsee gseet gseet	gseeji	gsääch	gsee
'to go'	gaa	gang!	gange (5) geisch geit	gange (5) ganget gange	gangi	gieng	ggange
'to stand'	staa	stand!	stande (5) steisch steit	stande (5) standet stande	standi	ständ *or* stüend	gstande
'to let'	laa	laa!	laa laasch laat	löi löit löi	löiji	liess	glaa la (7)
'to pull'	zie	züch! zie!	zie ziesch ziet	zie ziet zie	zie	zieti zöög	zoge

Notes

(1) After *z* the inf. is mutated (a relic of the MHG gerund *ze tüenne*).

(2) The rural forms are *faa* or *föö*.

(3) The rural forms are *gää/-t*, *nää/-t*.

(4) Like *gsee* goes *gschee* 'to happen'.

(5) The countryside has *gaa* or *göö*, *staa* or *stöö*. New compromise forms have arisen: *gönge, stönde*, etc., so that in Berne itself four different forms are current: *mir gaa, gange, göö, gönge; mir staa, stande, stöö, stönde*. (See Baumgartner, pp. 27–30, 46 f., 95–9.)

(6) Pres. subj. and conditional take the regular endings given in §§ 27, 28.

(7) When used as an auxiliary.

§ 32

On Particles, see chap. ii, § 48.

PHONETIC TRANSCRIPTION[1]

For the principles of this transcription, see the phonetic transcription of Zt. (p. 71).

t lyt štan·dən‿ɔf tər gas ɷmənan·dərən‿ɔnd lɷəgə də ræːt ɷnd bɔrgər naɣə, wɪ sɪ t raːthuːsštægən‿u·f gaŋŋə. mə wɛɪs hyk‿kɪts ən uzmɑxxətə. əz ɪž næxtɪ nɔ laŋ· lɪəxt ksɪ ɪ də tsɷm·ftštɷbən‿ɔnd ɪ də wɪːrtshyzər.

abər waz wɛttɪ daː tsksɛː ziː? zɪ rɛdə nɪd əma·ł mɪtənan·d. mə wɛɪs nɪd, wær hɪn·dər, vɔr ɔnd næbən‿ɛɪm tštægən‿u·f ɣɔn·t.

wɔ dər rɪttər vɔ špɪəts mɪt‿sinə herə ɪ dɪ grɔːssɪ raːtsštɷbə ɣɔn·t, hɔkxəts žɔ daː wɪ mɣttɪgɪ zɛkx ɪmənə špiɣər, ɛɪ ɣlɷm·pə. mə kšpɣːrt wɪ daz lɛɪɣət. əz dɷn·štət nɷmə zɔ. dər her adrɪɑːn dæŋ·kxt, waz trɛɪts ɑp ɑ dæ· bɔrgərmɷttəɣ anə tsrɛdə? ɪ hættɪ æbəzɔmæːr ga špɪəts uvə ɣɷennə, abər ɪttəm, ɔps œppɪz pattət ɔdər niːd, khœːrə mɣəssə zɪz!

wɪł dər žɔł·thɛɪs partɛɪ ɪž, præzɪdɪərt hɣt‿tər vennər ɣɪštlər. ær rezɣmɪərt, waz gɛštər kaŋŋən‿ɪž. hɣt sœł ərɣen·t wæːrdə, ɔp tsræxt, dər lɑm·pfrɪdə ustsrɣəffə, ɔnd tsræxt, pɷəssə fɣr‿ə vrɪdəsprɷx iːtstsɪə, dər štak‿khœːrɪ ɔdər də twɪŋ·herə. dɪ herɔ hɛɪz vərbrɪəvət, abər dər bɔrgərɣlɷm·pə wɷts an·dərz. dər vennər ɣɪštlər, dɪkx ɔnd rɔːt, glæn·tst nɪd nɷmə vɔr žmæːr, žɪər nɔ mɛː vɔr štapfættərləx- kxɛɪt ɔnd bɔrgərbræːvɪ, wɔnər phertət jɪts zɪks nɣmmə blɔs ɷm taːšprɣx vɔm her nɪkxlɔɷz vɔ dɪəspɑx tstɣə, əz gaŋŋɪ ałłɪ twɪŋ·herə aː. denə mɣəs jɪts ɛɪnɪž ksɛɪt si waz gattɪks. ɪm· zig ə drɛɪtægɪgə bæːrnər nɔ laŋ· lɪəbər, wɔ də ɔ dər štak‿kœnnɪ, waz ɪrə khœːrɪ ałz dɪ ał·tə bæːrnər, wɔ geŋ· nɷmə ts wassər ɷf ɪrɪ mɣlɪ rɛɪzə. da raŋ·kləts ɪ də rɛɪə vɔ də twɪŋ·herə. dər štatšribər pfiːft tswɣššə zinə tsæn·də dyrə, ɔnd dər zɛkxəlmɛɪštər vræŋ·kxlɪ, wɔ dər ɣɪštlər nən‿ɷm zi mɛɪnɷŋ vrakt, zɛɪt nɷməː ,,mə zɷettɪ mɛɪnə, dər gan·ts raːt wæːrɪ ɣbəlkhœːrɪg. ɪ ha mɪ zax ksɛɪt.'' ɛɪnt ɷnd an·dərə han·dwærxsmaː , wɔz nɪk‿xa vərwɔrkkə, daz dər zɛkxəlmɛɪštər tsɷ də twɪŋ·herə štɛɪt, laxxət. abər jɪts wɪːrts štɪł·. dər vennər het‿təm her adrɪɑːn ts wɔrt kæː . žɔ t‿ɑːrt, wɪ dæ· da·štɛɪt ɷntsə mɪt‿sinə izəgraːuwən‿ ɔɷgən‿ɑːlɷəkt, kšwɛɪkkət dɪ raːtsmannə.

[1] A phonetic transcription of the Bernese dialect of Langenthal is given in O. Gröger, *Schweizer Mundarten. Sitzber. d. Kais. Akad. d. Wiss. in Wien.*, Phil. hist. Kl., 176.3, 1914, pp. 25–8.

RUDOLF VON TAVEL: FROM *RING I DER CHETTI* [1][1]

D'Lüt standen uf der Gass umenanderen und luege de Räät und Burger nache, wi si d'Raathuusstägen uuf gange. Me weiss, hütt git's en Üsmachete [2]. Es isch nächti no lang Liecht gsi i de Zunftstuben und i de Würtshüser.

Aber was wetti da z'gseh sy? Si rede nid emal mitenand. Me weiss nid, wär hinder, vor und näben eim d'Stägen uuf chunnt.

Wo der Ritter vo Spiez mit sŷne Herren i di groossi Raatsstube chunnt, hocket's [3] scho da wi müttigi Seck i mene Spŷcher, ei Chlumpe. Me gspüürt, wi das leichet. Es dunschtet nume so. Der Herr Adrian dänkt, was treit's [4] ab, a dä Burgermuttech ane z'rede? I hätti äbesomähr ga Spiez üfe chönne. Aber item, ob's öppis pattet oder niid, ghööre müesse si's!

Wil der Schultheiss Partei isch, präsidiert hütt der Venner [5] Chischtler. Er resümiert, was geschter ggangen isch. Hütt söll erchennt wäärde, ob ds Rächt, der Landfriden üsz' rüeffen, und ds Rächt, d'Buesse für e Fridesbruch yz' zieh, der Stadt ghööri oder de Twingherre. Di Herre hei's verbriefet, aber der Burgerchlumpe wott's anders. Der Venner Chischtler, dick und root, glänzt nid nume vor Schmäär, schier no meh vor Stadtvätterlechkeit und Burgerbräävi, wo-n-er bhertet, jitz sŷg's nümme bloss um d'Aasprüch vom Herr Niklous vo Diesbach z'tüe, es gangi alli Twingherren aa. Dene müess jitz einisch gseit sy, was Gattigs. Im sŷg e dreitägige Bäärner no lang lieber, wo de o der Stadt gönni, was ire ghööri, als di alte Bäärner, wo geng nume ds Wasser uf iri Müli reise. Da rangglet's i de Reie vo de Twingherre. Der Stadtschrŷber pfyft zwüsche sŷne Zähnde düre, und der Seckelmeischter Fränkli, wo der Chischtler ne-n-um sŷ Meinung fragt, seit nume: ,,Me sötti meine, der ganz Raat wääri übelghöörig. I ha mŷ Sach gseit." Eint und andere Handwärchsma, wo's nid cha verworgge, dass der Seckelmeischter zu de Twingherre steit, lachet. Aber jitz wiird's still. Der Venner het dem Herr Adrian ds Wort ggää. Scho d'Aart, wi dä dasteit und se mit sŷne ŷsegrauwen Ougen aaluegt, gschweigget [6] di Raatsmanne.

,,Dir heit's ghöört, mŷni gnäädige Herre", seit er zum Burgerchlumpe, ,,wi's der Venner Chischtler meint. Was vo den alte Gschlächter no da isch, söll nüt meh gälte. Aber i möcht ech gfragt ha: Wäm verdanket d'Stadt meh, den alte Gschlächter oder dene

1 Rät. 2 Rat-. 4 Wirts-. 7 grossi. 9 gspürt, laichet. 12 nid, ghöre. 14 gangen. 15 wärde, rüefen. 18 rot. 19 Schmär. 20 -brävi, Asprüch. 21 Niklaus. 22 ihm, Bärner. 23 ihre. 28 wäri. 31 gä, Art. 32 -grauen. 33 gnädige.

---

[1] See §§ 3 and 11 on spelling. All signs ˇ for short, close vowels are introduced by me. Where I have altered the spelling to express vowel length this is indicated at the bottom of the page with line number, but only on the first occurrence of the word.

Dreitägige, wo sech nume z'Bäärn ypurgeret hei, für vo der Stadt
z'profitiere? Dir vergässet, wi's ggangen isch! Hätte nid di Ritter uf
de Herrschaften um d'Stadt ume Mannschaft und Gäld häärggää für
d'Stadt, so wüürdet diir nid hie tage. Si sy üsgrückt für Bäärn, si hei
d'Chriege gfüehrt und o ds Gäld derfüür ggää. Ohni sii ghöörti keis
Land zur Stadt. Si hei's eroberet, und mit irem Gäld isch no meh
derzue gchouft woorde. Und was si der Stadt und de Chlööschter und
fromme Stiftunge vermacht hei, vo däm wei mer nume gaar nid
rede. Me cha wohl säge: di Gschlächter hei us Bäärn gmacht, was es
hütt isch. Und jitz chömet diir, wo warm ўneghocket sўd und no
nŭt ta heit für d'Stadt, und weit ŭs andere cho [7] Rächt vorhaa
und Freiheite, wo Cheiser und Chünige der Stadt sölle ggää haa, diir,
wo vo Rächt und Gsetz weder gix no gax verstandet! — Was heit
dir afange für d'Stadt taa? Wenn alben euereine vorŭse gschickt
wird und öppe ga Stettlen oder Höchstette [8] muess rўte, so ver-
rächnet dr dem Stadtseckel jedes Wurschtschўbli, wo dr frässet.
Aber wenn's de drum z'tüe isch, zum Cheiser, a d'Fürschtehööf,
nach Frankrych, Burgund, i d'Niderland oder nach Savoye z'rўte,
wo me de muess e Gattig mache, wenn me wott Ghöör überchoo, ja,
da derfüür sy mir de hurti guet. Und zale dörffe mer's us ŭsem Sack!
Wär isch i dene letschte Jahre ggange? — Der Herr Niklous vo
Diesbach, ŭse Herr Schultheiss, der Herr alt-Schultheiss vo Ring-
goltingen und ig. Was mi aageit, so han i sit dem Tood vo mўm Vatter
— i chan ech's nachewўse — füfhundert rhynischi Taaler für
d'Stadt verritten und nŭt umeghöische. Es reut mi nŭt. Ŭsi Vätter
hei no meh taa für se. Es isch mer nume leid, dass i de Hand-
wärchslŭte, wo mir d'Ŭsrüschtung gmacht hei, ha müesse Gäld
schuldig blўbe. So isch es, und di andere drei Herre hei allwäg nid
minder tieff i Sack greckt.

Und jitz chömet diir und weit is ŭsi Rächt näh! Dir nähmtet is am
liebschten alles wägg, damit mer nŭt meh chönnte tue für d'Stadt
und dir is emel ja kei Dank schuldig wääret! Mir sötte nŭt meh sy,
aber under euch syn ere [9], wo grüüslech gäärn als Junker und
gnäädige Herr möchten aagredt sy. Dir wüsset wohl, warum dr ekei
Blick heit welle tue i ŭsi Briefen und Urchunde. Dir möchtet lieber
nid schwarz uf wyss und versiglet gseh, was ech nid i Chraam passet,
damit dir ŭs descht unverfroorener chönnet vorhaa, mir trўbe
Muetwille mit der Stadt und tüejen ech ŭsnutze. — Säget is doch
einisch, mit was mir euch ŭsnutze! Säget's! — Säget's, ihr Herre
Handwärchsmeischter! — Verbruuche mir öppe nid ŭses Gäld hie i
der Stadt, i eune Wärchstatte? Verchouffe mir euch ŭses Chorn nid

---

1 yburgeret. 3 härgä. 5 derfür, si. 7 worde, Chlöschter. 8 gar. 13 ha 14 ta.
17 -höf. 19 Ghör, -cho. 20 dörfe. 22 Ringoltingen. 24 Taler. 29 tief. 31 wäg.
33 gärn. 34 agredt. 36 Chram. 37 unverfrorener. 41 verchoufe.

um zwe Plappart billiger als d'Buure, he? — Füehre mir nid üse
Wy i d'Stadt und zalen Ohmgäld und Böspfennig [10] druffe, wo mer
ne ja dusse grad so guet chönnten ychälleren und verchouffe?"
Der Herr Adrian gseht, dass si uf de hindere Bänke der Chopf
schüttlen und giechtig lache. Und eine ghöört er zwüsche d'Chnöi
abe bröösme: „Ja, ja, hie i der Stadt trybet dr ke Muetwille mit is,
aber was vorusse geit. . . ."
„Was geit vorusse? — Säget's nume, wenn öppis z'sägen isch! —
I weiss, was Dir meinet, Meischter. E jede trouet dem andere zue,
was er sälber gäärn täät. — Aber wenn eine da sitzt, wo döörfti
chlage, mir heigen ihm sy Sach gnoo oder Frou oder Tochter
aagrüehrt, so söll er davüre choo und 's fräveli säge. I bin ech guet
derfüür [11], es isch keine daa. Hindenum Verbrüelen und vor
Züge Härestah isch äbe zwöierlei!
Dir wüsset nume z'guet, dass es soo isch, und drum heit dr nid
lugg gla, d'Sach esoo z'drääje, dass mir alli im Handel vom Herr vo
Diesbach Partei sygen und müesse der Üstritt näh. Hinder üsem
Rügge weit dr bschliesse. Mir chönnten ech das verhaa, wenn mer
wette. Mir bruuchte numen üsi Lüt zsämez'rüeffe, und de chönnte
mer mit der Stadt mache, was üs gfiel. Aber das mache mir niid,
d'Stadt isch üs z'lieb. Mir wei se nid für nüt pouet und gmehret haa.
Mir schlaan ech vor, gnäädigi Herre, setzet es unparteiisches Gricht
zsäme. Tüet dry, wän dr weit, wenn's nume Rächtskundigi sy. Dene
wei mer der Handel vorlege, und mir verpflichten is scho jitz, ire
Spruch aaz'näh, er ma de üsfalle, wi-n-er wott. Mir hei derby nüüt
anders im Sinn als der wahr Nutze vo der Stadt."
Meh als hundert Chöpf hange tieff vorabe. D'Raatsstube gseht uus
wi ne ghaareti Bschüsi. Und me gspüürt: Under der Bschüsi heisst's
eifach: ä'ä! [12] Mir wei nid u fertig! — So geit's halt i der Demo-
kratie. Da isch nüt so glaashert, wi was i der Luft lyt. Da chönne
d'Ängel vom Himmel iri Gygen umhänken und gah, es wirft ne
niemer es „Dank heiget!" nache.
Di Herre vom Adel wäärde gheissen abz'trätte, und du tuet der
Venner Chischtler in ere hässige Reed alles düür, was der Ritter vo
Spiez gseit het. Me macht der Seckelmeischter no einisch z'rede. [13]
Wi froh wääre di Burger, wenn er ne doch nume wetti um das vor-
gschlagene Gricht ume hälffe! Zeerscht begährt er nid z'rede. Und
wo si-n-im nid Rueh löj, haltet er ne der Gotts Willen aa [14], si
sölle Vernunft aanäh und's nid muetwillig mit dene Herre verdeerbe;
aber syni Wort gangen under im Rurre, Üfbegähren und Lache vo
dene rootbrächte Gsichter, wo jitz wider d'Nasen I der Luft hei. Me
rangglet, steit uuf und brüelet dürenander. Der Venner muess scho

sỹ Metzgerstimm vürenäh, für la [15] abz'stimme. Di groossi Mehr-
heit wott's la druuf abchoo, wär Meischter blỹbi, und ds Gricht wiird
verworffe.

Der Tschuepp isch uus. Si machen im d'Stägen-Abgah meh
Läärmen als im Üfechoo, und bald druuf tschäderet's und chlin-
gelet's übermüetig i allne Trinkstube. — ,,Dene Donnere [16] hei
mer's gseit! Jitz nume fräveli wỹters! Mir löj nid lugg, gäb der
Chischtler Schultheiss und im Raat alls ǔses isch!''

Wo du aber i de nächschte Tage vor de Hǔser vom Adel gsattlet
und gschürret und packt woorden isch, wi für längeri Zỹt, het's du
scho i eint und anderer Boutique gheisse: ,,Es wär doch am Änd
gschỹder gsi, me hätti en andere Rank gsuecht!'' Dussen aber isch
vo Schloss zu Schloss d'Abreed ggange: ,,Löjt se mache! Si wärde
de scho murbe!''

Bald na Ooschtere sy irere nes paar [9] gägen Aaben i der Trinkstube vo Metzgere [17] binenandere gsässen und hei sech's la wohl
sy bi nere Channen Inselwy [18]. Si hei uf e Meischter Chischtler
gwaartct. — Wo blỹbt cr o?

Ändlech geit d'Türen uuf, und hinder zweene Manne fallt si
unnöötig ruuch i ds Schloss. Me het der Chischtler sünsch als e
gspräächige Ma gkennt, und sỹ Fründ, der Gäärber Irreney, het o
für eine ggulte, däm [19] geng öppen öppis z'Sinn chunnt; aber hütt
hocke si zueche, me hätti chönne meine, si heige di böschte Händel
mitenand.

,,Wo fählt's?'' fragt du afange der Venner Chuttler. Antwort
überchunnt er keini. Hätte si öppe söllen erzelle, was ne vori am
Stadtbach passiert isch? Dert hei Wyber a mene Troog gwäsche,
und juscht, wo di beide Raatsmanne vorby chöme, schüttet eini ne
Züber uus, und das eso, dass der Meischter Chischtler bis a Buuch
üfe versprützt wiird.

,,Hee'', het der Venner üfbegährt, ,,channsch nid luege?''

,,Üsereis het nid derwyl, gassuuf und gassab z'luusse, ob nid öppe
grad so ne nǔtnutzige Bschüsiträppeler chunnt cho z'pflaule.'' Und
wi mit mene Hahnen aaglaa [20] isch es um e Troog ume gloffe. E
jedi het so nes Sprüchli gwüsst.

,,Wüsset dir nid, mit wäm dr redet?'' het der Irreney se z'Reed
gstellt. ,,Das isch der Herr Schultheiss Chischtler!'' — ,,Soo?'' het's
über e Troog ewägg g'antwortet, ,,mir kenne dä nǔt. Öppe der
Metzger Chischtler het me gkennt.'' En anderi het dry ggää:
,,Wurschteti dä i sỹr Schaal statt im Raathuus!'' Und e dritti het ob
em Üsdrääje vo mene Hemli ghulfe: ,,Jowäger, voranen isch er no
Meischter gsi, jitz isch er nume no e Krouteri.'' Di beide Manne sy

2 wird. 5 Lärmen, Ufecho. 10 gschirret, worden. 15 Oschtere, Abe. 18 gwartet.
21 gsprächige, Gärber. 22 gulte. 27 Trog. 34 agla.

scho schier bim Zўtgloggen [21] obe gsi, so het's am Brunne no gsprützt und brätschet und gwäffelet, dass di ganzi Gass under d'Loubeböge choo isch.

Der Peter Chischtler het im eerschten Aalouff nŭt Schlächts welle; aber wi's de so geit, wenn eim i der Töubi über vermeintlechs Unrächt ds Häärz dürebrönnt, so vergisst me, der Sach uf e Grund z'gah, und de isch me verchouft und verraate.

Bi der Schultheisse-Wahl am Ooschtermääntig het der Herr vo Scharnachthal nume vierzig Stimme gmacht, der Ritter vo Spiez gar nume no öppis zu zwänzig, und äär, Metzger Chischtler, der grooss Huuffe. Da het er gmeint, wolle, er heig am rächte Trom zoge; aber wo du di Twingherren alli bis uf vier us der Stadt abgreiset sy, het er sech doch in aller Heimlechkeit müesse zuerede: Jitz, Peeter, häb di derzue [22], sünsch . . . ! — Und jitz chöme si mer dääwääg, het er sech du uf em Wääg zur Metzgere-Zunft gseit. Da leit me sech i ds Gschiirr für se, und ds Tüüfels Dank het me. Aber — ,,Meischter bisch gsi, und jitz nume no Krouteri" — jitz, wo du den andere der Meischter zeige söttisch! Isch nid öppis dranne? — Het nid o der Dokter Stadtschrўber gseit, a däm Ooschtermääntig sўge böösi Zeichen am Stäärnehimmel gsi? Han im gseit: ,,I tät Ech druuf!" [23] Aber am Änd isch doch öppis dranne.

Drum schwўgt hütt der Schultheiss i der Trinkstube. Dass im ds Volk nid meh druffe het [24], das ma ne. Aber die da am Tisch mache sech keini settige Sorge. Si hei numen ei Gedanke: jitz, wo me di Junker dusse het, muess me zuefahre! Der Peeter Chischtler weiss ganz guet, wenn er liess la merke, wi's ihm z'Muet isch, so siege si: ,,Schultheiss, du bisch es Chalb!" [25] Und richtig geit's nid lang, so isch der neugwählt Venner Boumgaartner mit mene guete Raat zur Hand, wi me de Twingherren und dem ganzen Adel wўter chönnti nes Bei stelle. ,,Het nid vor füf Jahre, wo di groossi Monstranz mit dem Heiltum isch gstole woorden [26] und 's gheisse het, das sўgi e Straaff vo Gott für en Übermuet vo de Bäärner — wott säge vo dene Junker — der Raat es Mandaat erlaa gäge di unanständige churze Chleider vom Mannevolch, gäge di länge Schleppen a de Frouechleider und gäge di länge Spitzen a de Schueh? Und wär het sech draa gchehrt? Es paar frommi Lŭtli, wo sowiso kei Hoffert trўbe! Der ganz ander Adel het grad deschtmeh no aagwändet, für z'zeige, dass d'Stadt ine nüüt z'befäle heigi. — Das Mandaat muess wider vüre!"

,,Rächt hesch, Boumgaartner", seit der Chuttler, ,,das muess erneueret sy. Traage si mira duss, uf de Schlösser, was se luschtig düecht! — I der Stadt. . . ."

,,Dusse traage si nŭt Settigs", fallt im der Irreney i ds Wort,

4 Alouf. 6 Härz. 8 Oschtermäntig. 10 är. 13 Peter. 14 däwäg. 15 Wäg. 19 bösi. 20 Stärne-. 28 Baumgartner. 32 Straf. 33 Mandat, erla. 35 dra. 40 Trage.

„nume hie i der Stadt, für d'Lüt z'ergere, wo kei Hoffert vermöj.
Mit däm äbe wei si-n-is ungere [27] tue, di Donnere!"
Dä Vorschlaag het zündtet.

„Was meinsch, Schultheiss?" Si fraage ne no; aber ob ja oder nei,
d'Sach isch üsgmacht, er muess. Miir hei ne-n-uf e Schümel glüpft, u
miir chlepfe mit der Geisle, wenn er bocket. Der Peeter Chischtler
läbt nid wohl dranne. Er gseht eigetlech, dass es esoo isch, dass er uf
mene frömde Schümel sitzt und dass die d'Geisle hei, wo hinder ihm
zueche standen und hetze; aber er nimmt nid die uf d'Latte [28].
Er schwört dem Adel Hass, dää isch d'schuld. Er gloubt, der Adel
gieng sicherer z'Grund, wenn me ne liess la machen oder no zu
wȳterem Übermuet verfüehrti; aber das gieng z'lang, der Burgerchlumpe möcht's no erläbe, er wott öppis gseh. Was i der Luft lȳt,
muess düre. Und drum wird ds moorndrisch im Raat bschlosse, ds
Chleidermandaat z'erneueren und z'verscheerffe. Es muess dene
Junker und irne Wyber a ds Läbige gah!

Mit groossem Mehr isch es bschlosse. Si möge sech schier nid
ebhaa z'juze, wo si us der Raatsstube chömc. — „Heit dr gseh, der
alt Fränkli grännet schier!"

Nei, ds Plääre chunnt ne-n-erscht aa [29], wo am Taag druuf e
burgundischi Gsandtschaft [30] aarückt und nam Schultheiss fragt,
Es isch um nes Bündnis z'tüe. — „O du grundgüetigi Muetter
Maria!" süüfzet der Seckelmeischter. Di burgundische Herre
chönne nid bäärndütsch und der Schultheiss vo Bäärn nümme
wältsch, und der Seckelmeischter und der Dokter Stadtschrȳber
müesse dene Herre raate, si sölle sech a d'Eidsgenosse wände.

Wo de der *chevalier de Bubenbert* sȳgi und der *chevalier de Char-
natal, ci-devant écuyer de Son Altesse*, möchte di Herre wüsse. Der
Schultheiss steit mit dem Rügge halb gäge di Gsandten und luegt
zum Fänschter uus. „Göht se mira ga sueche!" brummlet er.

Dem Seckelmeischter schiesst ds Bluet under di wysse Haar. Er
seit de Burgunder, di Herre sȳgen alli über Land, währed der
Stadtschrȳber dem Meischter Chischtler zuesteckt: „So cha me nid,
Herr Schultheiss! Dänket doch o, mit wäm mer da rede!"

„He nu, so göht mit nen i d' ‚Chroonen' überen u stellet nen uuf
bis gnue!"

„Das wei mer o", seit der Seckelmeischter.

Wo si dusse sy und d'Türe fescht im Schloss, lüpft der Schultheiss
dcr Fuess zu mene Stupf und rurret: „Was bruuche mir Burgunder?"
Und uf der Stägen usse seit der eint Burgunder zum andere: „*Quel
drôle de gouvernement!*"

Der Meischter Chischtler het nid gueti Läbtig ghaa uf em Schult-

3 Vorschlag. 4 frage. 5 mir. 14 morndrisch. 15 verscherfe. 20 Tag. 35 Chronen.
42 gha.

heisse-Stuehl. Sÿni Fründe hei ds Unmügleche von im erwaartet.
Vor ine het er sech nüüt dörffe vergää. Er hätti nie sölle la merke,
dass er über öppis nid Bscheid weiss. Zum Glück sy no es paar
Manne da gsi, wo-n-im us Liebi zur Stadt hei ghulffe ds Rueder haa:
näbem Vatter Fränkli und dem Stadtschrÿber der Herr Urban vo
Muelere, der Junker Hetzel, der alt-Venner Brüggler und der
Junker Matter, ds böscht Muul zwar vo Bäärn. Vo däm het er sech
mängs müesse la gfalle. Da het's geng ggulte, tue, wi wenn me nüüt
vo denen anähm und de doch mache, was si aaggää hei. Im Ougschte
hätti me du söllen öpper a d'Tagsatzung ga Luzärn schicke wäge
de burgundischen Umtriibe. Da hei di Herre gseit: ,,Jitz hilft alles
nüüt, Herr Schultheiss, da muess öpper reise, wo sech i der Sach
üskennt, und zwar der Herr Adrian vo Buebebäärg!"

,,So? Meinet dr" — Da wird's de wider heisse: Han i's nid gseit,
wenn gritte sy muess, so isch üsereine de wider guet gnue?"

,,Das müesset Dr halt schlücke, Herr Schultheiss!" seit der Herr
Urban. ,,Dir wäärdet's öppe nid welle la druuf abchoo, dass under
Euem Regimänt öppis vo Bäärn uus verchaflet wird, wo di ganzi
Eidsgenosseschaft aageit! — I will scho mit im ga rede."

,,Mira, so machet!"

13 -bärg.

NOTES

Points of syntax and morphology which are discussed in the *Notes*
to the Zt. text are not repeated here.

[1] *Rudolf von Tavel.* Born 21 December 1866 in Berne, died 19
October 1934, journalist. Most successful and important Bernese
and Swiss dialect writer. His realistic historical novels, imbued with
a strong moral and religious conviction, cover the development of
Berne and its people from the fifteenth to the nineteenth centuries;
outstanding among these are *Der Houpme Lombach*, 1903, *Der Stärn
vo Buebebärg*, 1907, *D'Haselmuus*, 1922, *Unspunne*, 1923, *Ring i der
Chetti*, 1931. A special number of *Schwyzerlüt* (i, 1–2, 1938/9) is
devoted to his work. *Bibl.* Hugo Marti, *Rudolf von Tavel* (biogr.),
Berne, 1935; E. M. Bräm, *R. v. Tavels Werk als Ausdruck schweizerischen Denkens und Empfindens*, Berne, 1944; A. Senn, 'R. v. Tavels
historische Romane', *Monatshefte für den deutschen Unterricht*,
xxxvii, 1945, 565–70, Helene von Lerber, *Bernische Landsitze aus
R. v. Ts. Werken; id., Das christliche Gedankengut in der Dichtung R.
v. Tavels*, Berne.—An excellent recent survey of Swiss dialect
literature is by A. Senn in H. Smith, *Columbia Dictionary of Modern
European Literature*, N.Y., 1947, p. 801 f.

Our extract (*Ring i der Chetti*, pp. 242–54, Francke, Berne, 1953) describes a scene during the social disturbances in the fifteenth century, the so-called *Twingherrenstreit*. The citizens of Berne, organized in their craft guilds, demand the rights which hitherto had been the prerogatives of the aristocratic families, the *Twingherren*. Von Tavel, himself a member of the old ruling patriciate, while accepting democracy, stresses the importance of responsibility, selfless service and of placing patriotism above sectional interests.

[2] The ending *-ete* forms fem. nouns from verbs denoting (*a*) an undesirable and irksome action, e.g. *e Truckete* 'a pressing together of crowds'; (*b*) (concrete) a sufficient amount for a certain process, e.g. *e Chochete Öpfel* 'apples just enough for one cooking', *e Lismete* 'knitting'. *Usmachete* is 'a settlement, a working out'. See O. F. Hodler, *Beiträge zur Wortbildung und Wortbedeutung im Berndeutschen*, Berne, 1911; Stalder, pp. 216–20; Szadrowsky, *BSG*, xviii, 1933, 77–81.

[3] 3rd pers. sg. impersonal.

[4] See Note 9 to Zt. text.

[5] The officers of state mentioned here are the *Venner* 'councillor in charge of the armed forces', *Twingherre*, the aristocratic overlords with certain privileges, *Stadtschrÿber* 'town clerk', *Schultheiss* 'president of the council and the head of the City and state of Berne'.

[6] 'To make silent', causative verb from *schwÿge* 'to be silent'. The WGmc. doubling of consonants before *j* (of *-jan*) is sometimes preserved even after a long consonant or a diphthong, cf. Braune-Mitzka, § 96, Anm. 1.

[7] See Note 18 to Zt. text.

[8] Two villages not far from Berne.

[9] This is the genitive of the pers. pron., 3rd pers. pl., retained in a few set phrases.

[10] Two medieval taxes.

[11] 'I guarantee.'

[12] Negation; inverted comma stands for a glottal stop.

[13] *Z rede mache*—gallicism.

[14] 'Begs them for heaven's sake.'

[15] See Note 18 to Zt. text and [26] below.

[16] Term of mild abuse. Initial fortis or 'potenzierte Fortis' (see chap. ii, § 14.4).

[17] Seat of the guild of the butchers.

[18] Wine from the *Petersinsel* in the Lake of Bienne.

[19] This rel. pron. is not correct dialect; better *won em*.

[20] Simile is that of running water turned on by a tap, i.e. 'rapidly'.

[21] *Zÿtgloggeturm* 'clock tower' is a famous landmark in the centre of old Berne. The streets in the city are flanked by arcades (*Loube*).

[22] 'Look out!'

[23] 'That is a likely story!'

[24] 'That the people do not like him better, is a great disappointment to him.'

[25] 'You are a fool!'

[26] In the subordinate clause the finite verb often precedes the p.p., cf. Note 2 of Zt. text.

[27] The author marks carefully the lower class (or rural) accents of the craftsmen. Thus *ungere* for *undere*; *düecht* for *dunkt*; *u* for *und*, *vermöj* for *vermöge*, *göht* for *ganget*. See § 1.

[28] 'To dislike, to tackle.'

[29] 'They come to tears.'

[30] The Duchy of Burgundy was Berne's neighbour to the west and became both aggressive and dangerous under Charles the Bold. But the Swiss Confederation (*D'Eidsgenosseschaft*) won four decisive battles in the last of which Charles the Bold met his death. The hero of this novel, Adrian von Bubenberg, won fame by his heroic defence of the beleaguered frontier town of Murten.

GLOSSARY

See the introductory remarks to the *Glossary* on p. 84. Words given in that *Glossary* which have the same meaning in Bd. are not included here. As to the plural formation of nouns (A, B, C, D), see chap. ii, § 20, and § 13 of this chapter; for verbs consult chap. ii, § 38, and § 26 of this chapter. For details the reader is referred to the *Idiotikon* (*Id.*).

Aabe, A. evening.
aagää, p.p. *ggää*, demand, indicate.
aawände, C. spend on dress.
abchoo, *druff* (= p.p.) cf. NHG *darauf ankommen*.
ä'ä [æ'æ] no!
a'fange, at last.
albe, sometime, ever, usually.

bherte, C. confirm.
bocke, C. shy, rear.
böschte, sup. most wicked.
Boutique, (French) workshop.
brätsche, C. gossip, (*Id.*, v, 1014).
bröösme, C. utter piecemeal, reluctantly.
Bschüsi, cobbled surface. (Zt. *Bsetzi*).

chlepfe, B. crack the whip.
chlingele, C. clatter.
Chlumpe, B. lump, crowd.
Chnöi, A. knee.

dääwääg, this way.
de, *du* unstressed *doo*, then.
derwyl, adv. time.
düür, adv. through.

ebhaa, refl. refrain from.
einisch, once.
emel ja, certainly.
euereine, one of you.

fräveli, adv. openly, without hesitation.
frömd, strange.

ga, unstressed prep. to, towards.
gäb, until (*Id.*, ii, 69–9).

Gattig (*Id.*, ii, 499–501), *e G. mache*, look elegant to impress; *was G. s* what is befitting.
geng, always.
ghaaret, hairy.
giechtig, malicious, angry.
gix no gax, *weder-*, nothing at all.
gnue, enough.
gränne, C. cry (*Id.*, ii, 742).
grüüslech, very.

hässig, angry.
Handel, B. quarrel.
hocke, C. sit.
Hoffert, luxury.
hurti, quickly.

jowäger, excl. well, indeed.
juze, C. shout with joy.

Krouteri, muddler (*Id.*, iii, 917).

leiche, C. summer lightning.
Liecht, light.
lüpfe, B. lift.
lugg laa, to give in.
luusse, C. look out (*Id.*, iii, 1455).

Määntig, Monday.
mira, < *mir an*, as far as I am concerned, cf. *meinetwegen*.
moorndrisch, in the morning, or tomorrow.
müttig, < *Mütt*, a large measure.
murbe, soft.
Muttech, lot, crowd (*Id.*, v, 575).

na, prep. after.
nache, adv. after.
nächti, last night.

nümme, no longer.
nume, only.

o, also.
Ougschte, August.

patte, C. be of use.
pflaule, cry with face contortions.
plääre, howl, of animals or like animals (*Id.*, v, 136).
Plappart, fifteenth-century coin.

ranggle, C. indistinct muttering.
Rank, en andere R. sueche, look for another way out.
recke, B. reach.
reise, C. lead, *uf d Müli r.* turn something to one's advantage (*Id.*, vi, 1311).
rootbrächt, ruddy.
rurre, C. grumble.
ruuch, rough, loud.

Schaal, f. butcher's shop (*Id.*, viii, 530–4).
schlücke, B. swallow.
Schmäär, fat, grease.
Schümel, A. white hors
settig, such.
Stäge, f. A. stairs.
Stupf, m. B. push.
sünsch, otherwise.

Tagsatzung, Diet of the Old Swiss Confederation.
Töubi, f. anger.
Trom, n. thread.
tschädere, C. chatter, clatter.
Tschuepp, m. upheaval.

übelghöörig, hard of hearing.
umehöische, demand the return of.
umhänke, hang up (round).

verbrüele, C. decry, accuse.
verchafle, C. muddle (*Id.*, iii, 155).
vergää, sech öppis v., to show a weakness.
verhaa, dat. of pers. to stop a person.
versprütze, B. splash.
verworgge, C. swallow.
vor'abe, down in front.
vorane, before.
vorhaa, reproach.
vori, a moment ago.

wäffele, natter.
wältsch, French.
wolle, well then.

yburgere, naturalize.

Züber, A. bucket.
zueche, adv. near.

CHAPTER IV

ALSATIAN

§ 1. Area and Status

1.1 The two French *départements* of *Bas-Rhin* and *Haut-Rhin* are almost entirely German-speaking. Historically and geographically they form a traditional unit, a province, or, as the inhabitants would call it themselves, *e Landl*. Linguistically Alsace occupies a unique position among German-speaking territories, in so far as dialect is here not exclusively, or even primarily, in competition with and confronted by standard German.[1] The function which elsewhere is fulfilled in varying degrees by NHG is here carried out by French. As the *langue de culture* it is the medium of learned, cultural or written commercial and administrative intercourse. This is more so since the Second World War than ever before. It is true, the *haute bourgeoisie* adopted French before the middle of the nineteenth century and stuck to it throughout almost half a century of annexation to the German *Reich* as a *Reichsland*. All other classes, i.e. 90 per cent of the population, have retained their native German dialect as the everyday spoken medium. Even after the stirring experience of the French Revolution and the Napoleonic Empire had made the Alsatians Frenchmen in spirit, NHG played an important part as a literary medium. The Churches, newspapers, periodicals and higher literary works to a large extent made use of NHG rather than of French, which required a much greater mental effort to acquire than NHG. With the exception of the fact that the *haute bourgeoisie* and aristocracy spoke and wrote in French, which gave the linguistic scene in Alsace an eighteenth-century appearance, the language situation in Alsace up to 1871 was hardly different from that which prevailed in Switzerland, Luxemburg and parts of Austria and Germany. The annexation to the *Reich* in 1871 meant first of all a severe cutting back of French. From now on only the upper classes had access to French and among them the use of French even increased during 1871–1918.[2] The bulk of the population grew up practically

---

[1] Pennsylvania German dialect with English as its cultural language is in a similar situation. In East and South-East Europe there were, and perhaps still are, German dialect areas with foreign languages, e.g. Hungarian, as written medium. Here it is through lack of knowledge of standard German, in Alsace through choice and political reasons, that a foreign language serves as written and cultural medium.

[2] See P. Lévy, *Histoire linguistique d'Alsace et de Lorraine*, Paris, 1929, ii, 458.

ignorant of the language of the nation to whom they continued to feel spiritually linked.

For the first time the dialect acquired an importance as a written and cultural medium. There had been little dialect literature before 1870, although one of the masterpieces of dialect literature, G. D. Arnold's *Der Pfingstmontag*, appeared as early as 1816. Now in 1898 an Alsatian theatre was founded in Strasbourg.[1] It had an immediate success. Colmar and Mulhouse and even smaller country towns followed the example of Strasbourg. A continuous stream of dramatic works, especially in the lighter vein, from the pens of the masters Gustave Stoskopf and Ferdinand Bastian and of many others inspired and kept the love, interest and admiration of the Alsatian public. It was a kind of national demonstration. It gave the Alsatians a chance to retire into themselves, to show their difference from the tens of thousands of German immigrants who flooded into Alsace after 1871. At the same time as NHG had for the first time become the daily medium of large numbers of inhabitants of Alsace, albeit only of immigrants,[2] the dialect rose to a level it had never occupied before.[3]

After 1918 and especially after 1944 French replaced NHG very rapidly as the literary and cultural language of the educated. The Church is to-day the mainstay of NHG; the press, popular literature and the cinema are further channels of communication in NHG for the not so highly educated. If the running sore of irredentism is allowed to heal up completely and for good there is little doubt that a happy if somewhat complicated state of balance between French and NHG will be achieved, while the dialect will continue to flourish behind this neutralizing shield. It is true, dialect is not used in discussions of cultural, scientific and intellectual topics and to that extent the conditions are different from those obtaining in Switzerland or Luxemburg. But as its antagonist is now French rather than NHG its immediate survival is as assured as is that of the dialects

---

[1] See Lévy, *op. cit.*, ii, 455; G. Koehler, *Das Elsass und sein Theater*, 1907; D. Lutz, 'Das elsässische Theater, seine Entwicklung und Literatur' (*Wissenschaft, Kunst und Literatur in Elsass-Lothringen 1871–1918*, 1934); F. Maisenbacher, 'Bühne und Leben in Strassburg', *Jahrbuch der Els.-Lothr. Gesellschaft*, v, 1933; H. Reich, 'Elsässer Theater', *Strassburger Monatshefte*, vi, 1940; Schoen, 'Le théâtre alsacien', 1902; W. Teichmann, 'Elsässische Dialektliteratur' in *Reallexikon der deutschen Literaturgeschichte*, i. 265–9, 1925–26.

[2] P. Lévy, ii, 457, fn., quotes the *Strassburger Post*, 1907, 'Ein Elsässer, ein wirklicher Elsässer, der in seinem Hause hochdeutsch redet? Das hiesse ja geradezu seinen Landsleuten Ärgernis geben.' See also W. Kahl, *Mundart und Schriftsprache im Elsass*, Zabern, 1893; H. Menges, *Volksmundart und Volksschule im Elsass*, Gebweiler, 1893.

[3] Much dialect writing is found in *Elsässische Volksschriften*, Verlag Heitz und Mündel, Strassburg. Extracts in dialect in K. Gruber, *Zeitgenössische Dichtung des Elsasses*, Strassburg, 1905; R. Siegrist, *Lebende elsässische Dichter*, 1938, and *Lebende Dichter um den Oberrhein, Lyrik und Erzählung*, 1942.

I

in Switzerland and Luxemburg. It is unlikely that French will replace *Elsässisch* in the ranges where it now thrives in the near future, as some intellectuals demanded after the bitter experiences of occupation and oppression.[1] Public opinion again favours the retention and cultivation of this characteristic heritage. Dialect literature is still flourishing on a modest scale, especially in the theatre.[2] There is at least one publishing house (Editions Salvator, Mulhouse) which specializes in the publication of dialect plays for amateur dramatic societies, and the classics of the Alsatian stage, such as Stoskopf's *Dr Herr Maire*, of which even a film was made in the post-war years, do not fail to attract the Alsatian public.

1.2 Linguistically 'Alsatian' is, of course, split up into a multitude of local dialects. If one singles out certain phonological and morphological features one can say that Alsatian as a whole belongs to the dialect type of Low Alemannic.[3] Only the border areas in the south, the Sundgau, and those in the north are excluded. On the other hand the dialects spoken in the plain on the right bank of the Rhine in Baden are closely related to Alsatian. In the north it is primarily the *pfund/pund* -isogloss which divides the Alem. dialects from the Franconian of Lorraine and the Palatinate[4] (*DSA*, 62). It runs from the Donon in the Vosges, on the German–French linguistic border, north-eastwards along the hills to the River Lauter near Wissembourg and thence along the Lauter to the Rhine.[5] It is known in German dialectology as the *Selz-Lauterschranke*. Other isoglosses which run roughly in the same direction are Alem. (MHG) diphthongs *ie, uo (üe)* against Franc. monophthongs (*DSA*, 12, 96); Alem. palatalization of MHG *û, uo, ou* (*DSA*, 24, 71); Als. *laase* against Franc. *lēse* (< MHG *ē*) 'to read'; Alem. (MHG) *i, û* before consonants against Franc. diphthongs (*DSA*, 24, 74); Alem. *hesch, het*, against Franc. *hasch, hat*, i.e. mutated forms of 2nd and 3rd pers. sg. pres. indic. of 'to have'.[6]

In the east the *Is/Eis* isogloss (*DSA*, 74) running along the

[1] E.g. A. Biedermann, 'L'Alsace littéraire et intellectuelle' in *Visages de l'Alsace*, Paris, 1948.
[2] E.g. in the years 1921–26 there appeared 97 plays, 14 vols. of stories, 8 vols. of lyrics.
[3] Mitzka, *DPhA*, i, 686 'Oberrheinisches Nordalemannisch'.
[4] The Alsatians show themselves aware of this linguistic difference by nick-naming the Lorrainians *Pägser*, i.e. 'people speaking a *p*'.
[5] See the maps in Martin-Lienhart, *Elsäss. Wörterbuch*, ii; Lévy, *op. cit.*, i; Jutz, *Alem. Maa.*; Maurer, *Oberrheiner etc.*; O. Stoeckicht, *Sprache, Landschaft und Geschichte des Elsass* (DDG, 42), Marburg, 1942; Bohnenberger, *Alem. Ma.* where a detailed description of the isogloss is given.
[6] For the Franc.-Als. boundary between Alsace and Lorraine see especially E. Beyer, 'A la limite des dialectes alsaciens' in *Lorraine, Alsace, Franche-Comté*, Société Savante d'Alsace et des Régions de l'Est, Strasbourg-Paris, 1957, pp. 335–83.

Schwarzwaldschranke, separates Low Alem. from Swabian. The
Swabian diphthongization affects also the MHG vowels *û* and *iu*.
The chief isogloss separating Low Alem. from High Alem. is the
k-/ch- isogloss (*DSA*, 17) which forms the *Sundgau-Bodenseeschranke*.
Here lies also the boundary between northern unrounding in *Hîser*
against southern *Hṻser*.

What characterizes the Alsatian dialectal scene is the degree in
which it has been subjected to infiltration by northern, Franconian
forms. Thus the most important isoglosses run from west to east across
the Rhine plain, lying usually farther south in Alsace than in Baden.
The towns frequently represent more northern forms than the surrounding countryside.[1] As a number of important isoglosses run
roughly through the middle of Alsace one speaks of a southern type
(*Haut-Rhin*) and a northern type (*Bas-Rhin*). Here the northern type
has been chosen for more detailed description. The text is written in
Strasbourg dialect, which is distinguished by a number of features
which we find again in the Franc. dialects to the north. Strasbourg
is to some extent a Franc. linguistic enclave in Alem. territory. For
this reason I have preferred the more characteristically Alsatian
speech of Barr for the phonetic description. Again it must be pointed
out, however, that while the differences are easily noticed by the
native speakers and the trained phonetician, to the outsider these
local dialects present a fairly homogeneous picture. It is, of course,
such factors as the basis of articulation, stress and intonation
patterns, and the consonantal system which give the local *patois* the
typical Alsatian appearance. For the detailed knowledge of local
groupings and internal divisions one must await the forthcoming
Linguistic Atlas of Alsace, now in preparation at Strasbourg University.[2] Most studies published up to now are based on the material
of the *DSA* (e.g. Maurer, Stoeckicht).

GENERAL CHARACTERISTICS OF LOW ALEMANNIC
(NORTHERN ALSATIAN)

§ 2. PHONOLOGICAL FEATURES[3]

2.1 *The Vowels*

(1) The MHG long vowels *î*, *û*, *iu* are preserved as monophthongs
though frequently shortened, see § 2.2. *î* and *iu* have coincided through

---

[1] This emerges from Maurer and Stoeckicht. The former states, p. 215, 'So
überwiegt im Rheinland der Eindruck des Staffelraums, die einheitliche
Ausprägung rückt in die zweite Linie, . . .'
[2] See E. Beyer, 'Deux entreprises, un même esprit: L'Atlas linguistique de la
Suisse alémanique et celui de l'Alsace' in *L'Alsace et la Suisse à travers les
siècles*, pp. 429–62, Strasbourg, 1952.
[3] See fn.(1), p. 32.

unrounding of the latter. In hiatus position, however, they form new diphthongs *ei* and *öi* similar to those of High Alem.[1]

(2) The MHG diphthongs *ie, ue, üe* are preserved as diphthongs, but *ie* and *üe* have coincided. Strasbourg makes an exception in so far as it has, like Franc., long monophthongs: [iː] and [yː].

(3) The MHG diphthong *ei* is generally *ai* in Upper Alsace, but in Lower Alsace varies locally between *ai, ei*, and monophthongs of an open *e-* quality. Strasbourg monophthongized *ei* and *ou* before nasals and liquids to *ā* like the Franc. dialects to the north but appears to be abandoning this peculiarity.[2] In most of Alsace MHG *ou* is palatalized to *öi*.

(4) L. Alem. distinguishes MHG *ē* and *e*, the former having been opened to a very advanced *a* in much of Alsace, while the latter is more close. In Strasbourg the former is *ē̆*.

(5) MHG *â* is generally rounded to *ō*; *a* is a back vowel. Before *sch* (< Gmc. *sk*) *a* is generally palatalized.

(6) MHG *ê* and *ô* are generally preserved, the latter having coincided with MHG *â*, the former with MHG *œ*.

(7) MHG *i* and *u* are opened but *u* is generally retained in those cases where NHG has now *o*, e.g. *d Sunn* 'sun'.

(8) General unrounding of MHG *ü, iu, ö, œ, öu* which fall together with the reflexes of MHG *i, î, e, ê, ei*.

(9) A characteristic feature is the palatalization of MHG *û, uo, ou* > *ü, üe, öi*. But the palatalization of *ou* > *öi* is not as widespread as that of the other two vowels.[3]

(10) Lengthening of originally short vowels has given rise to a new series of long vowels: [eː, ɒː, oː].

(11) Initial vowels have a smooth onset. Glottal stop is unknown and *liaison* is general.

(12) [j] < *g, h, w* has often had a palatalizing effect on preceding back vowels.

---

[1] See J. F. Kräuter, 'Die schweizerisch-elsässischen *ei, öy, ou* für alte ī̆, ū̆, ǖ', *ZfdA.*, xxi, 1877, 258–72.

[2] E. Beyer (by letter): 'La monophthongaison … est en voie de régression en strasbourgeois. Ainsi on dit actuellement plutôt *haim* et *Baum* que ha:m et Ba:m.'

[3] See L. Tesnière, 'Le ü du dialecte alsacien', *EG*, iii, 1948, 147–56, *id.*, 'Le ü alsacien outre-Rhin', *EG*, ix, 1954, 153 f.; J. Fourquet, 'La palatalisation spontanée de l'alsacien *hüs, brüeder, köife'*, *Essais de philologie moderne*, Paris, 1953, pp. 181–8; E. Beyer, 'A propos de l'ü alsacien en pays de Bade', *EG*, xi, 1956, 240–4. E. Haendke, *Die mundartlichen Elemente in den elsässischen Urkunden des Strassburger Urkundenbuches, 1261–1332*, Strassburg, 1894, adduces evidence of the palatalization of MHG *hûs* occurring as early as 1286. The question of a Celtic substratum has been frequently raised, as well as the connection with the palatalization found in Highest Alem., e.g. in Valais.

2.2 Vowel Quantity

(1) Some MHG short vowels in open syllables are lengthened, although this *Leichtinnendehnung* is frequently prevented by certain following consonants. This lengthening is more widespread in Upper Alsace than in Lower Alsace.

(2) The high-tongue vowels have been generally shortened before former fortis stops and fricatives.

(3) Certain consonantal clusters (especially *cht*) have frequently had a lengthening effect.

2.3 Vowels in Unstressed Syllables

(1) The MHG prefixes *be-* and *ge-* retain their unstressed vowels except before certain consonants and before vowels, where they are dropped.

(2) Unstressed *i* occurs in adjectival endings (< MHG *iu*), and has arisen as an excrescent vowel in certain consonantal clusters.

(3) MHG unstressed final *-e* has generally been dropped.

2.4 The Consonants

(1) The consonantal system consists of a single series of semi-fortis stops and fricatives without significant voicing. Only the sonants are voiced. All consonants are short.

(2) While initially WGmc. *þ* and *d*, MHG *b* and *p* are not distinguished, *g* and *k* are distinguished before vowels only. Initial *k* is represented by the velar aspirated semi-fortis *kh-*. Gmc. *f*, *s* and HG *ff*, *ss* have coincided.

(3) In the cluster *-nk-* the stop is unaspirated and unaffricated in contrast to High Alem.

(4) The fricative *ch* has usually velar and palatal allophones, distributed as in NHG. The palatal one has in some areas become identical with the *sch-* sound.

(5) *st* and *sp* are, within one morpheme, always *scht* and *schp*.

(6) Medially between vowels and after *l, r* MHG *-b-* and *-g-* become semi-vowels (*w, j*). MHG final *-g* disappears altogether in a large part of Lower Alsace.[1]

(7) The liquids *r* and *l* are usually preserved, the former is frequently uvular and on the point of coalescing with /x/.

(8) Final *-n* after unstressed *e* is dropped but reintroduced if the next word begins with a vowel. Lower Alsace in contrast to Upper Alsace has preserved *-n* after stressed vowels, cf. *gsii-gsin* 'been'.

(9) A number of ancient sound changes are now found only in relic areas, e.g. *ss* < *hs* (*wååsse* 'to grow'); disappearance of *n, m*

[1] Cf. E. Ochs, 'Der Lautwandel b > w in Baden', *Beitr.*, xlvi, 1922, 147–56.

before *s, f* with diphthongization of preceding vowel (*feif* 'five'); diphthongization of short vowels before *mb, nd, ld* (*heiner* 'behind', *weil* 'wild'); velarization of *nd* > *ng*.

§ 3. Morphological Features

3.1 Noun and Article

(1) The noun has no special endings for cases, but there are local dialects which distinguish a dative plural. No distinction is made between subjective case and objective case.

(2) Plural formation in *-er* is more widespread than in NHG or H. Alem.

(3) The general diminutive ending is *-(e)l*, but in Lower Alsace many nouns form a second, more intimate dim. in *-ele*; both forms with mutation.

3.2 The Adjective

(1) In the strong declension the plural common case and the fem. sg. common case end in *-i*.

3.3 The Pronouns

(1) The personal pronouns distinguish dative and accusative.

(2) NHG *uns* is *uns*.

(3) The possessive pronouns NHG *unser, euer* have forms with *-r*.

(4) The possessive pronouns *mўn*, etc., have the ending *-er* in masc. common case, and *-s* in neuter common case. Cf. *dўner grooss Hund, dўns junge Kalwel*: NHG *dein grosser Hund, dein junges Kälbchen*: High Alem. *dyn groosse Hund, dys jung Chälbli*.

(5) The relative pronoun is *wo* (*wu*).

3.4 The Verbs

(1) The tense system consists of a present, a perfect and a pluperfect. The pres. subj. has generally vanished.

(2) The subjunctive preterite serves as a conditional. Strong forms exist of only few strong verbs, otherwise forms in *-t, -ti* or expressions with the verb for 'to do' are used.

(3) There is a uniform plural ending for all tenses in *-e*.

(4) *Rückumlaut* is unknown.

(5) The verb NHG *haben* has mutated forms in 2nd and 3rd pers. sg.

(6) Mutation occurs only in those strong verbs with root-vowel *-e-*. It goes through the whole singular.

(7) For NHG *gewesen gsi/gsin* is used south of a line which runs

through *Bas-Rhin* just north of Saverne-Wasselonne-Strasbourg. North of this line the past participle is *gewan*.

(8) The verbs for 'to go' and 'to stand' are reflexes of MHG *gên, stên*, not *stân, gân*. These forms derive from the northern Franc. dialects.

(9) The infinitive of regular verbs ends in *-e*, that of irregular ones in *-n*.

PHONOLOGY [1]

THE VOWELS

§ 4. THE VOWEL PHONEMES

The number and character of the MHG vowel phonemes has been substantially changed by the processes of lengthening of originally short vowels and shortening of originally long vowels. Although these processes were conditional, quantity is now phonemic owing to the obliteration of the difference between former lenis and fortis consonants. Long and short vowels may occur in the same surroundings, e.g. *lyde* 'to suffer'—*lẏde* 'to ring', *süüfer* 'clean'—*Süfer* 'drunkard'. (For details, see § 10.) Of further far-reaching consequence were the processes of unrounding and palatalization, both spontaneous and before [j] < *g*.

Front	Front rounded	Back	Diphthongs
i(:)	y(:)		
ɪ(:)		ɔ(:)	iə yə
e(:)	ø(:)	o(:)	
ɛ:	œ(:)		
a(:)		ɒ(:)	

(:) indicates that a phoneme occurs both long and short.
[u:] occurs only in French loan-words. There is also a short central vowel [ə] which is always unstressed. The diphthongs are stressed on the first element.

Distributional restrictions are found above all in the case of /ø, ø:, œ/, which occur in stressed conditions only before /j/. On the other hand, none of the long- or short back vowels occur before /j/. On grounds of complementary distribution it would, therefore, be possible to regard [ø, ø:, œ] as allophones of the back vowels.

---

[1] I wish to express my gratitude to Monsieur Roger H. Reinbold of Barr, whose thesis for the *Diplôme d'Etudes Supérieures* on the dialect of Barr, 1959, although it came to my notice only after the conclusion of my MS, helped me to correct a number of errors, especially with regard to the occurrence of the long vowels /ɪ:, e:, ɔ:, o:/. M. Reinbold willingly answered questions and ungrudgingly put his great knowledge at my disposal.

But since the back–front opposition is otherwise distinctive, i.e. phonemic, and as /œ:/ is distributionally unrestricted, it is preferable to posit them as separate phonemes, on grounds of distinctiveness, phonetic as well as structural.

Only the back vowels and /a(:)/ occur before /x/ and no long vowels occur before /ŋ/. Before /j/ the phoneme /ɛ:/ has a short allophone [ɛ].

Examples: /fi:l/ 'much': /bil/ 'swelling': /mɪ:l/ 'mill': /bɪl/ 'pill': /e:l/ 'oil': /hel/ 'hell': /dɛ:l/ 'part': /ma:l/ 'flour': /šal/ 'bell': /mɷ:l/ 'time': /šɷldi/ 'guilty': /so:l/ 'sole': /sol/ 'shall': /bɒ:l/ 'soon': /fɒl/ 'trap': /šdiəl/ 'chairs': /šdyəl/ 'chair': /jy:li/ 'July': /fyl/ 'rotten': /wø:jə/ 'to dare': /bøjə/ 'to build': /wœ:jə/ 'cart': /hœjə/ 'to beat'.

§ 5. Spelling

Ferdinand Bastian, the author of our specimen text, did not work out a consistent spelling system based on the vowel phonemes of his dialect.[1] On the whole he follows NHG orthography, with arbitrary departures here and there. It has, therefore, been necessary to alter the spelling to make it more phonemic. The sound values which the letters have are those of the dialect of Barr. The dialect of Strasbourg has many sounds which differ from these, but as the differences are more phonetic than phonemic the alterations in spelling are an improvement for Bastian's dialect as well. The letter *e*, for instance, serves, in Bastian's spelling, both for /e/ and /a/, (Strasbourg [e] and [ɛ]). Here the two phonemes are expressed by *e* and *a* respectively. The signs *ie* are only used for the diphthong /iə/, which is [ɪ:] in Strasbourg, and *üe* only for /yə/ = [ʏ:] in Strasbourg, but never for /i:/ for which Bastian uses it occasionally as well. For this phoneme I have generalized *y* which Bastian uses sporadically. The short phoneme /i/ is distinguished by the mark ˘ for shortness. In all other cases length is expressed by doubling, except where Bastian retains the NHG length sign *h*.

The correspondences are as follows:

Phoneme	*Letter*	*Phoneme*	*Letter*	*Phoneme*	*Letter*
i, i:	y̆, y	y(:)	ü, üü	ɒ(:)	å, åå
ɪ(:)	i, ee	ɷ(:)	u, oo	iə	ie
e(:)	e, ëë	o(:)	o, ôô	yə	üe
ɛ:	èè	œ(:)	œ, œœ		
a(:)	a, aa	ø(:)	ö, öö		

[1] Alsatian dialect spelling is on the whole rather confused. See H. Schneegans, *Über die orthographische Anarchie im Schrifttum des Strassburger Dialekts*, 1896.

§ 6. Stressed Short Vowels

6.1 [i] this is a close, high-front vowel. It is a product of shortening and is the most frequent representative of

(i) MHG *î*: *wÿtt* 'wide', *Pfÿff* 'pipe'.

(ii) MHG *iu*: *dÿtsch* 'German', *dÿte* 'to point'.

6.2 [ɪ] is a very open i- sound, approaching close [e]. Most Alsatians with the French value of *i* in mind regard this sound as an e- variety. It is the regular correspondence of MHG *i* in positions where lengthening did not occur.

(i) MHG *i*: *Milich* 'milk', *isch* 'is'.

(ii) MHG *ü*: *Glick* 'luck', *iwer* 'over', *Kinni* 'king'.

(iii) MHG *î* in *gsin* 'been' where shortening occurred early.

6.3 [e] is a slightly open and lax, mid-front vowel, in most positions about [ẹ].

It represents:

(i) MHG *e* (the so-called primary umlaut) where lengthening has not occurred: *ermer* 'poorer', *geje* 'against', also in *Mensch* 'human being'.

(ii) MHG *ö*: *Lecher* 'holes', *Vejel* dim. 'bird'.

(iii) MHG *i* and *ü* before MHG *g*: *Ejel* 'hedgehog', *Flejel* 'wing', *steje* (< MHG *î*) 'to climb'.

(iv) MHG *î*, *iu* stressed in hiatus position, *î*, *iu öu* before *j*, *w* > *e* + *j*: *frej* 'free', *schneje'* 'to snow', *trej* 'faithful', *nej* 'new', *freje* 'rejoice'. It is possible to regard this sound as a diphthong but owing to the phonetic character of [j] it is preferable to take the second element as a semi-consonant. Before a consonant (always belonging to another morpheme) [j] becomes more vocalic, e.g. *gheje* 'to fall'— *er gheit*, *frej—freis*. See the identical case in § 6.8.

6.4 [a] is a very advanced, low-tongue vowel, phonetically about [a⁺]. It is one of the most characteristic vowels of Alsatian but does not occur in Strasbourg. There it is less open (more like [ɛ]) but nevertheless distinguished from the preceding vowel (6.3). Bastian shows himself aware of this Strasbourg peculiarity by pointing, in his spelling, to Barwel's rural [a] in *gasse* 'eaten', *ewack* 'away', *gewann* 'been', [a:] in *Spitzewaaderi* 'ribwort' against Jüstinel's Strasbourg [ɛ:].

It derives from:

(i) MHG *ë*: *Fald* 'field', *halfe* 'to help'.

(ii) MHG *ä*: (the so-called secondary umlaut) and analogical umlaut: *Hand* 'hands'.

(iii) MHG *a* before *sch* (< *sk*): *Asch* 'ashes'.

(iv) MHG *e* (primary umlaut) before nasal clusters in some words: *danke* 'to think', *ang* 'narrow'.

6.5 [ɒ] is a low-back vowel, slightly rounded, but varying in the degree of o- colouring. It stands for MHG *a* where no conditional changes have occurred: *Nâme* 'name', *lâng* 'long'.

6.6 [o] is a close, rounded, back vowel representing MHG *o* where no conditional changes have occurred (e.g. before MHG *-cht*, *-g-*): *Morje* 'morning', *Ofe* 'stove', *Bode* 'floor'.

6.7 [ꭥ] is an open, rounded, high-tongue back vowel. It continues MHG *u* except where conditional changes have occurred (e.g. before MHG *g*): *Schmutz* 'kiss', *kumme* 'to come', *Sunn* 'sun'. Before the velar stops Als. has frequently non-mutated forms, e.g. *Bruck* 'bridge', *Muck* 'midge', *bucke* 'to bend', *verruckt* 'mad'. Before the liquids and nasals Als. has [ꭥ] for MHG *o*: *furt* 'away', *genume* 'taken'.

6.8 [ø] is a close, rounded, mid-front vowel occurring only before *j*. It derives from:

(i) MHG *û* in stressed hiatus position or before *w, j*: *böje* 'to build', *Söj* 'sow', *tröje* 'to trust'.

(ii) MHG *u* and *o* before *g*: *Köjel* 'bullet', *Böje* 'bow', *gflöje* 'flown'.

6.9 [œ] is an open, rounded, mid-front vowel. It represents MHG *ou* where shortened, especially before MHG *j, w* > /j/: *ich glæb* 'I believe', *Oej* 'eye', *hœje* 'to beat', *kœje* 'to chew', *genœj* 'enough'.

On the phonemic interpretation of [ø] and [œ], see § 4.

6.10 [y] is a close, rounded, high-front vowel. It is a product of shortening representing MHG *û* in the majority of cases: *üss* 'out', *ich brüch* 'I need', *Strüss* 'bunch of flowers'.

§ 7. Long Vowels

7.1 [iː] occurs in those rather rare cases where shortening of the MHG high-tongue vowels has not taken place.

(i) MHG *î*: *Wywele* 'woman' dim., *er blyt* 'he stays'.

(ii) MHG *iu*: *Hyser* 'houses', *Byrl* 'small farmer'.

(iii) MHG *i* lengthened in *vyl* 'much'.

7.2 [ɪː], for quality, see § 6.2. It derives from:

(i) MHG *ê*: *Seel* 'soul', *Schnee* 'snow'.

(ii) MHG *œ*: *bees* 'wicked', *heere* 'to hear'.

(iii) MHG *i* lengthened: *Gseecht* 'face', *Beer* 'pear'.

(iv) MHG *ü* lengthened: *Meel* 'mill'.

7.3 [eː] is a close, mid-front vowel, and relatively rare, deriving only from MHG *e* and *ö* under conditions of lengthening: *Nëëjel* 'nails', *schëële* 'to peel', *Mëër* 'sea', *Dëëchter* 'daughters', *Ëël* 'oil'.

Other Als. dialects derive this phoneme also from §7.2 (i) (ii).

7.4 [ɛː] in the dialect of Barr corresponds to a diphthong of *ai*- or *ei*- quality in most of Alsace. *DSA*, 16 *heiss* shows *häss* for Barr as an enclave, occurring also north of Strasbourg. The *heiss/häss* (Franc.) isogloss runs more or less parallel to the river Lauter. Strasbourg has *aa* in certain surroundings (e.g. before *m*). It derives from:

(i) MHG *ei*: *gemèènt* 'meant', *Mèèschter* 'master'.
(ii) MHG *öu*: *getrèèmt* 'dreamed', *Bèèm* 'trees', *Frèèd* 'joy'.
In front of /j/ it is short: *zèje* 'to show'.

7.5 [aː] is a very advanced, low-front vowel and occurs for:
(i) MHG *æ*: *strahle* 'to comb', *naaje* 'to sew'.
(ii) MHG *ē*, *ä* when lengthened: *Waaj* 'way', *Daaj* 'days', *laase* 'to read', *Gelaajehèèt* 'occasion'.

7.6 [ɒː] has the same quality as the corresponding short vowel and is the product of lengthening of MHG *a*: *Råååd* 'wheel', *Hååfe* 'pot'.

7.7 [ɔː] is a very open, rounded, high to higher mid-back vowel and derives from:
(i) MHG *ô*: *Broot* 'bread', *Bohn* 'bean'.
(ii) MHG *â*: *Hoor* 'hair', *schloofe* 'sleep'
(iii) MHG *u* lengthened: *Sohn* 'son'.

7.8 [oː] is a close, rounded, mid-back vowel and derives from MHG *o* where lengthening has taken place: *Dôôchter* 'daughter', *gstôhle* 'stolen', *vôr* 'before', *wôhne* 'to dwell'.

7.9 [øː] is a close, rounded, mid-tongue front vowel deriving from: MHG *â*, *ô*, before *g* and *w*: *frööje* 'to ask', *wööje* 'dare', *Trööj* 'trough', *blööj* 'blue', *grööj* 'grey'. (See § 4.)

7.10 [œː] is an open, rounded, mid-front vowel deriving from:
(i) MHG *ou*: *kææfe* 'to buy', *glææwe* 'to believe'.
(ii) MHG *a* before *g*: *Dææ* 'day', *Wææje* 'waggon', *sææje* 'to say', *Nææjel* 'nail'.

7.11 [yː] is a close, rounded, high-tongue vowel deriving from MHG *û* in those comparatively few cases where shortening has not occurred: *Müür* 'wall', *süür* 'sour'.

§ 8. DIPHTHONGS

8.1 [iə] begins with an unrounded, high-front element which bears the stress and ends in the neutral, central, unstressed vowel. It represents:
(i) MHG *ie*: *lieb* 'dear'.
(ii) MHG *üe*: *Fiess* 'feet', *mied* 'tired'.
The dialect of Strasbourg has a monophthong [iː] in these cases.

8.2 [yə] begins with a rounded, high-front element which bears the stress and ends in the neutral, central, unstressed vowel. It stands for:

(i) MHG *uo*: *güet* 'good', *Küe* 'cow', *Brüeder* 'brother'. In Strasbourg speech a monophthong of open quality [ʏ:] or [ø:] replaces this usual Alsatian diphthong.

§ 9. UNSTRESSED VOWELS

Except in foreign words and compounds only *i* and the neutral, central vowel [ə] occur in unstressed positions. Unstressed *u* is confined to the ending *-ung*.

9.1 [ɪ] is lax and open. It derives from the following sources:

(i) MHG *i* in the following suffixes: *-lih nàtyrli* 'naturally'; *-ig ungaddi* 'impolite'; *-isch*.

(ii) MHG *iu* in adjectival endings: *jungi Mèèdle* 'young girls'.

(iii) An excrescent vowel *i* is found between *r* and *l* and *g*, *k*, *ch*: *durich* 'through', *Milich* 'milk'.

(iv) In final position in some nouns: *Tschooli* 'fool'.

9.2 [ə] does not continue final unstressed MHG *-e*, for this has dropped generally. Where [ə] is in final position it was followed by *-n* in MHG.

It occurs in the following instances:

(i) In the prefixes *ge-* and *be-* except before *h*, *s*, *št*, *š* and the vowels, and in the case of *ge-* also before *f*. Cf. *gereecht, gemèènt—gsin, bstellt*.

(ii) In the suffixes *-er*: *Hyser* 'houses', *-em*, *-el*, and where originally covered by *-n*, e.g. inf. *halfe* 'to help'. In the masc. art. the *-r* is syllabic: *dr*, as in the prefix *ver-*: *verliebt* 'in love'. The suffix *-el* has also a syllabic *l*, so that there is frequently no vocalic element.

(iii) In the diminutive suffixes *-el* (< *lin*), *-ele*, and the plural *-le*.

(iv) In the feminine suffix *-e* (< MHG *-inne*), *Kèche* 'woman cook', *Brèète* 'width'.

(v) In unstressed elements of compounds, e.g. *erüss* 'out' < *her-*, *Krànket* 'illness'.

§ 10. VOWEL QUANTITY[1]

10.1 Before single consonants, except /ŋ/, both long and short vowels occur. Thus the distribution of length is not restricted and it can only be understood from the historical development.

Before consonantal clusters only short vowels are normally found with the exception of the clusters *-cht*, *-ršt*, and to a much more limited extent *-rt*. The first one in particular has had a definite lengthening effect on the preceding vowels, e.g. *raacht* 'right',

---

[1] J. Fourquet published a similar account of vowel quantity in Alsatian in 'Phonologie und Dialektforschung am Elsässischen', *Phonetica*, iv (Supplement), 1959, pp. 85–92, which came to my notice only after my manuscript had gone to press.

Gseecht 'face', *Gåårte* 'garden', but *Frucht* 'corn', *Burscht* 'lad', *Flucht* 'flight'.

10.2 Two processes have fundamentally altered the MHG vowel quantity distribution and account for the present status. The first affected the long, high-tongue vowels which were reduced before all MHG fortis consonants and MHG clusters. As this shortening occurred also before all liquids and nasals except *r* it may indicate that these consonants were formerly fortis. Not only the products of the HG sound-shift and of doubling count as fortis but also those former lenes which were hardened in final position (*Auslauts-verhärtung*). It appears that at one time long, high-tongue vowels were tolerated only before lenes. E.g. *rўte* 'to ride', *lўte* 'to ring', *grўfe* 'to seize', *wўss* 'white', *Büch* 'belly'; before *m, l, n*: *Pflüm* 'plum', *Mül* 'mouth', *brün* 'brown'; *sch* < *sk* counts as fortis, hence *Rüsch* 'state of being drunk'; clusters: *st Füscht* 'fist'; final hardening of former lenis: *Hüss* 'house', *Müss* 'mouse', but pl. *Hyser, Mys, Ỹss* 'ice' but *Yse* 'iron'. Long, high-tongue vowels are thus found before the former lenis consonants *s, f, (v)* (*Yfer* 'eagerness', *süüfer* 'clean'), *d* (*Syd* 'silk', *lyde* 'to suffer'), *b* (*Lyb* 'body', *trywe* 'to drive', *Trywel* 'grapes').

10.3 As a corollary to this former distributional pattern prevailing among the high-tongue vowels can be seen the *Leichtinnendehnung*, a widespread phenomenon and fundamental for NHG. However, this process of lengthening of short vowels before lenis consonants was a very inconsistent shift, especially in Lower Alsace, while in Upper Alsace and other L. Alem. dialects (including that of Basle) this process was carried through fairly regularly. In Lower Alsace it was limited both with regard to the vowels affected and to the lenis consonants which followed. Before single *r* and single *l* all vowels were lengthened, but before *m* none were affected. In the case of all the other lenis consonants only preceding MHG *a* and *ē*, *ä* were generally lengthened; the other vowels remained short. E.g. *Beer* 'pear', *Kôhle* 'coal', *Speel* 'game'; *Nåme* 'name'; *Håås* 'hare', *Baase* 'broom', *laawe* 'to live', *Lååde* 'shop', *Naawel* 'mist', *Hååfe* 'pot', *Bååd* 'bath', *laase* 'to read', but *Esel* 'donkey', *Hewel* 'lever', *Ofe* 'stove', *rede* 'to talk'. Exceptions occur, e.g. *Kafer* 'beetle', *Schadel* 'skull', *Lawer* 'liver' and in Strasbourg also *Nawel* 'mist'. In view of the continuous influences of one local dialect upon another and of the standard language upon all dialects it is not surprising that what emerges are tendencies rather than rules without exception.

10.4 The obliteration of the difference between lenis and fortis consonants has deprived this distributional pattern of its former *raison d'être*. It is possible that this consonantal development arrested the process of the redistribution of vocalic quantity before it could be carried through to its logical conclusion.

§ 11. Comparison with the NHG Vowels

(1) The quantity distribution in Als. shows only certain features in common with that of NHG, e.g. the fragmentary *Leichtinnendehnung*.

(2) The lengthening effect of certain consonantal clusters, e.g. *cht*, is characteristic of Lower Als. but absent in NHG.

(3) Two diphthongs continue the MHG diphthongs *ie, uo, üe* which are monophthongized in NHG.

(4) The NHG diphthongs *ei, au, eu/äu* (MHG *î, û, iu; ei, ou, öü*) do not occur in Als. and the two MHG sources which have coalesced in NHG are kept apart.

(5) Unrounding has obliterated the MHG and NHG differences between short and long *i—ü*, short and long *e—ö, ei—eu/äu* (< *öü*).

(6) Palatalization has produced a new set of rounded front vowels in Als. which are opposed to back vowels in NHG.

(7) The *e-* series in Als. differs sharply from that of NHG. It is still based largely on the MHG opposition *e:ē* (*ä*).

(8) The NHG rule that short vowels are lax does not apply; there are short, tense, close vowels in Als.

(9) The Als. *ō* derives, as distinct from the NHG *ō*, from two sources (MHG *ô* and *â* though not from MHG *o* lengthened), but when mutated these are distinguished: [i:] and [a:].

(10) In its retention of unstressed *e* in the prefixes *ge-* and *be-* except before a limited number of consonants, Als. stands nearer to NHG than to H. Alem. The occurrence of unstressed *-i* in the adjectival declension is a common Alem. feature and stands in contrast to the NHG declension.

Chief Vowel Correspondences

Als.¹	e a	y, ẙ üü, ü	èè œœ	ej öj	ie üe	ee oo
MHG	e ē, ä	î iu û	ei öü ou	-î/ -iu/ -û/	ie üe uo	ê, œ ô â
NHG	e, ä	ei eu, äu au	ei äu au	ei eu au	ie[i:] ü u	e, öh, oo, aa
			eu			

NHG	e, ä	ei	au	eu/äu	ie[i:] ü u	ee, öh, oo, aa
MHG	e ē, ä	î, -î/ ei	û -û/ ou	iu -iu/ öü	ie üe uo	ê, œ ô â
Als.	e a	y, ẙ ej èè	üü, ü öj œœ	y, ẙ ej èè	ie üe	ee oo

---

¹ For the phonetic value of the letters, see § 5. MHG and NHG sounds are given in their respective orthography.

THE CONSONANTS

§ 12. THE CONSONANTAL SYSTEM

Stops	Fricatives	Aspirates,	Affricates	Sonants	
b	f	(bf	ph)	m	w
d	s š	(ds | th | dš)	n	l	j
g	x	(kh)		ŋ	R	h

The historical consonantal system has been substantially reduced. The opposition of fortis and lenis is completely abandoned. For one place of articulation Als. has but one stop and one fricative.[1] Phonetically speaking it is in most circumstances a voiceless semi-fortis. The phonetic signs used here have been chosen for their simplicity; they must always be understood as semi-fortes, unless another allophonic value is indicated. They are unsatisfactory if they are compared with those used in the transcription of other dialects unless one keeps in mind their special significance. The stops [b, d, g] share the voicelessness of the SGm. lenes but are less relaxed. On the other hand they are neither as long nor as energetically articulated as the SGm. fortes. Alsatian scholars have seen the nearest cognates in the unaspirated French stops [p, t, k]. Martin-Lienhart's *Elsässisches Wörterbuch* therefore uses these signs to indicate the semi-fortes.

The affricates are more relaxed than the NHG affricates and both shorter and more relaxed than the H. Alem. fortis affricates. Phonemically they are clusters of a stop plus fricative, similarly the aspirates [kh, ph, th].[2]

Initially and medially stops and fricatives are normally realized as semi-fortes. Finally they are fortis after short stressed vowels but usually semi-fortis after long vowels, cf. *Müss—Mys* sg.-pl. 'mouse'. The fortis allophones are expressed, where this is necessary, by: [p, t, k, ff, ss, šš, xx].

As far as the distribution is concerned /s/ does not occur before consonants in the same morpheme; /x/ does not occur initially in native words, and in many Als. dialects it is restricted to the position

---

[1] Als. thus participates, like Rhen. Franc. (chap. v, § 12), in the *binnenhochdeutsche Konsonantenschwächung* (see Primus Lessiak, *Beiträge zur Geschichte des deutschen Konsonantismus*, Vienna, 1933) which W. Mitzka now calls the *deutsche Konsonantenschwächung* since it affects all dialects except the peripheral ones: Low Franc., Westphal., West Middle Franc., H. Alem., South Bav., Silesian, East Pommeranian ('Die dänische und die deutsche Konsonantenschwächung', *ZfMaf.*, xxii, 1954, 65–87).

[2] See L. Bloomfield, 'Initial *k* in German', *Language*, xiv, 1938, 178–86.

after back vowels, being replaced by /š/ in all other positions;[1] [kh], which is fortis phonetically, occurs only initially before stressed vowels. /h/ occurs only initially, including the position after a prefix. /w/ does not occur finally and /ŋ/ of course not initially. /j/ occurs initially before vowels, medially and finally only after front vowels and liquids. The only voiced consonants are the sonants. All consonants are short.

§ 13. SPELLING

In view of the great simplicity of the consonantal system the NHG orthography can be retained without much harm. Bastian's departures from it, arbitrary and illogical as they often are, can therefore also be left.

The following spellings are most frequent:

Phoneme	Letter	Phoneme	Letter	Phoneme	Letter
b	b, p, bb, pp	f	f, v, ff	m, n, ŋ, l, R	m, n, ng, l, r; mm, nn
d	d, t, dd, tt, dt	s	s, ss (1)		ll, rr
g	g, k, gg, ck	š	sch, ch (2)	w, j, h	w, j, h
		x	ch		
bf	pf	ds	z, tz	kh-	k-, c-

Notes

(1) It has to be remembered that s before t or p if in the same morpheme is always [š].

(2) ch represents [š] in all cases where in NHG the ich-Laut would apply.

§ 14. THE CONSONANT PHONEMES

14.1 [b] is a semi-fortis voiceless stop. It derives from:

(i) MHG b in initial and final position: blywe 'to stay', ich hǎb 'I have'.

(ii) MHG p and -pp-: Bǎbbe 'papa', bǎbbele 'to talk', Spack 'bacon'. In loan-words initial MHG or NHG p is usually followed by h as in native words where an unstressed vowel is dropped: Pharson 'person', Phǎǎr 'pair', cf. bhǎlte 'to keep'.

(iii) It is the result of assimilation in ebber 'somebody'. In final position after a short vowel it becomes fortis.

14.2 [d] is a semi-fortis voiceless stop deriving from:

(i) MHG d: Syd 'silk', rede 'to talk'.

---

[1] See E. Beyer, 'La prononciation de l'ich-Laut', Les Langues Modernes, xlix, 1955, pp. 214–21.

(ii) MHG *t* and *tt*: *ferdig* 'finished', *bate* 'to pray', *Dœœ* 'day'. In final position after a short vowel it becomes fortis.

14.3 [g] is a semi-fortis voiceless stop, deriving from:

(i) MHG initial *g-*: *geje* 'against', *gehn* 'to go'.

(ii) MHG *-gg-* and *-ck-*: *Spack* 'bacon', *schmecke* 'to taste', *Eck* 'corner'.

(iii) MHG initial *k* before a consonant, medial and final *k*: *Krieg* 'war', *stårik* 'strong', *trinke* 'to drink'.

(iv) MHG *ch* in the cluster *chs*: *Ochs* 'ox'. In final position after a short vowel it becomes fortis.

14.4 [f] is a semi-fortis, voiceless, labio-dental fricative and continues both MHG *f(ff)* and *v*:

(i) MHG *-ff-* (< Gmc. *p*): *schåffe* 'to work', *halfe* 'to help', *offe* 'open'.

(ii) MHG *-v-* (< Gmc. *f*): *Hååfe* 'pot', *Ofe* 'stove'. Finally after a short vowel it is fortis.

14.5 [s] is a semi-fortis, voiceless, fricative articulated with the tip of the tongue and derives from:

(i) MHG *s* (Gmc. *s*): *loos* 'loose', *Nåås* 'nose', *süür* 'sour'.

(ii) MHG medial and final *z* (Gmc. *t*): *Füess* 'foot', *besser* 'better'. It does not occur before other consonants of the same morpheme. Finally it is fortis after a short vowel, e.g. *Hüss—Hyser* 'house(s)'.

14.6 [š] is a semi-fortis voiceless fricative articulated with the blade of the tongue. It derives from:

(i) MHG *s* before consonants in the same morpheme: *Mèèschter* 'master', *Schnüer* 'string', *Nescht* 'nest', but *gewisst* 'known'.

(ii) MHG *sc, sch* (< Gmc. *sk*): *scheen* 'beautiful'.

(iii) MHG *ch* except after back vowels. Originally this was, and still is with the older generation, a palatal allophone of the /x/ phoneme. The younger generation speaks generally [š]: *Strèèch* 'trick', *ich* 'I'.

14.7 [x] occurs only as a velar fricative in the younger generation where the palatal variant has become [š]. It does not occur initially. It continues MHG *ch* after back vowels: *noch* 'after', *Wuch* 'week'.

14.8 The affricates [bf] and [ds] derive from the same sources as the corresponding NHG affricates: *zåhle* 'to pay', *Kåtz* 'cat'.

14.9 [dš] results from juxtaposition of the dental stop and [š]: *wottsch* 'want' 2nd pers. sg., *Handschi* 'glove'.

14.10 [kh] this is a fortis-aspirated stop which occurs only initially before a stressed vowel and is derived from MHG *k-*: *Kind* 'child', *Küe* 'cow', and MHG *geh-*: *gheert* 'heard'. Phonemically it is /g + h/, see § 12.

K

14.11 The nasals [m n ŋ] and the liquids [l] and [R] occur in the same positions as in NHG and derive from the same sources. The liquids function also as syllabics. *r* is a uvular trill and in some positions (especially final) difficult to distinguish from [x]. In contrast to H. Alem. and the dialects of Haut-Rhin final *-n* after stressed syllable is generally preserved (*gsin* 'been'), but in unstressed syllables it becomes 'mobile' (see chap. ii, § 18, ii, iii), cf. *üss den Œje* 'out of the eyes': *mit de Hand* 'with the hands'.

14.12 [w] is a voiced, labio-dental semi-consonant with little friction. It occurs initially and medially before vowels and derives from the following sources:

(i) MHG *w* initially: *wann* 'when', *zwèi* 'two'; medially *eewig* 'eternal', *farwe* 'to colour'.

(ii) MHG *-b-* medially after vowels and *r, l* : *iwer* 'above', *blywe* 'to stay', *Barwel* 'Barbara', *ëëwe* 'flat'.

In many Als. dialects especially those of Lower Alsace [w] has also developed from MHG *-g-* after *a*: Strasbourg *saawe* 'to say', *Waawe* 'waggon'.

14.13 [j] is a voiced, palatal semi-consonant produced without friction. It occurs initially before any vowel, but medially and finally only after front vowels and *r* and *l*. It derives from:

(i) MHG *j* initially: *jung* 'young', *Joor* 'year'; medially *draaje* 'to turn', *blieje* 'to flower'.

(ii) MHG *-g-* medially after vowels and *r, l* (but see § 14.12 (ii)): *frööje* 'to ask', *Waaj* 'way', *Œj* 'eye', *Morje* 'morning'.

(iii) MHG *-w-*: *ejer* 'your', *erfreje* 'to rejoice', *Frœj* 'woman', *reje* 'to regret'. In the dialect of Barr it regularly has a palatalizing effect on preceding back vowels.

14.14 [h] occurs only initially before vowels or after stops and is derived from:

(i) MHG *h*: *håån* 'to have'; after the prefixes *b-, g-* (< *be-, ge-*): *bhålte* 'to keep', *gheert* 'heard'.

(ii) in loan-words after initial stops: *Khårt* 'card', *The* 'tea', *Thomåt* 'tomato', *Phåår* 'pair' and after MHG *k-*.

§ 15. ASSIMILATION

15.1 Historical assimilations, no longer felt as such, are frequent, e.g. *Jumfer*: *mf* < *-ngf-*, *Mumfel*: *mf* < *ndf*, *ebber*: *bb* < *tw*.

15.2 In quick speech, progressive assimilations are frequent, e.g. *n + w*: *wann mer* > *wammer* 'if one' or 'if we'; *b + m*: *gib mir* > *gimmer* 'give me'; *d + b* or *g* > *b* or *g*: *nid güet* > *ni güet*; *nid kumme* > *ni kumme*. But they are not nearly so universal as in H. Alem. In our text, for example, the following instances, where H. Alem.

would assimilate, are left unassimilated by the informants: *d Milich,
d Bèèn, er het bees getrèèmt, ken Frœj.*

§ 16. COMPARISON WITH THE NHG CONSONANTS

The most salient differences are:

(1) The NHG opposition of voiced/voiceless stops and fricatives
has no parallel in Als. There is only one series of voiceless stops and
fricatives, mainly semi-fortis in character but with fortis allophones.
There are, as in NHG, but in contrast to H. Alem., no long consonants.

(2) Als. departs from the MHG consonantal system even more
radically than NHG: it no longer distinguishes between MHG *d* and
t, s and *zz, f(v)* and *ff, g* and *k* before consonants, *b* and *p* initially
and finally.

(3) The semi-consonants *w* and *j* play a large part, the MHG
incidence having been substantially increased by the shift of MHG
b and *g* after vowels and liquids to *w* and *j*.

(4) The distinction between velar and palatal allophones of NHG
ch is on the point of disappearing through fusion of the palatal
variant with the sound represented by *sch*.

(5) The loss of final *n* in unstressed syllables in Als.

(6) The clusters [šp] and [št] in medial and final position are
characteristic of High and Low Alem. but absent in NHG.

(7) The absence in Als. of the glottal stop before stressed initial
vowels and, in consequence, the liaison of words; frequent breaking
of hiatus.

MORPHOLOGY

NOUNS AND ARTICLES

§ 17. FORMATION OF THE PLURAL

As in the plural formation of H. Alem. the important features are
the loss of former unstressed final *-e* and of former final *-n* in unstressed syllables. The three chief means of expressing plurality are
the endings *-e* (< *-en*),[1] *-er*, and mutation, which may be used alone
or in combination with a plural ending. There are thus four main
types of plural formation:

Type A: without ending or mutation;
Type B: by mutation alone;
Type C: by adding *-e* in the plural;

---

[1] As in H. Alem. this historical *-n* reappears frequently before words beginning with a vowel. See § 14.11. It is not indicated in this section.—Cf. fn.(1),
p. 55.

Type D: by adding *-er* and with mutation where the root-vowel is mutatable.

Note: As mutation is an important morphological device it is necessary to know in which way the mutatable vowels mutate:

Basic mutatable vowel:	å	o	oo	ô	u	ü/üü	œœ	üe	öi
Mutated vowel:	a/e	e	aa/ee	ĕē	i	ў/y	èè/aa	ie	ei

For the phonetic value of these letters, see § 5. In the case of *å* (long or short) the historical or primary umlaut is *e*, e.g. *Glåås—Glēēser* 'glass'; *Grååb—Grēēwer* 'grave'; *Rååd—Rēēder* 'wheel'; the modern and analogical umlaut is *a*, e.g. *Raadel* 'wheel' dim., *Fååde—Faade* 'thread', *Grååwe—Graawe* 'ditch'. The umlaut of *oo* is *aa* if it is from MHG *â*, e.g. *Hoor—Haarel* 'hair' (dim.), but *ee* if it is from MHG *ô*, e.g. *root—reeter* 'red'. Likewise the umlaut of *œœ* (< MHG *ou*) is *èè*, of *œœ* (< MHG *a*) is *aa*, or *ēē*, (primary umlaut), e.g. *Bœœm—Bèèm* 'tree', *Wœœje—Waaje* 'cart', *Nœœjel—Nēējel* 'nail'.

Type A. To this type belong:

(i) Some neuter nouns, incl. diminutives, especially those of the second degree:[1] *Fanster* 'window', *Gewidder* 'thunderstorm', *Johr* 'year', *Hysele* 'house' dim.

(ii) Most masculine nouns with a non-mutatable root-vowel: *Epfel* 'apple', *Bèèn* 'leg', *Waaj* 'way', *Jaajer* 'hunter'.

(iii) Those feminine nouns ending in *-e* in the sg.: *Keche* 'cook', *Lehrere* 'woman teacher'. The number of nouns belonging here is small, i.e. considerably smaller than in High Alem., cf. *Blüem* 'flower', *Supp* 'soup', *Guf* 'pin', *Stirn* 'forehead', which belong to Type A in Zt.

Type B. To this type belong:

(i) Most masculine nouns with a mutatable vowel: *Bock—Beck* 'billy-goat', *Büch—Bŷch* 'belly', *Schüeler—Schieler* 'pupil', *Dœœ—Daaj*[2] 'day', *Strüss—Strŷss* 'bunch of flowers', *Nåme—Name* 'name'.

(ii) Most of those feminine nouns which mutate in NHG: *Küe—Kiej*[2] 'cow', *Dôôchter—Dēēchter* 'daughter', *Müss—Mys*[3] 'mouse'.

This type of plural formation is more frequent in Als. than in NHG owing to the loss of former final *-e*.

Type C: ending *-e*. To this type belong:

(i) The majority of feminine nouns: *Nåås—Nååse* 'nose', *Zwaal—Zwaale* 'towel', *Blüem—Blüeme* 'flower', *Schrüüb—Schrüüwe* 'screw'.

---

[1] See Note 3, p. 157.

[2] MHG final *-g* has disappeared; MHG medial *-g->j*; MHG *-j* is preserved, *Küeje > Kiej*.

[3] This shows vowel shortening before MHG fortis (*mûs*) but preservation of long vowel before MHG lenis (*miuse*).

(ii) The majority of masculine nouns denoting animate beings: *Büe—Büewe* 'boys', *Büür—Büüre* 'farmer' and some other masc. nouns, e.g. *Stâchel—Stâchle* 'quill'.

(iii) The neuters *Oej—Oeje* 'eye', *Ohr—Ohre* 'ear' and the diminutives of the first degree: *Hindl—Hindle* 'dog' dim.

Type D: ending in -*er* with mutation where possible.

(i) The majority of the neuter nouns: *Hüehn—Hiehner* 'hen', *Kamin—Kaminer* 'chimney', *Bett—Better* 'bed', *Harz—Harzer* 'heart', *Mül—Mŷler* 'mouth', *Tier—Tierer* 'animal'.

(ii) A few masculine nouns: *Mânn—Manner* 'man'.
More nouns belong to this type in Als. than in NHG or H. Alem.[1]

§ 18. CASE FORMS

Only a few local Als. dialects distinguish a case, the dative plural, by means of an ending.[2] The majority do not possess any special case forms except as occasional relic forms.

Possession is rendered by the same dative paraphrase as in High Alem. See chap. ii, § 21.

§ 19. GENDER[3]

The majority of nouns have the same gender as in NHG but the following are among those with a different gender: *Fâhne* m. 'flag', *Farsche* m. 'heel', *Bânk* m. 'bench', *Bâgge* m. 'cheek', *Egg* n. 'corner'.

§ 20. THE DECLENSION OF THE DEFINITE ARTICLE

The definite article is the least stressed form of the demonstrative pronoun. There are two case forms.

	m.	.	*n.*	*pl.*
Common Case	dr (1)	d (4)	s	d (4)
Dative	im, m (2)	dr (1)	im, m (2)	de(n) (3)

Notes

(1) In the most reduced form of the article the *r* is syllabic, in other positions an unstressed [ə] appears: *der. e* is always [ə]. Occasionally this form is reduced to *de*.

(2) In the dative this least stressed form is used especially after prepositions. Before nouns we frequently find *im*, e.g. *im Barwel*; *im Mössjö Jean isch sŷner Nâmesdœœ*; f. *in dr*, pl. *in de*.

(3) Mobile -*n* inserted before words beginning with a vowel.

(4) This form is also used before an adj. in contrast to H. Alem. (where it is *di*), e.g. *d latz* 'the wrong one', *d groos Kâtz* 'the big cat'.

---

[1] See Lienhart, p. 44.   [2] E.g. see Lienhart, pp. 42–6.
[3] Cf. the interesting article by E. Beyer, '*Die Bach* en alsacien', *Bulletin de la Faculté des Lettres de Strasbourg*, xxxiii, 1954, 113–34.

§ 21. The Declension of the Indefinite Article

	m.	f.	n.
Common Case	e	e	e
Dative	eme	enere	eme

Notes

(1) e is [ə].

(2) The dative forms are also shortened to *me* and *nere* generally after a prep. ending in a vowel.

(3) The masc. c. c. is *en* before vowels. If no prep. precedes the forms *ime, inere* are often found.

§ 22. Agglutinations

In addition to the fusions of prepositions and articles known in NHG there are, e.g., these: *áme* (NHG *an einem*), *ime* (NHG *in einem*), *býme* (NHG *bei einem*), also in the fem. *ánere*, etc., *waajem* (MHG *wegen dem*).

ADJECTIVES

Adjectives are inflected for gender, number and case only when used in attributive position or when substantivized. There are only two case forms. The weak and strong declensions are used according to the same rules as in NHG.[1]

§ 23. The Strong Declension

	m.	f.	n.	pl.
Common Case. . .	junger (2)	jungi	jungs (1)	jungi
Dative . . .	jungem	junger	jungem	junge

Notes

(1) Other Low Als. dialects have an endingless form. If the adjective ends in a sibilant the ending is often *-es* (*e bees Kind* or *e beeses Kind*).

(2) The ending *-er* in the direct object case is an analogical extension. Traces of the former accusative still exist: *güete Morje, ich winsch dr e gsunde Áppetit*.

(3) Where the undeclined form ends in *-i* (*ungaddi*) the former final consonant is restored before endings (*ungaddigi*).

(4) Adj. ending in *-el* drop their *-e-* before inflexional endings, e.g. *dunkel—dunkler* 'dark'; a former final *-n* is restored in these cases, e.g. *offe—offeni* 'open'.

---

[1] Cf. chap. ii, *Adjectives*. In many Als. dialects the poss. pron. has strong endings for all genders in the common case, hence the following adj. is weak.

§ 24. THE WEAK DECLENSION

			m.	f.	n.	pl.
Common Case	.	.	jung	jung	junge⎫	junge
Dative	.	.	junge	jung (1)	junge⎭	

Notes

(1) Forms in *-e*, general farther north (e.g. Strasbourg), occur also: *gib s enere groosse Kåtz.*

§ 25. COMPARISON

The endings of the second and third degrees are: *-er*, *-st*: *wåårm—wermer—wermscht* 'warm', *grooss—greesser—greescht* 'big'. Umlaut occurs wherever the root-vowel is mutatable (see § 17). *Å* mutates to *e*. The comparative particle is *ås*.

NUMERALS
§ 26

Êener declines like a possessive pronoun (see § 29) and can be used both as a noun (in the sense of 'somebody') and as an adjective. The unstressed forms are the indefinite article. The numerals for 'two' and 'three' do not distinguish genders or cases.

PRONOUNS
§ 27. PERSONAL PRONOUNS

The same relationship between stressed and unstressed forms exists as in High Alem. (See chap. ii, § 31.)

	1st Person			*2nd Person*		
Nom. sg.	ich	ech	i	düü	dü	de
Acc. sg.	mich	mech	mi	dich	dech	di
Dat. sg.	miir	mer	mr	diir	der	dr
Nom. pl.	miir	mer	mr	iir	er	r
Acc. pl.	uns	es		eich	ech	i
Dat. pl.	uns	es		eich	ech	i

	3rd Person										
	m.			*f.*			*n.*			*pl.*	
Nom.	aar	er	r	sii	si	er	as	es	s	sii	si se
Acc.	iine		ne	sii	si	se	as	es	s	sii	si se
Dat.	iim	im	em	iire	ere	err	im	em		iine	ne

Notes

(1) The letter *e* stands always for [ə], *ii* for [ɪː].

(2) In inversion the pron. of the 2nd pers. sg. is omitted unless stressed: *Hesch mer's güet üssgereecht?*

(3) For the use of the stressed and unstressed forms, see our text.

(4) Agglutinations with prep. occur also: *gfellt mer âm* cf. NHG *an ihm*. The indefinite personal pronoun is *mer*, dat. *èèm*, acc. *èène*.

(5) If the neuter acc. refers to a female person, it is *ins*.

§ 28. Reflexive Pronouns

There is only one special form *sich, si* for the 3rd pers. sg. and pl. acc. and dat. Some dialects still use the pers. pronouns for the dative or generally after prepositions.

§ 29. Possessive Pronouns

They are *mÿner, dÿner, sÿner, unser, ejer, iir.*

(i) *mÿner, dÿner, sÿner.*

	m.	f.	n.	pl.
Common Case . .	mÿner	mÿni	mÿns	mÿni
Dative . . .	mÿm	mÿnere	mÿm	mÿne

Notes

(1) The above forms are also used as nouns but they are not preceded by the definite article as in NHG, e.g. *es isch mÿner*. This applies also to the pronouns listed below under (ii).

(2) As all these forms have inflexional endings attributive adjectives are weak, e.g. *mÿner scheen Strüss*: NHG *mein schöner Strauss*.

(3) In the dat. the particle *e* or *i* is frequently prefixed to the poss. pron. This applies also to the pronouns below.

(ii) *unser, ejer, iir.*

	m.	f.	n.	pl.
Common Case .	unsere	unseri	unsers	unseri
Dative . .	unserem	unsere	unserem	unsere

§ 30. Demonstrative Pronouns

For 'this' Als. uses *dar, die, dis* with two degrees of stress.

		m.	f.	n.	pl.
Common Case .	Nom.	dar	die, di	des, dis	die, di
	Acc.	dane			
Dative . .		dam	dare	dam	dane

Notes

(1) In the case of the masc. dem. pron. a distinction is made

between subject case and direct object, e.g. *stelle die Schissel uf dane Tisch* 'put this dish on this table'.

For 'that':

		m.	f.	n.	pl.
Common Case	. .	saler	sali	sal	sali
Dative	. .	salem, sam	salere	salem, sam	sale

Note

Alternative forms with *ds-*, e.g. *dsaler, dsal*, are also heard.

For 'such' the dialect uses *eso e*, pl. *sonig*; for 'such, so' *dåse* (NHG *so*).

§ 31. INTERROGATIVE PRONOUNS

	Common Case	Dative
who?	*wer*	*i wem*
what?	*wås*	
which?	*weler, weli, wels*	*i welem, welere,*
	pl. *weli*	*wele*
	sg. *wås fir e (èèner)*	
	pl. *wås firichi*	

§ 32. INDEFINITE PRONOUNS

èner, -i, -s; dat. *èèm, èènere*, acc. masc. *èène*
   (§§ 26, 29)   }   somebody
eber
nieme, niemes   nobody
ebs, adj.: *e bisl, e bisele, weni*   something, some
nix (1)   nothing
vyl(i) (2), as a noun: *vyli*, dat. *vyle*   much, many
månicher, -i, -s, pl. *månichi*   many
epådr   a few
jeeder (3), *-i, -s*, dat. *jeedem, jeedere*   each, all
åll, ålli, dat. *ålle* (pl.)   all
ålles, dat. *ållem, ållere* (sg.)   all
ken, ke (4) (adj.)—*kener, -i, -e* (noun)   no, none

Notes

(1) The vowel is [i]

(2) The vowel is short if the word is less strongly stressed: *vўli* or *vili*.

(3) Often with prefixed indef. art. *e jeeder, eme jeede, enere jeedere.*

(4) The adj. *ken* is indeclinable, e.g. *ken Månn, ken Wort, ken Daaj. Kener* used as a noun is declined as follows:

		m.	f.	n.	pl.
Common Case	. . .	kener	keni	kene	keni
Dative	. . .	kenem	kenere	kenem	kene

§ 33. RELATIVE PRONOUNS

Like High Alem. Alsatian uses *wu*: *frommi Kinder, wu d Seel uffhèètere.*

VERBS

§ 34. FORMS AND CLASSIFICATION

The verb has the following form classes: infinitive, imperative, past participle, present indicative and a past subjunctive (= conditional), and the compound tenses perfect and pluperfect, and a passive. The infinitive ends in *-e(n)* except in the case of the monosyllabic verbs, which end in *-n*. The infinitive particle is *ze*, e.g. *d Hànd ze drucke* 'to squeeze one's hand'.

The *imperative* is in the sg. identical in form with the 1st person sg. and in the pl. with the plural of the present, e.g. *Heer!* 'listen' (sg.); *hôôle mer ebbs ze bicke* 'fetch me something to eat' (pl.).

According to the way the past participle is formed two classes can be distinguished: a weak class: p.p. ending in *-t*, and a strong class: p.p. ending in *-e(n)*.

The *past participle* is characterized by the prefix *ge-*, *g-* (before vowels, fricatives or *h*), except the p.p. of *gehn* 'to go', *kumme* 'to come': *gànge, kumme*, and the p.p. of the modal auxiliaries and the verbs with prefixes. The verbs in *-iere(n)* take *ge-* in the p.p. in contrast to the practice in NHG, e.g. *gedrumbiert < drumbiere* 'to err'.

§ 35. STRONG VERBS

Verbs belonging to this class form their p.p. in *-e*; the majority have a different root-vowel in the p.p. from that of the infinitive; those with *a* as the root-vowel of the infinitive change to *i* in the sg. of the present.

According to stem alternants we can distinguish the following classes, leaving out of account the monosyllabic verbs (§ 40):[1]

I. Identical vowel in the inf. and p.p.:
  (i) [ɒ:] *fàhre* 'ride', *gràdwe* 'dig' (Ii).
  (ii) [ɔ:] *bloose* 'blow', *stoosse* 'push' (Ii).
  (iii) [ɒ] *hàlte* 'hold' (Iii).
Isolated cases are *hèèsse—ghèèsse* 'to be called', *böje—geböje* 'build', *schlœœje—geschlœœje* 'beat', *drœœje—gedrœœje* 'carry', *kumme—kumme* 'come', *laase—gelaase* 'read', *wasche—gewasche* 'wash'.

---

[1] As these classes are similar to those of H. Alem. the reader should compare chap. ii, § 39, where more examples are given. Reference to the relevant class in H. Alem. is made in brackets.

II. Vowel alternation [i or i: /ɪ]:

(i) [i:/ɪ] *schnyde—gschnitte*[1] 'cut', *blywe—gebliwe* 'stay' (II).

(ii) [i/ɪ] *rўde—geritte* 'ride on horseback', *dyte—gedite* 'point' (II).

III. Vowel alternation [iə/ o]: *biete-gebote* 'offer'; with long vowel before *r*: *friere—gfrôôre* 'freeze'; with palatalized vowel before *j* < *g*: *flieje—gflöje* 'fly' (III and X).

IV. Vowel alternation [ɪ/ɷ]: *finde—gfunde* 'find', *schwimme—gschwumme* 'swim', *ginne—gegunne* 'grant' (IV).

V. Vowel alternation [a/o] with root-vowel *i* in the sg. pres.: *halfe—gholfe* 'help'; with *u* in p.p. before nasal: *name—genume* 'take'; with long vowels before *l, r*: *stahle—gstôhle* 'steal', *flaachte—gflôôchte* 'weave'.

VI. Identical vowel [a] but with *i* in the sg. pres. as in preceding class V: *asse—gasse* 'eat' (VII).

VII. Vowel alternation [ɪ/a]: *sitze—gsasse* 'sit' (VIII).

VIII. Vowel alternation [y/o]: *süffe—gsoffe* 'drink' (IX).

A number of isolated vowel alternations: *leje—gelaaje* 'lie flat' (VIII), *schwëëre—gschwôôre* 'swear', *verschrecke—verschrocke* 'frighten', *dresche—gedrosche* 'thresh', *lœœfe—geloffe* 'run', *schўne—gschune* 'seem', *wëëje—gewööje* 'weigh', *steje—gstöje* 'climb'.

A small number of verbs which were weak in MHG have become strong and some formerly strong ones have become weak. They are on the whole the same ones as those which have changed classes in H. Alem. (For details, see also Lienhart, p. 71.)

§ 36. The Present

The endings are: sg. 1 -, 2 *-sch*, 3 *-t*, pl. *-e*, e.g. *heere* 'hear':

ich heer   mer⎫
du heersch   ir ⎬*heere*
ar heert   si ⎭

Notes

(1) The pl. of the pres. is always identical with the infinitive. Before words beginning with a vowel, especially enclitic pronouns, an *n* is inserted, e.g. *ir liewi Baasle, welle-n 'r?*

(2) If the root ends in a sibilant there is assimilation in the 2nd pers. sg.: *loon* 'to let, leave'—*dü loosch* (1st *loos*). In the 3rd pers.

---

[1] The grammatical change is, of course, only apparent because of the retention of the NHG orthography. There is only one dental stop, a semi-fortis, see §§ 12; 14.2.

sing. there is assimilation if the root ends in a dental stop, e.g. *rede* 'to talk', *ar red*.

(3) There are no traces of a present subjunctive. Als. dialects use the indicative also in indirect speech. Cf. *Hesch dü mer nit gsœœt, dü wèèsch weli?* Cf. Zt.: *Häsch mer nid gsäit, du wüssisch weli?* 'Did you not say you knew which one?'

§ 37. THE CONDITIONAL

37.1 Only a very few verbs of the strong class still form strong past subjunctive forms, e.g. *name* 'take': *ich naam, dü naamsch, ar naam, mer naamte.* See § 40, Monosyllabic Verbs.

37.2 The majority of verbs, both strong and weak, which form a synthetic past subjunctive take the ending *-t*, e.g. *kœœfe* 'buy', *ich kœœft, mer kœœfte.* Occasionally this ending is also added to strong forms. Thus Bastian has: *ar gabt; s isch mer als gangd'i durich e Wåld.*

37.3 In Barr by far the most frequent way of forming the conditional is the paraphrase of infinitive with the auxiliary *gaad, gaadsch, gaade.* E.g. *wann numme ålli såpeurs d'r Güxel gaad hole; ich gaad gehn; si gaad s wisse.* In Strasbourg the auxiliary is usually the past subjunctive of *tüen* 'do'.

§ 38. THE COMPOUND TENSES AND THE PASSIVE

Like H. Alem. the Als. dialects have two compound tenses for the past, both formed by means of the auxiliaries *sin* 'be' and *håån* 'have' and the past participle. There are no traces of the MHG imperfect tense.

Perfect: *ar isch gånge; ar het gekœœft.*
Pluperfect: *ar isch gånge gsin; ar het gekœœft ghet.*

Future time is usually expressed by adverbs of time and the present tense of the verb. The auxiliary *waare* (= NHG *werden*) indicates an assumption or supposition if used with the infinitive of the verb. But the passive is formed with *waare* and the p.p. as in NHG: *do wurd gekocht.* The forms of *waare* are: pres. sg. *wur, wursch, wurd,* pres. pl. *waare* p.p. *wore.*

§ 39. THE MODAL AUXILIARIES

In contrast to H. Alem. the modal auxiliaries in Als. have not an identical form for past part. and infinitive. But the infinitive is always identical with the pl. of the pres. The following forms must therefore be distinguished:

	Inf. Pl. Pres.	1, 3 Sg. Pres.	2 Sg. Pres.	Condit.	P.P.
'to be able'	kenne	kånn kåå	kånnsch kååsch	kennt	gekennt
'should like' or 'be able'	meeje	måå	mååsch	mecht	gemecht
'must'	mien	müess	müesch	miesst	gemiesst
'to want'	welle	will	witt	wott	gewellt, gewott
'shall, should'	solle	soll	sollsch sotsch	sott	gesollt, gsott
'to be allowed'	derfe	derf	derfsch	derft	gederft

Notes

(1) In the perfect and pluperfect tenses the infinitive is used as in NHG before a main verb in the infinitive, but the auxiliary precedes the main verb as in H. Alem., e.g. *hån mer denn nit solle kumme?*

(2) The pres. of *meeje* occurs only in the negative, e.g. *ich måå-nit.*

§ 40. Monosyllabic Verbs

These verbs end, in contrast to all other verbs, in *-n* in the infinitive and the pl. of the present. The verbs corresponding to NHG *nehmen, kommen, ziehen* which in Zt. belong to the monosyllabic verbs are regular strong verbs in L. Alem. (*name, kumme, zieje,* but Barr has *zyn-gezöje*). The following forms must be distinguished:

	Inf. Pl. Pres.	Imp.	Sg. Pres.	Condit.	P.P.
'to have'	hån	heb! hewe!	håb (1) hesch het	hatt	ghett
'to be'	sin	sei! seje!	bin bisch isch	waar pl. waarde waare	gsin
'to do'	düen (2)	düe!	düe düesch düet	daat	gedoon
'to give'	gaan	gib! gan!	gib (1) gisch git	gaab (1) pl. gaabe or gaawe	gaan
'to see'	saan	(lüej!)	seh sehsch seht	—	gsaan
'to go'	gehn (4)	geh! gehn!	geh gehsch geht	gangt gaad gehn	gånge
'to let'	loon	loss! loon!	loos loosch loost	liess	geloon

Notes

(1) Before enclitic personal pronouns these forms ending in *-b* change to *-w*, e.g. *hăwi, giwi, giw ere, giw uns.*

(2) Initial *d* is here adopted because it is frequent in dialect writings. It represents of course the semi-fortis.

(3) Like *gehn* goes *stehn,* 'to stand' p.p. *gstănde.*

PARTICLES

§ 41

In Upper Alsatian dialects the use of particles of place is equally developed as in SGm. (see chap. ii, § 48) and the forms are more or less the same. The Lower Alsatian dialects are nearer NHG in their usage. Thus reinforcement of the prepositions of place by a following adverbial particle is no more frequent than in NHG where it is, of course, not unknown. As in NHG a difference is made in the case of the adverbs of place between movements towards the speaker and movement away from the speaker. But a similar difference is also made in the case of adverbs denoting rest.

Preposition	*Movement*		*Rest*	
	(a) *away from speaker*	(b) *towards speaker*	(a) *not with speaker*	(b) *with speaker*
in (drin) (2)	nỹn	erin, rin	drinne	hinne (3)
üss (1) (drüss)	nüss	erüss, rüss	drüsse	hüsse
uff (druff)	nuff	eruff, ruff	drowe	howe
— (drăb)	năb	erăb	} drunde	hunde
under (drunder)	nunder	erunder		
iwer (driwer)	niwer	riwer	driwe	hiwe
hinder (dhinder)	hinderi, (6) dehinder	hindere, dehinder	dhinde, dehinder	hinde do hinde dhinde
vôôr, fer (4) (devôôr)	vôôri (6) devôôr, feere	erfeer, evôôr	devôôr, vorne	vorne, do vorne, dvorne
um (drum)	num	erum, rum	drumerum	—
ze (derzüe)	—	—	—	—
ăn (4) (drăn)	ăne (5)			

Notes

(1) No difference in vowel length between prep. and adv. *üss, uff,* cf. SGm. *uf* (prep.) *uuf* (adv.).

(2) The forms with *dr-* correspond to NHG *dar-*, e.g. *darin*, etc.

(3) Cf. NHG *hier drin, hier draussen.*

(4) Here the adverbs have long vowels *vôôr, ăăn.*

(5) *Ăne* is NHG *hin*, e.g. *wo gehsch ăne?* 'where are you going?' NHG *her* is *har.*

(6) Like *dne* this is a relic of the older way of forming the adverbs of direction, < *hinder hin, an her* (cf. SGm.), e.g. *er isch hinderi kumme* 'he has been put into prison' (Martin-Lienhart, *Els. Wtb.*). Examples: *üss em Hüss, ich kumm nid drüss, geh nüss; kumm erüss; er isch drüsse, er isch hüsse.*

PHONETIC TRANSCRIPTION

While this transcription is essentially phonemic, it takes account of the chief allophones. A description of the individual vowels and consonants is given in §§ 6, 7, 8, 9, 14. [b, d, g, f, s, š, x] are voiceless semi-fortes. Finally they are generally more fortis than initially or medially, but only after short vowels is the fortis character definite and indicated in the transcription by means of the symbols [p, t, k, ff, ss, šš, xx]. The affricates [bf, ds, dš] are also semi-fortes, while initial prevocalic [kh] is more clearly fortis. [ʀ] is uvular.

Words of two or more syllables have the main stress on the first syllable except where marked otherwise.

wɔ nɔmə dʀ khɒšbʀ so lɒŋ bli:d? jɔmfʀl

andlɪš — hęšmərs gyəd ˌyssgəʀɪ:šd? khɔmd s ba:sələ? so: , dɪss wa:ʀ dʀ ɪ:ʀšd šdʀɛ:š.

o: , ɪ‿šɒff gejə dɪss ɒʀšl mɪd hand ɔ fiəs. dy hęš mər dɒx diə bšdęld, wɔ ɪš gəmɛ:nd hɒb? ha: jo:

hɪ:ʀ, khɒšbʀ — dywɔʀš mər dɒx nɪdlads — bi węm bɪš da gsɪn·? bi ɒlə.

dʀ sibɪl, šysdɪnəl, ɒmeli, baʀwəl?

ɪš hɒbs nɪm ə'ʀa:xd gəwɪsd weli, no: — jęsəs, jęsəs — khɒšbʀl ɪš fʀdswi:fəl — hęš dy mʀ nɪ gsœ:d, dy wɛ:š weli?

jo: , ɒ:wəʀ bęsʀ ɪš bęsʀ.

ɪš wɛ:s mər nɪm dsə halfə. wɒs hęš dan yssgəʀɪ:šd?. šløi, ɪš hɒb ɪm baʀwəl gsœ:d, əs ɪš mər, wɪ wan dʀ mɛ:šdər hi:ʀɔ:də sɒd.

dɪss hęš gsœ:d? s wɔʀd mʀ aŋ, ɪš myəs ɒ d lɒfd. — bęsʀ ɪš bęsʀ.

bɪš dɔ: , khɒšbʀ? jęds had ɪš dɪ bɒl yššalə lɔ:n.

bɪš bim ɒʀšəl gsɪn·, khɔmd s? šnyəʀšdʀɒgs ɪw'ɔʀ dʀ faldwa:j. sɪš gyəd, khɒš gɪ:n.

nɪd əmɔ·l ə šnabsəl bəkhɔmd mʀ.

hɒns, hɒns, dmɪlɪš ɪš dɔ: .

wan‿nɔmə əmɔ:l ə mɪljo:n kha:m.

gyədə mɒʀjə, hɒns. dęʀd šdɪ:d‿mɪlɪš mɪd əmə pɪn dœ butik. wɒs mɒxš da wɪdʀ fɪʀə gsɪ:šd, mʀ mɛ:nd jo d hiənəʀ hɒn dʀ s bʀɔ:d əwak gəbɪgd. khę męnš daŋgd ɒn minʀ nɒməsdœ: .

ɪš wɪnš dʀ ə fɛʀmi frœj ɒn fʀšdɒnd dsyəm nɒməsdœ: . hɪmələsɒgɒff, ɪš bʀyš khę fʀœj ɒn khę fʀšdɒnd.

ej, gyədə mɒʀjə, hɒnsl. ɪš hɒb dɪš šɒn dʀysə gsyəšd. fi:l glɪk ɒn ə liəbs wi:wələ ɪn dʀ hysšdɒnd. ɒmbędiəʀə dɒx ɛ:nə nɪt. dis gšmɒds — jo: , wans jęds nɒx jɒŋi mɛ:dlə wa:ʀə. — los nə, aʀ hęd bɪ:s gədʀɛ:md. — dy ɒʀməʀ. dɛʀfs ɒŋənəs dɒndl nɪt əʀfɒ:ʀə, wɒs dʀ gɒldhɒnsl gədʀɛ:md hęd? wan ɪš nɔmə ə ejəl wa:ʀ mɪd

FERDINAND BASTIAN : *D'R HANS IM SCHNOOKELOCH* [1]

(Extract from Act II)

Angenes (sonntäglich aufgeputzt, eine Rose im Haar, sitzt auf dem
Sofa, mit einer Spitzenarbeit beschäftigt)*:* Wu numme der
Câsper so lång blyt? (seufzt)

Casper (in abgetragenem Gehrock, rote Kravatte, grosser Strohhut.
— Mitteltüre)*:* Jumfer! [2]

Angenes (eilig)*:* Andlich! — Hesch mer's güet üssgereecht? Kummt's
Baasele? [3]

Casper: Hmh!

Angenes: So, dis waar d'r eerscht Strèèch. O, i schåff geje dis Urschel
mit Hand un Fiess. Dü hesch mer doch die bschtellt, wu ich
gemèènt håb?

Casper (zögernd)*:* Haa — joo.

Angenes: Heer [4], Câsper — dü wursch mer doch nit d'latz — bў
wem bisch da gsin?

Casper: Bў ålle.

Angenes: D'r Sўbille, Jüstinel, Amelie, Barwel?

Casper: Ich håb's nim eraacht gewisst welli, no —

Angenes (händeringend)*:* Jesses, Jesses — Câsper! ich verzwyfel —
Hesch dü mer nit gsœœt, dü wèèsch welli?

Casper: Jo — åwer, besser isch besser.

Angenes: Ich wèèss mer nim ze halfe. Wås hesch dann üssgereecht?

Casper: Schlöi! Ich håb im Barwel gsœœt, es isch mer, åls wi wann
d'r Mèèschter hyroote sott.

Angenes: Dis hesch gsœœt? — 's wurd mer ang, ich müess å d'Luft
(eilig Mitteltüre ab).

Casper (schaut ihr verblüfft nach)*:* Besser isch besser. (Schüttelt den
Kopf.)

Lehn (von links hintere Seitentüre mit einer Tasse Milch)*:* Bisch doo,
Câsper? Jetz hatt ich di båll üssschalle loon. Bisch bўm Urschel
gsin, kummt's?

Casper: Schnüerstråcks iwer d'r Faldwaaj.

Lehn: 's isch güet, kåsch gehn.

Casper: Nit emol e Schnapsel kreijt [5] mer (ab).

Lehn (geht zur vorderen Seitentüre links und klopft)*:* Håns, Håns!
d'Milich isch doo.

For spelling, see §§ 5 and 13. Where alterations have been made Bastian's
original spelling is given at the bottom of the page, but only on the first occurrence. For *d* Bastian has *a*. The numbers refer to the cues, not the lines.

1 wo, bliet. 2 Jumpfer. 3 Endlich, guet, üssgericht, Bäsele. 5 wär, erscht,
Streich, ich, Händ und Füess, gemaant. 6 Ha, jo. 7 Horch, letz, bie, bisch de
denn. 10 erecht, wölli. 11 gsaat waisch. 13 waiss, helfe. 14 Schlöüi, wie, wenn,
Maischter, hirothe. 15 eng, an. 17 do, hätt, dich, schelle, lon, biem. 18 Schnuer-,
üewer, Feldwäj. 18 kannsch.

Hans (tritt auf, sonntäglich gekleidet, weisses Hemd, Vatermörder, schwarze Binde, dunkle kurze Hose, rotes Gillet mit Silberknöpfen, weisse Wadenstrümpfe, Schnallenschuhe): Wann numme emool e Million kaam. (Legt sich missmutig lang hin aufs Sofa, das Kinn auf beide Hände gestemmt).

Lehn: Güete Morje, Håns. Dert steht d'Milich mit eme pain de boutique [6]. Wås måchsch da widder fir e Gseecht, mer mèènt jo d'Hiehner hån d'r s'Brood ewackgebickt.

Hans: Ke Mensch dankt ån mỹner Nåmesdœœ.

Lehn: Ich winsch d'r e fermi Frœj un Verstånd züem Nåmesdœœ.

Hans (erhebt sich): Himmelsåckuff, ich brüch ken Frœj und ken Verstånd.

Angenes (Mitteltüre): Ai, güete Morje Hånsel. (Küsst ihn stürmisch.) Ich håb dich schun drüsse gsüecht. Vyl Glick un e liebs Wywele in d'r Hüssstånd.

Hans: Åmbediere doch èène nit. Dis Gschmutz [7] — joo, wann's jetzt noch jungi Mèèdle waarde [8] (setzt sich).

Lehn: Loss 'ne, ar het bees getrèèmt (rechts von ihm).

Angenes: Dü årmer (links von ihm). Derf's Ångenes Dåntel nit erfåhre, wås d'r Goldhånsel getrèèmt het?

Hans: Wann ich numme e Ejel waar mit meterlånge Ståchle (steht erregt auf). Dåss'rs gråd wisse, ich bin nit verliebt, ich kå d'Wybslỹtt nit schmecke. D'r Båbbe Gerôme isch e n'ålter Ållefånz, dar het e Kraan im Hirn, e Gschtunz, zwèj het'r.

Lehn: Oho, wie gilt's dann doo?

Hans (gegen die Mitteltüre gehend): Diss Zuck [10] hån'r ejch in mir gedrumbiert, ich bin e Månn un ke Wœœjerååd.

Angenes: Ei, dü Herrjee.

Lehn: Håns, do haar, wås isch loos?

Hans: Wås nit ångebunde n'isch (rasch ab).

Angenes: Er isst schu widder nit. Hånsele heer! (ihm nach, ab).

Lehn: Ei se schlœœ [11], wås kennt do d'r hinter stacke? Sott mich mỹni fyn Nåås im Stich geloon hån? (Tippt sich sinnend an die Nase.)

Urschel (hübsches, junges Mädchen im Bauernkostüm von links, hintere Seitentüre): Güete Dœœ, Jumfer Lehn, wås het Si [12] so brassånts?

Lehn: Kumm Urschel, setz dich. Hesch mer die zwèj Roosesteckle mitgebrôôcht?

Urschel: Herrjee, die håwi im Dummle gånz vergasse (will ab).

---

1 emol, käm. 2 dort, for, Gsicht, maant, Hühner, Brod, eweck-. 3 ken, denkt, miner, -daa. 4 wüensch, Frau, zuem. 6 gsuecht, Viel, Glück, Wiewele. 7 aane. jo, Maidle, wärde. 8 er, bös, getraamt. 9 hett. 10 Wiebs-, der, Krän, zwai. 12 Waauerad. 13 Herrje. 14 her, los. 16 esst, schun, horch. 17 schlaa könnt, stecke, mini, Nas, gelon. 18 bressants. 19 Rosestöckle, gebrocht. 20 vergesse.

Lehn: Urschel, blyb. (Räuspert sich mehrmals und streicht ihre Schürze zurecht.) Ich håb dich welle frööje [13], wås dü vun unserem Håns håltsch?

Urschel (steht auf): Jumfer Lehn!

Lehn: Gall, dü mechscht's nit sœœje.

Urschel (wiegt sich in den Lenden): E Mollekopf isch'r, e wieschter, wo nix wèèss, åls èène üsszepflecke, ze knübbe [14].

Lehn: So ungaddi? [9]

Urschel: No sœœet'r åls, wann ich mӯner Vetter, d'r såpeur, hyroot kœœft'r mir e Schwåånebelz üss Kåtzehoor [15]. Jå, Jumfer Lehn, un Liedle singt'r uff mich, dåss ich schun meh wi èènmool gegrine [16] håb.

Lehn: Wie singt'r åls?

Urschel: 's Urschel mit-em kålte Harz,
d'Giftkrott mit d'r Spinnezung;
Båcke wie e Unschlitkerz,
Un e gsundi Båbbellung.
Ållåbonheur,
Sålü såpeur! (Salutiert)

Lehn: Ei, wås!

Urschel: Waaje dem lüej ich 'ne schun zwèj Wuche nim ån. O Gott! (Seufzt). Åwer bӯ d'r eerschte beschte Gelaajehèèt zåhl ich's em erüss mit Zinseszinse.

Lehn: Dåss-em d'Œje Wåsser gann. Datsch dü im œj d'r Sundœnåme åm Wardi sœœje [17].

Urschel: Ich sœœe Ihre, Jumfer Lehn, wann dis mӯner Månn gabt, der miesst mer sich um d'r Finger erumwickle.

Lehn: Bon, ålles nooch mӯm Idee. Wås will ich sœœje, — wottsch dü d'r Håns?

Urschel: Ich? (Wird verlegen — kleine Pause, weint plötzlich in ihre Schürze).

Lehn: Ååwer, Urschel, ich glœb dü pfupfsch?

Urschel: Wann ich dis gewisst hatt, dåss Sy mich so ebbs frööjt, waar ich går ni kumme.

Lehn: Nå, nå, dü bisch doch ken brigitte de soie, e Sydebriedel [18]. Urschel, redd, jå odder nèèn?

Urschel: Ich wott 'ne schun, åwer (weint heftig). D'r Båbbe will hån, dåss ich mӯner Vetter, d'r såpeur, hyroot.

Hans (erregt zur Mitteltür herein): In dam Råttenescht isch ålles Herr un Mèèschter. Do wurd kummediert, kåjatzt, d'Bèèn

---

1 frööje. 3 Gell, du, saaue. 4 wüeschter. 6 kauft, gegrienne. 10 waje, Gelejeheit. 11 Aue, genn, ihm, au, Sundaaname, Werdaa. 12 min, müesst sich mer. 15 Awer, glaab. 16 nit. 17 Siede-, naan. 19 dem, Baan, verwechselt, rauche, narrächt, Kueh, wicht, Lüe.

verwachselt [19], gekocht, ålli Kaminer rœœche wi nit raacht,
d'r Dokter huckt bў d'r Küeh und wўcht nim. Ich bin doo Herr
un (erblickt Urschel, verwundert) — Lüej doo, 's Urschel!
(Kleine Pause.)

Urschel (wendet sich verlegen ab): Håns!

Lehn: Wås will d'r Herr un Mèèschter?

Hans: Wås måcht dann d'Måmsell Munkedrissel [20] do?

Lehn: Mössjö Kopfhanker, d'Måmsell Ursch verzelt m'r grååd vun
ihre Hochzўtt mit-em Vetter.

Urschel: Aåwer, Jumfer Lehn.

Lehn: Ursch, ke Wort!

Hans: Ursch, isch's wohr, mit-em såpeur? — Ich glœb gåår dü
grynsch ha? [16]

Lehn: For Frèèd nåtyrli, for Frèèd.

Hans: 's Urschel mit-em kålte Harz,
      d'Giftkrott mit d'r Spinnezung?

Urschel: Heert Si's, Jumfer Lehn, wie'r stupft u fobbt, der Mollekopf?

Hans: Do kånn mer danne Schwåånebelz üss Kåtzehoor kœœefe?
(Kleine Pause.) Åch, wann numme ålli såpeurs d'r Güxel daat
[20] hôle (ab).

Urschel: Un ich will ken Schwåånebelz üss Kåtzehoor mit zåmmten
såpeur nit.

Lehn: Also, dü mechscht d'r Håns, bon, dis isch d'Hœptsåch. Åwer
èèns will ich d'r gsœœet hån, wunderfitzigi Wybslўtt kånn'r nit
verbutze, drum uffgebåsst vor der Hånd. Dis hèèsst, e wunderfitzigi Frœj isch kèène Waaj ze verååchte, dann si bringt
Såches [21] ån d'r Dœœe, wu d'r Månn nit trèèmt, verstehsch,
nit trèèmt. Du reste, wann's emool so wўtt isch, wursch-em
schu d'Hoor üss de n'Œje strahle [22] un mўni Parson hesch
uff dўnere Sўtt, ça suffit. Soo, kumm jetz mit miir, ich gib d'r
noch instruction de famille un wås d'r såpeur ånbelångt, mit
dam wur ich schu ferdi. (Ursch trocknet ihre Augen. Lehn
nimmt die Tasse, beide linke hintere Seitentüre ab.)

(Angenes und Sybille Mitteltüre. — Sybille, schlanke Blondine,
etwas gezwungen vornehm, spricht exaltiert, geblümtes Sommer-
kleid, trägt Chignon; in der Hand einen hellfarbigen Sonnenschirm,
Fächer anhängen.)

Angenes: Wås hett'r da üssgereecht, d'r Cåsper? Kumm, Harz, gib
dis Dings, kumm. (Ist sehr um sie beschäftigt.) Mon Dieu, wie
dü hўtt natt bisch [23].

4 -henker, verzählt, grad, Hochzitt. 7 gar, griennsch. 8 Fraid, natierli.
10 Hört. 11 denne dät. 13 Haupt-, verachte, haisst, Person, mit mer, gieb.
14 denn, hitt, nett.

Sybille: Nur hÿtt? Avec ça, Frœj Båås.

Angenes: Kumm, setz di, liebs Sybillele, dü bisch ållewÿl scheen, jo dann.

Sybille: Jå, dankt Si, Frœj Båås, d'r Cåsper sœœt, es daat grysser- lich brassiere, ar gschbyrt so ebbs, åls wi [24] wann sÿner Mèèschter hyroote miesst, pensez, isch dis e politesse.

Angenes: Ååwer, ååwer — (abseits) nå, wann'r dis de n'åndere œj gsœœt het.

Sybille: D'r Mössjö Jean du trou des cousins [25] isch joo e schår- månter Mensch, mit sovyl Phåntåsie un derno het'r so bsunderi Gedånke un dis gfellt mer åm. Er kummt mer vôôr wie e ungelaases poème.

Angenes: Oui, dis müess mer sœœeje, e poème. — Vun jeehaar isch's mÿner Harzwunsch gewese [26] — wann Ihr Zwèj — wann ich's erlaawe daat [20] —

(Bärwel, junges, strammes Bauernmädchen Schlupfkappe auf, mit einem grossen Feldblumenstrauss, Mitteltüre.)

Bärwel: E scheener Büjür vun d'r Mieadder [27]. Büjür Båås Ångenes, bisch œ do Sÿbille, wie geht's d'r dann? Hu, bisch du im Stood!

Angenes (ihr entgegen eilend): Barwel! — Jesses, wås het mer der Cåsper ångereecht?

Sybille (herablassend): Bonjour, Barwel.

Bärwel: Danke numme, d'Mieadder und d'r Vodder hön naachti ze veel Süürkrüt un Spack gasse, no hån se gånz Noocht 's Grimme ghett. Wo isch denn d'r Höns?

Angenes: Barwel, e Momant, ich håb mit d'r Måmsell Sÿbille noch ebbs ze redde. Chérie, kumm, mer welle do nyn gehn.

(Jüstinel, ein lebhaftes, fürwitziges Ding, spricht übersprudelnd schnell, sommerlich gekleidet, Schäferhut auf, Sonnenschirm, hat einen Blumenstrauss in der Hand, kommt Mitteltüre herein- gestürmt.)

Jüstinel: Bonjour, Frœj Båås, bonjour, bonjour Sÿbille, lüej doo, 's Barwel. (Küsst alle rasch ab.)

Sybille: Dü hesch œj e Strüss, wie kummt's?

Jüstinel: Ei, im Håns sÿner Nåmesdœœ ischs hÿtt. Sahn'r, scheeni Mårgrittle. Blåbberroose un Spitzewääderi, Spitzewääderi, dis het'r garn, züe garn.

Angenes: Bisch dü åwer e Båchstalz [28].

Bärwel (nachäffend): Spitzewääderi, Spitzewääderi.

Sybille: Tiens, im Mössjö Jean isch sÿner Nåmesdœœ, do müess mer gråtüliere. Lèèder fahlt's mer åm e Strüss.

2 dich, allewiel, schön. 3 griesserlich, bressiere, gschbiert. 5 jo, gfallt, vor, ungeleses. 6 jeher, Herzenswunsch, erlewe. 7 ö. 10 nachti, Speck. 13 kommt's. 14 sin Namesdaa isch hitt, Sehn, -wäderi, gern. 15 Bachstelz. 16 -waderi. 17 Leider fehlt.

Jüstinel: 's Åmelie kummt œj no. Sunsch geht's güet, Frœj Båås, un bў diir Sÿbille, Barwel, joo, mer brücht nit ze frööje, nit ze frööje.

Angenes: Ihr exküsiere — (abseits) isch mer dis e Strèèch.

(Amelie, etwas älter, fast mannhaftes Auftreten, starke Stimme, spricht etwas gedehnt, einfach gekleidet, trägt Chignon, einen Strauss in der Hand.)

Amelie: Sålü bisåmme. Wie geht's, wie steht's? (Drückt allen kräftig die Hand.)

Sybille: Du nimmsch ålli Daa ungadderigi Måniere ån, so èèm d'Hånd ze drucke.

Jüstinel: Jo, d'Måme sœœet ållewÿl, 's isch e Rossgettel.

Amelie: Ich bi hålt üss d'r Schifferzunft [29] un nit so gschlååcht wie Ihr, Ihr, wi sœœet åls d'Båås Lehn, Ihr åme de hareng.

Angenes: Ååwer, Åmelie, schamm di, so ze pårliere [30].

Amelie: Frœj Båås, wås gitt's dann hÿtt by Eich ze verrÿsse, dåss mer extrå ÿngelååde sin worre?

Angenes: Ÿngelåådc?

Sybille: Frœj Båås?

Bärwel: Isch d'r Cåsper œj bÿ Eich gewann?

Angenes: Dis isch e mal entendu?

Bärwel: Nè, Frœj Båås, ken målåntåndü. Heere, Båås, wèèss-r's, d'r Höns, dåss'r hyroote sell? [27]

Angenes: Hyroote? Wer sœœet dann so ebbs?

Amelie: Wås, d'r Håns will hyroote so buntiwerex? — Jetz krejt d'r Moond e Loch!

Jüstinel: Er will hyroote, unsere Goldvetter, wo isch'r dann? Wèèss mer's Frœj Båås, wer? [31] Åmand gåår èèns vun sÿne Baasle. Redd si, sœœet Si, Frœj Båås.

Angenes: Ums Himmelswille, sœœeje nÿx eso züem Håns, ich bitt Eich.

Sybille: O nè, dis war jo geje d'politesse.

Bärwel: Ich sœœe nit hÿscht un nit hott. Åwer d'r Cåsper het's gsœœet, dåss —

Hans (vordere linke Seitentüre, ganz erstaunt)*:* Åh — Dunderschiess — wi —

Jüstinel: Liewer Vetter, bonjour, bonjour, vyl Glick, Gsundhèèt, e långs Laawe, un do isch e Strüss mit Spitzewääderi, Spitzewääderi, (Küsst ihn.)

Bärwel: Ewack, dåss ich-em œ èèner gann kå. (Küsst ihn stürmisch

1 noch. 4 nemmsch, alle Daa, aim. 5 Rossgöttel. 6 bin, gschlacht. 7 dich. 8 Euch, verrisse, yngelade. 13 Nä, Horche, wäiss. 15 buntüewerex, Mond. 16 Amend, Bäsle. 17 nix. 18 naan. 19 söö, gsäjt. 21 Gsundheit, Lewe. 22 Ewack, äner, gann, kann, ware, Vieh.

und drängt ihm den Strauss auf.) Dü sellsch so ålt waare wi d'r
Mådusålem, 's Veeh sell d'r gsünd blywe un sell sich vermehre
wi d'r Sönd åm Meer.

Amelie: Sålut bien, mon vieux! (Schlägt ihm auf die Schulter.) Ich
winsch d'r e gsunder Åppetit, d'r Rast isch Naawessåch —
voilà Håns, e Strüss.

Hans (wischt sich die Wange): Wås isch dann Eich ins Mül gfåhre?
[32]

Sybille: Mössjö Jean du trou des cousins! (Knixt.) Mÿni Winsch solle
ålli wohr waare un e harzigs Wywele mecht d'r d'r Laaweswaaj
versiesse.

Jüstinel: Dis isch widder geredd, geredd.

Hans: Versiesse. (Knixt.) Ich sœœ Eich vÿlmools merci — ååwer
s waar mer liewer gsin, Ihr hatte mer nÿx gewunsche, da wås
sin Winsch? Wann's numme ken Nåmesdaj gaabt [33].

Sybille: Winsch sin frummi Kinder, wo d'Seel uffhèètere un nur
's Beschte bringe, wås's Menscheharz erfreje kå.

Hans (träumerisch): Winsch sin Kinder, frummi, wo d'Seel uffhèètere — Sÿbille! (Drückt ihr innig die Hand) — nur 's Beschte
bringe wås — (sich abwendend) åch — wås bringe si dann —
Stryss!?

Lehn (von links hintere Seitentüre): Wås müess mer sahn?

(Alle Mädchen begrüssen stürmisch Lehn: Bonjour, Frœj Båås,
bonjour, liewi Båås!)

Angenes (abseits): Jesses, d'r Schåndårm kummt [34], courage,
courage.

Lehn (abwehrend): Heere, isch dann ebbs åbårds gschahn, dåss Ihr
hÿtt ålli doo sin?

Jüstinel: Jå hån mer dann nit solle kumme?

Sybille: Parfaitement, e Bsüech måche, Frœj Båås?

Amelie: Verschtell Si sich numme nit.

Bärwel: Ei, mer welle im Höns d'r Nåmesdœœ ånwinsche — un
lüschtrå [35], wås'r fir èni hyroote sell [27].

Angenes: O — oh, (Sinkt aufs Sopha.)

Sybille: Ååwer, Barwel!

Amelie: Håhå, nit iwel.

Hans (ist scheu rückwärts getreten): Wås hesch gsœœet, Barwel?

Bärwel: Galle, ich håb's gsœœet, er wèèss-es salwer nit?

Lehn: Ich find ke Wort meh, mÿni Zung isch stÿff und stårr.

Angenes: Gott sej Dånk! (Erhebt sich.)

Hans: Ich soll — håhå, håhåhå! Wer hett den Ejch so ebbs gsœœet?

---

1 e gsunde, Rest, Newessach. 2 Müül. 3 versüesse. 5 vielmols. 6 frommi,
uffheitere, erfraje. 7 sie. 8 sehn. 9 Gendarm. 10 horche, gschehne. 12 Bsuech.
14 for åni. 17 üewel. 19 selwer.

Bärwel: Ei, d'Båås Ångenes, so vўl i wèèss.

Lehn: So, so — ai wås! (Wirft einen zornigen Blick auf Angenes.)

Hans: Un Ihr Ålli welle mich hyroote?

(Die Mädchen schauen verlegen umher.)

Jüstinel: Mer wèèss-es nit.

Sybille: Ich glœb, nur 's Harz het do e Wort ze redde. 'S isch delicååt, e so ne Frööj.

Hans: Ich kumm mer vôôr, wi e n'espèce Kinnij [36]. (Klatscht vergnügt in die Hände.) Wann ich ebbs vum Hyroote heer, krej ich Hunger. Hôôle mer ebbs ze bicke un ebbs ze mamle, Ihr liewi Baasle, well-n'r? Dånte Lehn, reecht ebbs, wi mèènsch?

Jüstinel: Båås Lehn, derfe mer? — E Tartele, Håns?

Sybille: E Brootwirschtel vўllicht mit Spinååt?

Amelie: Odder e Mimpfele Båschteet — e süürs Fischele?

Bärwel: Odder e Fatze Spack? [37]

Hans: Jo, joo, gehn mit d'r Båås Lehn. (Setzt sich schmunzelnd mitten ins Zimmer.) 'S isch doch ebbs drå åm Nåmesdœœe.

1 ich. 5 hätt, delicat, eso e Frööj. 6 vor, hole. 8 Brotwürstele, Spinat. 9 Mumpfel, Baschtet. 10 Fetze Speck. 11 dran.

NOTES

(See the remarks to the *Notes* on p. 80.)

[1] *Ferdinand Bastian* was born in Strasbourg in 1869, where he lived till his death in 1944, a respected and beloved master of dialect drama. A writer of light comedy farces (from 1898 onwards), he won respect first with *D'r Hans im Schnookeloch* (1903). It was the idyllic old-time world of Alsatian good living which attracted him and which he brought to life in many lively sketches and plays. After the First World War he opened up a new field for Alsatian dialect drama with his fairytale plays and phantasies, especially for children. The more noteworthy among his over four dozen plays are: *D'r Dorfschmidt* (1901), *E Serenädel* (1905), *D'r schwarz Kaffee* (1907), *'S Deifele* (1909), *Prinzess Fleurette* (1918), *D Wundergej* (1922), *Strüwelpeter* (1933), *'s Zauberhorn* (1934).—Hans im Schnookeloch had long been a Strasbourg legendary figure, a wealthy spoilt young man, ever at the mercy of his moods and never satisfied, the subject of a popular cautionary tale, when Adolf Stöber wrote a song *Hans im Schnokeloch* (1862) which made Hans a popular figure far beyond Alsace. This well-known folk-song goes:

> Der Hans im Schnokeloch hett Alles was er will!
> Unn was er hett, diss will er nitt,
> Unn was er will, diss hett er nitt,
> Der Hans im Schnokeloch hett Alles was er will!

Er isch e richer Bür, unn's gfallt em nim sin Hüs;
    Abrisse losst er sin Gebei
    Unn stellt sich funkelnauelnei
E Hüs mit Schir unn Stall an's Gallebriechel nüs.

Unn in der erste Naacht, uff einmol rufts: Fyrio!
    Sin Hüs verbrennt unn d'Stallung mit —
    Unn was er will, diss hett er nitt.
Jez leit sin neier Beau — e Kohlehüffe — do.

Er hett e süfri Frau, getreu in Glück unn Nod,
    Rechtschaffe, so wie's weni gitt:
    Doch was er hett, diss will er nitt —
Er losst sie sitze dheim, bis sie sich grämt ze Dod.

Jez bli't em noch sin Güet. Was macht er? Schla uff Schla
    Verkauft er Alles, Matt unn Feld,
    Unn macht sin ganzi Hab ze Geld,
Unn setzt sich uff e Schiff for nach Amerika.

Was gschicht? E Sturm bricht los unn in de leschde Nod
    Küm schwimmt er selbst an Ufer noch;
    Kummt bettelarm ins Schnokeloch,
Unn schafft als Bureknecht bedrüebt ums däjli Brod.

Unn ze Sank-Galle drüs, dort hett er jetzt sin Grab;
    Unn was er hett, diss müess er han,
    Unn was er will, er kann's nit han —
Drum leb zefridde doch mit Gott unn diner Hab!

This Alsatian folk-legend attracted, apart from Bastian, also the much greater dramatic talent of René Schickelé. Bastian's play is a series of amusing and witty episodes. In the second act the two old maiden aunts, fussy Angenes and energetic Lehn, for ever spoiling their melancholy and moody nephew Hans, the rich farmer in the Schnookeloch, take steps to cure him of his depressions by finding him a wife. Lehn has Urschel in mind, Angenes Sybille, both cousins of Hans. But the scatter-brained messenger, Casper, forgets which one he is to invite and to be on the safe side invites all Hans's cousins to celebrate his *Nâmesdœœ*, the day of the saint he is named after.

[2] Obsolete for 'Miss', now *Mamsell*.

[3] Als. has a great predilection for diminutives, of which the dialects of Lower Alsace have two degrees. The first ordinary dim. ends in *-l* (*-el*), pl. *-le*, e.g. *Liedl, Handl, Dântel, Hânsel*; the second degree expressing that something is specially small, neat and sweet

ends in *-ele*, sg. and pl., e.g. *Handele, Wirschtele, Fischele*. Both degrees take umlaut, e.g. *Hund—Hindle—Hindele* 'dog', *Rock—Reckl—Reckele* 'frock'. As in H. Alem. even verbs and particles can take a diminutive ending, e.g. *kechle* 'to simmer' < *koche* 'to cook'; *wddsele?* 'what is it, dear child?' < *wdds* 'what'.

[4] Bastian has *Horch*, but both a group of Strasbourg students and my informants from Barr stated that this word is not genuine dialect but imported from NHG.

[5] My informants from Barr would not use *kreje* 'to get' but *bekumme* (see also pp. 154, 156, *Kreijt der Moond e Loch, Krej ich Hunger*).

[6] Bread bought in a shop counts as a special treat.

[7] *Schmutz* 'kiss', *Gschmutz* a collective noun, cf. NHG *Küsserei*.

[8] Pl. cond. of 'to be' (see §§ 38, 40) arising from confusion between *waar* (cond. of *sin*) and *waare* 'to become', NHG *werden*. Informants use *waare*.

[9] One informant replaced *ungaddi* by *ungnaadi*.

[10] 'This time', one informant would say *diss Mool*.

[11] Unknown to informant. According to Martin-Lienhard, *Els. Wtb.*, short for *ei, so schlaa dich der Dunder*, exclamation of astonishment.

[12] Obsolete use of 3rd pers. sg. as the form of polite address.

[13] Note the word-order. The p.p. of the auxiliary precedes the inf. of the main verb in Alem. dialects.

[14] 'To pinch', informant from Barr would say *pfatze*.

[15] Something impossible, hence ridiculous.

[16] Bastian has the verb *gryne—gegrine* 'to cry' instead of which my informants would say *hyle—ghylt*. One informant would further alter to: Liedle singt r *iwer* mich, dåss ich schun meh *dås* èènmool ghylt håb. See also p. 152, 'Ich glœb gåår dü grynsch (hylsch)'.

[17] 'Give him a piece of your mind.'

[18] A weak, touchy person.

[19] 'Trip over your own feet with rushing around.'

[20] *Munkedrissel* 'a glum, sulky person', *Kopfhanker* 'a melancholy, depressed person'. The informants use the Barr form *gaad* (see § 37.3).

[21] 'Things', i.e. secrets, scandals.

[22] 'Make him see clearly.'

[23] Bastian has 'wie natt dü hy̆tt bisch' which one of my informants considers undialectal word-order.

[24] Informant suggests *wi wann* rather than *als wi wann*.

[25] French pun on the meaning of *cousins*, i.e. 'cousins' and 'large mosquitoes'. Both informants have *gfellt*, although otherwise only strong verbs with root-vowel *a* mutate (§ 35).

[26] Strasbourg lies within the *gsin* 'been' area. It is rather strange that Bastian should make Angenes say *gewese*. Bärwel, the country girl from the Kochersberg region, characteristically says *gewann*. The *gewese* form testifies to the dialect mixture in Strasbourg in this respect. Barr has *gsin*.

[27] Bärwel's dialect shows the following country dialect characteristics: the use of *Mieadder* (rather *Miädder*) and *Vodder* instead of urban *Mâme* and *Bâbbe*; *veel* not *vyl* 'much'; palatalizations before -*ns*-, -*nd*: *Höns, Sönd, gsünd* (*Hans, Sand, gsund*); *gewann* for *gsin*; *Stood, Noocht* for *Stâdd, Nâdcht*. On rural [a] against Strasbourg [ɛ], see § 6.4. Bärwel's conversation is characteristically concerned with food and her idioms are expressions of the farmyard: *nit hÿscht un nit hott sœœje* (*hÿscht* 'left', *hott* 'right'—orders for horses and cattle). One informant would say *geschtert Oowe* for *naachti*. Both say *soll* rather than *sell*.

[28] Lit. wagtail, an affected, overdressed person.

[29] 'Down-to-earth, unaffected.'

[30] The interspersion of French words is generally ridiculed and meant to have a comic effect here (*rede* is the genuine dialect word).

[31] Bastian has *wenne*.

[32] 'What's come over you?'

[33] Informants says *gaab* for Bastian's *gäbt*.

[34] Person of authority who is generally disliked.

[35] 'Hear', informant does not use this vb., suggests *lüeje*.

[36] 'Like a king.'

[37] Informants would say *Stickel Spack* for *Fatze Spack*.

GLOSSARY

See the introductory remarks to the *Glossary* on p. 84 and for full information Martin-Lienhart.

Àllefànz, simpleton (obs.).
àls, each time.
àmbediere, wv. bore.

Bàbbelung, gift of the gab, mouth.
bàll, soon.
Bàschteet, C. pie.
bicke, wv. eat (slang).
Blàbberoose, peony.
buntiwerex, precipitately.

dummle, wv. hurry.
Dunderschiess, swear word (damn).

Ejel, hedgehog.
e'wack, away.

ferm, strong, reliable.
fobbe, wv. tease, mock.

gall, pl. *galle*, NHG *nicht wahr*.
Graan, pl. -*e*, fishbone.
grysserli(ch), terrible.
Gschtunz, fat, old woman (obs.).
Güxel, devil (< cuckoo).

Herrjee, exclam. of fear, consternation.
Himmelsàckuff, swear word (damn).

Jesses, exclam. of fear.

ka'jatze, wv. rush to and fro.

latz, wrong.
lüeje, wv. look.

mamle, wv. drink (slang).
Mimpfele, dim.—lit. 'a mouth-full'
Mollekopf, fathead, boor.

naachti, last night.
nim, no longer.
numme, only.

pfupfe, wv. sob.

Rossgettel (*Gettel* = godchild), wild, rough girl.

Schlöi, excl. (damn).
schnüerstràcks, straight.
Spitzewäàderi, ribwort.
Stàchel, p. *Stàchle*, quill.
stràhle, wv. comb.
stupfe, wv. (lit. push) tease, incite.
Sunndi, Sunday.

üsspflecke, wv. mock, torment.
ungàddi, impolite, rough.
Unschlitkerz, tallow candle.

verbutze, tolerate, stand.
verrÿsse, p.p. *verrisse*, pull to pieces.

Wàrdi, weekday.
wunderfitzig, curious, inquisitive.

CHAPTER V

DARMSTADT

§ 1. AREA AND STATUS

1.1 This dialect has been chosen as an example of Rhenish Franconian and because one of the classics of German dialect literature, the delightful comedy *Der Datterich*, by E. E. Niebergall, is written in Darmstadt dialect. The linguistic situation in a town like Darmstadt is, however, very different from that found in many other areas included in this book. The dominant feature is that the standard language is overwhelmingly strong and the dialect, although pertinacious, in full retreat. The most conservative form of speech, regarded as 'genuine dialect', is spoken by only a small minority of the population, while also a minority speak a form of speech which owes nothing to the local dialect. The large majority of the population speak *Umgangssprache* or *Halbmundart* with from slight to strong dialect features. To single out the 'genuine' dialect for treatment does therefore not do justice to the linguistic situation of Darmstadt. A number of studies[1] have dealt with this problem, and it can therefore here be left aside. It is, of course, not only in recent decades that the dialect of Darmstadt has been assailed by outside influences, above all that of the standard language. It probably lost its status of being the linguistic medium of a whole society centuries ago. Thus, not being homogeneous in itself, it has not been a rallying point for a whole area but rather a channel through which corrosion of native dialects has been guided into the surrounding countryside. Genuine dialect in Darmstadt represents an older form of speech compared with the current semi-dialect of the majority of the inhabitants, but it is in itself less conservative than the dialect of some suburbs, e.g. Bessungen, which in its turn is less conservative than certain country dialects. These may indicate what Darmstadt dialect formerly was like, just as the semi-dialect of today's majority may indicate what 'genuine' dialect will be like in the future. Both Rudolph and Born have attempted a definition of genuine dialect and of semi-dialect, e.g. by drawing the line between dialectal *Fraad, laad, Baam* and semi-dialectal *Fraid, laid, Baum* (NHG *Freude, leid, Baum*)[2] and by

---

[1] Cf. O. Rudolph, 'Über die verschiedenen Abstufungen der Darmstädter Mundart', *Hessische Blätter f. Volkskunde*, xxvi, 1927, 10–17; Grund, and above all Born.

[2] One informant stated that the *a*- pronunciation in these words now often has a facetious, humorous, burlesque effect.

establishing numerous other criteria. Born has also pointed out the salient Darmstadt features which delimit urban dialect against the surrounding rural dialects but which are frequently also found in the smaller country towns. One of the most noticeable features is urban intervocalic -d- in words which have d in NHG compared with rural -r-. In spite of numerous isoglosses which run through the Darmstadt area and which Born has strongly emphasized, dialect geography has shown the Hesse-Darmstadt region to have a certain homogeneity which sets it apart from other Rhenish Franconian dialects.[1]

1.2 Rhenish Franconian is the name given to a great variety of dialects which have, however, at least two phonological features in common. In the south and east they are bounded by the p–pf isogloss separating Upper German from Middle German dialects. At its western end it divides the Franconian dialects of Lorraine and the Palatinate from the Low Alemannic of Alsace (see chap. iv, § 1.2). Farther east it marks off the South and East Franconian dialects, and running northwards between the rivers Fulda and Werra it separates the West Middle German dialects from the East Middle German dialects of Thuringia.[2]

The second isogloss, the dat–das line, distinguishes Rhenish Franconian from the other West Middle Franconian dialects and runs from Saarbrücken in the south-west in a north-easterly direction through the Rhineland and Hesse to the Rothaargebirge, the dividing line between HG and LG.[2]

This vast area falls into at least two large regions: the Palatinate west of the Rhine and Hesse north of the river Main. In between, east of the Rhine and bordered by the Main in the north and east and the Odenwald in the south-east, lies the territory of the Hesse-Darmstadt dialect. While sometimes Hesse-Darmstadt dialect goes with the dialects of the Palatinate (e.g. DSA, 106, geh) on other occasions it differs from them (e.g. DSA, 16, heiss) and sometimes it asserts its independence from both (e.g. Mitzka, Wortatlas, iii, Maulwurf = H.Dst. Mollbert).[3]

---

[1] Cf. F. Maurer, Sprachschranken, Sprachräume und Sprachbewegungen im Hessischen, Giessen, 1930, also: Hess. Blätter f. Volkskunde, xxviii, 1929, 43– 109: 'So entsteht im Mainzer und Darmstädter Raum eine neue Sprachland- schaft zwischen dem Oberhessischen und Pfälzischen' (p. 106). F. Wrede in his Einteilungskarte (DSA, 56) divides Nordrheinfränkisch (Hessisch) into Mittel- hessisch and Mainz-Darmstadt-Aschaffenburg. I shall refer to this dialect region as Hesse-Darmstadt.

[2] See Apfel -isogloss DSA, 3, Pfund DSA, 62, and the maps in Mitzka, Maa., Hdb.; O. Behaghel, Geschichte der deutschen Sprache, 5th ed., 1928; Wagner, Sprachlandschaften; id., Die Gliederung der deutschen Mundarten, 1954.

[3] For details, see the dialect geographical studies of G. Bertaloth, Zur Dialektgeographie des vorderen Odenwaldes u. des nördlichen Rieds, Erlangen, 1935; P. Freiling, Studien zur Dialektgeographie des hessischen Odenwaldes,

GENERAL CHARACTERISTICS OF RHENISH FRANCONIAN (HESSE-DARMSTADT)

§ 2. PHONOLOGICAL FEATURES[1]

2.1 The Vowels

(1) The MHG long vowels *î, û, iu* are represented by diphthongs similar to those of NHG (*ai, au*), the reflexes of *î* and *iu* having coincided.

(2) The MHG diphthongs *ie, uo, üe* are monophthongized as in NHG, with *ie* and *üe* again coinciding owing to unrounding of the latter.

(3) The MHG diphthongs *ei* and *ou* are monophthongized and have coincided in a long front *ā*. (Cf. *DSA*, 16, Dst. *hăss*/NHG *heiss*.) Under NHG influence *ai* and *au* are advancing, prevailing already in semi-dialect.[2]

(4) The representative of MHG *e* (primary umlaut) is on the whole still distinguished from the reflexes of MHG *ē* and *ä* except in the positions before *r* and nasals.

(5) The reflex of MHG *a* is generally a back vowel, with some rounding before nasals and liquids. MHG *â* has become *ō* in genuine dialect and has coincided with MHG *ô*, but is kept distinct from the dialectally lengthened MHG *a*. In the urban centres this state of affairs is much disturbed and sounds approaching the NHG equivalents have made considerable progress. Before *sch* (< Gmc. *sk*) mutated forms are still common.

(6) MHG *ē* and *ô* are generally preserved in the H.Dst. area in contrast to surrounding dialects with *î, äi* and *ū, ou*. They have coincided with the reflexes of MHG *œ* and *â*.

(7) MHG *i* and *u* are to-day mainly represented, except before *r*, by *i* and *u*. But the phenomenon known as *Mitteldeutsche Senkung* (*i, u > e, o*) seems to have been common in late medieval times (see Born, p. 128 f.). Relics are more common in rural areas than in the urban centres.

(8) Unrounding of the MHG rounded vowels *ü, iu, öu, ö, œ* is general.

(9) Before nasals diphthongs (present and former) are usually nasalized, in semi-dialect frequently more so than in genuine dialect.

DDG, xii, Marburg, 1929; W. Seibt, *Zur Dialektgeographie der hessischen Berg-strasse* (*Giessener Beitr. z. dt. Phil.* 27), Giessen, 1930; F. Valentin, *Geschicht-lich- geographische Untersuchungen zu den Mundarten rings um Mainz*, Erlangen, 1934; Born, and Maurer, *Sprachschr. Hessen.*

[1] See fn. 1, p. 32.

[2] See Born, p. 89: 'Im ganzen Gebiet altes *flăsch* neben jungem *flaisch*' 'meat'.

(10) Before a vocalized *r* (see § 14.13) the reflex of MHG *ë, e, i, ö, ü,* is [ε], of *u, o,* and *a* [ɔ].

(11) Glottal stop before initial stressed vowel in unknown. But there is no *liaison,* e.g. *en/Appel* 'an apple'.

2.2 Vowel Quantity

(1) Lengthening of MHG short vowels in open syllables is the rule (*Leichtinnendehnung*) except before [j] and [w] and the endings *-er, -el.* There are also other isolated exceptions.

(2) Originally long vowels are shortened in the same cases as in NHG (e.g. before consonantal clusters). Shortening is also fairly general before [j] and [w], and of MHG *uo* before [x].

(3) There are still traces of lengthening before historical *cht* (Cf. chap. iv, §§ 2.2; 10.1).

2.3 Vowels in Unstressed Syllables

(1) The NHG prefixes *be-* and *ge-* retain their vowels except before *s* and *f* where they may be dropped (cf. chap. iv, §§ 2.3; 9.2).

(2) MHG unstressed final *-e* has generally been dropped.

2.4 The Consonants

(1) The stops and fricatives are voiceless lenes. Initially before vowels there are also aspirated fortis stops. All consonants are short. Only the sonants are voiced.

(2) In initial position the HG sound-shift affected only Gmc. *t,* the other stops have remained unshifted; medially and finally Gmc. *-pp-* was also unaffected. MHG *d* and *t* have coincided.

(3) The velar fricative *ch* has no longer a palatal counterpart, the latter having coincided with *sch.*

(4) MHG *s* before consonants has developed as in NHG.

(5) Medial *-b-* and *-g-* have become fricatives.

(6) Gmc. *f* and HG *ff* have not coincided.

(7) Final *n* in the MHG—NHG unstressed ending *-en* and after long root-vowels has dropped.

(8) *r* occurs in Dst. only initially (incl. beginning of a syllable) and after consonant, otherwise it is vocalized.

(9) Medially after vowels MHG *d, t* have become *r* in the whole region. The urban centres have restored a stop.[1]

(10) The assimilation of original *nd* > *n, ld* > *l* is general, though urban speech often restores the original clusters under NHG influence.[2]

---

[1] Cf. *DSA,* 12, *Bruder;* Born, p. 103 f.
[2] Cf. *DSA,* 60, *hinten;* Mitzka, *Wortatlas,* iii, *Holunder,* Rh.-Franc. *Holler.*

§ 3 MORPHOLOGICAL FEATURES

3.1 Noun and Article

(1) The noun has no special endings for cases. The articles have a common form for subject and direct object.

(2) There are five types of plural formation.

(3) Nouns form a diminutive by means of *-chen* [-šə].[1]

3.2 The Adjective

(1) The weak declension distinguishes traditionally between an objective case and a nominative. The latter is endingless. No distinction is made for gender.

(2) Under NHG influence *-er* is being introduced into the masc. nom. case of the strong declension.

3.3 The Pronouns

(1) The personal pronouns distinguish three cases.

(2) The demonstrative pronoun neuter (nom. and acc.) has a mutated vowel (*däs*).

(3) The possessive pronouns NHG *unser, euer* have forms with *-r*.

(4) The possessive pronouns masc. and neutr. have different forms in nom. and acc. sg. for use as an adjective and as a noun.

(5) The relative pronoun is *wo* or *der, die, däs wo*.

3.4 The Verb

(1) The tense system consists of a present, a perfect, a pluperfect and a few isolated forms of a preterite. There is no present subjunctive.

(2) A synthetic subjunctive preterite (functioning as a conditional) exists only for a few verbs.

(3) The conditional is otherwise formed by means of the auxiliary for 'to do', i.e. subj. pret., *deed*.

(4) There is a two-form plural as in NHG (1st and 3rd pers.; 2nd pers.).

(5) There is no *Rückumlaut* in genuine dialect.

(6) The verb NHG *haben* has unmutated forms throughout the present.

(7) The 2nd and 3rd pers. sg. of all strong verbs show umlaut provided the root-vowel is mutatable (i.e. *e, ä, a, oo*).

(8) For NHG *gewesen* H.Dst. uses *gewäse*.

(9) The dialect verbs for NHG *gehen, stehen* are reflexes of MHG *gên, stên*.

(10) The infinitive of regular verbs ends in *-e* or *-rn* ⌐-ən⌐ (corresponding to NHG verbs in *-ern*).

---

[1] See Born, p. 115 f.; *DSA*, 59, *Schäfchen*.

M

PHONOLOGY

THE VOWELS

§ 4. THE VOWEL PHONEMES

The process of unrounding has done away with the MHG rounded front vowels. Nasalization accompanied by the loss of a final nasal consonant is widespread in the case of certain vowels but seems to be voluntary in many words. It is also to some extent tied up with the social stratification of dialect and semi-dialect. In monosyllabic words ending in a vowel these nasalized vowels contrast, however, with all the other vowels and it is therefore advisable to regard them as separate phonemes.[1] E.g. *See* 'lake': *sei* 'be' imp.: *seĩ* 'be' inf.: *so* or *bei* (NHG *bei*): *Bã* (NHG *Bein* sg.): *Baĩ* (NHG *Beine* pl.). However only three such nasalized phonemes are frequent and well established: /ɒ̃:, ɒĩ, aõ/. In other cases nasalization may be regarded as a voluntary alternative, e.g. *scheen—schee—scheẽ* (NHG *schön*). Before nasal consonants many vowels, especially /ɒ:/, are slightly nasalized, in semi-dialect even more so than in genuine dialect.

Front	Back	Diphthongs
i(:)	u(:)	
e(:)	o(:)	
ε(:)		ɑɪ ɑω
a:	ɑ ɒ: ɒ̃:	ɒĩ aõ

(:) indicates that a phoneme occurs both long and short. The central vowels [ɜ, ə] occur only in unstressed positions; [ɜ] is a vocalic realization of *r* after vowels (see § 9).

§ 5. SPELLING

In order to make the spelling of our text in H.Dst. dialect phonemic only comparatively minor rearrangements are necessary. There are two vowel qualities not distinguished in NHG which must be orthographically indicated in dialect: [e—ε, a—ɒ]. The author of our text, Robert Schneider, uses the letters *e* and *ä* in the NHG way, i.e. largely etymologically, rather than phonemically. The two letters will have to be employed to distinguish two phonemes. Then there are two long vowels of the a- type. Where Schneider does not indicate the length of the back variety I propose to use *h*, i.e. *ah*, for the long vowel. The spelling *aa* stands only for the long, front vowel. In the case of the short, low-tongue vowel /ɑ/ no attempt is made to indicate the exact phonetic realization, i.e. [ɔ, ɒ, ɑ, a], as this varies from speaker to speaker and often also from word to word. Nasalization is indicated by the diacritic mark ˜, but not before a nasal

[1] See fn. 3, p. 46.

consonant: ã, aĩ, aũ. The greatest spelling difficulty arises, as usual, in connection with vowel length. Robert Schneider makes little attempt to indicate length except where the NHG orthography expresses it. Occasionally he indicates a dialectal short vowel by doubling of the following consonant (*hawwe* 'to have', *awwer* 'but'). As the quantity distribution in dialect is rather close to that of NHG with fairly regular exceptions there is no need to depart substantially from the NHG spelling rules. Thus the following spelling rule operates: in open syllables all monophthongs are long and in closed syllables all monophthongs are short. Shortness in open syllables is expressed by doubling the following consonant, except in the case of *j*, before which all monophthongs are short. Length in closed syllables is expressed by doubling where Schneider does not already indicate it in some other way.

The correspondences are as follows:

Phoneme	Letter	Phoneme	Letter
i:	ie	u(:)	u
i	i	o(:)	o
e(:)	e	ɑ, ɒ: ɔ̃:	a, ah, ã
ɛ(:)	ä	a:	aa
ɑɪ; ɒĭ	ei, ai; aĭ	ɑɷ ɑ̃õ;	au; aũ

§ 6. STRESSED SHORT VOWELS

6.1 [i] is a high-tongue vowel, slightly open, but more close than [ɪ] in English or NHG. It derives from:

(i) MHG *i* in positions unaffected by lengthening (see § 10. This precondition is assumed as understood for the rest of this §): *hinner* 'behind', *geschriwwe* 'written'.

(ii) MHG *ü*: *Glick* 'luck', *iwwer* 'over'.

(iii) MHG *ie, üe* in cases of shortening: *zije* 'to pull', *Bischer* 'books'.

It does not occur before *r*. But see § 6.3 (ii).

6.2 [e] this is a close, tense, mid-front vowel representing:

(i) MHG *e* in many cases: *besser* 'better', *letzt* 'last'.

(ii) MHG *ö*: *Drebbsche* 'drop' dim.

(iii) MHG *e, ē, ä* before nasals: *schenke* 'to make a present', *Fenster* 'window'.

(iv) MHG *ê, æ* where shortening occurred: *hett* 'had', *meje* 'to mow'.

It does not occur before *r*.

6.3 [ɛ] is a lax, open vowel about like NHG *e* in *Bett*. It derives from:

(i) MHG *ē, ä: räscht* 'right', *gäwwe* 'to give'.

(ii) MHG *e, ē, ä, i, ö, ü* before *r*:[1]*Bärsch* 'mountain', *Wärt*, 'innkeeper,' *Wärtsche* 'word' dim., *Schärz* 'apron'.

It does not occur before nasals. (See § 6.2.)

6.4 [ɑ] is a low-back vowel. It is the most unstable vowel of the whole system. NHG influence tends to advance it to [a], while in many words it is [ɒ] or still nearer [ɔ]. One is not entitled to posit two short phonemes, say /ɒ/ and /ɑ/, since the realizations cannot be said to contrast. They vary from speaker to speaker. The isogloss (ɑ/ɔ) runs through our region and also accounts for the generally unsettled state of affairs. (See Born, pp. 49–61; 141.) This vowel derives from:

(i) MHG *a: anner* 'other', *Blatz* 'room'.

It does not occur before *r* of the same syllable, but occasionally represents MHG -*ar*- before certain consonants. Cf. *schwazz* 'black', *asch* NHG *arg*.

6.5 [o] is a more tense and close rounded, mid-back vowel than the corresponding NHG *o*- sound. It represents:

(i) MHG *o: Gott* 'God', *odder* 'or'.

(ii) MHG *â* where shortened: *hot* 'has', *losse* 'to leave'. There is a more open allophone before *r*: [ɔ], in which position all the back vowels are neutralized just as the front vowels are neutralized in the same position: *Wort* 'word', *gewort* 'waited' p.p., *Dorscht* 'thirst'.

6.6 [u] this is again a rather tense, close vowel. It represents:

(i) MHG *u: gucke* 'look'.

(ii) MHG *o* before nasals in most words, in genuine dialect at least: *vun* 'of', *schun* (< MHG *ô*) 'already'.

(iii) MHG *uo* in some words where shortening has occurred, e.g. *Mutter* 'mother', *Duch* 'cloth', *Buch* 'book', *Blum* 'flower'.

(iv) MHG *û* in *uff* 'up, on' and its compounds.

It does not occur before *r* of the same syllable.

§ 7. Long Vowels

7.1 [iː] is a tense, close, high-front vowel. It derives from:

(i) MHG *ie: verdiene* 'to earn', *liewer* 'dear'.

(ii) MHG *üe: Kiefer* 'cooper', *Brieder* 'brothers'.

(iii) MHG *i* under conditions of lengthening: *spiele* 'to play'.

(iv) MHG *ü* under conditions of lengthening: *Dier* 'door', *spiern* 'to sense'.

---

[1] In semi-dialect at least [i] is also heard before *r*.

7.2 [e:] is a tense, close, mid-front vowel deriving from:

(i) MHG *ê*: *Seel* 'soul', *ewisch* 'eternal'.

(ii) MHG *œ*: *schee* 'beautiful', *bees* 'wicked'.

(iii) MHG *e* lengthened: *hewe* 'to lift', *schele* 'to peel'.

(iv) MHG *ö* lengthened: *Eel* 'oil', *Ewe* 'stoves'.

(v) MHG *æ*: *speet* 'late', *geeb* cond. 'to give', *keem* cond., 'to come'.

7.3 [ɛ:] is a lax, open, mid-front vowel deriving from:

(i) MHG *ē* in cases of lengthening: *Wähg* 'way', *läwe* 'to live', *stähle* 'to steal', *dräde* 'to tread'.

7.4 [a:] is a low-front vowel resulting from monophthongization of:

(i) MHG *ei*: *er waass* 'he knows', *blaasch* 'pale'.

(ii) MHG *ou*: *Aach* 'eye', *laafe* 'to run', *kaafe* 'to buy', *Fraad* 'joy' (beside *Fraid*).

Before former or present nasal this vowel does not occur.

7.5 [õ:] is a low, nasalized, back vowel arising from

(i) MHG *ei* before *n* or *m*: *Bã* 'leg', *glã* 'little', *Stã* 'stone', *kã* 'no, none', *deham* 'at home'.

(ii) MHG *ou* before *n* or *m*: *Bam* 'tree', *Tram* 'dream'.

(iii) MHG *an-* in the prefix: *ã'geguckt* 'looked at'.

7.6 [ɒ:] is a low-back vowel with a variable amount of rounding. Under the influence of NHG it tends to be more advanced in semi-dialect (or only in individual words) than in genuine dialect. It represents:

(i) MHG *a* where lengthening has occurred: *Glahs* 'glass', *ablade* 'to unload', *sahche* 'to say', *Wahche* 'wagon'.

(ii) MHG *â* in an increasing number of words where the representation by [o:] no longer applies: *Sprahch* 'language', *Frahch* 'question', *Dade* 'deeds'.

7.7 [o:] is a rounded, mid-back vowel representing:

(i) MHG *ô*: *blooss* 'only', *Dood* 'death'.

(ii) MHG *â* in a diminishing number of words: *bloose* 'to blow', *Owend* 'evening', *nooch* 'after'.

(iii) MHG *o* where lengthening occurred: *Owe* 'stove', *gezooche* 'pulled' p.p.

7.8 [u:] is a rounded, high-back vowel deriving from:

(i) MHG *uo*: *duhn* 'to do', *Bluut* 'blood'.

(ii) MHG *u* where lengthening occurred: *Kuuchel* 'bullet'.

§ 8. DIPHTHONGS

All diphthongs begin with a low central vowel and move in the direction of either an open, high-front or an open, high-back vowel.

The first element is considerably longer than the second, especially when the word is strongly stressed.

8.1 [ɑɪ] derives from:
(i) MHG *î*: *Eis* 'ice', *bei* 'at'.
(ii) MHG *iu*: *deitsch* 'German', *Haiser* 'houses'.
(iii) MHG *öu*: *Hai* 'hay', *fraije* 'to enjoy'.

8.2 [ɒĩ] this nasalized diphthong derives from the same sources as the preceding diphthong in cases where it preceded a nasal. As minimal pairs exist it is necessary to posit an independent phoneme rather than to regard this as an allophone of the preceding diphthong (cf. [nɑɪ/ nɒĩ] 'new/nine').
(i) MHG *î*: *deĩ* 'yours', *greine* 'to weep'.
(ii) MHG *iu*: *Zaĩ* 'fences', *naĩ* 'nine', *Fraind* 'friend'.
(iii) MHG *öu*: *draime* 'to dream'.

8.3 [ɑω] derives from:
(i) MHG *û*: *aus* 'out', *saufe* 'to drink'.

8.4 [ɑω̃] see § 8.2 It is rare; e.g. *braũ* 'brown'.

§ 9. Unstressed Vowels

In simple words the same unstressed vowels [*i, ə, u*] appear as in NHG, but with distributional differences in the case of [ə].

9.1 [ə], where it appears in final position, goes back to a MHG -*en*, for MHG -*e* in this position has been dropped. Where it was once followed by -*r* it has developed into [ɜ].

9.2 [ɜ] is an unstressed vowel of open, mid- to low-central quality. It has arisen in unstressed syllables where a former *r* has disappeared.
(i) -*er*: *Laader* 'ladder'.
(ii) *ver*-: *verlore* 'lost'.
(iii) -*ren*, -*ern*: *uffheitern* 'to cheer up'.

In stressed syllables it occurs also after the short vowels [ɛ] and [ɔ] or any of the long vowels and diphthongs excluding the nasalized ones (see §§ 6.3, 6.5).[1]

§ 10. Vowel Quantity

Vowel quantity is not automatically tied to any specific position or dependent on certain surroundings. But the MHG quantity distribution has been radically changed by the general tendency to lengthen all short vowels in open syllables. As in NHG there are,

---

[1] On its phonemic position, see § 12.

however, a number of circumstances which have prevented the complete realignment on this basis. These circumstances are not the same in H.Dst. dialect as in NHG.

10.1 Before [j] < MHG *g, h, j,* the dialect tolerates only short vowels. NHG influence is responsible for long vowels now often occurring also in this position, especially in semi-dialect.

10.2 Before [w] < MHG *f, b, w,* short vowels are much more frequent than long ones, but *gäwwe* 'to give': *läwe* 'to live'.

10.3 The endings *-er* and *-el* seem to have often prevented the operation of *Leichtinnendehnung* (see § 2.2).

10.4 Among the consonants which have prevented it both in H.Dst. and in NHG *ch* should be specially noted (cf. *Knochen, gebrochen*). In H.Dst. there are traces of a corresponding law of shortening of long vowels (notably *ū* < MHG *uo*) before *ch,* see § 6.6. There are also traces of certain consonantal clusters, notably former *-cht,* having produced lengthening, e.g. *schlääscht* 'foolish', 'simple', *Gnääscht* 'farm labourer'.

§ 11. Comparison with the NHG Vowels

The most noteworthy differences are:

(1) The *Leichtinnendehnung* has less radically operated in H.Dst. than in NHG. Therefore we frequently meet with short vowels where NHG has long ones.

(2) The absence of rounded front vowels in H.Dst. and the consequent falling together of the vowels corresponding to NHG *i—ü, e—ö* (long and short), *ei—eu.*

(3) The development of nasalized long vowels and diphthongs in H.Dst.

(4) The existence of the two mid-front phonemes /e/ and /ɛ/ both short and long being a reflex of certain MHG features.

(5) The development of an unstressed vowel from postvocalic *r* and the accompanying lowering and coalescence of all short-front vowels (> [ɛ]) and of all short-back vowels (> [ɔ]).

(6) The continued differentiation between MHG *ei* and *î,* MHG *ou* and *û,* which have coalesced in NHG.

(7) On the other hand the dialectal coalescence of the reflexes of MHG *ei* and *ou,* which are kept apart in NHG.

(8) The coalescence in dialect of the reflexes of MHG *â* and *ô,* although under NHG influence the former distinction seems to be in the process of being restored.

(9) The absence of final *-e* deriving from MHG final *-e,* which is frequently retained in NHG.

Chief Vowel Correspondences

Dst.*	e	ä	ei	au	aa	ie[i:]	u(:)	e, ee		i
MHG	e	ë, ä	î	iu, öu	û	ei ou	ie	üe uo	ê, e œ, ö	i ü
NHG	e, ä[ɛ]		ei eu, äu	au	ei au	ie[i:] ü	u(:)	e	ö	i ü

NHG	e, ä [ɛ]		ei	au	eu/äu	ie(i:)ü	u	e	ö	i ü
MHG	e	ë, ä	î ei	û ou	iu öu	ie	üe uo	ê, e œ, ö		i ü
Dst.	e	ä	ei aa au aa		ei	ie[i:]	u	e, ee		i

* For the phonetic value of the letters, see § 5. MHG and NHG sounds are given in their respective orthography.

THE CONSONANTS

§ 12. The Consonantal System

Stops		Fricatives		Aspirates,	Affricate	Sonants	
b		f			(ph)		m	w
d		s	š	(th)		(ds)	n	l	j
g		x			(kh)		ŋ	r	h

The consonantal system is very similar to that of Als. (see chap. iv, § 12) although phonetically speaking the stops and fricatives are more relaxed, i.e. they are lenes compared with the Als. semi-fortes. Only the sonants are voiced. In the case of the stops and fricatives the amount of voicing is negligible and irrelevant. All consonants are short.

The aspirates consist of a fortis stop with slight aspiration. They occur only in initial position before stressed vowels, cf. *Bahd—Pahd* 'bath—path'. Both they and the affricate [ds] can be regarded as phoneme clusters.

In final position after short vowels the fricatives have generally fortis allophones.

In their distribution the stops (including *ds*) are unrestricted in voiced surroundings. Of the fricatives /x/ occurs only after a back vowel. Initially /s/ does not occur before consonants and /f/ only before vowels and liquids. /h/ occurs only initially, but /ŋ/ never. /w/ and /j/ do not occur finally. /r/ occurs only before vowels. In all other positions where it is historically justified it is represented by an unstressed vowel, a vocalic *Ersatzlaut*. This could be regarded as an allophone of /r/, being in complementary distribution with [r], although phonetically it is more closely related to [ə] with which it contrasts in some positions.

§ 13. SPELLING

The author of our specimen text attempts to bring out only the most salient consonantal differences between his dialect and NHG. Thus the bilabial semi-consonant [w] is usually indicated where it corresponds to NHG *b*, e.g. *schreiwe—schreiben*. The correspondence of lenis labial stop [b] to NHG *pf* in certain cases is also brought out, e.g. *Drobbe—Tropfen* 'drop'. The lenis character of the stops and fricatives on the other hand is only inconsistently hinted at, e.g. *gud: gut* 'good', *drinke—trinken* 'to drink', but also *gut, Seit* 'page', *Gutdhat* 'good deed'. It would, of course, be easy to systematize so simple a consonantal system as that of H.Dst. dialect, but the connection with NHG would be endangered and needlessly so. Only contrasts need be brought out. Otherwise regularity may be sacrificed to easy recognizability. Thus in initial position *b, d, g* stand for lenis stops, *p, t, k* for aspirated fortis stops. In all other positions Schneider's spellings may be retained. Dang, *Darmstädter Wörterbuch*, introduces *b, d, g* in all positions. Some rearrangement is also necessary with regard to the letters *g* and *ch*; the former stands only for [g] and the latter for [x]. By using *sch* for [š] everywhere except initially before consonants, where the NHG spelling convention *st, sp* can be retained, the regularization goes farther than is strictly necessary. But it helps to reduce the number of rules to be remembered when reading. Thus we have the following spellings:

Phoneme	Letter	Phoneme	Letter	Phoneme	Letter
b	b, (1) p, bb, pp	f	f, v, ff	w, j	w, j
d	d, (1) t, dd, dt, tt	s	s, ss	m	m, mm
g	g, (1) k, gg, ck	š	sch (2)	n	n, nn
ph-	p-	x	ch	ŋ	ng, n(k)
th-	t-	ds	z, tz	l, r	l, ll, r, rr (3)
kh-	k-			h	h

Notes

(1) Initially only *b, d, g* to mark the contrast with the aspirated fortis stops.

(2) Initially before *t* and *p* I have retained the NHG spelling *st*, *sp*.

(3) I have retained the spelling with *r* where the *Ersatzlaut* occurs (see § 14.13), for it functions allophonically.

§ 14. The Consonant Phonemes

14.1 [b] is a voiceless lenis bilabial stop deriving from:

(i) MHG *b* initially and finally: *bleiwe* 'to stay', *Stubb* 'living room'.

(ii) MHG and foreign *p* initially before liquids, in the cluster MHG *sp*: *Blatz* 'room', *Abrill* 'April', *Esbe* 'aspen'.

(iii) WGmc. -*pp*- and -*bb*-: *Drobbe* 'drop', *Ribbe* 'rib'.

(iv) assimilation in *äbbes* 'something'.

14.2 [d] is a voiceless lenis dental stop deriving from:

(i) MHG *d*:[1] *däss* 'that', *Dorschd* 'thirst'.

(ii) MHG *t*: *draurisch* 'sad', *Dodegräwer* 'gravedigger', *dräde* 'to tread'.

(iii) MHG *tt*: *wedde* 'to bet', *bidder* 'bitter'.

14.3 [g] is a voiceless, lenis palato-velar stop and derives from:

(i) MHG *g* in initial position or before a dental after a front vowel: *gäwwe* 'to give', *er segd* 'he says'.[2]

(ii) MHG *k* initially before consonants, i.e. sonants: *globbe* 'to knock', *grank* 'ill'.

(iii) MHG -*gg*- and -*ck*-: *Sack* 'bag', *gucke* 'to look'.

(iv) MHG *h* before *s*: *Fugs* 'fox', *wagse* 'to grow'.

14.4 [f] is a voiceless, lenis labio-dental fricative deriving from:

(i) MHG *f*, *ff* (< Gmc. *p*): *färschde* 'to be afraid', *saufe* 'to drink', *uff* 'on'.

(ii) MHG *pf* in loan-words from NHG: *Fennisch* 'penny', *Flischt* 'duty', *Kamf* 'fight'.

In semi-dialect MHG *v* (< Gmc. *f*) in medial position is also represented by this sound: *Ofe* 'stove', see § 14.14.

14.5 [s] is a voiceless, lenis alveolar fricative deriving from:

(i) MHG *s* and *z* (*ss*, *zz*): *wos* 'what', *Nahs* 'nose'.

In the positions where MHG *s* developed to NHG *sch* this dialect has also *sch* as well as in a few cases after *r*, e.g. *Dorschd* 'thirst'.

14.6 [š] is a voiceless, lenis alveolar-palatal fricative articulated with the blade of the tongue. It is nearer [ç] than the NHG [š]. It derives from:

(i) MHG *s* initially before consonants: *schwazz* 'black'.

(ii) MHG *s* in the final cluster *rst*: *Worscht* 'sausage'.

---

[1] In the country dialects, intervocalic position is excluded, for there MHG *d* > *r*. On assimilations, see § 15.

[2] In final position it is very rare, but it occurs in the words *Wähg*, 'way', *Dahg* 'day', *Schlahg* 'blow'. (Cf. §§ 14.6 (iv); 14.7 (ii).)

(iii) MHG *ch* medially and finally after palatal vowels: *Leisch* 'funeral', *u'heeflisch* 'impolite'; in the diminutive suffix: *Drebbsche* 'little drop'.

(iv) MHG *g* in the adjectival ending NHG *-ig*: *draurisch* 'sad'. In semi-dialect this sound is frequently also found to represent MHG *g* after palatal vowels medially or finally: *Wähsch* 'way' for dialectal *Wähg, Rieschel* 'bolt' for dialectal *Riejel*.

14.7 [x] is a voiceless lenis velar fricative. It occurs only finally and medially after back vowels. It derives from:

(i) MHG *ch* after back vowels: *Duch* 'cloth', *brauche* 'to need'.

(ii) MHG *g* after back vowels: *Aach* 'eye', *geflooche* 'flown'.[1]

14.8 [ph] is a bilabial fortis stop with slight aspiration occurring only initially before vowels. It derives from:

(i) WGmc. *p-*: *Pund* 'pound', *Pahd* 'path', *peife* 'to whistle', in words which have not been influenced by NHG, e.g. *Flischt* 'duty', *Fennisch* 'penny'.

14.9 [th] is an alveolar-dental fortis stop with slight aspiration occurring only initially before vowels. It derives from NHG and is found only in recent loans, e.g. *Titel* 'title', *turne* [2] 'to do gymnastics'.

14.10 [kh] is the corresponding palato-velar aspirated fortis stop. It occurs only initially before vowels and represents MHG *k-* in this position: *koche* 'to cook'.

14.11 [ds] is a lenis alveolar affricate deriving from the same sources and occurring in the same places as the corresponding NHG affricate *z*: *zwanzisch* '20', *Katz* 'cat'.

14.12 The nasals [m, n, ŋ] occur in the same positions and derive from the same sources as in NHG with the following exceptions:

(i) [n] does not occur in final unstressed syllables after [ə], cf. *si hawwe—sie haben*. It occurs, however, after [ɜ].

(ii) In conservative dialect it does not occur finally after stressed long vowels or diphthongs, cf. *Rheĩ—Rhein*. The nasalized vowels and diphthongs have arisen in this position. (See §§ 7.5; 8.2; 8.4.)

(iii) MHG final *m* which has become *n* in several NHG words is frequently still preserved in H.Dst., e.g. *Schwaddem* 'vapour'.

14.13 Of the liquids [l] occurs as in NHG but [r] is severely restricted in range. In Dst. it is a slightly rolled trill occurring only before a vowel either initially or medially at the beginning of a syllable. In all other positions the historical *r* is regularly represented by the unstressed vowel [ɜ]. (See §§ 9; 12.)

---

[1] Very conservative (and rural) dialect has here a semi-vocalic glide of *u—w* character, cf. Als. and Born, pp. 58–60. See also § 14.3 (i).

[2] Initial /d/ is also heard.

14.14 [w] is in genuine dialect a voiced bilabial fricative; under NHG influence it becomes frequently labio-dental. It derives from the following sources:

(i) MHG *w* initially and after initial consonants: *waasch* 'soft', *schweer* 'heavy'.

(ii) MHG *w* intervocalically or after liquids in medial position: *Fawe* 'colours' (sg. *Fab*), *Schwalwe* 'swallows'.

(iii) MHG *b* medially after vowels and liquids: *stärwe* 'to die', *Läwe* 'life'.

(iv) MHG *v* (< Gmc. *f*) medially: *hewe* 'to lift', *sauwer* 'clean'. It does not occur finally.

As a representative of intervocalic MHG *g* after back vowels Dst. now has usually [x], but see § 14.7 and Born, pp. 58–60, 108–12.

14.15 [j] is a voiced palatal fricative with very little friction. It never occurs finally. It represents:

(i) MHG *j* initially and medially between vowels: *jahche* 'to chase', *neje* 'to sew', *dreje* 'to turn'.

(ii) MHG *g* medially after front vowel: *räjene* 'to rain', *geje* 'against'; after *l* or *r*: *Galje* 'gallows', *Morje* 'morning', but see § 14.6. Semi-dialect has usually [š] in the cases mentioned under (ii).

14.16 [h] occurs only initially and corresponds to NHG *h*.

§ 15. ASSIMILATION

15.1 Two kinds of historical assimilation are widespread in Rh.-Franc.: former medial *-nd-* > *n* and former *-ld-* > *l*, e.g. *hunnert* '100', *anner* 'other', *hinne* 'behind', *Wannel* cf. NHG *Wandel*; *schullisch* 'guilty', *Holler* 'elder-tree'. In urban speech the NHG cluster *ld* or *lt* > *ld*, is now usually restored, e.g. our text *Falde*, *zugehalde* (cf. Born, p. 51).

15.2 A former *r* after *a* is occasionally assimilated to a subsequent consonant, e.g. in our text *schwazz* 'black' (cf. Born, pp. 53–6); and in the former ending *-ern* or *-ren* the *r* is assimilated to *n* and has helped to preserve *n* in a position in which it has otherwise dropped.

15.3 In rapid, especially vulgar, speech progressive assimilations are frequent, especially in the form of dropping of consonants in unstressed words. Our text provides the example *mi' nanner* 'with one another'. Also *wammer*: NHG *wenn man*; *kammer*: NHG *kann man*, *gu-mol*: NHG *guck mal*; *gumorje*: NHG *guten Morgen*.

§ 16. COMPARISON WITH THE NHG CONSONANTS

The most salient differences are:

(1) The NHG opposition of voiced/voiceless stops and fricatives has no parallel in Dst. There is only one series of voiceless lenis stops

and fricatives. Only initially they contrast with aspirated fortis stops.

(2) Dst. dialect departs from the MHG consonantal system even more radically than NHG. It has abandoned the distinction between MHG *d* and *t*, initial *b* and *p*, *s* and *z* (*zz*), *g* and *k* before consonants. Unlike Als. it distinguishes between medial MHG *f* (*v*) and *ff* (< Gmc. *p*).

(3) Medial *w* and *j* correspond to MHG -*b*- and -*g*-, to which there is no parallel in NHG.

(4) The velar fricative *ch* is not matched by a palatal allophone as in NHG. On the other hand, the occurrence both of velar *ch* and of *sch* is much increased through the development of MHG *g* > *ch* after back vowels and *ch* > *sch* after front vowels.

(5) The loss of final *n* in unstressed syllables where it is not protected by the assimilation of a former preceding *r*.

(6) The dialect lacks the glottal stop onset and has, unlike NHG, no hardening in final position as a neutralization of consonantal stop and fricative contrasts.

MORPHOLOGY
NOUNS AND ARTICLES
§ 17. FORMATION OF THE PLURAL

Since there is no inflexion for case, nouns can only be grouped according to the way in which they form their plural. The five types of plural formation are conditioned by three historical processes: (a) loss of former final -*e*, (b) loss of former final -*n*, unless (c) assimilation with a preceding *r* occurred.

Type A: plural not marked by ending or mutation.

Type B: plural marked by mutation alone.

Type C: plural marked by ending -*e*.

Type D: plural marked by ending -*er* [3] with mutation where possible.

Type E: plural marked by ending -*n*.

Note: All back vowels are mutatable. The correspondences are as follows:

Basic mutatable vowel:	a	o	u	au
Mutated vowel:	ä/e	e	i	ai

For the phonetic values of these letters, see § 5. Long vowels mutate correspondingly. The morphologically active umlaut of *a* is *ä*, e.g. *Grawe—Gräwe* 'ditch', *Katz—Kätzje* 'cat' and dim., but a few historical mutations in *e* occur, e.g. *Abbl—Ebbl* 'apple', *Ast—Est* 'twig', and, of course, there are the distributional limitations, e.g. in *Hand—Hend* 'hand' (see § 6.2–3).

Type A. To this type belong:

(i) Many neuter nouns: *Zimmer* 'room', *Pund* 'pound'.

(ii) Most masculine nouns including most of those ending in -*e* in the pl. in NHG: *Fraind* 'friend', *Drobbe* 'drop', *Wähg* 'way'.

(iii) As there are practically no fem. nouns ending in -*e* in the sg. this sub-group of Type A, sizeable in H. Alem., is confined to one noun *Bärn* 'pear'.[1]

Type B. To this type belong:

(i) A number of masc. nouns with mutatable root-vowel, especially those which also mutate in NHG, with the addition of a few masc. nouns which belong to other classes in NHG: *Bruder—Brieder* 'brother', *Stuhl—Stiehl* 'chair', *Arm—Ärm* 'arm', *Worm—Wärm* 'worm', *Gaul—Gail* 'horse', *Schlahch* (or *Schlahg*)*—Schlehsch* 'blow'.

(ii) Most of those fem. nouns which mutate in NHG: *Bank—Benk* 'bench', *Maus—Mais* 'mouse'.

Type C. To this type belong:

(i) The majority of feminine nouns: *Leisch—Leische* 'funeral', *Stubb—Stuwe* 'sitting-room', *Sind—Sinde* 'sin'.

(ii) The majority of masculine nouns denoting animate beings: *Kumbahn—Kumbahne* 'pal', *Buub—Buwe* 'boy', and a few other masculines.

(iii) The neuter noun *Aach—Aache* 'eye'.

Type D. To this type belong (mutation occurs in the case of back root-vowels):

(i) The majority of the neuter nouns: *Loch—Lescher* 'hole', *Buch—Bischer* 'book', *Ding—Dinger* 'thing', *Määdsche—Määdscher* 'girl', *Stick—Sticker* 'piece', *Mensch—Menscher* 'girl'.

(ii) Those masculines which form their plural in -*er* in NHG with the addition of a few others.

(iii) Diminutives in -*sche*: *Drebbsche—Drebbscher* 'little drop', *Säckelsche—Säckelscher* 'little bag', *Staasche—Staascher* 'stone'.

This type is more frequent than in NHG. Phonetically speaking, the difference between Types C and D is that between unstressed [ə] and [ɜ] in the case of most speakers.

Type E. To this type belong:

(i) Those nouns of Type C the roots of which end in -*r* in NHG: *Ohr—Ohrn* 'ear', *Dier—Diern* 'door'.

(ii) In analogy to those under (i) other nouns with former final -*r*: *Dier—Diern* 'animal', *Door—Doorn* 'door', *Babier—Babiern* 'paper', *Hoor—Hoorn* 'hair', *Joor—Joorn* 'year'.

---

[1] One informant has pointed out that he says *Birn* [bɪɜn] (see § 6.3 (ii)) in the sg. and *Bärn* [bɛɜn] in the pl. He also has the pl. *Baʔ* of the sg. *Bã* 'leg'.

§ 18. Case Forms

Case forms which occur, e.g. in our text *vun Härze gegunnt*, derive from NHG. The dialect makes no case distinctions. For the possessive there is the usual dative paraphrase, e.g. *unserm Datterich sei Härz*. Other genitival functions are expressed by *vun*, e.g. *im Beiseĩ vun zwaa Dodegräwer* 'in the presence of two gravediggers'.

§ 19. Gender

Among those few nouns with a different gender from that of NHG are: *Frolein* f. 'Miss', *Bagge* m. 'cheek', *Mensch* n. in the sense of 'woman' (pejorative), *Bach* f. 'brook'.[1]

§ 20. The Declension of the Definite Article

There is a common case and a dative. No distinction is thus made between subject and direct object.

	m.	*f.*	*n.*	*pl.*
Common Case	de	di	s	di
Dative	em	de	em	de

Notes

(1) *e* represents everywhere [ə].

(2) These forms are the least-stressed forms of the demonstrative pronoun and demonstrative forms are occasionally used with little demonstrative force, e.g. *däss letzte Drebbsche, an dem Engel vorbei*.

(3) Agglutinations as in NHG, e.g. *vum, ans*, etc., and also *an* (NHG *an den*), *newem* (*neben dem*), *mim* (*mit dem*), etc.

§ 21. The Declension of the Indefinite Article

	m.	*f.*	*n.*
Common Case	en, e (2)	e	e
Dative	eme	ere (4)	eme (4)

Notes

(1) e stands everywhere for [ə].

(2) The two masc. forms are not used to make a case distinction but, it appears, largely for euphonic reasons and reasons of stress, e.g. *e guder Drobbe, en klaane Engel, e dicker Schwaddem, en samfte Ribbestumber. En* is regularly used before a noun beginning with a vowel.

(3) Agglutinations as in NHG; see also *wien*, NHG *wie ein*.

(4) After prepositions ending in a vowel this is reduced to *re, me*, e.g. *bei-re*.

---

[1] See O. Philipp, '*Die Bach*. Ein Beitrag zur Geographie der deutschen Mundarten', *ZfdMaa.*, 1907, pp. 1–18; 210–17; 1908, pp. 55–66; 333–45; 1906, pp. 373–9.

ADJECTIVES

Under the influence of NHG the strong declension now usually distinguishes between a nom. and an acc. masc. The weak and strong declensions are used according to the same rules as in NHG.

§ 22. THE STRONG DECLENSION

		m.	*f.*	*n.*	*pl.*
Common Case	.	junge (1)	jung (2)	jung (2)	} junge
Dative	. .	jungem (3)	junger	jungem	

Notes

(1) Semi-dialect usually has -*er* for nom. and -*e* for the objective case, e.g. Schneider: *en klaane Engel* but *e guder Drobbe, e dicker Schwaddem* (nom.).

(2) *E nei Seit* (f.), *e gross Buch* (n.).

(3) Also endingless forms, e.g. *mit kalt Wasser*.

§ 23. THE WEAK DECLENSION

	m.	*f.*	*n.*	*pl.*
Nom.	jung, -e (1)	}jung	jung, -e (1)	}junge
Acc. }	junge		}junge	
Dat. }		junge		

Notes

(1) In conservative dialect masc. and neuter have an endingless nom., e.g. Schneider: *de grobb Bengler, di schwazz Katz*, but *der iwwerrenzige Dorscht.*

(2) Acc. *de gleische Wähk, däss letzte Drebbsche.*

§ 24. COMPARISON

The endings of the second and third degrees are: -*er* [3], -*st* [sd]. Umlaut occurs in most cases where the root-vowel is mutatable. Special forms occur of *klä* 'small'—*klenner*—*klennste*. The comparative particle is *wie*, e.g. *weider wie dorsch s Galljevärdel.*

NUMERALS

§ 25

As in NHG only the word for 'one' is still declined:

	Strong Declension			Weak Declension		
	m.	*f.*	*n.*	*m.*	*f.*	*n.*
C.C.	aan, aaner	aa	aa	aa(2), aane	aa	aa(2), aane
Dat.	aam	aaner, aam		aane	aane	aane

Notes

    (1) *aa* stands for [ɒ:] or [ɒ̃:].

    (2) In conservative dialect for nom. only.

    (3) The unstressed forms serve as the indefinite article.

PRONOUNS

§ 26. PERSONAL PRONOUNS

The forms of the pronouns are dependent on the sentence stress. The second form given is the one used in unstressed position.

	1st Person	*2nd Person*	*3rd Person* m.	f.	n.
Nom. sg.	isch	duu, de	er, e	sie, se	es, s
Acc. sg.	misch	disch	ihn, en, n	sie, se	es, s
Dat. sg.	mier, mer	dier, der	ihm, em, ne	ihr, ere	ihm, ne
Nom. pl.	mier, mer	ihr, er	sie, se		
Acc. pl.	uns	eisch	sie, se		
Dat. pl.	uns	eisch	ihne, en		

Notes

    (1) *r* is everywhere vocalized, see § 14.13.

    (2) In inversion and after prepositions the least-stressed forms are used, e.g. *hoste* 2nd pers. sg. 'have'; *un dann hawwe-sen zugeschebbt* 'and then they covered him over'.

    (3) Agglutination with prepositions occur also, e.g. *hot uff Hochdeitsch zurer gesacht*, cf. NHG *zu ihr*.

The indefinite personal pronoun is *mer*, dat. *aam*, acc. *aane*.

    (4) In the 3rd pers. pl. the dem. pron. *die* is frequently used where one would expect the pers. pron. *sie*. The latter is felt to be more polite and is always used in the polite address.

§ 27. REFLEXIVE PRONOUNS

There is only one special form *sisch* for the 3rd pers. sg. and pl. objective case.

§ 28. POSSESSIVE PRONOUNS

They are: *mein, dein, sein, ihr, unser, eier, (dene) ihr.*

(i) *mein, dein, sein.*

	m.	f.	n.	pl.
Common Case . .	mei (1) mein (2)	mei	mei	mei
Dative . . .	meim	meine	meim	meine

N

Notes

(1) The form *mei* is an alternative only in the nom., if *mei* is used a difference is thus made between nom. and acc., e.g. Schneider *sei Fraind Spirwes* (nom.), *sein Säje gäwwe* (acc.) 'give his blessing'.

(2) When used as a substantive the masc. nom. has the special form *meiner* and the neuter common case the form *meins*.

(3) Many speakers use nasalized diphthongs.

(ii) *unser, eier, dene* (5) *ihr*.

	m.	f.	n.	pl.
Nom. . .	unser (1)	⎫unser	⎫unser (2)	⎫unser
Acc. . .	unsern	⎬	⎬	⎬
Dat. . .	unserm	unsere (3)	unserm	unsere (3)

Notes

(1) This nom. form has arisen under NHG influence, the older common case form being *unsern*.

(2) When used as a substantive the masc. nom. has a special form *unserer* and the neuter common case the form *unsers*.

(3) Besides these forms there are alternative ones: *unserne*.

(4) On vocalized *r*, see § 14.13.

(5) In the 3rd pers. pl. the poss. pron. is nearly always accompanied by the demonstrative *dene*, in the 3rd pers. sg. frequently by *dem, dere*; and the polite form is *ihne ihr*.

§ 29. DEMONSTRATIVE PRONOUNS

For 'this' the forms are:

	m.	f.	n.	pl.
Nom.	der	die	däss	die
Acc.	den			
Dat.	dem	dere	dem	dene

Notes

(1) Before *r* the letter *e* represents [ɛ].

(2) Vowels in open syllables are all long and are therefore not specially marked.

For 'that' the dialect has *säller*, which declines like an adjective in the strong declension, e.g. Schneider *däss Wädder an sällem Dahg* 'the weather on that day'.

§ 30. INTERROGATIVE PRONOUNS

	Nom.	*Acc.*	*Dat.*
who?	wer	wen	wem
what?	wos		
which?	weler,	welen	welem (semi-dialect uses *welscher*)
	wel (f.)		weler
	weles (n.)		welem
	wele (pl.)		
	wos fir (with indef. article)		

§ 31. INDEFINITE PRONOUNS

aaner, aa (f.n.), dat. *aam, aaner*	} somebody, one
jemand	
kaaner, kaa, kaans, niemand	nobody
ebbes, wos	something
nix	nothing
viel	much, many
mansch aaner, etc. *manscher*, etc.	many a
jeder, jeed, jeedes, dat. *jedem, jedere*	each
epahr	a few
all, dat. *alle* pl.	all
alles, dat. *allem, allere* sg.	all
kaa (adj.)	no

Note: The adj. *kaa* (nom. sg. and pl., all genders) has the following forms: *kaan* (acc. sg. m. n.), *kaam* (dat. sg. m. n.), *kaaner* (dat. sg. f.), *kaane* (dat. pl.). *Aa* in *kaa, aa* is usually nasalized.

§ 32. RELATIVE PRONOUNS

The relative pronoun *wo* is usually linked with the demonstrative pronouns, e.g. Schneider: *er is unnerwähks mansch-ere annere orme Seel begäjend, die wo de gleische Wähk hatt als wie er.*

Wo is also a conjunction, cf. NHG *als: domols, wo.*

VERBS

§ 33. FORMS AND CLASSIFICATION

The verb has the following simple form classes and tenses: infinitive, imperative, past participle, present indicative, a few isolated forms of the past indicative and past subjunctive (= conditional), occasionally a present participle, which is usually borrowed from NHG. The compound tenses and forms are the perfect, pluperfect, a passive and a conditional. The infinitive ends in *-e* except in the case of three monosyllabic verbs (*geh, steh, seï*) and in the case of verbs ending in a vocalized *r* which has preserved the former *-n*, e.g. *abflattschern* 'to depart, die'.

The infinitive particle is *zu.*

The imperative corresponds in formation to that of NHG. According to the way the past participle is formed two classes can be distinguished: a class of weak verbs, p.p. ending in *-t* [d] and a class of strong verbs with a p.p. ending in *-e.*

The past participle is characterized by the prefix *ge-*, which is, however, absent in the case of some verbs beginning with a velar stop, e.g. *gange* 'gone', *gäwwe* 'given', *grigd* 'got', *kumme* 'come', and (*wärn* >) *worn* 'become'. Weak verbs ending in a dental stop lack the participial ending -*t*, e.g. *gered* 'talked', *gewort* 'waited'. Vowel alternation between pres. and p.p. occurs only in strong verbs and one weak verb: *bringe—gebracht* 'bring'. Those other weak verbs which have the so-called *Rückumlaut* in NHG have levelled in genuine dialect, e.g. *denke—gedenkt*, 'think', *brenne—gebrennt* 'burn'.

§ 34. STRONG VERBS

The majority of the verbs whose p.p. ends in -*e* have a different root-vowel in the p.p. from that of the infinitive. Mutation of the root-vowel in the 2nd and 3rd pers. sg. pres. is much more widespread than in Alem. affecting nearly all verbs with the root-vowels *a, e, ä, oo, aa.*

Regular strong verbs do not possess a simple past tense and only those few mentioned in § 36 form a simple past subjunctive. We can thus best group the classes according to the stem alternants in the infinitive and past participle.[1]

I. Identical vowel in the inf. and p.p.:

(i) [ɒ:] *drahche* 'carry', *lade* 'load', *fahrn* 'ride' (OHG VI).

(ii) [o:] *schlofe* 'sleep', *brode* 'roast', *stoosse* 'push' (OHG VII).

(iii) [ɑ] *falle* 'fall', *fange* 'catch', *halde* 'hold' (OHG VII).

(iv) [a:] *haache* 'hit', *laafe* 'run' (alternative p.p. *geloffe*), *haasse* 'be called'.

All these verbs mutate to *e* (*ē*) in the 2nd and 3rd pers. sg. pres., except *haasse, haache.*

(v) [ɛ] *ässe* 'eat', *gäwwe* 'give', *mässe* 'measure', *säje* 'see' (OHG V).

(vi) [ɛ:] *läse* 'read', *dräde* 'tread' (OHG V).

The verbs of the last two sub-groups mutate to *i* in the 2nd and 3rd pers. sg. pres.

(vii) Isolated cases are *kumme* 'come' with the mutated forms *kimst, kimt*, and *ruffe—geruffe* 'call'.

II. Vowel alternation [ai/i]: *schneide—geschnitte* 'cut',[2] *bleiwe—gebliwwe* 'stay' (OHG I).

III. Vowel alternation [i:/o or o:]:

(i) *fliesse—geflosse* 'flow', *giesse—gegosse* 'pour', *verliern—verlorn* 'lose', *friern—gefrorn* (the last two with long vowel in p.p.) (OHG II).

(ii) Before *j* the vowel is short: *flije—geflooche* 'fly', *bije—gebooche* 'bend', *bedrije—bedrooche* 'cheat' (OHG II).[3]

---

[1] Cf. the classes in chap. ii, § 39.

[2] There is, of course, no grammatical change phonetically. It is only apparent because of the traditional spelling. See §§ 12; 14.2.

[3] A new kind of grammatical change has here arisen: [j—x] or in semi-dialect [š—x].

(iii) An analogical formation: *sitze—gesotze* 'sit' (but also *gesässe* < NHG).

IV. Vowel alternation [i/u]: *drinke—gedrunke* 'drink', *gewinne— gewunne* 'gain', *winsche—gewunsche* 'wish' (OHG III).

V. Vowel alternation [ɛ/o]:

(i) *hälfe—geholfe* 'help', *wärn—worn* 'become', *bräche—gebroche* 'break', *stäche—gestoche* 'sting' (OHG III and IV).

(ii) With *e*, probably under the influence of a weak verb, *schmelze —geschmolze* 'melt', *henge—gehongge* 'hang'; with close vowels before nasals: *nemme—genumme* 'take'.

(iii) With long vowels before liquids: *stärwe—gestorwe* 'die', *befähle—befohle* 'command', *stähle—gestohle* 'steal', *schwärn— geschworn* 'swear' (OHG III).

All these verbs mutate to *i* in the 2nd and 3rd pers. sg. pres. But see § 6.3 on vowels before *r*.

Some isolated vowel alternations: *saufe—gesoffe* 'drink', *hewe— gehowe* 'lift', *leije—geläje* 'lie' (or *lieje, liesche—gelääsche* under NHG influence).

A number of formerly strong verbs have become weak, notably *bitte* 'beg', *reije* 'regret'.

§ 35. THE PRESENT

The endings are: Sg. 1 -, 2 -*st*, 3 -*t*; Pl. 1, 3 -*e*, -*rn*, 2 -*t*, e.g.

isch drink	*mir drinke*
du drinkst	*ihr drinkt*
er drinkt	*sie drinke*

Notes

(1) *t* stands, of course, always for the lenis.

(2) A verb ending in -*r* has -*rn* in the 1st and 3rd pers. pl.: *mir, sie friern* 'be cold'. Rural dialects have this ending also in 1st pers. sg., e.g. *isch fahrn* or *isch fahn* 'I ride' (see Born, p. 118).

(3) A verbal root ending in *j* (MHG *g*) before vocalic endings, has a *g* before consonantal endings, e.g. *isch flie, mir flije—er, ihr fligt* 'fly' (semi-dialect with *sch* everywhere). Sometimes *g* is found also in the 1st pers. sg., e.g. *isch grig* 'I get', *du grigst, er grigt, mir, sie grieje.*

(4) A verb ending in *w* (MHG *b*) before vocalic endings, has *b* in all other cases, e.g. *isch bleib, du bleibst, er bleibt, mir, sie bleiwe.*

(5) For mutation in the 2nd and 3rd pers. sg., see § 34, where details are given. Some weak verbs also mutate by analogy, e.g. *hole* 'fetch': *helst, helt*; *sahche* 'say' : *segst, segt*; *frooche* 'ask' : *fregst, fᵳegt* (p.p. *gefroocht*). Former *g* has not become *ch* after palatal vowel and before dental.

§ 36. The Conditional

36.1 Only very few verbs of the strong class still form synthetic past subjunctive forms, e.g.

bleiwe 'stay'—*blieb*　　　　　*nemme* 'take'—*nehm*
gäwwe 'give'—*geeb*　　　　　*kumme* 'come'—*keem*

36.2 Even these few strong verbs usually take the weak ending and form alternative conditionals: *geebd, nehmd, keemd.* This also applies to the monosyllabic verbs:

geh 'go'—*gin(d)*　　　　　*dun* 'do'—*deht*
steh 'stand'—*stind*　　　　*sei* 'be'—has a different root form: *weer.*

36.3 The few weak verbs with a synthetic past subjunctive have the regular endings -*t(d)* (1, 3 sg.), -*st* (2 sg.), -*te* (1, 3 pl.), -*t* (2 pl.): *brauche* 'need'—*braicht*, and *hawwe* 'have' has *hett.* The modal auxiliaries form their conditional in the same way (see § 39).

36.4 By far the most frequent way of forming the conditional is the analytical form of the past subj. of 'do' (*deht*) and the infinitive, e.g. Schneider *sie hawwe erst gedenkt, er deht widder mol uff de Pritsch sitze.*

§ 37. The Past Indicative[1]

In contrast to the Alem. dialects, which have no trace whatever of this tense, the Franc. dialects form a past indic. of at least a few verbs. These are in H.Dst. *hawwe* 'have' and *sei* 'be' and the modal auxiliaries (see § 39).

§ 38. The Compound Tenses and the Passive

Most verbs express past time by a compound tense consisting of the auxiliaries *hawwe* or *sei* (pres. or past indic.).

Perfect: *er is gange; sie hawwe gedenkt.*

Pluperfect: *er woor gange; sie hadde gedenkt.*

In contrast to the Alem. dialects, H.Dst. uses *hawwe* for the perfect of *steh* and *sitze*, e.g. Schneider *hot gesässe, hot gestanne,* see also: *hot mit der Hand iwwer e voll Seit . . . gefohrn* (p. 194).

For future time the dialect nearly always uses the present tense. Only if an assumption is made or a probability expressed is *wärn* (NHG *werden*) used, e.g. Schneider *wie wärd mir's geh.*

The passive is formed with *wärn* and the p.p. as in NHG, e.g. Schneider *bis se uffgeruffe wärn dehte* (= condit. of *wärn*).

---

[1] H. Reis, *Beiträge zur Syntax der Mainzer Mundart,* 1891; *id.,* 'Der Untergang der einfachen Vergangenheitsform', *GRM,* ii, 1910, 382–92; K. Jacki, 'Das starke Präteritum in den Mundarten des hochdeutschen Sprachgebiets', *Beitr.,* xxxiv, 1909, 425–529; A. Kaiser, *Studien zur Bildung des Präteritums in den heutigen deutschen Mundarten,* Giessen, 1910; Ph. Kaiblinger, 'Ursachen des Präteritumverfalls im Deutschen', *Teuth.,* vi, 1929/30, 269–78.

§ 39. The Modal Auxiliaries and Irregular Verbs

39.1 Four or five basic forms are distinguished in the case of the modal auxiliaries. All the others are derived from these in a regular way.

	Inf.; 1, 3 Pl. Pres.	1, 3 Sg. Pres. (3)	2 Pl. Pres.; Condit.	Past Indic.	P.P. (4)
'to be able'	kenne	kann	kennt	konnt	gekennt
'should like'	meje	mahch	meescht (2)	mocht	gemocht
'must'	misse	muss	misst	—	gemisst
'to want'	wolle	will	wollt	wollt	gewollt
'shall, should'	solle	soll	sollt	sollt	gesollt
'to be allowed'	därfe	därf	därft	—	gedärft

Notes

(1) The ending *t* represents everywhere a lenis.

(2) For the 2 pers. pl. pres. there is an alternative *meegt*.

(3) The 2 pers. sg. pres. takes the ending *-st*.

(4) In the perfect and pluperfect tenses the infinitive is used before a main verb as in NHG, e.g. Schneider *wo en de grobb Bengler hot abkammisole wolle*. This is also the case with *losse* 'let'.

39.2 A number of verbs must be classed as 'irregular':

	Inf.	Pres.		Past Indic.	Past Subj. (Condit.)	P.P.
'to be'	seī imp.: sei!	bin (3) bist is	sin seid sin	woor (1)	weer	gewäse (4)
'to have'	hawwe imp.: hab!	hab (7) host hot	hawwe habt hawwe	hat	het	gehatt
'to know'	wisse	waass waasst waass	wisse wisst wisse	wusst	wisst	gewisst (gewusst)
'to do'	duhn imp.: duh!	duh (5) duhst duhd	duhn duhd duhn	—	deht	gedo gedān
'to go'	geh (6) imp.: geh!	geh gehst geht	gehn gëht gehn	—	ging	gange

Notes

(1) 1st and 3rd pers. pl. end in *-rn, woorn, weern*. Alternative forms: *wah, wahn* (pl.).

(2) *-t* is a lenis.

(3) In much of the territory, though not in Darmstadt, the 1st pers. sg. pres. is *sein*, see Born, p. 118 and map 4. This form replaces also urban *sin* in 1st and 3rd pers. pl. pres.

(4) Born, map 3, shows *gewääst* west of Dst.

(5) Only the towns have *duh*, otherwise *duhn*.

(6) The same forms for *steh* 'stand', except p.p. *gestande* condit. *stind*.

(7) In inversion *haww-isch*.

PARTICLES

§ 40

Adverbs of place are differentiated like those of NHG according to the direction of the motion. In the case of rest H.Dst. has also some synthetic forms, e.g. *unne*, NHG *dort unten*; *hunne*, NHG *hier unten*, but these are not so well developed as in Lower Als.

Preposition	*Movement* (a) *away from speaker*	*Adverb of Place* (b) *towards speaker*	*Rest*
in (drinn)	nei, enei, (1) (enin)	erei (1) (erin)	drinn
aus (draus)	naus	eraus	draus (2)
uff (druff) (3)	nuff	ruff	drowwe
unner (drunner)	nunner	runner	drunne (4)
			unne
iwwer (driwwer)	niwwer	eriwwer	driwwe
hinner (dehinner)	hinner	hinner	hinne
voor (devoor)	(voor)	ervoor	
um (drum)		rum	
zu (dazu)			
an (dran)	(ane) (5)	(ane) (5)	

Notes

(1) The presence of initial *e-* depends on sentence stress and the extent of NHG influence.

(2) *Haus* for NHG *heraus*, *hier draussen*.

(3) The form used in commands is *auf*.

(4) *Hunne* for NHG *hier unten*.

(5) These forms occur only in conservative dialect.

PHONETIC TRANSCRIPTION

For the principles of this transcription, see pp. 71, 148. A description of the individual sounds is given in §§ 4, 6–9, 12, 14. [b, d, g, f, s, š, x] are voiceless lenes, tending more towards fortis in final position after stressed short vowels. It might have been more logical to use the signs [v, z, ž, γ] for the lenis fricatives, but as these are not opposed to fortes like [b, d, g] to [ph, th, kh] it appeared unnecessary.

Words of two or more syllables have the main stress on the first syllable except where marked otherwise.

wi də dadəriš in də himl khumə is

dsum gə'deŋgə ɒn də 'do:dəs͵dɒ:g fun unsəm ɛɜnsd e'lias 'ni:wɜ͵gɑl,
gə'šdɔɜwə ɒm 'nɒĩn͵dse:ndə a'bril 'ɑxdse:hunɜ'drɑıun͵fɛɜdsiš, bə'-
grɒ:wə ɒm dswɒndsišdə a'bril, o:wənds, im bɑısɒĩ fun dswa:
'do:də͵grɛ:wɜ.

šon drɑı dɒ:g hodɜ jedsd də'hɒ̃:m uf əm sag gə'lɛjə, unsɜ gu:dɜ
dadəriš. ɜ hod͜swɒ:ɜ ned so· rɛšd gə'wisd, wos əm ɑıšəndliš wo:ɜ,
awɜ das ɜ aləwɑıl ufəm ledsdə lox phɑıfd, dɛs hodɜ dox gə'šbi:ɜd.

sis a:x khɒ̃: dogdɜ khumə, dɛɜn bə'hɔɜšə un bəglobə un s əm hed
sɒ:xə odɜ go:ɜ ebəs hed fašrɑıwə khenə. du li:wə šdro:sag, ɒn unsəm
gu:də dadəriš khond khɒ̃: dogdɜ un khɒ̃: abo'de:gɜ wɒs fɛdi:nə.
no'ja: , un do wa:s mɜ šon . . .

sɒĩ saʊfkhumbɒ:nə un šga:dbri:dɜ hawən a:x šon drɑı dɒ:g lɒŋ
fəmisd; si hawə ɛɜsd gədeŋgd, ɛɜ de:d widəmol uf də bridš sidsə.
ɒm fɛɜdə dɒ:g o:wənds, do hod siš dox sɑĩ frɒĩnd šbɛɜwəs əmo·l
ufgərabəld, um no·xəm dsu gugə. ɜ is ɒlso dɛ:rə wagəlišə hiŋglsla:dɜ
ənuf in di daxgaʊb, wo ɛɜ loši:ɜd hod (nox imɜ o:nə rijəl ɒn də
šduwədi:ɜ), no un wi do də šbɛɜwəs sɒĩn frɒĩnd dadəriš hod do:lijə
sɛ:jə, do hodɜ glɑıš gəmɛɜgd: dismo·l fašdeldɜ siš ned, wi do·mo·ls,
wo ən də grob beŋlɜ hod abkhamiso·lə wolə, dismo·l is əs ɛɜnsd.

sɒĩ frɒĩnd šbɛɜwəs, ɜ moxd sonsd sɒĩ, wi ɜ wold, awɜ ə gu:d hɛɜds
hodɜ imɜ gəhad, ɒlso də šbɛɜwəs hodən drum gəfro:xd, ob ɛɜm nox
wos du: khend. un do hodən də dadəriš mid gɒnds fəlo:rənə a:xə
ɒ̃:gəgugd un hod gəsaxd: ɒləwɑıl is aʊsgədrumbd, ɒləwɑıl maxd ən
ɒnɜrɜ də ledsdə šdiš! awɜs we:rəm jedsd ɒləs wɔɜšd, hodɜ gəmɒ̃:nd,
blo:s dasɜ so drɑʊrıš abfladšən misd, wo ɜ dox dɛs gɒndsə lɛ:wə so
lusdiš gənumə hed, do hedɜ dox ən lusdišərə abši:d fun də wɛld
fədi:nd. — ax, un də dɔɜšd, dɛɜ iwɜrendsišə dɔɜšd, hodɜ gəšde:nd . . .

dɛs hod sɒĩm frɒĩnd šbɛɜwəs fasd s hɛɜds abgədrigd. ɜ is drum fɜɜd
un hodəm ə flaš asmanshɑısɜ gəho:ld, ɒ̃: fun dɛ:rə sɔɜd, wo di šwads
khads druf sidsd, de·n, wo unsɜ dadəriš fɔɜ sɒĩ lɛ:wə gɛɜn gələbəd
hod. di flaš hawə sə dɒn a:x dsum abši:d minɒnɜ gədruŋgə; dɛs
ha:sd, gədruŋgə hod ɑıšəndliš blo:s də dadəriš, un sɒĩ frɒĩnd šbɛɜwəs
hodsəm fun hɛɜdsə gəgind.

ROBERT SCHNEIDER:

WIE DE „DATTERICH" IN DE HIMMEL KUMME IS [1][1]

Zum Gedenke an de Dodesdahg vun unserm Ernst Elias Niebergall [2], gestorwe am nainzehnte Abrill achtzeh'hunnertdreiunvärzisch, begrawe am zwanzischste Abrill, owends, im Beiseï vun zwaa Dodegräwer.

Schun drei Dahg hot-er jetzt dehaam uff-em Sack geläje, unser guder Datterich. — Er hot zwoor net so räscht gewisst, wos-em eischendlisch woor, awwer dass er alleweil uff-em [3] letzte Loch peift, däss hot-er doch gespiert.

's is aach kaã Dokter kumme, der [4] en behorsche un beklobbe un 's em hett sahche odder goor äbbes hett verschreiwe kenne. Du liewer Strohsack, an unserm gude Datterich konnt kaã Dokter un kã Abbodheker wos verdiene. Noja, un do waass mer schun . . . [5]

Seï Saufkummbahne un Schkaadbrieder hawwe'n aach schun drei Dahg lang vermisst; sie hawwe erst gedenkt, er deht widder mool uff de „Pritsch" sitze [6]. Am värrte Dahg owends, do hot sisch doch seï Fraind Spirwes emol uffgerabbelt, um nooch em zu gucke. Er is also dere wackelische Hinkelslaader enuff in die Dachgaub, wo er loschiert hot (noch immer ohne Riejel an de Stuwwedier) [7], no un wie do de Spirwes [8] sein Fraind Datterich hot do-lieje säje [9], do hot-er gleisch gemärkt: dissmool verstellt er sisch net, wie domools, wo-en de grobb Bengler [10] hot abkammisole wolle, dissmool is es ärnst — —

Seï Fraind Spirwes, er mocht sunst seï, wie er wollt, awwer e guud Härz hot-er immer gehatt [11], also de Spirwes hot-en drum gefroocht, ob er-em noch wos duh kennt. Un do hot-en de Datterich mit ganz verlorene Aache ã'geguckt un hot gesacht: „Alleweil is ausgedrumbt, alleweil macht-en annerer de letzte Stisch!" — Awwer es weer-em jetzt alles Worscht, hot er gemaant, blooss dass er so draurisch ab-flattschern misst, wo er doch däss ganze Läwe so lustisch genumme hett, do hett-er doch en lustischere Abschied vun de Wält verdient.—„Ach, un de Dorscht, der iwwerrenzische Dorscht!" hot-er gestehnt ...

Däss hot seïm Fraind Spirwes fast 's Härz abgedrickt. — Er is drum fort un hot-em e Flasch „Assmannshaiser" [12] gehoolt, aã vun

1 -dag. 2 neun -verzig. 3 zwanzichste. 4 geleje. 5 zwor, recht. 6 eigendlich wor. 7 dess. 8 behorche. 9 sage, gor ebbes. 12 Schkad- 13 dhet, mol. 14 verrte, sich. 15 Freund. 16 wackelige. 17 Stuwe-. 18 sehe. 19 gleich gemerkt. 21 ernst. 22 gud. 23 Herz, gefrogt. 24 dhu. 25 Aage, gesagt. 26 Stich. 27 bloss, draurig. 28 Lewe,lustig. 29 Welt. 30 iwwerrenzige. 32 geholt.

---

1 See *Notes*.
For spelling, see §§ 5, 13. Where alterations have been made, Schneider's original spelling is given at the bottom of the page, but only on the first occurrence. All ˜ are mine.

dere Sort, wo die schwazz Katz druff sitzt, deen, wo unser Datterich
for sei Läwe gärn geläbbert hot. Die Flasch hawwe se dann aach zum
Abschied mi'nanner gedrunke; däss haasst, gedrunke hot eischendlisch blooss de Datterich, un seï Fraind Spirwes hot-sem vun Härze
gegunnt. [13]

Un de Datterich hot aä iwwer's annermool mit de Zung geschnalzt
un hot gesacht: ,,Ach, de Weï schleischt so samft bei aam!" — Un
wie er däss letzte Drebbsche [14] hot enunnerlaafe losse [15], do hot-er
sisch mit-eme wohlischte Seifzer ausgestreckt un hot gesacht: ,,'s
woor doch e guder Drobbe, de Assmannshaiser . . . !", un aus
woor's. — —

De Spirwes hot-em die Aache zugedrickt un hot aach die Leisch
for-en bestellt. Un's woor aach de aanzische, wo hinnenooch gange
is. — 's woor e goor ormseelisch Leisch; de aäne Dodegräwer hot
flischtgemäss e Vadderunser gemormelt, un dann hawwe-sen zu-
geschebbt. . . .

Middlererweil is em Datterich seï ,,verdribbelt Seel", wie de
u'heeflisch Bengler gesacht hot, langsam em Himmel zugeflooche [16].
's woor Ende Abrill un däss Wädder an sällem Dahg grod net zum
beste. — Un de Wähk woor weit, asch weit — weider wie dorch's
Galljevärdel. . . . [17]

Däss haasst, langweilisch woor's jo grod net, dann er is unnerwähks
mansch-ere annere orme Seel begäjend [9], die wo de gleische Wähk
hatt als wie er. No, un wie däss so is, die orme Seele sin mi'nanner ins
Gebabbel kumme, mer hot sisch mi'nanner bekannt gemacht un sisch
gäjeseidisch [9] vorgestellt un hot sisch äbbes vun seim verwischene
Läwenswannel verzehlt: wos un wie mer's gedriwwe hot, un schliesslisch aach vun seim letzte End. — No, un do hot sisch's so gesprääschs-
weis erausgestellt, dass doch die meiste vun dene orme Seele uff's
Stärwe guut vorbereit woorn un konnte dässwäje die letzte Wähk mit
Gottverdraue a'dräde. — Blooss unser guder Datterich, der konnt
mit seim ,,letzte End" kaän Staat mache, dann niemand hot-em sein
Säje gäwwe, un seï letzt Eelung woor, streng genumme, e Flasch
Assmannshaiser.

,,Aujeh!" hot-er gedenkt, ,,isch will doch emool säje, wie der Spass
ausgeht." — Dann, offe gestanne, seï ewisch dorschdisch Seel hot uff
zehe Meder gäje de Wind nooch Weï' gestunke wie e Kieferschärz.

,,Soosche [14], do weern mer!" hot uff aämool aä vun dene orme
Seele gesacht, wie se ans Himmelsdoor kumme sin. E' anner vun dene
orme Seele hot an de Schäll gezobbelt [18], wo näwe gehonke hot, un

1 den. 2 gern, gelebbert. 7 schleicht. 8 Drebbche. 9 wohlichte. 12 Leich.
13 aanzige. 14 ormseelig. 15 gemess. 18 u'heeflich, gefloge. 19 Wedder, sellem.
21 -verdel. 22 -weilig. 23 begejend, gleiche. 26 gejeseidig, verwichene.
28 gesprächs-. 30 Sterwe, dessweje. 31 a'drede. 33 Seje gewwe. 36 ewig,
dorschdig. 38 Sooche. 39 -dor. 40 Schell, newe.

do is dann aach glei en klaäne Engel kumme, hot uffgeriejelt un hot
gesacht, die Härrschafte meschte ereikumme. Also sin se 'neï; aach
de Datterich. Un wie der an dem klaäne Engel vobeigeht, do hot
der-en emool grooss ã'geguckt un hot sisch die Nahs zugehalte.
„Noja“, hot de Datterich gedenkt, „däss kann jo guut wärrn.“ —

Gleischdruff is e annerer Engel [19] kumme un hot gesacht, die
Härrschafte sollte einstweile im Wortezimmer Blatz nemme, bis se
uffgeruffe wärrn dehte, es ging strickte de Nummero nooch, un es
deht kaäns iwwerhibbelt [18] wärrn. Un wie sisch de Datterich
haamlisch an dem Engel vobeischlengele wollt, do hot sisch der aach
die Nahs zugehalte un hot-en emool streng gemustert, so als gotter-
sprisch [20]: wie kimmt dann der do ereï . . .

Do is awwer doch unserm Datterich seï Härz in die Hose geritscht,
wann mer bei-ere orme Seel so sahche kann, un er hot sisch drum ganz
hinne uff die Owebank gesetzt, wo schun so e anner orm verhuzzelt
Seel gesässe hot; un do hot er dann gewort. Nooch un naach is dann
aä um die anner vun dene orme Seele uffgeruffe worrn, däss Wortezimmer is immer leerer worrn, un schliesslisch hot unser Datterich mit
dere annere orme Seel noch allaäns dogesässe. Un die hot geziddert
wie Esbelaab un hot in aäm fort gestehnt zum Staäerwaasche, un
drum hot se de Datterich gefroocht: „No, wos is, worum jaunert Ihr
dann so?“

„Ach, du liewer Gott“, hot die druff gesacht, „ach, wie wärd mir's
geh, wann ich jetzt vor unserm Härrgott steh, un er rächent [21] mit
mer ab!“

„Habt dann Ihr so viel uff-em Kärbholz?“, hot se de Datterich
gefroocht.

„O, du liewer Heiland!“ hot die anner orm Seel gesacht un wollt
grod ã'fange, dem Datterich ihr Schanddade zu beischte, awwer do
is widder en Engel kumme un hot die zwaa letzte Seele uffgeruffe.
Un do hot em Datterich seï Nachbarseel es Heile un Zehneklabbern
krigt, weil's zur letzte Abräschnung gange is.

Aach unserm Datterich is es jetzt e Portzion annerster [22] worrn,
dann in seim Gedäschnis sin allerhand Erinnerunge uffgedaucht un
Straasch, mit dene mer sisch alles, blooss kaän Stuhl im Himmel verdiene kann. Un rischtisch, wie er sisch an dem dritte Engel vobei-
schlengle wollt, hot der-en aach emool uff's Korn genumme un hot
sisch mit-eme Zibbel vun seim Faltehemd die Nahs zugehalte.

Jetzt is awwer doch em Datterich sei vielgeriehmt Kuraasch mit
Grundeis gange [23], er is zusammegeklabbt wie'n lahme Froschgiexer, un eh er nor wusst wie, do hawwe se vor unserm liewe Härr-

2 Herr-, mechte. 4 gross, Nas. 5 werrn. 7 Warte. 8 uffgerufe. 11 gottersprich.
16 gesesse. 23 werd. 24 rechent. 26 Kerb. 28 o'fange, beichte. 32 Abrechnung.
34 Gedächtnis. 36 richtig.

gott seim Drohn gestanne. De Datterich hot gornet uffgucke kenne
vor so viel Lischt, un er hot nor aã iwwers annermool iwwer sei root
Knuwwelnahs nooch unserm Härrgott geblinzelt. —

De-ärst is die anner orm Seel drã'genumme worrn, un de liewe
Härrgott hot in e grooss Buch eneïgeguckt un hot dann mit zusamme-
gezoochene Aachebraune [24] die anner orm Seel uff's Fissier genumme
un hot uff Hochdeitsch zurer gesacht: „Du hast auf Erden Sünde
um Sünde auf dich gehäufet, du hast deine armen Eltern schlecht be-
handelt und deine Geschwister um ihr Erbteil betrogen; du hast Geld
ausgeliehen gegen hohe Zinsen und Wucher getrieben zum Nachteile
deines Nächsten, du hast die Armen darben lassen, während du im
Überflusse lebtest, du hast . . ." un so is es fortgange, Seit um Seit,
un net aã aãnzisch Guutdaht wor vun dere Seel in unserm Härrgott
seim Buch nodiert. Un schliesslich hot unser liewer Härrgott zornisch
gesacht: „Du bist nicht wert, dass du in meinen Himmel aufgenom-
men wirst — fort mit dir zur Hölle!" — —

Vier odder fimf Engel hawwe jetzt die orm Seel am Schlawittsche
genumme, hawwe e eisern Falldier uffgerisse, wo gleich e dicker
schwäwwelischer Schwaddem eraufkumme is, un hawwe die sindisch
Seel enunner gestumbt in die Hell. — —

Den Datterich hot's orndlisch geschuckert, wie er däss gesäje hot.
Awwer schun hot jetzt unser liewer Härrgott ihn ã'geguckt un hot
dann bloos gesacht: „Aha — der Datterich!" — un hot e nei Seit
uffgeschlahche vun dem dicke Buch.

„Komm näher heran", hot de liewe Härrgott zum Datterich gesacht un hot mit de Hand iwwer e voll Seit vum Datterich seim
Schuldkonto gefohrn. Der awwer hot sich gornet gedraut nejerzugeh,
bis-em so zwaa Ärzengel en samfte Ribbestumber gäwwe hawwe,
dass er fast hiegedorzelt weer. Un do hot unser liewer Härrgott mit
seine Nahs aach emool in de Luft erum geschnubbert, hot seï Aachebraune hoochgezooche un hot blooss gesacht: „Hm — hm — Ass-
mannshäuser!" — sunst nix . . .

Un dann hot er ã'gefange un hot unserm Datterich seï Sinderegister
vorgeläse: „Datterich", hot-er widder uff hochdeitsch gesacht, „Datterich, warum hast du auf Erden ein Faulenzerleben geführt, warum
hast du arme, brave Handwerker um ihren Verdienst betrogen und
das Geld in den Wirtshäusern verprasst und verspielt; warum hast
du nur immer in Wolfgang Reiters zweiunddreissigblätterigem Gebetbuch [25] geblättert, anstatt deine Seele auf den Himmel vorzube-
reiten, warum hast du den Kuppler gespielt und gute Menschen auf
Abwege gebracht? Warum . . ." un so is es fortgange in aaner

---

2 Licht, rot. 4 erst, dro'. 5 gross. 6 gezogene. 13 Gutdhat. 17 Schlawittche.
19 schwäwweliger, sindig. 20 Höll. 21 orndlich, gesehe. 24 uffgeschlage.
27 neher. 28 Erz-, gewwe. 31 hochgezoge. 34 gelese.

Duur [26]. Kaã Vergehe, un weer's aach däss klennste gewäse, is iwwerhibbelt worrn, un de Datterich hot schun uff däss Dunnerwort gewort: „Fort mit dir zur Hölle!" —

Awwer doo is uff aãmool unserm Datterich e reddender Gedanke kumme. Die ganz Zeit hot unser liewer Härrgott blooss vun seine schläschte Seite geredd, wo awwer sin die gute gebliwwe? – Un wie unser liewer Härrgott grod emool e Peisje gemacht hot, do hot de Datterich ã'fange zu redde, ärst e bissje leis un zahghaft, awwer dann immer lauder, un hot gesacht, dass er doch aach seï gude Seite gehatt hett, vor allem sein Humor, mit dem er doch so viel Mensche zu-ere frohe Stund verholfe hett, un ob däss net uffgeschriwwe weer, in dem Buch do, hot-er unsern Härrgott gefroocht. Odder ob däss valleischt nix weer, wann mer die Mensche uffheidern deht, un ob däss Freehlischseï net äwe so gottgefellisch weer wie däss Greine un Driebsalbloose, un ob net die gelachte Drehne aus-em sällwe Säckelsche kemte wie die gegreinte, un ob blooss die Haamduxer un Duckmaiser guut ã'geschriwwe weern bei unserm Härrgott; un ob's net schun in de Schrift haasse deht: „Der Wein erfreut des Menschen Herz!" — un ob unser Härrgott die gude Drobbe net däshalb wochse losse deht, um damit dass se aach gedrunke werrn solle; un ob net er, de Datterich, schun manschen, der schun verzweifle wollt, widder uffgerischt hett mit seim Humor? — Die pahr klaäne Klebberschulde, die wo er hinnerlosse hett, die kennte doch so schweer net ins Gewischt falle, un iwwrigens hett-em doch der bidderbees Bengler zuletzt noch emool dermaasse ins Kreiz gehaache [27], dass domit schun allaãns all seï Sinde abgegolte weern. . . .

Immer lauder is unser Datterich worrn, un zuletzt is er de A'klääscher gewäse, un unser liewer Härrgott hot muxmaisjestill dogesässe un hot nor aã-iwwer'sannermool iwwer sei Brill ewäck ganz verdutzt bald seï zwaa Ärzengel un bald den vorschnäwwlische Datterich ã'geguckt. — Awwer uff aãmool is e hell un heider Läschle iwwer unserm liewe Härrgott seï A'dlitz gewittscht, un er hot in seine milde un fraindlische Art zu seine zwaa Ärzengel näwe seim Drohn gesacht: „Nun denn, in Gottes Namen, lasset ihn eingehen in des Reiches Herrlichkeit!" —

„So, däss maãn ich-derr Ihne awwer aach!" [28] hot de Datterich druff gesacht un is groossmogelisch [29] hinner dene zwaa himmlische Amtswalter härgange . . .

Un so is-er zuguderletzt doch noch in de Himmel kumme. Noja, es misst net de Datterich gewäse seï . . .

---

1 Dur, gewese. 6 schlechte. 7 Peische. 8 zaghaft. 13 valleicht. 14 Freehlichsei, -gefellig. 16 Säckelche. 17 o'geschriwwe. 21 manchen. 22 uffgericht, paar. 23 schwer, Gewicht. 25 dermasse, gehaage. 28 A'kläger, muxmaische. 29 eweck. 31 Lächle. 33 freundliche, newe. 38 her-.

NOTES

(See the remarks to the *Notes* on p. 80)

[1] *Robert Schneider*, born 6 Dec. 1875, died 1945, lived and worked all his life in Darmstadt as a lithographer and later a local government official. Over the years he built up a considerable local reputation as a humorous writer in dialect, evoking successfully and affectionately the particular local spirit and sense of humour of his *Heiner* (i.e. people of Darmstadt). As it was Schneider who launched the appeal for a memorial to Darmstadt's great dialect writer, Niebergall, it is befitting that Schneider's own short story on Niebergall's *Datterich* should represent him. His works include: *Heinerblut, Gedichte in Darmstädter Mundart*, 1908; *Lyrisches und Lustiges. Gedichtercher in Hessen-Darmstädter Mundart*, 1920; *Die Wildsau un annern lustige Sache in Hesse-Dst. Mundart*, 1921; *Därrobst. Gedichter un Geschichtcher*, 1940; *Des un Sell von Bienchen Bimbernell*, collected and publ. after his death, 1949; *Kraut un Riewe*, 1951. The publishing house of Roether, Darmstadt, began to republish all his works in 1951. Our specimen text, one of Schneider's most successful short sketches, appeared in *Därrobst*. It deals with the unforgettable figure of *Datterich*, the hero of Niebergall's play, on the day of his death and ascension to heaven. Datterich, ever living on his wits, amoral, always cheerful, never-to-be-got-down, wine-soaked, an endearing crook, is not at a loss even in the most crucial situation.

[2] The *Datterich* of E. E. Niebergall is one of the classics of German dialect drama. Niebergall (13 Jan. 1815–19 Apr. 1843) wrote his *Datterich, Localposse in der Mundart der Darmstädter in 6 Bildern*, in 1841. His biographers do not agree as to how much Datterich is a self-portrait of the author, an unsuccessful student of theology, afterwards eking out a meagre existence as a private coach. See K. Esselborn, *E. E. Niebergalls Erzählende Werke*, i, ix–xxiv, Darmstadt, 1925, and H. von der Au in the most recent ed., Darmstadt, 1950, Wittich.

[3] MHG *ûf* was shortened before the diphthongization of *û* > *au*, cf. *druf, enuf, eruf, hinne-uf* (NHG *hinten hinauf*) and *DSA*, 128.

[4] Relative pronoun borrowed from NHG.

[5] Allusion to Datterich's failure ever to pay a bill. Informants tend to say *schon, sonst* (p. 191, l. 22, cf. § 6.6 (ii)).

[6] Reference to *Datterich*, vi, 9, when he was in prison, sitting on a wooden pallet.

[7] Each time a creditor comes to see Datterich about his debts, he says he will have a bolt fitted, but of course he never does anything about it.

[8] *Spirwes* is his best drinking companion.

[9] Informants use a long vowel under the influence of NHG; cf. § 10.1.

[10] Bengler, an angry bootmaker, whom Datterich owes money, despairing of ever getting his money, decides to give Datterich a beating. But the ever-resourceful Datterich pretends to be critically ill and in a fever delirium. Bengler therefore spares him but later encounters him in the street and beats him up thoroughly.

[11] Informants state that *gehatt* is slightly archaic and that *gehabt* is now common.

[12] *Assmannshausen* is a famous wine-producing village on the Rhine, not far from Rüdesheim; of its wine Datterich (vi, 1) says: '*Der Wei schleicht so samft bei amm*' (*Schleiche* 'flow down', NHG *schläuchen*).

[13] *Gegunnt* is archaic. Informants use *geginnt*.

[14] The common diminutive ending is *-sche*, after *s* and *sch* it is *-je*, e.g. *Drebbsche, Peisje, bissje, Kneibsche* 'small kitchen-knife', *Kobbsche Kaffee* 'cup of coffee'. The pl. is either identical or ends in *-scher*. After a final [g] or [x] the dim. ending is usually *-elsche*, e.g. *Säckelsche, Bischelsche* 'booklet', but this ending is also common as a second degree of diminution with most nouns, e.g. *Hindsche* and *Hundelsche* 'dog', *Aachelscher* dim. of 'eyes', *Knechelsche* of 'bone, ankle'. See *DSA*, 59, *Schäfchen* (pl.): H.Dst. *-ercher*, Lux. *-erchen*, Westphal. *-kes*, SGm. *-li*, Als. *-le*, Upper Austrian *-l*. As in many other dialects diminutives can also be formed of other parts of speech, e.g. Schneider *soosche* (< *so*) 'well, that's done', 'here you are', cf. SGm. *sooli*; Niebergall *gutsche* (*gut*); *bloddsche* from *blodd* 'broke'.

[15] Informants have *lasse*.

[16] Informants syncopate: *gflooche, gsacht, gstanne*, cf. § 2.3 (1).

[17] In iv, 2, Datterich, up to one of his deceiving tricks, takes the way through the thieves' quarter (*Galljevärdel*), where, he thinks, nobody will see him.

[18] *Zobbele* 'pull repeatedly', cf. NHG *zupfen*. The verbal ending *-ele* indicates that an action takes place in repeated small bouts; it has thus diminutive-iterative function. Cf. *hibbele*—NHG *hüpfen* 'jump', *schnuddele* 'gossip', *giggele* 'giggle', *sisch kibbele* or *kiwwele* 'tease', *abschnibbele* 'cut off', *puddele* 'splash about in water, paddle'; also with the meaning of smelling of something, e.g. *becksele* 'smell of goats'.

[19] One informant prefers *en annern Engel*, which is more genuine.

[20] 'So to speak', 'as if', Dang, p. 59, explains its origin as '*als besser sprechend*'; see J. Franck, 'Godersprech und Verwandtes', *ZfdMaa.*, 1908, pp. 289–302 (< OHG *quedan* 'to speak').

[21] The NHG ending *-net* corresponds to Dst. *-ent*, cf. *druckend*: *trocknet*; *begäjend*: *begegnet*.

o

[22] *Mir wird's annerster* (listening to what somebody says) 'makes me sick'.

[23] Colloquial German for 'to be in a blue funk'.

[24] Informants have *Aachebraae* or *Aachebraue*.

[25] Datterich refers to a pack of cards as 'Wolfgang Reiters zweiunddreissigblättrigem Gebetbuch'.

[26] *In aaner Duur* 'on and on'.

[27] Idiomatic expression for 'give him a thorough beating'.

[28] A kind of double ethic dative, combining the personal pronoun of intimate address (*derr*) with that of formal address (*Ihne*). This blend occurs also in the direct object, e.g. *isch sahch-derr Ihne* 'I tell you'.

[29] This adj. derives from *Grossmogul*. It is used by Niebergall and is said to be still current to-day in colloquial Darmstadt speech.

GLOSSARY

See the introductory remarks to the *Glossary* on p. 84. Dang, *Darmstädter Wörterbuch* is not arranged in alphabetical order and therefore of limited use.

Aachebraune, eyebrows.
abflattschern, wv. die (slang).
abkammisole, wv. beat up.
äbbes, something.
alleweil, now.
als, always, usually.
asch, very (NHG *arg*).

Dachgaub, f. attic room.

Froschgiexer, m. small knife.

Gebabbel, n. chattering.
greine, wv. cry.

Haamduxer, m. sneak.
hiedorzele, wv. stumble and fall down.
Hinkel, n. A. chicken.

iwwerrenzisch, superfluous.

jaunern, wv. lament.

Kieferschärz, f. C. cooper's apron.
Klebberschulde, small debts. See Grimm, *Wtb.*, v, 976.

Knuwwelnahs, C. bulbous nose.

läbbern, wv. tipple.
Leisch, f. C. funeral (see Mitzka, *Wortatlas*, iv).

muxmaisjestill, absolutely quiet (like a mouse).

Ribbestumber, a dig in the ribs.
ritsche, wv. slide.

säje, sv. see.
Schkaad, German card game *Skat*.
Schlawittsche, am S. nemme, take by the scruff of the neck.
schuckern, wv. shudder with cold or fright.
Schwaddem, m. vapour.
Stisch, m. A. trick (cards).
stumbe, wv. push.

uffrabbele, sisch, wv. brace oneself.

verdribbele, wv. dribble, waste.
verhuzzele, wv. dry up, shrivel.
vorschnäwwlisch, pert.

CHAPTER VI

UPPER AUSTRIAN

§ 1. AREA AND STATUS

1.1 Austria and Bavaria stand linguistically between the extremes of North Germany and the Alemannic areas. Taking society as a whole, it can be said that the linguistic scene in North Germany is characterized by a deep gulf between a rather small rural and urban working-class population speaking dialect and the standard-speaking middle and upper classes. This northern standard owes relatively little to the local dialects. The Alemannic areas, on the other hand, are basically dialect-speaking with no superstratum of native standard-speakers. In Austria no gulf separates the classes linguistically, only shades of subtly graded distinctions. The transition between genuine dialect and standard is gradual, socially as well as geographically. Standard owes relatively much to the local dialects. Dialect features colour the speech much higher up the social scale than in Central and North Germany. This gradualism is characteristic not only within one locality but also from the big urban centres outwards into the remoter rural districts. Gradualism characterizes, it is true, not only Austria and Bavaria but the whole south, notably also Swabia, but excluding the Alemannic areas in the narrower sense. Thus it is typical that of all the Austrian provinces the Alemannic-speaking province of Vorarlberg alone does not participate in this gradualism but has a wholly dialect-speaking native society embracing all classes.

The reasons for this gradualism lie in the history of the NHG standard language. Linguistically Austro-Bavarian contributed to the rising standard language more than any other area except the East Middle German home area itself. Historically Austria, with its seat of the imperial government and as the centre of imperial policy and society, took a great part in its promotion. With its monarchic and aristocratic society Austria has always had a supraregional upper-class language (a *Herrensprache*) of great importance which has for centuries had a strong impact on the peasant dialects, as Kranzmayer has shown repeatedly.[1] The ideal of a socially and culturally elevated and refined standard language has impressed itself on Austria in a way it never has on the Alemannic areas. It is, paradoxically, this strong participation in the making of the NHG standard language

---

[1] See fn. 3 on p. 16 and *Lautgeogr.*, p. 2.

which endowed the local dialectal phonology—and vocabulary—with
a remarkable resilience. It was possible to profess the ideal of the
rising standard language and yet retain one's own local pronunciation; after all, it was, so to speak, one's own standard language. Thus
the Austrian standard of the old imperial aristocracy and bureau-
cracy took as its spoken pattern forms developed on its own soil, e.g.
in Vienna, and above all in Prague and Laibach, centres which
lacked a local German peasant dialect. It is only relatively recently,
i.e. in the last few decades, that this Austrian standard has moved
more and more and deliberately in the direction of the accepted
Bühnenaussprache.

Gradualism as an approach to language shows itself also in the
willingness to meet one's partner half way. The peasant speaking to
a townsman or an upper-class official will drop the local features of
his dialect and attempt to speak the current colloquial of the region,
the *Verkehrssprache,* just as much as the normally standard-speaking
official will adopt the forms of the *Verkehrssprache* when speaking to
a person he assumes to be normally a dialect speaker. The resulting
situation is that the peasantry in Austria everywhere still speaks
dialect but that it readily and rapidly adopts forms percolating into
the countryside from the market towns. Naturally there are regions
of greater resistance and wide areas, especially those near the pro-
vincial capitals, which are less conservative than the average. The
inhabitants of the country towns also speak dialect but in a diminishing degree of genuineness.

Upper Austria is linguistically the most conservative of the
Danubian provinces. Naturally the Alpine regions are more conservative still.[1] My informants were an Upper Austrian dialect writer of
65, now living in Linz, and a girl in her twenties from Gmünden.
They can be said to represent the dialect of the small country
towns, which is somewhat less archaic than the speech of the rural
districts.[2]

1.2 As large a province as Upper Austria is, of course, not uniform
in its dialect. The author of our text writes in the dialect of the
centre, roughly speaking the area west of the Krems river and east
of the Hausruck mountains. The River Traun runs more or less
through the middle of our area, which covers politically the Haus-
ruckviertel, the western Traunviertel, and the northern Salzkammer-
gut.[3]

[1] Kranzmayer, *Lautgeogr.*, p. 5, states as a principle 'Je höher die Landschaft
überm Meeresspiegel liegt, desto altertümlicher sind die Sprachschichten'.
[2] For details, see §§ 2.1 (12); 4; 7.7 (iii); 7.10 and Note 4; § 10.1.
[3] See the maps by A. Haasbauer in *Teuth.*, i. 1924–5; M. Hornung—F.
Roitinger, *Unsere Mundarten*, p. 57; Kranzmayer, *Lautgeogr.*, maps 8 (*Dorf*),
10 (*rot*), 12 (MHG *iu*), 24 (MHG *-en*) and *Hilfskarte* 2.

The territory where Bavarian dialects[1] are spoken is inhabited by over eight million people and is one of the largest clearly marked German dialect areas. It is surrounded on three sides by Slav-, Magyar-, and Romance-speaking populations. Only in the west and north-west are Bavarian dialects confronted with other German dialects: Alemannic from the Alps to the Danube and East Franconian on the north-western sector. Probably the most incisive dialect boundary in Austria is that running across the Arlberg Pass. Some of the isoglosses which here divide Alemannic from Bavarian are: Alem. monophthongs *ī, ū* for MHG *ī, ū* against Bav. diphthongs *ai, au*; MHG *a* preserved in Alem. against Bav. *o*; MHG *æ, ä* represented as *ē, ä* in Alem. against a front *a* in Bav.; MHG *ei* becomes *ai* or is monophthongized in Alem. against Bav. *oa*; Alem. *füüf* (with dissolution of *n* before fricative) against Bav. *fimf*; rounded vowels for MHG *ü, ö, öü* in Alem. against unrounded vowels in Bav.; Alem. forms for 'you' deriving from MHG *ir, iuch* against Bav. *es, enk*; Alem. forms for the verbs 'go', 'stand' derived from MHG *gân, stân* against Bav. forms from MHG *gên, stên*; Alem. *Zischtig* or *Aftermontag* (Swabian) against Bav. *Ertag* for 'Tuesday' (*DSA*, 26); MHG unstressed *-en* > *e* in Alem. but *-n* in Bav. (*DSA*, 121, (*dresch*)*en*). These and many other isoglosses run in a narrow or sometimes wider belt northwards along the River Lech, the old tribal frontier between Alemanni and Bavarians, to the Danube and northwards beyond. The dialects spoken north of the Danube as far as Regensburg and thence to the Czech frontier are called *North Bavarian*.[2]

The wide, flat plateau along the Isar and Danube stretching eastwards from Munich and Regensburg to beyond Vienna, embracing the provinces of Upper and Lower Bavaria and Upper and Lower Austria, is the territory of the most progressive and homogeneous Bavarian dialects known as *Middle Bavarian* or *Danubian Bavarian*. Southwards Middle Bavarian extends as far as the foothills of the Alps beyond which the much more conservative *South Bavarian* or *Alpine Bavarian* dialects are spoken. The heartland of these are the provinces of Tyrol and Carinthia, while Salzburg and Styria are, linguistically speaking, transition zones.[3] Isoglosses which divide Danubian from Alpine Bavarian are: the vocalization of the liquids, e.g. *l* (Kranzmayer, *Lautgeogr.*, maps 26, 4 *Felder*, 7 *Holz*), *r* (Kranzmayer,

---

[1] See Mitzka, *DPhA*, i, 721–52, with maps on p. 721; E. Kranzmayer, 'Der bairische Sprachraum', *Jb. d. dt. Sprache*, ii, 1944, 169–80, and, of course, *Lautgeogr.*

[2] Kranzmayer, *Lautgeogr.*, map 15, shows North Bav. *ou* in *Blut* against *ua*, *ui*, etc., in Middle Bav.

[3] E. Kranzmayer, *Sprachschichten und Sprachbewegungen in den Ostalpen*, 1931, and *Lautgeogr.*, *Hilfskarte* 1; I. Reiffenstein, *Salzburgische Dialektgeographie* (Beitr. z. dt. Philologie, vi), Giessen, 1955.

Lautgeogr., 6 *merken*, 8 *Dorf*); the phenomenon known as the Middle Bavarian lenition of consonants (see § 10.2), *id.*, map 21; Mid. Bav. monophthong *o* in *Hosen*, *e* in *Peter* against South Bav. diphthongs (*id.*, maps 5 and 9); MHG *-en* > *-n* in South Bav. but > *-a* after certain consonants in Middle Bav. (*DSA*, 30 (*gebroch*)*en*).

GENERAL CHARACTERISTICS OF MIDDLE BAVARIAN (CENTRAL UPPER AUSTRIAN)

§ 2. PHONOLOGICAL FEATURES[1]

2.1 The Vowels

(1) The MHG long vowels *î*, *û*, *iu* (mutated) are represented by diphthongs *ai*, *au*. The reflexes of *î* and mutated *iu* have fallen together in *ai*. While modern colloquial no longer distinguishes between mutated MHG *iü* and unmutated MHG *iu*, the conservative rural dialects have *ai* only for the former and *eo* for the latter.[2]

(2) The MHG diphthongs *ie*, *uo*, *üe* are preserved as diphthongs (*ia*, *ua*), but through unrounding the reflexes of *ie* and *üe* have coincided.

(3) The MHG diphthong *ei* has become *oa*, but MHG *ou* has now generally coincided with the development of MHG *û* in *au* (except before *m*, *f*: > *ā*).

(4) Of the three different MHG *e*- sounds (*e*, *ē*, *ä*) the secondary umlaut (MHG *ä*, *æ*) is everywhere strictly distinguished from the others. But the reflexes of MHG *e* and *ē* have been widely confused—with a clear tendency in favour of close *e*—even where there are still two distinct *e*- phonemes.[3]

(5) MHG *a* and *â* have become the same type of open *o*- sound (*å*), which is kept apart from the reflexes of MHG *o*, *ô*.

(6) For MHG *ê* Middle Bav. has in contrast to North and South Bav. a long monophthong. But in the case of MHG *ô* diphthongal reflexes seem to have been general at one time although Upper Austrian with the reflex *eo* is now isolated among the Middle Bav. dialects of Austria.

(7) MHG *i* and *u* are generally preserved.

(8) All MHG rounded front vowels (*ö*, *œ*, *ü*, *iu*, *üe*, *öü*) have become unrounded. But a new series of rounded front vowels has arisen through the vocalization of *l*: *ü*, *ö*, *œ*.

(9) A whole new series of nasalized vowel phonemes has arisen

---

[1] See fn. 1, p. 32.
[2] Cf. E. Mertes, 'Ahd. iu ohne Umlaut im Dialektgebiet des Deutschen Reiches', *Teuth.*, vi, 1929–30, 161–234; vii, 1930–31, 43–120, 268–87.
[3] Kranzmayer, *Lautgeogr.*, p. 26 f., speaks of *verworrene e-Mundarten*.

through the nasalization of every vowel (in certain cases with accompanying modification in vowel quality) before a MHG nasal consonant.

(10) The vowel developments have been generally affected by following consonants other than stops and fricatives, e.g. by the nasals (nasalization), by *l* (labialization and vocalization leading to new diphthongs), by *r* (vocalization leading to diphthongs), and by *h* (opening effect).

(11) Initial vowels have a smooth onset, a glottal stop being unknown in that position.

(12) Svarabhakti vowels between liquids and other consonants are now largely confined to the old speakers of the most conservative dialects.

2.2 Vowel Quantity

(1) Full participation in the lengthening of short vowels in open syllables or, in other words, before lenis consonants (*Leichtinnendehnung*).

(2) Originally short vowels are also lengthened in originally monosyllabic words both before original lenis consonants (*Leichtschlussdehnung*) and original fortis consonants and even certain consonantal clusters (*Schwerschlussdehnung*).

(3) Vowel quantity is no longer phonemically distinctive. Every vowel before a lenis or a nasal plus lenis is long, every vowel before a fortis or a nasal plus fortis is short.

2.3 Vowels in Unstressed Syllables

(1) The NHG prefixes *be-* and *ge-* generally lose their vowel.

(2) The NHG unstressed syllable *-er* usually corresponds to the unstressed low central vowel [ɒ].

(3) MHG *-e* has everywhere disappeared. Where it was once followed by nasal consonants these have become syllabic, except after certain consonants, especially nasals and velars, where *-en* has become [-ɒ].

(4) The MHG adjectival ending *-iu* is preserved as *e* or *i*.

(5) Excrescent vowels have arisen in certain consonantal clusters.

2.4 The Consonants

(1) The consonantal system is based on an opposition of fortis and voiceless lenis sounds except in initial position. Only the sonants are voiced.

(2) In initial position MHG *d* and *t*, *b* and *p* are not distinguished, *g* and *k* only before vowels.

(3) In a general way it can be said that present lenes correspond

to MHG fortes and present fortes to MHG geminates in dissyllabic words.

(4) The fricative *ch* is more or less velar, even after palatal vowels.

(5) MHG *s* before consonants has developed as in NHG except before *p* and after *r* where it has become *sch*.

(6) Medial *-b-* has frequently become a fricative or, if followed by former *n*, been assimilated to *m*; medial *-d-* has disappeared when followed by *l* or *n*.

(7) Final *ch* has often disappeared.

(8) Final *n* in the MHG and NHG ending *-en* has not generally disappeared as in other Upper German dialects but is usually preserved as a nasal consonant.

(9) The liquids *r* and *l* generally occur only before vowels; syllabic *l* also finally, particularly after dentals.

§ 3. Morphological Features

3.1 Noun and Article

(1) There is one class of masc. nouns which distinguishes in the sg. an objective case from the nom. by means of an ending. The dat. pl. is also generally marked by an ending.

(2) A distinction between subject and object is made in the case of the masc. sg. articles, but no distinction between direct and indirect object. The fem. and neuter articles, however, distinguish a dative from a common case.

(3) The noun class without distinction for number is much larger than in NHG (intrusion of *-n* into sg.).

(4) The diminutive ending is *-l* (vocalized in certain cases), with the second degree *-al*.

3.2 The Adjective

(1) In the strong declension the plural common case and the fem. sg. common case end in *-e* [e].

(2) In the fem. sg. often no distinction is made between a weak and strong declension.

3.3 The Pronouns

(1) Most personal pronouns distinguish between dative and accusative. There is a genitive form after certain prepositions.

(2) The personal pronouns of the 2nd pers. pl. go back to old dual forms (*es, enk*).

(3) The personal pronoun for NHG *uns* goes back to a mutated form (*ins*).

(4) The possessive pronouns pl. have forms with *-r* (*insa, enka, ihra*).

(5) The demonstrative pronoun neuter (common case) is *des*.

(6) The demonstrative pronoun *dea*, etc., functions also as a relative pronoun.

3.4 The Verbs

(1) The tense system consists of a present, a perfect, and a pluperfect (rare). There is no present subjunctive.

(2) The conditional is expressed by means of the past subjunctive in the case of a few strong verbs, otherwise by means of the suffix *-ad*.

(3) Modern dialect has a two-form plural like NHG, conservative dialect continues the MHG three-form pl.

(4) The 2nd pers. pl. has a suffixed pers. pron. (*es kemmts*: NHG *ihr kommt*).

(5) There is no *Rückumlaut*.

(6) The verb NHG *haben* has unmutated forms in the sg. pres.

(7) Mutation occurs only where the root-vowel of a strong verb is *e*. It goes through the whole sg.

(8) For NHG *gewesen* Upper Austrian has *gwen*.

(9) The dialect verbs for NHG *gehen, stehen* are reflexes of MHG *gên, stên*.

(10) Verbal endings corresponding to MHG *-en* are realized as: *-n, -m, -ng, -a*, depending on the preceding sound (present or former).

PHONOLOGY

THE VOWELS

§ 4. THE VOWEL PHONEMES

As the quantity of vowels is dependent on the syllabic structure and the nature of the following consonants, there are three ways of interpreting the vowel and consonant phonemes. Firstly, vowel length could be regarded as the primary distinctive feature, secondly, the intensity of articulation of the consonants (lenis or fortis), and thirdly, two prosodic features of syllabic structure could be distinguished to which vowel length and consonantal intensity would be subordinate. With good reason Pfalz and Koekkoek[1] regard the opposition of fortis and lenis consonants as phonemically most im-

---

[1] A. Pfalz, 'Zur Phonologie der bayrisch-österreichischen Mundart', *Lebendiges Erbe, Festschrift Reclam*, Leipzig, 1936, pp. 9–19; B. J. Koekkoek, *Zur Phonologie der Wiener Mundart, Beitr. zur dt. Philologie*, vi, Giessen, 1955.

portant.[1] It follows that vowel length is phonemically irrelevant. Every vowel phoneme has two variants: a long one in an open syllable or if followed by one or more lenis consonants including a nasal plus lenis consonant, and a short one if followed by one or more fortis consonants including a nasal plus a fortis consonant. This applies to the simple vowel phonemes as well as the diphthongs and the nasalized vowels. In unstressed positions in the sentence long vowels before lenes may be reduced.

The nasalized vowels occur mainly before nasal consonants, but they are nevertheless not mere positional variants of the non-nasalized vowels. In certain positions they occur also without a subsequent nasal consonant and contrast with the non-nasalized vowels, e.g. *sche(n)* 'beautiful': *See* 'lake', *stum* 'dumb': *Stu'm* 'living-room', *rena* 'to run': *re'n* 'to talk'. The four phonemes of the mid-tongue position (back and front) contrast with only two nasalized mid-tongue vowels (back and front). To some extent nasalization is dependent on sentence stress. In unstressed positions it is often lacking in conditions where it is to be expected.

The rounded front vowels, having arisen from labialization, are to be regarded as phonemes and not as positional variants before *l* because the *l* is vocalized, at least in rural dialect. Urban dialect has restored a thick, velar *l* in some words, especially after [ø] and [œ], but less frequently after [y].

Front	Front rounded	Back
i ī	y	u ũ
e ⎫	ø	o ⎫
ε ⎭ε̃	œ	ɔ ⎭ɔ̃
a ã		

The unstressed vowels, the most frequent of which are [ɒ, e], can be regarded as unstressed allophones of the stressed vowels.

There are numerous diphthongs, all of which must, however, be considered as unit phonemes since they are subject to the same quantity rules as the simple phonemes.

iɒ ⎫	ay	aε	ãε̃
εɒ ⎭ãε̃	oe	(eo)[2]	
ɔɒ ⎫	ɔe	(εo)[3]	
uɒ ⎭ɔ̃ɒ̃	ui	ɑo	ɑ̃õ

---

[1] H. L. Kufner, 'Zur Phonologie einer mittelbairischen Mundart', *ZfMaf.*, xxv, 1957, 175–84, regards the quantity of the fortis consonants as phonemically more relevant than the intensity of articulation, hence he interprets the fortis consonants as clusters, e.g. [t] as /dd/. This assumption is possible in his Upper Bavarian dialect since there are no contrasting lenis and fortis clusters (cf. Up. Austr. *Kobf*: *Kepf*). In such Upper Austrian clusters quantity distinctions are not made.

[2] See §§ 7.1 (i); 7.7 (iii). [3] See §§ 6.6 (iii); 7.9.

Instead of the diphthongs [ay, oe, ɔe, ui], which have arisen through the vocalization of a former *l*, many urban speakers now use a monophthong followed by a thick velar *l*.

§ 5. SPELLING

The author of our specimen text follows the NHG orthography as closely as possible. Although certain spellings are traditional in Austrian dialect literature our author employs only one, that of *ö* for [e]. For the front vowels he uses both *i—ü* and *e—ö* according to the NHG distribution, thus depriving himself of the possibility of distinguishing between the dialectal rounded and unrounded front vowels. He also fails to distinguish between /a/ and /ɔ/, although for the latter Austrian dialect writers have often used *å*.[1] It is clear that a certain number of alterations have had to be made to make the spelling phonemic and thus both regular and meaningful.

Since nasalization of the vowels before a nasal consonant is regular there is no need to indicate it. Where no nasal consonant follows, the nasalization of the vowel is indicated by an *n* in brackets. If a vowel is not nasalized, although now followed by a nasal consonant, an apostrophe is inserted, cf. *re'n, hi(n), Hen* (NHG *reden, hin, Henne*).

Vowel length does not have to be expressed since it is linked to the nature of the following consonants. Thus before *b, d, g, bf, z, s, r, l, n, m* vowels are normally long, before *p, t, k, pf, tz, ch, sch* short. But where, in the corresponding NHG word, vowel length is indicated by *h* or doubling this is retained in our text. Before lenis *sch* and *ch* the vowel symbols are doubled. Phonemes and letters correspond as follows:

Phoneme	Letter	Phoneme	Letter	Phoneme	Letter
i	i, ie	y	ü	iɒ	ia
e, ε	e, ë	ø	ö	εɒ	ea
a	a	œ	œ	aε	ai
u	u	ay	ei(l), äu(l)	ɑo	au
o	o	oe, ui	oe, ui	uɒ	ua
ɔ	å	ɔe	åe	ɔɒ	oa, åa

Unstressed [ɒ] is spelt *a*, unstressed [e] is *e*.

[1] It is noteworthy that one of my informants—a layman in dialectology—in preparing the text for a tape-recording introduced this distinction herself by altering *a* to *å* where this was required.

§ 6. The Stressed Monophthongs

6.1 [i] this close, tense, high-front vowel represents:[1]

(i) MHG *i*: *Gsichd* 'face', *sitzen* 'to sit'.

(ii) MHG *ü*: *Glick* 'luck', *Schissl* 'bowl'.

The nasalized counterpart derives from the same sources before every MHG nasal consonant.

6.2 [e] is a close, tense, mid-front vowel. It represents:

(i) MHG *e* (the primary umlaut): *Seck* 'sacks', *fest* 'firm'.

(ii) MHG *ē*: *Weda* 'weather', *Segn* 'blessing', *vagessn* 'to forget'. A large majority of MHG *ē* have thus coincided with the reflex of MHG *e*. This coincidence is very characteristic of Austro-Bavarian dialects and is very rarely found outside this dialect area. Some MHG *ē*,[2] especially those before *h* and *ch*, are, however, represented by [ε].

(iii) MHG *ö*: *megn* 'to like', *Reck* 'skirts'.

6.3 [ε]. This open, mid-front vowel stands for:

(i) MHG *ê*: *Schnēē* 'snow', *gēht* 'goes'.

(ii) MHG *œ*: *Hēh* 'height', *stēssn* 'to push'.

(iii) MHG *ē* in a few cases, especially before *h*, *ch*: *sēhgn* 'to see', *Knēchd* 'farm labourer'.

6.4 [ε̃]. There is only one nasalized mid-front vowel. The above-mentioned opposition is thus neutralized. This nasalized vowel is the correspondence of MHG *e*, *ē*, *ö*, *ê*, *œ* before former or present nasal consonants, e.g. *kema* 'to come', *geh(n)* 'to go', *sche(n)* 'beautiful'.

6.5 [a] is a very advanced front a- sound. It derives from:

(i) MHG *ä*, *æ*: *stad* 'quiet', *schlaffri* 'sleepy'. Nasalized [ã] before former or present nasal consonants: *i kam* 'I should come'.

(ii) MHG *ou*, *û* before *f*: *af* 'on', *laffa* 'to run', *kaffa* 'to buy', and before *m*: [ã] *kam* 'hardly', *Bam* 'tree'.

6.6 [ɔ] is a lax, rounded, low-back vowel and derives from:

(i) MHG *a*: *åft* 'then', *Någl* 'nail'.

(ii) MHG *â*: *blåsn* 'to blow', *schlåffa* 'to sleep'.

(iii) MHG *ô* in case of those dialect speakers who have abandoned the Upper Austrian diphthong *eo* (see § 7.9): *Tåd* 'death', *gråss* 'big'.

6.7 [o] a close, tense, mid-back vowel. It derives from:

(i) MHG *o*: *Hof* 'farm', *o'm* 'upstairs'.

6.8 [ɔ̃]. Before a nasal consonant (< MHG) the opposition between lax and tense, mid-back vowels is neutralized. This nasalized vowel

---

[1] The position before MHG *l*, *r*, *n*, *m*, *ng* is excluded in such general statements throughout this paragraph.

[2] A. Pfalz, *Die Mundart des Marchfeldes*, Vienna, 1913, p. 31, estimates the incidence as comprising about 23 per cent of MHG *ē* for his dialect. See also the very full treatment in Kranzmayer, *Lautgeogr.*, pp. 25–34.

thus derives from MHG *a, â, o, ŏ*: *Hånd* 'hand', *tå(n)* 'done', *scho(n)* 'already'.

6.9 [u] is a tense, close, high-back vowel deriving from MHG *u*: *bussn* 'to kiss', *Buda* 'butter'. The nasalized counterpart derives from the same source before every MHG nasal consonant, e.g. *jung* 'young'.

6.10 [œ]. This rounded, lax, mid-front vowel has arisen conditionally from MHG *ë, œ, ê* before *l*: *Gœld* (rural *Gœd*) 'money', *Sœ'n* 'souls'.

6.11 [ø] is a higher, tenser, rounded, mid-front vowel than the preceding one and has arisen from MHG *e, ö* before *l*: *Ködn* 'cold', *Gsö* 'companion'.

6.12 [y] is a rounded, tense, high-front vowel deriving from MHG *i, ü, üe* before *l*: *vü* 'much', *Müh* 'mill', *küh* 'cool'.

§ 7. THE DIPHTHONGS

All diphthongs are stressed on the first element. According to the final element they can be grouped into (a) diphthongs ending in the low central vowel [ɒ], and (b) diphthongs ending in a high or mid vowel. Group (a) has been greatly increased through the vocalization of a former postvocalic *r* and group (b) through the vocalization of a former postvocalic *l*.

7.1 [iɒ] derives from:

(i) MHG *ie*: *liab* 'dear', *schia'm* 'to push', *friasn* 'to freeze'.[1]

(ii) MHG *üe*: *miad* 'tired', *Briada* 'brothers'.

(iii) Vocalization of *r* in MHG *ir, ür, er*: *Gschia* 'crockery', *fiachtn* 'to fear', *fiati* 'finished'.[2]

(iv) MHG *i* in: *ea siacht* 'he sees', *Schriad* 'step'.

7.2 [ɛɒ] derives from:

(i) MHG *ë, ê, ö, œ* with vocalization of following *r*: *weaffa* 'to throw', *Deaffa* 'villages', *hea'n* 'to hear'.

(ii) MHG *i* in the pronouns *eahm* 'him', *eahna* 'them'.

(iii) Mutated dialectal *oa* (< MHG *ei*): *Breadn* 'width'.

7.3 [ẽɒ̃] has developed from MHG *ie, üe, ei* (mutated) before MHG nasals: *dean* 'to serve', *grea(n)* 'green', *gleana* 'smaller'.

7.4 [ɔɒ] derives from:

(i) MHG *ei*: *broad* 'broad, wide', *Goas* 'goat'.

---

[1] Conservative dialect has *eo* in the case of the strong verbs of the OHG III class (< Up. Gm. unmutated *iu*) on account of levelling within the paradigm, thus *scheo'm, freosn* (see Note 4).

[2] Both informants use this diphthong in the words *fiati, Iada* 'Tuesday', *miaka* 'to notice', which are the forms of the Danubian *Verkehrssprache*. According to Kranzmayer, *Lautgeogr.*, map 6, Upper Austria has [ɛɒ] in the words *merken, Ergetag* in contrast to Bav. and Lower Austrian [iɒ].

(ii) MHG *o, ô, a, â* with vocalization of following *r*: *Doaf* 'village', *Joa* 'year'.

7.5 [uɒ] derives from:

(i) MHG *uo*: *Huad* 'hat', *Schua* 'shoe'.

(ii) MHG *ur, uor*: *Duascht* 'thirst'.

7.6 [ɔ͂ɒ] has developed from MHG *ei, uo* before MHG nasals: *hoamli* 'secret', *tua(n)* 'to do'.

7.7 [aε] derives from:

(i) MHG *î*: *Wai* 'woman', *baissn* 'to bite'.

(ii) MHG *ei* in certain words under the influence of church language and NHG or upper-class speech: *Gaisd* 'spirit', *Flaisch* 'flesh, meat', *Kaisa* 'emperor'.

(iii) MHG *iü*: *daidsch* 'German', *Haisa* 'houses', *nai*[1] 'new'.

(iv) MHG *öu*: *Hai* 'hay', *Kaiffa* 'buyer'.

Nasalized [a͂ε] derives from the same sources before MHG nasals, e.g. *Wai(n)* 'wine'.

7.8 [ɑo] derives from:

(i) MHG *û*: *Maus* 'mouse', *Brau* 'custom', but see § 6.5 (ii).

(ii) MHG *ou*: *ea haud* 'he strikes', *Schaua* 'shower', see § 6.5 (ii).

Before MHG *n*: [ɑ͂o] *brau(n)* 'brown'.

7.9 [εo] is a typically rural, central Upper Austrian diphthong, for which urban speech usually has [ɔ], see § 6.6 (iii) and Note 6. It derives from:

(i) MHG *ô*: *Teod* 'death', *greoss* 'big'.

(ii) MHG *o* before *r, cht, chs*: *Teochta* 'daughter'.

7.10 The following four diphthongs have arisen through the vocalization of a former *l* after certain MHG vowels.[2] They are still general in rural dialects, but urban speakers frequently restore a velar *l* under the influence of NHG, especially after *a* and *o* in stressed positions.

(i) [ay] < MHG *î, û, iu, æ, ei, ou, öu* + *l*, e.g. *hei'n* 'to cure', *Tei(l)* 'part', *Mäu(l)* 'mouth', *wei(l)* 'because', *fahln* 'to go wrong'.

(ii) [oe] < MHG *ol*: *Goed* 'gold', *voe* 'full'.

(iii) [ɔe] < MHG *a, â* + *l*: *Tâe* 'valley', *Mâhe* 'meal'.

(iv) [ui] < MHG *ul, uol*: *Schuid* 'guilt', *Schui* 'school'.

---

[1] MHG *iu* was unmutated in Bav. before *r, w*, hence conservative rural speech has *eo*: *neo, deo* 'dear'.

[2] Cf. C. Selmer, 'Velarization and u- vocalization of l in German dialects', *PMLA*, xlviii, 1933, 220–44; 'Palatalization and i- vocalization of l in present German dialects', *GR*, viii, 1933, 124–36; 'Die Herkunft der Palatalisierung und Mouillierung des l- Lautes in deutschen Dialekten', *PMLA*, i, 1935, 1200–22.

§ 8. Unstressed Vowels

In native simple words only the following unstressed vowels occur frequently: [ɒ, i, y, e].

8.1 [ɒ] is the most frequent unstressed vowel. It occurs in the following cases:

(i) In the prefixes *da-* (NHG *er-*), *va-* (NHG *ver-*): *dafriasn* 'to freeze', *valia'n* 'to lose'.

(ii) In the endings: (*a*) -*a* (NHG -*er*): *Muada* 'mother', *schena* 'more beautiful'; deriving from former -*en* after the nasal consonants and after *k*, *ch* and *f*:[1] *nema* 'to take', *tringga* 'to drink', *stecka* 'stick', *låcha* 'to laugh', *kaffa* 'to buy'; in reduced compounds, e.g. *Sunnda* 'Sunday'; (*b*) -*ad*: in the past subjunctive *håedad* 'to hold', *zindad* 'to set alight'; in the pres. part. *låchad* 'laughing'; (*c*) -*al*, the diminutive (< -*erl*): *Heatzal* 'heart'; (*d*) -*ast*, superlative ending after *sch*, *st*, *z*: *kiazast* 'shortest'; (*e*) -*an*, adjectival ending denoting materials, e.g. *saidan* 'silken'.

8.2 [y] deriving from -*el* mainly after labials: *Gåwü* 'fork', *Kepfü* 'head'.

8.3 [i] in the endings -*i* (< MHG -*ic*, -*ec*): *ledi* 'unmarried'; -*li* (< MHG -*lîh*) *gmiadli* 'jolly'; -*isch*, -*ing*, -*in* (*Bairin* 'farmer's wife'), -*nis*.

8.4 [e] (i) in adjectival endings generalized from MHG -*iu*: *en å(n)gsëhgne Bairin* 'a respected farmer's wife', and in *ohne* 'without'.

(ii) In the prefixes *be-* and *ge-* under certain conditions in which the vowel has not been dropped, e.g. *bedriagn* 'to cheat' (mainly under NHG influence); *Geduid* 'patience', *geboa'n* 'born' (only before labial and dental stops).

8.5 [u] in the ending -*ung*: *Zaidung* 'newspaper'.

§ 9. Comparison with the NHG Vowels

(1) In Upper Austrian, quantity is now a function of the syllabic structure, which permits length also before consonantal clusters provided these are lenis. Seen historically Middle Bav. and NHG share the *Leichtinnendehnung*, but the *Schwerschlussdehnung* is typical of the former.

(2) Two diphthongs continue the MHG diphthongs *ie, uo, üe*, which are monophthongized in NHG.

(3) Although MHG *î, û, iu* are diphthongized as in NHG, the product of MHG *î* is distinguished from the reflex of MHG *ei* in contrast to NHG.

---

[1] After *f*, conservative central Upper Austrian has a nasal ending, thus *kaffm* 'to buy', *Pfaiffm* 'pipe', *Ofm* 'stove'. Our author has the eastern Upper Austrian and general Mid.-Bav. -*a*, e.g. *kaffa*, etc. See Kranzmayer, *Lautgeogr.*, § 46h and map 24.

(4) Unrounding has obliterated the MHG and NHG differences between long and short *i*—*ü* (but see (5)), short and long *e*—*ö*.

(5) In rural dialect a distinction is still made between mutated MHG *iu* (> *ai*) and unmutated MHG *iu* (> *eo*) which both become *eu* in NHG.

(6) Vocalization of postvocalic *l* has produced a new set of rounded front vowels in Upper Austrian.

(7) The e- series is characterized by a sharp difference between the reflexes of MHG *e*, *ē* on the one hand and *ä* on the other, which have all coalesced in NHG.

(8) There are many short, tense vowels in Upper Austrian.

(9) In conservative dialect the reflex of MHG *ô* (a monophthong in NHG) is diphthongized (*eo*).

(10) General nasalization of all vowels before nasal consonants in Upper Austrian.

(11) Absence of umlaut of OHG *u* in many words before velar fortis stops. Cf. *rucka*: NHG *rücken*.

(12) The Upper German apocope of final -*e* distinguishes Upper Austrian from NHG.

Chief Vowel Correspondences

U.Au.[1]	e(ē) a	ai (eo)	au eo oa	ia ua	ē i
MHG	e, ē, ö ä, æ	î öu, iü(iu)	û, ou ô ei	ie, üe uo	ē, ē̆, œ i, ü
NHG	e(ä) ö e(ä)	ei eu/äu	au o ei	ie[i:]ü u	e ö i, ü

NHG	e, ä	ei eu/äu	au o	ie[i:]ü u	ee, öh i ü
MHG	e, ē ä, æ	î ei öu iü(iu)	û ou ô	ie, üe uo	ē, ē̆, œ i ü
U.Au.	e(ē) a	ai oa ai (eo)	au eo	ia ua	ē i

[1] For the phonetic value of the letters, see § 5. MHG and NHG sounds are given in their respective orthography.

THE CONSONANTS

§ 10. THE CONSONANTAL SYSTEM

Stops		Fricatives		Affricates		Sonants		
fortis	lenis	fortis	lenis	fortis	lenis	nasals	liquids	semi-vowels
p	b	f	v	(pf	bv)	m		w
t	d	s š	z ž	(ts, tš	dz, dž)	n	l, r	j
k	g	x	γ	(kh)		ŋ		h

P

10.1 Stops, fricatives and affricates lack any significant amount of voicing, while the sonants are voiced (except *h*). The opposition of fortis : lenis is limited to medial and final position. Initially it is neutralized in a semi-fortis sound. [kh] occurs only initially before vowels. It stands clearly outside the phonemic pattern and is best regarded as a cluster of a fortis allophone of /k/ + /h/. The affricates can also be regarded as clusters. The liquids, in rural dialects at least, are severely restricted in occurrence: /l/ occurs only initially before vowels, medially after consonants and between vowels, and finally after dental consonants and after vowels as a syllabic (the morpheme -*l* in the diminutive);[1] /r/ shares these positions except the final one.[2] /h/ and /j/ occur only initially before vowels, /h/ also initially after [k]. The bilabial /w/ does not occur finally.

Similar restrictions are imposed on some fricatives: /x/ does not occur initially[3] and /s/ does not occur initially before consonants.

The fortis consonants, which are longer than the corresponding NHG voiceless consonants, occur only after a short vowel (including a short diphthong), the lenis consonants only after a long vowel. (On the phonemic interpretation, see § 4.) In final clusters only lenis consonants can combine with lenis and only fortis with fortis. But with nasals both lenis or fortis are possible.

10.2 The present-day distribution of lenis and fortis and their link with vowel quantity has come about in consequence of two late-medieval processes. One affected vowel quantity and the other the character of the consonants. The MHG vowel quantity was radically altered by lengthening of short vowels in open syllables (*Leichtinnendehnung*) and by lengthening of short vowels in all monosyllabic words (*Leichtschlussdehnung* before lenis, *Schwerschlussdehnung* before fortis). The corollary was the shortening of long vowels before fortis consonants in dissyllabic words. After 1300, four-fifths of all word-forms became affected by the Middle-Bavarian lenition,[4] which changed the inherited Bavarian consonantism fundamentally. This lenition shares a number of features with the *binnenhochdeutsche Konsonantenschwächung*[5] but is also different in many ways. The Middle-Bavarian lenition involves the following changes: (1) initially

---

[1] But see §§ 4; 6.10; 7.10.

[2] Conservative rural dialects have *r* also in final post-vocalic position, cf. *lar*: urban *la* 'empty'; *Baur*: *Baua* 'peasant'.

[3] Since [h] and [x] are in complementary distribution Koekkoek, *op. cit.*, p. 44, regards [h] as an allophone of [x]. But the phonetic dissimilarity is considerable (palato-velar against glottal), and no other fricatives have a similar allophonic distribution. However, there is no doubt that [h] fills a gap in the pattern, which in the case of the other fricatives does not exist.

[4] Kranzmayer, *Lautgeogr.*, p. 95.

[5] See chap. iv, § 12, and P. Lessiak, *Beiträge zur Geschichte des deutschen Konsonantismus*, 1933.

all fortes coalesce with the former lenes in a series of semi-fortes, except the former affricate *kh-* (< Gmc. *k*) which is, in prevocalic position, still distinguished from the reflex of MHG *g*; (2) all MHG fortes and geminates in final position become lenes; all MHG fortes in medial position become lenes. Where we now have a medial or final fortis consonant it derives from a MHG medial geminate *pp, tt, kk, ss, zz, tz, ff, pf, hh, kch,* or *sk, st, ft, cht,*[1] or medial or final *sp, hs.* E.g. *Fuas—Fiass* 'foot—feet'; *Kobf—Kepf* 'head—heads'; *Bog—Beck* 'buck'; *Weda* 'weather', *Bett* 'bed'. (3) MHG lenes are preserved as lenes, or, in the case of *b* and *d,* lost medially and occasionally finally, e.g. *re'n* 'to talk', *Re'gn* 'rain', *ge'm* 'to give', *Bua* 'boy', *Wai* 'woman'. (4) Vocalization of former *r, l* after a vowel.

§ 11. SPELLING

In initial position, where there is no contrast between lenis and fortis, the NHG orthography can be safely retained. *K* before a vowel is an aspirated fortis, all other letters represent semi-fortes. Medially and finally fortis and lenis consonants will have to be carefully marked, not only because they contrast, but also because they are to indicate the length of the preceding vowel. The orthography of our author has had to be amended correspondingly.

The following spellings are adopted.

Phoneme	Letter	Phoneme	Letter	Phoneme	Letter
b	b	v	v, f	bv	bf
d	d	z	s	dz	z
g	g	γ	ch	m, n, ŋ	m, n, ng (gn) (3)
p	p	f	ff	pf	pf
t	t, dt	s	ss (1)	ts	tz
k	k, ck	x	ch (2)	l, r	l, (4) r
kh	k	ž, š	sch (2)	w, j, h	w, j, h

Notes

(1) The spelling *st* has the same values as in NHG; *sp* is always [šp].

(2) In order to avoid doubling of those combinations of letters the lenis consonants are marked by the doubling of the preceding vowels. Diphthongs are marked by a length sign in such cases.

---

[1] A. Pfalz, 'Die Mundart des Marchfeldes', *Sitzungsberichte der Akad. d. Wiss. in Wien,* Phil.-hist. Kl., 170, 1913, describes the distribution of vowel quantity before these last three clusters as being dependent on the number of syllables in the MHG word, but Roitinger states that in the dialect of Weibern there is half-length with semi-fortis, irrespective of the number of syllables in the MHG word. The practice of my informants seems to follow the dialect of the Marchfeld.

(3) Where [ŋ] is the product of assimilation of a former *g* + *n* or *h* + *n* the spelling *gn* is retained to facilitate recognition.

(4) Where *l* occurs in the text in postvocalic-preconsonantal position it is pronounced even by the more conservative of my informants.

§ 12. THE CONSONANT PHONEMES

12.1 [p, t, k] are unaspirated fortis stops occurring medially and finally and deriving from:

(i) MHG stop geminates in medial position: *tråppm* 'to stump', *spottn* 'to mock', *keck* 'impertinent'.

(ii) MHG stops after nasals, especially before further consonants: *Lampü* 'lamb', *hintn* (*t* with nasal release, or replaced by a glottal stop), *singst* 'sing' 2nd pers. sg. pres.

(iii) MHG stops in certain other consonantal clusters: *Wuascht* 'sausage', *miaka* 'to notice' (< *rk*), *wåchsn* 'to grow' [*ks* < *hs*], *Kestl* 'kettle' (arisen as a glide between *s* and *l*).[1]

(iv) NHG: *Datum* 'date'.

12.2 [b, d, g] are voiceless lenis stops. In initial position they are semi-fortis and do not contrast with fortis stops. They represent:

(i) The MHG fortis stops in those positions not mentioned in § 12.1: *Bred* 'board', *Vedan* 'cousins', *Schriad* 'step', *Speg* 'bacon', *Ködn* 'cold', *baidln*[2] 'to shiver'.

(ii) The MHG lenis stops which have not been dropped (see § 10.2): *Bruada* 'brother', *liab* 'dear', *Tåg* 'day', *Waiba* and *Waiwa* 'women'.

12.3 [f, s, š, x] are fortis fricatives which continue the MHG fortis (geminate) fricatives in medial position: *kaffa* 'to buy', *Wåssa* 'water', *Fiass* 'feet', *Fresch* 'frogs', *båcha* 'to bake', *låcha* 'to laugh'.

12.4 [v, z, ž, γ] are the corresponding lenis fricatives. In initial position they (excluding *ch*) are semi-fortes and do not contrast with fortis fricatives. They represent:

(i) MHG final fortis fricatives: *Fuas* 'foot', *Ros* 'horse', *Froosch* 'frog', *wōach*[3] 'soft'.

(ii) MHG lenis fricatives *f* and *s*: *Ofa* 'stove', *Hof* 'farm', *losn* 'to listen', *friasn* 'to freeze'.

12.5 The distribution of the lenis and fortis affricates, which are preferably regarded as clusters rather than as unit phonemes, corresponds to that of the fricatives and stops. Thus: *Kobf* 'head' but pl. *Kepf*, *Såez* 'salt', *Siz* 'seat', *sitzn* 'to sit'.

---

[1] On the fortis *t* in the def. art., see § 13.

[2] In syllables deriving from MHG *-ten*, *-tel* the character of the dental stop varies according to the carefulness of the articulation. It may be replaced by a glottal stop or be realized merely as a syllabic ŋ or a syllabic velar ļ.

[3] MHG *ch* in final position has usually dropped, e.g. *Bå* 'brook', *Jo* 'yoke'.

12.6 [kh] corresponds, historically speaking, to MHG initial *k* before vowels: *kåed* 'cold', but *gloa(n)* 'small'; and to MHG *geh-*, e.g. *ghoam* 'secret'.

12.7 The occurrence of the nasals and liquids has much changed in comparison with MHG. Assimilation and loss in final position in monosyllabic words has determined the history of the nasals, and vocalization in any but pre-vocalic position that of the liquids.

(i) Final [m] has resulted from assimilation of *b* + *n*: *ge'm* 'to give'; *w* + *n*: *schnai'm* 'to snow'; *f* + *n*:[1] *Ofm* 'stove'; *p* + *n*: *Kåppm* 'cap'.

(ii) Final [ŋ] has resulted from assimilation of *g* + *n*: *saugn* 'to suck'; *h* + *n*:[2] *gschëhgn* 'to happen'.

(iii) Nasalization of the root-vowel is the only trace of a former final *n* in monosyllabic words, e.g. *Må(nn)* 'man', *i kå(nn)* 'I can'.

(iv) On the occurrence of the liquids, see §§ 4; 7.10; 10.1. Both are frontal except [l] which after consonants is velar. An historically unjustified *r* is frequently used to break the hiatus, e.g. *wia-r-i*: NHG *wie ich*.

12.8 [w] is a voiced bilabial semi-vowel without lip-rounding. It represents:

(i) MHG initial *w*: *Winta* 'winter', and medial *w* in *ewi* 'eternal'.

(ii) MHG *b* before *-el*, *-er*: *Waiwa* 'women'.

12.9 [j] is a voiced palatal semi-vowel occurring only initially before vowels. It represents MHG *j* in that position, e.g *Jo* 'yoke'.

12.10 [h] continues MHG *h* only in initial position, e.g. *Hoamad* 'home'.

§ 13. ASSIMILATION

Bavarian dialects are particularly prone to assimilations. The changes brought about in the case of nasal suffixes are discussed in § 12.7. For the rest we have to distinguish between (1) historical assimilations, e.g. *Braigga* 'bridegroom', *mumpfeln* 'mumble', *Pfiat di God* 'may God protect you' (*bh-* > *pf-*), *fimf* 'five'; and (2) sandhi assimilations. The latter are to some extent dependent on the speed with which the sentences are spoken, but in compounds and in the case of the article *d* (a fortis) assimilations are general. The dental stops and the dental nasal are assimilated to labials and velars either by being changed to labials or velars, i.e. *n* and *d* before *f*, *m*; *n* before *g*, *k*, or by being absorbed, i.e. *d* before *b*, *g*, *k*. Resulting from this

---

[1] Assimilation after *f* holds good only for those Upper Austrian areas where former *-en* has not become *-a* (see § 8.1 (ii)).

[2] This assimilation is urban. Rural speech has *-a* < MHG *-en* after velars, e.g. *sëha: sëhgn* 'to see'.

absorption we get initial long fortis stops,[1] e.g. *d'Bairin* 'the farmer's wife' [p-], *d'Dean* 'the maid' [t-], *d'Goas* 'the goat' [k-], *mid̮gēh(n)* 'to accompany' [-k-], *d'Kuchl* 'the kitchen' [kh-], *d'Cilli* 'Cecilia' [ts-]. The dental stop or nasal is made homorganic in: *d'Fåschingszaid* 'carnival' [pf-], *d'Muada* 'mother' [pm-], *fain' Glaseln* 'fine glasses' [-ŋg-], *koan Fraid* 'no joy' [-mv-], *gehn ma* 'let's go' [-m-], *miass ma* ($< n + m$) 'we must'.

§ 14. COMPARISON WITH THE NHG CONSONANTS

The most salient differences are:

(1) Intensity plays, to a limited extent, the part which intensity and voice together play in NHG. In initial position there is only one series of voiceless semi-fortis stops and fricatives. Medially the inherited contrast of fortis and lenis is less well preserved in Upper Austrian than in NHG. Only the formerly medial geminate fortis is regularly distinguished from the lenis.

(2) The historical NHG distinction between initial *d* and *t* (*Dach*, *Tag*), *b* and *p* (*bar*, *Paar*) or *g* and *k* before consonants (*grob*, *Krug*) is not retained.

(3) Where NHG has a medial lenis *b*, *d*, *g* before a nasal suffix, Middle Bavarian has generally dropped the stops.

(4) Where NHG has a final *ch* this has frequently been lost in Upper Austrian (NHG *Bach*: *Bå*).

(5) A final nasal is generally assimilated to the preceding consonant.

(6) The final position is not marked by neutralization of the two stop and fricative series.

(7) The fortis stops are unaspirated in Upper Austrian.

(8) The liquids *r* and *l* are severely restricted in distribution.

(9) The dialect lacks the glottal stop onset.

MORPHOLOGY

NOUNS AND ARTICLES

§ 15. FORMATION OF THE PLURAL

Three historical processes have determined the plural formation

---

[1] See A. Pfalz, 'Phonetische Beobachtungen an der Mundart des Marchfeldes in Niederösterreich', *ZfdMa.*, 1911, pp. 244–60; F. Roitinger, 'Zur Partizipialbildung in den eo- Mundarten Oberösterreichs', *ZfMaf.*, xx, 1951, 114–17, describes these long fortes as follows: 'Leniseinsatz zur Fortisstärke anschwellend und explodierend.' He adds that these long fortes (cf. *potenzierte Fortis*, chap. ii, § 14.4) arise also in the case of the syncopated prefix MHG *ge-* before *d*, *b*, *g*, *z*, *pf*, *k*, e.g. *dengga—dtenkt* 'to think', *baissn—bpissn* 'to bite' (p. 116), but only in conservative dialect, while Middle Bav. generally has no trace of this verbal prefix before stops. Further examples in G. Weitzenböck, *Die Mundart des Innviertels besonders von Mühlheim, ZfMaf. Beiheft 17*, Halle, 1942, pp. 112–14.

of the present dialect (*a*) the loss of a former final *-e*, (*b*) the preservation of the MHG ending *-en* as a nasal suffix and the extension of
the use of this nasal suffix, (*c*) the Middle-Bavarian lenition (§ 10.2).
Five types of plural formation can be distinguished:

Type A: plural not marked by ending or mutation.
Type B: plural marked by mutation.
Type C: plural marked by change of lenis to fortis.
Type D: plural marked by nasal suffix.[1]
Type E: plural marked by ending *-a* (< *-er*) with mutation where
possible.

Note: All back vowels are capable of mutating. The correspondences are:

Back vowel:	å	o	u	au	ua	oa
Mutated vowel:	a/e	e	i	ai	ia	ea

For the sound values of these letters, see § 5. The morphologically
active and most frequent umlaut of *å* is *a*, e.g. *Grå'm—Gra'm* 'ditch',
but a few mutations go back to the primary umlaut of OHG (see
§ 6.2), e.g. *Åsd—Est* 'branch', *Ståd—Sted* 'town'.

Type A. To this type belong:
(i) Many neuter nouns: *Schåf* 'sheep', *Tåe* 'valley'.
(ii) A few masc. nouns, especially those with a front vowel: *Schriad*
'step', *Weg* 'path', *Bam* 'tree', and *nomina agentis* in *-a*.
(iii) A few masc. nouns ending in a nasal in the sg., e.g. *Besn*
'broom', and the two neuters *Augn* 'eye', *Oa'n* 'ear'.
(iv) A large number of fem. nouns, i.e. those ending in a nasal in
the sg.: *Flåschn* 'bottle', *Nåsn* 'nose', *Suppm* 'soup', *Gåssn* 'lane',
Stiagn 'stairs'.

Type B. To this type belong:
(i) A fairly large number of masc. nouns, especially those with a
mutatable root-vowel: *Ståb—Stab* 'stick', *Wågn—Wagn* 'carriage',
Hof—Hef 'farm', *Nåm—Nam* 'name'.
(ii) Most of those fem. nouns which mutate in NHG: *Braud—Braid*
'fiancée', *Maus—Mais* 'mouse'.
(iii) A special sub-group is formed by those nouns which have a
lenis in the sg. and a fortis in the pl.: *Flus—Fliss* 'river', *Rog—Reck*
'skirt', *Tånz—Tantz* 'dance', *Kobf—Kepf* 'head', *Plåz—Platz* 'square',
Bå—Bach 'stream'.

Type C. To this type belongs a small group of masc. nouns where
the pl. is indicated by a change of final consonant only: *Grif—*

---

[1] This nasal (< MHG *n*) may for historical or contextual reasons be either
dental, labial or velar (see § 12.7).

Griff 'grip', *Füsch—Fisch* 'fish', *Tüsch—Tisch* 'table', *Fleg—Fleck* 'spot'.

Type D. To this type belong:

(i) All those fem. nouns not showing mutation and not having a nasal ending in the sg. (see Type A): *Roas—Roasn* 'journey', *Goasl—Goasln* 'whip', *Zaid—Zaidn* 'time', *Wocha—Wochan*[1] 'week'. A few fem. nouns ending in a nasal root have an extended pl. ending *-an*: *Muam—Muaman* 'aunts'.

(ii) The majority of masc. nouns denoting animate beings: *Gsö—Gsö'n* 'fellow', *Veda—Vedan* 'cousin', *Bua—Bua'm* 'boy', *Dokta—Doktan* 'doctor'.

Type E. To this type belong:

(i) The majority of the neuter nouns: *Guad—Giada* 'farmstead', *Büd—Büda* 'picture', *Bred—Breda* 'board'.

(ii) A few masc. nouns: *Må(nn)—Måna* 'man'. Some nouns show evidence of the Mid.-Bav. lenition: *Då—Dacha* 'roof'.

§ 16. Case Forms

(i) There is one group of masc. nouns (Type D (ii)) which distinguish in the sg. between a subject (nom.) and an object case by adding a nasal suffix in the latter function. E.g. Nom. *Bua* 'boy', *Våda* 'father', *Baua* 'farmer': obj. case *Bua'm, Vådan, Bauan*. This applies also to the masc. names, e.g. *Frånz—Frånzn*, and the neuter *Heatz* 'heart', e.g. *ban Heatzn* (27).[2]

(ii) A nasal suffix also distinguishes the dat. pl. from the other pl. forms except in Type D fem. nouns, e.g. A *mid n Diabm* 'with the thieves'; B *ban Kia'n* 'with the cows'; C *aff n Tischn* 'on the tables'; E *aff n Giadan* 'on the farms'. After a vowel or a nasal the ending is *-an*, e.g. *Bam* 'tree': *Baman; mid n Augnan* 'with the eyes'. Conservative dialect has a secondary dat. pl. suffix *-a* or *-an* also in the case of Type D nouns, esp. masc., e.g. *va de Bua'ma* or *Bua'man*.

(iii) Relic forms show the old genitive, e.g. *um Gods Wü'n*, cf. NHG *um Gottes Willen*; otherwise the usual dat. paraphrase is used for the possessive, e.g. *en Lenzbauan sai(n) Rosal*. Other genitival functions are expressed by prepositions, e.g. *de Nåchbauan van Lenzhof*.

§ 17. Gender

A number of nouns have a gender different from that of the corresponding NHG word, e.g. *Eck* n. 'corner', *Zipfü* n. 'tip', *Krippü* n.

---

[1] This noun once belonged to Type A (iv). After *ch* former *-en* > *-a* (§ 8.1 (ii)); *-an* in the pl. is thus historically a double pl. ending.
[2] Such bracketed numbers refer to the stanzas of the text.

'cripple', *Tölla* n. 'plate', *Huastn* f. 'cough', *Mensch* n. 'female servant', *Laid* in the sg. in the sense of 'person' is n.

§ 18. THE DECLENSION OF THE DEFINITE ARTICLE

Each gender distinguishes only between two cases, but while masc. has a common object case and a subject case, the other genders mark a dative and have a common case for subject and direct object.

	m.	*f.*	*n.*	*pl.*
Nom.	da⎫	d, (3) de (2)⎫	s, des (2)⎫	d, (3) de (2)
Acc. Dat.	⎬ en ,(4) den (2)	da	en, (4) den (2)	en, (4) den (2)

Notes

(1) *E* is [e], *a* is [ɒ].

(2) The forms *de, den, des* are used before an adjective, e.g. *de liab Frau* but *d Frau*.

(3) The syncopated form *d* (a fortis) is used in unstressed positions before nouns and is assimilated to labial and velar initial consonants (see § 13). Conservative dialects have a more restricted use, usually confining the short form to the position before vowels and sonants.

(4) A more reduced form *n* is used after prepositions, e.g. *mid n Fränzn*. Sandhi assimilations occur in rapid speech, e.g. *em Vddan, eng Kindan* (pl.).

(5) Personal names regularly take the def. art., e.g. *da Fränz, d Cilli*. Altogether the art. is indispensable with most nouns, e.g. *A Glick soe e hâm!*, NHG *Glück soll er haben! Des gibt iha en Muad* (7), NHG *das gibt ihr Mut*, cf. Note 19.

§ 19. THE DECLENSION OF THE INDEFINITE ARTICLE

	m.	*f.*	*n.*
Nom.	a ⎫	⎫	a
Acc.	⎬	a ⎬	
Dat.	an ⎭	⎭	an

§ 20. AGGLUTINATIONS

Prepositions fuse with the def. art. *en* (§ 18) in the following way: *in* (NHG *im, in den*), *zan, van, ban, an* or *en, am, iban* (NHG *zum, zu den, vom, von den, beim, bei den, am, an den, auf dem, auf den, über dem*, etc.).

ADJECTIVES

The weak and strong declensions are used according to the same rules as in NHG.

§ 21. The Strong Declension

	m.	f.	n.	pl.
Nom.	schlechda	} schlechde	} schlechds	} schlechde
Acc. }	schlechdn			
Dat. }		schlechdn	schlechdn	schlechdn

Notes

(1) The nasal suffixes are realized as -*a* after *m* or *ng* (see § 8.1 (ii)), or assimilated to labial and velar consonants (see § 12.7), e.g. *ban hausheochn Fåll* (39), *am långa Weg*. Adjectives ending in -*n* fuse the nasal ending with the root consonant and those ending in -*s* or -*sch* fuse the *s*- suffix of the neuter, e.g. *a greoss's miass ma håm* (22).

(2) After prepositions the attributive adj. in the pl. has the form of the nom., e.g. *mid goedane Ranftln* (69).

§ 22. The Weak Declension

	m.	f.	n.	pl.
Nom.	schlechd	} schlechd, -e (2)	} schlechd, -e (2)	
Acc. }	schlechdn			} schlechdn
Dat. }		schlechdn	schlechdn	

Notes

(1) Note 1 of the preceding paragraph applies here as well, e.g. *de å(n)gsēhgna Laid*; *fia de åama Sœ'n*; *de fain Glaseln* (69).

(2) Fem. and n. common case can also end in -*e*, cf. *de wåhre Liab, des schene Gschia* (69) but *de liab Frau*. After the indef. art. *a* strong forms are used, e.g. *a soetsåme Håtzat* 'a strange wedding'.

§ 23. Comparison

The comparative ends in -*a*, and root-vowels capable of mutating usually mutate, e.g. *gloa(n)—gleana* 'small'. The superlative ends in -*st* (or -*ast*), e.g. *grēsst* 'biggest', *schenst* 'finest', but the form of the comparative is preferred to that of the superlative, so that the context alone indicates the degree, e.g. *fia mi is s am bessan* (44) = sup., *du hettst mi en liaban* (47) = sup. The comparative particle is *des*.

NUMERALS

§ 24

The numeral for 'two' distinguishes between the genders *zwe* or *zwen* (m.), *zwo* (f.), *zwoa* (n.), but *zwoa* is gaining ground. *Oa* 'one' declines like a strong adj. when used attributively and like a weak adj. when used as a noun with the def. art., e.g. *da oa*, etc. When referring to hours the numerals end in -*i* or -*e*, e.g. *naini* '9 o'clock'.

PRONOUNS

§ 25. PERSONAL PRONOUNS

		1st Person	2nd Person	3rd Person		
Nom.	sg.	i	du, d, - (1)	ea, e, a	}se, si, s	}es, s, as
Acc.	sg.	mich, mi	dich, di	n (2)		
Dat.	sg.	mia, ma	dia, da	eahm	iha	eahm
Gen. (3)	sg.	maina	daina	saina	(saina)	saina
Nom.	pl.	mia, ma	es, s, -	}se, si, s		
Acc.	pl.	}ins (4)	}enk			
Dat.	pl.			eahn (-a)		

Notes

(1) In inversion and after prepositions the least stressed, most re-duced forms are used,[1] e.g. *håsd*: NHG *hast du*; *håma*: NHG *haben wir*; *des wissts ēh*: NHG *das wisst ihr ja*.

(2) This occurs only enclitically, e.g. *es druckt n* (27), otherwise *eahm* is used, e.g. *fia eahm* 'for him', *wei(l)s eahm håed ned . . . måg* (8).

(3) The genitive sg. occurs only after the prepositions *ne'm, gegn, wegn, iba, unta, hinta, voa, nåch, ohne*, especially when stressed.

(4) The form *uns* borrowed from NHG is now an alternative.

(5) The indefinite personal pronoun is *ma* (before vowels often with inorganic -*r*: *mar*), object case *oan*.

§ 26. REFLEXIVE PRONOUNS

The special form *si, se*, 3rd pers. sg. and pl., occurs only in un-stressed positions in the acc., otherwise the personal pronouns in the dat. serve as reflexive pronouns, e.g. *drum låssens eahn Zaid*: NHG . . . *lassen Sie sich Zeit*; *si kennd si guad aus* (10); *hiatzt büd a eahm ai(n)*: NHG *jetzt bildet er sich ein*.

§ 27. POSSESSIVE PRONOUNS

They are *mai(n), dai(n), sai(n), iha, insa, enka, eahna*.

(i) *Mai(n), dai(n), sai(n)* decline as follows:

	m.	*f.*	*n.*	*pl.*
Nom.	mai(n) }	mai(n) }	mai(n) }	maine
Acc. }	main	main	main	
Dat. }				

[1] Cf. A. Pfalz, 'Suffigierung der Personalpronomina im Donaubairischen', *Sitzungsberichte der Akad. d. Wiss. in Wien*, Phil.-hist. Kl., vol. 190, Vienna, 1919.

Notes

(1) The fem. sg. common case being endingless, a following adjective is strong, e.g. *mai(n) oanzige Teochta*.

(2) The substantivized form *da mai(n)* or *da maine* is preceded by the def. art. as in NHG.

(ii) *Insa, enka, iha* (3rd pers. sg. fem.), *eahna* (3rd pers. pl.) take the suffix *-n* in the same cases as *mai(n)* and *-e* in the pl., e.g. *za enkan Paarl*: NHG *zu euerem Pärchen*; *eahne Stiahl sand laa*: NHG *ihre Stühle sind leer*; but *eahn* in the oblique cases, e.g. *in eahn Zimma* (dat.).

§ 28. DEMONSTRATIVE PRONOUNS

There are no forms corresponding to NHG *dieser, jener* and the chief dem. pron. is:

	m.	f.	n.	pl.
Nom.	dea	de	des (3)	de
Acc.	dcn	de	des (3)	de
Dat.	dcn	dea	den	den (2)

Notes

(1) The length of the vowels varies with the amount of emphasis. The unstressed forms function as the def. articles.

(2) There is also an extended form *denan*, and all forms can be combined with *då*, e.g. *de då*.

(3) In the sense of 'that' *dås* is used, and *dasoebig* or *dasel* (NHG *der selbe*) function also as demonstratives.

(4) For 'such' the dialect uses *aso a, so a, sotta, secha*.

§ 29. INTERROGATIVE PRONOUNS

	Nom.	*Obj.*
who?	wea	wen
what?	wås	
which?	wela, -e, -es	welen (m. n. sg.)
	wås fira	

§ 30. INDEFINITE PRONOUNS

oana, -e, oas; acc. m., dat. m., n. *oan*, dat. f. *oana* } somebody
eamd, wea
koana (goes like *oana*) } nobody
neamd
wås   something
a weng   some, a little
nix   nothing
vü   much, many
månig, menig   many

etla	some, several
e pȧȧa	a few
eniada, -e, -s	each, every
ȧlle, dat. *ȧen, ȧesȧnd* (pl.)	all
ȧess, dat. *ȧen* (sg.)	all
koa(n) (goes like *mai(n)*, § 27)	no

§ 31. Relative Pronouns

Like NHG Up. Austrian uses the dem. pron. in this function. The use of *wo* is also known.

VERBS

§ 32. Forms and Classification

The verb has the following simple form classes and tenses: infinitive, imperative, past participle, present indicative, past subjunctive (= conditional), present participle. The compound tenses and forms are: perfect, pluperfect, a passive and a conditional.

32.1 The infinitive ends in a nasal consonant, in *-a*, or is endingless.

(i) *Nasal.* The character of the nasal is determined by the preceding sounds (see §§ 8.1 (ii); 12.7). It is *-m*: after present or former labial stops or fricatives, e.g. *trai'm* 'drive', *trȧppm* 'stalk', *schlȧffm*[1] 'sleep'; *-ŋ*: after former *g* or *h*, e.g. *sȧgn* 'say', *sēhgn* 'see'; *-n*: after present or former dentals or liquids, e.g. *raidn* 'ride', *lesn* 'read', *spia'n* 'sense', *moan* 'mean'.

(ii) *-a*, if the root ends in *k, ch, m, n* (< *nn*), *ng*, or *f* (see § 8.1 (ii)), e.g. *stecka* 'stick', *mȧcha* 'make', *kema* 'come', *rena* 'run', *singa* 'sing', *schlȧffa* 'sleep'.

(iii) *Endingless*, with the root ending in a nasalized vowel, e.g. *gēh(n)* 'go', *stēh(n)* 'stand', *tua(n)* 'do', *drah(n)* 'turn', *mah(n)* 'mow', *nah(n)* 'sew', *wah(n)* 'blow', *bliah(n)* 'flower', *bemiah(n)* 'trouble', *gfrai(n)* 'please', *schau(n)* 'look', *hau(n)* 'hew', *schrai(n)* 'yell'.

The infinitive particle is *z*.

32.2 The imperative is identical with the pres. (in the sg. with the 1st pers. sg. pres.).

32.3 The present participle ends in *-ad* and declines like an adj., e.g. *lȧchad* 'laughing', *schraiad* 'yelling'.

32.4 The past participle ends either in *-d* (*weak verbs*) or *-n, -m, -ŋ, -a*, according to the rules applying to the infinitive ending (*strong verbs*). Verbs beginning with a vowel, a sonant or a fricative have the prefix *g-*. Before stops Mid-Bav. has generally no prefix, but the most conservative Up.-Aust. dialects have a fortis as a reflex of the former suffix (see § 13). Verbs in *-ian* (NHG *-ieren*) also have the prefix before the appropriate initial sound. *Wea'n* 'become' and

[1] Eastern Upper Austrian has *-a* after *f* (§ 8.1 (ii)).

låssn 'let' are without *g-*, as are the verbs with prefixes. Vowel alternation between pres. and p.p. occurs only in strong verbs and one weak verb (*bringa—bråchd* 'bring'); there is no *Rückumlaut*.

§ 33. Strong Verbs

Only strong verbs with *e* as the root-vowel of the inf. change to *i* (or *ü* before former *l*) in the sg. of the pres. According to stem alternants the following classes can be distinguished, leaving out of account the verbs ending in a nasalized vowel (§ 38):

I. Identical vowel in the inf. and p.p.:

(i) [ɔ] *wåchsn* 'grow', *blåsn* 'blow' (OHG VI and VII).

(ii) [ɔe] *fåen* 'fall', *måen* 'grind'.

(iii) [ɔɒ] *fåhan* 'ride'.

(iv) [e] *essn* 'eat', *ge'm* 'give', *kema* 'come' (OHG V). With mutation to *i* in the whole sg. of the pres.

(v) [ɛ] *sëhgn* 'see', *gschëhgn* 'happen' with the forms *i siag* or *siach*, *du siagst, e siacht* (*gschiacht*).

II. Vowel alternation [aɛ/i]: 22 verbs, e.g. *laidn—glidn* 'suffer', *blai'm—bli'm* 'stay' (OHG I).

III. Vowel alternation [iɒ/o]: 16 verbs, e.g. *biagn—bogn* 'bend', *schia'm—gscho'm* 'push'; with grammatical change and *oa* in p.p.: *friasn—gfroa'n* 'freeze', *valiasn—valoa'n* 'lose' (OHG II).

IV. Vowel alternation [ɪ/u]: 18 verbs, e.g. *bindn—bundn* 'bind', *singa—gsunga* (OHG III a).

V. Vowel alternation [e/o]: 8 verbs, all with mutation to *i* (or *ia*) in the sg. of the pres., e.g. *brecha—brocha* 'break', *dreschn—droschn* 'thresh'; with diphthong resulting from *r-* vocalization: *weaffa—gwoaffa* 'throw', *wea'n—woa'n* 'become' (OHG III and IV).

VI. Vowel alternation [œ/oe]: 6 verbs, with mutation to *ü* in the sg. pres., e.g. *stœ'n—gstoe'n* 'steal', *hœffa—ghoeffa* 'help' (OHG III and IV).

VII. Some isolated vowel alternations: *sauffa—gsoffa* 'drink', *nema—gnuma* 'take', *liegn—glegn* 'lie flat', *sitzn—gsessn* 'sit', *hoassn—ghoassn* 'be called'.

A number of formerly strong verbs have become weak, notably *bittn* 'beg', *pflegn* 'care'.

§ 34. The Present

The endings are: Sg. 1 -, 2 *-sd*, 3 *-d*; Pl. 1 *-n* (*-m, -an*), 2 *-ts*, 3 *-n* (*-m, -an, -and*), e.g. *nema* 'take':

i nim	*mia neman* (5)
du nimsd (3)	*es nemts* (6)
e nimd (4)	*si neman* (7)

Notes

(1) In the 1st pers. sg. strong verbs have generally a lenis (i.e. they are treated like MHG monosyllabics), e.g. *i bais* (*baissn* 'bite'), *i bid* (*bittn* 'beg'), but weak verbs with a fortis retain the fortis: *i griass* (*griassn* 'greet').

(2) The endings of the 2nd and 3rd pers. sg. are lenis after vowels and sonants but usually fortis or semi-fortis (with short root-vowel) after other consonants, especially clusters.

(3) If the root ends in a sibilant the ending is *-d*.

(4) If the root ends in a fortis dental stop there is no ending.

(5) The ending is *-n* after a dental (*mia lesn*); *-m* if the root of the sg. ends in *-b* (*mia ge'm*); *-an* after *k, ch, ng, m, n* (*mia måchan, mia bringan*). In inversion the ending is assimilated: *miass ma, re'ma; mia miassn, mia re'n*.

(6) Always with suffixed pronoun, also in the imperative, e.g. *kemmts Våda* (NHG *kommt Vater!*), *losts!* 'listen' (see § 25).

(7) Our author uses a two-form pl. Conservative dialects have a 3rd pers. pl. in *-nd* after dentals and *-and* after velars, labials and nasals (*si lesnd, si måchand*).

§ 35. THE CONDITIONAL[1]

35.1 Only a few strong verbs still form a strong past subj., e.g. *wea'n* 'become': *i wuad; nema* 'take': *i nam; ge'm* 'give: *i gab; liegn* 'lie flat': *i lag; gëh(n)* 'go': *i gang*.

35.2 The majority of strong verbs form their synthetic conditional in *-ad* in analogy to the weak verbs. The endings are: sg. 1, 3 *-ad*, 2 *-asd*; pl. 1, 3 *-adn*, 2 *-ats*. Some of the strong verbs given above have also weak forms, e.g. *nemad, gangad*. The conditional of *bringa* 'bring' is *bracht*. E.g. *schmeckad* (71), *sëhad* (80), *åes drahad si d Stu'm* (90).

35.3 There is also a periphrastic conditional consisting of inf. and past subj. of the auxiliaries *tua(n)* or *wea'n*, e.g. *es tad mi gfrai(n)* (NHG *es würde mich freuen*).

§ 36. THE COMPOUND TENSES AND THE PASSIVE

There are two compound tenses for the past, both formed by means of the auxiliaries *sai(n)* and *håm* and the p.p.

Perfect:	*es is gschëhgn;*	*si håd kennd*
Pluperfect (rare):	*es is geschëhgn gwen;*	*si håd kennd ghåbd.*

The auxiliary *wea'n* and the infinitive form a future tense which

---

[1] See J. Mindl, 'Der Konjunktiv in der Mundart des oberen Landls', *Teuth.*, i, 1924, 108–49.

is, however, mainly used to express a probability or to make an assumption, e.g. *wiad ma sëhgn* (63).

The passive is formed with *wea'n* as in NHG, e.g. *da Biadlmå(nn) wiad bstimmd* (5).

§ 37. THE MODAL AUXILIARIES

As in H.Alem. the modal auxiliaries have a common form for the inf. and the p.p. The following forms must be distinguished:

	Inf., P.P.	Sg. Pres. 1, 3	2	Pl. Pres. 1, 3	2	Condit.
'be able'	kina	kå(nn)	kånnsd	kinan (1)	kints	kunnd
'should like'	megn	måg	mågst	megn (2)	megts	mechd, megst
'must'	miassn	muas (3)	muast	miassn (1)	miassts	miassad(4)
'want'	woe'n (5)	wü	wüsd	woe'n	woets	wöd
'shall'	soe'n	soe	soesd	soe'n (1)	soets	soed
'may'	deaffa (6)	deaf	deafd	deaffa (1)	deafts	deaffad

Notes

(1) Obsolescent form in the 3rd pers. pl. ends in *-nd*.
(2) There is also an extended form *megnan* [meŋɒn].
(3) A more archaic form is *mua*.
(4) Also *miasst*.
(5) The older form is *wö'n* (< MHG *wellen*).
(6) The older form is *deffa*.

§ 38. VERBS WITH VOCALIC STEM

A number of verbs end in a nasalized root-vowel and are thus endingless in the inf. (see § 32.1 (iii)). These forms are:

	Inf.	Imp.	Sg. Pres.	Pl. Pres.	Condit.	P.P.
'to be'	sai(n)	sai!	bi	san	wa	gwen
			bisd	sats		
			is	san(d) (1)		
'to do'	tua(n) (2)	tua!	tua	tuan	tad	tå(n)
			tuasd	toats		
			tuad	tuan(d) (1)		
'to go'	gëh(n)	gëh!	gëh	gëhn	gang	gå
			gëhsd (3)	gëhts		
			gëhd (3)	gëhn(d) (1)	(gangad)	

Stëh(n)—gståndn 'stand' goes like *gëh(n)*, as do the other verbs of this type.

The verb *håm* 'have' may be added here:

'to have'	håm	håb!	hå(n)	håm	hett	ghåbd
			håsd (3)	håbts		
			håd (3)	håm	(hed)	also: ghåd

Notes

(1) The forms with *-d* are obsolete. Of *gëh(n)*, *stëh(n)* there are extended forms *gëhngan*, *stëhngan* (1st, 3rd pers. pl.).

(2) It has to be remembered that initial *t-* indicates a semi-fortis and that the spelling *ua(n)* expresses the nasalized diphthong [ŏ͂b].

(3) These forms occur also with short vowel + fortis consonant.

§ 39. PARTICLES

The particles of motion resemble, in their formation, those of H. Alem., but, unlike H.Alem., Bav. distinguishes like NHG between movement away from the speaker and movement towards the speaker (cf. chap. ii, § 48).

Preposition	Adverb of Place		Rest
	Movement away from speaker	*Movement towards speaker*	
in (drain)	aini	aina	drin, drinnad
aus (draus)	aussi	aussa	drausst
af (draf)	affi	affa	o'm, dromad
å(b) (drå(b))	åbi, åwi	åba, åwa	}drunt
unta (drunta)	unteri	untera	
iba (driba), ob	iberi	—	dri'm, drent
hinta	hinteri	—	hint
voa	viri	vira	voran
um (drum)	umi	uma	umadum
nåch	nåchi	nåcha	—
z (zua)	zuawi	zuawa	—
å(n) (drå(n))	å(n)i	åna	—

Q

PHONETIC TRANSCRIPTION[1]

For the principles of this transcription, see pp. 71, 148. A description of the individual sounds is given in §§ 6, 7, 8, 12. In initial position [b, d, g, v, z, ž, γ] are voiceless semi-fortes, in all other positions they are voiceless lenes. This also applies to the affricates [bv, dz] while initial [kh] is an aspirated fortis.

Words of two or more syllables have the main stress on the first syllable except where marked otherwise.

> dɒ wĭntɒ iz ūmi
> ūm pfɔšĭŋz dza·ɛd dɔ:
> ez lɔst ɔbɒ zwe:dɒn
> ūn‿tšna·ɛm no netnɔ: .

> haɛt khɔ̃:z əz me· wi:dɒ
> dro:m zānz haɛt gu·ɒd gri:γd,
> khãm zɛ:ŋ mɔkst, zo hɑ·odz dɒ
> dez drɔtšwa: īnz gzi:γd.

> dɔbaɛ no: de khø:dn
> dɒvri·ɒzn mekst ži·ɒ.
> haɛt brakst, wõnz ned zã·ɛn mu·ɒz
> nɛ̃ɒmd ɑosi vɔɒ ti·ɒ.

> en my:nɒ, dən dikŋ
> mɔ:g niks zo la·ɛγd ɔ̃:
> ūn tsili, zã·ɛ dɔxtɒ
> de lɔxt, wɔsnɒ khɔ̃: .

> zi lɔxt, wayz iɒn glik
> ɔeway nɛ·ɒdɒ khĭ·md
> haɛt wi·ɒd jɔ ban lɛ̃ntsbɑ·oɒn
> dɒ bi·ɒdlmɔ̃: bždĭ·md.

> dɒ bi·ɒdlmɔ̃:? — vra·ɛli,
> əz išɔ̃: zo· wa:ɛd!
> iz jɔ thɔtsɒd žɔ̃: ɔ̃·'gzetst
> nɔ· dɒ e:zdɒliŋ dza:ɛd.

---

[1] A transcription of an Upper Austrian dialect is given in A. Götze, *Proben hoch- und niederdeutscher Mundarten*, p. 42 f. and in J. Seemüller, *Sitzungsberichte der Akad. d. Wiss. in Wien*, Phil.-hist. Kl., vol. 167, iii, 21–5, 1911.

For spelling, see §§ 5 and 11. Where alterations have been made the original spelling is given at the bottom of the page, but only on the first occurrence. The numbers refer to the stanzas. All *d* and *ě* are introduced by me, as are the brackets for nasalized vowels not followed by a nasal consonant.

KARL MAYER-FREINBERG: *DE WÅHRE LIAB* [1]

(Chapter iv and most of chapter v)

1   Da Winta is [2] ummi
    Und d'Fåschingszaid då,
    Es låsst åba 's Wedan
    Und 's Schnai'm noh ned nåh.

2   Hait [3] kå(nn)s es me wieda,
    Dro'm sands hait guad g'richd',
    Kam sëhgn mågst, so haud's da
    Des Tråtschwa in's Gsichd.

3   Dåbai noh de Ködn,
    Dafriasn [4] megst schia.
    Hait brachst [5], wånn's ned sai(n) muas,
    neamd aussi voa d'Tia.

4   En Mü(ll)na, den dicken,
    Måg nix so laichd å(n)
    Und d'Cilli, sai(n) Teochta,
    De låcht, wås s' na kå(nn)!

5   Sie låcht, wei(l)s iha'n Glick
    Åewei(l) nëhada kimmd:
    Hait wiad jå ban Lenzbauan
    Da Biadlmå(nn) b'stimmd!

6   Da Biadlmå(nn)? — fraili,
    Es is scho(n) so waid!
    Is jå d'Håtzat [6] scho(n) å(n)gsetzt
    Nåh da esdalign Zaid.

7   Und d'Cilli wiad Bairin
    Am wunderschen' Guad!
    A å(n)gsëhgne Bairin! —
    Des gibt iha en Muad . . .

1 Winter, -zeit, Wödan, Scheibn, nöt.
2 Heunt, ös, mö, wieder, drobn, guat, g'richt, haut, dös, -schwer, Gsicht.
3 Dabei, dö, Kältn, mögst, schier, sein, muass, vor, Tür.
4 Ön, Müllner, leicht, sein, dö.
5 ihrn, Glück, allweil, nähada, kimmt, wird, -baurn, Biatlmann, b'stimmt.
6 freili, weit, Heohzat, österlign.
7 Bäurin, -schön', ang'sehgnö, dös, Muat.

8 Wei(l)s eahm [7] håed, en Frånzn,
   Ned gåa so rëchd måg;
   Åba nå(n), an „Lenzhofer"
   Kriagt ma ned ålle Tåg . . .

9 So bai zwoahundad Jo [8]
   Und en Beag dro'm gmua Wåed . . .
   Des hitzend iha 's Heatz,
   Dåss da Braigga ah g'fåed.

10 Vaninfdi is d'Cilli! —
   Sie kennd si guad aus:
   Sie håd rëchd vü Gœld
   Und dazua g'head a Haus!

11 Da Bruada kriagt 's Hoamad
   Und sie braucht an Må(nn),
   Mid den sie se ibaråc
   Sëhgnlåssen kå(nn).

12 Da Hof gibt eascht 's Å(n)sëhgn,
   Iha Våda sågt's ah.
   Und dea låsst si ned spottn,
   Ea zåhlt'n scho(n) schwa! —

13 Hiatzt is de Zaid då.
   Sie kemman hait zåmm,
   Wei(l)s noh wegn da Håtzat
   Vü ausz'måcha håm. —

14 De åed Lenzbairin tråhld
   Åesa gånzi in Gsichd . . .
   Damids unscheniad san,
   Håts in Stibal [9] dro'm g'richd.

15 Und da sitzens banånd:
   Da Mü(ll)na gånz wōach,
   De Waiba voe Rebing,
   Da Frånz völli blōach.

8 halt, gar, recht.
9 bei, -hundert, Joch, Berg, gnua, Wald, Herz, Bräugga, g'fallt.
10 Vernüfti, kennt, hat, viel, Geld, g'hört.
11 Hoamat, mit, sö, überall.
12 erst, der, er, schwar.   13 wögn.
14 alt, strahlt, alsa ganze, unscheniert, Stüberl.   15 voll.

16 ,,I gfrai mi" sågt d'Bairin,
 ,,Dåss d'Cilli båe kimmd
 Und hå(n) ma åes Auszug
 Des Stibal då bstimmd."

17 Åft re'ns wegnan Datum.
 ,,Wia d'Cilli håed mechd."
 ,,Jå", moant de, ,,en Iada [10]
 Nåh Osdan wa's rëchd."

18 ,,I hå(n) nix dagegn . . ."
 Sågt d'Muada glai draf;
 Da Frånz åba mumpfelt:
 ,,Gëts, schia'm ma's noh af!

19 Es fœhld umadum noh,
 I kriag eascht en Wågn
 A viazehn Tåg speda,
 Und d'Ros san ned b'schlågn . . ."

20 Na schliassli wea'ns aini(g),
 Åft re'ns iba 's Måhe,
 Då redt si da Mü(ll)na
 So laichd wia ned båe:

21 ,,Is ëh laichd, des Måhe,
 Des håma ban Stea'n.
 I frim enk's scho(n) å(n),
 Des tua i gånz gea'n.

22 A greoss's miass [11] ma håm,
 Dåss s'es umadum sëhgn,
 Wås zwoa, de a Gœld håm,
 Åes ausrichtn megn! —

23 Mid'n Gœld, des wissts [12] ëh,
 Måg da Cilli neamd å(n).
 Mai(n) oanzige Teochta
 Kriagt åess wås i hå(n).

16 gfreu, bal, als.
17 rödns, wögnan, halt möcht, Örta, Ostern.
18 dagögn, glei, Gehts, schiabn.
19 fahlt, vierzehn, spöda, Ross.
20 Schliessli werns, üba, Mahl.
21 Stern, gern.   22 müass, Alls.

24 Und des is hipsch vü! —
    Ba mia in da Müh,
    Wo da Hund åewei(l) kœhld,
    Stët a Kupfa voe Gœld . . ."

25 Da Frånz, dea vabaisst si,
    Es wiad eahm frai schlëchd —
    Wånn d'Cilli sai(n) Rosal wa,
    Åft wuad scho(n) åess rëchd! —

26 's Rosal! — Me is s' denn
    Ah aini i(n) d'Ståd?
    Sie håt's jå doh kennd [13],
    Dåss ea s' gea'n g'håbt håd . . .

27 Es druckt'n ban Heatzn,
    Blaischwa is sai(n) Gmiad . . .
    ,,I schau drunt a weng nåh",
    Sågt e, ,,wei(l) si nix riad . . ."

28 Und kam dåss ea's sågt,
    Is ea drausst ba da Tia
    Und drin stöd eahn d'Muada
    Hiatzt Glåskråpfa [14] via.

29 Da Frånz åba schlaichd si
    Hint aussi ban Haus,
    Ea håedad's in Maian drin
    Gåa nimma aus. — —.

30 Es is scho(n) rå'mfinsta,
    Am Bo'n z'gëht da Schnëë,
    A wårma Wind waht hiatzt
    Dåhea iba d'Hëh.

31 Es wiad håed van Friahling
    A Åmåtza sai(n) . . .
    En Frånz, den baidlt's:
    Fia eahm gibt's koa(n) Gfrai(n) — —

24 hübsch, mir, Mühl, kehlt, Steht.
25 vabeisst, frei, schlecht, war, wurd.
26 Mö, eini, Stadt.   27 Bleischwar, Gmüat, rührt.
28 stöllt, vür.   29 schleicht, haltat, Mäuern.
30 rabnfinster, Bodn, Daher, Höh.
31 Früahling, beitlt's, Für.

32   Fia eahm gibt's koan' Friahling — —
      Sai(n) Heatz is so schwa,
      Åes wånn d'Ållersœnzaid [15],
      De traurige wa. — —

33   Ea loahnd si å(n) d'Maua å(n),
      Åes wa ea strah-miad . . .
      Då is 's eahm, åes hett si
      Ne'm saina [16] wås g'riad.

34   Hm! — Zindad eahm oana
      Sain' Hof epa å(n),
      Voa Miadigkaid lag eahm
      Hait ah ned vü drå(n).

35   Da head ea's hiatzt wieda . . .
      Es flennd wea ban Haus . . .
      Da Wehdåm schlågt ah håed
      In Ausweats [17] oft aus!

36   Ea tåppt nåh da Maua hi(n),
      Då rennd wea dåvo(n) . . .
      A Schroa! — und åft springd ea
      Ah nåchi scho(n)

37   Und schraid völli b'sessn:
      „Håed aus! [18] låss di sëhgn,
      Sunst is's um mai(n) Heatzruah
      Af Ewigkaid [19] g'schëhgn!" — — —

38   Und dåni in d'Wiesn
      Und åbi zan Båh
      Rennd 's Waibsbüd voa saina
      Und ea hintn nåh . . .

39   Und . . . „Bisd as, mai(n) Liabste? —"
      Då rauscht scho(n) da Schwåll,
      Då fångt ea s' gråd af noh,
      Ban hausheochn Fåll.

32 Allerseelnzeit.
33 loahnt, Maur, strah-müad, hätt, Nöbn, g'rührt.
34 zündat, öbba, Müadigkeit.
35 hört, flennt, wer, Auswärts.
37 schreit, Ewigkeit.
38 Weibsbild.   39 bist.

40 Und 's Heatz af da Zung
   Druckt ea s' zuwa zan Laib . . .
   „Mai(n) Rosal, mai(n) Liabe —
   Mai(n) Liabste — mai(n) Waib!" —

41 Wia teod hengts af eahm o'm . . .
   E straimeld iha d'Hååa
   Und bussts und bussts wieda:
   „Mai(n) Rosal! — is's wåha?

42 Du bist as! — I hå(n) di
   In Teod hiatzt å'gjågt — !"
   Sie redt nix und schaud'n
   E'm å(n), kloa(n) vazågt,

43 Åft nimmts'n ban Håes
   Und busselt'n z'teod,
   Danåh stëssts'n dåni
   Und saifzt: „Liaba God,

44 Wås hån i denn tå(n) hiatzt . . .
   I bi(n) di ned wead! —
   Fia mi is's am bessan [20],
   Es deckt mi de Ead' . . .

45 Oa(n)måe åba håt's mi
   Noh trie'm za dain' Haus;
   Hiatzt — dåss i di gsëhgn hå(n),
   Is's gfœhld und is's aus!

46 I hån jå bis hait ned
   De wåhre Liab kennd,
   Hiatzt woass i's wås's is,
   Wei(l) da Teod dåhea rennd . . .

47 Jå, Franzl, du hettst as
   So guad mid mir gmoand:
   Du hettst mi en liaban!" [20]
   Sågt s' hoamli und woand.

40 Leib, Liabö.
41 teot, hängts, streimelt, Haar, wahr.
42 rödt, schaut, Öbn.
43 Hals, stösst, seufzt, Gott.
44 wert, bössan, dö Erd'.   45 triebn, gfahlt.
46 daher.   47 hätt'st, gmoant, woant.

48   „Und schau — in mia sœlba
     Gët lång scho(n) wås via . . .
     I kenn mi ned aus rëchd,
     Åba des såg i dia:

49   Mai(n) Heatz schlågt fia di! —
     Åba untabai schlågt
     A kloa(n)s Heatzal fia mi,
     Des mi sœlba å(n)klågt — — —

50   I måch mi ned bessa.
     — Va eahm hån i's Kind,
     Fia des i koa(n) Haidl,
     Koa(n) Hoamad meha find'.

51   I bid di, håb stad [21],
     Låss mi noh a weng re'n! —
     Du bist jå åewei(l)
     So vü guad mid mia gwen . . .

52   Du soest åesånd wissen! —
     Des Kind is mai(n) Teod — — —
     O mai(n) God — warum
     Bin i aini i(n) d'Håd! — — —

53   Mia håm uns rëchd gea'n g'håbt;
     Då håd ea's eafåhan,
     Dåss's aso mid mia stët
     Und is — gånz — åndas woan. —

54   Wås hån i åess g'lidn! . . .
     Ea is woass God wo . . .
     Wia guad håst ma's du gmoand . . .
     Gråd sain wü's ah so! — [22]

55   Gëh, låss mi — Gœll Franzl,
     Du denkst scho(n) af mi [23],
     Wånn i — jå, wånn i —
     Åft nimma bi! — — "

48 selba, vür, dir.
50 mehr.   51 bitt.
52 sollst, allsand.
53 erfahrn, steht, anders, worn.
54 g'littn, will's.
55 Gelt, bi(n).

56 Då druckt eas fest zuwa
    Und sågt: ,,Wiad's wia's wiad! — [24]
    I måch ohne daina
    In Le'm meha koan' Schriad.

57 Du bist ma mai(n) Liabas! —
    Und håst fia dai(n) Kind
    Koan Vådan, koa(n) Hoamad,
    So nimm mi håed g'schwind! —

58 Wås nutzt oan' da Raichtum
    Und 's Å(n)sëhgn, d'gross' Eha,
    Mai(n) Heatz braucht dai(n) Liab
    Und verlångt si ned meha!

59 Dai(n) Liab måcht mi glickli,
    Und wånnst [25] mi kånnst megn,
    So gibt uns da Heagott
    Aus Fraid scho(n) sain' Segn!"

60 Gånz g'schreckt und frai ståa
    Schaud'n 's Rosal hiatzt å(n) . . .:
    Dåss's denn af da Wœld
    So a Liab ge'm kå(nn)? . . . ! — — —

61 In Stibl o'm wåatens
    Am Frånz scho(n) hipsch lång,
    Da Mü(ll)na wiad schlaffri,
    Da Cilli wiad bång.

62 Wås d'Bairin vazöhld — mai(n),
    Då losens kam zua,
    So Vedan und Muaman
    Håms eh sœlba gmua!

63 Und wia's amåe wea'n wiad?
    Und wås åess wiad gschëhgn?
    Des wiad ma, wånn d'Cilli
    Am Hof is, scho(n) sëhgn.

56 ers, föst, ohnö, Schriatt.
57 Vadern.   58 Reichtum, Ehr.
59 glückli, Herrgott, Freud, Sögn.
60 g'schröckt, starr, schaut, Welt.
61 Ön, Stübl, wartens, schlafri.
62 vazählt, Vödan, Moaman.   63 wer(d)n.

64 Da Mü(ll)na raisst 's Mäu(l) af:
   „Åft wiad ma's scho(n) sëhgn!"
   Und d'Cilli, de denkt si:
   „Åft miassts ah åess megn" [26].

65 Åesånd håms scho(n) ausgred.
   's Måhe wiad ban „Stea'n".
   Hiatzt mechten sie's håed ah
   Vån Frånzn noh hea'n,

66 Wen ea ainlådnt dazua . . .
   Jå, wo ea denn blaibt? —
   Da Mü(ll)na mecht hoamfåhan,
   Wei(l)'s eh nimma schnaibt . . . [27]

67 'n Kaffee håms scho(n) g'håbt,
   Bacht und Kråpfa dazua —
   Es traibt'n nix hoam,
   Åba — ea håd scho(n) gmua.

68 Da Cilli is's fraili
   Ned trabi, denn d'Braud,
   De siacht si in Glåskåsten
   Haifti und schaud

69 Des schene Kaffee-Gschia å(n)
   Und de schen' Schåe'n,
   Mid goedane Ranftln
   Und umadum gmåe'n.

70 Då schau, de fain' Glasaln!
   Dane'm de liab Frau,
   „Kemmts [28] Våda [29], schauds hea då:
   A goedana Pfau

71 Zwischen da Muattagottes
   Und an Waihbrunnkestl,
   Dane'm a g'schliffas Glås,
   Då schmeckad da håed's Mestl!"

65 ausgröd, hörn.
67 treibt.
68 freili, Braut, häufti, schaut.
69 Gschirr, Schaln, goldanö, gmaln.
70 fein, Glaseln, Vater.
71 Weihbrunnköstl, schmöckad, Möstl.

72 Da Mü(ll)na gët zuwi
Und d'Bairin sågt: „Glai
Kimm i auffa mid'n Frånzn,
Schaud's å(n) åess dawei(l)!"

73 Sie laft iba d'Stiagn åbi,
Aini in d'Stu'm,
Pröllt aussi in d'Kuchl
Und schaud umadum.

74 Schraid aussi in Hof
Und frågt d'Dia'n [30] und en Knëchd
Und frågt 's Mensch und en Buam
Und schraid åft eascht rëchd:

75 „Frånz! — d'Cilli brauchd di!"
Und gaustad in Ståe
Und zruck iba's Viahaus,
Voe Gift scho(n) und Gåe.

76 Då knagatzt hiatzt 's Haustoa,
'Wea kimmt denn so spåd?
Wea stësst's denn so dåni? —
Wås gibt's denn na gråd? — —

77 Da Frånz mid an Waibsbüd! —
Jå — is denn wås gschëhgn? — —
Sie hengt eahm am Håes,
Ma måg's Gsichd gåa ned sëhgn'.

78 „Frånz! — " . . . Und ea dait'
Mid da Hånd za da Stiagn:
„In d'Hëh gëhn ma affi!"
Und sie låsst si ziagn.

79 „Um Gods wü'n! — Wås gibt's denn?" —
Und dro'm in da Stu'm
Drahd si d'Cilli ban Glåskastl
Hiatzt frai gach um,

74 Schreit, Dirn, Knecht.
75 braucht, Stall, Vorhaus, Voll, Gall.
76 spat, stösst.   77 Hals.
78 deut', auffi.
79 Gotts willn, draht.

80 Spraitzt d'Augn af und schaud,
   Åes wånns Gspensta sëhad:
   Wås is des? — Wås kimmt iha
   Denn då in d'Nëhad? — — —

81 A Pååa stët voa iha då ...
   Sie kennd si gschwind aus! ...
   Låcht spettisch und is scho(n)
   Davo(n) in oan' Saus.

82 Da Mü(ll)na schraid nåchi:
   „Wås håsd denn? — Blaib då!"
   Åft schaud ea und schaud ea —
   Und gëhd iha stad nåh.

83 „Pfiat di God!" sågt ea „Bairin,
   Sai du håed doh gschaid! —
   Fead is s' Dia'n gwen ban enk,
   Gœll — i miak ma scho(n) d'Laid!"

84 Haud d'Tia zua, tråppt åbi,
   Heast 's Ainspånna scho(n),
   Mid da Goasl an Schnåeza
   Und hiatzt fåhans davo(n)! ...

85 In Stibl dro'm gibt's hiatzt
   Wås hochwichtigs å(b) ...
   Mai(n)! — D'Bairin schlågt d'Hend
   Iban Kobf zåmm — håed jå! —

86 „Wås soe denn des hoassn?"
   Sågts entli, „Hå(n) Bua?
   I hå(n) va den Gspü, desst uns
   Viamåchst hiatzt gmua!"

87 Und gifti und gah fåhats
   Auf's Rosal und schraid:
   „Hiatzt låsst en Bauan aus,
   Du kecks Doan, hëchste Zaid!"

80 Spreitzt, Nähad.   81 Paar, spöttisch.
82 hast, geht.
83 Pfüat, gscheid, Ferd, gwön, mörk, ma's, Leut.
84 Haut, Hörst, Einspanna, Schnalza.
85 Händ, Üban, Kopf.
86 soll, endli, Gspiel, dösst, gnua.   87 Baurn, köcks, höchste.

88 Da bamd si da Frånz af,
    Druckts zuwa voa ihra,
    Und bussts und bussts wieda,
    Und håd koan' Scheniera:

89 ,,Umasunst is åess, Muada —
    Mia hairåtn zåmm! —
    I kunnt ohne iha då
    Koa(n) Fraid nimma håm! — "

90 Då is's gach da Bairin
    Åes drahad si d'Stu'm,
    Da Tiisch und de Kåstn
    Um sie umadum . . .

91 Da Baua redt aso? —
    Jå, wia wiad iha denn gschwind?
    Stëhd wiakli iha Bua då?
    Is's wiakli iha Kind? — —

92 Ea fiabad voe Fraid
    Und de Schånddia'n tuad ah,
    Åes wånn's de grësst Gnåd'
    Und koa(n) Unglick ned wa.

93 Denn 's Unglick wa fiati,
    Wånn de då kam hea!
    Wås is denn a Haus
    Ohne Å(n)sëhgn und Eha? — —

94 Sie hået' eahm åess via,
    Und sie bitt' und sie red:
    ,,Es gëhd uman Hof, Frånz,
    Begraifst es denn ned? —

95 Dain' Vådan, den tad's noh
    Ins Gråb aini wëh,
    Und d'Fraindschåft, de greoss',
    Wia de is, woasst ëh! —

88 bamt, auf.
89 heiratn.
90 Do, Tisch.
91 Baur, wirkli.
92 fibbert, tuat.   93 förti.
94 Begreifst.   95 tat.

96 Und nåcha eascht d'Laid . . . !"
Då låcht ea höllaud,
Dåss d'Bairin si frai nix
Meha z'sågn håd traud.

97 ,,I hairåd ned d'Fraindschåft,
I hairåd ned d'Laid,
I hairåd wen i wü,
Gët's guad oda gfœhld! —"

96 hellaut, traut.
97 heirat, guat.

NOTES

(See the remarks to the *Notes* on p. 80)

[1] *Karl Mayer-Freinberg* was born 24 August 1875 in Steyr and died 17 August 1949 in Linz, where he had spent most of his life. From 1908, when with others he founded the *Bund oberösterreichischer Mundartdichter*, he was active in the Upper Austrian dialect movement. After the publication of his early poems, *Griasnocka, foaste und sperö, wias ös wöllts!*, 1905, he contributed to the year-books *Hoamatgsang*, 1910, 1920, 1930, of the *Bund*. Members of the *Bund* and contributors to *Hoamatgsang* were the dialect poets Anton Matosch, Norbert Hanrieder, Leopold Hörmann, Josef Krempl, Eduard Samhaber, Franz Klein, Georg Wagnleithner. Mayer published literary biographies of Matosch, Hörmann, Krempl and of others and wrote three short epic poems, *s' Paradeisgsangl* (1919), *Da Franzl im Himmel* (1919) and *Dö wahre Liab* (1949). His wide knowledge of Upper Austrian dialect poetry becomes evident in his bibliographies "Oberösterreichische Mundartbücher", *Volksbildung*, Vienna, ix, 1929, 77–85; *Die oberösterreichische Mundartdichtung*, Linz, 1949. The following anthologies contain poems by Mayer: Hans Commenda, *Meister der Mundart. Ein Hausbuch oberösterreichischer Dichtung. Die Altmeister von Lindemayr bis Reischl*. Schärding, Vienna, 1948; Joh. Hauer, *Am Quell der Muttersprache, Österreichische Mundartdichtung der Gegenwart*, Vienna, Stiasny, 1955. Stelzhamer's works have been edited in the series *Aus da Hoamat* (31 *Hefte*). In 1946 the *Bund*, dissolved in 1939, was reconstituted as the *Stelzhamerbund der Freunde oberösterreichischer Mundartdichtung*.

Dö wahre Liab is a ballad-like poem dealing with a social problem of an old farmer aristocracy where marriage and the passing on of the homestead becomes a dynastic problem of overriding importance.

Franz, heir to the *Lenzhof*, has fallen in love with a servant girl, Rosal. She has left the farm, however, attracted by the splendour of the city and its socially freer atmosphere. In the meantime a marriage has been arranged between Franz and Cilli (Cecilia), the daughter of the wealthy flour miller. Our extract opens with the preparations for this wedding, which are interrupted by Franz's procrastination and Rosal's sudden reappearance. In swift and poignant strokes the author develops the dramatic clash between the irrational claims of love and the conventional demands of family and society.

[2] Mayer has *war*, a loan from NHG, instead of which my informants preferred *is*.

[3] Mayer's spelling *heunt* [haɛd] points to the more archaic pronunciation with nasalized vowel which derives from *hinacht*, lit. 'to-night'. The now usual pronunciation [haɛt] is influenced by NHG *heute*.

[4] Mayer has *dafroisn*. The diphthong *oi* is the eastern and western correspondence of central Upper Austrian *eo* (§ 7.1). Mayer uses the archaic eastern form (Steyr) while my informants use the more modern colloquial *ia*. Note that the grammatical change has not been levelled out as in NHG, cf. English *freeze*: MHG *friesen*. The prefix *da-* corresponds to NHG *er-*.

[5] Before *s* or *sch* every former *ch* (< *k, h*) > *k*, hence [brakst], *megst* but *mecht* (§ 37).

[6] *Hătzat* 'wedding'. Mayer writes *Heohzat*, thereby indicating the archaic central Upper Austrian diphthong *eo* (< MHG *ŏ*), see also *greoss* (22, 95) but *gross* (58), *heochn* (39), *teot* (41), *Teod* (42, 46, 52), *Teochta* (4, 23). I have retained these spellings, except here, although both my informants have the vowel [ɔ] (see § 6.6 (iii)). It is interesting to note that Mayer rhymes *Teod* with *Stăd* (52), indicating a pronunciation identical with that of my informants. His *eo* may thus be only traditional spelling.

[7] The stressed pers. pron. *eahm* is the common object case, thus corresponding to NHG *ihn* and *ihm*, cf. *fia eahm*: NHG *für ihn*. (See § 25.)

[8] *200 Jo*: One *Jo* (NHG *Joch*) is a measure of land, as much as can be ploughed in a day; 200 *Jo* corresponds to about 280 acres.

[9] The diminutive ending with the strongest sense of diminution and affection is *-al*. Historically it is the ending *-l* after a root ending in *-er*. The primary diminutive suffix *-l* has now hardly any diminutive force, thus we have *Dia'n* or *Dia'ndl* 'girl' but *Dia'ndal* as a term of affection and as a diminutive. After velars the more conservative dialects realize the primary ending *-l* as *-i* or *ü*, e.g. *Biachü* 'book'. This ending (without umlaut of the root-vowel) functions also as a sort of third degree of diminution which belongs to childish or

nursery language. Thus for 'head' we have *Kobf, Kepfü* or *Kopfl, Kepfal* and childish *Kopfü*.

[10] *Iada* 'Tuesday' is one of those Austro-Bav. names of the days of the week which derive from the Greek (day of Ares), cf. *Pfinztag* 'Thursday', and see *DSA*, 26 (*Ertag*), E. Kranzmayer, "Die Namen der Wochentage in den Mundarten von Bayern u. Österreich". *Arbeiten zur Bayerisch-österr. Dialektgeographie*, I, Vienna-Munich, 1929; on diphthong, see § 7.1 (iii).

[11] See § 34 (5).

[12] See § 25 (1).

[13] Note the use of *kenna* here where NHG would use *wissen*.

[14] Informants use the pl. *Glåskråpfan* 'doughnuts'.

[15] The 2nd November, the day after All Saints' Day, is All Souls' Day in the Roman Catholic calendar. It is celebrated in memory of the dead.

[16] See § 25 (3).

[17] 'Spring', the season leading away (auswärts) from winter. The term is mainly Lower Bavarian and Upper Austrian, cf. Mitzka, *Wortatlas*, iv, 15.

[18] 'Wait a minute', 'Stop'.

[19] Informants put the def. art. before the noun; the expression without the art. appears to be borrowed from NHG (see § 18 (5)).

[20] See § 23.

[21] 'Quiet, please, listen!', cf. *maisalstad*: NHG *mäuschenstill*.

[22] 'But now it will have to be like this.'

[23] The use of *auf* (*af*) after *denken* is also found in Austrian standard in place of NHG *an*.

[24] 'Come what may.'

[25] The ending of the 2nd pers. sg. is often anticipated in dialects and added to adverbs, cf. O. Weise, 'Die sogenannte Flexion der Konjunktionen', *ZfdMaa.*, 1907, pp. 199–205.

[26] 'Afterwards you will have to like it.'

[27] The former fricatives *w, h*, which have disappeared in inter-vocalic position, have become fortis *p* or *ch* before stops, e.g. *schnaibt*: *schnai'm, sěhgn*: *siacht* (68).

[28] See §§ 25 (1), 34 (6).

[29] The words *Våda* and *Muada* are usually spelt with *d* by Mayer and pronounced with a lenis by my informants, probably following the spelling. Both Roitinger and Grau state that a fortis stop in these words is now usual, while a lenis is felt to be coarse.

[30] *Dia'n* is the senior female servant and *Kněchd* the senior male farm labourer, while *da Bua* and *s Mensch* are the juniors.

R

GLOSSARY

See the introductory remarks to the *Glossary* on p. 84, and for further information Joh. And. Schmeller, *Bayerisches Wörterbuch*, 2nd ed., 1872 ff.

a, ah, also.
àesànd, all, everything.
àewei(l), always.
àft, then, after.
Áinspànna, A. one-horse carriage.
a'màe, in future, some time.
Ámàtza, m. breath of air.
a'so, such.
Auszug, m. retreat.

Bacht, n. NHG *Gebäck*.
bàe, soon.
Bàh, B. brook.
baidln, wv. shake, shiver.
bama, si, wv. rear, rebel.
ba'nànd, together.
Biadlmà(nn), person who invites the wedding guests.
Braigga, m. bridegroom.
bussn, wv. kiss.
  busseln (iterative).

dàni, away.
Doan, f. person (derog.).
drahn, wv. turn.

eascht, first, all the more.
ëh, indeed.
e'm, even, straight.
enk, you (see § 25).
epa, perhaps, NHG *etwa*.

fahln, wv. miss, go wrong.
fead, last year.
fiaban, wv. tremble.
fiati, finished, complete.
flena, wv. cry.
frai, very, really.
fremma, order, arrange.

gach, gah, hasty, quick.
gànzi (àesa-), all over, everywhere.
gaustan, wv. search hastily and superficially.

gfrain, wv. be glad.
glai, straightaway.
Glàskràpfa, kind of doughnut.
gmua, enough.
Goasl, f. D. whip.
gœll, NHG *nicht wahr*.
gschreckt, frightened.
Gspü, n. (collective), playing.

Haidl, n. D. cradle.
haifti, quickly, much.
hiatzt, now.
Hoamad, n. homestead.

kema (ea kimmd), come.
knagatzn, creak.
Kòdn, f. cold.
kœhln, wv. bark.
Kràpfa, D. doughnut.
Kuchl, D. kitchen.
Kupfa, f. D. coffer.

loana, wv. lean.
losen, wv. listen.

Màhe, wedding feast.
me? why?
me, again, NHG *malwieder*.
Muaman, D. female cousins and aunts.
mumpfeln, wv. mutter.

na, only.
nà(n) (àba-), after all.
neamd, nobody.
nëhad, near.
Nëhad, f. vicinity.
nimma, no longer.

Pfiad di God! 'God protect you'.
pröllen, wv. hurry.

Ranftl, n. D. edge.
Rebing, f. activity, excitement.

246

re'n, si, state.

Scheniera, shame.
Schriad, A. step.
schwa, heavy.
Schwåll, whirl, waterfall.
spåd, late.
stad, slow, quiet.
Stiagn, f. A. stairs.
strah-miad, dog-tired.
straimeln, wv. stroke.

tåppm, wv. grope.
trabi, in a hurry.
tråppm, wv. stump.

Tråtschwa, n. 'load', blizzard.

umadum, everywhere, all round.
untabai, underneath.

Vedan, D. cousins and uncles.
vü, much.

wahn, wv. blow.
Waihbrunnkestl, D. holy-water
    stoup.
Wedan, n. (verbal noun), weather.
Wehdam, m. pain, unhappiness.

zåmm, together.
zruck, back.

CHAPTER VII

LUXEMBURGISH

§ 1. AREA AND STATUS

1.1 The whole population of the Grand Duchy of Luxemburg, with the exception of the immigrant Walloon inhabitants of one mining village, speak, in their daily life, Luxemburgish, a West Moselle Franconian dialect. Dialect is thus, as in Switzerland, the sole spoken medium of all classes in all informal and even some formal situations. Only the Court, the Church, the schools, and, to a lesser extent, Parliament and the law courts use one of the two official national standard languages, French or German, also for oral communication. These foreign standard languages are thus reserved almost exclusively for writing. While the Church and the press use NHG, the legal and political bodies, including the Court, prefer French. Education is conducted more in German in the lower forms and more in French in the higher forms. Both languages, however, are more or less foreign to the Luxemburger, who is by birth monolingual in his native dialect, bilingual or trilingual only through education. This situation is nothing new for Luxemburg. The medieval duchy with its *quartier allemand* and its *quartier wallon* was a bilingual state, and the modern Grand Duchy, confined to its Luxemburgish-speaking districts by the Treaty of London of 1839, has nevertheless continued the tradition of two national languages. Up to the First World War the pendulum swung in the direction of NHG, since then it has gone in the direction of French. The vicissitudes of twentieth-century history have bestowed some official recognition on the spoken dialect, while the claims of modern education and technological progress have made powerful inroads on its purity. Hundreds of loan-words and expressions from both standard languages[1] have invaded the dialect formerly geared exclusively to the simple requirements of a rural community. In 1912 Luxemburgish became by law a subject to be taught in the elementary schools, in 1945 also in the lower forms of the secondary schools. But in competition with an already heavy linguistic programme Luxemburgish has a difficult stand as an academic subject. In 1938 naturalization was made dependent on the knowledge of Luxemburgish. Attempts to make the dialect also a written language for everyday practical use, e.g. in newspapers, failed. But Luxemburg

---

[1] See F. C. Southworth, 'French Elements in the Vocabulary of the Luxemburg Dialect', *Bull. ling. et éth.*, 2, 1954, 1–20.

dialect literature, with its remarkable nineteenth-century classic *De Renert*, continues to flourish on a more modest level removed from the daily bustle.

Naturally Luxemburgish, like any other dialect, has many local variants. Since the beginning of this century, however, a national *koinè* has gradually taken shape. It is a product of levelling, amalgamation of local forms, and of the exclusion of rare regional features. It is a kind of average language spoken by all those whose career brings them into daily contact with people from all over the country. It is spoken by all classes outside their own narrow regional circle, where they may retain their local speech. The local dialects are pushed back more and more towards the remoter parts of the country while the *koinè*, the national spoken standard language, a kind of *überlandschaftliche Verkehrssprache*, makes rapid progress. It is true, every speaker carries his own local dialectal colouring into the *koinè* and the process of levelling is not complete. It must be emphasized that the *koinè* is a product of levelling between local dialects and not between dialect and NHG, as the term *Verkehrssprache* usually implies in Germany and Austria. Internal migration, urbanization and centralization have been powerful factors in the shaping of the *koinè*. Although the capital city has afforded the most fertile soil for its growth, the *koinè* is nevertheless distinct from the dialect of Luxemburg City itself. It happens to be closest to the local dialect of the Alzette valley north of the capital.[1]

1.2 The question of the position of Luxemburgish within the framework of West Middle German dialects was reopened with the publication of Rob. Bruch's *Grundlegung*, 1953, and *Das Luxemburgische im westfränkischen Kreis*, 1954. The older view, formulated by the Rhenish School under the leadership of Theodor Frings, interpreted the dialect area extending between the *Pfund/Pund* line in the south and the *ich/ik* line in the north in terms of the participation in the second soundshift. The Rhenish Fan,[2] thus established, was seen as the result of a linguistic thrust from south to north along the River Rhine. Luxemburgish appears thus as a relic area in the extreme west of Moselle Franconian, separated from Rhenish Franconian by the *dat/das* isogloss (*Hunsrück-Schranke*), from south-eastern Moselle Franconian by the *op/auf* isogloss, and from Ripuarian by the

---

[1] On the status of Luxemburgish and the rise of the *koinè*, see the *Einleitung* of the *Luxemburger Wörterbuch*, 1950; Bruch, *Grundl.*, pp. 62–97; Bruch, *Grammaire*, pp. 109–15.

[2] See *DSA*, 3; T. Frings, *Rheinische Sprachgeschichte*, 1922, republished with maps in *Sprache und Geschichte*, i, 1956, 1–54; and *Kulturströmungen und Kulturprovinzen in den Rheinlanden*, 1926, the chapter on language being republished with the title 'Sprache und Geschichte am Rhein' in *Sprache und Geschichte*, ii, 1956, 40–146; A. Bach, 'Die sprachl. Stellung Luxemburgs', *Lux. Jb.*, 1931–2, pp. 3–13.

Dorp/Dorf isogloss in the north (*Eifel-Schranke*). The medieval state of the archbishop-elector of Trier is regarded as the historical basis upon which Moselle Franconian came into existence.

This view has been repeatedly challenged by the Luxemburg scholar, Robert Bruch.[1] He demands a division of the Middle Franconian dialects based on internal evidence rather than on external criteria, i.e. the second soundshift, carried in from Upper German dialects. He further sees the linguistic history of the Rhinelands shaped by a powerful Frankish west–east expansion in Merovingian and Carolingian times creating a so-called Franconian Bay or triangle with its base resting broadly on the Franco-German linguistic frontier, its Moselle–Lahn axis pointing eastwards into Thuringia. The later north expansion of the Upper German dialects has caused the Franconian Bay to contract in stages graded differently for individual isoglosses. Luxemburg's peripheral position has facilitated the survival of the type of language which emerged from the linguistic symbiosis of West Franks and Romans in Northern Gaul after the Frankish conquest.[2]

The West Moselle Franconian relic area can be defined as enclosed by a fascicle or belt of isoglosses running from the Franco-German linguistic frontier west of St. Vith in the Eifel south-eastwards towards Bitburg, thence southwards to west of Trier and south-westwards to the Franco-German linguistic frontier south-west of Thionville (Diedenhofen) in Lorraine. Luxemburgish is thus not spoken only in the Grand Duchy but also by a dwindling number of people in the adjacent areas of Belgium (district of Arlon),[3] Germany (area of Bitburg), and France (district of Thionville);[4] altogether by more than 300,000 people. Isoglosses which frame this West Moselle Franconian dialect area are for instance *Kand* 'child'—Rip. *Kenk*, East Moselle Franc. *Kend* (*DSA*, 17, see also 19 and 20: *as* 'is', 60: *hann* 'behind' and Bach, *op. cit.*, map 3, *Wanter* 'winter'); (*ge*)*brach*(*en*) 'broken'—E. Mos. Franc. (*ge*)*broch*(*en*) (*DSA*, 29); *eis*[5] 'us'—Rip. and E. Mos. Franc. *us, os*, (*DSA*, 39); *Brudder* 'brother',

---

[1] In his books mentioned above and in 'Mittelfränkische Relikte des Zwischenstadiums der Affrikata', *ZfMaf.*, xxi, 1952–3, 149–58; 'A cheval sur la frontière linguistique: un circuit francique en Europe occidentale', *Orbis*, iii, 1954, 34–42; 'Die Lautverschiebung bei den Westfranken', *ZfMaf.*, xxiii, 1955, 129–47; 'Sprache und Geschichte', *ZfMaf.*, xxiv, 1956, 129–50; 'Westfränkische Sprachströmungen in Mitteldeutschland', *Festschrift Adolf Bach*, *Rheinische Vierteljahrsblätter*, xxi, 1956–7, 14–44.

[2] Some of the arguments are attacked by K. Heeroma, 'Fränkisch, Ingwäonisch und Luxemburgisch', *ZfMaf.*, xxv, 1957, 65–77.

[3] See A. Bertrang, 'Die sterbende Mundart', *Lux. Vjbl.*, vii, 1936, 135–52.

[4] See J. Tockert, 'Die luxemburgische Sprachgrenze', *Annuaire*, 1925, pp. 54 ff. with map 1 on p. 59; Bach, *op. cit.*, fn. 2, p. 249; for a description of the Franco-German linguistic frontier see Bruch, *Grundl.*, pp. 105–12.

[5] Luxemburg City has *ons*, imported from NHG.

(DSA, 12); *Dueref* 'village'—E. Mos. Franc. *Dorf*—Rip. *Dörp (DSA,*
47); *an* 'and'—general Rhenish form *on (DSA,* 67); the ending *-en* in
bauen (DSA, 64), *dreschen (DSA,* 121), etc., against E. Mos. Franc.
-e; *him, hem* 'him' (Bach, *op. cit.,* map 2). Isoglosses which separate
Moselle Franc. as a whole from other Rhenish dialect areas are e.g.
Eis 'ice'—Rip. *Is (DSA,* 74); *Haus* 'house'—Rip. *Hus (DSA,* 24);
Pond (DSA, 62) 'pound', *Hond (DSA,* 35) 'dog'—Rip. *Ponk, Honk*;
fleh(en), fleih(en) 'to fly'—Rip. *flēg- (DSA,* 124); *schwätzen* 'to talk'
(DSA, 55)—Rip. *kallen*; *wat* 'what' *(DSA,* 127)—Rh. Franc. *was.*[1]

GENERAL CHARACTERISTICS OF WEST MOSELLE FRANCONIAN (LUXEMBURGISH)

§ 2. PHONOLOGICAL FEATURES[2]

2.1 *The Vowels*

(1) The MHG[3] long vowels *î, û, iu* correspond to two series of
diphthongs (*ai-äi, au-âu*); but the reflexes of *î* and *iu* have coincided.

(2) The normal correspondences of MHG *ie, uo, üe* are *éi, ou,* the
reflexes of *ie* and *üe* again coinciding.

(3) The MHG diphthongs *ei* and *ou* correspond to monophthongs
ee and *aa.*

(4) No distinction is made between the reflexes of MHG *e, ē, ä.*

(5) The correspondence of MHG *a* in a closed syllable is a long
front *aa,* except when followed by *l, m, n* in final position or *l, m, n*
plus another consonant (> short *a*), or when followed by *ht* or
former *hs, ft* (> *ue*). In an originally open syllable the diphthong *ue*
is normally found. Before *sch* (< Gmc. *sk*) *a* is generally palatalized
to *ä. Long â* has generally become *o* (except before *ht* or *n*).

(6) The correspondences of MHG *ê, æ, œ,* and of *ô* are *éi* and *ou*
respectively.

(7) MHG *i* and *u* have been subjected to the *Mitteldeutsche
Senkung* which has lowered them in originally closed syllables to *a*
or *e* or *ē* in the case of the former and to *o* in the case of the latter.
In the same circumstances *o* has been lowered to *a.*

[1] The whole material of the *DSA* was scrutinized by Rob. Bruch and forms
the basis of the maps in his *Grundl.* For internal divisions in Luxemburgish, see
Bruch, *Grundl.* and *Grammaire*; Richard Huss, *Studien zum Luxemburgischen
Sprachatlas,* Luxemburg, 1927; Palgen, *Studien.*

[2] Cf. J. Feltes, 'Les efforts phonétiques d'un petit pays trilingue', *Proceedings
of the Third International Congress of Phonetic Sciences,* Ghent, 1938, pp. 424–6;
fn. 1, p. 32.

[3] This comparison, of course, in no way implies that Lux.—or any other
modern dialect—has at any stage of its development actually conformed to
'classical MHG'. Such an assumption would be certainly less justified in the
case of Lux. than in that of Upper German (esp. Alem.) dialects.

(8) MHG rounded front vowels appear as unrounded vowels, e.g. *ü* > *i*, *ö* > *ĕ*.

(9) A characteristic feature is the diphthongization of the originally short vowels *e* (MHG *e*, *ĕ*, *ä*) > *ie*; *o*, *a* > *ue* in originally open syllables.

(10) Nasalization is generally unknown.

(11) A new series of long monophthongs *i*, *e*, *ä*, *o*, *u* has arisen from lengthening of originally short vowels in certain limited contextual circumstances.

(12) Initial vowels have a smooth onset.

2.2 Vowel Quantity

(1) The Lux. vowel quantity has been fundamentally affected by the phenomena of circumflexion (*Zerdehnung*, *Trägheitsakzent*) resulting in lengthening and/or diphthongization, and of correption (*Korreption*, *Rheinische Schärfung*, *Rheinische Akzentuierung*) leading to shortening of long vowels and monophthongization of diphthongs and certain consonantal changes, see *Schwebelaut* (§§ 12.3; 14.17 ff.), *Gutturalisierung* (§ 10.3).

(2) The consonantal clusters *ht*, *hs*, *r* plus consonant and single *r* have generally had a lengthening effect on the preceding vowel.

(3) The nasals, the dental stops, *l* and *ch* have frequently had a shortening effect on preceding vowels, incl. diphthongs.

2.3 Vowels in Unstressed Syllables

(1) The NHG prefixes *be-* and *ge-* retain their vowels.

(2) MHG unstressed final *-e* has generally been dropped.

(3) Svarabhakti vowels have arisen in the surroundings of liquids.

2.4 The Consonants

(1) The consonantal system is based on an opposition of voiced and voiceless stops and fricatives except in absolute final position where only voiceless stops and fricatives occur. Before vowels in sandhi, on the other hand, only voiced stops and fricatives occur. There is also an opposition of small functional yield between simple *l*, *m*, *n*, *ng* and the *Schwebelaute l:*, *m:*, *n:*, *ng:*.

(2) Where NHG has *pf* Lux. has *p*. WGmc. *d* and *þ* have coincided (*đ*). Where Gmc. *t* is followed by the dental suffix of the past part. of weak verbs the second soundshift is not in evidence. Gmc. *t* is also unshifted in the so-called *Mittelfränkische Reliktwörter* (*dat*, *wat*, *ět*, *dĕt*, *-t*, n. adj.).

(3) The distribution of velar and palatal *ch* is identical with that of NHG, both occur also voiced, as does *sch*.

(4) *St* is, within one morpheme, and except in the ending of the superlative, *scht*.

(5) Gmc. *ƀ* is *b* in initial position, *w* in medial and *f* in final position. Gmc. *g* is *g* in initial position, *ch* in final and medial position after consonants. In intervocalic position it has disappeared.

(6) The liquids *r* and *l* are preserved. The former cluster *rs* has become voiced *sch* (hardened in absolute final position), and *rn* > *r*.

(7) Final *-n*, e.g. in the MHG–NHG unstressed ending *-en*, is preserved except before all consonants other than the dental stops (and affricate) and *h*.

(8) Under the so-called Ripuarian velarization *n* has changed to *ng* in certain contexts.

(9) General assimilation of former *ld* > *l* except before the suffix *-el*, *nd* > *n*, *hs* > *s*; the loss of *n* before fricatives and the change *ft* > *cht* are found in some words.

§ 3. MORPHOLOGICAL FEATURES

3.1 Noun and Article

(1) The noun has no special endings for cases, but there are relic forms of a differentiated dat. sg. and of a gen. sg. The articles have a common form for subject and direct object, but there is a form for the gen.

(2) There are three main types of plural formation.

(3) Nouns form a diminutive by means of *-chen*.

3.2 The Adjective

(1) There is only one declension for the attributive adjective, but in the masc. and n. dat. two different endings are used according to whether there is a preceding art. or not.

(2) There is a genitive case in *-er* in the pl.

(3) The comparative is formed analytically with the particle *méi* 'more'.

3.3 The Pronouns

(1) The personal pronouns of the 1st and 2nd pers. sg. distinguish four cases (incl. a gen.), those of the 3rd pers. sg. only three (common obj.–subj. case, dat., gen.) and those of the pl. also three (nom., common obj., gen.).

(2) Beside the *koinè* form *ons* 'us' there is still the older *äis* or *eis*.

(3) In the possessive pronouns of the sg. forms showing the *rheinische Gutturalisierung* alternate with those which do not (*mäi-méng* 'my' masc.-fem., etc.)

(4) The poss. pron. of the pl. have the ending *-t* in the neuter,

those of the sg. only when used pronominally but not when used as adjectives.

(5) Instead of the NHG pronouns *er, ihm, ihn, es, ihnen, ihr,* Lux. has the so-called Ingvaeonic pronouns *hien* 'he', *him, hatt* 'it', *hinen* 'them', *hir* 'her', *hiren* 'their'.

(6) The demonstrative pronouns *deen, déi, dat,* etc., serve also as relative pronouns.

3.4 The Verbs

(1) Most verbs have only the following tenses: a pres. ind., a perfect, a pluperfect. Some verbs have also a preterite ind. and a preterite subj. There is no present subj.

(2) Where there is no synthetic preterite subjunctive the conditional is formed by means of the auxiliaries *gin* 'to give', or *goën* 'to go', *doën* 'to do'.

(3) The passive is formed with *gin*.

(4) The future is occasionally expressed by *goën*.

(5) The 1st pers. sg. pres. shares the same ending with the 1st and 3rd pers. pl.

(6) A large number of strong verbs are endingless in the past participle.

(7) There are many more cases of *Rückumlaut* than in NHG.

(8) The verb corresponding to NHG *haben* has unmutated forms throughout the present.

(9) The 2nd and 3rd pers. sg. pres. of many strong verbs show umlaut.

(10) For NHG *gewesen* Lux. uses *gewiescht*.

(11) The dialect infinitives for NHG *gehen, stehen* are reflexes of MHG *gân, stân.*

PHONOLOGY

THE VOWELS

§ 4. The Vowel Phonemes

What makes the historical identification of the Lux. vowel phonemes difficult is not only the extent to which lowering, unrounding, lengthening and diphthongization have radically altered the historical WGmc. or MHG vowel system but above all the frequent contextual interferences. Thus one historical phoneme, e.g. WGmc. or MHG /i/, may now be found to have representatives in four different phonemes, e.g. /ɪ, iː, ɑ, ə/, the last with its two chief allophones [ə and e]. In every one of these modern Lux. phonemes it has furthermore coincided with some reflexes of other historical phonemes, e.g. in /ɑ/ with one of the reflexes of WGmc. or MHG *o* and *a*.

Front	Central	Back
i:		u:
ɪ		ʋ
e:		o:
ɛ	ə	ɔ
a:	ɑ	

Foreign phonemes occurring only in loan-words, e.g. /y/, are not included. The short vowels are generally more lax or open than the long vowels. Instead of [e:] many local dialects have [ɛ:], which is generally the variant used before *r*.[1] The central vowel /ə/, occurring in stressed as well as unstressed positions, has the chief allophones [e] before /ŋ, k, ç/ and [ə] in all other surroundings.

There are eight falling diphthongs:

iə uə

ei ou

ɛ:i ɑ:u

ɑi ɑu

The diphthongs /ei, ou, ɑi, ɑu/ are short, both elements being of equal length. /ɛ:i/ and /ɑ:u/ have always a long first element, while /iə/ and /uə/ have a very short second element with a first element of varying length according to context and conditions of stress.

§ 5. Spelling

Joseph Tockert, the editor of the *Jubiläumsausgabe* of Rodange's *Renert*, dropped Rodange's own spelling in favour of the Engelmann–Welter system.[2] This is on the whole a satisfactory orthography. The system used in the *Luxemburger Wörterbuch*, 1950,[3] is a further improvement, e.g. by introducing *éi, ou* for /ei, ou/ instead of the earlier *e', o'*. I have made the necessary alterations to make Tockert's edition conform to the practice of the *Lux. Wtb.*, e.g. by eliminating *h* as a length sign and by using *ē* for [ə] instead of *ö*. The quantity of a vowel is expressed according to the following rule: single vowel before single consonant or before hiatus is long, before a cluster (incl. double consonant) it is short unless spelt double, in which case it is long. This rule applies to stressed syllables only, and also to the members of compounds. The spellings *ch, sch, jh* [ž], *ng* count as clusters although they stand for a single consonant phoneme. *Z* [ts], however, counts as a single consonant. As the voiced fricatives [z, ɟ, γ] are spelt with single *s, g* even after short vowels in the spelling

---

[1] See Bruch, *Grammaire*, p. 23. [2] See p. 23.
[3] See also Bruch, *Grammaire*, pp. 8–40.

system of the *Lux. Wtb.* the quantity of the preceding vowel remains unexpressed. To help the reader I have used the sign ⌣ for a preceding short vowel. In monosyllabic particles and auxiliaries doubling of consonants is not felt to be necessary after short vowels.

The correspondences between phonemes and letters are as follows:

Phoneme	Letter	Phoneme	Letter	Phoneme	Letter
i(:)	i, ii	ə/e	ë é (2)	ei	éi
e:	e, ee	iə	ie (3)	ε:i	äi
ε(:)	ä, e-ä, (1) ää	uə	ue	ɑi	ei, ai (4)
a(:)	a, aa			ou	ou
u(:)	u, uu			ɑ:u	âu (5)
o(:)	o, oo			ɑu	au

Notes

(1) *ä* only for the umlaut of *a* or corresponding to NHG *ö*, otherwise *e*. The long, open allophone is always spelt *ä* or *ää*.

(2) For the allophone [e] before [ç, k, ŋ]: *é*, but not in unstressed suffixes.

(3) In final syllables of French loan-words *-ie* is retained for [iː].

(4) The umlaut of *au* is spelt *ai*, otherwise *ei*.

(5) The *Lux. Wtb.* uses *au* for the long as well as the short diphthong.

§ 6. STRESSED SHORT VOWELS

6.1 [ɪ] is an open, lax, high-front vowel deriving from:[1]

(i) WGmc.[2] *i* where lengthening did not occur (especially before [l, m, n]): *Wisebaach* 'brook in the meadow', *Biwwel* 'Bible'.

(ii) Mutated WGmc. *u* where lengthening did not occur: *Kinnek* 'king', *Millen* 'mill'.

(iii) WGmc. *ê*[2] and *eu* (= MHG *ie*) where shortening occurred (especially before dentals and velars): *Krich* 'war', *Lidd* 'song', *bidden* 'to offer'.

(iv) WGmc. *ô* (= MHG *uo*) mutated (under the same conditions): *midd* 'tired', *Bicher* 'books'.

(v) Shortened other diphthongs in isolated cases: *sin* 'to be', *ech stin* 'I stand', *ech gin* 'I give or go', *din* 'to do'.

---

[1] Only the native sources are indicated. Foreign phonemes in loan-words are usually assimilated into the Lux. system, but these foreign sources are left out of account.

[2] Reference to WGmc. is traditional in Lux. philology owing to the development of the Lux. sounds, some of which never went through the MHG stage.

6.2 [ɛ] is an open, lax, mid-front vowel, deriving from:

(i) WGmc. *e* in originally closed syllables: *Dreck* 'dirt', *treffen* 'to meet'.

(ii) WGmc. *a* mutated in originally closed syllables and before *sk* (> *sch*): *besser* 'better', *Äppel* 'apples', *Fläsch* 'bottle'.

(iii) WGmc. *o* mutated in originally closed syllables: *Fräsch* 'frogs', *Lächer* 'holes'.

(iv) WGmc. *ai* (MHG *ei*) before [ŋ] < *n*:[1] *Steng* 'stones', *mengen* 'to mean'.

6.3 [ə] is a short, stressed, mid-central vowel with neutral lip position. It derives from:

(i) WGmc. *i* in originally closed syllables, except before *l, m, n, ht,* or *r* and *r*- clusters.[2] In a minority of cases the correspondence is, however, *a* (see § 6.4 (ii)). E.g. *gewёss* 'surely', *Schrёft* 'writing'.

(ii) WGmc. *o* in originally closed syllables, especially before *l, ll, l* + cons., where mutated: *Drёpps* 'drop', *Wёllef* 'wolves'.

(iii) WGmc. *u* mutated in closed syllables: *Bёsch* 'wood', *dёnn* 'thin', *schёlleg* 'guilty'.

(iv) WGmc. *i, ô* mutated (= MHG *üe*), *eu* (= MHG *iu* and *ie*) before [ŋ] < *n*: *Péng* 'pain, torture', *gréng* 'green', *néng* 'nine', *déngen* 'to serve'.[3]

Before [ŋ, ç, k] the allophone [e], a short, close, tense, mid-front vowel, occurs, in all other cases [ə]. E.g. [e]: *ad* (i) *déck* 'thick', *sécher* 'sure', *sénken* 'to sink'; *ad* (iii) *Réck* 'back', *Stéck* 'piece'; and (iv) above.

6.4 [ɑ] is a neutral, central, low-tongue vowel. It corresponds to:

(i) WGmc. *a* in closed syllables before *l, m, n* + cons. or before *l, n* in final position: *Dall* 'valley', *Mann* 'man', *falsch* 'wrong'; in loans from NHG with *a*.

(ii) WGmc. *i* in originally closed syllables, except before *l, m, n, ht,* or *r*: *batter* 'bitter', *fannen* 'to find'.[4]

(iii) WGmc. *o* in originally closed syllables except before *l*: *Schlass* 'castle', *Kapp* 'head'; also before WGmc. tenuis (*p* > *ff, k* > *ch*, etc.): *affen* 'open', *kachen* 'to cook'.

6.5 [ɔ] is an open, lax, mid-back vowel. It represents:

---

[1] This is an example of the effect of the Rhenish velarization upon the Lux. dialects. After WGmc. *ai* (MHG *ei*) *n* followed by another syllable > [ŋ]. The vowel is affected by the Rhenish correption and becomes short. See Bruch, *Lux.*, p. 116 f.; Palgen, *Studien*, map 9, 'meinen'.

[2] The position before *r* is regularly left out of account in this paragraph, since all vowels in this position are now long.

[3] See fn. to § 6.2 and Palgen, *Studien*, maps 8, 10, 12.

[4] Bertrang (§ 76) assumes this to be the regular correspondence of WGmc. *i* and regards /ə/ as a product of Lux. mutation. Bruch, *Lux.*, pp. 62–5, reckons with the possibility of *Ablaut*.

(i) WGmc. *o* in originally closed syllables before *l, ll, l-* clusters: *Vollek* 'people', *Wollef* 'wolf'.

(ii) WGmc. *u* in originally closed syllables except before *r* and *h* + cons.: *Broscht* 'chest', *domm* 'stupid'.

(iii) WGmc. *ô* (MHG *uo*), *û* in conditions where the Rhenish velarization occurred (see §§ 6.2 (iv) and 6.3 (iv)): *Hong* 'hen', *Schong* 'shoe(s)', *brong* 'brown'.

6.6 [ɷ] is an open, lax, high-back vowel. It represents:

(i) WGmc. *u* in certain monosyllabic words mainly: *Stuff* 'living-room'; also *kucken* 'to peep'.

(ii) WGmc. *ô* (= MHG *uo*) under conditions of shortening, e.g. before *l, m, n, d, t, ch*: *Brudder* 'brother', *gutt* 'good', *Stull* 'chair'.

(iii) WGmc. *a* in originally open syllables before *n*: *Hunn* 'cock', *Bunn* 'railway'.

§ 7. Long Vowels

7.1 [i:] is a close, high-front vowel, deriving from:

(i) WGmc. *i* in originally open syllables in some words and in closed syllables before *r* and *ht*: *riicht* 'right', *Stir* 'forehead'.

(ii) WGmc. mutated *u* in the same conditions: *Dir* 'door', *Fiisschen* 'fox' dim.

(iii) Loans: *Piisch* 'peach'.

7.2 [e:] is a close, mid-front vowel. Before *r* a more open [ɛ:] occurs, which many local dialects use in general instead of [e:]. It derives from:

(i) WGmc. *ai* (= MHG *ei*), except before [ŋ]: *Been* 'leg', *Heed* 'heath'.

(ii) WGmc. *au* and *-awi-* mutated (= MHG *öu*): *Beem* 'trees', *Freed* 'joy', *Hee* 'hay'. Locally: *Bäm*, etc.

(iii) WGmc. *a, â* mutated: *Deeg* 'days', *Bleeschen* 'bubble' dim., *Ärem* 'arms'.

(iv) WGmc. *-agi, -ege-*: *Neel* 'nails', *We* 'way', *leën* 'to lay', *Meedchen* 'girl'.

(v) WGmc. *e* before *r*: *Här* 'Mr.', *Stär* 'star'.

7.3 [a:] is a very advanced, over-long vowel. It derives from:

(i) WGmc. *a* in closed syllables before *ll, mm, nn, l* (< *ld*), *n* (< *nd*), *ng, r* + cons. and all stops and fricatives[1] except *hs, ht* (incl. < *ft*): *Baach* 'brook', *Af* 'ape', *Plaz* 'place'.

(ii) WGmc. *au* (= MHG *ou*): *A* 'eye', *kafen* 'to buy'.

7.4 [o:] is a close, mid-back vowel, deriving from:

(i) WGmc. *â* except before *ht* and *n*: *Dot* 'deed', *Joër* 'year'.

(ii) WGmc. *-age-*: *kloën* 'to complain', *Nol* 'nail'.

---

[1] Also in WGmc. open syllables before tenuis, e.g. *maachen* 'to make'.

7.5 [u:] is a close, high-back vowel, deriving from:

(i) WGmc. *u* in closed syllables before *r* and *ht, ss* (< *hs*): *Fuuss* 'fox', *huurtech* 'quick'.

§ 8. DIPHTHONGS

8.1 [iə] has a first element of varying length according to context and stress and a very short final element. It represents:

(i) WGmc. *e* and *a* mutated (= MHG *ë* and *e*) in originally open syllables and in closed syllables before *hs, ht*, and before *r* and *r*-clusters (except original *rr, rt*) in some words: *hiewen* 'to lift', *iessen* 'to eat', *briechen* 'to break',[1] *Bierg* 'mountain', *Bier* 'bear'. But owing to various interferences: *Häärz*, 'heart', *Ärem* 'arms', *Bäärtchen* 'beard' dim., *Äärd* 'earth'.[2]

(ii) Mutation of Lux. *ue* (see § 8.2): *zielen*, to count', *Dierfer* 'villages', *Blieder* 'leaves', *Bieder* 'baths'.

8.2 [uə] has a first element of varying length according to context and stress and a very short final element. It represents:

(i) WGmc. *a* in originally open syllables[3] and in closed syllables before [s] < *hs*, [x] < *hl, ft*: *bueden* 'to bathe', *Hues* 'hare', *Nuem* 'name', *Nuecht* 'night', *bezuelen* 'to pay', but *aacht* 'eight'.

(ii) WGmc. *o* in originally open syllables[4] and before *r, r* + cons. and *cht*: *Dueref* 'village', *Duechter* 'daughter', *luewen* 'to praise'.

(iii) WGmc. *â* before *ht*: *bruecht* 'brought'.

8.3 [ei] both components are short and equivalent in length. It represents:

(i) WGmc. *ai* (= MHG *ê*): *Séil* 'soul', *méi* 'more'.

(ii) WGmc. *ê*[2] (= MHG *ie* < OHG *ia*): *Bréif* 'letter'.

(iii) WGmc. *eu* (= MHG *ie*):[5] *léif* 'dear', *schéissen* 'to shoot'; also in the borrowed suffix corresponding to NHG *-ieren*: *angajhéieren* 'to engage'.

(iv) Mutation of WGmc. *au* (= MHG *ô*), i.e. MHG *œ*: *béis* 'wicked'.

(v) Mutation of WGmc. *ô* (= MHG *uo*), i.e. MHG *üe*: *fréi* 'early', *séiss* 'sweet', *féieren* 'to lead'.

(vi) Mutation of WGmc. *â* (= MHG *æ*): *spéit* 'late', *schwéier* 'heavy'.

8.4 [ou] both components are short and equivalent in length. It represents:

(i) WGmc. *au* (= MHG *ô*): *dout* 'dead', *Brout* 'bread'.

---

[1] Also before original tenues WGmc. *p, t, k*. On this diphthongization and parallel developments in Romance languages, see Bruch, *Lux.*, pp. 78–88.
[2] On NHG influence, see Bruch, *Lux.*, p. 76. Lux. City has *Hierz*.
[3] But not before WGmc. tenuis, see § 7.3 (i).
[4] But not before WGmc. tenuis, see § 6.4 (iii).
[5] For shortening, see § 6.1 (iii) and (iv).

(ii) WGmc. *ô* (= MHG *uo*):[1] *Fouss* 'foot', *Bouf* 'boy'. Long *o* of foreign origin becomes also Lux. *ou*: *Kanounen* 'guns', *Natioun* 'nation'.

(iii) WGmc. *â* before *r*: *wouer* 'true'.

(iv) WGmc. *-og-*: *Bou* 'bow, bend'.

(v) All strong verbs which still have a preterite, form it with *-ou-*: *blouf* pret. of *bleiwen* 'to remain', *koum* < *kommen* 'to come', *souz* < *sëtzen* 'to sit'.

8.5 The following two pairs of diphthongs /ɛ:i/–/ɑi/ and /ɑ:u/–/ɑu/ have arisen from the same sources:

(i) The first pair from both WGmc. *î* and *iu* (*eu*), the latter coinciding with the MHG product of the mutation of *û* (*iu*);

(ii) the second pair from WGmc. *û*.

The division into two phonemes in each case is the result of an earlier system of accentuation which resulted in circumflexion (i.e. an over-long vowel) in some conditions and in correption (i.e. shortening) in some others. This has led to a difference in quality linked with a difference in quantity in present-day Lux. Morphological circumstances have frequently disturbed the historical development. But the following conditions reflect the normal development:[2]

(i) /ɛ:i/ and /ɑ:u/ are found in (*a*) monosyllabics if they are original monosyllabics, (*b*) in penultimate syllables before voiceless consonants.

(ii) /ɑi/ and /ɑu/ are found in (*a*) monosyllabics which have become monosyllabics through the loss of a former suffix, (*b*) in penultimate syllables before voiced consonants or in hiatus.

The two pairs of phonemes thus contrast mainly in present monosyllabics. If they now contrast also in polysyllabics this is brought about by morphological interference. Examples: (i) (*a*) *Käil* 'wedge', *Äis* 'ice'; *Zâun* 'fence', *Brâut* 'fiancée', *Hâut* 'skin'; (*b*) *wäissen* 'to whiten', *gräifen* 'to grip'; *sâufen* 'to drink', *bâussen* 'outside'; (ii) (*a*) *Feil* 'file', *Mais* 'mice'; *Laun* 'mood', *haut* 'to-day', *Dauf* 'dove'; (*b*) *weisen* 'to lead', *dreiwen* 'to drive'; *sauer* 'sour', *mausen* 'to catch mice'. The phonological difference has led to a semantic differentiation, even if etymologically not justified, e.g. in *fein* 'elevated': *fäin* 'decent', *faul* 'rotten': *fâul* 'lazy', *weit* 'wide' of clothes: *wäit* 'far'.[3] The last traces of the dative case of nouns go back to this

---

[1] For shortening, see § 6.6 (ii). On the problem of this diphthongization as a whole, see T. Frings, 'Germanisch ô und ê', *Beitr.*, lxiii, 1939, 1–116; Bruch, *Lux.*, 93–101.

[2] For shortening of the vowel before velar nasal < dental nasal (Rhenish velarization), see §§ 6.3 (iv); 6.5 (iv).

[3] See Bruch, *Lux.*, p. 9.

development, e.g. *Läif* 'body': *am Leif* dat.; *Hâus* 'house': *Haus* dat.; also *bäi* adv.: *bei* prep.

§ 9. UNSTRESSED VOWELS

Except in foreign words and compounds only /ə/—[e] in the endings *-echt, -ek*—is at all frequent in unstressed positions.

9.1 [ə] derives from MHG *-e* + cons. and *i* in suffixes, e.g. *Kinnek* 'king', *gespréicheg* 'talkative', *bedeien* 'to mean', *frĕndlech* 'friendly', *déckeg* 'very thick', *vergiessen* 'to forget', *Liddchen* 'song' dim., *rootsĕm* 'advisable', *Kächen* 'woman cook', *Wourecht* 'truth'. All MHG unstressed vowels not followed by a consonant have been dropped.

9.2 [ə] has developed as a svarabhakti vowel in the following circumstances:

(i) Between *l* and *m, f, ch, k*: *Mĕllech* 'milk', *hallef* 'half', *Vollek* 'people', and *r* and those consonants mainly after long vowels: *Tiremchen* 'tower' dim., *durech* 'through'.

(ii) After diphthong or long vowel before final *r*: *schwéier* 'heavy', *Déier* 'animal'.

(iii) After diphthong or long vowel before *n* in verbal forms: *freĕn* 'to rejoice', *froĕn* 'to ask'.

9.3 [ɔ] occurs in the suffix *-ong*: *Menong* 'opinion'.

§ 10. VOWEL QUANTITY

10.1 The distribution of vowel quantity is not restricted by position with the exception that in words ending in a stressed vowel the latter is normally always long and that before *r* and *-cht* short vowels are very rare and to some extent 'irregular'. Two seemingly contradictory processes have fundamentally affected the historical quantity distribution.

10.2 *Circumflexion*[1] (*Trägheitsakzent*)—the lengthening of originally short vowels, diphthongization of long or lengthened vowels—has affected in originally open syllables (*a*) WGmc. *a* > *ue*, but before WGmc. tenuis > *aa*; (*b*) WGmc. *e* incl. before WGmc. tenuis > *ie* (but WGmc. *a* did not mutate > *ie* before WGmc. tenuis); (*c*) WGmc. *o* > *ue* but not before WGmc. tenuis; - in originally closed syllables except before *l, m, n* + cons., final *l, n*, and *s* < *hs*, *cht* < *ht, ft*: (*a*) WGmc. *a* > *aa*. Lengthening has also affected all WGmc. short vowels before *cht* < *ht, ft, s* < *hs*, final *r* and *r* + cons.: (*a*) WGmc. *a* > *ue* + *s*, *cht*, > *aa* + *r*, *r* + cons.; (*b*) WGmc.

---

[1] On circumflexion and corrdption, see Bruch, *Lux.*, pp. 66–133, where the bibliography is given.

S

e > *ie*; (*c*) WGmc. *o* > *ue*; (*d*) WGmc. *i* > *ii*; (*e*) WGmc. *u* > *uu*.[1]
In the case of WGmc. short vowels before originally final *l* or nasal,
or clusters with *l* or nasals the circumflexion has not affected the
vowels but the following consonant and has produced the so-called
Schwebelaute /l:, n:, m:, ŋ:/. Diphthongization has also occurred in
the case of (*a*) WGmc. *ô* (= MHG *ô*, *uo*) > *ou*; (*b*) WGmc. *ê*, *eo*
(= MHG *ie*) > *éi*; (*c*) WGmc. *î*, *û* > *äi*, *âu*.

10.3 *Correption* (*Schärfung*) leads to shortening of originally long
vowels or diphthongs and may affect the development of consonants
(*Verengung*), e.g. the *Rheinische Gutturalisierung*, which has, however, affected Lux. little, with the exception of the dialects of the
northern province of the *Ösling*.[2] Shortening is found before dental
stops, nasals, *l*, *ch* and *s* and affects WGmc. *ê*, *eo* (*Krich* 'war', *Lidd*
'song'), *ô* (*gutt* 'good', *Brudder* 'brother', *Stull* 'chair'), *î*, *û* > *ai*, *au*.[3]
Shortening with change of former dental nasal to velar nasal is
found in the case of (*a*) WGmc. *î* + *n* in former penultimate syllable
(*dénger* NHG *deiner*, *Wäin* but *Wéngchen* (dim.) 'wine'); (*b*) WGmc.
û and *iu* + *n* (*brong* 'brown', *néng* 'nine'); (*c*) WGmc. *ô* + *n* (*Hong*
'hen', *Schong* 'shoe') and umlaut (*gréng* 'green'); (*d*) WGmc. *eo* + *n*
(*dengen* 'to serve'); (*e*) WGmc. *ai* (MHG *ei*) + *n* (*kleng* 'small').

§ 11. COMPARISON WITH THE NHG VOWELS

(1) Apart from the general tendency to lengthen short vowels in
open syllables Lux. and NHG go separate ways in the treatment of
vowel quantity.

(2) Characteristic of Lux. are the long vowels before certain
consonantal clusters, e.g. *r* + cons., *cht*.

(3) Lux. has diphthongs unknown to NHG: *éi* (NHG *ee*, *ie*, *ö*, *ü*),
ou (NHG *oo*, *u*), *ue* (NHG *a*, *o*), *ie* (NHG *e*, *ä*).

(4) Lux. has *äi* and *ai* corresponding to NHG *ei*, *eu*; *âu* and *au*
corresponding to NHG *au*.

(5) Unrounding has obliterated the NHG differences between
i–ü, *e–ö*, *ei–äu*.

(6) Like NHG, Lux. makes no distinction between the umlaut of
a and the historical *e*.

(7) Lux. keeps the reflexes of MHG *ou*, *ei* distinct from those of
MHG *û* and *î*, unlike NHG, but has monophthongs, *aa* and *ee*, for the
former.

(8) Like NHG, Lux. has lax, open short vowels and tense, close
long vowels.

---

[1] It is interesting to note that the high-tongue vowels are hardly affected by
lengthening but are, on the other hand, exposed to lowering.
[2] See R. Bruch, 'Die Mundart des Nordöslings', *Annuaire*, 1952, pp. 1–50.
[3] In contrast to *äi*, *âu*, see § 8.5.

(9) Lux. retains unstressed vowels in the prefixes *ge-* and *be-* like NHG, but unlike NHG drops former final *-e* not followed by a consonant.

Chief Vowel Correspondences

Lux. (1)	ue	ie	o	a	ĕ	ou	éi	ee	aa	äi	ai	áu	au
MHG	a, o (2)	e, ĕ, ä (2)	u o (3)	i	ü	ô uo ê, ie, æ, œ, üe		ei, öu ou		ī, iu		û	
NHG	a, o	e, ä	u o	i	ü	o u e, ie, ä, ö, ü		ei, eu ou		ei, eu,		au	

NHG	a, o	e, ä	u	i	ü	o u e, ie, ä, ö, ü		ei	eu, äu	au	
MHG	a o (2)	e, ĕ, ä (2)	u	i	ü	ô uo ê, ie, æ, œ, iu		ei	ī iu öu	û	ou
Lux.	ue, a	ie	o	a, ĕ, ĕ		ou	éi	ee	äi ai ee	âu, au	aa

Notes

(1) For the phonetic value of the letters, see § 5. MHG and NHG sounds are given in their respective orthography.

(2) In originally open syllables and before *-ht,* for details, see §§ 8.1; 8.2.

(3) In closed syllables, for details see § 6.4.

THE CONSONANTS

§ 12. THE CONSONANTAL SYSTEM

Stops		Fricatives		Affricates	Sonants	
voiceless	voiced	voiceless	voiced		nasals	liquids
p	b	f	v		m m:	
t	d	s š	z ž	(ts)	n n:	r
k	g	x	ɣ		ŋ ŋ:	l l: (h)

12.1 Stops and fricatives form oppositions of voice in initial and medial positions—with some restrictions—while in final position the laws of hardening in absolute final position and of lenition in sandhi before vowels apply. Those restrictions concern the fricatives other than the labial ones. Of the dental fricatives only /z/ occurs initially before vowels. No dental occurs before consonants in initial position. Only the alveolar-palatal /š/ is tolerated in that position. The palato-velar fricatives have velar allophones [x] and [ɣ] after short and long *a, o, u, au* and palatal allophones [ç] and [ʝ] after all other phonemes. The voiced palatal allophone [ʝ] occurs also initially but the voiceless palato-velar is unrepresented in that position unless we choose to regard [h], which occurs only initially, as an allophone of /x/. The initial voiceless stops are slightly aspirated.

12.2 In absolute final position and in sandhi before consonants only voiceless stops and fricatives occur (NHG *Auslautsverhärtung*), cf. *gudder* /d/: *gutt* /t/ 'good'; *Bouf* /f/: *Bouwen* /v/ 'boy(s)'. On the other hand in sandhi before a word beginning with a vowel all final stops and fricatives are voiced, even clusters,[1] cf. *kuckt*: *kugd ewech*[2] 'looks', 'looks away'; *riicht* 'straight': *riijd als*; *wat* 'what': *wad as*. This law applies also before unstressed *ĕt* (< *hat*) 'it', but not before the unstressed personal pronouns the stressed forms of which begin with *h*. (See § 27.)

12.3 The contrast between short /l, n, m/ and long /l:, n:, m:/, the so-called *Schwebelaute*, occurs only after short vowels in final position or before a final consonant, e.g. in final *-ls*, *-lt*, *-mt*, *-mp*, *-ns*, *-nsch*, *-nt*. For instance: *Brĕll* 'spectacles', *Fall* 'fall', *Spill* 'game', *voll* 'drunk', *Mann* 'man', *Sall* 'hall', *Hals* 'neck', *Feld* 'field', *Kand* 'child', *Mënsch* 'human being', *dir kënnt* 'you would be able to', *komm* 'come' p.p., but: *komm!* 'come' imp., *Still* 'stem', *Säll* 'halls', *voll* 'full', *dir kënnt* 'you can'. Before *k ng* is also a *Schwebelaut*, e.g. *dengken* 'to think', so is *m* before *p*, e.g. *Damp*, 'steam'. Medially the *Schwebelaut* loses much of its character and appears to be non-phonemic.[3]

§ 13. SPELLING

Since all consonants with the exception of the *Schwebelaute* are short the orthography of the *Luxemburger Wörterbuch* follows the NHG practice of using double consonants to indicate vowel short-ness. On the whole the NHG spelling conventions are followed:

Phoneme	Letter	Phoneme	Letter	Phoneme	Letter
p	p, pp	f	f, ff, v (2)	x-ç	ch, g (5)
b	b, bb	v	v, w	ɣ-ʝ	g, j
t	t, tt	s	ss	ts	z, tz
d	d, dd	z	s (3)	m, n, ŋ	m, n, ng
k	k, ck, kk	š	sch (4)	l, r	l, r
g	g, gg (1)	ž	jh	n:, l:	ņ, ļ
				etc. (6)	

[1] See Bertrang, § 218; Bruch, *Lux.*, pp. 46–8.

[2] This sandhi-lenition is not indicated in the orthography of the *Lux. Wtb.*, 1950, nor in the specimen text given here, but see the phonetic transcription.

[3] Professor R. Bruch has kindly stated in a letter: ,,Nach einer mehrjährigen Überprüfung komme ich zum Schluss: Am stärksten ausgeprägt ist die

Notes

(1) *G* has this sound value primarily in initial position.

(2) *V* only in initial position where the corresponding NHG word has *v*.

(3) In initial clusters *st-*, *sp-*, it stands for *sch*.

(4) In French loan-words also *ch*.

(5) The spelling conforms to that of NHG where there is a NHG parallel, but after a short vowel in stressed final position only *ch* is used.

(6) The *Schwebelaute* are indicated by ., but not in the specimen text.

(7) The hardening in final position is indicated only in words which have no parallel in NHG, otherwise the NHG practice is followed. Sandhi-lenition is not indicated as it is obvious from the context.

§ 14. The Consonant Phonemes

14.1 [p] is a fortis, voiceless, bilabial stop representing:

(i) WGmc. *p* in initial position and medially and finally in the WGmc. cluster *mp*: *Pond* 'pound', *Tromp* 'trump card'.

(ii) WGmc. *-pp-* and *-bb-*: *Apel* 'apple'.

(iii) WGmc. final *p* only in *op* 'on', cf. NHG *auf*.

14.2 [t] is a fortis, voiceless, alveolar stop representing:

(i) WGmc. *dd*: *Mëttel* 'means'.

(ii) WGmc. *t* in those positions where it is unshifted in NHG: *batter* 'bitter', *Nascht* 'nest'; and in the so-called *Mittelfränkische Reliktwörter*: *wat* 'what', *dat* 'that', *hat*, *ët* 'it', *dët* 'this', the neuter ending *-t*: *schéint*, cf. NHG *schönes*; in the pret. and past part. of weak verbs the inf. of which has *tz* (< *t*): *geschwat—schwätzen* 'to talk'.

14.3 [k] is a fortis, voiceless, velar stop representing:

(i) WGmc. *k* in those positions where it is unshifted in NHG: *Kanner* 'children'.

(ii) WGmc. *-kk-* and *-gg-*: *plécken* 'to pick', *Bréck* 'bridge'.

(iii) WGmc. *hs* > *ks* in some words: *sechs* 'six', *Ochs* 'ox', but see § 14.9 (iii).

The following three voiced stops do not occur in final position except in sandhi before vowels (see § 12.2). The three voiceless stops can, in final position, therefore also derive from the sources given in the next three paragraph sections.

Konsonantendehnung in den umschriebenen Fällen im Auslaut, abgeschwächt ist sie im Wortinlaut; Sandhierscheinungen können sie im Wortinnern ganz verschwinden lassen. In *van:t* „Wind" ist die Dehnung länger als in *man·təl*, noch kürzer (kaum merklich) ist sie in *mɛn(·)təlçən*."

14.4 [b] is a voiced, bilabial stop representing:

(i) WGmc. initial *b-*: *Baach* 'brook', *Brout* 'bread'.

(ii) WGmc. *-bb-* in some words: *babbelen* 'to gossip'.

14.5 [d] is a voiced, dental-alveolar stop representing:

(i) WGmc. *d*: *Deel* 'part', *néideg* 'necessary'.

(ii) WGmc. *þ*: *Daum* 'thumb'.

14.6 [g] is a voiced, palato-velar stop representing:

(i) WGmc. initial *g-*: *goën* 'to go', *Gedold* 'patience'.

(ii) Medially it derives from loans: *Waggon*.

14.7 [f] is a voiceless, labio-dental fricative representing:

(i) WGmc. *f* except in intervocalic position (> [v]): *Fuuss* 'fox', *Wollef* 'wolf'.

(ii) WGmc. *þ* in medial and final position after vowels, *l* or *r*: *Schëff* 'ship', *Af* 'monkey'.

(iii) in final position WGmc. *ð*: *Bouf* 'boy', *Graf* 'grave'.

14.8 [v] is a voiced, labio-dental fricative, with bilabial articulation after [k, š, ts]. It derives from:

(i) WGmc. *ð* in medial position: *Liewen* 'life', *selwer* 'self'.

(ii) WGmc. *f* in intervocalic position: *Uewen* 'stove'.

(iii) WGmc. *w* in initial and medial position: *wénken* 'to wave', *wëschen* 'to sweep'.

14.9 [s] is a voiceless, dental fricative, deriving from:

(i) WGmc. *s* in final position, and WGmc. *-ss-*: *Hues* 'hare', *këssen* 'to kiss'.

(ii) WGmc. *t* in medial and final position after vowels: *Noss* 'nut', *wäiss* 'white' (but see § 14.2 (ii)).

(iii) WGmc. *-hs-* in many words: *Wuess* 'growth', *Fuuss* 'fox'.

14.10 [z] is a voiced, dental fricative, deriving from:

(i) WGmc. *s* in prevocalic initial and medial position between vowels: *soën* 'to say', *Eisen* 'iron'.

14.11 [š] is a voiceless, post-alveolar, grooved fricative representing:

(i) WGmc. *sk*, WGmc. *s* in initial position before all consonants and in medial and final position also generally before *t* (except in the superlative ending): *Bësch* 'wood', *stoussen* 'to push', *Nascht* 'nest', *Duuscht* 'thirst'.

14.12 [ž] is a voiced, post-alveolar, grooved fricative, representing:

(i) WGmc. *-rs-* in medial position: *gehoojhem* 'obedient'.

(ii) French loan-words: *angajhéieren* 'to engage'.

14.13 [x] is a voiceless, palato-velar fricative, velar after back vowels, palatal in other surroundings. It derives from:

(i) WGmc. *k* in medial and final position after vowels: *Saach* 'thing', *Mëllech* 'milk'.

(ii) WGmc. *g̣* in final position: *Dag* 'day', *ewech* 'away'.

(iii) WGmc. *h* before *t*: *dichteg* 'busy', *Nuecht* 'night'.

(iv) WGmc. *ft* > *cht* in a few words: *Luucht* 'air', *uechter* 'after'. (See Note 15.)

14.14 [ɣ] is a voiced, palato-velar fricative, velar after back vowels, palatal in other surroundings, including the initial position. It derives from:

(i) In initial position: WGmc. *j*: *Joër* 'year'.

(ii) In medial position from WGmc. *g̣*, e.g. after *l*, *r*: *Bierger* 'mountains', *verdilgen* 'to wipe out', after vowels in such words where a former WGmc. *g̣* has not disappeared altogether (cf. *Nol* 'nail', *Ren* 'rain'):[1] *Spigel* 'mirrors', *Vigelchen* 'bird', *Kinnegin* 'queen', *Jugend* 'youth', *Dugend* 'virtue'.

14.15 [ts] is the only affricate in Lux. It derives from the same sources as the corresponding affricate in NHG, thus: WGmc. *t* in initial position before vowels and *w*: *Zong* 'tongue', *Zäit* 'time', in medial and final position after *l*, *r*, and *-tt-*: *Kaz* 'cat', *späizen* 'to spit'.

14.16 [h] the glottal aspirate occurs only in initial position and derives from WGmc. *h*: *Heed* 'heath'.

14.17 [m] is a bilabial nasal deriving from the same sources as the corresponding NHG nasal. Before *p* we find generally the *Schwebelaut*:[2] *schwammen* 'to swim', *Damp* 'steam'.

14.18 [n] and [n:] contrast only in the positions indicated in § 12.3. Historically, WGmc. *n* has been affected by (*a*) loss before fricative,[3] e.g. *siecht* 'soft', *ais* 'us'; (*b*) velarization (> ŋ), e.g. *Steng* 'stones', see § 10.3; (*c*) sandhi assimilation (see § 16); (*d*) loss in final position after *r*: *Bur* 'spring', cf. *burn—bourne*.

14.19 [ŋ], the velar nasal occurs as *Schwebelaut* before other consonants, e.g. *fenken* 'to catch'; and has developed in many cases from a former *n* (see § 10.3).

14.20 [l] is a palato-velar lateral deriving from WGmc. *l* and contrasting with the *Schwebelaut* [l:] in final position only (§ 12.3). The *Schwebelaut* occurs also before other consonants, e.g. *Gol̦d* 'gold'.

14.21 [r] is a frontal trill and derives from WGmc. *r*, except before *s* where it has been assimilated, e.g. *Freed* 'joy'.

---

[1] See Bruch, *Lux.*, pp. 34–7; *Grundl.*, p. 172 f.

[2] Phonetically the *Schwebelaut* is a lengthened nasal or *l* where the voice is withdrawn before the end of the articulation, giving the impression of a suspended phonation or a pause.

[3] On this 'Ingvaeonism', see Bruch, *Lux.*, pp. 15–20; *Grundl.*, pp. 156, 166.

§ 15. Assimilation[1]

Historical assimilations are frequent, e.g. *e kënt* 'he comes' (*mt* > *nt*); *eppes* 'something' (*tw* > *p*); *Gromper* 'potato', cf. NHG *Grundbirne* (*ntb* > *mp*). Some assimilations form historical sound laws:

(i) Intervocalic *-ld* > *l*: *bal* 'soon', *halen* 'to hold'.

(ii) Intervocalic *-nd-* > *n*: *fannen* 'to find', *Kanner* 'children' but *Kand* 'child'; but not before the suffix *-el*: *Bändel* 'garter'.

(iii) Other assimilations are, e.g. *rs* > *š*, *ž* (see § 14.11, 12), *rn* > *r* (see § 14.18), *hs* > *s* (see § 14.9 (iii)).

(iv) For assimilation (voicing) in sandhi, see § 12.2.

§ 16. The Mobile *-n*[2]

Final *n* is dropped in sandhi and at the juncture of compounds if the next word begins with a consonant other than *h, d, t, n* or *z*, e.g. *den Dag* 'the day', *den Af* 'the monkey', *den Hunn* 'the cock', but *de Wanter* 'winter', *de Wollef* 'wolf', *de Mann* 'the man', or *mäin Hâus* 'my house', but *mäi Brout* 'my bread'. The lengthened *n* [n:] is exempted, as well as the *n* which is the product of assimilation and reduction < *-nn, -nd-*, e.g. *dënn* 'thin', *blann* 'blind'. But the *n* of *an* 'and' is 'mobile'. The prefix *on-* retains its *n* everywhere. Before *si, se* 'she, they' the *n* is frequently preserved.

§ 17. Comparison with the NHG Consonants

The most salient differences are:

(1) While Lux. shares with NHG a consonantal system based on a difference between voiced and voiceless consonants, which is neutralized in final position, the Lux. final consonants are affected by sandhi lenition.

(2) Lux., unlike NHG, does not distinguish between WGmc. *þ* and *d* (NHG *d* and *t*).

(3) Lux. has *p* where NHG has *pf*.

(4) Where NHG has medial and final *b* and *g* Lux. has fricatives *v* or *f*, *ch* or *j*, or, especially in the case of *g*, has completely lost the consonant.

(5) Final *n*, especially in inflexional endings, is 'mobile', i.e. dropped before all consonants other than *h, d, t, n* or *z*.

(6) Lux. has so-called *Schwebelaute*, i.e. long nasals and a long lateral.

(7) Certain NHG clusters, notably *-nd-, -ld-, -lt-, -rs-*, have been exposed to total assimilation in Lux.

(8) Lux. lacks the glottal stop onset.

[1] See Bruch, *Lux.*, pp. 6–15.
[2] See Bruch, *Lux.*, pp. 25–8; *Grammaire*, p. 43; *Lux. Wtb.*, 1950, p. 5.

MORPHOLOGY

NOUNS AND ARTICLES

§ 18. Formation of the Plural

Lux. possesses only two endings to express plurality in nouns, a former final -*e* having dropped. Mutation can also indicate plurality either alone or in conjunction with the ending -*er*. In one class of nouns number emerges from the context only. The laws of assimilation of former medial -*ld*- and -*nd*- have created a number distinction based on a difference in the root consonants. Thus there are the following types of plural formation:

Type A: plural not marked by ending or mutation.
Type B: plural marked by difference in root consonant.
Type C: plural marked by mutation alone.
Type D: plural marked by ending -*en*.
Type E: plural marked by ending -*er* with mutation where possible.

Note: All back and low-tongue vowels are mutatable. The correspondences are as follows:

Basic vowel:	a	aa	o	oo	u	ue	ou	au	âu
Mutated vowel:	ă/ë/ie	ä/ee	ĕ	ee	i	ie	éi	ai	äi/ai

For the phonetic value of these letters, see § 5. There is often a change in length as well, e.g. *aa* (< *a*) mutates to *ä*, e.g. *Apel*— *Äppel*. The umlaut of *a* < WGmc. *o*, *i* is *ĕ* (*é*), e.g. *Kaṇd* 'child'— *Kĕndchen*. The umlaut *ie* of *a* presupposes an earlier *ue* in the mutated form (see § 8.1 (ii)), e.g. *Blat* 'leaf'—*Blieder*. The umlaut of *au* usually follows the rules set out in § 8.5, thus *Hâus*—*Haiser* 'house', *Mâul*— *Mailchen* 'mouth', *Hâut*—*Hait* 'skin', but before voiceless consonants in (former) penultimate syllables: *Bâuch*—*Bäich* 'belly', *Fâuscht*—*Fäischt* 'fist'.

Type A. To this type belong:
(i) Nouns ending in -*en* (except dim. -*chen*): *Millen* 'mill', *Familjen* 'family'.
(ii) Some neuter nouns: *Schwäin* 'pig', *Been* 'leg'.
(iii) Some masc. nouns in -*er* or -*el* or with non-mutatable root-vowel: *Fĕscher* 'fisher', *Wierfel* 'dice', *Fanger* 'finger' (but also *Fangeren* after Type D (ii)), *Fĕsch* 'fish'.

Type B. To this type belong mainly masc. nouns with non-mutatable root-vowel ending in -*nd* or -*n*: *Frĕnd*—*Frĕnn* 'friend', *Hond*—*Honn* 'dog', *Steen*—*Steng* 'stone'.

Type C. To this type belong:
(i) Most masc. nouns with a back root-vowel: *Moo*—*Mee* 'stomach', *Krou*—*Kréi* 'jug'; those ending in -*nd* change to *n* in the pl. *Band*— *Bänn* 'volume'.

(ii) Those fem. nouns which mutate also in NHG: *Kou—Kéi* 'cow', *Mâus—Mais* 'mouse', and with consonantal change *Wand—Wänn* 'wall', *Hand—Hänn* 'hand'.

Type D. To this type belong:

(i) The majority of fem. nouns: *Kaz—Kazen* 'cat', *Geess—Geessen* 'goat', *Baach—Baachen* 'brooks'.

(ii) Many masc. nouns: *Af—Afen* 'monkey', *Bouf—Bouwen* 'boy', *Stéier—Stéieren* 'bull'.

(iii) Some neuters: *A—Aen* 'eye', *Ouer—Oueren* 'ear', *Huer—Hueren* 'horn', *Déier—Déieren* 'animal'.

Type E. To this type belong:

(i) The majority of neuter nouns: *Enn—Enner* 'end', *Hong—Hénger* 'hen', *Kand—Kanner* 'child', *Bild—Biller* 'picture'.

(ii) A larger number of masc. nouns than in NHG: *Abléck—Ablécker* 'moment', *Mond—Ménner* 'mouth', *Bësch—Bëscher* 'wood'.

(iii) All diminutives in *-chen* take *-ercher* in the pl., those in *-elchen* take *-elcher* (see Note 2 to text).

§ 19. CASE FORMS

Lux. nouns are without any case endings, except for the genitive ending *-s* in certain fixed formulas, e.g. *Zäits genuch* 'enough time', and dat. pl. *-en* in obsolescent usage, e.g. *de Leiden* 'people' for *de Leit*. The laws of assimilation (see § 15) and of correption giving rise to a *Schwebelaut* (see §§ 12.3; 14.17 ff.) have further left traces of dative sg. forms,[1] e.g. nouns ending in *-nd*: common case *Hond* 'dog', *Mond* 'mouth', *Kand* 'child', *Pond* 'pound', dative *Honn*, *Monn*, *Kann*, *Ponn*; nouns in *-l*: c.c. *Hals* 'neck', *Stall* 'stable', dative *Haals*, *Stal*; nouns with diphthongs *Hâus* 'house', *Läif* 'body' dat. *am Haus*, *am Leif* 'in the house', etc. Possession is expressed by the usual dialectal dative paraphrase, e.g. *dem Af séng Fra* 'the monkey's wife'; other genitival functions by *vun*.

§ 20. GENDER

The majority of nouns have the same gender as in NHG, but the following are among those with a different gender: *Bak* m. 'cheek', *Eck* m. 'corner', *Botter* m. 'butter', *Pobeier* m. 'paper', *Baach* f. 'brook', *Fënster* f. 'window', *Plaz* f. 'place'.

§ 21. THE DECLENSION OF THE DEFINITE ARTICLE

	m.	f.	n.	pl.
Common Case	den (2)	d	d	d
Dative	dem (3) } der		dem (3)	den (2)
Genitive (4)	des }		des	der

[1] See Bruch, *Lux.*, p. 9; *Grammaire*, p. 50.

Notes

(1) *e* is [ə], when stressed [e:].

(2) With mobile *-n*, see § 16. Historically speaking, the common case derives from the accusative.

(3) After prepositions often shortened to *em*, e.g. *hannerem* 'behind the . . .'.

(4) On the use of the genitive, see Note 6 to the text.

(5) The def. art. is also used before personal names.

§ 22. The Declension of the Indefinite Article

	m. n.	*f.*
Common Case	en (1)	eng
Dative	engem	enger
Genitive	enges	enger

Notes

(1) With mobile *-n*, see § 16.
(2) Stressed *e* is [ɛ].

§ 23. Agglutinations

In addition to the fusions of prepositions and articles known in NHG there are e.g. also *mam* (NHG *mit dem*), *nom* (NHG *nach dem*).

ADJECTIVES

§ 24. Declension

Adjectives are inflected only when used in attributive position or when substantivized. The frequent use of the genitive is characteristic. Only traces have survived of the Gmc. distinction between strong and weak declensions (see Note 2).

	m.	*f.*	*n.*	*pl.*
Common Case	jongen	jong	jongt (3)	jong
Dative	jongen/-em (2)	jonger	jongen/-em (2)	jongen (4)
Genitive	jongen	jonger	jongen	jonger (5)

Notes

(1) Final *-n* is mobile, see § 16.

(2) The ending is *-em* only if the adjective stands alone before a noun.

(3) If no art. or pron. precedes the adj. can be endingless, e.g. *schéi Wieder* 'fine weather'. As a noun after *wat* or *eppes* 'something', *näischt* 'nothing' it takes *-es*, *-s*, e.g. *näischt Gutts*, cf. NHG *nichts Gutes*.

(4) Often endingless, especially if alone or preceded by a numeral.

(5) The gen. is used especially after numerals, words of quantity or measure or the partitive pronoun *där*, cf. the three possibilities *mat dräi grousse* (or: *grouss*, see 4) *Kierf* 'with three big baskets' dat., or *mat dräi grousser Kierf* gen. The gen. occurs also when the adj. is substantivized, e.g. *dräi Grousser*; especially when alone, e.g. *dat si Schlechter* 'these are bad ones'.

§ 25. Comparison

The comparative is formed analytically with the particle *méi*, e.g. *méi laang* 'longer', except in the case of the anomolous *besser* 'better', *léiwer* 'rather', *manner* 'less'. Comparatives in *-er* of other adjectives, used rarely, indicate the relative degree, Engl. 'rather'. The indef. art. follows *méi*, e.g. *méi e laangt* (n.). The comparative particle 'than' is *wéi* or *ewéi*.

The superlative ends in *-st* with mutation where possible, e.g. *de längst, am längsten*. The suffix *-eg* has the meaning 'very', e.g. *grouss* 'big'—*gréisst* 'biggest'—*grousseg* 'very big'.

NUMERALS

§ 26

Een, with mobile *-n*, has a special form for use as a noun only in the common case neuter: *eent*, e.g. *dat kënnt op eent eraus* 'it's the same thing'. The forms are the same as those of the indef. art., except that the common case masc. and neuter has a long vowel. The forms for 'two' distinguish *zwee* n., *zwéi* m., *zwou* f. in conservative use.

PRONOUNS

§ 27. Personal Pronouns

The stressed and unstressed forms are:

	1st Pers.	2nd Pers.	3rd Person m.	f.	n.
Nom. sg.	ech	du, de	hien, en (2)	si, se	hatt, et, t
Gen. sg.	ménger	dénger	sénger	hirer	sénger, ës
Dat. sg.	mir, mer	dir, der	him, em	hir, er	him, em
Acc. sg.	mech	dech	hien, en (2)	si, se	hat, et, t
Nom. pl.	mir, mer	dir, der		si, se	
Gen. pl.	onser (3)	ärer		hirer	
Dat. pl.	}ons (3)	}iech		hinen, en	
Acc. pl.				se, si	

Notes

(1) The vowel in *ech, dech, mech,* is [e]; otherwise *e* stands for [ə].

(2) With mobile *-n*, but a hiatus before it and after *de* or *se* is often filled with *n*, e.g. *Hues de n e kannt?* 'Did you know him?'

(3) This is the form in the capital, otherwise Lux. has *äis* or *eis, eiser.*[1]

(4) The gen. is used e.g. after certain verbs: *ech bráuch dénger nēt* 'I do not need you'.

The indefinite personal pronoun is *een* (*mer* is obsolescent), which always follows the verb, being replaced before it by *et*, e.g. *'T heescht een an engem Dag méi, wéi een an enger Woch kritt.* Cf. NHG 'Man verlangt (heischt) an einem Tag mehr, als man in einer Woche kriegt.'

§ 28. REFLEXIVE PRONOUNS

There is only one special form *sech* [e] for the 3rd pers. sg. and pl., nom. and acc.

§ 29. POSSESSIVE PRONOUNS

They are: *mäin, däin, säin, hiren, onsen (eisen), ären.*

(i) *mäin, däin, säin.*

	m.	f.	n.	pl.
Common Case	mäin	méng	mäin/mäint (1)	méng
Dative	méngem ⎫	ménger	méngem	méngen
Genitive	ménges ⎭		ménges	ménger

Notes

(1) The form *mäint* is used in pronominal function (without article), *mäin* in adjectival. As to local variants, see Bruch, *Grammaire*, p. 65 and map 9.

(2) Final *n* is always mobile, e.g. *mäin Hâus, mäi Brout.*

(ii) *hiren, onsen (eisen), ären.*

	m.	f.	n.	pl.
Common Case	hiren	hir	hiirt	hir
Dative	hirem ⎫	hirer	hirem	hiren
Genitive	hires ⎭		hires	hirer

Notes

(1) Final *n* is mobile.

(2) In the neuter common case no difference is made between pronominal and adjectival use.

---

[1] E. Rooth, 'Ist die Form *us* im Ripuarisch-Moselfränkischen "Ingwäonisch"?', *Neuphilologische Mitteilungen*, liii, 1952, 258–76.

(3) In the 3rd pers. pl. the poss. pron. is often accompanied by the pers. pron., e.g. *hinen hiren.*

§ 30. DEMONSTRATIVE AND PARTITIVE PRONOUNS

The def. art. (§ 21) is the unstressed form of the dem. pron.:

		m.	*f.*	*n.*	*pl.*
Common Case	. .	deen	déi	dat	déi
Dative	. . .	deem ⎫	där	deem	denen
Genitive	. . .	dees ⎭		dees	där

Notes

(1) Final *n* is mobile.

(2) In contrasting the particles *hei, elei* for 'this' and *do, elo* for 'that' are added, e.g. *deen Apel hei—deen do.* For *deen—hei,* i.e. for something that is near, Lux. uses also *dĕsen, dĕs, dĕst* which declines like an adj. (§ 24).

Lux. possesses also a partitive pron., the function of which corresponds more or less to that of the part. pron. of French. It is *däers* (m., n.), *där* (f. and pl.).

§ 31. INTERROGATIVE PRONOUNS

For 'who?' Lux. has *wie(n)* (common case) and *wiem* (dat.), for 'what?' it uses *wat,* for 'which?' *wat fir,* followed by the indef. article.

§ 32. INDEFINITE PRONOUNS

een, eng, eent (declines like *mäin*)	somebody
keen, keng, keent, pl. *keng*	nobody, no, none
eppes	something, a little
näischt	nothing
vill	much, many
e puer	a few
etlech	several
jeder, jidereen, jidwidereen	each, every
all, dat. *allen* (pl.)	all, every
alles (sg.)	all

§ 33. RELATIVE PRONOUNS

The dem. pron. *deen, déi, dat* is used as the relative pronoun.

VERBS

§ 34. FORMS AND CLASSIFICATION

The Lux. verb has the following form classes: infinitive, imperative, past participle, present indicative, and a limited number of verbs have a preterite indicative and a preterite subjunctive (= conditional). The compound forms are: perfect, pluperfect, conditional, passive.

The infinitive ends in -*en* (mobile -*n*) except in the case of the monosyllabic verbs *hun* 'have', *sin* 'be', *gin* 'give, become', *din, dun* 'do'. The infinitive particle is *ze*.

The imperative is in the sg. endingless, but otherwise identical with the form of the 2nd pers. sg. pres. and in the pl. it is identical with the form of the 2nd pers. pl. pres.

The past participle[1] is characterized by the prefix *ge-*, which is absent, however, in the case of the modal auxiliaries, verbs with prefixes, and the following verbs: *bliwwen* 'remained', *bruecht* 'brought', *font* 'found', *gaang* 'gone', *gin* 'given', *kaaft* (*kaf*) 'bought', *kannt* 'known', *kascht* 'cost', *komm* 'come', *kritt* (*krut*) 'got'. The ending is -*en* for the strong verbs; but a large number of strong verbs are endingless. Weak verbs end in -*t* in the past part. Weak verbs with *z* in the root of the inf. have a -*t* which is a product of the assimilation of a former, unshifted -*t*- and the participial ending -*t*. Difference in root-vowels between inf. and p.p. is characteristic of the strong verbs, but a considerable number of weak verbs have this difference as well on account of *Rückumlaut*.

§ 35. Strong Verbs

Verbs belonging to this class have the ending -*en* in the p.p. or are endingless; the majority have a different root-vowel in the p.p. from that of the inf. Apart from the special form (mutation) in the 2nd and 3rd pers. sg. there are two stem forms for the majority of strong verbs, and three or four forms in the case of about a dozen verbs. These latter verbs still form a pret. ind. and a pret. subj. The root-vowel is uniformly -*ou*- for the pret. ind. and -*éi*- for the pret. subj. The following have four forms: *bleiwen-blouf-bléif-bliwwen* 'remain', *kommen-koum-kéim-komm* 'come', *gesinn-gesouch-geséich-gesinn* 'see', *leien-loug-léig-geleën* 'lie', *sëtzen-souz-séiz-gesiess* 'sit', *fänken-foung-féing-gefaang*(*en*) 'catch' (also *hänken* 'hang'), *halen-houl-héil-gehalen* 'hold', for others, see § 41 (ii). Some have only three forms, e.g. *schlofen-schléif-geschlof* 'sleep', *stoussen-stéiss-gestouss* 'push', *loossen-léiss-gelooss* 'let' (when used as an auxiliary the p.p. is *loosst*).

Owing to the numerous conditional vowel changes which have affected the historical Lux. vowels a classification of the strong verbs according to the stem alternants would demand over two

---

[1] H. Suolahti, 'Die Luxemburger Partizipformen', *Annales Academiae Scientiarum Fennicae*, Ser. B. Tom L, Helsinki, 1942.

dozen classes, many of which would consist of one or two verbs only. The following are the most important classes:[1]

I. Identical vowel in the inf. and p.p.:
(i) *a*: *fallen—gefall* 'fall';
(ii) *o*: *droën—gedroën* 'carry';
(iii) *ä*: *wäschen—gewäsch* 'wash';
(iv) *ie*: *friessen—gefriess* 'eat';
(v) *u*: *ruffen—geruff* 'call';
(vi) *ue*: *wuessen—gewuess* 'grow'.

II. Vowel alternation *äi* (or *ei*)/*a*: *bäissen—gebass* 'bite'.

III. Vowel alternation *éi*/*o*, *ue*, *u*: *fléissen—gefloss* 'flow', *verléieren—verluer* 'loose', *léien—gelunn* 'tell a lie'.

IV. Vowel alternation *a* or *ē*/*o*: *bannen—gebonn* 'bind', *drénken—gedronk* 'drink', *hëllefen—gehollef* 'help'.

V. Vowel alternation *e*/*a*: *treffen—getraff* 'meet'.

VI. Vowel alternation *ie*/*ue*: *stierwen—gestuerwen* 'die'.

VII. Vowel alternation *ie*/*a*: *briechen—gebrach* 'break'.

§ 36. Weak Verbs

Weak verbs are characterized by the dental suffix in the past participle and in the preterite in the case of those verbs which still form a preterite. They are divided into three categories: (*a*) the large majority with two forms only and no vowel change, e.g. *laachen—gelaacht* 'laugh'; (*b*) six verbs with four forms; (*c*) three verbs with three forms; (*d*) a number of verbs with two forms but with vowel change (*Rückumlaut*).

36.1 The following verbs still form a pret. ind. and a pret. subj.

		Pret. Ind.	*Pret. Subj.*	*P.P.*
bréngen	'bring'	bruecht	briecht	bruecht
denken	'think'	duecht	diecht	geduecht
froën	'ask'	frot	freet	gefrot
soën	'say'	sot	seet	gesot
kréien	'get'	krut	krit (kréig)	kritt (krut)
fannen[2]	'find'	font	fënt	font

36.2 The verbs *huelen* 'fetch', *kafen* 'buy', *maachen* 'make' form a synthetic conditional in the manner of the strong verbs: *héil*, *kéif*, *méich*. Rodange uses also the strong form *mouch(en)* for the pret. of *maachen*. The 3rd pers. sg. pres. has a mutated vowel: *mecht*.

36.3 *Rückumlaut* is found in over a dozen weak verbs, e.g. *leën—geluegt* 'lay', *schëdden—geschott* 'pour'. Those with *z* in the root have

---

[1] For reference to the OHG classes, see chap. v, § 34.
[2] This originally strong verb is in this category for phonological reasons (see § 15 (ii)).

t in the past part. (see § 14.2 (ii)), e.g. *jäizen—gejâut* 'yell, cry', *schätzen—geschat* 'estimate', *schwätzen—geschwat* 'talk', *setzen—gesat* 'set'.

§ 37. THE PRESENT

The endings are: Sg. 1 *-en*, 2 *-s*, 3 *-t*; Pl. 1, 3 *-en*, 2 *-t*, e.g. *kucken* 'look':

ech kucken	mir kucken
du kucks	dir kuckt
en kuckt	si kucken

Notes

(1) Final *n* is mobile (§ 16).

(2) Strong verbs have a mutated root-vowel in the 2nd and 3rd pers. sg. (see § 18 Note). Verbs which in NHG alternate between *e* and *i*, e.g. *essen*, have *ie* and *ē(é)* in Lux.

(3) Before dentals certain diphthongs were shortened in Lux. (see § 10.3). This has resulted in the change of *éi—i* in the verbs *fléien* 'fly', *léien* 'tell a lie', *zéien* 'pull', *kréien* 'get', *geschéien* 'happen', e.g. *en zitt* 'he pulls'.

§ 38. THE CONDITIONAL

38.1 Only a limited number of strong and weak verbs still form a synthetic conditional (see §§ 35; 36.1). The endings are: Sg. 1st and 3rd: -, 2nd: *-s* (*-t* of the weak verbs being absorbed), Pl. 1st and 3rd: *-en*, 2nd: *-t*.

38.2 The majority of verbs form the conditional analytically by means of the conditional of the auxiliary *gin* plus the inf. of the main verbs, e.g. *ech géif kucken* 'I should look'. The auxiliaries *goën* and *doën* can also form the conditional and are used especially when a wish is expressed, e.g. for NHG *würde gerne, möchte*.

§ 39. THE PRETERITE INDICATIVE

The endings of the forms are the same as for the synthetic conditional (= preterite subjunctive). The verbs which still form a preterite indicative in the *koinè* are given in §§ 35; 36.1. In the dialects of the northernmost district the pret. ind. is much more frequent, and Rodange borrowed a number of such forms for the *Renert*, e.g. in our extract *wénkten* < *wénken* 'wave', *schwaten* < *schwätzen* 'gossip', *jâuten* < *jäizen* 'yell', *soungen* < *sangen* 'sing'.

§ 40. THE COMPOUND TENSES AND THE PASSIVE

The two compound tenses for past time are formed with the auxiliaries *hun* and *sin* and the past participle.

Perfect: *hien as gaang; hien huet gesot.*
Pluperfect: *hie war gaang; hien hat gesot.*

T

Generally the future time is expressed by the present, but *göen* is occasionally used, e.g. *wat geet een maachen?* cf. English *what is she going to do?*

The passive is formed by means of the auxiliary *gin* and the past participle, e.g. *keng Wourecht gouf gesot.*

§ 41. THE MODAL AUXILIARIES AND IRREGULAR VERBS

The following forms are distinguished:

41.1 Modal auxiliaries

	Inf.	Sg. Pres.	Pl. Pres.	Pret.	Cond.	P.P. (2)
'to be able'	kĕnnen (1)	1, 3 kann 2 kanns	1, 3 kĕnnen 2 kĕnnt	konnt (1)	kĕnnt (1)	konnt (1)
'must'	mussen	1, 3 muss 2 muss	1, 3 mussen 2 musst	musst	misst	musst
'want to'	wĕllen	1 wĕll 2 wĕlls 3 wĕllt	1, 3 wĕllen 2 wĕllt	wollt	wĕllt	wollt
'shall' 'should'	sollen	1, 3 soll 2 solls	1, 3 sollen 2 sollt	sollt	sollt	sollt
'may'	däerfen dierfen	1, 3 däerf 2 däerfs	1, 3 däerfen 2 däerft	duerft	dierf	duerft

41.2 Other auxiliaries and irregular verbs

	Inf.	Imp.	Sg. Pres.	Pl. Pres.	Pret.	Cond.	P.P.
'to have'	hun	hief! hut!	hun hues huet	hun hut hun	hat	hätt	gehat (gehuet)
'to be'	sin	sief! (4) sid!	sin bas as	sin sid sin	war	wäer (wier)	gewiescht
'to become'	gin (goën)	gĕf! gitt!	gin gĕs gĕt	gin git gin	gouf	géif	gin
'to do'	din	déi! dit!	din (doën) dees deet	din dit din		déit	gedon (gedunn)
'to stand'	stin (3) (stoën (5))	stéi! stit!	stin (stoën) stees steet	stin stit stin	stoung	stéing	gestan (gestangen)

Notes

(1) Final *n* is everywhere mobile. In the pret., cond., and p.p. *-nn-* is /n:/.

(2) The modal auxiliaries are used in the inf. when linked with the inf. of a main verb. The part. in *-t* stand alone.

(3) *Gin (goën)* 'to go' goes like *stin*. The p.p. is *gaang(en)*.

(4) On this interesting form, see Bruch, *Lux.*, pp. 55–60.

(5) The forms *goën, stoën* are replacing the other, now obsolescent, forms.

PARTICLES

§ 42

Adverbs of place are not distinguished as to the direction of the motion, but those denoting rest are frequently more closely defined by further particles, e.g. *do* 'there' or *hei* 'here'.

	Preposition	Movement	Adverb of Place	Rest
'in'	an (dran) (1)	erann	bannen	dobannen, hei-
'out'	aus (draus)	eraus, raus	bâussen	dobâussen, hei-
'on'	op (drop)	erop	uewen	doenobben
'off'	of, af	erof	} ënnen	dodrënnen
'under'	ënner (drënner)	erënner		donidden
'over'	iwwer (driwwer)	eriwwer	driwwen	dodriwwen
'behind'	hanner (dohanner)	—	hannen	dohannen
'before'	vir	ervir	vir	
'about'	ëm (drëm)	erëm	drëm	ronderëm

Note

(1) These bracketed forms correspond to NHG *darin*, etc. Compounds with *do-*, *hei* are also formed of these, e.g. *heiran, doran*, etc., and of the adverbs of motion, e.g. *doeriwwer, heieriwwer*, etc.

PHONETIC TRANSCRIPTION

For the principles of this transcription, see pp. 71, 148. A description of the individual sounds is given in §§ 4, 6–9, 12, 14. [b, d, g, v, z, ž, γ, ɟ] are voiced lenes.

Words of two or more syllables have the main stress on the first syllable except where marked otherwise.

am šlas hiəft fu:s də švɛn·tsçən
zou ri:ɟd a·ls vei ə phoul,
ge:t matsən du·rç zeŋ faindən
e:ri:çt tsʊm khɪneksštɔl· .

ə zɛtst seç du:r ɔp tkneiən,
də khɪnek khʊgd‿əvɛç.
də fu:s fɛŋ:d ʊn tsə leiən,
a·n al a:blek mei frɛç:

hɛ:r khɪnek, khən:t di:r li·əzən
ɔp je·dəm zeŋər šti:r,
a šteiŋ hir šɔl·t gəšrɪvən
ɔp alən hi:rər di:r;

khən:t di:r an thiərtsər khʊkən
vɪ an ɛŋ vɪzəba:x :
da kheim ə'lo meŋ ɔnšɔl·t
hai hu:rteç ʊn dən da:x.

da geif di:r meŋə faindən
hir fal·šhe:t klo:r gəzɪn
dei frei a špeit hai geint meç
mat hi:rə klo·ə štɪn.

ha:l štəl: ! du šlɛçtə khiərəl,
zou zo·t də khɪnek beis,
deŋ do:tən dei zɪ batər
deŋ riədən nəmə zeis.

eç hʊn nu·n deŋər lɪɟən
gənʊx an de:s gəšwɛts;
du gəs mər nu fəru:rte·lt
no· la:ut ɔx fʊm gəzɛts.

MICHEL RODANGE: *RENERT*

Oder de Fuuss am Frack an a Maansgréisst[1]

XI. GESANK

DE FUUSS AM KINNEKSPALAIS. DEM RENERT SENG ERKLÄRONGEN.
SENG HERAUSFURDERONG. SENG VERTEIDIGONG DURCH D'FRA BABEL
AN D'KINNEGIN.

Am Schlass hieft Fuuss de Schwänzchen[2]
sou riicht als wéi e Poul,
geet matzen duurch séng Feinden
eeriicht zum Kinneksstull [3].

E setzt sech dur op d'Knéien,
de Kinnek kuckt [4] ewech.
De Fuuss fängt un ze léien,
an all Abléck méi frech:

,,Här Kinnek, kënnt Dir liesen
op jedem sénger Stir,
a stéing hir Schold geschriwwen
op allen hirer Dir;

kënnt Dir an d'Hierzer kucken
wéi an eng Wïsebaach:
da kéim elo méng Onschold
hei huurteg un den Dag.

Da géif Dir ménge Feinden
hir Falschheet klor gesinn [5],
déi fréi a spéit hei géint mech
mat hire Kloe stinn.''

,,Hal stëll! du schlechte Kierel,''
sou sot de Kinnek béis,
,,déng Doten, déi si batter,
déng Rieden nëmme séiss.

Ech hun nun dénger Lïgen [6]
genuch an dees Geschwätz;
du gëss mer nu verurtelt
no Lâut och vum Gesetz.'' [7]

---

[1] The spelling is that of the *Lux. Wtb.*, 1950. The extent to which it differs
from that of the *Jubiläumsausgabe* is slight and the details are given in §§ 5
and 13. See *Notes*.

„Genéidgen Här a Kinnek,“
sot Renert do zum Léiw,
„bedenkt, wat ech gemaacht hun
méng Deeg laang Iech zu léif!

Wann aner Râute wénkten [8],
da stoung de Renert fest;
a wann Dir mech verurtelt,
't wier nët fir Iech dat Best.

A mengt Dir, wier ech schëlleg,
ech stéing dann och elei?
Am Éisléck [9] fënd ech Plazen
méi sécher wéi déi hei.

De Grimpert koum mech ruffen,
da koum ech da gelaf;
um Plankebierg bei Blaaschent [10]
begéinte mer den Af.

Dee sot: „Här Fuuss, gitt hardi,
a wiert Iech, wéi Der kënnt.“
„Ech weess mech,“ sot ech, „Komper,
ganz fräi vun aller Sënd.“

Nu fannen ech, 't Kanengchen,
dat huet mech hei verklot,
an Dir sit béis: ech denke,
keng Wourecht gouf gesot.

Ech souz mat ménger Biwwel
bei ménger Dir doheem,
an d'Vigelcher déi [11] soungen
an Hecken an op Bäm.

Ech sin e Frënd vum Fréijoer,
an't mecht mer ëmmer Freed,
wann d'Réi do ëm mech sprangen
wi d'Lamer op der Heed;

wann d'Huese stinn de Männchen
an d'Duurteldaifche séngt;
wann d'Dréischel hire Jongen
am Nascht hirt Iesse bréngt,

Den Hunn geet mat den Hénger
am Bësch dann op an zou;
an op dem Milleweier
do schwammen d'Inte frou.

Wie soll dann nët vergiessen
de Wanter an séng Nout?
Ech souz an deer Betrachtonk
ëm d'Zäit vum Owebrout.

Du koum dohier den Duckler [1],
an 't ass e brave Mann:
E gréisst. „Ma," sot ech, „Komper,
Dir gitt dach mat erann?

Dann huelt Der eppes un Iech,
frësch Kraider [12] an eng Kuuscht;
ech weess, Dir iesst keng Fleeschspeis,
soss briecht ech och eng Wuuscht [13]."

Hie koum. En ësst, mir sproochen,
mer hun nach vill gelaacht,
an alles huet dem Komper
och séier [14] gutt geschmaacht.

Mä wësst Der, Här, méng Kanner,
déi si, wi aner sin;
se wëllen ëmmer iessen,
soubal s'e Ruecht [15] gesinn.

Se kucken dem Kanengchen
a sénge Mäifel no;
entfoul em dann eng Grimmel,
wupp, war mäin Eelsten do.

Mäin Eelsten ass e flénken,
de Jéngsten ass nët fâul;
op eemol hät de Komper
deem Klengen eng op 't Mâul.

Do gouf deen Eelste rosen,
en hëllt de Mann mam Krag,
an 't goung em fir en Ouer;
Här Kinnek, do ass d'Saach.

Et war mäin Hâus, méng Guttheet,
méng Kanner a mäi Brout;
ech hätt se losst gewäerden [16],
da war 't Kanengchen dout.

Ma ech erwëschen d'Jongen,
a weider nët gefaxt,
ech werfen s'ënner d'Siddel
dee Klengen huet gequackst.

Kuckt, wann een ass onschëlleg,
dann deet 't Verkloe wéi,
an 't wiert een séch op 't ongescht [17]
géint Kaarmësch oder Kréi.

Se wëlle mech verdillgen
mat Fra a Kand a Knuob.
Sou goung et mam Kanengchen;
wéi goung et mat dem Kuob?

De Gakhans huet 't lëscht traureg
op eiser Fiischt gesiess,
e sot, séng Fra déi hätt sech
u Fëschen [18] dout gefriess.

Ma wou, a wann? wat weess ech?
ech gouf nët weider uecht;
wat gëlt [19], en huet nach selwer
dat Mënsch ëm 't Liewe bruecht!

'T ass liicht e Mann verkloën,
ech fuerdren hei Bewäis;
ech loosse mech nët féieren
als wi e Schof op 't Äis.

Wie wëllt mech nach verkloën?
dee komm, nu stinn ech hei!
a kann en näischt beweisen,
da schlo mer äis elei."

Nu stounge sénger Feinden
vill do mat laanger Nues [20] ;
déi haart sonst géint e jâuten,
se schwaten nu feng lues.

Du Kuob an och 't Kanengchen,
déi mouchen [21] sech ewech,
se soten sech: „Dat Déngen
dat richt verfluucht nom Pech.

Wi sollte mir äis meeschtren
mam Fuuss? dat ass kee Spaass!
mir missten do jo bäissen
dach ounéi Feel an 't Gras."

Ma béis stinn do ze kucken
de Wollef an de Bier.
De Kinnek sot: „Wie Kloen
nach huet, dee komm nun hier!"

Du duechten déi zwéin Helden,
datt Fiechte leit kee Läif [22].
De Renert ass e Flénken,
ma Bier a Wollef stäif.

Se stoungen do ze récken
a maachen d'Fâuscht am Sak;
dem Renert säi Gewëssen
blouf haart als wi e Wak.

„Gesitt Der," sot en hardi,
„mir maulen s'op de Réck,
ma sollten s'et beweisen,
da sin se nët méi fléck."

„Abee," sot drop de Kinnek.
„Da bass de nach nët lass.
Wien huet deem brave Lampert
de Kapp erofgebass

an deen zum Spott mam Widder
geschéckt am Ranzel mir?
Ech louss de Widder déiten [23],
an d'Schold bleift, Schellem, dir.

Du hues mech frech beluen
mat Bittgäng a mat Geld;
kurzëm, esou en Näischnotz
dee schafft een aus der Welt."

„Här Kinnek," sot de Renert,
„wo steet mer mäi Verstand?
Ass Lampert dout? O Bläckert,
wars du dat do amstand!

Konns du den Hues ermuerden?
O miserabelt Gold!
Ech hat em jo de Ranzel
mat Iedelsteng gefollt [24]

a mat de schéinste Saachen
fir Iech an d'Kinnegin.
Wiem soll een nu nach trauen,
wa Bläckert dat konnt dinn?"

Nët héiere konnt de Léiw méi
dem Phariseier no:
e goung a séng Gemaacher
a fondt séng Fra och do.

A bei hir war och 't Babel,
dem Af séng aartlech Fra;
si huet en dichtegt Mondstéck,
de Léiw op si en A.

Déi sot: „Mäin Här a Kinnek,
Der maacht Iech vill Verdross
an 't wäer, mech unzehéieren,
vleicht gur nët ëmmesoss.

De Renert ass mäi Koseng,
an 't ass e kluge Mann,
an deen een an dem Konzel
nët gutt entbiere kann.

Et ass an deer Familjen,
säi Papp war och gescheit;
an 't koumen och wuel Kloe
géint hie vu falsche Leit.

Mä 't konnt een op en zielen
als Diplomat am Rot,
an Ire Papp huet allzäit
séng Menonk him gefrot.

A brâucht en och eng Schlëmmtchen,
wéi dat jo dack geschitt,
de Fiissche bruecht et fierdeg,
wéi Lentz an Dicks e Lidd [25].

Esou ass och de Renert,
E riedt als wéi gedréckt.
Wou huet Dir fir Gesandten
een, deen sech besser schéckt?

De Bier an och de Wollef,
se suerge blouss fir sech,
a géif et näischt ze schlécken,
se léissen Iech am Stéch.

Se schmiren 't Vollek ëmmer
mat séngem egne Fett.
Se schreiwe grouss Artikeln
an dëss an déi Gazette:

Do wëssen se ze plangen
fir 't Land bal dët an dat,
an hun um Enn dach ëmmer
fir d'egen Täsch geschwat.

'T ass een als wi deen aner,
wéi d'ganz Familjen ass,
an iwwerall erkennt Der
dann och hir Wollefsrass.

Dir kennt se, wann se pléien:
do fierchten se keng Maark.
Schwaach sin s'och am Bezuelen,
am Fuerdren owwer staark.

Dir kennt se, wann se delen:
du hun se guer keng Mooss;
de Wollef hëllt sech d'Brocken,
deen aanre léisst en d'Zooss.

Beim Wanen läit Säint hanne,
beim Dreschen owwer vir.
Dir sit eng Klensch him schëlleg,
da bréngt en Iech ëm d'Dir.

A fällt e gudde Kirel
de Lëmmlen an 't Gegrëpps,
deem drécke se dann 't Hierzblutt
eraus bis op eng Drëpps.

Sin s'eemol an der Schamber,
dann hun s'et an der Hand:
se kéiren op hir Millen
sech d'Buren all vum Land.

Op 't Gripsen an op 't Grapsen
hun s'allzäit hirt Gebiichts;
a mecht een deer [26] ee Koschter,
da stielt e säi Geliichts.

E schwätzt da géint de Mammon,
a fiddert sech de Krapp;
e weist mam Daum géint Himmel
an hält de Su am Grapp.

Ech kënnt Iech der verzielen
vum Wollef bis zur Kaz.
Déi Mëttel [27], déi déi wielen!
Ma hei ass nët di Plaz!

De Renert ass onggiedlech,
hie kuckt dem Déngen no:
a mecht dann een eng Foutaise,
dann ass de Fiisschen do.

Hie schreift sech op hir Spichten,
mä guer nët un den Héil [28],
Här Kinnek, do ass d'Ursaach,
hie läit en op der Séil.''

,,D'Fra Babel huet nët onrecht,''
sot drop och d'Kinnegin,
,,de Bier als wi de Wollef,
't ass näischt op déi ze gin.

Se hun ersierklech Mënner,
grouss Mee a greilech Zänn.
Mä wann Der déi dann ofzielt,
da sit Der och um Enn.

Well wou et heescht ze halen
fir 't Land am haarde Sträit,
dann zéien d'Schwänz se widder
an drécken sech op d'Säit.

A gëtt et eemol Brïgel,
a gräift een se mam Fleesch,
se huelen dann hir Deel alt [29],
an nach mat gräisslech Kreesch.

E Wollef an enger Festonk,
dee kënnt nët aus der Bretz,
bis datt en dran erhéngert.
Wéi goung et deem zu Metz? [30]

Mat honnertachtzeg Dausend
nach wosst en sech kee Rot;
du louss en sech da fänken:
et wor fir d'Welt eng Schmot [31].

Mam Renert ass et anescht.
Geschitt him och eng Fapp,
hie weess se gutt ze maachen,
ewell bei him ass Kapp.

Verzeit him! Wann de Wollef
sech dann och vun Iech scheedt,
de Fuuss ass een, mat deem een
zeng aner siche geet.

En huet eng grouss Familjen,
dat losst nët aus der Wo!
Dohin, wou déi hinzéien,
do gi vill aner no.

Dir huet nach vill ze maachen,
bedenkt et wuel, main Här!
Kee Büdget ass votéiert,
Dir héicht nach d'Schätzeng gär."

,,'T ass wouer," sot de Kinnek,
,,de Renert huet vill Frënn;
an zéien déi sech vu mer,
da sti méng trei Leit dënn.

Trei Männer hun ech néideg,
well 't Geld ass eeschtlech rar,
e jidden [32] hält et un sech,
an ech, ech bräicht et bor.

D'Arméi ass schlecht montéiert,
an dura geet eng Zomm [33].
De Biere fele Kapen,
De Fräschen uen er [34] Tromm.

Nei Mäntel bräichten d'Raten,
an d'Béck och méi laang Schwänz,
och d'Mâulefen nei Bröllen,
an d'Wëllef méi kleng Pänz.

Ech schaaft de Kaze gieren
ganz aner Kloen un,
de Ochse [35] méi grouss Hueren,
laang Spueren och dem Hunn.

de Schwéngen [18] eise Schnëssen,
den Huose fënnef Been;
e fonkelneit Gewëssen
hätt néideg jidwereen.

A Chassepot a Kanounen,
Zëndnolen, Muerd an Doud,
Dat huet d'Arméi méi néideg
als wi de Bauer 't Brout [31]."

„An dat och nët, Här Kinnek,"
sot durop d'Kinnegin.
„Et bleift jo, ouns d'Arméi, Iech
vill Bessres nach ze dinn.

D'Zaldoten, déi verzieren,
den Aarbechtsmann erniert;
wa kee méi Krich wëllt féieren,
da brâuch ee keen, dee wiert.

Mä d'Stroosse sin ze bauen;
de Schleek ass iwwel drun,
wann hien e Schrack [36] wëllt fueren,
da muss e Virspan hun.

Besonnesch huet Der d'Schoulen,
do bräicht Dir nach vill Geld,
fir 't Vollek gutt z' erzéien,
dat Néidegst vun der Welt.

Do si jo d'Schwäin an d'Stéieren,
an d'Ieselen, d'Honn an d'Béck,
se si jo ounéi Léier
a schleechvoll Ongeschéck.

Se sâufen als wéi Béischten,
se rolzen op der Gaass,
se klappe Fra a Kanner,
dat nennen se da Spaass.

Se hu keng eenzeg Iddee;
eng liewe fir hir Pänz,
déi aner gläwe ferrem,
't géif Daiwele mat Schwänz.

An huet ee säin Diplëmmchen
fir d'Lïge vun der Échel,
dee kann dem Véi verkafen
als Riichtschäit och eng Séchel.

Se loossen all sech féieren,
wi d'Schof, an ounéi Fro;
e Schallek zitt den Hiemsläpp,
da läft d'ganz Häerd em no.

Se gläwe schéine Spréch,
ma méi nach dem Geschmaach;
a bleift hir Gurgel dréchen,
da war kee gudden Dag.

Mat engem fette Mâufel
scho féiert een s'an d'Fal;
dann huelt se mat de Schwänzen [18]
a fuert dermat an d'Wahl!

Do stëmmt den Ochs den Tiger,
de Widder stëmmt de Wollef;
se kréien 't éischt e Friessen
an hannendrop de Kollef.

Do, Här, do ass nach Aarbecht,
se läit do laang a breet.
Alle Männer mussen hëllefen,
am meeschten déi gescheit.

Mä bréngt Dir ëm de Renert,
da gin séng Frënn Iech grobb.
Se sin elo nach mat Iech,
da stinn [37] se géint Iech op."

,,Ech weess wuel," sot de Kinnek,
,,ma kuckt, en ass ze schro:
kâum huet een him verziën,
da kënnt eng aner Klo.

Dach wëllt Dir mech berieden! [38]
dem Schellem halt Der zou.
Mä schwéier ass beweisen,
eng Schierbel sief [39] e Krou.

Dir Fraleit huet dach Mënner!
Dir maacht dat Schlecht ons léif;
Dir maacht et hei mam Renert
als wéi mam Apel d'Éiv."

NOTES

(See the remarks to the *Notes* on p. 80)

[1] *Michel Rodange* (1827–76) became intimately acquainted with the people of his small country first as a schoolteacher and later as an inspector in the civil engineering department of the Grand-Ducal civil service. His humanitarian compassion and strong democratic conviction, nurtured on the liberal ideas of 1848, led him between 1866 and 1871 to participate passionately in the excited discussions and negotiations about Luxemburg's future. Napoleon III's desire for annexation and the rising tide of German nationalism found their advocates in Luxemburg, while a third party stood for complete independence. Human behaviour in its manifold manifestations is the subject of his epic *Renert*, 1872, ('Renard the Fox, or the Fox in the Frockcoat and in Human Size'), written with a passion for truth and justice, pulsating with wit, humour and satire. Rodange's only literary source was Goethe's *Reineke Fuchs*, itself a re-creation of the medieval *Renard the Fox* legend. Rodange places the story in Luxemburg and in the time of the Franco-Prussian war.

The *XI. Gesank*, corresponding roughly to Goethe's ninth, contains allusions to the capitulation of the French army at Metz, and expresses for instance Rodange's own hatred of militarism, his demand for peaceful development of the country and for universal education to raise the crude standards of the populace. It centres on the defence of *Renert* before the King (*de Léiw*) in the presence of the Queen and her friend Babel, the wife of the monkey (*den Af*), who take his side. Other animals playing a part are *Grimpert*, the badger, Renert's nephew; *Duckert* or *den Duckler*, the rabbit; *Lampert*, the hare; *Bläckert*, the ram; *Gakhans*, the crow; *de Wollef* (wolf), and *de Bier* (bear), while others are merely mentioned.

Rodange's language is a mixed rural dialect, but he makes the individual animals speak the dialects of the various parts of the country where they come from. This is not very noticeable in the *XI. Gesank* since none of the speakers come from the more distant parts. King, Queen and Babel speak the dialect of the capital while Renert talks Rodange's own mixed rural dialect.[1] A literary appreciation is given by F. Léger-Arlon, *M. Rodanges Tierepos Renert*, Lux. 1927, Verlag Jonghemecht.

[2] The standard diminutive ending of nouns is *-chen* in the sg., *-ercher* in the pl. Back vowels are mutated, e.g. *Schwanz—Schwänz-chen—Schwänzercher*. Nouns ending in *-k*, *-g*, *-ch* (or occasionally also in *-sch* or *-z*) take the dim. suffix. *-elchen*, pl. *-elcher*, e.g. *Abléck* 'moment'—*Abléckelchen*. Nouns which end in *-el*, *-em* or *-er* take in pl. only *-cher*, e.g. *Vigelcher* 'birds'. All diminutives retain, in contrast to NHG, the gender of the noun from which they are derived, e.g. *de Schwänzchen* m., *d Duurteldaifchen* f. See R. Bruch, 'Zur Diminutivbildung im Luxemburgischen', *Revue Trim.*, xxxi–xxxii, 1949, 169–79.

[3] The *koinè* has *Stull* while Rodange used a dialect form *Stoul* to rhyme it with *Poul*.

[4] This widespread colloquial form is generally regarded as a contamination between HG *gucken* and LG *kiken* 'to look'.

[5] This is the possessive dative paraphrase, 'the falsehood of my enemies' (see § 19). The verb is in the passive (§ 40), 'would be seen'.

[6] Articles, personal, demonstrative and possessive pronouns are in the genitive after a number of verbs, e.g. *sech schummen* 'be ashamed of', *bräuchen* 'need', and after certain adjectives and adv., e.g. *sécher* 'sure', *midd* 'tired of', *genuch dénger Ligen* 'enough of your lies'. Cf. *sénger Feinden vill* (p. 284), see § 27.

[7] 'According to the [content of the] law.'

---

[1] See J. Tockert's introduction and commentary in the *Jubiläumsausgabe von Rodanges Werken*, 1927, or the shortened ed. of 1939, a reprint of which appeared in 1954 (Editions du Centre).

U

[8] 'To say no, or to waver', lit. 'move one's head towards the window panes'.

[9] NHG *Ösling*, the Lux. Ardennes, a remote region.

[10] Hill near *Blascheid*, central Lux.

[11] Original text has *se*.

[12] Original text gives *Krädder* as the pl. of *Krâut*.

[13] Informant said *Wurscht*. According to Bruch, *Grundl.*, map 40, p. 244, *Wuuscht* is the form of the north. The form with *r* is influenced by NHG.

[14] Instead of the Germanism *séier* informant used *ganz recht*.

[15] *Ruecht* 'crust' NHG *Ranft* (cf. Up. Austr. *Ranftl*, p. 239) shows the Low Franc. (Dutch), Ripuarian and north-west LG soundshift *ft > cht* which has left certain traces in Lux. Cf. NHG *achter* (< LG): E. *after*. See J. P. Paulides, 'Das Luxemburgische im Spiegel des Niederländischen', *Annuaire*, 1952, pp. 68–72; R. Schützeichel, 'Der Lautwandel von ft zu cht am Mittelrhein', *Rhein. Vierteljahrsblätter*, xx, 1955, 253–75 (= *Ad. Bach Festschrift*).

[16] In Lux. word order the infinitive is placed after the past part. of a modal auxiliary (incl. *loossen*) in contrast to NHG.

[17] Obsolete expression, 'defends himself tooth and nail'.

[18] This dat. pl. is no longer usual in the *koinè*, thus informant says *u Fësch*. Also *de Schwäin* for *de Schwéngen*; *mat de Schwänz* for *Schwänzen*.

[19] Cf. NHG *was gilt es?* 'I bet'.

[20] 'Embarrassed.'

[21] See § 36.2.

[22] Lit. 'fighting bears no life' i.e. there is no future in fighting.

[23] Informant says *dout maën* (= *maachen*) for *déiten*.

[24] This form with *Rückumlaut* is replaced in the *koinè* by the analogical *gefëllt < fëllen* 'to fill'.

[25] Lentz and Dicks (i.e. Edmond de la Fontaine) are nineteenth-century Lux. dialect poets.

[26] Gen. pl., see § 30.

[27] Informant says *Mëttlen*.

[28] Hearth iron, MHG *hahel*, the place where debts would be marked.

[29] 'They go down like a pricked balloon.'

[30] This is a reference to Marshall Bazaine's hasty surrender of Metz on 27th Oct. 1870, thought to be an impregnable fortress and defended by over 170,000 men and 1,400 heavy guns. After the war Bazaine was sentenced to death for treason and cowardice, but escaped to Spain.

[31] This stanza was deleted by the German censorship in the 1941 edition.

[32] Informant has *jedereen*.

[33] 'This runs into a [pretty] sum.'

[34] Instead of 'without their drums' informant has *eng Menge Tromm*.

[35] The phonologically correct form *Uess* has been replaced in the *koinè* by NHG *Ochs*.

[36] *Schrack*, NHG *Schritt*, exemplifies the phenomenon known as *Rheinische Gutturalisierung*, in consequence of which a dental stop or nasal is changed into a velar, e.g. Ripuarian *Lük*, NHG *Leute*, *Zik*, NHG *Zeit*. This development has affected Lux. only to a limited extent, but the northern dialects much more than the rest. See Bruch, *Lux.*, pp. 109–20; "La vélarisation ripuaire des occlusives dentales", *Revue Trim.*, xxix–xxx, 1949, 78–90; Frings, *Sprache u. Geschichte* I and II under *Gutturalisierung* in the index.

[37] Informant has *dann sti se . . .*

[38] Informant says *Dach Dir wëllt . . .*

[39] Informant says *wier*.

GLOSSARY

See the introductory remarks to the *Glossary* on p. 84, and for full information *Luxemburger Wörterbuch*, 1906, or the *Lux. Wtb.*, 1950 ff.

A, D. eye.
Aarbechtsmann, E. worker.
Abee, < Fr. *ah bien*, well.
Abléck, E. moment.
an, in, and.
aner, other(s).
anescht, otherwise.

batter, bitter.
Béischt, beast.
Bēsch, E. wood.
besonnesch, specially.
Bretz, f. quandary.
Brigel, blows.
Bur, m. D. spring, well.

Chassepot, rifle invented by C.

dack, often.
delen, wv. share, divide.
Déngen, n. pl. *Dénger*, thing.
dichteg, quick, hardworking.
Dir, D. door.
dréchen, dry.
Dréischel, f. thrush.
Drëpps, f. D. drop.
drop, then.
dur, there.

Echel, f. D. owl.
eeriicht, straight, at once.
eeschtlech, terribly.
éischt, *t-*, at first.
eisen, iron.
e'lei, here.
e'lo, now, there.
ëmmesoss, in vain.
Enn, E. end.
ënner, under.
erhéngeren, wv. starve.
ersierklech, horrible (obs.).
e'wech, away.
e'well, because, for.

Fal, trap.
fänken, § 35, catch.

Fapp, f. lie, error.
faxen, wv. joke.
féieren, wv. lead.
feng, fine, very.
ferrem, < Fr. *ferme*, strongly.
fidderen, wv. stuff, feed.
Fiischt, f. D. roof-ridge.
fléck, quick.
Foutaise, Fr. howler.
Fräsch, D. frog.

gär, NHG *gerne*.
Gebiichts, n. intention.
Gegrëpps, grabbing hands.
géint, against.
Geliichts, n. lights.
geschmaacht, tasted.
gesinn, § 35, see.
gieren, see *gär*.
gläwen, wv. believe.
gräisslech, terrible.
Grapp, m. grip.
grapsen, wv. grip, grab.
greilech, terrible.
Grimmel, f. D. crumb.
gripsen, grasp, grab.

haart, loud.
haën, gehaën, hit.
halen, § 35, hold, endure.
hannen, behind.
hannendrop, afterwards.
hardi, Fr. brave.
heeschen, wv. beg, demand, be called.
hei, here.
héichen, wv. increase.
héieren, wv. hear, listen.
hëllt < *huelen*, wv. § 36, fetch, take.
Hiemsläpp, m. tail of the shirt.
hier, NHG *her*.
Hond, pl. *Honn*, B. dog.
Hong, pl. *Hénger*, E. hen.
Huer, D. horn.
Hues, D. hare.
Hunn, D. cock.

Iedelsteng, jewels.
Int, D. duck.

jâuten < *jäizen*, §§ 36; 39; cry, yell.
jidwereen, each one.

Kaarmēsch, f. white-cap, dunnock.
Kand, pl. *Kanner*, E. child.
Kap, D. cap.
Kapp, C. head.
kēnnt < *kommen*, comes.
klappen, wv. beat.
Klensch, f. < Fr. *clenche*, door handle.
Klo, D. (a) complaint, (b) claw.
Kollef, D. rifle butt.
Komper, < Fr. *compère*, relative.
Konzel, council.
Koschter, verger.
Koseng, cousin.
Knueb (obs.), boy.
Krapp, C. crop, throat.
Kreesch, yells.
Kréi, D. magpie.
kréien, wv. § 36, get.
Krou, C. jug.
Kueb, m. crow.
Kuuscht, f. crust, slice of bread.

läit, 3rd pers. sg. pres. < *leien*, § 35, lie.
lass, loose, free.
léien, be-, § 35, tell a lie.
Léier, f. instruction, knowledge.
léif, dear.
lēscht, t-, recently.
liicht, easy.
loossen, § 35, let.
lues, quiet, soft.

Ma, *mä*, < Fr. *mäis*, but.
Maark, D. boundary stone.
mat, with.
matzen, middle, through.
Mäufel, pl. *Mäifel*, mouthful.
Mäulef, m. D. mole.
maulen, wv. brag.
meeschteren, fight for mastery.
mengen, mean, believe.
Milleweier, millpond.
Mo, C. stomach.
Mond, pl. *Mēnner*, E. mouth.

Mondstéck, cf. NHG *Mundwerk*, gift of the gab.
montéieren, wv. equip.

nach, yet.
Näischnotz, good-for-nothing.
näischt, nothing.
Nascht, n. E. nest.
nēmme, only.
nēt, not.
Nues, D. nose.

och, also.
onggiedlech, not lazy.
ouns, without.

Panz, f. < Fr. *panse*, C. belly.
Papp, D. father.
plangen, wv. plan.
Plaz, f. D. place.
pléien, wv. plough.
Poul, m. C. pole.

quacksen, wv. squeal.

Ranzel, m. C. haversack.
Réck, D. back.
récken, wv. withdraw, move.
Réi, roe-deer.
Riichtschäit, ruler.
rolzen, wv. fight, quarrel.
rosen, angry, raging.

Schamber < Fr. *chambre*, parliament.
Schätzeng, taxation.
schēlleg, guilty.
Schierbel, piece of broken pottery.
schlécken, wv. swallow, bite.
schleechvoll, brim-full.
Schleek, m. D. snail.
Schlēmmtchen, f. E. trick.
schloēn, § 35, beat, fight.
Schmot, f. disgrace.
Schnēss, f. D. snout.
schro, wicked, shrew.
schwaten, < *schwätzen*, §§ 36; 39; talked.
sichen, wv. look for.
Siddel, f. D. settle.
soss, otherwise.
soubal, as soon as.
Spichten, tricks.
sproochen, wv. talk.

Spuer, D. spur.
Stéier, D. bull.
Stir, D. forehead.
Su, < Fr. *sous*, penny.

Tromm, drum.

uecht gin, cf. NHG *achtgeben*.
un, at.

Véi, cattle.
verkloën, wv. accuse.
vleicht, perhaps.
votéieren, wv. vote.

Wak, m. hard stone.
Wanen, winnowing.
well, because, but.
wien, who.
Wo, f. scales.
Wourecht, f. truth.
wupp, quickly, cf. NHG *-flugs*.

Zaldot, D. soldier.
zéien, § 35, pull.
Zëndnol, f. D. firing-pin
zeng, ten.
zielen, wv. count.
Zooss, < Fr. *sauce*.

CHAPTER VIII

WESTPHALIAN: MÖNSTERLÄNSK PLATT

§ 1. AREA AND STATUS

1.1 Who speaks dialect? is a question of crucial and vital importance everywhere in North Germany. No German dialect has as impressive a past literary and political significance as Low German and yet is so sorely threatened with extinction. Nowhere is the movement for the preservation and cultivation of dialect stronger or more convincingly supported by writers of talent. The greater need seems to be calling for a greater effort.

Low German gradually lost its proud status as a language of importance in Northern Europe, which it held during the later centuries of the Middle Ages, after 1500. A century later it could no longer be called a written language. Hand in hand with its decline as a written medium went its decline as a spoken language. The nobility and the patriciate of the North German cities had abandoned Low German by 1800 and the *bourgeoisie* followed in the nineteenth century. In its descent down the social ladder Low German has now reached the lowest rungs. In the twentieth century even the working class, especially in the larger industrial areas, and the wealthier farming communities have begun to abandon their native dialect with its stigma of social inferiority. By and large, only the remoter farming regions still cling to Low German. Two pre-war studies[1] give the results of statistical investigations concerning the vitality of Low German. Their picture shows Low German as strong only in the last social and geographical retreats. War and post-war resettlement of refugees have dealt further blows to Low German.[2] K. Schulte Kemminghausen showed that Low German is still the daily medium of the rural population of the Münsterland. Industrialization usually leads to the abandonment of dialect. Parents will often speak standard German with their children in order to help them in their school careers. Some of these children will later, after leaving school, revert to Low German. In the towns it was found that the workplace of the breadwinner is often the safer refuge for dialect than the family

---

[1] K. Schulte Kemminghausen, *Mundart und Hochsprache in Norddeutschland*, Neumünster, 1939 ('Der heutige Stand des Plattdeutschen in Westfalen', pp. 68–101); H. Janssen, *Leben und Macht der Mundart in Niedersachsen*, Hanover-Göttingen, 1943.

[2] H. Wesche, 'Die Lage der Mundarten in Niedersachsen', *Festschrift Boeck*, pp. 282–92, surveying the situation in the fifties states: 'Alles in allem, die Lage der Mundarten scheint trost- und hoffnungslos', p. 288.

circle. Both Janssen and Kemminghausen stated that women were less faithful to dialect than men and that girls liked giving themselves an air of sophistication by adopting standard German. Janssen further found that the poorer the soil, the smaller the farms, the lower the income and the larger the families the stronger was Low German. A firm and closely-knit society would cling to dialect much more tenaciously even in the vicinity of large towns than regions where there was much internal migration. As to North Saxon, it is the areas between the rivers Ems and Weser and the heathland and fen districts between the Weser and the Elbe and the rural and fishing villages of Holstein which are its strongholds.

Between genuine dialect on the one hand and standard NHG on the other there are various shades of mixtures generally known as *Missingsch*, i.e. NHG spoken with a strong dialect admixture by speakers with a deficient knowledge of NHG, or *Patentplatt*, the Low German attempted by a speaker of NHG.

The movement for the protection and preservation of Low German started in the eighties of the last century and led to the formation of a large number of associations and clubs, linked together in the *Allgemeine Plattdeutsche Verband* with its periodical *De Eekboom*. Low German theatres were opened in several centres and frequented mainly by the townspeople who did not normally speak Low German. Chairs of Low German philology were founded at the universities of Kiel, Hamburg, Münster, Rostock and Göttingen. New editions of the classics of Low German, Klaus Groth, Fritz Reuter, John Brinkman, Johann H. Fehrs, Ferdinand Krüger, were joined by remarkably good works of younger writers such as Augustin Wibbelt, Karl Wagenfeld, Fritz Stavenhagen, Hermann Bossdorf, Gorch Fock, Rudolf Kinau and many others. Their public was and is almost entirely urban and no longer dialect-speaking. The newspapers published articles in dialect until in 1937 the *Reichspressechef* forbade the publication of contributions in Low German, in spite of the fact that many active supporters of the Low German movement had embraced the Nazi ideology. Today the press rarely contains any articles in Low German, but the radio with its broadcasts of Low German plays, stories and sermons enjoys widespread popularity.

In the heyday of the *Niederdeutsche Bewegung*[1] there were advo-

---

[1] See H. Bossdorf, 'Das Problem der niederdeutschen Schriftsprache', reprinted *Niedersachsenbuch* 1924/5, pp. 37–41; H. Brömse, 'Was ist uns das Niederdeutsche?', *ZfDk.*, 1935, pp. 698–709; Kurt Gassen, *Die Niederdeutsche Bewegung der Gegenwart*, Greifswald, 1933; R. Mehlem, *Um Wesen und Würde der plattdeutschen Sprache*, Hildesheim, 1941; H. Teuchert, 'Plattdeutsche Schriftsprache und plattdeutsche Dichtung', *De Eekboom*, 1925, pp. 76 ff., 110 ff.; *id.*, 'Der Schicksalsweg der niederdeutschen Sprache', *NdJb.*, lxxvii, 1954, 120–33; W. Niekerken, 'Zu den Problemen der Zweisprachigkeit im nieder-

cates of the revitalization of Low German as a standard written language. Endless and tedious discussions ensued as to the desirability
or otherwise, its place in the educational system and the orthography[1]
to be adopted. The post-war years have brought a resurgence of the
literary movement.[2] Münster, Hamburg and many other towns have
their Low German theatres. But these literary endeavours are still
mainly supported by intellectuals and townspeople who do not normally speak Low German themselves. The rural population, whose
daily language Low German still is, is largely unaffected by these
efforts at resuscitation. They have therefore had little success in
stemming the tide, which runs powerfully against Low German.

1.2 The Westphalian dialects belong to the Low Saxon dialects.
The isogloss -e(n)/-(e)t for the ending of the 1st and 3rd pers. pl. pres.
of the verb is generally regarded as separating the Franconian dialects of the Rhineland from the Saxon dialects of Westphalia. In the
south the *Benratherlinie* of the second soundshift runs eastwards
along the Rothaar mountains separating the Hessian dialects from
Westphalian. In the east, Westphalian gives way to Eastphalian
west of the River Weser. Westphalian as a whole is thus encircled
by a belt of isoglosses running southwards from Bentheim on the
German–Dutch frontier along the eastern fringe of the Ruhr district
to the Rothaargebirge in the south, thence eastwards in the direction
of the Weser which it follows towards Minden. From there a wide
sweep north of Osnabrück brings it back to Bentheim.[3] Such isoglosses are e.g. Westphal. diphthong *uo* or *ua* in the words NHG
(ge)*broch(en)* (*DSA*, 29), *Dorf* (*DSA*, 47); Westphal. *küren* for 'to talk'
against Ripuarian *kallen*, Hessian *schwätzen* and North Saxon
snacken (*DSA*, 55); Westphal. *Rüe* for 'dog' against Rip. *Honk*, Hess.
Hond, NS *Hund*. Other Westphal. characteristics are e.g. the distinction between the reflexes of WGmc. *ā* and *ă* which was lengthened
subsequently; preservation of intervocalic WGmc. -*sk*- (*wasken* 'to

deutschen Raum', *NdJb.*, lxxvi, 1953, 64–76; *id.*, 'Zur Lage des Niederdeutschen in unserer Zeit', *NdJb.*, lxxi–lxxiii, 1948–50, 337–47; *id.*, 'Von den
Grenzen der niederdeutschen Sprache', *Festschrift Boeck*, pp. 214–22; R.
Mehlem, W. Seedorf (ed.), *Niederdeutsch. Ein Handbuch zur Pflege der Heimat-
sprache*, Hanover, 1957. Numerous articles on the aims of the movement
appeared in the *NdJb*.

[1] See chap. i, pp. 24–5.

[2] K. Schulte Kemminghausen, 'Literaturbericht über plattdeutsche Dichtung
in Westfalen 1939–1952', *Westfälische Forschungen*, vi, 1943–52, 246–53,
mentions about eighty books of novels, short stories, plays or lyrics in Westphalian dialect. In Hamburg the *Bookkring* and *Fehrs-Gilde* devote themselves
to the publication of books in Low German. See further *Übersicht über die
wichtigsten niederdeutschen Vereine, Heimatbünde, Heimatvereine, Arbeitskreise,
Kulturgemeinschaften u. ä.* and *Zeitschriften-Übersicht* in *Niederdeutsch* (fn. 1
above), pp. 201–12.

[3] Cf. the maps in Foerste, *DPhA*, p. 2003; Mitzka, *DMaa.*, p. 60

wash').[1] The most important internal boundary runs along the River Lippe, separating North Westphal. from South Westphal. The *Münsterland* forms the heart of the North Westphal. area. With Münster as its centre it stretches out to Dülmen in the west, Beckum and Warendorf in the east and Rheine in the north. *DSA*, 16, *heiss* 'hot' shows Westphal. north of the Lippe with monophthong, south of the Lippe with diphthong, while *DSA*, 41, *Wiesk* 'meadow' and *DSA*, 45, *Geis* 'geese' coincide roughly with the *Münsterland*. The maps in Mitzka, *Wortatlas*, for 'horsefly' (vol. v) giving *Blinde*, for 'pin' (vol. iv) *Koppnadel*, for 'jay' (vol. iii) *Hiekster*, for 'elder' (vol. iii) *Büssenholt*, show the extent of the *Münsterland* dialect in lexical features.

The *Münsterland* has produced an impressive number of good dialect writers, notably Augustin Wibbelt, the author of our specimen text, Karl Wagenfeld from Lüdinghausen, Ferdinand Krüger from Beckum, Anton Aulke from Senden, Friedrich Castelle from Appelhülsen, Franz Giese and Hermann Landois from Münster.[2]

GENERAL CHARACTERISTICS OF WESTPHALIAN (MÜNSTERLAND DIALECT)

§ 2. PHONOLOGICAL FEATURES[3]

2.1 The Vowels

(1) The WGmc.[4] long vowels $\bar{i}$, $\bar{u}$ and the later mutated $\bar{u}$ are preserved as long monophthongs.

(2) WGmc. $\bar{e}^2$ and *eo* (> MHG *ie*) are represented by a diphthong *ai*, but WGmc. $\bar{o}$ (> MHG *uo*) is preserved as *o*.

(3) WGmc. *au* (> MHG *ou*, $\bar{o}$) is *au* (but was $\bar{o}$ in OS); WGmc. *ai* (> MHG *ei*, $\hat{e}$) is *e* or *ai* (if mutated).[5]

(4) All the originally short high- and mid-tongue vowels have developed differently according to whether they were in closed syllables or in open syllables and before an *r*- cluster. In the latter case they

---

[1] For further details, see Foerste, *DPhA*, p. 2004 f; E. Bussmann, 'Die Abgrenzung und Einteilung der westfälischen Mundart', *Münsterland*, 1921, pp. 18–23; T. Baader, 'Probleme der westfälischen Dialektgeographie', *Zfd-Maa.*, 1923, pp. 188–204; E. Nörrenberg, 'Die Grenzen der westfälischen Mundart', *Westfälische Forschungen*, vii, 1953–4, 114–29.

[2] J. Bergenthal, *Westfälische Dichter der Gegenwart*, 2nd ed., Münster, 1954, p. 29, speaks of a 'besondere plattdeutsche Dichter-Landschaft': the region between Münster and Warendorf, Lüdinghausen und Beckvm.

[3] See fn. 1, p. 32.

[4] In historical studies LG is usually compared with MLG, OS or WGmc. As a knowledge of MLG or OS cannot be generally assumed for students of German I have preferred making reference to WGmc.

[5] See H. Behrens, 'Beobachtungen zur Geschichte der niederdeutschen Diphthongierung', *NdJb.*, lxxvii, 1954, 84–110.

have become diphthongized and the reflexes of WGmc. *i* and of the primary umlaut of *a* have coincided, as have the reflexes of WGmc. *e* and of the secondary umlaut of *a*.[1]

(5) WGmc. *ā* and WGmc. *ă* subsequently lengthened are kept apart, the former being a slightly rounded back vowel, the latter a front vowel.

(6) The WGmc. short vowels in closed syllables have been generally preserved.

(7) Mutation has produced rounded front vowels.

(8) The mutated reflex of WGmc. *ā* ($>$ *ai*) has coincided with mutated WGmc. *au, ai*, and with *eo*.

(9) Nasalization is generally unknown.

(10) Initial vowels have a smooth onset.

2.2 Vowel Quantity

(1) All originally short vowels in open syllables have either been lengthened or diphthongized; correspondingly, originally long vowels before consonantal clusters have been shortened.

(2) *R*, alone or as a first member of a cluster, has generally had a lengthening effect on the preceding vowels.

2.3 Vowels in Unstressed Syllables

(1) The prefix corresponding to NHG *be-* retains an unstressed vowel, but the former participial prefix *ge-* has generally vanished.

(2) The medieval final -*e* is generally preserved.

2.4 The Consonants

(1) The consonantal system is based on an opposition of voiced and voiceless stops and fricatives except in final position where only voiceless stops and fricatives occur.

(2) WGmc. *p, t, k* are preserved. WGmc. *d* and *þ* have coincided (*d*).

(3) The velar fricative (*ch*) occurs also initially, where it represents WGmc. *g*.[2]

(4) WGmc. *s* before other consonants incl. initial *k*, is now preserved only in the most conservative dialects. Otherwise NHG *š* has been adopted.

(5) WGmc. *ð* is *b* in initial position and before a nasal, otherwise it is a labio-dental fricative. WGmc. *g* is generally preserved as a fricative.

---

[1] H. Teuchert, 'Der Lautstand der kurzen Stammsilben im Westfälischen', *ZfdMaa.*, 1921, pp. 97–124.
[2] Cf. Th. Frings, 'Vom g, von seinen Lautwerten und von germanischen Sprachlandschaften', *Festschrift Adolf Bach* (= *Rheinische Vierteljahrsblätter*, xx, 1955, 170–91).

(6) *L* is generally preserved, but *r* is often vocalized in post-vocalic and pre-consonantal positions.

(7) Final *-n* in inflexional suffixes is preserved.

(8) General assimilation of former *-nd- > n, -ld- > l.*

(9) The WGmc. cluster *hs* is reduced to *ss*; the loss of *n* before fricatives and the change of *ft > cht* are found in some words.

§ 3. Morphological Features

3.1 Noun and Article

(1) Only one group of masc. nouns still distinguishes a nom. sg. from the oblique cases, otherwise the noun has no special endings for cases. Among the articles only masc. distinguishes between a nom. and a common objective case.

(2) There is in addition to the usual pl. suffixes also a plural ending *-s*.

(3) Nouns form a diminutive by means of *-ken*.

3.2 The Adjective

(1) The strong declension makes no distinction for cases.

(2) The weak declension distinguishes in the sg. the nom. from the common objective case (masc.).

3.3 The Pronouns

(1) The personal pronouns of the 1st and 2nd pers. have a common objective case. The pers. pron. of the 3rd pers. masc. makes a distinction between stressed and unstressed forms (stressed *em*, for common objective case, unstressed *en*). The pers. pron. of the 3rd pers. pl. distinguishes between dat. and acc.

(2) In the 2nd pers. pl. the forms of the pers. pron. are the 'Ingvaeonic' *ji* (nom.), *ju* (obj.).

(3) The poss. pron. make no distinction for case, except in the masc. gender.

(4) The dem. pron. *dee*, etc., serve also as rel. pron.

3.4 The Verbs

(1) The tense system consists of a present, a preterite indicative and subjunctive, a perfect and a pluperfect. There is no present subjunctive.

(2) Most strong verbs use different stem forms for the sg. (1st, 3rd pers.) and the pl. (incl. 2nd pers. sg.) of the pret. The pl. form is mutated, deriving from the pret. subj.

(3) There is a uniform ending for the pl.: *-t* in the pres., *-n* in the pret.

(4) The future is expressed by means of the auxiliaries *sollen* and *wollen*.

(5) Past participles have no prefix (NHG *ge-*).

(6) There are a small number of weak verbs with *Rückumlaut*.

(7) The verb corresponding to NHG *haben* has mutated forms throughout the present.

(8) The 2nd and 3rd pers. sg. pres. of strong verbs show umlaut.

(9) For NHG *gewesen* Westphal. uses *west*.

(10) The verbs corresponding to NHG *gehen*, *stehen* have a root vowel deriving from WGmc. *ā*.

PHONOLOGY
THE VOWELS
§ 4. The Vowel Phonemes

The main developments which have led to the present phonemic system have been the processes of lengthening or diphthongization of short vowels in originally open syllables and of shortening of long vowels in originally closed syllables. Vowel quantity is, however, not tied to syllabic structure in modern Westphalian. Rounding in labial surroundings has further had important phonetic effects. In the case of the high-tongue vowels and of back vowels, vowel length is linked to a difference in quality, the short vowels being more open and lax than the corresponding long ones.

Front	Front Rounded	Back
i:	y:	u:
ɪ	ʏ	ʊ
e(:)	ø:	o:
ɛ	œ(:)	ɔ
a(:)		ɒ:

(:) means that a vowel occurs both long and short. There is also an unstressed central [ə].

The difference between /e/ and /ɛ/ is phonetically slight, and under NHG influence the phonemic character of the distinction is being undermined. While the distinction between, e.g., /hen/ and /mɛn/ is still perceptible, in most words with /e/ the vowel is frequently opened to be almost indistinguishable from /ɛ/. The feeling for the functional difference seems to have disappeared.

There are eight diphthongs:

ɪə	ʏə	ʊə
ɪɛ	ʏœ	ʊɒ
ɑɪ		ɑʊ

§ 5. Spelling

The author of our specimen text, Augustin Wibbelt, employs the basic rule of NHG spelling, i.e. a short vowel is followed by a double consonant or a cluster, and in an open syllable a vowel is long. Before a single final consonant a long vowel is usually indicated by doubling and a short vowel is usually followed by a double consonant, except in the case of unstressed particles. Wibbelt's spelling is thus more consistent than that of NHG. The two short, unrounded, mid-front phonemes are not distinguished, i.e. *e* and *ä* are used etymologically rather than phonetically, following the NHG practice. By using *e* and *ä* for sound values the necessary distinction can be made. To some extent the use of *ie* for both long *i* and for the diphthong *ie* is unsatisfactory. However, the distinction emerges from the consonants which follow: if there is only one, *ie* is long *i*; if there is a cluster, it is the diphthong *ie*. The use of the two letters *ao* for a monophthong might also be considered misleading. As it is traditional in Westphalian and as it is used unambiguously it can be retained.

The correspondences are:

Phoneme	Letter	Phoneme	Letter	Phoneme	Letter
i:	ie, ih, ii	y:, Y	ü, üh	ɪə	ie (3)
ɪ	i	ø:	ö, öh	ɪɛ	iä
e	e	œ	ö	Yə	üe
e:	e (1), ee, eh	œ:	äö	Yœ	üö
ɛ	ä	u:, ʊ	u, uh, uu	ʊə	ue
ɛ:	ä, ää, äh	o:	o, oh, oo	ʊɒ	uo
a(:)	a, aa, ah	ɔ	o, ao (2)	ɑɪ	ai, ei
		ɒ:	ao	ɑʊ	au

Notes

(1) Single letters for long vowels apply only in open syllables.

(2) This spelling is used before *l* or *l* + cons. where the vowel corresponds to NHG *a*.

(3) If *ie* indicates a diphthong it is always followed by more than one consonant.

§ 6. Short Stressed Vowels

6.1 [ɪ] is an open, lax, high-front vowel deriving from:

(i) WGmc. *i* in closed syllables (but see § 6.2): *Kind* 'child', *Fisk* 'fish'.

(ii) WGmc. *ī* before consonantal clusters: *licht* 'light'.

6.2 [e] is a close, tense, mid-front vowel representing:

(i) WGmc. *a* mutated in closed syllables: *Menske* 'human being', *Bedde* 'bed', but see § 6.3 (ii).

(ii) WGmc. *e* in a few words: *Stemme* 'voice', *Geld* 'money'.

(iii) WGmc. *i* before a single consonant in: *met* 'with'.

(iv) WGmc. *ai* and *eu* (OS *eo*) before clusters: *ment* 'meant'.
On the distinction between /e/ and /ɛ/, see § 4.

6.3 [ɛ] is an open, lax, mid-front vowel representing:

(i) WGmc. *e* in closed syllables: *hälpen* 'to help', *slächt* 'bad'.

(ii) WGmc. *a* mutated in closed syllables, either as the secondary umlaut or in words where the connection with the a-root vowel is still obvious: *Hänn* 'hands', *Snäpsken* < *Schnapps*.

6.4 [a] is an advanced low-tongue vowel deriving from:

(i) WGmc. *a* in closed syllables except where followed by *l*: *lang* 'long', *namm* 'took'.

(ii) WGmc. *ā* before clusters: *dachte* 'thought'.

6.5 [ɔ] is an open, lax, mid-back vowel deriving from:

(i) WGmc. *o* in closed syllables: *Hoff* 'farm', *Klock* 'clock'.

(ii) WGmc. *o* and WGmc. *au* in conditions of shortening before consonantal clusters: *socht* 'sought', *koft* 'bought'.

(iii) WGmc. *a* before *l* in certain words: *aolle* 'old'.

6.6 [ɷ] is an open, lax, high-back vowel and derives from:

(i) WGmc. *u* in closed syllables: *wunnen* 'won', *Schuller* 'shoulder'.

(ii) WGmc. *ū* under conditions of shortening: *lustern* 'to listen'.

6.7 [œ] is an open, lax, rounded, mid-front vowel deriving from:

(i) WGmc. *o* mutated in closed syllables: *Pöst* 'posts'.

(ii) WGmc. *ō* and *au* mutated under conditions of shortening: *mössen*, NHG *müssten*, *grötter* 'bigger'.

(iii) WGmc. *a* before *l* mutated: *häöllt* 'holds'.

(iv) WGmc. *e* in labial surroundings in: *söwst* 'self', *Hölp* 'help'.

(v) OS *iu* under conditions of shortening: *söchten* 'to sigh'.

6.8 [y] is an open, lax, rounded, high-front vowel deriving from:

(i) WGmc. *u* mutated before clusters: *lück* 'little', *Püllken* 'bottle' dim.

(ii) WGmc. *ū* and *eu* mutated before clusters: *Frünt* 'friend'.

(iii) WGmc. *i* in labial surroundings: *tüsken* 'between'; a similar process of rounding has produced *düt* 'this', *ümmer* 'always'.

§ 7. Long Vowels

7.1 [i:] is a close, tense, high-front vowel and represents WGmc. *ī*: *Tied* 'time', *gliek* 'like'.

7.2 [e:] is a close, tense, mid-front vowel representing:

(i) WGmc. *ai* not affected by mutation: *Been* 'leg', *bleek* 'pale'.

(ii) in the verbal ending corresponding to NHG *-ieren*: *kureeren* 'to cure', and for OS *ē* in *he* 'he', *de* 'this, the'. Before *r* there is an open, lax variant: *mähr* 'more', *äher* 'before'; also in the case of:

(iii) WGmc. *e* lengthened before *r*: *wäern* 'to become'.

7.3 [a:] is an advanced, tense, low-tongue vowel representing WGmc. *a* in originally open syllables: *maken* 'to make', *hahlen* 'to fetch'.

7.4 [ɒ:] is rounded, low-back vowel deriving from:

(i) WGmc. *ā*: *slaopen* 'to sleep', *Maot* 'measure'.

(ii) WGmc. *o, a* before *r* + dentals: *Waort* 'word', *Gaoern* 'garden'.

(iii) WGmc. *au* before *r*: *Aohr* 'ear'.

7.5 [o:] is a close, tense, mid-back vowel deriving from WGmc. *ō*: *Moot* 'courage', *noog* 'enough'.

7.6 [u:] is a close, tense, high-back vowel deriving from:

(i) WGmc. *ū*: *buten* 'outside', *duern* 'to last'.

(ii) WGmc. *u* before former *rr*: *gnuern* 'to growl'.

7.7 [ø:] is a close, tense, rounded, mid-front vowel deriving from:

(i) WGmc. *ō* mutated: *Fööt* 'feet'.

(ii) WGmc. *ā* mutated in: *wöern* 'were'.

7.8 [œ:] is an open, lax, rounded, mid-front vowel deriving from:

(i) WGmc. *ā* mutated (active umlaut of [ɒ:]): *mäötig* < *Maot* 'measure', *gefäöhrlick* 'dangerous'.

(ii) WGmc. *au* mutated in: *häören* 'to hear', *häöchter* 'higher'.

7.9 [y:] is a close, tense, rounded, high-front vowel deriving from:

(i) WGmc. *ū* mutated: *Hüser* 'houses', *Krüüs* 'cross'.

(ii) WGmc. *u* mutated with loss of former following *d*: *küern* 'to talk', *Rüe* 'dog'.

(iii) WGmc. *eu* mutated: *Düwel* 'devil', *Lüe* 'people', *bedüern* 'to assert', in the 2nd and 3rd pers. sg. pres. of strong verbs of the WGmc. II class and in analogy to these in *sühs* 'you see' < *seihen* 'to see'.

§ 8. DIPHTHONGS

Of the eight diphthongs two start with a low-tongue element and are phonetically very similar to the NHG diphthongs [ɑo, ɑe]. Three diphthongs are falling, ending in a neutral central element and three diphthongs are rising, ending in a lower mid-tongue element.

8.1 [ɑɪ] represents:

(i) WGmc. *ai* mutated: *klein* 'small', *rein* 'clear'.

(ii) WGmc. *eu*: *leif* 'dear', *geiten* 'to pour'.

(iii) WGmc. *ē* (OHG *ia*): *slaip* 'slept', *raip* 'called'.

(iv) WGmc. *au* mutated: *draimen* 'to dream', *glaiben* 'to believe', *naidig* 'necessary'.

(v) WGmc. *ā* mutated (historical umlaut): *leig* 'bad', *naihm* 'would take'.

8.2 [ɑɷ] represents WGmc. *au*: *Baum* 'tree', *daut* 'dead', *graut* 'big'.

8.3 [ɪə] represents WGmc. *i* in originally open syllables: *siecker* 'sure', *viell* 'much', *wietten* 'to know', *Niewwel* 'mist', *giebben* 'to give', *niemmen* 'to take'.

8.4 [ɪɛ] represents:

(i) WGmc. *e* in originally open syllables and before *r* + consonant: *biädden* 'to pray', *Hiärfst* 'autumn', *Hiätt* 'heart', *Wiähr* 'weather'.

(ii) WGmc. *a* mutated: *Miägde* 'maids', *Tiänn* 'teeth'.

8.5 [ɷə] represents WGmc. *u* in originally open syllables: *kuemmen* 'to come', *Kuegel* 'ball'; WGmc. *ō* after shortening to former *u* in *guett* 'good'.

8.6 [ɷɒ] represents:

(i) WGmc. *o* in originally open syllables and before *r* + consonant: *Knuocken* 'bone', *Guott* 'God', *wuoll* 'well', *befuollen* 'ordered', *muorgen* 'to-morrow', *stuorben* 'died' p.p.

(ii) WGmc. *u* in an open syllable in some words: *Stuowe* 'living-room'. Informant uses this diphthong also in *Suohn* 'son'.

8.7 [ʏə] represents WGmc. *u* mutated in originally open syllables: *Sprüeckwaort* 'proverb', *Küeck* 'kitchen'.

8.8 [ʏœ] represents:

(i) WGmc. *o* mutated in originally open syllables: *Hüöwe* 'farms', *Hüöppnunk* 'hope'.

(ii) WGmc. *u* mutated before *r*: *düör* 'through', *Düör* 'door', *füördern* 'to demand', and in *üöwer* 'over'.

§ 9. Unstressed Vowels

Except in foreign words and compounds only [ɪ] and [ə] occur in unstressed positions. Unstressed *u* is confined to the ending *-ung*.

9.1 [ɪ] occurs only in suffixes, e.g. *-ig*: *trurig* 'sad'; *-lick*: *wüerklick* 'really'; *-ink*: *Lewink* 'lark'.

9.2 [ə] continues in many cases medieval final unstressed *-e*.

(i) e.g. in the plural of nouns: *Dage* 'days', *Föte* 'feet'; in the sg. of nouns: *Bedde* 'bed', *Wiele* 'while'; in adjectival and pronominal endings: *met iähre gesunne Natur*; in the 1st pers. sg. pres. of verbs: *ick wünske* 'I wish'; in the ending of the pret. of weak verbs: *lachede*

x

'laughed'; in adverbs: *lange* 'a long time', *liese* 'softly'. There is, however, a good deal of variation and there are local differences as well. Thus in Wibbelt we find *Stemm* 'voice' for *Stemme*, *Stuof* for *Stuowe* 'living-room', *ik glaif* for *ik glaiwe* 'I believe', *ik häff* for *ik häwwe* 'I have'.

(ii) It occurs in the prefix *be-*: *begieggnen* 'to encounter', and in the prefix *ge-*, which is, however, mainly a nominal prefix, the participial *ge-* having been lost in late medieval times: *Gewietten* 'conscience'.

(iii) In the suffixes *-en*, *-em*, *-el*, *-er* [-ɛr] the vowel is often elided in rapid speech and the consonants become syllabic. In more deliberate speech it is preserved.

§ 10. Vowel Quantity

Westphalian follows, like NHG, the general rule that in open syllables only long vowels or diphthongs occur and that before consonantal clusters only short vowels are tolerated. On the whole the exceptions to this rule are less numerous than in NHG. Originally short vowels before *r* have either been lengthened or diphthongized (before *r* + consonant). *R* has now, however, no automatic lengthening effect. Short vowels before *r* occur, perhaps under NHG influence.

§ 11. Comparison with the NHG Vowels

(1) The quantity distribution follows the same principles as in NHG.

(2) Diphthongization before *r* + consonant in Westphalian.

(3) The NHG diphthongs *ei*, *au*, *eu* have at least double correspondences, as old differences, which have been removed in NHG, are preserved.

(4) Like NHG Westphalian distinguishes between unrounded and rounded front vowels, the effects of the historical mutations thus being still structurally significant.

(5) Characteristic tendency to rounding in labial surroundings in Westphalian.

(6) The NHG rule that short vowels are lax and long vowels tense generally applies, with exceptions in the case of the *e-* phonemes.

(7) Westphalian has three characteristic falling diphthongs and three rising diphthongs unknown to NHG.

(8) The two diphthongs *au* and *ai* are phonetically the same in NHG and Westphalian.

(9) Historical long *a* and lengthened *a*, which coincide in NHG, are kept apart in Westphalian.

(10) With regard to the occurrence of unstressed *-e* Westphalian is nearer NHG than almost any other dialect.

Chief Vowel Correspondences

West-phal.[1]	ie	iä	ue	uo	üe	üö	ie[i:]	u	ü	au	ai		oo	ee
WGmc.	i	e(a)	u	o	u-[i]	o-[i]	ī	ū	iu, ū	au eu(eo), ē[2]			ō	ai
NHG	i	e	u	o	ü	ö	ei	au	eu	au, o	ie		u	ei, e

NHG	i	e	u	o	ü	ö		ei	au	eu	u
WGmc.	i	e(a)	u	o	u-	o-[i]		ī ai	ū au	iu au-[i] ō	
West-phal.[2]	ie, i iä, e	ue, u	uo, o	üe, ü	üö, ö		ie[i:]ee	u au	ü ai	oo	

[1] For the phonetic value of the letters, see § 5. NHG sounds are given in their usual orthography.

[2] Different development according to whether the sound was in an originally open syllable or not.

THE CONSONANTS

§ 12. THE CONSONANTAL SYSTEM

Stops		Fricatives		Sonants		
voiceless	voiced	voiceless	voiced	nasals	liquids	semi-vowels
p	b	f	v	m		
t	d	s (š)	z	n	l, r	j
k	(g)	x	ɣ	ŋ		h

The opposition of voice among stops and fricatives obtains only in initial and medial position. In final position, including the penultimate in consonantal clusters, only voiceless stops and fricatives occur. In initial position the voiceless stops are slightly aspirated. The voiced stops /b/ and /d/ are frequent only in initial position. /g/ is a marginal phoneme being introduced in NHG words, above all in the prefix ge- (e.g. Gedanken) where it is, however, still a free variant of /x/. It is also heard as a variant of /ɣ/ after short vowels and before /ŋ/, e.g. in seggen 'to say', liggen 'to lie'. Another new phoneme is /š/. It is in the process of establishing itself as a separate phoneme in initial position. As a phonetic variant of the /s/- phoneme it now occurs before other consonants in initial position and before /k/ in medial and final position. But many speakers have /š-/ now for /šx-/, e.g. informant said *S-choppen* 'barn' but *Schulte* 'village mayor or squire'. The opposition of /s/ and /z/ occurs only in intervocalic position. Only the voiceless alveolar fricative is used initially or finally. /v/ is a labiodental voiced fricative in the majority of cases, but after initial /k, t, d, s/ it is bilabial. The palato-velar fricatives have velar allophones [x, γ] after (or initially before) back vowels (like NHG) and palatal allophones [ç, ʝ] in all other circumstances. The contrast between the voiceless ones and the voiced ones is confined to the intervocalic position and dependent on very few words with /x/ in that position, e.g. *lachen* 'to laugh'. Were it not for these few examples of intervocalic /x/ (see § 14.9 (ii)) the distribution could be said to be complementary, /γ/ occurring only intervocalically. The semi-vowel /j/ and the glottal /h/ occur only in initial position.

§ 13. SPELLING

The NHG spelling system can be retained. It has to be remembered that doubling of consonants indicates only that the preceding vowel is short. There are the following correspondences between phonemes and letters:

Phoneme	Letter	Phoneme	Letter	Phoneme	Letter
p	p	f	f, v (1)	m	m
t	t	v	w	n	n
k	k, ck	s (š)	s, sch (2)	ŋ	ng
b	b	x	g, gg, ch	l, r	l, r
d	d	γ	g, gg, ch (3)	j	j
(g)	g	z	s	h	h (4)

Notes

(1) The letter *v* for /f/ occurs only in initial position in the same words as in NHG, e.g. *Vader* 'father'.

(2) Before consonants in initial position and before medial and final *k* Wibbelt retains the earlier LG spelling with *s* although phonetically the sound is [š]. Initial *sch* may represent /sx/ or /š/, the latter being now much more general.

(3) *G* and *ch* are used as in NHG. *G* represents a fricative except in the rare cases mentioned in § 12. An intervocalic *ch* indicates the voiceless sound, an intervocalic *g* the voiced one.

(4) *H* in any other than initial position is merely a sign for vowel length.

§ 14. The Consonant Phonemes

14.1 [p, t, k] are the representatives of:

(i) WGmc. *p, t, k* in all positions. Westphalian is unaffected by the HG soundshift. E.g. *Kopp* 'head', *slaopen* 'to sleep', *teihn* 'ten', *laoten* 'let', *biätter* 'better', *maken* 'to make', *bruocken* 'broken'.

(ii) *T* is also the representative of WGmc. *d, þ* in final position, and *k* of WGmc. *g* after *ng*: *Moot* 'courage', *gonk* 'went'.

14.2 [b] is a voiced, bilabial stop deriving from:

(i) WGmc. *b* initially and *bb* medially: *biädden* 'to pray', *Ribbe* 'rib'.

(ii) WGmc. *ƀ* medially before *m* (< *-ben*): *blieben* [bli:bm] 'to stay', *Liäben* 'life'.

14.3 [d] is a voiced, alveolar stop deriving from WGmc. *d* and *þ*: *möde* 'tired', *Liäder* 'leather', *daip* 'deep'. In intervocalic position the stop is often found only in deliberate and careful articulation. In more rapid and careless speech it may be replaced by *r* (< *dd*), e.g. *Berre* or *Bedde* 'bed', *har* 'had'. In many words a former stop has disappeared altogether, e.g. *Wiär* 'weather', *Broer* 'brother', *Lüe* 'people', *mö'e* 'tired'. (See also § 15.)

14.4 [g] is a voiced, palato-velar stop, occurring before /ŋ/ < *n* in certain words, e.g. *liggen* 'to lie', *leggen* 'to put' and in some NHG loans.

14.5 [f] is a voiceless, labio-dental fricative deriving from:

(i) WGmc. *f* in initial and final position: *viell* 'much', *Hoff* 'farm'.

(ii) WGmc. *ƀ* in final position and before voiceless consonants: *Wief* 'wife', *giffs* '[you] give'.

14.6 [v] is a voiced, labio-dental fricative (bilabial after consonants) deriving from:

(i) WGmc. *w* in initial position: *ik weet* 'I know', *quamm* 'came', *twintig* 'twenty'.

(ii) WGmc. *ƀ* in medial position but not before *m*: *leiwer* 'rather', *owwer* 'but', *Düwel* 'devil'.

(iii) WGmc. *f* in intervocalic position: *Hüöwe* 'farms'.

14.7 [s] is a voiceless, alveolar fricative except before consonants initially and before *k* medially and finally when it is a grooved dorsal fricative [š]. It derives from WGmc. *s*: *Suohn* 'son', *sweeten* 'to sweat', *vers-cheiden* 'different', *Mensk* 'man', *staohen* 'to stand'. From WGmc. initial *sk-* a new phoneme /š/ is now arising: *Schell* 'bell'.

14.8 [z] is a voiced, alveolar fricative deriving from WGmc. *s* medially in voiced surroundings: *brusen* 'to storm', *Rausen* 'roses'.

14.9 [x] is a voiceless, palato-velar fricative (as to chief allophones, see § 12) deriving from:

(i) WGmc. *g* in all positions except medially between vowels: *gaohen* 'to go', *leig* 'bad'.

(ii) WGmc. *h* medially and finally: *lachen* 'to laugh', *Dochter* 'daughter', *saog* 'saw'.

(iii) WGmc. *f* before *t* in a few words: *ächter* 'after'.

14.10 [ɣ] is a voiced, palato-velar fricative (as to chief allophones, see § 12) deriving from WGmc. *g* medially in voiced surroundings: *Siägen* 'blessing', *jagen* 'to hunt'.

14.11 The nasals [m, n, ŋ] derive from the same sources as the nasals in NHG. As to assimilation, see § 15. [r] is an alveolar, rolled liquid representing WGmc. *r*. In final unstressed position the articulation is weak in rapid speech. In conservative dialect it also represents WGmc. *-dd-*: *Berre* 'bed'. [l] is a middle-tongue lateral deriving from WGmc. *l*.

14.12 [j] is a voiced, palatal semi-vowel, occurring only in initial position and deriving from WGmc. *j*: *Jaohr* 'year'.

14.13 [h] occurs before vowels initially and as an aspirate after initial voiceless stops. It represents WGmc. *h* initially before vowels: *Huus* 'house'.

§ 15. ASSIMILATION

The following historical assimilations are characteristic of Westphalian:

(i) *-ld-* > *l*: *haollen* 'to hold', *Schuller* 'shoulder'.

(ii) *-nd-* > *n*: *Enne* 'end', *schennen* 'to grumble'.

(iii) *r* before *t* in some words: *Hiätt* 'heart', *diättig* 'thirty'.

(iv) *n* before fricatives:[1] *us* 'us', *Gaus* 'goose', *fief* 'five'.

(v) *-hs* > *s*: *wesseln* 'to change', *Osse* 'ox'.

(vi) *n* before *s* in the unstressed suffix *-ken*: sg. *Snäpsken*, pl. *Snäpskes*.

(vii) *t, d* before *s* in the 2nd pers. sg. pres.: *löss* '(you) let'.

(viii) *t* after *p, k, f, g, s* in the 3rd pers. sg. pres.: *he segg* 'he says'.

Sandhi assimilations, which are to some extent dependent on the speed and carefulness of speech, are:

(i) unstressed *n* after labials > *m*: *bliebm* 'to stay'.

(ii) unstressed *n* after velars > [ŋ]: *Knuockng* 'bone'. This occurs also at the juncture of words, e.g. *Ruh un Plege* > *Ruh um Plege*.

§ 16. COMPARISON WITH THE NHG CONSONANTS

The most salient differences are:

(1) Westphalian preserves the WGmc. consonantism, i.e. is unaffected by the HG soundshift.

---

[1] On this 'Ingvaeonic' sound change, see p. 52.

(2) Westphalian is less conservative than NHG in one respect: it obliterates the difference between WGmc. *d* and *þ* in initial and medial positions, where NHG preserves it.

(3) The velar fricative in initial position and the voiced velar fricative in medial position are alien to NHG.

(4) The NHG affricates *pf* and *tz* are alien to Westphalian.

(5) Traditional Westphalian lacks the NHG sounds *g* and *sch*.

The most noteworthy similarity lies in the fact that the consonantal system rests on the opposition of voice and lack of voice, which is neutralized in final position.

MORPHOLOGY

NOUNS AND ARTICLES

§ 17. FORMATION OF THE PLURAL

In addition to the usual plural suffixes found in German dialects, i.e. *-e* and/or *-en* and *-er*, Westphalian has a suffix *-s*. Since the addition of a plural suffix often affects the syllabic structure, certain vocalic and consonantal changes accompany the formation of the plural apart from the usual mutation in certain types. Thus there are subgroups of nouns with changes from short vowel (sg.) to long vowel (pl.), from monophthong (sg.) to diphthong (pl.), from root consonantal clusters *-nt, -lt, -nk* in the sg. to *-n-, -l-, -ng-* in the pl., from a final voiceless consonant to the corresponding voiced consonant before a plural suffix.

The following types of plural formation can be distinguished:

Type A: plural not marked by ending or mutation.

Type B: plural marked by mutation alone.

Type C: plural marked by suffix *-e* (with or without vocalic and consonantal changes).

Type D: plural marked by suffix *-e* plus mutation (with or without vocalic and consonantal changes).

Type E: plural marked by suffix *-en* (or nasal suffix in general).

Type F: plural marked by suffix *-er*, with mutation where possible.

Type G: plural marked by suffix *-s*.

Note: All back vowels and low-tongue vowels are capable of mutating. The correspondences are:

Back vowel	a	ao	o	oh	u	uh	au	uo
Mutated vowel	ä/iä	äö	ö/üö	öh	ü/üe	üh	ai	üö

Where two possible mutated vowels are given the second is the result of diphthongization in open syllables.

Diphthongization and lengthening in altered syllabic conditions imply the following changes:

sg.	a	e	i	o	u	ü	ö
pl.	ah	iä	ie	uo	ue	üe	üö

Type A. To this type belong:
(i) Very few masc. nouns, e.g. *Finger* 'finger'.

Type B. To this type belong:
(i) A number of masc. nouns, especially dissyllabic ones: *Nagel—Niägel* 'nail', *Vuegel—Vüegel* 'bird', and those masc. ones which are affected by apocope: *Foot—Fööt* or *Föte* 'foot', *Tahn* or *Tand—Tiänn* or *Tiänne* 'tooth'.
(ii) A few fem.: *Dochter—Döchter* 'daughter', especially those affected by apocope: *Hand—Hänn* or *Hänne* 'hand'.

Type C. To this type belong:
(i) A number of masc. nouns, especially those with non-mutatable root-vowels: *Wind—Winne* 'wind', *Knächt—Knächte* 'labourer', *Daif—Daiwe* 'thief', *Dagg—Dage* 'day'.
(ii) A number of neuter nouns: *Jaohr, -e* 'year', *Piärd, -e* 'horse'.

Type D. To this type belong:
(i) A large number of masc. nouns, mainly those which also mutate in NHG: *Hoff—Hüöwe* 'farm', *Baum—Baime* 'tree', *Slagg—Sliäge* 'blow'.
(ii) A fair number of fem. nouns, mainly those which also mutate in NHG: *Magd—Miägde* 'maid', *Muus—Müse* 'mouse', *Gaus—Gaise* 'goose', *Ko—Köe* 'cow'.
(iii) One or two neuters: *Fatt—Fiäte* 'barrel'.

Type E. To this type belong:
(i) The majority of fem. nouns: *Saak—Saken* 'thing', *Straot—Straoten* 'street', *Sünn(e)—Sünnen* 'sin'.
(ii) The majority of masc. nouns denoting animate beings (except those in *-er*): *Buer—Buern* 'farmer', *Mensk(e)—Mensken* 'man'.
(iii) The neuters: *Aug(e)—Augen* 'eye', *Aohr—Aohren* 'ear', *Hiätt—Hiätten* 'heart'.

Type F. To this type belong:
(i) The majority of the neuter nouns: *Glass—Gliäser* 'glass', *Land—Länner* 'land', *Glidd—Gliedder* 'limb'.
(ii) A few masc.: *Wuorm—Wüörmer* 'worm'.

Type G. To this type belong:
(i) Masculine nouns ending in *-r, -l, -n*: *Druoppen—Druoppens* 'drop', *Spaigel—Spaigels* 'looking-glass', *Bäcker—Bäckers* 'baker'.

(ii) A few neuters and all diminutives in -*ken*: *Fenster*—*Fensters* 'window', *Blömken*—*Blömkes* 'flower'.

(iii) Fem. nouns in -*er*: *Süster*—*Süsters* 'sister'.

§ 18. CASE FORMS

Münsterland dialects have only one subclass of nouns which distinguish cases. Type E (ii) masc. nouns take the ending -*n* in the objective case. Eastphalian dialects, however, indicate a dat. sg. and a dat. pl., and Wibbelt, coming from the eastern fringe of the Münsterland, employs dat. endings occasionally although rather irregularly. Thus we find *in'n Huse* and *in'n Huus, nao besten Kräften*. NHG influence may be held responsible for the latter expression.

A genitive sg. ending -*s* is found in fixed formulas, e.g. *eenes Aobens, Guotts Hölp* and with proper names, e.g. *Hellkamps Hoff*. Otherwise the usual dative paraphrase is used for the possessive, e.g. *har Vader siene Schell gaohen?* (father's bell).

§ 19. GENDER

A number of nouns have a gender different from that of the corresponding NHG word, e.g. *Biecke* f. 'brook', *Aor* n. 'ear of corn'.

§ 20. THE DECLENSION OF THE DEFINITE ARTICLE

The masc. article alone distinguishes between subject and object.

	m.	*f.*	*n.*	*pl.*
Nom.	de	} de	} dat	} de
Objective Case	den (1)			

Notes

(1) After prepositions the art. is reduced to -*n*, e.g. *up n Hoff*, which is assimilated to a preceding nasal: *an'n Grund* 'on the ground'. This is also the case with neuter nouns. Thus *in'n Hus(e), in'n Hiätten, in'n Bedde*.

(2) Westphalian does not use the art. before personal names, e.g. *Wilm, Anna, Vader*, etc.

(3) *Tom, tor* (*tom Ekel, tor Stelle*) retain a dative form, cf. NHG *zum, zur*.

§ 21. THE DECLENSION OF THE INDEFINITE ARTICLE

There are only two forms and no case distinctions are made:

m.n.	*f.*
en, n	ene, ne

The reduced forms are used in the least stressed positions, e.g. after prepositions.

ADJECTIVES

§ 22. The Declensions

The Strong Declension

m.	f.	n.	pl.
jungen	junge	jung	junge

The Weak Declension

	m.	f. n.	pl.
Nom.	junge	junge	jungen
Obj. C.	jungen		
(Dat.		jungen)	

The historical distinction between a weak and a strong declension has been reduced radically. Thus it can be stated that:

(i) The adjective before a masc. noun ends in *-en* except, in the subject case, after the def. article *de*, the dem. pron. *düsse*, the possessive pronouns and in the vocative with or without pers. pron. In those exceptional cases it ends in *-e*. E.g. *en griesen Niewwel, gueden Moot*, but *de leiwe Häer* or *leiwe Häer!*

(ii) The adjective before a fem. noun ends in *-e* except in expressions where a dat. def. art. occurs, e.g. *tor rächten Tied*.

(iii) The adjective before a neuter pronoun is endingless except after the def. article *dat*, the dem. pron. *düt* and the possessive pronouns, in which cases it ends in *-e*. In circumstances where a prep. has absorbed a former dat. def. art. the ending is *-en*, e.g. *en guett Dink, dat halwe Püllken, an'n lesten Enne*.

(iv) Before nouns in the plural it ends in *-en* if preceded by an article or a pronoun, if not it ends in *-e*.

§ 23. Comparison

The endings of the second and third degrees are: *-er, -(e)st*. E.g. *jung—jünger—jüngste* or *möde—möder—mödeste* 'tired'. The adjective *graut* 'big' has shortened vowels in the comp. and sup.: *grötter, grötste*. The comparative particle is *äs*.

NUMERALS

§ 24

The only numeral which distinguishes between genders is *een* (m.n.), *eene* (f.). It is used as an adjective or a noun. Like the strong adj. it does not distinguish cases.

PRONOUNS

§ 25. PERSONAL PRONOUNS

	1st Person	2nd Person	3rd Person		
Nom. sg.	ick, 'k	du, -te, (2) -	he, e	se	et, 't
Obj. sg.	mi	di	em, en, n (3)	iähr	et, 't
Nom. pl.	wi	ji (6)	se
Obj. pl.	us	ju	iähr, se (4)

Notes

(1) In inversion and after prepositions the least stressed, reduced forms are used. In the 2nd pers. sg. the pers. pron. may be left out altogether, e.g. *wo bliffs so lange?*

(2) The form *-te* is enclitic, e.g. *wees-te?* 'do you know?'

(3) The general rule is: *em* for the objective case when stressed; *en, 'n* when unstressed, e.g. *et wör biätter för em un us* 'it would be better for him and for us', but *Vader hadd'n vörlaoten* 'father had let him in'. Occasionally Wibbelt seems to be influenced by the NHG practice.

(4) In the 3rd pers. pl. a distinction is made between the dat. *iähr* and the acc. *se*.

(5) The indefinite personal pronoun is *man*.

(6) *Ji* and *ju* are also the polite form of address (sg.).

§ 26. REFLEXIVE PRONOUNS[1]

The special reflexive pronoun *sick* for the 3rd pers. sg. and pl. corresponds in its use to the NHG *sich*. For the other persons the personal pronouns are used.

§ 27. POSSESSIVE PRONOUNS

They are *mien, dien, sien, iähr, use, ju, iähre.*

(i) *Mien, dien, sien, iähr, ju* decline as follows:

	m.	*f.*	*n.*	*pl.*
Nom.	mien	miene	mien	miene
Obj.	mienen	miene	mien	miene

(ii) *Use* and *iähre* differ from the above forms only insofar as they end in *-e* in the nom. masc.

Note: Apocope in the fem. form is occasionally found, e.g. *mien siäg' Moder.*

---

[1] Cf. H. Reichhelm, *Das Reflexivpronomen im Niederdeutschen*, Diss. Greifswald, 1921.

§ 28. DEMONSTRATIVE PRONOUNS

(i) *De, dat*. The unstressed forms of this demonstrative pronoun serve as the definite article. The demonstrative forms are:

	m.	*f.*	*n.*	*pl.*
Nom.	dee }	dee	dat	dee
Obj.	den }			

An extended form pointing to something distant is: *jiender de,* etc.

(ii) *Düsse, düt* is used to point to something close.

	m.	*f.*	*n.*	*pl.*
Nom.	düsse }	düsse	düt	düsse
Obj.	düssen }			

For 'such' the dialect uses *son*, pl. *söcke*.

§ 29. INTERROGATIVE PRONOUNS

who?	*well* (obj.: *wen*)
what?	*wat*
which?	*well*
	wat-för

§ 30. INDEFINITE PRONOUNS

een, eene (see § 24)	somebody
nich een	nobody
wat	something, a little
nicks	nothing
viell	much, many
mannich (-een)	many a
iälke ⎫ *wat* ⎭	several, some
jeder (NHG)	each, every
alle (pl.)	all
alles (sg.)	all
kinn, kinne (goes like *mien*, § 27)	no

§ 31. RELATIVE PRONOUNS

Like NHG, Westphalian uses the dem. pron. in this function, replacing, however, the dem. *dat* by *wat*.

VERBS

§ 32. FORMS AND CLASSIFICATION

The verb has the following simple form classes and tenses: infinitive, imperative, past participle, present indicative, preterite indicative and preterite subjunctive. The compound tenses and forms are: perfect, pluperfect, passive, and future.

The infinitive ends in -*en*. In rapid speech this tends to be reduced to a syllabic nasal: a dental after vowels or dentals, a labial after labials, a velar after palato-velars, e.g. *bietn* 'to bite', *driebm* 'to drive', *sliekng* 'to creep'. The infinitive particle is *te*.

The root of the imperative is identical with that of the 1st pers. sg. present. In the sg. it is endingless, in the pl. it ends in -*t*.

The past participle ends either in -*en* (with the same assimilations as in the case of the infinitive) or in -*t*. In contrast to NHG there is no prefix *ge*-.

§ 33. STRONG VERBS[1]

The conjugation of the strong verbs is in no dialect more conservative and more complex than in Westphalian. The common factor is the *n*- suffix in the past participle and the vowel alternation in the root. There may be as many as six different vowel alternants in one verb. Usually there are five. As in Lux., to group the strong verbs according to the stem alternants would lead to a complicated system of over two dozen possibilities. The following grouping is based on the strong verbs occurring in our specimen text. It gives a representative picture of the possible alternants as well as of their relative importance. The following stem forms have to be distinguished:

1 Sg. Pres. Inf. Pl. Pres.	2, 3 Sg. Pres.	1, 3 Sg. Pret.	Pl. Pret. 2 Sg. Pret.	P.P.
I. ie[i:]	i	ee	ie	ie

12 verbs: *kieken, blieben*,[2] *smieten, schienen, wiesen, kriegen, schrieben, strieken, slieken, bieten, swiegen, stiegen* (OHG I).

II. ei	ü	au	üe	uo

2 verbs: *geiten, fleiten* (OHG II); with *seihen* as a subgroup (ei-üh-ao-äö-ei).

III. i	i	a	ü	u

3 verbs: *drinken, winnen, singen* (OHG IIIa).

IV. e/ä	e/ä	o	ö	o

4 verbs: *hälpen, gellen, trecken, wäern* (OHG IIIb).

V. iä	ä	a	üö	uo

2 verbs: *stiärben, verdiärben* (OHG IIIb).

VI. iä/ie	i	a	ai	ue/uo

4 verbs: *niemmen, liäsen, spriäcken* (with *üe* instead of *ai*), *befiällen*, and similarly *kuemmen* with *ue-ü-a-ai-ue* and *u* in the imp. and *qu-* in the pret. (Mainly OHG IV.)

VII. ie	i	a	ai	ie

1 verb: *giebben* (OHG V).

[1] See also A. Kaiser, *Studien zur Bildung des Präteritums in den heutigen deutschen Mundarten*, Giessen, 1910; J. Pickert, *Das starke Verbum im Münsterländischen*, Progr. des Gymn. von Attendorn, 1908; H. Behrens, 'Niederdeutsche Präteritalbildungen', *Beitr.*, xlviii, 1924, 145–222; id., *Die Bildung der starken Praeterita in den niederdeutschen Mundarten*, Hamburg, 1922.

[2] Verbs in -*ben* have -*f* in final or preconsonantal and -*w* in prevocalic position.

	1 Sg. Pres.			Pl. Pret.	
	Inf. Pl. Pres.	2, 3 Sg. Pres.	1, 3 Sg. Pret.	2 Sg. Pret.	P.P.
VIII.	i	i	a	ai	iä
	2 verbs: *liggen, sitten* (OHG V).				
IX.	ao	ö	ō	ö	ā
	1 verb: *slaon* (OHG VI).				
X.	a/ao	ä	o	ö	a
	4 verbs: *fangen, hangen, fallen, haollen* (OHG VII).				
XI.	ao/o/au	ö	ai	ai	ao/o/au
	4 verbs: *laoten, slaopen, ropen, laupen* (OHG VII).				

§ 34. Weak Verbs

The large majority of weak verbs are characterized by an unalterable root-vowel for all tenses and a suffix -(*e*)*de* in the pret., -(*e*)*t* in the past part. (on the distribution of -*de*/-*ede*, see § 36).

Departures from this normal pattern arise through (*a*) *Rückumlaut*, (*b*) shortening of long vowels or diphthongs in the root, (*c*) assimilation of dental suffix to the root. Irregular weak verbs occurring in our text are:

	Inf.	*Pret.*	*P.P.*
'to say'	seggen	sagg	sagt
'to lay'	leggen	lagg	lagt, legt
'to tell'	tellen	tall	tallt
'to abuse'	schennen	schann	schannt
'to think'	denken	dach	dacht
'to bring'	bringen	broch	brocht
'to feel'	föhlen	foll	folt
'to seek'	söken	soch	socht
'to ask'	fraogen	frogg	frogt
'to make'	maken	mook	maakt
'to mean'	meinen	menn(de)	ment
'to share'	deelen	deelde	delt
'to believe'	glaiwen	gloff	gloft
'to hear'	häöern	haor (häörde)	haort

§ 35. The Present

The endings are: sg. 1 -*e*, 2 -*s*, 3 -*t*; pl. -(*e*)*t*, e.g. *niemmen* 'take':

ick niemme (1)   *wi*⎫
du nims (2)   *ji* ⎬ *niemmet* (4)
he nimp (3)   *se* ⎭

Notes

(1) In inversion the final -*e* is usually dropped: *niemm-ick*.

(2) Strong verbs have a mutated root-vowel in the 2nd and 3rd pers. sg. The vowels are generally shortened before consonantal clusters, e.g. *griepen—gripp* 'grasp', *laigen—lügs* 'tell a lie'. Where

there is a diphthong in an open syllable the closed syllables of the 2nd and 3rd pers. sg. have a monophthong, e.g. *giewwen—giffs* 'give'.

(3) The ending *-t* is subject to assimilation, e.g. > *p* after *m*. After *t, p, k, ch, s* there is complete assimilation, e.g. *he gifft* 'he gives', *he gripp* 'he grasps'.

(4) Syncope of the *-e-* in the suffix is not unusual, e.g. *wi griept* for *griepet*. Before an enclitic pers. pron. in inversion the ending is dropped.

§ 36. The Preterite Indicative

(i) Strong verbs have the following endings:

1, 3 pers. sg. -, 2 -(*e*)*s*, pl. -*en*. The pl. ending -*en* is subject to the same assimilations as the -*en* ending of the inf. (see § 32).

E.g.

$$\left.\begin{array}{l} ick \\ he \end{array}\right\}namm \qquad \qquad \left.\begin{array}{l} wi \\ ji \\ se \end{array}\right\}naimen$$

du naims

(ii) Weak verbs have the following endings:

1, 3 pers. sg. -(*e*)*de*, 2 pers. sg. -(*e*)*des*, pl. -(*e*)*den*. The suffix -*de*- is found after liquids and nasals, -*ede*- primarily after stops and fricatives, cf. *kloppede, frenskede, plaogede* but *hühlde, gnuerde, mende*. In rapid careless speech -*d*- may be realized as -*r*-.

E.g.

$$\left.\begin{array}{l} ick \\ he \end{array}\right\}plaogede \qquad \qquad \left.\begin{array}{l} wi \\ ji \\ se \end{array}\right\}plaogeden$$

du plaogedes

§ 37. The Preterite Subjunctive and the Conditional

As far as endings are concerned forms of a pret. subj. different from those of the pret. indic. exist only in the 1st and 3rd pers. sg. of strong verbs, which end in -*e*, e.g. *ick, he naime*. Owing to differences in the stem vowel some weak verbs also distinguish between a pret. indic. and a pret. subj.

§ 38. The Compound Tenses and the Passive

The two compound tenses for the past are formed by means of the auxiliaries *sien* and *häbben* and the p.p. The latter is used also in the case of verbs of motion accompanied by a complement.

Perfect: *he hät küert*;   *he is kuemmen.*
Pluperfect: *he hadde küert*;   *he was kuemmen.*

The auxiliary *sollen* with the inf. is used to form the future tense if an action is caused by external circumstances, but *wollen* with the

inf. expresses future where the will of the agent is involved. E.g. *et sall wull biätter sien* 'it will be better'.
The passive is formed with *wäern* as in NHG (§ 33 IV).

§ 39. THE MODAL AUXILIARIES

	Inf.	Sg. Pres.	Pl. Pres.	Sg. Pret.	Pl. Pret.	Condit.	P.P.
'be able'	können	kann (1, 3) kanns (2)	könnt	konn (1, 3) könns (2)	können	könn	konnt
'may'	müegen	magg (1, 3) maggs (2)	müeget	mogg (1, 3) möggs (2)	möggen	mögg	mocht
'must'	mötten	mott (1, 3) moss (2)	mött't	moss (1, 3) möss (2)	mössen	möss	mosst
'want'	wollen	will (1, 3) wuss (2)	willt	wull (1, 3) wuss (2) (wulls)	wullen	wüll	wullt
'shall'	sollen	sall (1, 3) sass (2)	söllt	soll (1, 3) soss (2)	sollen	söll	sollt
'may'	drüeben	draff (1, 3) draffs (2)	drüewet	drof (1, 3) dröfs (2)	dröffen	dröff	drofft

Notes

[1] In the inversion the *-t* in the pl. pres. is usually dropped, e.g. *nu will wi nich alles verdiärben* (p. 329).

[2] The p.p. is also used after an infinitive, in contrast to NHG practice, cf. *wenn he hädd' seggen sollt*, NHG *wenn er hätte sagen sollen*.

§ 40. AUXILIARIES AND IRREGULAR VERBS

	Inf. Imp.	Sg. Pres.	Pl. Pres.	Sg. Pret.	Pl. Pret.	Cond.	P.P.
'to be'	sien sie! siet!	sinn bis is	sind	was (1, 3) wös (2)	wören	wör	west
'to have'	häbben	häff [2] häss hät [2]	häfft	hadd(e) (1, 3) hädds (2) hadd(e)	hädden	hädde	hatt
'to do'	dohen doh! doht!	doh(e) döhs döht	dohet	daih (1, 3) dais (2)	daihen	dai	daohen
'to go'	gaohen gaoh! gaoht!	gaoh geihs geiht	gaoht	gonk (1, 3) göngs (2)	göngen	gönk	gaohen
'to stand'	staohen staoh! staoht!	staoh steihs steiht	staoht	stonn (1, 3) stöns (2)	stönnen	stönn	staohen
'to know'	wietten	weet wees weet	wiettet	wuss (1, 3) wüss (2)	wüssen	wüss	wusst
'to become'	wäern	wäre wäss wätt	wät	wor (1, 2) wors	wäern	wüer	worn

Notes

[1] In the pl. pres. the -*t* is dropped in inversion, e.g. *häff wi.*

[2] These forms have replaced former *häwwe, häff(t).*

PARTICLES

§ 41

Westphalian is reticent in its use of adverbs in conjunction with prepositions of place. No distinction is made, in the case of the adverbs of motion, between movement towards and movement away from the speaker.

Prepositions	Adverbs of Place Movement	Rest
in (drin)	harin	binnen
ut (derut)	harut	(to)buten
up (dorup, drup)	harup	buoben
af (deraf)	haraf	} unnen
unner (derunner)	harunner	
üöwer (drüower, dor-)	harüöwer	derüöwen
ächter (derächter)		ächten
vör (dervör)	harvör	vörn

Y

PHONETIC TRANSCRIPTION[1]

For the principles of this transcription, see pp. 71, 148. A description of the individual sounds is given in §§ 6–8, 14.

Words of two or more syllables have the main stress on the first syllable except where marked otherwise.

xɔət dɪŋk vat sɪk bɪɛtərt sęç dat šprүəkvɔrt. ɔn dat vɔrt çelt soxar fɔn n laɪç dɪŋk, den dat ɪs үmər no ən xɔət dɪŋk, vęn t sɪk bɪɛtərt. de menšk khan fɪəl u·thɔln, so laŋ ɛs he hүœpnɔŋk hɛt; vęn he mɛn ən ęnt afkhi:kŋ khan ɔf ən bɪətkən bɪɛtərɔŋk ɔn ɛrlɪçtərɔŋk mɪɛrk, dan maxt su:r si:n, ɔn ət max laŋə du:rn, de menšk sętət dүœr, vęn he ən lүk mark ɪn de knɔɒkŋ hɛt.

dat har vɪlm vɪsə, ɔvər he mɔs_sɪk sęgŋ: met fa:dər vɛt althi:t laɪjər, ɔn do ɪs xar khɪn ęnt an. vęl khan dɔbi xɔədən mo:t bəhɔln?

fa:dər ble:f ɪn bedə, ɔn ɛs de dɔktər sax, ət vø·r əm fɪəl bɪɛtər, van he ɒp'štœn, do daɪ he·t ɛrst reçt nɪç. de phas'to·r vas dər vɛst, ɔn fa:dər hadn šɪɛmshalvər fүœrlɒ:tn ɔvər ət ble:f ɛst vas. ɛrst hadə phas'to·r fɔn fərsaɪn khy·ərt, mɛn dat šme:t de ɔlə vi:t fɔn sɪk; he xœŋk no nɪç daɒt, ɔn vęn sə aɒk alə dru·p lu:ərdən. dan har de phas'to·r męnt, ət še:n əm aɒk, dat əm nɪks faɪldə, he sœl mɛn ɒpštɒ:n. dat ve:s de ɔlə aɒk af; he vɔl si:nə ru:ə hɛbm ɒm ple:çə, dat kœn he dɔx vɔl fərlaŋən.

mœt ju dər so met hendo:n, sax de hɛ·ro·mə to de baɪdn jɒŋə ly:ə, he ɪs ɪn de khɪnthaɪt, çɪftəm blo·s khɪnən šnaps!

dat ɪst xra·də, sax vɪlm tru:rɪç, he fүœrdərt ət ɔn vɛt va:n, van he khɪnən krɪç.

dan ɔvər met mɒ:t — fərnүmftɪç tode:ln. twe· šnɛpskəs upm dax ɪs no:x.

domet ɪs he nɪç tofrɪɛə, he vɪl de phɔl hɛbm.

dat çaɪt nɪç, raɪp de phas'to·r i:vrɪç, ɒp khɪnən fal! he ɪs ən khɪnt, ɔn so mɔt he bəhanəlt vɛ·rn.

dat vas lɪçt gəsęçt. de ɔlə çnu·ərdə ɔn šan so laŋə bɪs vɪlm nɒ:xaf ɔn əm de phɔl үœvərlaɪt. dən anərn dax mɔs he sə əm vi:r vęçnɪəmən, ɔn nu· vas de dy:vəl lɔs. de ɔlə špγətərdə fɔn çɪft, vęn he vɪlm mɛn sɒ:x, ɔn mo:kən so šlęçt bi· ana, ɛs he ɪɛbm khɔn.

[1] A transcription of a *Mönsterlänsk* dialect is given in A. Götze, *Proben hoch- und niederdeutscher Mundarten*, pp. 86–8. See also E. Nörrenberg, 'Zehn Wenkersche Sätze in dreizehn westfälischen Ortsmundarten', *NdKbl.*, xlvi, 1933, 38–45; B. Holtmann, *Ostbevern* (Bibliogr., p. 387).

AUGUSTIN WIBBELT: *DAT VEERTE GEBOTT* [1][1]

(Extract: Chapter XX and beginning of Chapter XXI)

Guett Dink, wat sick biättert, segg dat Sprüeckwaort. Un dat Waort gellt sogar von en leig Dink, denn dat is ümmer no en guett Dink, wenn't sick biättert. De Mensk kann viell uthaollen, so lang' äs he Hüöppnunk hät; wenn he män en End afkieken kann of en biettken Biätterunk un Erlichterunk miärkt, dann magg't suer sien, un et magg lange duern, de Mensk sett't et düör, wenn he en lück Mark in de Knuocken hät.

Dat hadde Wilm wisse, owwer he moss sick seggen: ,,Met Vader wät't alltied leiger, un do is gar kinn End an [2]." Well kann dobi gueden Moot behaollen?

Vader bleef in'n Bedde, un äs de Dokter sagg, et wör em viell biätter, wenn [3] he upstönn, do daih he't erst rächt nich. De Pastor was der west, un Vader hadd'n schiämshalwer vüörlaoten, owwer et bleef äs't was. Erst hadd' de Pastor von Verseihen küert, män dat smeet de Aolle wiet von sick; he gönk no nich daut [4], un wenn se auk alle drup luerden. Dann hadde de Pastor mennt, et scheen em auk, dat em nicks feihlde, he söll män upstaohen. Dat wees de Aolle auk af; he wull siene Ruh un siene Plege häbben [5], dat könn he doch wull verlangen.

,,Mött't ju der so met hendohen" [6], sagg de Häerohme [7] to de beiden junge Lü'e, ,,he is in de Kindheit. Gifft em bloss kinnen Snaps!"

,,Dat is't grade", sagg Wilm trurig, ,,he füördert et un wät wahn, wenn he kinnen krigg."

,,Dann owwer met Maot — vernümftig todeelen. Twee Snäpskes [8] up'n Dagg is noog."

,,Domet is he nich tofriä'e, he will de Pull häbben."

,,Dat geiht nich", raip de Pastor iiwrig, ,,up kinnen Fall! He is en Kind, un so mott he behannelt wäern." —

Dat was licht geseggt [9]. De Aolle gnuerde un schann so lange, bis Wilm naogaff un em de Pull üöwerlait. Den annern Dagg moss he se em wier wäggniemmen, un nu was de Düwel laoss. De Aolle spüetterde von Gift, wenn he Wilm män saog, un mook en so slächt bi Anna, äs he iäben konn.

Anna hadd' [10] de Plege üöwernuemmen un holl sick tapper. Se

5 sieen. 10 guetten. 11 wöer. 13 halber. 17 soll. 21 Giefft. 23 truerig. 35 haoll.

---

1 See *Notes*.
For spelling, see §§ 5, 13. Where alterations have been made to the spelling of the text in the *Gesammelte Werke*, vol. iv, the original spelling is given at the bottom of the page, on the first occurrence.

lait den Aollen küern un schennen un bleef ümmer iäbenmäötig rühig [11], tolest hadd' sick Schultenvader so an iähr nätte Wiäsen wüent, dat he se gar nich missen konn. De junge Frau met iähre gesunne Natur un iähren lichten Sinn hadd' sick üöwer de ganze lästige un hässlicke Saak vullstännig wäggsett't: se broch't sogar feddig, dat se mankst en Leedken sank met iähre helle Lewinksstemm, un dat was ümmer, äs wenn en Sunnenstraohl düör Wolken föllt.

Wolken tröcken buten an'n Hiemmel. Et stürmde un riängede, de Hiärfst was kuemmen, so rächt rugg un untömig. Wolken höngen auk üöwer Hellkamps Hoff. Wilm was gieggen fröher rein utwesselt: Wenn he auk von Natur en lück ärnst was, so satt doch en frisk Liäben in em, owwer nu wor he ümmer luriger. He gonk gar nich mähr so stramm un risk, sonnern lait sick hangen, un mankst konn he ne ganze Wiele still in een Lock kieken. Anna smeet faken en besuorgt Aug up em un versoch, em uptomuntern [11], so guett äs't gonk. Dann wull he sick uprappeln, owwer et glückede nich.

Et wör all no wat west [12], wenn de Aolle nich so fiindsiälig un so gehässig gieggen em west wör. Wilm foll, dat sien eegen Hiätt auk lanksam kaolt un bitter wor, un he moss sick mankst nütten to-samenniemmen, üm nich en scharp Waort to seggen, wenn sien Vader em aohne allen Grund so höhnsk begieggnede.

,,Anna", sagg Wilm eenes Aobends, äs de beiden alleen wöern, ,,ick häff gar nich mähr dat Geföhl, dat he mien Vader is. He wät mi alle Dage früemder un — wenn'k et seggen sall — mähr un mähr tom Ekel.''

,,Oh, Wilm — "

,,Ick kann't nich ännern, et is so. Ick weet söwst, dat et nich rächt is; et stimmt nich met dat veerte Gebott, un mien siäg' Moder — "

He konn nich wieder un lagg dat Gesicht in de Hänn. Anna lagg em de Hand up de Schuller:

,,Laot män, Wilm, dat döht nicks [13], do kanns du nich vüör [2].''

Wilm keek sick up [14], he was bleek in't [15] Gesicht un sagg met heesterige Stemm:

,,Un dat is't leigste no nich — owwer ick kann de Gedanken nich laosswäern, ick magg mi wiähren, et hölpt nicks — ick häff wüerklick den Wunsk, Vader mögg stiärben — jä äher, jä leiwer — "

Anna verschrock sick [14]: ,,Still, Wilm, spriäck dat gar nich ut!''

,,Doch, ick mott't seggen, un wenn'k et di nich seggen sall, well dann? Et is so wiet met mi kuemmen, dat ick mienen eegen Vader uprichtig den Daut wünske. Un segg söwst — wat döht he no up de Wält? Is he nich sick un annere en Krüüs, un wör't nich viell biätter — "

2 nette. 7 fällt. 11 ernst. 12 woer, lueriger. 17 fiendsiälig. 18 faoll. 35 helpt. 41 Welt.

„Nu kinn Waort mähr!" sagg Anna bestimmt un keek em an met graute, ärnste Augen. „Dat so'n Gedanke kümp, is nich diene Schuld, owwer du draffs en nich hiägen. Wenn du di do harindenks, Wilm, dann is dat Sünn, Wilm." Se namm siene Hand: „Wi häfft us met Guotts Hölp doch so wiet düörslagen, un ick mein, use Plicht daohen nao besten Kräften [16], nu will wi [17] nich alles verdiärben an'n lesten Enne no — "

„An'n lesten Enne, meins du, et wör baoll to Enne?"

„Dat will wi Guott üöwerlaoten. Owwer wi mött't et düörhaollen. Ick will di jä hälpen, so guett äs ick kann — "

„Anna, dat döhs du, un wenn'k di nich hädd' [10], ick weet nich — — — "

He stonn up: „In Guotts Namen! Et mott gaohen un sall gaohen. He is mien Vader, un ick will em Suon sien."

Tobuten hühlde de Wind üm de Pöst, un de Riängen sloog gieggen de Ruten, dat et kliätterde. Düör all dat Brusen un Susen haor man tieggenan Schultenvader siene Schell [18], un Anna gonk hen, üm to fraogen, wat he wull. —

Erst hadd' de Aolle füördert, et soll stännig een bi em sitten un auk nachts bi em waaken. Tolest was he domet tofriä'e, dat se em ne Schell henstellden, owwer nu hadden se Dagg un Nacht kinne Ruh. Jeden Augenblick gonk de Schell [4], un wenn dann nich faots een anlaupen quamm, dann was he verdreitlick. Anna moss stännig up'n Draff sien, denn Drüke konn't den Aollen sälten rächt maken un Wilm siliäwe nich. Et quamm faken vüör, dat de Aolle nachts schellde, un wenn Anna dann in alle Iile upstonn un hengonk, sagg he: „Legg mi de Küssens höchter [19]." Oder he frogg: „Wu Tied is't?"

Et was en Glück, dat de junge Frau so'n lichten Slaop un so'n glau Aohr un so'n flink Wiäsen hadde, dat se ümmer gau tor Stelle was. Un doch quamm se nich ümmer gau noog. Dann gnuerde Schultenvader: „Wo bliffs so lange, wull Wilm di nich gaohen laoten?"

Anna mogg betüern, soviell äs se wull, dat Wilm kinn Waort dovon seggt hädde [20], de Aolle bleef dobi: „He häöllt di alltied trüg, he hät kinn Hiätt för mi — en nätten Suon!"

To verwünnern was, dat de junge Frau alltied de Geduld bewahrde. Drüke kreeg alle Dage gröttern Respäkt vüör iähr un sagg to Wilm: „Unner düsse Ümstänne wöern wi aohne iähr gar nich feddig, se is en Siängen in'n Huse [21] un artet ganz up de siäge Frau, bloss dat se wat munterer un zärtlicker [22] is."

Drüke verstonn sick met Schultenvader gar nich mähr, un se mook

4 ues. 5 uese. 10 helpen. 25 selten. 28 fraogg.

sick kinn Gewietten dorut, jeden Aobend en Rausenkrans to biädden
in de Meinunk, dat de leiwe Häer em den Hiemmel giebben mögg —
„et wör biätter för em un us", dach se, „wenn du dat doch män
inseihen wuss, leiwe Häer!"

In de leste Tied konn Schultenvader nich mähr slaopen. He plaogede den Dokter so lange, bes de em Druoppens verschreef.

„Nu owwer upgepasst" [9], sagg de Dokter, „düt is kinne Medzin,
de man liäppelwiese nimp. Dat geiht met Druoppens, un de mött't
nätt aftellt wäern — teihn, na, de eelfte un twiälfte is auk no nich
gefäöhrlick. Wenn de junge Frau dat üöwernaihm! Fraulü'e häfft
düör de Bank [23] ne genauere Hand un sind auk mährstied iäben
gewiettenhaft."

„Na", menn Wilm, „en Gewietten häff ick apatt auk."

„Dat hät jeder Mensk", lachede de Dokter. „De Gewiettens sind
bloss verscheiden. Spass [24] bisiete, ick mein met Gewietten Vüör-
sicht un Akraotheit, un dat is hier naidig."

„Könn dat gefäöhrlick wäern?"

„Gefäöhrlick? Den Düwel auk! Wenn de Aolle dat halwe Püllken
up eenmol naihm — un so viell bruuk't no gar nich to sien —, dann
krigg he'n Slaop, ut den [25] ick en nich wier wecken könn. Na, up
en paar Druoppens kümp et nich an, ji sind jä kinne Kinner, owwer
laot em nich söwst derbi, he is in de Kindheit."

„Häer Dokter, seggt em dat leiwer nich, süss häff wi kinne Ruh
mähr in'n Huse [21], denn he is so ängstlick un truet annere Lü'e
alles to."

„Dat bruukt he jä auk gar nich to wietten." —

De Druoppens daihen guett, un Anna moss se aftellen; an Genauig-
keit lait se't wisse nich feihlen, un dat was weinigstens wunnen, dat
de Schell nachts nich gonk, wenn Vader aobends de Druoppens
krieggen hadd'.

De Hiärfst was unfröndlick.

Alle Dage datsölwe Wiähr, alle Dage datsölwe Elend.

De Welt was gries tobuten, un dat Liäben was gries binnen de Pöst.
Schultenvader lagg in'n Bedd [26] un gnuerde un schann up Wilm.
Wilm saog en mankst den ganzen Dagg nich, dann gonk he wier in
de Kammer un frogg: „Vader, wu geih't?" Un dann kreeg he faken
nich äs ne Antwaort.

Drüke biädde [27] alle Aobende iähren Rausenkrans, dat de leiwe
Häer „em" den Hiemmel giebben mögg. Söwst de Knächte un
Miägde wöern still un lurig woern de leste Tied, et lagg en griesen
Niewwel nich bloss buten, auk in't Huus [15].

Un Anna?

„Du sühs leig ut, is et di nich guett?" frogg Wilm.

6 bis. 9 elfte. 32 datselwe. 39 Knechte.

„Ick mott mi verköhlt häbben, et ligg mi so swaor in de Gliedder."

„Dann bliffs du muorgen liggen. Dat feihlde bloss no, dat du krank wörs — et is so all baoll nich uttohaollen."

„Well küert faots von Krankheit? Drüke sall mi gliek Kamellen upgeiten [28], dann sin'k muorgen kureert."

De Niewwel steeg. Alles was gries: dat Fäld, de Wiesk, de Gaoern, alls gonk unner in Niewwel, un dat kleine Ühlken, dat Liekenhöhnken, satt in den aollen Wiehenbaum ächtern Schoppen un raip met grelle Stemm: „Kumm met! Kumm met!"

„So, Frau", sagg Drüke, „nu drinkt Ju [29] den Tee un dann seiht to, of Ji nich sweeten könnt. Up de Art giff't sick am besten. Wenn Ji wat bruukt vanacht, dann laot de Schulte mi män wecken. Ick häff doch kinnen fasten Slaop, ick sin viell wach, un dann biädd' ick — Guott, et giff der soviell to biädden, un ick häff en besonner Anliggen — wenn de leiwe Häer dat män inseihen wull!" — —

De Klock sloog teihn.

Wilm hadd' alleen in de Stuof siätten un in de Tiedunk luosen, owwer wenn he hädd' seggen sollt, wat he luosen hädd' [30], dann wör em dat nich müeglick west, un wenn't em den Kopp kost't hädd'. Nu satt he do to draimen [31], wildess de Klock in de Küeck met iähren hatten Slagg de Sekunnen tall un dat Ühlken in'n Wiehenbaum allmankst raip: „Kumm met! Kumm met!"

De ganze Tied, siet dat sien siäg' Moder stuorben was, trock vüör em vörbi, un he söchtede. Up sien junge Glück was viell Schatten fallen, un well konn wietten, wat no quamm. Vader was jä nich krank äs bloss an Inbellunk, un wenn he wier upstonn, dann was't gar nich to beriäcken, wat he för Unsinn [32] möök. So wat wät jä mährstied leiger met de Tied. Et wör biätter, wüerklick biätter —

Wilm streek sick üöwer de Bless, äs wenn he de Gedanken verjagen wull.

Do foll em in, dat Anna so fröh nao'n Bedde gaohen was, un dat Vader siecker siene Druoppens nich krieggen hädd'. Soll he se em giebben? Dann was weinigstens Ruh in de Nacht.

En lichten Schudder laip em üöwer. Teihn Druoppens — oh, he wuss't ganz genau — un wenn't auk en Dutz [33] was — of twintig wull — ? Diättig siecker —

„Guott staoh mi bi!" söchtede Wilm un stonn up. Hadde de Aolle nich stüent? He slaip tieggenan. Soll he haringaohen in de Kammer? Dann wüll he wisse siene Druoppens häbben — twintig mössen't sien — üm Guotts willen ne! Bloss teihn — „Kumm met!" raip dat Ühlken.

Wilm puussede de Lamp ut un sleek sick lanksam düör de Küeck; he gonk sachte an Schultenvader siene Kammer vörbi.

6 Feld. 17 Stuow. 42 pussede.

De Wind was upstaohen, en swacken, söchtenden Wind, de
ümmer wier anfonk, liese to günseln un ümmer wier inholl, äs wenn
he mö'e wör. Wilm slaip swaor un deip, unrühig, denn he was an't
draimen [31]. Up'nmaol richtede he sick up — hadd' Vader siene
Schell gaohen? Un wat was't? Anna wull doch nich upstaohen, so
elend äs se was?

„Anna — bis du up?"

„No nich", sagg Anna, „owwer wat slöpps du! [34] Vader hät
tweemaol schellt, ick konn di nich wach kriegen un wull gerade
söwst gaohen."

Wilm was all ut'n Bedd [26] un trock sick gau an:

„Dat geiht nich — du könns di jä wat hahlen, wo du so verköhlt
bis — ick gaoh söwst."

„Et sall wull biätter sien [35]. Teihn Druoppens, Wilm! He hät
sienen Slaopdrunk nich krieggen. Pass owwer guett up!"

„Sie aohne Suorge!"

He beet de Tiänn tohaup, denn se slögen em anenanner, dat et
klapperde.

„Hier steiht ne Kärsse, Wilm, Sticken staoht [36] der tieggen."

He mook Lucht.

„Mien alles," raip Anna, „du bis auk nich wuoll — wat sühs du
krank ut! [34] Ick glaif, dann is't biätter — "

Se hadd' sick upricht't.

„Nicks", Wilm wiährde af, „du bliffs, un ick gaoh! Mi feihlt nicks,
et is bloss dat bleeke Lecht."

„Teihn Druoppens", sagg Anna no eenmaol, „un dann maak,
Vader schellt all wier."

Wilm gonk met blaute Fööt de Düör harut, sacht äs ne Katt, un
de Kärsse flackerde in siene Hand. Dat Flämmken was so unrühig
äs ne arme Siäll, de no wat guettomaken hät. He gonk düör de
Küeck; em ducht, sien Hiätt kloppede no hätter äs de aolle Klock
met iähr Ticktack. Wat sagg de aolle Klock?

„Teihn — Stück — teihn Stück — teihn Stück — "

Et was düütlick to häöern, unwillkürlick bleef he staohen un
lusterde.

Ne — nu was't anners:

„Giff — mähr — giff mähr — giff — mähr — "

Was he dann verrückt woern, dat he sowat häörde? Un he haor't
düütlick: „Giff mähr — "

Nu was't wier anners:

„Twintig — diättig — twintig — diättig — vättig — füftig —
sässtig — "

Ick gaoh wier trüg, dach Wilm, Vader sall sick wull giebben [37].

2 inhaoll. 34 düetlick. 41 fiftig.

Do schellde't, dütmaol stärker un länger — Wilm stonn still.

Et schellde wier, et steeg em venienig up in'n Hiätten — kinne Ruh bi Dagg un Nacht — alltied verwendt — en Elend fört Huus, en Elend för sick söwst — worüm no up de Welt, för wen un för wat? „Twintig — diättig — vättig — füftig — " sagg de aolle Klock. Do schellde't un schellde un schellde — Wilm gonk harin. —

„Ick häff mi Suorge maakt", sagg Anna, „du blieffs so lange ut, un dat Schellen häörde gar nich mähr up. Is Vader nu still?"

„He is still", sagg Wilm.

„Hät he nich schannt?" frogg Anna.

„Ne — un nu laot us slaopen."

Se swieggen. De Wind gonk liese üm't Huus un günselde üm de Ecken äs en klein krank Kind. Drüke was auk lengst wach woern un hadd' iähren Rausenkranz krieggen — „och, leiwe Häer, wenn du't em doch män günnen wuss! Wör't denn nich biätter?"

De Muorgen was anbruocken. Grao keek he düör't Fenster. Anna lagg wach un lusterde up dat Wiärken, wat [38] nu in'n Huse den Anfank namm, en Tratt up de Träpp, en Düöernklappen, en Rappeln in de Küeck, en Ropen up de Diäll, en verstuollen Fleiten up'n Hoff, un dotüsken kreihede de Hahn un frenskede en Piärd, et wor ümmer liänniger. Süss was se alltied de erste; owwer nu, bi iähre Verköhlunk, hadde Wilm iähr anbefuollen, dat se liggenblieben soll. Wilm was all upstaohn.

Äs se so lagg un naodach, quamm iähr in den Sinn, dat Schultenvader soviell schellt hadde in de Nacht. Of he no slaip? Wilm hadd' em jä de Druoppens giebben. Un of Drüke wull tor rächten Tied nao em keek? Up Drüke konn man sick verlaoten.

In den Augenblick quamm Drüke in de Kammer, so liese, äs wenn se iähr nich wecken wull; se gonk up Strümp.

„Bis du't, Drüke? Ick sin lengst wach."

Drüke sagg nicks un quamm an't Bedde; Anna richtede sick up, un äs se de aolle, trüe Siäll in't Gesicht keek, verschrock se sick. Un doch mook Drüke en rühig un tofriä'en Gesicht; owwer ärnst was't, so ärnst, dat Anna up de Stell Bescheid wuss:

„Drüke — wat is — is Vader — ?"

„Verschreckt Ju nich, Frau! De leiwe Häer hät wüerklick en Inseihen bruket un em to sick nuemmen. Mien alles — et wät Ju slächt!"

14 längst.

NOTES

(See the remarks to the *Notes* on p. 80)

[1] *Augustin Wibbelt*, born 19 September 1862 at Vorhelm, Kreis Beckum, died 14 September 1947, after a busy life as a priest, journalist and popular story writer, on his ancestral farm, where he had retired in 1935. With Karl Wagenfeld and Ferdinand Krüger he stood in the forefront of Westphalian dialect writing and was the most successful writer. As a story-teller he excelled in the description of rural life. In *Drüke Möhne* he created a collection of vivid sketches of *Mönsterlänsk* society, which has deservedly become a regional classic. His other works include *Wildrups Hoff*, 1901; *De Strunz*, 1902; *Hus Dahlen*, 1903; *Schulte Witte* (2 vols.). *Dat veerte Gebott*, 1913, is probably his best novel. It combines a rural setting with a profound moral problem: the physical and mental decline of a father and the suffering thus created for his son. Chapter XX, given here, shows old Schulte Hellkamp confined to bed, while his son Wilm and his daughter-in-law Anna are at the end of their tether. The faithful maid Drüke is no longer tolerated by the old man and the son, although mindful of the Fourth Commandment, cannot help wishing for the end. Is he to hasten it?

See further: W. Bachmann, *Aug. Wibbelt. Des Dichters Leben und Werk*, Essen, 1932; A. Baldus, *Augustin Wibbelt. Sein Leben und sein Werk*, Leipzig, 1921; J. Bergenthal, *Westfälische Dichter der Gegenwart*, Münster, 1954 (2nd ed.); G. Schalkamp, *Wibbelt und die Dorfgeschichte*, Bonn, 1933; B. Haas-Tenckhoff, *Augustin Wibbelt. Mit einem Verzeichnis der Schriften von und über Wibbelt*, Essen, 1948. Readers and handbooks on Westphalian literature: R. Eckhart, *Handbuch zur Geschichte der plattdeutschen Literatur*, Bremen, 1911; W. Lehnhoff, *Westfälische Mundarten*, Dortmund, 1920; H. Schönhoff, *Geschichte der westfälischen Dialektliteratur*, Münster, 1914; W. Uhlmann-Bixterheide, *Das plattdeutsche Westfalen*, Dortmund, 1921. G. Henssen, *Volk erzählt. Münsterländische Sagen, Märchen und Schwänke*, Münster, 1935, 2nd ed. 1952; *id.*, *In de Uhlenflucht. Plattdeutsche Schwänke und Märchen aus Westfalen*, Münster, 1939. Wibbelt's *Gesammelte Werke*, Münster, Heckmann Verlag, vols. i–vi, 1953–57, were edited by Jos. Tembrink.

[2] This separation of demonstrative adverb and preposition, which is the rule in MHG but no longer in NHG, is characteristic of LG. Cf. *do kanns du nich vüör*, p. 328.

[3] Informant says usually *wann* for *wenn* in Wibbelt's text.

[4] *Gaohen* 'to go' is used in many idioms. Cf. this expression with English 'go mad' and see *gonk de Schell*, p. 329, *de Wind gonk liese üm't Huus*, p. 333.

[5] Informant said: *he wull siene Ruhe häbben un Plege*, which, bringing the verb forward, is better dialect.

[6] 'You will have to put up with it.'

[7] *De Häer* generally refers to the priest. *Ohm* is an uncle or a friend of the family.

[8] The diminutive suffix of nouns is *-ken* (sg.), *-kes* (pl.). Cf. *Ühlken*. See also E. Nörrenberg, 'Das westfälische Diminutivum', *NdJb.*, xlix, 1923, 1–42.

[9] The past participle has the prefix *ge-* only in formulas or when an auxiliary is omitted. Cf. *nu owwer upgepasst*, p. 330.

[10] Where Wibbelt spells *hadd'* or *hadde* informant usually pronounces *har*; p. 329 *här*.

[11] Here and elsewhere informant uses an unmutated vowel (*ruhig*); on the other hand he says *uptomüntern* with a mutated vowel.

[12] 'It would have been bad enough.'

[13] Cf. NHG *das macht nichts*.

[14] LG has a number of reflexive verbs which have no parallel in NHG, cf. *sick verschrecken*.

[15] As Münsterland dialect has no dat. case one would expect an invariable neuter art. *t* for subject and object. Wibbelt is inconsistent. Here he has the common case as also *in't Hus* (p. 330). At other places he has the art. *n* for the dat., e.g. *in'n Huse* (p. 329), *in'n Hiätten* (p. 333), *nao'n Bedde* (p. 331). Neighbouring dialects and NHG are responsible for this inconsistency. My informant read *in'n* in all these cases.

[16] This dat. pl. is borrowed from NHG.

[17] On the dropping of final *-t* in inversion, see §§ 35 (4), 39 (1).

[18] Dative paraphrase for possessive, see § 18.

[19] Informant says *häöchter*.

[20] NHG would use the pres. subj. of *haben*. Westphal. having no pres. subj. must make use of the pret. subj. where the subj. is required.

[21] Wibbelt occasionally distinguishes a dat. sg. from the common case: *Huus—Huse*, a distinction which is made by the more conservative of Westphalian dialects although not by that of central Münsterland. Informant says *Huus*.

[22] A loan-word from NHG.

[23] 'Always.'

[24] The vowel in *Spass* is short. This pronunciation is often heard when Westphalians speak NHG—as it is with Swiss people and Bavarians. The idiom *Spass bisiete* is borrowed from NHG.

[25] Instead of Wibbelt's relative clause, informant has the more genuine *n Slaop, dat ick en nich wier wecken könn*.

[26] Informant always uses *Bedde*.

[27] Pret. of *biädden* with assimilation of the pret. suffix *-de*.

[28] A brew made with camomile is believed to bring down the temperature.

[29] *Ju* is objective case. This kind of ethic dative is also found with *iäten*, e.g. *et di wat!* 'eat something'.

[30] Informant says *har* instead of *hädd*.

[31] 'He sat there dreaming', cf. *he was an't draimen*.

[32] Informant reads *för en Unsinn möök*.

[33] Informant says *Dutzend*.

[34] The interrogative pronoun *wat* is used for NHG *warum*, e.g. *wat slöpps du?* and NHG *wie*, e.g. *wat sühs du krank ut?*, p. 332.

[35] See § 38.

[36] The difference between sg. and pl. of *staohen* lies in the vowel only: *steiht* (sg.), *staoht* (pl.), § 40. As to *Sticke* 'match' see Mitzka, *Wortatlas*, iii, 'Streichholz'.

[37] 'Father will have to be patient.'

[38] See § 31.

GLOSSARY

See the introductory remarks to the *Glossary* on p. 84, and for further information Woeste, *Wörterbuch der westfälischen Mundarten.*

ächter, behind.
Akraotheit, accuracy.
all, already.
apatt, indeed.
äs, as.

baoll, soon.
beriäcken, wv. § 36 (ii), assess.
binnen, inside.
blaut, naked.
Bless, f. forehead.
buten, outside.

der, there.
Diäll, f. F. hall.
Draff, m. trot.

faken, often.
faots, at once.
feihlen, wv. § 36 (ii), be amiss. *et feihlde em nicks*, nothing was wrong with him.
fleiten, wv. § 36 (ii) whistle
frensken, wv. § 36 (ii), neigh.
füördern, wv. § 36 (ii), demand.

Gaoern, B. garden.
gau, quick.
Gift, anger, ardour.
glau, sharp.
gnuern, wv. § 36 (ii), grumble, growl.
gries, whitish grey.
günseln, wv. § 36 (ii), howl.

hahlen, wv. § 36 (ii), fetch, catch.
hatt, hard.
hiägen, wv. § 36 (ii), cherish.
Hiätt, F. heart.

iiwrig [iːvrɪç], eager, excited.

Kärsse, F. candle.
kieken, sv. § 33, I, look.
klappen, wv. § 36 (ii), knock, bang.

kliättern, wv. § 36 (ii), rattle, clatter.
Klock, f. F. clock.
Krüüs, C. cross.
küern, wv. § 36 (ii), talk.

leige, bad.
Lewink, m. lark.
liännig, lively.
Liekenhöhnken, G. bird of death.
Lucht, light.
lück, little.
luern, wv. § 36 (ii), wait.
luosen p.p. < *liäsen*, sv. § 33, VI, read.
lurig, bad-tempered, distrustful.
lustern, wv. § 36 (ii), listen.

mährstied, mostly.
män, only.
mankst, sometime.

nätt, exactly.
no, still.
noog, enough.
nütten, very much.

of, or; if.

Post, m. B. post.
Pull, f. F. bottle.
puussen, wv. § 36 (ii), clean.

rappeln, wv. § 36 (ii), clatter.
riängen, wv. § 36 (ii), rain.
risk, upright.
rugg, rough.
Rute, f. F. window-pane.

schennen, wv. § 34, abuse, grouse.
schiämshalwer, because he was ashamed.
Schoppen, m. G. barn.
Schudder, m. shudder, tremble.
Schulte, mayor, squire

seggen, wv. § 34, say.
siäge, blessed, late.
sick, sick, ill.
siliäwe nich, never.
smieten, sv. § 33, I, throw.
söchten, wv. § 36 (ii), sigh.
spüettern, wv. § 36 (ii), spit.
Stuof, F. living-room.
süss, otherwise.
swaor, heavy.

Tand, B. pl. *Tiänn*, tooth.
tieggen, against.
  der tieggen, over there.
  tieggenan, next door.
tobuten, outside.
tohaup, together.
tolest, at last, finally.
totüsken, in between.
Tratt, m. step.
trecken, sv. § 33, IV, draw.

trügg, back.

ümmer, always.
untömig, unruly, wild.
uprappeln, sick -, wv. § 36 (ii), pull
  oneself together.

vanacht, to-night.
venienig, angry, poisonous.
verseihen, sv. § 33, II, err, make a
  mistake.
verwendt, put upon.
vüörlaoten, sv. § 33, XI, let in.

Wiähr, weather.
Wiehenbaum, D. willow.
wier, again.
Wiesk, f. F. meadow.
wildess, whilst.
wisse, certainly.
wu, how.

CHAPTER IX

NORTH SAXON: LOWER ELBE

§ 1. Area[1]

The Low Saxon dialect area is usually divided into West Low Saxon and East Low Saxon. The former is spoken mainly in the old tribal territories of the Saxons east of the Ems river up to a line running southwards from the Baltic coast near Lübeck to Magdeburg.[2] East Low Saxon are the dialects spoken in the eastern, formerly Slav provinces which were Germanized in the course of the Middle Ages.

The West Low Saxon dialects form three large subgroups: Westphalian (see chap. viii), Eastphalian and North Saxon. North Saxon thus stretches from the Ems to the above-mentioned line east of Lübeck. In the north it gives way to Danish or Frisian dialects in the area of Flensburg. Dialects spoken south of a line running eastwards from Meppen on the Ems to the Elbe south-east of Lüneburg belong to the Westphalian or Eastphalian groups. Isoglosses which separate North Saxon from Westphalian are, among others, those of NS monophthong *o* or *a* against Wph. diphthong *uo* or *ua* in 'broken' (*DSA*, 29), in the word for village (*DSA*, 47, *Dorf*).[3]

Eastphalian dialects are distinguished by the forms *mik*, *dik* from NS *mi*, *di* 'me, thee'. Eastphalian and Mecklenburgish to the east of the Lübeck–Lüneburg line are also characterized by the diphthong *ei* against NS *e* [εI] in 'he' (*DSA*, 48), in NHG *weh* (*DSA*, 33) and *DSA*, 103, *zwei*: *twei* against NS *twee*. Eastphalian has *ei* against NS *e* in NHG *fliegen* (*DSA*, 122). *DSA*, 12, *Bruder* shows the Mecklenburgish and Eastphalian diphthong *au* against NS *o* [ɔɑ]. The morphological feature of the ending *-t* for the 3rd pers. pl. pres. is typical for West Low Saxon (Eastphalian *-et*), while East Low Saxon has *-en* (see *DSA*, 126, *fliegen* and *DSA*, 7, *-en*).

Among the lexical features the following maps show the characteristic boundaries of the NS dialect area: *DSA*, 55, *snacken* 'to talk'; Mitzka, *W'tatlas*, iv, *Heister* 'magpie', *Grashüpper* 'grasshopper'; Mitzka, *W'tatlas*, vii, *Wort* 'drake' (see also Foerste, *DPhA*, p. 1967).

It is, of course, to be expected that an area as vast as that of NS should be split up into numerous local dialects.[4] Those west of the Weser (Emsland, Oldenburg) have close links with the dialects of

---

[1] As to the status of the dialect, see chap. viii, § 1.
[2] See the maps in Mitzka, *DMaa.*; Foerste, *DPhA.*, p. 2002.
[3] The isogloss is described in Foerste, *DPhA.*, p. 2000.
[4] See the map in Foerste, *DPhA.*, p. 2033.

Dutch East Friesland and Westphalia. In the north the dialect of Schleswig goes its own way in many respects. The core of NS is thus formed by the dialects spoken between Weser and Elbe (North Hanover) and those spoken in Holstein. The specimen text, one of W. Wisser's fairy-tales, is in the dialect of Holstein. The speaker who made a tape-recording of it speaks a NS which is representative of the Lower Elbe district (Harburg), but of the variety spoken in the higher-lying sandy areas known as the *Geest*. In some ways this deviates from the dialect of the *Elbmarschen*. The phonological and grammatical description of NS is based on his variety of NS.[1]

GENERAL CHARACTERISTICS OF NORTH SAXON
(LOWER ELBE)

§ 2. PHONOLOGICAL FEATURES[2]

2.1 The Vowels

(1) The WGmc.[3] long vowels *î*, *û* and the diphthong *iu* correspond to the long vowels *ie*, *u*, *ü*, except in hiatus positions where diphthongization has usually occurred.

(2) WGmc. *io* and *ê²* (= MHG *ie*) and *ai* (= MHG *ei*) have coalesced in a diphthong [ɛɪ], spelt *e*, *ee* (but see § 7.8).

(3) WGmc. *ô* (= MHG *uo*) and *au* (= MHG *ou*, *ô*) have coalesced in a diphthong [ɔɷ] spelt *o*, *oo* in the *Elbmarschen*. For the *Geest*, see §§ 7.9–7.10. The mutation of this (= MHG *üe*, *öü*) is [œɪ] spelt *ö*, *öö*.

(4) The reflexes of WGmc. *e* and of mutated WGmc. *a* have coincided.

(5) The reflexes of WGmc. *â* and of WGmc. *a*, *o*, *u* in formerly open syllables have coincided.

(6) WGmc. short vowels have been generally preserved in closed syllables. Conditional changes have been brought about in labial surroundings (rounding) and before *r*.

(7) The results of the medieval umlaut are preserved as rounded front vowels.

(8) There is a general tendency to diphthongize long vowels except the high-tongue vowels. Thus the old long vowels are now diphthongized (except *î*, *û*), but a new series of long vowels has arisen through the lengthening of originally short vowels in originally open syllables. These are generally less, if at all, affected by the tendency to diphthongize.

[1] See C. Borchling, 'Hamburg und die niederdeutsche Sprachlandschaft', *Niederdeutsche Welt*, x, 1935, 56 f.; Agathe Lasch, 'Beiträge zur Geschichte des Neuniederdeutschen in Hamburg', *NdJb.*, xliv, 1918, 1–50.

[2] See fn. 1 on p. 32.

[3] See fn. 4 on p. 302.

(9) Nasalization occurs locally.

(10) Initial vowels have in many areas a glottal stop onset.

2.2 Vowel Quantity

(1) Originally short vowels have been lengthened in originally open syllables but have remained short in closed syllables.

(2) Originally long vowels have been shortened before consonantal clusters in the same syllable.

(3) Before r and r- clusters short vowels have been lengthened.

(4) So-called over-long vowels have arisen in monosyllabic morphemes ending in originally voiced v, s, d, g or in a vowel, through the apocope or syncope of a former unstressed e.

2.3 Vowels in Unstressed Syllables

(1) The prefixes corresponding to NHG be-, ge-, insofar as they occur, retain their vowels.

(2) Medieval unstressed final -e has generally dropped.

(3) An unstressed vowel has resulted from the vocalization of a former r in all positions except at the beginning of a syllable.

2.4 The Consonants

(1) The consonantal system is based on an opposition of voiced and voiceless stops and fricatives except in final position, where only voiceless stops and fricatives occur.

(2) In medial voiced surroundings the opposition of the stops is neutralized after short vowels and slurred after long vowels. In initial position WGmc. p, t, k are preserved. WGmc. d and þ have coincided in all positions.

(3) WGmc. g is represented by a stop [g] except in final position and before voiceless consonants where it is a voiceless palato-velar fricative [x, ç].

(4) WGmc. s has become voiced in initial and intervocalic positions. It is preserved in initial position before consonants, but WGmc. sk has become sch.

(5) WGmc. ð is now a stop in initial position and before a nasal, but a voiceless fricative before voiceless consonants and in final position.

(6) L is generally preserved, but r is usually vocalized in postvocalic and preconsonantal positions.

(7) Final -n in inflexional suffixes is preserved as a nasal suffix assimilated to the preceding consonants.

(8) The nasal consonants occur both short and long (in final position only).

(9) The WGmc. cluster hs is reduced to ss; the loss of n before fricatives and the change of former ft > cht are found in some words.

z

(10) WGmc. *j* in initial position has become a slightly affricated voiced palatal fricative [dž].

§ 3. MORPHOLOGICAL FEATURES

3.1 Noun and Article

(1) Only one group of masc. nouns still distinguish a nom. sg. from the oblique cases; otherwise the noun has no special endings for cases. Only the masc. article (sg.) distinguishes between a nom. and a common objective case (but see § 20, Note (2)).

(2) There is, in addition to the usual German pl. suffixes, also a plural ending *-s*, and a plural formation based on the *Überlänge* (see §§ 4, 9.3).

(3) Nouns do not usually form a diminutive.

3.2 The Adjective

(1) The strong declension makes no distinction for cases.

(2) The weak declension distinguishes in the sg. the nom. from the common objective case (masc.).

3.3 The Pronouns

(1) The personal pronouns have a common objective case.

(2) In the 1st pers. pl. obj. case the HG form *uns* has prevailed over the earlier form without *n*. The forms of the 2nd pers. pl. are the 'Ingvaeonic' *ji, ju.*

(3) In the 3rd pers. sg. neuter the stressed form is *dat* (for earlier *et*).[1]

(4) The dem. pronouns *dee*, etc., serve also as relative pronouns.

3.4 The Verbs

(1) The tense system consists of a present, a preterite, a perfect and a pluperfect. There is no subjunctive.

(2) Strong verbs have in the preterite only one stem form.

(3) There is a uniform ending for the pl. : *-t* in the pres. (provided it is not assimilated), *-n* (or *-m*, *-ng*) in the pret.

(4) The future is expressed by means of the auxiliaries *schoelen* and *wüllen.*

(5) Past participles have no prefix (NHG *ge-*).

(6) There are only two weak verbs with *Rückumlaut.*

(7) The dental suffix (ending of the pres. pl., 3rd pers. sg. pres., and of the pret. of weak verbs) has been subjected to widespread assimilation resulting in complete loss.

(8) The verb corresponding to NHG *haben* has mutated forms throughout the present.

---

[1] See map in Foerste, *DPhA.*, ii, p. 1987.

(9) The 2nd and 3rd pers. sg. pres. of strong verbs show umlaut.

(10) For NHG *gewesen* NS uses *wään*.

(11) The verbs corresponding to NHG *gehen, stehen* have a root-vowel deriving from WGmc. *ā*.

PHONOLOGY

THE VOWELS

§ 4. THE VOWEL PHONEMES

There are seven short vowels and seven (or ten) long vowels. The short ones, at least among the front and high ranges, are more open and lax than the corresponding long ones. In many local dialects the long vowels of the mid range tend to be slightly diphthongized, especially when in a prominent position in the utterance. In other local dialects, especially those of the towns, they are close [eː, øː, oː]. The three, bracketed, long close mid-vowels are, as separate phonemes, found only in the *Geest* dialects in a limited number of words where the other dialects have the mid-tongue diphthongs. The length of the long vowels is to some extent dependent on the character of the following consonants. Before voiceless consonants the long vowels are slightly shorter than before voiced ones.

Front	Front rounded	Back	Diphthongs
iː	yː	uː	
ɪ	Y	ɔ	
(eː)	(øː)	(oː)	
ɛ(ː)	œ(ː)	ɔ(ː)	ɛɪ œɪ ɔɔ
a(ː)			a·ɪ a·ɔ

(ː) indicates that a phoneme occurs both long and short. There is also a short central vowel [ə] which is always unstressed.

There are five falling diphthongs. All have a long and clearly stressed first element. In unstressed positions in the sentence they tend to become monophthongal, cf. [hɛːɪ] 'he' stressed: [hɛ] unstressed.

A peculiarity of the North Saxon dialects is the occurrence of over-long vowels (*Überlänge, Schleifton*) in monosyllabic morphemes ending in lenis [v, z, d, γ] or a vowel, e.g. *Stuuv'* 'parlour', *Wies'* 'manner', *Sied'* 'silk', *Oog'* 'eye'. *Schleifton* is always linked with lenis character of the following consonant.[1] Lenis consonants occur inversely only

[1] Professor W. Niekerken has kindly confirmed this by letter: 'Meine Meinung geht dahin: Die ursprünglich stimmhaften stammschliessenden Konsonanten, vor denen sich die Überlänge eingestellt hat, sind im Gross-Hamburger Bereich (Holstein und Nordhannover) stimmlos. Da sie aber nicht mit der Spannung gebildet werden wie Laute nach einfacher Länge, könnte man sie stimmlose Lenes nennen.' See also § 9.3.

after *Schleifton*. Before fortis consonants *Schleifton* is found only if these consonants do not belong to the same morpheme, e.g. *he bruu't* 'he brews': *Bruut* 'fiancée'. After ordinary long vowels in monosyllabic morphemes final stops and fricatives are fortis, e.g. *stuuf* 'blunt', *wies* (*warrn*) 'to become aware', *siet* 'since', *Ploog* 'plough'. *Schleifton* may therefore be regarded as a separate phoneme, or, as an allophone of the unstressed phoneme /ə/. This solution recommends itself for historical reasons and for reasons inherent in the linguistic situation of North Saxon speakers. The *Schleifton* occurs in dialect where NHG, with which all speakers are conversant, has /ə/.

§ 5. SPELLING

Wisser spelt his LG as much according to the rules of NHG as possible. For distinctions he considered necessary he used diacritic marks. The latest edition of his works[1] dispenses with those and is therefore highly unsatisfactory from a phonemic point of view. The rules agreed to under the auspices of the *Fehrs-Gilde* (see p. 25) represent a satisfactory compromise between a radically phonemic system and that of NHG. I have therefore brought the text into line with the rules of the *Fehrs-Gilde*, with some minor additions.

The correspondences between phonemes and letters are as follows:

Phoneme	Letter	Phoneme	Letter	Phoneme	Letter
i(:)	i, ie	œ	ö	ɛɪ (5)	e, ee
ɛ	e, ä	œ:	oe	œɪ	ö, öö
ɛ:	ä, ää	u(:)	u, uu	ɔᴏ	o, oo
a	a	ɔ	o	a·ɪ	ei, ai
a:	ā (2)	ɔ:	a, aa	a·ᴏ	au
y(:)	ü, üü				

Notes

(1) In open syllables a single letter expresses a long vowel; in closed syllables a long vowel is indicated by doubling, except in the cases of *oe* and *ā*. This rule applies also to the diphthongs /ɛɪ/ and /œɪ/.

(2) The rules of the *Fehrs-Gilde* do not distinguish between /a:/ and /ɔ:/.

(3) *Schleifton* is indicated by an apostrophe, e.g. *de Lüüd'*.

(4) In monosyllabics which occur mainly in unstressed positions in the sentence the letters are not doubled, e.g. *ok* 'also', *vör* 'for', *wat* 'what', instead of (more correctly) *ook*, *voer*, *watt*.

[1] Wisser's spelling is, of course, retained in the photographic reproduction of his *Plattdeutsche Volksmärchen* by the Fehrs-Gilde, Hamburg, 1959.

(5) The rules of the *Fehrs-Gilde* do not distinguish between the long, close monophthongs [e:, ø:, o:] of the *Geest* dialects and the diphthongs [ɛɪ, œɪ, ɔʊ].

§ 6. Stressed Short Vowels

6.1 [ɪ] is an open, lax, high-front vowel deriving from:

(i) WGmc. *i* in closed syllables: *binnen* 'to bind'.

(ii) WGmc. *a* mutated before *n* in *Minsch* 'man'; WGmc. *e* mutated in *gistern* 'yesterday'.

(iii) WGmc. *ai, i, io* under conditions of shortening (cf. § 10.1): *licht* 'easy', *du kriggs* 'you get'.

6.2 [ɛ] is an open, lax, mid-front vowel deriving from:

(i) WGmc. *e* in closed syllables: *trecken* 'to pull', *weg* 'away'.

(ii) WGmc. *a* mutated in closed syllables: *seggen* 'to say', *vertellen* 'to tell'.

(iii) WGmc. *ai, â* mutated under conditions of shortening: *he lett* 'he lets'.

(iv) WGmc. *i* in isolated cases, e.g. *wedder* 'again', *hen* 'to'.

6.3 [a] is a low-tongue front vowel deriving from:

(i) WGmc. *a* in closed syllables: *achter* 'behind', *Kassen* 'chest, box'.

(ii) WGmc. *a, a* mutated, *e, i* followed by an original *r* and original voiceless dental: *swatt* 'black', *hatt* 'hard', *Hatt* 'heart'.

(iii) WGmc. *â* under conditions of shortening: *ik dach* 'I thought'.

6.4 [ɔ] is an open, lax, mid-back vowel. It represents:

(i) WGmc. *o* in closed syllables: *Hoff* 'yard', *Dochter* 'daughter' (see § 6.5 (ii)).

(ii) WGmc. *o, u* followed by *r* and an original voiceless dental: *Bost* 'breast', *kort* 'short'.

(iii) WGmc. *a* before *lt*: *Solt* 'salt'.

(iv) WGmc. *ô, au* under conditions of shortening: *Hochtiet* 'wedding'; from *û* in *op* 'on'.

6.5 [ʊ] is an open, lax, high-back vowel representing:

(i) WGmc. *u* in closed syllables: *Luss* 'desire', *bunnen* 'bound'.

(ii) WGmc. *o* in closed syllables especially before *l-* clusters: *vull* 'full', *Hult* 'wood' and in some other cases, e.g. *vun* 'of'.

(iii) WGmc. *û, ô* where shortened: *mutt* 'must'.

6.6 [œ] is an open, lax, rounded, mid-front vowel deriving from:

(i) WGmc. *o* mutated in closed syllables: *hölten* 'wooden', *Döchter* 'daughters'.

(ii) WGmc. *u* mutated before original *r* plus voiceless dental: *dösti* 'thirsty', *körter* 'shorter'.

(iii) WGmc. *ô, au, â* mutated with shortening: *he röppt* 'he calls', *he stött* 'he pushes', *he fröcht* 'he asks'.

6.7 [ʏ] is an open, lax, rounded, high-front vowel deriving from:

(i) WGmc. *u* mutated in closed syllables: *plücken* 'to pick', *ünner* 'under'.

(ii) WGmc. *i*, *e*, *a* mutated in labial surroundings: *twüschen* 'between', *ik bün* 'I am', *sülben* 'self'.

(iii) WGmc. *ô*, *û* mutated with shortening: *he stünn* 'he stood', *he süppt* 'he drinks'.

(iv) WGmc. *iu*, *io* in conditions of shortening: *Fründ* 'friend', *ümmer* 'always', *he flüggt* 'he flies'.

§ 7. Long Vowels

7.1 [i:] is a close, high-front vowel deriving from:

(i) WGmc. *î* (but see § 8.3 (v)): *blieben* 'to stay', *Tied* 'time'.

(ii) From various sources in *hier* 'here', *Papier* 'paper', *Fieg* 'fig'.

7.2 [ɛ:] is an open, mid-front vowel deriving from:

(i) WGmc. *i*, *e*, *a* mutated in open syllables and before original single *r*: *bäten* 'a bit', *bräken* 'to break', *bäter* 'better', *Slääg* 'blows', *ähr* 'her'. Before *r* it is more close: [e:].

7.3 [a:] is a low-tongue front vowel, identical with NHG [a:]. It derives from:

(i) WGmc. *i*, *e*, *a*, *a* mutated before original *r* plus labial or velar: *Kärk* 'church', *Bärg* 'hill', *Ārm* 'arm' (see § 9.4).

(ii) WGmc. *i*, *e*, *a*, *a* mutated, sporadically in other conditions, e.g. *wärrn* 'to become'.

(iii) WGmc. *a*, especially before *l*, e.g. *Sālv* 'ointment', *Hāls* 'neck'.

7.4 [ɔ:] is an open, lower-mid back vowel and derives from:

(i) WGmc. *a*, *o*, *u* in open syllables and before single *r*: *Water* 'water', *apen* 'open', *kamen* 'to come', *gar* 'quite'.

(ii) WGmc. *â*: *slapen* 'to sleep', *laten* 'to let'.

7.5 [u:] is a close, high-back vowel deriving from:

(i) WGmc. *û*: *Buuk* 'stomach', *Kuul* 'ditch'.

(ii) Various sources: *Juud* 'Jew', *Kur* 'cure'.

7.6 [œ:] is an open, rounded, mid-front vowel deriving from:

(i) WGmc. *o* mutated, *u* mutated in open syllables and before single *r*: *Koenig* 'king', *Soehn* 'son', *doer* 'through', *spoeren* 'to sense', *voer* 'before'. Before *r* it is more close: [ø:].

(ii) WGmc. *i*, *a* mutated in open syllables with labialization: *soeven* 'seven', *Foet* 'barrels'.

(iii) WGmc. *â* mutated and labialized: *Droehd* 'wires'.

7.7 [y:] is a close, rounded, high-front vowel and derives from.

(i) WGmc. *û* mutated: *Füüst* 'fists', *schümen* 'to foam'.

(ii) WGmc. *iu*: *bedüden* 'to mean', *düür* 'dear'.

The following three close, higher-mid vowels [e: o: ø:] occur as separate phonemes only in the *Geest* dialects and even there only in a limited number of words which vary from place to place. The *Elbmarschen* dialects have everywhere the diphthongs /ɛɪ ɔɷ œɪ/.

7.8 [e:] derives from:

(i) WGmc. *ai* in some words, e.g. in our text *menen* 'to mean', *wenen* 'to weep'. Professor Niekerken (Bibl., 120, p. xxi) speaks of 'letzte Reste, die der fortschreitenden Diphthongierung noch widerstehen . . .'

(ii) WGmc. *â* mutated, e.g. *leeg'* 'bad', *Scheper* 'shepherd'.

7.9 [o:] derives from:

(i) WGmc. *ô* in some words, e.g. *noog* 'enough'.

(ii) WGmc. *au* generally: *Broot* 'bread'.

7.10]ø:] derives from:

(i) WGmc. *ô* in some words, e.g. in our text *bedröövt* 'sad', *fröh* 'early'.

(ii) WGmc. *au* mutated: *köpen* 'to buy'.

§ 8. Diphthongs

In quality the elements correspond to the single vowels as described in § 7.

8.1 [a·ɪ] derives from:

(i) WGmc. *â* + *i* followed by a vowel: *dreihen* 'to turn', *kreihen* 'to crow', also WGmc. *â* + *i* in *he geiht, steiht* 'he goes, stands'.

(ii) WGmc. *ai* in some words (sometimes under NHG influence): *Arbeit* 'work', *beide* 'both', *meist* 'most', in the suffix *-heit*.

(iii) WGmc. *e* before *i* of the following syllable where an intervening consonant has dropped: *teihn* 'ten', *Seil* 'sail'.

(iv) WGmc. *-ajj-*: *Ei* 'egg'.

8.2 [a·ɷ] derives from: WGmc. *â* or *au* plus original *w*: *blau* 'blue', *klauen* 'to steal', *Dau* 'dew', *drauhen* 'to threaten', *gau* 'quick'.

8.3 [ɛɪ] derives from:

(i) WGmc. *ê* (= OHG *ia*): *he sleep* 'he slept', *Breef* 'letter'.

(ii) WGmc. *ai* (= OHG *ei* or *ê*): *Eed* 'oath', *Steen* 'stone', *See* 'sea' (but see § 7.8).

(iii) WGmc. *io* (= OHG *io*): *Deef* 'thief', *deep* 'deep'.

(iv) WGmc. *â* mutated: *Kees* 'cheese', *ik neehm* 'I took' (but see § 7.8).

(v) WGmc. *i* in hiatus position: *free* 'free'.

(vi) WGmc. *-eh* + *a* or *u*: *Veeh* 'cattle', *sehn* 'to see'.

(vii) WGmc. *i, e, a* mutated before original *r* plus original voiced dental: *Steern* 'forehead', *Weert* 'innkeeper', *Eer* 'earth', *Peerd* 'horse'.

—Before *r* it is realized as a close monophthong, see § 7.8, e.g. *Deern* 'girl'.

8.4 [ɔɑ] derives from:

(i) WGmc. *ô* (= OHG *uo*): *goot* 'good', *klook* 'clever' (but see § 7.9).

(ii) WGmc. *au* (= OHG *ou* or *ô*) in the *Elbmarschen* generally, in the *Geest* only in a few words (see § 7.9): *lopen* 'to run'.

(iii) Medieval *ô* of various sources: *froh* 'glad', *Roos'* 'rose'.

(iv) WGmc. *û* in hiatus position: *trooen* 'to trust', *booen* 'to build'.

(v) WGmc. *a* before original *ld*: *holen* 'to hold', *oolt* 'old'.

(vi) WGmc. *o, u* before original *r* plus voiced dental: *foorts* 'at once', *Woort* 'word' (phonetically realized as a close monophthong).

8.5 [œɪ] derives from:

(i) WGmc. *ô* (= OHG *uo*) mutated: *klöker* 'cleverer' (see § 7.10).

(ii) WGmc. *au* (= OHG *ou* or *ô*) mutated in the *Marschen* dialects, e.g.: *köpen* 'to buy', *schöön* 'beautiful' (see § 7.10).

(iii) Medieval *ô* of various sources: *Töhn* 'toes'.

(iv) WGmc. *o* or *u* mutated before original *r* plus voiced dental: *Höörn* 'horns', *vertöörn* 'to anger' (phonetically realized as a close monophthong [ø:]).

§ 9. Unstressed Vowels

Except in foreign words and compounds only [ɪ] and [ə] are at all frequent in unstressed positions.

9.1 [ɪ] is lax and open. It derives from the following sources:

(i) The medieval suffixes *-ig, -ag*: *oevrig* 'remaining'.

(ii) The medieval suffix *-ing*: *Missing* 'brass'.

(iii) The medieval suffix *-lik*: *täämlich* 'rather'.

(iv) The medieval suffix *-ling*: *Hüüsling* 'pauper'.

9.2 [ə] is a neutral, central vowel and occurs in the following affixes:

(i) In the prefix *be*: *bemöten* 'to meet'.

(ii) In the rare prefix *ge-*: *gemeen* 'common'.

(iii) In the adjectival suffix *-e* (see § 22): *dat groote Huus* 'the big house'.

(iv) In the suffix *-de*: *Längde* 'length'.

The suffixes *-el* and *-en* consist of a syllabic consonant without an unstressed vowel.

9.3 The *Überlänge* (*Schleifton*)[1] has been classified as an allophone of the unstressed vowel /ə/ (see § 4). *Überlänge*, which manifests itself by over-length of the root-vowel and lenis character of the final consonant, of course never occurs where [ə] is present. Historically

[1] See Otto Bremer, 'Der Schleifton im Nordniedersächsischen', *NdJb.*, liii, 1928, 1–32.

it has arisen where a medieval unstressed *e* has dropped[1] after a vowel or the voiced consonants *d*, *g*, *s*, *v* preceded by a long root-vowel, e.g. *Lüüd'* (MLG *lūde*) 'people', *Druuv'* (MLG *drūve*) 'grapes', *Müüs'* 'mice', including those long vowels which had developed from former short vowels in open syllables, e.g. *Nääs'* (MLG *nese*) 'nose', *Roed'* 'wheels'. Morphological analogies have often interfered with the *Überlänge*, but, by and large, it is now found in the following cases: (i) In the sg. of many fem. nouns of the medieval *ô-* and *n-* classes, e.g. *Leev'* 'love' (but *leef* 'dear'); (ii) In the sg. of a few masc. nouns of the *n-* class, e.g. *Lööv'* 'lion'; (iii) In the pl. of many nouns with former *-e* suffix, e.g. *Daag'* 'days', *Hoev'* 'yards', *Wääg'* 'ways'; (iv) In some adjectives of the former *ja-* class, e.g. *mööd'* 'tired'; (v) In some cases with former adverbial ending *-e*, e.g. *luud'* 'loudly'; (vi) In some verbal forms, e.g. 1st pers. sg. pres. *ik gääv'* 'I give', *ik lääv'* 'I live'; in the pl. pres. *wi gääv't*, *wi bliev't*; in the sg. pret. *ik bleev'*, *du bleev'st*, *he bleev'* 'stay', *ik lääv'*, *du lääv'st*, *he lääv'* 'live'; in the p.p. of weak verbs *lääv't*.

9.4 [ɜ] is an unstressed vowel of open mid to low central quality, more frontal after mid and front vowels and more retracted after back vowels. It is a vocalic realization of /r/[2] in postvocalic positions, occurring in the following unstressed positions:

(i) In the prefix *ver-*: *verleren* 'to lose'.
(ii) In the suffix *-er*: *bäter* 'better'.
(iii) In the verbal suffix *-ern*: *bätern* 'to better'.

It occurs also as an *r-* realization after all long vowels and diphthongs except /a:/, cf. [va:m] 'warm', [vɔɒm] 'worm', [ve·ɜt] 'innkeeper'.

§ 10. Vowel Quantity

10.1 Vowel quantity is not automatically tied to any specific position or dependent on the surroundings. Historically the distribution of vowel quantity has been profoundly affected by the late medieval lengthening of short vowels in open syllables and the shortening of originally long vowels before consonantal clusters. The dialect has on the whole followed these complementary tendencies strictly and has avoided analogical levellings. Thus we have short vowels in the originally closed syllables *Dag* 'day', *Slag* 'blow' but long vowels in the originally open syllables *Daag'*, *Slääg'*; long vowels in *griepen* 'to seize', *legen* 'to tell a lie', but before clusters the historically long vowels are shortened: *he grippt*, *he lüggt*. Where the

---

[1] It is true, the over-long vowel is heard also where a former liquid is vocalized, at least in especially conservative dialect, e.g. *ārg'* 'bad', *Ārm* 'arm', *Bāl* 'ball'.

[2] On its phonemic position, see § 12.2.

cluster arose after the historical quantity shift historically long vowels are tolerated: *wi griept, wi leegt.* Before voiceless consonants the long vowels are on the whole shorter than before voiced ones.

Exceptions to the historical lengthening process occur above all in words ending in the suffixes -*er* and -*el.*

10.2 Before single *r* or *r* plus consonant except a voiceless dental all originally short vowels have been lengthened.

10.3 *L* has often had a lengthening effect, e.g. *Hāls* 'neck'.

§ 11. COMPARISON WITH THE NHG VOWELS

(1) As to vowel quantity NHG and NS follow the same principles, but there is less morphological interference in NS.

(2) The long vowels before *r*- clusters are characteristic of NS.

(3) NS has two diphthongs unknown to NHG: /ɛɪ/ and /ɔɑ/ for NHG *ee, ie* and *ei* or *u, o* and *au* respectively.

(4) NS has long open mid vowels.

(5) NS has long high vowels *ī, ū, ṻ* where NHG has diphthongs *ei au, äu/eu.*

(6) Like NHG, NS makes no distinction between the umlaut of *a* and the historical *e.*

(7) Like NHG, NS has only open, lax, short vowels.

(8) NS has frequently rounding of front vowels in labial surroundings.

(9) Except in the declension of adjectives NS has dropped an original final unstressed -*e*, unlike NHG. As a compensation for this apocope NS has *Überlänge.*

Chief Vowel Correspondences

NS	ie[i:]	uu	üü	(2) aa[ɔ:]	ää[ɛ:]	oe[œ:]	ee[ɛ̆ɪ]	oo[ɔɑ]	öö[œɪ]
MHG	î	û	iu	â, a, o, u	i, ĕ, e ö, ü	ei, ie, ĕ	ou, uo, ô	öü, üe, oe	
NHG	ei	au	eu/äu	a o u	i e, ä ö	ü	ei, ie, e	au, u, o äu	ü, ö

NHG	ei	au	eu/äu	(2) ie	e, ä	a	o	u	ö	ü
MHG	ei î	ou û	öü iu	ie, i	ê, e, äê	â, a	ô, o	uo u	oe ö	üê ü
NS	ee ie	oo uu	öö üü	ee, ää	ee, ää	aa	oo	aa oo aa	öö oe	öö oe

Notes

(1) For the phonetic value of the NS letters, see § 5. MHG and NHG sounds are given in their respective orthography.

(2) In these tables the NS and NHG sounds are, insofar as they correspond to medieval short vowels, the reflexes in originally *open* syllables.

THE CONSONANTS

§ 12. The Consonantal System

Stops		Fricatives		Sonants	
voiceless	*voiced*	*voiceless*	*voiced*	*nasals*	*liquids*
p	b	f	v	m (m:)	
t	d	s š	z	n (n:)	l, r
k	g	x	ɉ	ŋ (ŋ:)	h

12.1 The system as it is set out holds good for initial position with the exception of /s/ and /x/ and the long nasals. In initial position the opposition /s/—/z/ is neutralized. Before vowels only [z] occurs and before consonants only [s].[1] /x/ with its two chief allophones [x] and [ç] occurs only in medial and final positions, i.e. only in positions where [h] is not found. It is therefore possible to regard [h] and [x], [ç] as allophones of one phoneme, [h] being its realization in initial position, [x] medially and finally after back and low vowels and [ç] in all other conditions medially and finally. [ɉ] occurs only in initial position. Phonetically it is a fricative rather than a semi-vowel, in fact in many local dialects, especially those near Hamburg, it is slightly affricated [dž].

12.2 In medial position the opposition of voiced and voiceless stops and fricatives is neutralized in the position before voiceless consonants. It is clearly marked only after long vowels although phonetically reduced to an opposition between voiceless lenes and voiced lenes, supported, however, by a slight variation in vowel length, e.g. [ri:dn] 'to ride'—[ri·ḍn] 'to pull', [ɔ:bm] 'stove'—[ɔ·ḅm] 'open', [ɛɪgŋ] 'own'—[ɛɪǥ̊ŋ] 'oaks'. In all positions other than before vowels /r/ is realized as a vocalic *Ersatzlaut*. This vowel [ɜ] (see § 9.4) contrasts in final position with unstressed /ə/, e.g. *leve, lever* 'dear' attributive and comparative. Since [ɜ] corresponds to [r] in NHG, speakers are liable to regard it as an *r*- realization. It can therefore be interpreted as an allophone of /r/ in spite of the phonetic dissimilarity.

[1] Where [s] occurs initially, e.g. in *süh!* 'look', it can be interpreted as a cluster. Cf. Niekerken (*Bibl.*, 120), 'Heute ist diese Spirans gewöhnlich zur Affrikata verschärft', p. xviii.

12.3 In absolute final position the contrast between voiced and voiceless consonants is neutralized. All consonants are voiceless. The stops which are strongly aspirated in initial position are unaspirated and on the whole weakly articulated. /t, f, s, x/ have lenis allophones after the over-long vowels (see §§ 4; 9.3). The final position is the only position in which the normal nasals contrast with long nasals, e.g. *ik kann* 'I can': *Kann'* 'pot'.

12.4 The occurrence of the phonemes and their chief allophones can be summarized as follows:

Phoneme	Initially bef. vowels	Medially betw. vowels	Finally	Überlänge
p	ph	b̦		
b	b	b̦ (5)	p	
t	th	d̦		
d	d	d̦ (5)	t	ḍ
k	kh	g̊		
g	g	g (5)	k	
f	f	f		
v	v (w) (1)	v	f	v̦
s	z (s) (2)	s		
z		z	s	z̦
š	š (3)	š	š	
ɟ	dž			
h	h (4)	x (6) ç	x (6) ç	ɣ (6) ɟ
m	m	m	m	
m:			m:	
n	n	n	n	
n:			n:	
l	l	l	l	
r	r	r	ɛ	

Notes

(1) After the consonants /d, t, k, s/ bilabial [w].

(2) Before consonants, e.g. *sl, sm, sn, st, sp, sw* (but see § 14.9).

(3) Does not occur before consonants.

(4) Only before vowels.

(5) Very rare; where /d/ is the reflex of former geminate *dd* or *tt* it is often in intervocalic position replaced by /r/, see § 14.4 (ii).

(6) After back and low vowels.

(7) ɟ indicates neutralization.

§ 13. Spelling

The spelling system worked out under the auspices of the *Fehrs-Gilde* (see p. 25), which I have adopted for the specimen text, has the following correspondences:

Phoneme	Letter	Phoneme	Letter	Phoneme	Letter
p	p, (2) pp (1)	f	f, v, (3) ff	x (6)	ch, g, gg
b	b, bb	v	v, w (4)	m, m:	m, mm'
t	t, tt	s	s, ss	n, n:	n, nn'
d	d, dd	z	s		ng, ng'
k	k, ck	š	sch	l	l, ll
g	g, gg (6)	ʝ	j	r	r (7)
		h	h		

Notes

(1) Doubling is used to indicate that the preceding vowel is short.

(2) The spellings *p*, *t*, *k* are also used for the voiceless lenis (see § 12.4) in intervocalic position.

(3) *V* only in initial position where the corresponding NHG word has *v*.

(4) *W* only in initial position including after initial consonants.

(5) In final position hardening is not indicated; the spelling thus follows NHG practice. But the presence of *Überlänge* is indicated by ', e.g. *d'*, *g'*, *s'*, *v'*.

(6) The least satisfactory decision is that of the retention of *g* where NHG has *g*. This means that *g* renders two phonemes, /g/ and /x/, while the latter is also spelt with *ch*, namely in those words where NHG has *ch*. Before a consonant except -*t* of pl. pres. and in final position *g* always represents /x/, but in initial position and medially it represents /g/.

(7) The spelling with *r* is retained even where it is vocalized.

(8) The assimilations of the nasal suffix (see § 14.15) are not expressed. The spelling is always -*en*.

§ 14. The Consonant Phonemes

The phonetic realizations of the consonant phonemes are given in § 12. The descriptions here refer to the initial position.

14.1 [p] is a voiceless, fortis, aspirated, bilabial stop representing WGmc. *p*: *Pann'* 'pan', *Päper* 'pepper'.

14.2 [b] is a voiced, lenis, bilabial stop representing:

(i) in initial, and medial, originally intervocalic positions (before a nasal) WGmc. *b*: *Broot* 'bread', *äben* 'even'.

(ii) WGmc. -*bb*-, -*pp*-: *rabbelen* 'to talk quickly'.

14.3 [t] is a voiceless, fortis, aspirated, alveolar stop deriving from: WGmc. *t*, *tt*: *Tiet* 'time', *lütt* 'small'.

14.4 [d] is a voiced, lenis, alveolar stop deriving from:

(i) WGmc. *d* and *þ* in initial position: *dien* 'thy', *Dochter* 'daughter'.

(ii) WGmc. *d* and *þ* in medial originally intervocalic positions provided it has not been vocalized: *Büdel* 'bag', *Lüüd* or *Lü* 'people', *Vadder* 'father'. The loss of the stop or replacement by an *r*-like flap in the case of a former geminate *-dd-* is more frequent in rural, careless articulation whereas in careful speech a *d* is usually heard.

14.5 [k] is a voiceless, fortis, aspirated, palato-velar stop deriving from: WGmc. *k*: *kieken* 'to look', *maken* 'to make'.

14.6 [g] is a voiced, lenis, palato-velar stop deriving from:

(i) WGmc. *g* in initial position: *graben* 'to dig', *gahn* 'to go'.

(ii) WGmc. *g, gg* in medial originally intervocalic position (before a nasal): *kriegen* 'to get', *bedragen* 'deceived'.

14.7 [f] is a voiceless, labio-dental fricative deriving from:

(i) WGmc. *f*: *finnen* 'to find', *Füür* 'fire', *Hoff* 'yard'.

(ii) WGmc. *b̄* before voiceless consonants and in final position: *du driffs* 'you drive', *Wief* 'woman'.

14.8 [v] is a voiced, labio-dental fricative (but with bilabial articulation after initial /d, t, k, s/). It derives from:

(i) WGmc. *w* in initial position: *wieder* 'farther'.

(ii) WGmc. *f, b̄* in intervocalic position except where a nasal follows: *Stävel* 'boot'.

14.9 [s] is a voiceless, alveolar fricative deriving from:

(i) WGmc. *s* in initial and medial position before consonants and in final position: *snacken* 'to talk', *du büss* 'you are'. Before *m, n, w* and especially before *l* [š] is now often heard instead of [s].

(ii) WGmc. *-ss-*: *küssen* 'to kiss'.

(iii) WGmc. *-hs-*: *wassen* 'to grow'.

14.10 [z] is a voiced, alveolar fricative deriving from: WGmc. *s* in initial position before vowels and in intervocalic position: *sehn* 'to see', *läsen* 'to read'.

14.11 [š] is a voiceless, post-alveolar, grooved fricative deriving from: WGmc. *sk*: *Schuuf* 'drawer', *Escher* 'spade'.

14.12 [j] is a voiced, palatal fricative deriving from: WGmc. initial *j*: *jung* 'young', *ji* 'you'.

14.13 [x] is a voiceless, palato-velar fricative, velar after back and low vowels, palatal in other surroundings. It derives from:

(i) WGmc. *g* before consonants in medial and in final positions: *du kriggst* 'you get', *Weg* 'way'.

(ii) WGmc. *gg* in final position: *Rüch* 'back'.

(iii) WGmc. *h* in final position: *hooch* 'high'.

(iv) WGmc. *ht*: *rech* 'right', *Nach(t)* 'night'.

(v) WGmc. *hh*: *lachen* 'to laugh'.

(vi) WGmc. *f* in the cluster *ft*: *achter* 'behind', *lichten* 'to lift'.

14.14 [h] is a glottal aspirate and derives from WGmc. *h-* in initial position: *Holt* 'wood'. On the phonemic interpretation, see § 12.1.

14.15 [m, n, ŋ] derive from the corresponding WGmc. single or double nasals.[1] Assimilation to the following or preceding consonant has frequently altered the place of articulation of the historical nasal. In particular the suffix *-en* is generally assimilated to the preceding consonant after the loss of the unstressed vowel. Thus syllabic *m* results from *-en* after labials, e.g. in *supen* 'to drink', *baben* 'above'; syllabic *ng* results from *-en* after velars, e.g. *liggen* 'to lie', *lachen* 'to laugh', *snacken* 'to talk'. For the assimilations in the case of homorganic nasals, see § 14.16.

14.16 [m:, n:, ŋ:]. These long nasals occur only in final position and have arisen under similar conditions to those which produced the *Schleifton* (see § 9.3). Nasals following on a short vowel are lengthened in compensation for the loss of a former *-e*, e.g. *Spinn'* 'spider', *Stimm'* 'voice', *bang'* 'afraid'. A further source of the long nasals are the assimilative changes which affected former *-en* after *n*, *m*, *ng*, e.g. *kamen* [kɔ:m:] 'to come', *singen* [zɪŋ:] 'to sing', *ahnen* [ɔ:n:] 'to suspect'.

14.17 [l] is a liquid which is alveolar or velar (in final and pre-consonantal positions) corresponding to WGmc. *l*, e.g. *Lief* 'body', *Pahl* 'pole'.

14.18 [r] is a frontal trill and continues WGmc. *r* before a vowel either initially or medially at the beginning of a syllable. In all other positions an historical *r* is represented by [ɜ], see § 9.4. E.g. *wringen* 'to wring', *riek* 'rich'.

§ 15. ASSIMILATION

Some historical assimilations form sound laws:

(i) Intervocalic *-ld-* > *l*: *holen* 'to hold', *Schuller* 'shoulder'.

(ii) Intervocalic *-nd-* > *n*: *binnen* 'to bind', *Kinner* 'children', but *Kind* (sg.).

(iii) Intervocalic *-rd-* > *r*: *Eer* 'earth', *Gaarner* 'gardener'.

(iv) *-hs-* > *ss*: *Voss*[2] 'fox'.

(v) In rapid speech *t* after voiceless consonants is usually completely assimilated, e.g. *Luss*, cf. NHG *Lust*.

(vi) As to the assimilation of *-en* to preceding consonants, see § 14.15 f.

---

[1] But WGmc. final *-ng* is now *-ngk*, e.g. *jung* 'young' but *Jung'* 'boy'.
[2] The spelling with *v* in this word is traditional in LG writing.

§ 16. Comparison with the NHG Consonants

The most salient differences are:

(1) While NS shares with NHG a consonantal system based on the opposition between voiced and voiceless consonants, which is neutralized in final position, the NS consonantism is characterized by general lenition in medial voiced surroundings. The *Auslautsverhärtung* does not operate in cases of *Überlänge*.

(2) NS, unlike NHG, does not distinguish between WGmc. *þ* and *d* (NHG *d* and *t*).

(3) NS lacks, of course, the affricates resulting from the HG soundshift and preserves the WGmc. stops which have become fricatives in HG (*p, t, k*). They are subjected to lenition in intervocalic position.

(4) NS has the WGmc. fricatives in final and preconsonantal position where NHG has stops (spelt *b, g*).

(5) NS has initial *st, sp* where NHG has *scht, schp*.

(6) NS has long nasal consonants in final position.

(7) The NS equivalents of certain NHG consonantal clusters have, in certain positions, been simplified. NHG *-nd-, -lt-, chs* correspond to NS *n, l, ss*.

(8) A final nasal is usually made homorganic with the preceding consonant in NS.

(9) NS has a vocalized variant of *r* in preconsonantal and final positions.

MORPHOLOGY

NOUNS AND ARTICLES

§ 17. Formation of the Plural

The loss of the former unstressed *-e* has deprived NS of one of the historical German plural suffixes, but the phenomenon of *Überlänge* has created a new means of expressing plurality. The quantity laws (see § 10) and the historical consonantal assimilations (see § 15) are also significant in the formation of the plural. In addition to the common German plurality marks (mutation, *-er, -en*) NS has the characteristically LG *s-* suffix. Thus there are the following types of plural formation:

Type A: plural not marked by ending or mutation.

Type B: plural marked by *Überlänge*.

Type C: plural marked by difference in root-vowel other than mutation with *Überlänge* where possible.

Type D: plural marked by mutation alone.

Type E: plural marked by nasal suffix.

Type F: plural marked by ending *-er*, with mutation where possible.

Type G: plural marked by *-s*.

Note: All back and low-tongue vowels are mutatable.

The correspondences are as follows:

Basic vowel:	a	ā	o	aa[ɔ:]	u	uu	oo[ɔɷ]
Mutated vowel:	ä/ää/oe	ää	ö/oe	oe	ü/oe	üü	öö

For the phonetic value of these letters, see § 5. There is often a change in length as well as mutation. In the case of *a* the long mutated vowel *oe* presupposes a lengthened *aa* in the plural.

Changes in vowel quantity due to different syllabic structure entail the following: *a, o, u*: *aa*; *i, e*: *ää*; *ö, ü*: *oe*.

Type A. To this type belong:
A few masc. and n. nouns with collective meaning: *Fisch* 'fish', *Aal* 'eel', *Haar* 'hair', *Schaap* 'sheep' and the fem. *Noet* 'nut'.

Type B. To this type belong:
A few masc. nouns with long root-vowels: *Breef—Breev'* 'letter', *Deef—Deev'* 'thief'.

Type C. To this type belong:
(i) A few masc. nouns: *Dag—Daag'* 'day', *Weg—Wääg'* 'way'.
(ii) A few neuters: *Schip—Schääp* 'ship', *Brett—Brääd'* 'boards'.

Type D. *Überlänge* and consonantal changes occur where appropriate, see §§ 9.3; 15. To this type belong:
(i) A considerable number of masc. nouns, especially the old *i*-stems, with many analogical formations: *Boom—Bööm* 'tree', *Hoff—Hoev'* 'yard', *Grund—Grünn'* 'ground'.
(ii) A fair number of fem. nouns, especially those which also mutate in MHG: *Bruut—Brüüd'* 'fiancée', *Hand—Hänn'* 'hand'.
(iii) A number of neuters in analogy to the above: *Huus—Hüüs'* 'house', *Rad—Roed'* 'wheel'.

Type E. To this type belong:
(i) The majority of fem. nouns: *Nääs'—Näsen* 'nose', *Eek—Eken* 'oak'.
(ii) Many masc. nouns: *Appel—Appeln* 'apple', *Buur—Buurn* 'farmer', *Bärg—Bärgen* 'mountain'.
(iii) A fair number of neuter nouns: *Hatt—Hatten* 'heart', *Jahr—Jahren* 'year', *Stück—Stücken* 'piece'.

As to the phonetic realization of the nasal suffix, see § 14.15 f.

Type F. To this type belong:
(i) A good number of neuter nouns but not as many as in NHG: *Bild—Biller* 'picture', *Kind—Kinner* 'child', *Wief—Wiever* 'woman'.
(ii) One or two masc. nouns: *Mund—Münner* 'mouth'.

A A

Type G. To this type belong:

(i) A large number of masc. nouns, especially those ending in *-er* or *-el* which denote animate beings, and nouns ending in a nasal: *Bäcker—Bäckers* 'baker', *Sloetel—Sloetels* 'key', *Gaarn—Gaarns* 'garden'.

(ii) A few neuters ending in a nasal or a liquid: *Küssen—Küssens* 'pillow'.

(iii) A small number of feminines ending in a nasal or liquid: *Deern—Deerns* 'girl'.

§ 18. CASE FORMS

Apart from relic forms of a genitive sg. and a dative sg. and pl. there is only one case distinction which is alive in NS. The masc. nouns of Type E (ii), denoting animate beings, take *-en* in the common objective case sg., e.g. nom. *de Minsch*, obj. *den Minschen*, pl. *de Minschen*.

Possession is expressed by a paraphrase with the possessive pronoun, e.g. *de Prinzessin ähr Stuuv* 'the princess's drawing-room'.

§ 19. GENDER

The majority of nouns have the same gender as in NHG, but there are some noteworthy differences, e.g. *Dook* m. or n. 'cloth', *Tehn* m. 'toe', *Bääk* m. or f. 'stream', *Anker* m. or n. 'anchor', *Sark* m. or n. 'coffin'.

§ 20. THE DECLENSION OF THE DEFINITE ARTICLE

	m.	f.	n.	pl.
Nom.	de			
Obj.	den	de	dat (2)	de

Notes

(1) *De* is [dɛɪ], or, when least stressed, [də].

(2) After prepositions which take the dat. in NHG the neuter art. is usually an enclitic nasal (*-n* etc.).

(3) All art. are reduced after prepositions, e.g. *vun'n Kaiser, achter 't Holt, in 'e Mitt*.

§ 21. THE DECLENSION OF THE INDEFINITE ARTICLE

There is only one form for all genders: *'n (en)*. No case distinctions are made.

ADJECTIVES

§ 22. DECLENSION

Adjectives are inflected only when used in attributive position or when substantivized. The Gmc. distinction between a weak and a strong declension has been much reduced in scope. A case distinction (between subjective and objective) occurs only before masc. nouns in the weak declension.

m.	f.	n.	pl.
jungen/-e (2)	junge	jung/-e (3)	junge/-en (4)

Notes

(1) Wisser has only two adjectival forms: the ending *-en* and the endingless adjective. Most NS dialects, however, preserve the unstressed *-e*, at least in monosyllabic adjectives in (*a*) fem.; (*b*) weak masc. nom. (see 2); (*c*) weak neuter (see 3); (*d*) strong pl. (see 4).

(2) The weak form in *-e* is found in the nom. after the def. art., a pers. pron., a dem. pron., a poss. pron.

(3) The weak ending *-e* is found after the art. and prons. listed in (2).

(4) The weak ending *-en* is found in the circumstances listed under (3).

(5) After *nix* 'nothing', *wat* 'something', *vääl* 'much' adj. take *-s*, e.g. *wat Harrs* 'something hard'.

§ 23. Comparison

The comparative ends in *-er*, and the superlative in *-s(t)*, e.g. *jung—jünger—jüngst*. Fewer adjectives with root-vowels capable of mutating have umlaut than in NHG, e.g. *waarm—waarmer—waarmst*. In some cases vowel shortening occurs, e.g. in *oolt—öller* 'old', *groot-grötter* 'big'. The comparative particle is *as*.

NUMERALS
§ 24

The only gender distinction is that between *een* m., n. and *eene* f. No case distinctions are made.

PRONOUNS
§ 25. Personal Pronouns

The stressed and unstressed forms are:

	1st Person	2nd Person	3rd Person		
Nom. sg.	ik, -k	du, de	he, (1) -e	se, (1) -s	dat, (2) t
Obj. sg.	mi	di	em, m	ähr	dat, t
Nom. pl.	wi	ji		se, (1) s	
Obj. pl.	uns	ju		jüm (3)	

Notes

(1) The vowel in *he, se* is [ɛɪ] except when unstressed.

(2) Before the verb the full form *dat* is always used, *t* occurs only enclitically. *Dat*, originally a dem. pron., has replaced the historical pers. pron. corresponding to English *it*, NHG *es*.

(3) In the 3rd pers. pl. Wisser has *ähr*, the Lower Elbe dialects have *jüm*.

(4) The indefinite pronoun is *man*.

(5) For the obsolescent polite form *Ji*, *Se* is now common, often with the verb ending in *-en*, e.g. *hebben Se, seggen Se*.

§ 26. Reflexive Pronoun[1]

There is only one special form *sik* for the 3rd pers. sg. and pl., without case distinctions.

§ 27. Possessive Pronouns

They are: *mien, dien, sien, ähr* (fem. sg. and 3rd pers. pl.), *uns, juun*.

The only case which is specially marked by an ending (*-en*, with assimilation of nasal to preceding consonant) is the objective masc., e.g. *do lett he sienen Soehn to sik kamen*.

The substantivized form is *mieni*, etc., preceded by the def. art., e.g. *dat mieni*, cf. NHG *das meinige*.

§ 28. Demonstrative Pronouns

There are two dem. pronouns. The shorter one functions also as the def. art. (see § 20). The other is:

			m.	*f.*	*n.*	*pl.*
Nom.	.	.	.	.	düsse }	düsse }	düt }	düsse
Obj.	.	.	.	.	düssen }			

For 'such' the dialect uses *so* + indef. art.

§ 29. Interrogative Pronouns

For 'who?' NS has *keen, wokeen*; for 'what?' it uses *wat*; for 'which?' *wat 'n* or *wat för-n* and *welk, welkeen*.

§ 30. Indefinite Pronouns

wään, een, wer	somebody
keenen, nüms	nobody
wat, n bäten	something, a little
nix	nothing

---

[1] See fn., p. 319.

vääl, väle	much, many
männich, männicheen	many (a)
wenig, -e	a few
welke, weck	some, several
jedereen (noun.), *jeder*	each, every
all [aːl] (pl.)	all
allens (sg.)	all
keen	no (adj.)

§ 31. Relative Pronouns

The dem. pron. *de* is used as the rel. pron., e.g. *dat is de Gördel, den du di as Kind jümmer ümbunnen hess*. With prepositions *wo* is used, see Notes 27, 31.

VERBS

§ 32. Forms and Classification

Probably in no other German dialect has the verbal system been so radically simplified as in NS. The NS verb has the following form classes: infinitive, imperative, past participle, present and preterite. There is no subjunctive. The compound forms are: perfect, pluperfect, passive and occasionally a future.

The infinitive ends in *-en*, i.e. a syllabic nasal realized as a labial after labials, a velar after velars and a dental after the other sounds (see § 14.15 f.). The infinitive particle is *to*.

The imperative is in the sg. endingless but otherwise identical with the root of the 2nd and 3rd pers. sg. pres., and in the pl. it is identical with the form of the pl. pres.

The past participle lacks a special prefix. It either ends in a nasal suffix *-en*, which is realized in the same way as the infinitive suffix, or in a dental suffix *-t*. This dental is, in rapid and somewhat slovenly speech, dropped after all consonants other than liquids or nasals. Following the above distinction one can classify the verbs into strong verbs (p.p. *-en*) and weak verbs (p.p. *-t*). Difference in the rootvowel of the inf. and the p.p. is further characteristic of the strong verbs.

Verbs with inf. in *-ben* or *-gen* have fricatives in final or preconsonantal positions, e.g. *drieben* 'drive': *ik driev', he drifft*; *kriegen* 'get': *ik krieg', he kriggt*.

§ 33. Strong Verbs[1]

Strong verbs are distinguished from weak ones by the nasal suffix in the past participle and by vowel alternation. Owing to internal

[1] See fn. 1 on p. 321.

sound developments the possible vowel alternations have greatly increased, although the historical classes still stand out as the most numerous. The following stem forms have to be distinguished in NS:

Inf.; 1st Sg. Pres. *Pl. Pres.*	*2, 3 Sg. Pres.*	*Pret.*	*P.P.*
I. ie [i:]	i	ee [ɛɪ]	ä[ɛ:]
kieken 'look'[1]	*kick(t)*	*keek*	*käken*

This class, comprising 25 verbs, corresponds to Class I of OHG.

II. e[ɛɪ]	ü	oo[ɔɷ]	a[ɔ:]
flegen 'fly'	*flügg(t)*	*floog*	*flagen*

This class comprises 14 verbs and corresponds to the OHG Class II. *Legen* 'tell a lie', *tehn* 'pull' and *scheten* 'shoot' have mutated forms in the pret.: *löög*, *töög*, *schööt*. This mutated pret. is also found in those verbs (5) with *u* in the first stem-form:

u[u:]	ü	öö[œɪ]	a[ɔ:]
sluten 'shut'	*slütt*	*slööt*	*slaten*

and in *rüken* 'smell', *rück(t)—röök—raken.*

III. i		ü/u	u
binnen 'bind'		*bünn*	*bunnen*
spinnen 'spin'		*spunn*	*spunnen*

The majority of the 20 verbs belonging to this class (corresponding to the OHG Class III) have a mutated root-vowel in the pret., deriving, historically, from the former pret. subjunctive. This class has only three stem-forms. The following verbs with certain vowel differences can also be added to this class:

(*a*) a		ü/u	u
fangen 'catch'		*füng*	*fungen*
wassen 'grow'		*wuss*	*wussen*

also *fallen* 'fall', *hangen* 'hang', *waschen* 'wash'.

(*b*) e		ü/u	o
gellen 'cost'		*güll*	*gollen*
helpen 'help'		*hülp*	*holpen*

IV. ä[ɛ:]	i	oo[ɔɷ]	a[ɔ:]
bräken 'break'	*brick(t)*	*brook*	*braken*

and *spräken* 'speak', *dräpen* 'meet' (but also *drapen—dröpps(t)—dreep—drapen*), *drägen* 'carry', *bedrägen* 'behave'. Without mutated second stem-form: *stählen* 'steal', *befählen* 'command', and with

---

[1] The forms given in the examples are the inf., 3 sg. pres., 3 sg. pret., p.p.

different vowel in the first stem-form: *bögen* 'bend', *swoeren* 'swear'.

V. ä[ɛ:]   i   ee[ɛɪ]   ä
    äten 'eat'   *itt*   *eet*   *äten*

Five verbs belong to this class (corresponding to the OHG Class V);
and with *i* in the first stem-form: *liggen* 'lie', *sitten* 'sit'.

VI. o[ɔɷ]   ö   ee[ɛɪ]   o
    lopen 'run'   *löpp(t)*   *leep*   *lopen*

Also *ropen* 'call' and *(be)holen* 'hold', *slapen* 'sleep' and:

    laten 'let'   *lett*   *leet*   *laten*

A number of verbs are isolated, notably

kamen 'come'	*kümmt*	*keem*	*kamen*
nähmen 'take'	*nimmt*	*nehm*	*nahmen*
heten 'be called'	*heet*	*heet (heess)*	*heten*
sehn 'see'	*süht, sütt*	*seeg'*	*sehn*
trecken 'pull'	*treck(t)*	*trock*	*trocken*
starben 'die'	*starv(t)*	*storv'*	*storben*
verdarben 'go bad'	*verdarvt*	*verdörv'*	*verdorben*

A number of formerly strong verbs are now weak, notably *läsen*
'read', *piepen* 'whistle', *raden* 'advise', *swemmen* 'swim', *stöten* 'push';
others are 'mixed', see § 34.4.

§ 34. Weak Verbs

The common distinguishing mark of all weak verbs is the dental
suffix of the p.p. (subjected to assimilation, see §§ 15 (v); 32), e.g.
gapen—gaapt 'gape'. Verbs with roots ending in a vowel or /d, x, v,
z/ have *Überlänge* (see § 9.3), e.g. *freen—free't* 'woo', *läben—läävt*
'live'.

There are three types of irregular weak verbs.

34.1 With difference in vowel length: [œɪ/œ]

Inf., 1 Sg. Pres. Pl. Pres.	2, 3 Sg. Pres., Pret., P.P.
böten 'mend'	*bött*
blöden 'bleed'	*blödd*
föden 'bring up'	*fött*
höden 'look after'	*hödd*
möten 'drive'	*mött*
stöten 'push'	*stött*

34.2 With consonantal differences:

doegen 'be of use'	*döcht*
döpen 'baptize'	*döfft*
köpen 'buy'	*köfft*
seggen 'say' pret. *sä*	*seggt*
söken 'seek'	*söcht*

Those verbs have also a difference in vowel length, while the following are the only ones which preserve the *Rückumlaut*: *bringen—bröch—bröch(t)* 'bring', *denken—dach—dach(t)* 'think'.

34.3 In the following the *-en* is part of the root: *rägen—rägent* 'rain', *räken—räkent* 'reckon', *sägen—sägent* 'bless'.

34.4 The following verbs have a 'strong' pret. but a weak p.p.:

Inf. Pres.	Pret.	P.P.
fahren 'ride'	*föhr*	*fahrt*
fragen 'ask'	*fröög'*	*fraag't*
graben 'dig'	*groov'*	*graav't*
maken 'make'	*möök*	*maakt*
sluken 'swallow'	*slöök*	*sluukt*

§ 35. THE PRESENT

The endings are: sg. 1 -, 2 -*s*(*t*), 3 -(*t*); pl. -(*t*), e.g. *delen* 'share':

ik deel	*wi* ⎫
du deels(*t*) (3)	*ji* ⎬ *deelt* (4)
he deelt (5)	*se* ⎭

Notes

(1) Both strong and weak verbs have *Überlänge* (for the conditions, see § 9.3) in the 1st pers. sg. and pl.

(2) Strong verbs have a mutated root-vowel in the 2nd and 3rd pers. sg. and a short vowel, see § 33.

(3) The *-t* is dropped in rapid speech.

(4) The *-t* is dropped in rapid speech after all consonants other than liquids and nasals.

(5) After *m* the dental suffix may be realized as a labial (*p*).

§ 36. THE PRETERITE

The endings are the same for the strong and the weak verbs. The latter have lost the historical dental suffix corresponding to English *-ed*, HG *-te*. Endings: sg. 1st and 3rd pers. -, 2nd -*s*(*t*), pl. -*en*, e.g. *delen* 'share', *beden* 'offer':

ik deel	*wi* ⎫	*ik bood'*	*wi* ⎫
du deels(*t*) (2)	*ji* ⎬ *delen*	*du bood's*(*t*) (2)	*ji* ⎬ *boden*
he deel	*se* ⎭	*he bood'*	*se* ⎭

Notes

(1) Strong and weak verbs have *Überlänge* (for the conditions, see § 9.3) in the sg.

(2) The *-t* is dropped in rapid speech.

(3) The nasal suffix is realized in the same way as in the inf. (see § 32).

(4) In the case of weak verbs where the *-t* of the 3rd pers. sg. pres. is slurred there is no formal distinction between pres. and pret. in the sg.

§ 37. THE COMPOUND TENSES AND THE PASSIVE

Perfect: *he hett snack(t)*; *he is kamen*.
Pluperfect: *he harr snack(t)*; *he wöör kamen*.

Hebben is used as the auxiliary also with verbs of motion accompanied by a compliment, e.g. *wo schuss du süss wedder na Huus kamen hebben?* 'How would you have come home again otherwise?' *He hett n paar Stunnen gahn* 'he has walked a few hours'.

The future tense is formed with *schoelen* and *wüllen*, e.g. p. 369 *un ik will doot blieben* 'and when I shall be dead'.

The passive is formed with *warrn* as in NHG, e.g. p. 374 *he warrt mit de Polizei weg bröcht* 'he is taken away by the police'; p. 375 *de Nääs' mutt afsnäden warrn* 'the nose must be cut off'.

§ 38. THE MODAL AUXILIARIES AND OTHER AUXILIARIES

The following forms are distinguished:

38.1 Modal Auxiliaries

	Inf.	*Sg. Pres.*	*Pl. Pres.*	*Pret.*	*P.P.*
'to be able'	koenen	kann (1, 3) kanns(t) (2)	koent	kunn	kunnt
'may'	moegen	mag (1, 3) mags(t) (2)	moeg(t)	much	much(t)
'must'	moeten	mutt (1, 3) muss(t) (2)	moet	müss	muss(t)
'want to'	wüllen	will (1, 3) wullt (2)	wüllt	wull	wullt
'shall, should'	schoelen	schall (1, 3) schass (2) (schallst)	schüllt	schull schuss (2)	schullt
'to be allowed'	dörven *or* droeven	dörv' (1, 3) dörfs(t) (2) dröff (1, 3) (draffs) (2)	dörvt droevt	dörv' dröff	dörv(t) dröff(t)

38.2 Other Auxiliaries and Irregular Verbs

	Inf.	Sg. Pres.	Pl. Pres.	Pret.	P.P.
'to have'	hebben	heff (3) hes(t) hett	hebb(t)	harr	hatt
'to be'	sien wäsen wään	bün büs(t) is	sünd	wöör	wään
'to become'	warrn	warr warrs(t) warrt	warrt	wörr	worrn
'to do'	doon	do deis(t) deit	doot	dä	daan
'to stand'	stahn	stah steihs(t) steiht	staht	stünn	stahn
'to know'	wäten	weet weesst weet	wäät	wüss	wüsst or wäten

Notes

(1) As to -*t*, see § 35 (4).

(2) *Gahn* 'go' goes like *stahn* with *güng* in the pret.; so does *slaan* 'hit' with *slöög* in the pret.

(3) In inversion we have *heck* for *heff ik*, *hewwi* for *hebbt wi*, *heji* for *hebbt ji*.

§ 39. Particles

In general the use is similar to that of Westphalian (see p. 325).

Prepositions (1)	Movement	*Adverbs of Place* Rest
in (4)	rin	binnen (3)
ut (2)	rut	buten
up, op	rup	baben
ünner	rünner, raf, dal	ünnen, af, dal, nerrn
oever	roever	oever
achter	na achtern	achter(n)
vör		vörn

Notes

(1) These prep. are also adv., e.g. *dat geit all ünner un oever*, cf. NHG *es geht alles drunter und drüber*; *he hett Ogen achter un vör*, cf. NHG *er hat Augen hinten und vorne*.

(2) The vowel is long.

(3) These adv. are also prep., cf. NHG *innerhalb*, etc.

(4) For the NHG compound particles *darin*, etc., NS has *dar* plus *in*, etc., but the demonstrative remains separated from the prep. by the verb and other parts of the sentence. See Note 6.

PHONETIC TRANSCRIPTION

For the principles of this transcription, see pp. 71, 148. A description of the individual sounds is given in §§ 6–8, 14.

Words of two or more syllables have the main stress on the first syllable except where marked otherwise.

dɒɒ ɪs mɔ·ɫ n khœ:nɪ vɛ:n, dɛɪ hɛḍn zœ:n hat, dɛn heḍ hɛɪ ɒp ra·ɪzn šɪkt, daḍ hɛɪn bɛ·ḍn ɣnəšɛɪt heḍ le:ɜn šɒlt.

as hɛ wɛdɜ thɒɒ hu:s khɣmt, dɛɪ zœ:n, dɒɒ zɛçt hɛɪ thɒɒ zi·n: fɔ·dɜ, hɛɪ vɒɫ daḍ hɛɪ dɛ ri:kstə vø̈:ɜ ɒp dɛ ga·ntsə vɛɫt. ɔɒ, zɛçt dɛ ɔɒɫ, da khans du nɔx mɔ·ɫ va:n, dɒɒ ɪs rɔ·t vœr.

ja, fɔ·dɜ zɛçt hɛɪ, vɔ'dɛnɪ mɒḍɪk dadɛn an'gɔ:n? ja, mi·n zœ:n, zɛçt dɛ ɔɒɫ, da khanɪk dɪ nu nɔx nɪç zɛgɳ.

vɛnɪk mɔ·ɫ khraŋk va:n dɒɒ, ɒnɪk vɪl do:t bli:bm, dɛn vɪlɪk dɪ daḍ zɛgɳ.

dat du:aḍ ɔɒk nɪç laɳ: , dɒɒ va·t hɛɪ khraŋk, dɛɪ khœ:nɪ.

dɒɒ lɛt hɛɪ zi·n: zœ:n thɒɒ zɪk khɔ:m: ɒn zɛçthɒɒ ɛm : ɪk bɣn nu khraŋk, zɛçt hɛɪ, ɒnt khan vɛ:zn, daḍ ɪk do:t bli:bm dɒɒ: nu vɪlɪk dɪ daḍ zɛgɳ. ɪn dən zɛɪ dɒɒ gɣnt axtɜ thɒɫt, dɒɒ hɛvɪk ɪnə mɪt n šatɜ ɪn fɜgrɔ:bm lɔ·ḍn. vɛn du dɛn· fɪn: da·ɪs, ɒn du khrɪçs dat khlɒɒk, vadat mɪḍ‿ɛn šatɜ ɒp zɪk hɛt, dɛn bɣstu dɛ ri:kstə ɒp dɛ ga·ntsə vɛɫt. du mɒst dɒɒ ɔ·vɜ khɛɪn frɒɒnspherzɔn vat fɔn ɔ·ḅmbɔ:ɒn, dɛɪ zɣnt nɪç thɒɒ thrɒɒn.

nɛɪ, daḍ vɪɫ hɛɪ dɛn ɔɒk jə nɪç.

n phɔ·ɒ dɔ:·ɣ̊ nɔ·hɛɜ, dɒɒ blɪft dɛ khœ:nɪ do:t. ɒn dɒɒ va·t hɛɪ jɛ ɪn dɛɪ khaphɛl bizɛt, ɒn dɛɪ zœ:n va·t khœ:nɪ.

nu· vɪɫ hɛɪ jə fo·ɒts bi dən šatɜ. hɛɪ nɪmp zɪk n ba:x ly:·ḍ an ɒn lɛt‿ən zɛɪ aflɔɒḅm. ɒn as dɛ zɛɪ aflɔɒḅm ɪs, dat hɛɪ ga·ns drœɪ:·j ɪs, dɒɒ faɳ:t zɛ jə an thɒɒ grɔ:bm.

zɛɪ grɔ:·ɣt ɒn grɔ:·ɣt ɣmɜlɒɒs, ɔvɜ dɒɒ ɪs khɛɪn šatɜ ɒn khɣmp khɛɪn šatɜ. dɒɒ dɛɳkt hɛɪ: šɒɫ di:n ɔɒɫ fɔ·ɜ daḍ ɔɒk man zo zɛçt hɛbm, dat dɒɒ gɔ·ɒ khɛɪn šatɜ ɪs?

hɛɪ ga·ɪt na dɛ khaphɛl ɒn mɔ:kt daḍ za:k ɔ·ḅm. dɒɒ lɪçt zi·n ɔɒɫ fɔ·də dɒɒ ɒn zɣçt zo e:ɜbɒɒ u:t, ɛ:bm zo e:ɜbɒɒ, as hɛɪ ɣmɜ u·tzɛɪn hɛt.

ne:, dɛɳkt hɛɪ, bədrɔ:gɳ khan hɛɪ dɪ nɪç hɛbm, di·n ɔɒɫ fɔ·dɜ.

hɛɪ zɣçt zo e:ɜbɒɒ u:t : vaḍ hɛɪ zɛçt heḍ, daḍ mɒt vɔ:ɒ vɛ:n. hɛɪ lɛt dɛɪ ly:· jə vi:dɜ grɔ:bm, avɜ dɒɒ ɪs khɛɪn šatɜ thɒɒ fɪn:.

thɒɒlɛst, dɒɒ va·t əm daḍ gɛlḍ al knap, daḍ hɛɪ dɛ ly:· nɪç rɛç me:ɜ bəthɔ:ĩn khan.

WILHELM WISSER:

DE PRINZESSIN MIT DE LANGE NĀĀS' [1][1]

Dar is mal 'n Koeni wään [2], de hett 'n Soehn hatt, den' hett he up Reisen schickt, dat he 'n bäten Ünnerscheed hett lehren schullt. As he wedder to Huus kümmt, de Soehn [3], do seggt he to sien'n Vadder [4], he wull, dat he de riekste [5] wöör up de gänze Welt. Och, seggt de Ool, dat kanns du noch mal warrn, dar is Raat vör [6]. Ja, Vadder, seggt he, wodenni mut ik dat denn angahn? Ja, mien Soehn, seggt de Ool, dat kann ik di nu noch nich [7] seggen. Wenn ik mal krank warrn do [8], un ik will doot blieben [9], denn will ik di dat seggen.

Dat dur't ok nich lang', do warrt he krank, de Koeni [3].

Do lett he sien'n Soehn to sik kamen un seggt to em: Ik bün nu krank, seggt he, un 't kann wäsen, dat ik doot blieben do: nu will ik di dat [10] seggen. In den See dar günt achter 't Holt, dar heff ik in 'e Mitt 'n Schatz in [11] vergraben laten. Wenn du den' finnen deis [8], un du kriggs dat klook [12], wat dat mit den Schatz up sik hett, denn büss du de riekste up de gänze Welt. Du muss dar aver keen Froonsperson wat vun apenbaren, de sünd nich to trooen.

Ne, dat will he denn ok je [13] nich.

'n paar Daag' naher, do blifft de Koeni doot. Un do warrt he je in de Kapell bisett, un de Soehn warrt Koeni.

Nu will he je foorts bi [14] den Schatz.

He nimmt sik 'n Bārg Lüüd' an un lett den See aflopen. Un as de See aflopen is, dat he gänz dröög' is, do fang't se je an to graben.

Se graav't un graav't ümmerloos, aver dar is keen Schatz un kümmt keen Schatz.

Do denkt he: Schull dien ool Vadder dat ok man so seggt hebben, dat dar gar ken Schatz is?

He geiht na de Kapell un maakt dat Sark apen: do liggt sien ool Vadder dar un sücht so ehrbar ut, äben so ehrbar, as he ümmer [15] utsehn hett.

Ne, denkt he, bedragen kann he di nich hebben, dien ool Vadder. He sücht so ehrbar ut: wat he seggt hett, dat mutt wahr wäsen. He lett de Lüüd' je wieder graben, aver dar is ken Schatz to finnen.

Toletz, do warrt em dat Geld al knapp, dat he de Lüüd' nich rech mehr betahlen kann.

1 wess. 4 riks, wer, ganz. 5 ward'n. 7 ne. 10 uk. 17 Frunsperson. 32 (dat).

---

1 See *Notes.*

For spelling, see §§ 5, 13. It has been altered to conform with the rules of the *Fehrs-Gilde.* Where Wisser used a different dialect form from that of the informant, Wisser's form is given at the bottom of the page but only at the first occurrence.

Do denkt he: Wat stell's nu eenmal up? Wenn du keen Geld mehr hest, denn gaht de Lüüd' di je weg. Un denn büss du je gänz up nix [16]. Dat dur't nich lang', do warrt dat ok so. As se wedder 'n Tietlang graav't hebbt, un he kann em [17] nich mehr betahlen, do smiet se dal un gaht weg. Do geiht he hen sitten un weent. Wat fangs du eenmal an? denkt he. Nu büss du de Lüüd' so vääl Geld schülli un kanns jüm [17] nich betahlen. Un dat üm nix un wedder [4] nix. Wenn dar 'n Schatz vergraben wöör—se hebbt s o lang' graav't— [18], denn müssen se je doch wat funnen hebben. He geiht wedder hen na de Kapell: do sücht sien ool Vadder ja so ehrbar ut, as he ümmer utsehn hett.

Dar mutt doch wat an wään, denkt he. Du schass morn fröh sülben an to graben fangen.

Annern Morgen nimmt he 'n Escher in de Hand un geiht sülben bi [14] to graben.

He graav't een'n Dag, he graav't noch 'n Dag, aver ne, he dröppt nix.

Do vergeiht em de Moot, un he geiht wedder hen sitten un weent. Du muss dat man upgäben, denkt he, finnen deis du doch nix.

He geiht wedder hen na de Kapell: do sücht sien ool Vadder graad' so ehrbar ut as süss.

Ne, denkt he, bedragen kann he di nich hcbben. Dat kann gar nich angahn [19]. Du schass morn fröh noch mal wedder bigahn [14] un graben. Aver dröpps du denn ok noch nix, denn hölls du up. Annern Morgen geiht he je wedder hen mit sien'n Escher un fangt vun frischen wedder an.

He hett man eerst 'n Ogenblick graav't, do stött he mit den Escher up wat harts.

O, denkt he, dat 's je wul 'n ool'n Steen.

He graav't wieder: do is dat 'n hölten Kassen.

Süh, denkt he, dien ool Vadder hett doch Recht hatt. Aver wenn du den Kassen ok gänz vull Geld hädd's, de riekste up de gänze Welt wöörs du je liekes nich. So vääl geiht dar je gar nich rin.

He graav't wieder un graav't den Kassen ut de Eer herut.

Do is de Kassen aver toslaten.

He lett 'n Slösser [20] kamen un lett den Kassen apen maken.

Do is dar noch 'n iesern Kassen in. De iesern is aver ari 'n bäten lütter wään as de hölten.

Do denkt he bi sik sülben: Ja, wenn du den' ok gänz vull Gold un Edelsteen hädd's, de riekste up de gänze Welt wöörs du je liekes noch nich. So vääl geiht dar je gar nich rin. He lett den iesern Kassen

1 (nu). 2 hess. 12 (ja). 13 wesen. 24 un *instead of* to. 28 ers. 29 harrs. 32 Rech. 34 in.

na sien'n Sloss transporteren, un do mutt de Slösser bi un mutt den' ok apen maken.

As de Kassen apen is, un he sücht to, wat dar in is, do liggt dar so 'n lütten linnen Büddel [4] baben up.

Och Gott, denkt he, dat is de lütt Büddel, wo du as Kind ümmer dien Alabastern in hädd's [21] un spääls darmit. Wat dien ool Vadder dar wul ut hatt hett [22], da he den' hett vergraben laten? Schass doch mal tosehn, wat [23] dar nich noch mehr in is. Hier kanns je nix mit maken.

Do liggt dar'n Stück Papier baben up, dat nimmt he eerst räf.

Un do kriggt he dar so 'n lütt Kinnertrumpett rut.

Ja, denkt he, wat schass du dar denn nu mit? Dat is je de lütt Trumpett, wo du as Kind ümmer up blaast hest, wenn du Suldat spälen dääs [24]. Wat dien ool Vadder dar wul ut hatt hett, [22] de to vergraben!

Do liggt dar noch 'n Stück Papier up, dat nimmt he ok räf. Un do kriggt he dar so 'n lütten Gördel rut, mit 'n lütten Dolch in.

Süh, denkt he, dat is de lütt Gördel, den' du di as Kind ümmer ümbunnen hest, un de lütt Dolch, dar hest du je ümmer mit späält. Aver wat is di dar n u mit holpen? Dat is je äll' wat vör lütt Kinner to spälen. Un dien ool Vadder sä [25] je doch, du schuss de riekste warrn up de gänze Welt.

Do liggt dar noch 'n Papier gänz ünner up 'n Bodden [4]. He kriggt dat Papier rut un denkt: Schass doch mal sehn, wat [26] dar nix up to läsen steiht.

Do steiht dar up: De linnen Büddel, so vääl as he sik den' vull wünschen deiht, vull Geld, denn is he ümmer vull.

Un de lütt Trumpett, wenn he dar up blasen deit, denn kaamt dar so vääl Suldaten up 'n Dutt, as he hebben will.

Un de Gördel, wenn he sik den' ümbinnen deit, denn kann he sik allerwägens hen wünschen, wo he will [27].

O, denkt he, wenn dat äll' wahr wöör, dat wöör je wat. Schass dat doch foorts mal proberen.

He wünscht sik den' lütten Büddel vull Goldstücken, un richti, do is de Büddel mit eenmal vull. He schüdd't em [28] ut un wünscht sik em noch mal wedder vull. Un dat deiht he so lang', bet he de gänze Stuuv' vull Goldstücken hett. Süh, denkt he, du büss de Lüüd' noch so vääl schülli: nu kanns du jüm [17] je betahlen.

He lett de Lüüd' wedder kamen un betahlt em [17] ut. Un do lett he dat groote Lock, wat [26] se graav't hebbt, dat lett he wedder toschüffeln, un lett den See wedder vull lopen, un do is dat je äll' wedder liekut. Un he is je de riekste up de gänze Welt.

Nu lääv't he eerstan so loos mit sien Geld. He kann sik je allens

10 heraf. 11 herut. 23 Borm. 43 ersan.

köpen un anschaffen [29], wat he hebben will. Geld hett he je ümmer genoog'.

Dat dur't sien Tiet: do warrt em dat oever [30]. Du sitts hier ümmer so alleen, denkt he, un hest nüms, wo [31] du 'n bäten mit snacken kanns: du schass di 'n Fro nähmen.

Nu kriggt he to hörn, dat de Kaiser von Marokko, dat de so 'n hübsche Dochter hett. Un do denkt he: Süh, dat wöör am Enn' wat vör di. Schass doch mal sehn, wat [26] du de nich kriegen kanns. He stickt sik sien Taschen vull Goldgeld—sien'n lütten linnen Büddel nimmt he ok mit —, un do reist he je loos, na Marokko hen.

As he dar ankamen deit, do geiht he je hen na 'n Slot un lett sik anmellen bi de Prinzessin. Un warrt ok je vörlaten.

Do fraag't se em, wat he vör 'n Anliggen hett, wat he will.

Ja, seggt he, wat se ken Lust hett [32] un will em heiraten.

Ja, wer he denn is.

Ja, seggt he, he is de riekste Koeni up de gänze Welt.

Ja, wo he dat mit bewiesen kann, fraag't se.

Ja, seggt he, he hett so 'n lütten linnen Büddel. Wenn he sik den' vull Geld wünschen deit, denn is he ümmer vull. Wat sien ool Vadder to em seggt hett, he schull dar keen Froonsperson wat vun apenbaren, dar denkt he nich an.

Ja, seggt de Prinzessin, denn schall he ähr den lütten Büddel doch mal wiesen.

He lang't sik in de Tasch un gifft ähr den lütten Büddel hen. Un se probert em je mal. Un so as se em vull wünscht, is he ümmer vull. Ja, seggt se, riek noog' is he je, dat sücht se je. Denn will se mal mit ähr'n Vadder snacken, wat de dar to seggt. He schall ähr den lütten Büddel man mal mitgäben, denn will se ähr'n Vadder den' mal wiesen. Süss kunn he ähr dat am Enn' nich tolöben [33].

Na, he is je so dumm un lett sik den Büddel afsnacken.

Dat dur't nich so lang', do kümmt dar Oller vun 'n Kaiser, he schall sien Dochter nich hebben. He schall maken, dat he vun sien Verbeet kümmt [34]. Süss lett he em mit de Polizei weg bringen.

Sien'n lütten Büddel kriggt he nich wedder. Den' is he loos. Nu mutt he je maken, dat he weg kümmt. Is man goot, denkt he, dat du dien Taschen vull Geld stäken hest! Wo schuss du süss wedder to Huus kamen hebben? [35]

He nimmt sik 'n Wagen un föhrt wa' [36] hen to Huus.

Nu grüvelt de dar je ümmerloos oever na, wo he dat angahn schall, dat he sien'n lütten Büddel wedder kriggt.

O, denkt he, du muss dien lütt Trumpett man nähmen. Denn reis's du wedder hen un kümms ähr mit Suldaten to Liev'. As he

2 nog'. 11 kamen, Sloss. 13 fröcht. 40 gruwelt.

wedder dar kümmt, in Marokko, un he steiht vör 'n Door, do kriggt he sien lütt Trumpett ut de Tasch un fangt an to blasen.

Do kaamt dar so vääl Suldaten up 'n Dutt, dat he 'n gänze Armee hett.

De Kaiser vun Marokko, de weet je gar nich, wat dar loos is, de schickt een'n vun sien Ministers hen un lett em fragen, wat dat to bedüden hett mit āll' de Suldaten, wat he will.

Ja, he will sien Dochter spräken.

Ja, dat kann he ok gern, lett de Kaiser em wedder seggen. He schall man hen kamen.

As he bi ähr kamen deit, do sücht se je hoch up [37], dat he dar wedder is. Un do fraag't se em, wo he bi āll' de Suldaten kümmt. Ja, seggt he, he hett so 'n lütte Trumpett. Wenn he dar up blasen deit, denn kaamt dar so vääl Suldaten up 'n Dutt, as he hebben will.

Wat sien ool Vadder to em seggt hett, dar denkt he wedder nich an. O, seggt se, denn schall he ähr de lütt Trumpett doch mal wiesen. Ne, seggt he, eerst schall se em sien'n lütten Büddel wedder gäben; ehr kriggt se de Trumpett nich to sehn.

Ja, seggt se, dien'n lütten Büddel schass du gern wedder hebben. Ik will ok gern dien Fro warrn, seggt se, wenn du mi noch hebben wullt. Ik wull dat al glieks; mien Vadder wull dat man nich hebben. Aver wenn ik em de Trumpett wiesen do, un ik vertell' em dat, dat du dar so vääl Suldaten mit up 'n Dutt blasen kanns, denn warrt he dar ok wul nix mehr gägen hebben. Giff mi de lütt Trumpett man mal mit. Denn bring' ik di den lütten Büddel naher ok wedder mit.

Na, he denkt je, se meent dat so, un lett sik wedder besnacken. Un gift ähr de Trumpett hen. Un se geiht dar je mit af.

Dat dur't nich so lang', do kümmt dar Oller, de Kaiser will em sien Dochter nich gäben. He schall maken, dat he vun sien Verbeet kümmt [34], oder he warrt mit de Polizei weg bröcht [38]. Nu mutt he je so wedder weg. Un sien Trumpett is he to [39] loos'. Un he hett man knapp mal so vääl Geld mehr, dat he wa' hen to Huus reisen kann.

Nu sinn't he dar je ümmerloos oever na, wo he sien'n lütten Büddel un sien Trumpett wedder her kriegen schall, un do denkt he an sien'n Gördel.

He binn't sik den Gördel üm un wünscht sik na de Prinzessin ähr Stuuv'. Un mit 'n Maal is he dar un steiht vör ähr.

Herr Je! seggt se, wat verfeers du een'n! Wo kümms du eenmal her?

Ja, seggt he, he hett 'n Gördel. Wenn he sik den' ümbinnen deit, denn kann he sik allerwägens hen wünschen, wo he will. Nu fiechelt se je wedder bi em rüm un snackt em allerhand vör. Ähr Vadder, seggt se, de hett dar nu gar nix mehr gägen, un se will foorts hen un

35 (her).

BB

em halen. Un denn will se em sien'n lütten Büddel un sien Trumpett ok wedder mitbringen. Aver denn schall he ähr den Gördel nu doch ok mal wiesen. Se will em blots mal proberen, wat se sik dar wul mit hen wünschen kann na ähr'n Vadder.

Na, he is je wedder so dumm un lööv't ähr dat to [33]. Un gifft ähr den Gördel hen. Un se binn't sik em üm un wünscht sik hen na ähr'n Vadder. Un weg is se. Dat dur't nich so lang', do kümmt dar Oller vun 'n Kaiser, he schall maken, dat he vun sien Verbeet kümmt [34], oder he warrt mit de Polizei weg bröcht.

Nu hett he aver gar keen Geld mehr hatt, un do mutt he je to Foot weg.

He hett 'n paar Stunnen gahn [35], do warrt he so hungeri.

Do denkt he bi sik sülben: Hädd's [40] du di doch man 'n Stück Broot in de Tasch stäken! Hier is je wiet un siet keen Huus to sehn, un Geld hest du ok je nich.

He geiht noch 'n Flach, do kümmt he in 'n groot Holt.

Do steiht dar 'n Fiegenboom in 't Holt mit rech so 'n schöne Fiegen [41].

Süh, denkt he, de kaamt di goot to pass. Dar schass di todägen satt an äten.

He plückt sik weck vun de Fiegen af un geiht dar bi to äten: do fang't mit eenmal sien Nääs' an to wassen. Un wasst ümmerloos, bet se wul 'n Ääl' lang is.

Och, du lever Gott [42], denkt he, wo geiht di dat eenmal! [43] Dien'n lütten Büddel büss du los', dien Trumpett un dien'n Gördel büss du loos, un nu is dien Gesich ok noch to schänn't! He weet je gar nich, wat he upstellen schall: he geiht hen sitten un weent.

As he 'n Tietlang säten hett, do warrt he so dösti.

He steiht wedder up un will je mal sehn, wat dar nich war [44] 'n bäten Water to finnen is.

Do warrt he 'n lütten Bääk wahr, de löppt na so 'n depe Waterkuul rin.

He will sik mit de Hand 'n bäten Water utfüllen ut den Bääk, aver dat will nich rech gahn: de lange Nääs' is em ümmer in'n Weg.

O, denkt he, denn geihs du hen na de Kuul un leggs di dar an de Kant up 'n Buuk, un denn drinks du in 'n Liggen. Se is je so deep, de Kuul, an de Grund kümms du je nich mit de Nääs' [45].

As he de Nääs' in 't Water hett, mit 'n Maal krüppt de wedder in Dutt, un is nich länger, as se vörher wään is. Nu weet he je Bescheed, wat dat mit de Fiegen un mit dat Water up sik hett, un do denkt he: Töf! Du schass ähr dat wa' trüch betahlen! Hett dat Froonsminsch d i anföhrt: nu schass ähr wedder anföhrn!

2 (doch). 21 wilk. 26 (ok noch). 32 herin. 34 in Wegen. 38 krüppt se. 41 Nu schass.

He plückt sik āll' sien Taschen vull Fiegen un geiht wa' trüch na de Stadt. Dar kehrt he in 'n Weertshuus in. Un do lett he 'n Juden kamen, de mutt em 'n Gaarnerantog un 'n swarten Dokterantog besorgen. Sien'n Prinzenantog — dar is je allerhand Gold un Kraam an wään — den' lett he den Juden so lang' to Pand. Un do treckt he sik an as Gaarner un geiht mit sien Fiegen — de hett he in n' Kiep hatt — dar geiht he vör 'n Slot mit up un dal un röppt: Fröhtiedig Fiegen! Wer [46] will fröhtiedig Fiegen köpen? Den Kaiser sien Dochter, de steiht graad' vör 't Finster un kickt ut: de hört dat. Un do schickt se 'n Bedeenten dal, de schall ähr de fröhtiedigen Fiegen köpen.

As de Bedeenter ähr de Fiegen rup bringt: O, seggt se, wat sünd dat eenmal vör schöne Fiegen!

Se itt dar 'n paar vun up: do fangt ähr de Nääs' an to wassen, un wasst ümmerloos, un warrt 'n Ääl' lang.

Och, du lever Gott! Nu is Holland je in Noot.

Nu warrt je āll' de Dokters un Professers anseggt, de schüllt ähr de Nääs' je weg kureren.

Ja, seggt de een, he weet anners keen'n Raat, as de Nääs' mutt afsnäden warrn.

O bewahr 'n! Dar will s' je nix vun wäten.

Se is je bang' wään vör de Wehdaag'.

Ja, seggt se, denn moet se je wat anners proberen.

Nu verschriev't se ähr toeerst wa' Sālv, dar schall se de Nääs' dreemal an'n Dag mit inwrieben.

Na, dat deit se je. Un se hett de Nääs' āll so blank schür't toletz, dat se sik dar in speigeln kann. Aver helpen deit dat nix.

Do backt se ähr 'n Plaster up de Nääs', dat schall de Nääs' bet in Dutt trecken. Aver de Nääs' blifft so lang, as se is. Do versöokt se dat mit kole Ümslääg'. Un as dat ok nich helpt, do versöokt se dat mit warme. Un so doktert se ümmerloos bi de Nääs' rüm. Un de Nääs' warrt toletz al so füürrot utsehn, as wenn se de Roos' dar in hett [47].

Wiltdes geiht de Koenissoehn wedder na dat Holt hen un haalt sik 'n Buddel vull vun dat Water, wo he sien lange Nääs' mit los worrn is. Un do treckt he sien'n Dokterantog an un maakt sik bekannt as Näsendokter.

Dat snackt sik je bald herüm, un do mutt he je foorts hen na 'n Slot kamen.

As he dar kamen deit, ja, seggt he, dat 's man al 'n bäten lang' her. Weg to kriegen is se wul, de Nääs', aver dat dur't nu 'n bäten länger. He kann dar nich ehr bi anfangen, se mutt eers mal 'n

2 Wertshus an. 7 -tidi. 10 Bedenter, hendal. 24 'n Salw. 25 dreemal dag's. 27 spegeln. 29 versökt. 31 herüm. 32 für'nrot. 37 als. 42 (mal).

Hungerkur dörmaken, de Prinzessin. Ja, dat will s' ok je gern, wenn he ähr blots vun de lange Nääs' wedder abhelpen kann.

Nu lett he ähr je eers mal 'n Tietlang todägen hungern. Se dörf keen Spier äten, seggt he, un dörf nix drinken as Water. Na, se hoolt dat 'n ach Daag' [48] ut. Se ward dar aver so leeg' bi, dat se sik gar nich mehr ähnlich sücht.

Toletz, do dur't em dat je [49], un do seggt he to ähr, so, nu kann se wedder wat äten. Un denn wüllt se nu ok bi de Nääs' anfangen. Annern Morgen bringt he ähr in 'n lütt Glas 'n bäten vun dat Water, wat he sik ut den Bääk haalt hett, un dar wischt he ähr 'n paar Drüppen vun up de Nääs'. Do warrt ähr dat so trecken [50] in de Nääs', un de Nääs' löppt 'n bäten in, warrt 'n bäten kötter.

O, seggt se, dat helpt.

Annern Morgen wischt he ähr wedder 'n paar Drüppen up de Nääs', un so alle Morgen. Un as se na 'n Achtdagstiet mal namäten doot, do is de Nääs' āl 'n vittel Ääl kötter worrn.

O, seggt se, nu hett dat je al arig holpen.

Ja, seggt he, wenn se nu noch 'n veerteihn Daag' [48] so biblifft, denn is de Nääs' gänz wedder in Dutt krapen.

Do is se je so vergnöög't un seggt to em, he schall sik wat wünschen, un wenn he sik ok 'n groten Büddel vull Goldstücken wünscht.

Ne, seggt he, dat verlangt he gar nich. Se schall em blots āll' ähr gollen Ring' mal wiesen un all' ähr gollen Armbänner un Hālskäden. Dar hett he so vääl vun seggen höört, seggt he.

Ja, de will s' em je gern mal wiesen.

Se slütt ähr Kommood' apen un treckt de Schuufen ut. Un he maakt dar je 'n Helphool vun, wat dat eenmal vör schöne Ring' un Käden sünd. So wat schööns, seggt he, hett he sien Daag' noch nich sehn. As se dat neddelste Schuuf ok uttreckt, do liggt sien lütt Büddel dar in un sien Trumpett un sien Gördel.

Eeen tween dree grapst he sik de dree Deel ut dat Schuuf herut.

Süh so, mien Deern, seggt he, nu nähm ik dat mienige wedder an mi. De Nääs' will ik di laten: de kanns du to 'n Andenken beholen. Un weg is he, as wenn em de Wind weg weiht hett. Un se steiht dar je mit ähr Nääs' un kickt achter em an.

Do hett se ähr lange Nääs' je beholen. Un wenn dar keen kamen is, de ähr de Nääs' weg doktert hett, denn kann se dar moegli noch mit rüm lopen [51].

5 hölt. 6 ähnli. 11 Drüpp. 12 körter. 17 ari. 29 neddels, (ok). 32 dat mini.

NOTES

(See the remarks to the *Notes* on p. 80)

[1] *Wilhelm Wisser*, born 27 August 1843 near Eutin, died 15 October 1935 in Oldenburg, Holstein, having spent his whole life in Eutin and in Oldenburg in eastern Holstein as a grammar-school teacher, devoting himself to the task of collecting the legends and fairy-tales of his homeland. In his *Auf der Märchensuche*, 1926, he expounded his method. He noted down the fairy-tales as he heard them and then edited them in the true style of the LG story-tellers and their language. His most important publications are: *Wat Grotmoder vertellt. Ostholsteinische Volksmärchen*, 3 vols., Leipzig, 1904; *Plattdeutsche Volksmärchen. Ausgabe für Erwachsene*, 2 vols., Jena, 1914–27 (with an appendix on orthography); *De Wunschsteen un anner Märchen*, Oldenburg, 1933. The fairy-tales have been frequently re-published. The latest edition of *Wat Grotmoder vertellt* appeared in 1954–6 in four slender booklets at the Franz Westphal Verlag, Wolfshagen-Scharbeutz. Our specimen text is in vol. i, pp. 46–55.—See also K. Schulte Kemminghausen, *Das niederdeutsche Volksmärchen*, pp. 102–8, in *Niederdeutsch*, ed. by R. Mehlem and W. Seedorf, Hanover, 1957. O. Mensing, 'Wisser und das Plattdeutsche', *Mitt. a. d. Qu.*, xxix, 1935, 2 ff.

Fairy-tales were also collected by G. F. Meyer: *Dumm' Hans, Plattdütsch Volksmärchen*, 1921; *Broder Lustig un anner plattdütsch Volksmärchen*, 1925, 2nd ed., 1929; *Plattdeutsche Volksmärchen und Schwänke*, 1925; *De golln Vagel, Holsteensch Volksmärchen*, 1925; *Wunnern un Wünschen, Plattdeutsche Volksmärchen, Mittelschleswigsche Volksmärchen*, 1934. For further reading, see the LG readers mentioned in the Bibliography, p. 384, and the list of publications of the *Fehrs-Gilde* and the *Bookkring*, Hamburg-Wellingsbüttel, Waldingstr. 39.

[2] Wisser has *wess*. For the *wess/wē(s)en* isogloss, see Foerste, *DPhA*, p. 2027.

[3] Repetition of the subject (*he . . . de Soehn*) is characteristic of popular speech.

[4] The spelling *-dd-* indicates the very slight dental stop which often tends to be a kind of an *r*-like flap. See § 14.4 (ii).

[5] Wisser has endingless adjectives, e.g. *riks*, also *de lang' Nes', de ganz Welt*; see § 22.

[6] Demonstrative adverbs (*dar*) and prepositions (*vör*) which form a compound in NHG (*dafür*) are generally kept separate in LG, cf. Note (2) p. 334.

[7] Wisser has *ne* for *nich* throughout.

B B *

[8] The use of the auxiliary *doon* is frequent, especially in subordinate clauses.

[9] For 'to die' NS uses often *doot blieben*. On the future tense, see § 37.

[10] In NS the dem. pron. *dat* has taken the place of the pers. pron. 'it', see § 25.

[11] The repetition of the prep. is characteristic of popular style.

[12] 'To find out', cf. NHG *klug werden*.

[13] *Ok* and *je* are ubiquitous filling particles of little meaning.

[14] *Bi* has also the meaning of 'to', especially as an adv. with verbs of motion, cf. NHG *hin*.

[15] For the isogloss *ümmer/jümmer*, see Foerste, *DPhA*, p. 2026. Informant has *ümmer* although one would expect *jümmer*.

[16] 'Then you have nothing at all left.'

[17] See § 25. Wisser uses *ähr* for the 3rd pers. pl. obj. case. Cf. the map in Foerste, *DPhA*, p. 2034.

[18] Informant has *se hebbt so lang' graav't hatt*.

[19] 'That is not possible.'

[20] *Slösser, Sloss* are NHG loans. Informant says *Smett* and *Slott*.

[21] Informant has *hatt hest*.

[22] 'What had he in mind?'

[23] Informant has *wenn*.

[24] Informant has *späält hest*.

[25] See § 34.2. Informant has *hett doch seggt*.

[26] *Wat* is generally used for introducing indirect questions, where NHG has *ob*. It is often also used in relative clauses for *dat* and has altogether a wider function than *was* in NHG (see also Note (3)). See Käthe Scheel, *Untersuchungen über den Satzbau der niederdeutschen Volkssprache und Kunstprosa*, Hamburg, 1939, pp. 94–6.

[27] Informant has *wo he man hen will*.

[28] This is the common objective case of the masc. pers. pron. No distinction is made between direct and indirect object, see § 25.

[29] NHG loan-word.

[30] 'He became tired of it'; cf. NHG *überdrüssig*.

[31] *Wo* in a relative clause is possible also when the subject is a person, not only when it is a thing.

[32] Note the mood in these indirect questions. NS lacks a subjunctive.

[33] *Glöben*, or the older form *löben* 'believe', takes the form *tolöben* in the presence of an indirect object. Informant has *gar nich mal tolöben*.

[34] Informant has *rünner kümmt*.

[35] On the use of *hebben* with verbs of motion, see § 37. Informant omits *hebben* and says *na Huus hen kamen*.

[36] The indef. pron. *wat* is often used to make the statement less definite; cf. the use of *like* in substandard English.

[37] 'She sees from high up [in the castle].'

[38] Informant has *he lett em mit de Polizei weg bringen.*

[39] *To* as an adv. 'also'; cf. NHG *dazu.*

[40] Note that the ordinary pret. is used where NHG would have the pret. sub. (conditional).

[41] Informant has *mit son recht schöne Fiegen.*

[42] This exclamation is borrowed from NHG. See § 22.

[43] 'What is happening to you?'

[44] Informant has *enn Stääd* 'anywhere'.

[45] Informant has . . . *kümmt de Nääs' ja wul nich.*

[46] Informant has *keen* for *wer*. An informant from Stade had *keen* for *wer* everywhere.

[47] Informant has *as wenn de Roos'* (erysipelas) *dar in is.*

[48] *N ach Daag'* is a week, *n veerteihn Daag'* a fortnight.

[49] 'He feels sorry.'

[50] 'She has a feeling that her nose is contracting.'

[51] Informant has *moeglicherwies vondaag'* ('to-day') *noch mit rüm lopen.*

GLOSSARY

See the introductory remarks to the *Glossary* on p. 84; and for further information W. Jungandreas, *Niedersächsisches Wörterbuch*; O. Mensing, *Schleswig-Holsteinisches Wörterbuch*; Käthe Scheel, *Hamburgisches Wörterbuch*; J. Sass, *Kleines plattdeutsches Wörterbuch*.

achter, behind.
afsnacken, wv. talk sb. into giving sth.
al, already.
allens, all (abs.).
allerwägens, everywhere.
anföhrn, wv. trick, cheat.
angahn, § 38.2, tackle.
ankieken, sv. § 33, I, look at, follow with one's eyes.
anners, otherwise.
anseggen, wv. ask, consult.
ari, bad, very.

Bääk, m. f. E. brook.
baben, above.
backen, wv. stick, fasten.
Bärg, mountain, a lot of.
bäten, *n-*, a bit, a little.
besnacken, wv. persuade.
bet, until.
biblieben, sv. § 33, I, persist.
blots, only.
Buddel, m.G. bottle.

dal, down.
dar, there.
Deel, A. or E. part, piece.
Deern, G. girl.
dösti, thirsty.
drapen or *dräpen*, sv. § 33, IV, hit, strike.
dröög', dry.
Drupp, D. drop.
Dutt, m. D. heap, mass.
  up n D. or *in D.*, together.

Eer, earth.
eers(t), first, before.
eerstan, at first.
Enn', E. end.
Escher, m. G. spade.

fiecheln, wv. stroke, flatter.
Flach, n. D. plain, stretch.
foorts, at once.
fröhtiedig, early.
Froonsperson, f. woman.

Gaarnerantog, gardener's clothes.
glieks, at once.
Gördel, G. belt.
grapsen, wv. grab.
grüveln, wv. brood.
günt, yonder.

halen, wv. fetch.
Help'hool, yelling, to-do.
hendal, down.

je, yes, indeed.

Kassen, G. chest.
kieken, sv. § 33, I, look.
Kiep, f. E. skep.
köpen, wv. § 34.2, buy.
kriegen, sv. § 33, I, get, take.
krupen, sv. § 33, II, creep, shrink.
Kuul, f. E. ditch.

leeg', bad.
liekes, all the same, nevertheless.
liekut, straight.
lütt, small.

man, only, but.

Nääs', E. nose.
na-mäten, sv. § 33, V, measure.
neddelst, lowest.
noog, enough.
nüms, nobody.

Oller, f. order, command.
Ool, de Oole, the old man.

380

pass, to p. kamen, suit.

schüllig, guilty.
Schuuf, f. E. drawer.
sluten, sv. § 33, II, shut.
smieten, sv. § 33, I, throw.
snacken, wv. talk.
Spier, en S., a little.
süh > sehn, sv. § 33, see.
sülben, self.
süss, otherwise.

todägen, capable, robust.
  t. äten, tuck in; (adv.) much.
toschännt, disfigured.
toschüffeln, wv. fill up.
tosehn, sv. see.
töven, wv. wait.
trecken, sv. § 33, pull, move.
trüch, back, backwards.
Trumpett, f. E. trumpet.

ümmer, always.

ümmerloos, continuously.
ünner, under.
Ünnerscheed, m. E. difference.
  Ü. lehren, get to know other
    circumstances.
upholen, sv. § 33, stop.
upstellen, wv. begin, do.

Verbeet, n. territory, area.
verfeeren, wv. startle, frighten.
vertellen, wv. tell.
Viddel, quarter.

war, anywhere.
weck, some, several.
wedder, again.
Wehdaag', pl. pain.
weihen, wv. blow.
wiesen, wv. show.
wiet un siet, far and wide.
wiltdes, in the meantime.
wo, how.
wodennig, how.
wrieben, sv. § 33, I, rub.

SELECT BIBLIOGRAPHY

This is a selective list including only books which are repeatedly quoted and such recent works which are most helpful in the fields concerned. As most of these contain bibliographies only a few older works are given here. Items which are quoted in connection with a specific point are cited in full at their first occurrence in footnotes and are not repeated in this list.

CHAPTER I

1 *Bach:* Adolf Bach, *Deutsche Mundartforschung. Ihre Wege, Ergebnisse und Aufgaben,* 2nd ed., Heidelberg, 1950.

2 Anneliese Bretschneider, *Deutsche Mundartenkunde,* Marburg, 1934.

3 Gerhard Cordes, 'Niederdeutsche Mundartdichtung' in *DPhA,* ii, 1954, 313–52.

4 *DSA: Deutscher Sprachatlas auf Grund des von Georg Wenker begründeten Sprachatlas des Deutschen Reichs in vereinfachter Form* begonnen von Ferdinand Wrede, fortgesetzt von Walther Mitzka und Bernhard Martin, Marburg, 1926–56.

5 *Henzen:* Walter Henzen, *Schriftsprache und Mundarten. Ein Überblick über ihr Verhältnis und ihre Zwischenstufen im Deutschen,* 2nd ed., Berne, 1954.

6 A. Hübner, *Die Mundart der Heimat,* Breslau, 1925.

7 B. Martin, *Die deutschen Mundarten,* 2nd ed., Marburg, 1959.

8 *id.,* 'Die hochdeutsche Mundartdichtung' in *DPhA,* ii, 1954, 259–312.

9 *Mitzka, Maa.:* Walther Mitzka, *Deutsche Mundarten,* Heidelberg, 1943.

10 *Mitzka, DPhA: id.,* 'Hochdeutsche Mundarten' in *DPhA,* i, 1952, 655–784.

11 *Mitzka, Hdb., id., Handbuch zum Deutschen Sprachatlas,* Marburg, 1952.

12 *Mitzka, Wortatlas: id., Deutscher Wortatlas,* i–ix (in progress), Giessen, 1951 ff.

13 H. Reis, *Die deutschen Mundarten* (Göschen), 2nd ed., Leipzig, 1920.

14 F. Schön, *Geschichte der deutschen Mundartdichtung,* 4 vols., 1920–38.

15 *Schwarz:* Ernst Schwarz, *Die deutschen Mundarten,* Göttingen, 1950.

16 F. Stroh, *Probleme neuerer Mundartforschung, Giessener Beiträge,* xxiv, 1928.

17 *Wagner, Sprachlandschaften:* Kurt Wagner, *Deutsche Sprachlandschaften, DDG,* xxiii, Marburg, 1927.

18 Otto Weise, *Unsere Mundarten, ihr Werden und Wesen,* 2nd ed., Berlin, 1919.

19 V. M. Zhirmunskii, *Nemetskaja dialektologija,* Moscow, 1956.

383

Dialect Readers:

20   K. Bacher, *Oberdeutsche Mundartdichtung*, Vienna, 1925.

21   O. Dähnhart, *Heimatklänge aus deutschen Gauen*, 3 vols., Leipzig, 1901 f.

22   K. Ernst, *Proben deutscher Mundarten*, Leipzig, 1915.

23   J. M. Firmenich, *Germaniens Völkerstimmen*, 3 vols., Berlin, 1843–66.

24   A. Götze, *Proben hoch- und niederdeutscher Mundarten*, Bonn, 1922 (in phonetic script).

25   W. Kahl, *Deutsche mundartliche Dichtungen*, Leipzig, 1901.

26   *Lautbibliothek der deutschen Mundarten*, ed. Deutsches Spracharchiv, Heft I ff., Göttingen, 1958 ff. (phonetic and phonemic transcriptions and tape-recordings).

27   C. Regenhardt, *Die deutschen Mundarten. Auserlesenes aus den Werken der besten Dichter alter und neuer Zeit*, 3 vols., Berlin, 1895–97.

28   J. Schaeffler, *Das Mundartenbuch*, Berlin, Bonn, 1926.

29   H. Teuchert, *Niederdeutsche Mundarten. Texte aus alter und neuer Zeit*, Leipzig, 1934.

30   C. Borchling and H. Quisdorf, *Tausend Jahre Plattdeutsch*, 2 vols., Hamburg, 1927–9.

31   *De Eikboom. Eine Auswahl niederdeutscher Dichtungen*, ed. W. Baetke and E. Walter, Halle, 1953.

32   *Niederdeutsches Balladenbuch*, ed. Janssen and Schräpel, Munich, 1925.

33   *Hausbuch niederdeutscher Lyrik*, ed. Janssen and Schräpel, Munich, 1926.

For regional readers see: SGm.: items 40, 44 below; p. 22, fn. 4; p. 27; p. 81, Note (1); p. 111, Note (1); Als.: p. 117, fn. 3; Austrian: p. 243, Note (1); Lux.: p. 22, fn. 1; p. 28; Westphal.: p. 301, fn. 2; p. 334, Note (1); NS: p. 377, Note (1) and item 128 below.

CHAPTER II

34 Dictionary: *Schweizerisches Idiotikon, Wörterbuch der schweizerdeutschen Sprache*, begründet von F. Staub and L. Tobler, Frauenfeld, 1881 ff.

35 *Baur:* Arthur Baur, *Praktische Sprachlehre des Schweizerdeutschen*, 2nd ed., Zürich, 1941.

36 *Bohnenberger, Alem. Ma.:* Karl Bohnenberger, *Die alemannische Mundart. Umgrenzung, Innengliederung und Kennzeichnung*, Tübingen, 1953.

37   Otto von Greyerz, *Die Mundartdichtung der deutschen Schweiz*, Leipzig, 1924.

37a   Rudolf Joho, *Neuer dramatischer Wegweiser. Schweizer Bühnenwerke* 1: *Volkstheater*, Zürich, 1953.

38 *Jutz, Alem. Maa.:* Leo Jutz, *Die alemannischen Mundarten. Abriss der Lautverhältnisse*, Halle, 1931.

39 *Maurer, Oberrheiner etc.:* F. Maurer and others, *Oberrheiner, Schwaben, Südalemannen,* Strasbourg, 1942.

40   Gotthold O. Schmid, *Wägwyser dür ds Schwyzerdütsch* (Epik und Lyrik), 3rd ed., Fribourg, 1954.

41   Samuel Singer, *Schweizerdeutsch,* Frauenfeld, 1928.

42 *Stalder:* F. J. Stalder, *Die Landessprachen der Schweiz oder Schweizerische Dialektologie,* Aarau, 1819.

43   Karl Stucki, *Schweizerdeutsch. Abriss einer Grammatik mit Laut- und Formenlehre,* Zürich, 1921.

44   O. Sutermeister, *Sammlung deutschschweizerischer Mundart-Literatur,* Zürich, 1882.

44a   Regula Waser, *Bibliographie selbständiger Publikationen in zürichdeutscher Mundart 1798–1954,* Zürich, 1955.

45 *Weber, BSG:* Albert Weber, *Die Mundart des Zürcher Oberlandes, BSG,* xv, 1923.

46 *Weber, ZGr.: id.,* *Zürichdeutsche Grammatik und Wegweiser zur guten Mundart,* Zürich, 1948.

CHAPTER III

47 *Baumgartner:* Heinrich Baumgartner,´ *Stadtmundart. Stadt- und Landmundart,* Berne, 1940.

48   *id., Die Mundarten des Berner Seelandes, BSG,* xiv, 1922.

49   Hedwig Haldimann, 'Der Vokalismus der Mundart von Goldbach', *ZfhdMaa.,* iv, 1903, 295–351; v, 1904, 225–44.

50   W. Henzen, *Die deutsche Freiburger Mundart, BSG,* xvi, 1927.
See also Chapter II above.

CHAPTER IV

51 Dictionary: E. Martin and H. Lienhart, *Wörterbuch der elsässischen Mundarten,* 2 vols., Strasbourg, 1899–1907.

52   H. Heimburger, 'Grammatische Darstellung der Mundart des Dorfes Ottenheim', *Beitr.,* xiii, 1888, 211–47.

53   V. Henry, *Le dialect Alaman de Colmar en 1870,* Paris, 1900.

54   P. Lévy, *Plaudereien über elsässische Sprache und Literatur,* Strasbourg, 1932.

55 *Lienhart:* H. Lienhart, *Laut- und Flexionslehre der Mundart des mittleren Zorntales im Elsass,* Strasbourg, 1891.

56   W. Mankel, *Laut- und Flexionslehre der Mundart des Münstertals im Elsass,* Strasbourg, 1886.

57   E. Martin, 'Sprachverhältnisse und Mundarten im deutschen Sprachgebiet von Elsass-Lothringen' in *Das Reichsland Elsass-Lothringen. I Landesbeschreibung,* 1898–1901, 91–7.

58   O. Stoeckicht, *Elsässische Dialektgeographie,* Bamberg, 1927.

59   *id., Sprache, Landschaft und Geschichte des Elsass, DDG,* xlii, Marburg, 1942.

60   A. Sütterlin, *Laut- und Flexionslehre der Strassburger Mundart in Arnolds 'Pfingstmontag'*, Strasbourg, 1892.
See also 36, 38, 39 above.

CHAPTER V

61 Dictionary: J. S. Dang, *Darmstädter Wörterbuch*, 2nd ed., Darmstadt, 1953.

62 *Born:* E. Born, *Die Mundart in Darmstadt und in seinem Umland*, Fränkische Forschungen, xii, Erlangen, 1938.

63   K. Bräutigam, *Die Mannheimer Mundart*, Heidelberg, 1934.

64   P. Freiling, 'Über die Mundart rund um Frankfurt', in *Rund um Frankfurt*, ed. H. Bingemer, W. Fronemann, R. Welcker, Frankfurt, 1924, 178–210.

65 *Grund:* H. Grund, *Die Mundart von Pfungstadt und ihre sprachliche Schichtung*, Heidelberg, 1935.

66   W. Haster, *Rheinfränkische Studien: Der Konsonantismus in Rheinhessen und der Pfalz*, Darmstadt, 1908.

67   Anni Pfeifer, *Beiträge zur Laut- und Formenlehre der Mainzer Mundart*, Giessener Beiträge, xix, 1927.

68   H. L. Rauh, *Die Frankfurter Mundart in ihren Grundzügen dargestellt*, Frankfurt, 1921.

69   H. Reis, *Die Mundarten des Grossherzogtums Hessen*, Halle, 1910. Also: *ZfdMaa.*, 1908, 302 ff.; 1909, 97 ff., 193 ff., 289 ff.

70   W. Seibt, 'Der hessen-darmstädtische Sprachraum', *Volk und Scholle*, xi, 1933, 50–55.
See also the dialect-geographical studies quoted p. 162, fn. 3.

CHAPTER VI

71 Dictionary: J. A. Schmeller, *Bayerisches Wörterbuch*, 2nd ed., 4 parts, Munich, 1872–7.

72   H. Grau, *Mundart und Kultur im Eisenland*, Linz, 1942.

73   *id.*, *Die mundartlichen Sprachräume Oberdonaus*, typescript diss., Vienna, 1939.

74   A. Haasbauer, 'Die oberösterreichischen Mundarten', *Teuth.*, i, 1924–25, 81–107.

75   M. Hornung, F. Roitinger, *Unsere Mundarten, Eine dialektkundliche Wanderung durch Oesterreich*, Vienna, 1950.

76 *Kranzmayer, Lautgeogr.:* Eberhard Kranzmayer, *Historische Lautgeographie des gesamtbairischen Dialektraumes*, Vienna, 1956.

77   J. Lachner, *999 Worte Bayrisch*, Munich, 1955.

78   Franz Roitinger, *Die Mundart von Weibern in Oberösterreich*, typescript diss., Vienna, 1933.

79   G. Weitzenböck, *Die Mundart des Innviertels besonders von Mühlheim*, Halle, 1942 (*ZfMaf. Beiheft*, 17).

CHAPTER VII

80 Dictionaries: *Wörterbuch der luxemburgischen Mundart*, 1906.

81   *Luxemburger Wörterbuch*, 1950 ff.

82 *Bertrang:* Alfred Bertrang, *Grammatik der Areler Mundart*, Brussels, 1921.

83 *Bruch, Grundl.:* Robert Bruch, *Grundlegung einer Geschichte des Luxemburgischen*, Luxemburg, 1953.

84 *Bruch, Lux.: id.*, *Das Luxemburgische im westfränkischen Kreis* (= Part iii, vol. ii of *Grundl.*), Luxemburg, 1954.

85 *Bruch, Grammaire: id.*, 'Précis populaire de grammaire Luxembourgeoise', *Bull. ling. et éth.*, iv–vi, 1955.

86 R. Engelmann, *Vokalismus der Viandener Mundart*, Diekirch, 1910.

87 J. Hess, *Die Sprache der Luxemburger*, Luxemburg, 1946.

88 L. Koenig, *Auf dem Wege zu einer Grammatik der luxemburgischen Mundart*, Luxemburg, 1928.

89 *Palgen, Studien:* Hélène Palgen, *Studien zur Lautgeographie Luxemburgs*, Luxemburg, 1948.

90 *id.*, *Kurze Lautlehre der Mundart von Echternach*, Luxemburg, 1931.

91 *id.*, 'Untersuchungen zur Grammatik der Echternacher Mundart', *Lux. Jb.*, 1931–32, 14–31.

92 *id.*, 'Vokalismus der Mundart von Knaphoscheid', *Lux. Jb.*, 1933, 3–18.

93 Nik. Welter, *Mundartliche und hochdeutsche Dichtung in Luxemburg*, Luxemburg, 1929.

94 *id.*, *Das Luxemburgische und sein Schrifttum*, latest ed., 1947.

CHAPTER VIII

95 Dictionary: F. Woeste, *Wörterbuch der westfälischen Mundarten*, Norden and Leipzig, 1882, 2nd ed., by E. Nörrenberg, 1930.

96 H. Büld, *Volk und Sprache im nördlichen Westfalen*, Münster, 1939.

97 *Foerste, DPhA:* William Foerste, 'Geschichte der niederdeutschen Mundarten', *DPhA*, ii, 1905–2062 (Neuniederdeutsch, 1970–2062).

98 H. Grimme, *Niederdeutsche Mundarten*, 2nd ed., T. Baader, Göschen, Berlin, 1922.

99 F. Herdemann, *Versuch einer Lautlehre der Westmünsterländischen Mundart*, Münster, 1921.

100 B. Holtmann, *Deutsche Mundarten. Mundart des Dorfes Ostbevern, Westfalen* (Institut f. Lautforschung, Lautbibliothek 41), Berlin, 1939.

101 J. Kaumann, *Entwurf einer Laut- und Flexionslehre der Münsterischen Mundart*, Münster, 1884.

102 Ch. Sarauw, *Vergleichende Lautlehre der niederdeutschen Mundarten im Stammlande*, Niederdeutsche Forschungen I, Copenhagen, 1921.

103 H. Wix, *Studien zur westfälischen Dialektgeographie im Süden des Teutoburgerwaldes*, DDG, ix, Marburg, 1921.

See also fn., pp. 299, 300, 302.

CHAPTER IX

104 Dictionaries: W. Jungandreas, *Niedersächsisches Wörterbuch*, Neu-
     münster, 1953 ff.

105 O. Mensing, *Schleswig-Holsteinisches Wörterbuch*, 5 vols., Neu-
     münster, 1927–35.

106 Käthe Scheel, *Hamburgisches Wörterbuch*, Neumünster,
     1956 ff.

107 Joh. Sass, *Kleines plattdeutsches Wörterbuch*, Hamburg, 1957.

108 J. Bernhardt, 'Lautstand der Glückstädter Mundart', *NdJb.*,
     xviii, 81–105; xx, 1–40.

109 Heinrich Bollmann, *Mundarten auf der Stader Geest*, Oldenburg,
     1942.

110 Paul Bröcker, *Kleine Wort- und Formkunde des Plattdeutschen.
     Ein Lehr- und Lernbüchlein*, Hamburg, 1938.

111 Rudolf Eckhart, *Handbuch zur Geschichte der plattdeutschen
     Literatur*, Bremen, 1911.

112 Otto Furcht, *Die Mundart des Alten Landes bei Hamburg*,
     Stade, 1934.

113 H. Heigener, *Niederdeutsche Mundarten im Kreise des Herzog-
     tums Lauenburg*, Hamburg, 1937.

114 Margarete Horn, *Die Mundarten im holsteinischen Niederel-
     beraum*, typescript diss., Göttingen, 1955.

115 Peter Jørgensen, *Die dithmarsische Mundart von Klaus Groths
     Quickborn*, Copenhagen, 1934.

116 *id.*, 'Formenlehre der dithmarsischen Mundart', *Teuth.*, v, 1928,
     2–38.

117 Gesinus Kloeke, *Der Vokalismus der Mundart von Finkenwärder
     bei Hamburg*, Hamburg, 1913.

118 Hugo Larsson, *Lautstand der Mundart der Gemeinde Alten-
     gamme in den Vierlanden bei Hamburg*, Hamburg, 1917.

119 Gustav F. Meyer, *Unsere plattdeutsche Muttersprache*, Kiel,
     1921.

120 Walther Niekerken, *Das Feld und seine Bestellung im Nieder-
     deutschen, Sprache und Volkstum*, v, Hamburg, 1935.

121 *id.*, *Die Sprache des werktätigen Volkes im niederdeutschen Raum*,
     Hamburg, 1948.

122 W. Pessler, *Plattdeutscher Wortatlas für Nordwestdeutschland*,
     Hanover, 1928.

123 H. Quisdorf and J. Sass, *Hilfsbuch für den Unterricht im Platt-
     deutschen*, Hamburg, 1937.

124 Th. H. F. Rabeler, 'Niederdeutscher Lautstand im Kreise
     Bleckede', *ZfdPh.*, xliii, 1911, 141–202, 320–77.

125 W. Seelmann, 'Die plattdeutsche Literatur des 19. und 20.
     Jahrhunderts', *NdJb.*, xli, i, 1915.

126 R. Stammerjohann, 'Die Mundart von Burg in Dithmarschen
     mit besonderer Berücksichtigung der Quantitätsverhältnisse',
     ZfdMaa., 1914, 54 ff.

127 *Zwischen Elbe, Seeve und Este. Ein Heimatbuch des Landkreises*

Harburg. Ed. Heinrich Laue and Heinrich Meyer, 2 vols., Harburg, 1925.

128 *Festschrift Boeck:* G. Hoffmann, G. Jürgensen (ed.), *Hart, warr nich mööd. Festschrift für Christian Boeck,* Hamburg-Wellings-büttel, 1960.

See also 97, 98, 102 above.

INDEX

Abstract nouns, 83
accusative, 60, 122, 138, 180, 182, 271, 319
adjectives, 58–9, 98, 138, 180, 221–222, 224, 271, 318, 342, 358–9
 comparison of, 59, 139, 180, 222, 272, 318, 359
 substantivized, 272
affricates, 45, 47, 49, 51, 131, 133, 214, 216, 267, 356
agglutination, 58, 98, 138, 140, 179, 181, 221, 271
allophone, 36 fn. 3, 38, 47–8, 53, 95, 124, 133, 135, 170, 172, 207, 214, 254–5, 257, 264, 311–12, 344, 348–9, 351–2
alphabetical writing, 17–18
Alsace, 30–1
Alsatian theatre, 117–18
an-, prefix, 52, 169
analogy, analogical, 34, 41, 54, 56, 59, 100–1, 138, 178, 185, 227, 294, 308, 349
Anglo-Frisian, 52
apocope (of -e), 43–4, 213, 316, 319, 341 (see also -e, final)
archaic, 32, 34–5, 121–2, 197, 228, 244
argot, 6
article, definite, 57–8, 61–2, 81, 97, 137, 140, 179, 217, 220, 224, 270, 317–18, 342, 358, 360
article, indefinite, 57, 59, 97, 138, 141, 179, 182, 221–2, 271, 274, 317, 358
aspirates, 131, 172
aspiration, 49, 50, 54, 121, 175, 311, 352
assimilation, 46–7, 49, 50 fn. 1, 53–4, 57, 64, 134–5, 143–4, 164, 176, 205, 216–18, 227, 253, 267–9, 275, 304, 314, 317, 321–3, 336, 342, 355, 360
Association phonétique internationale, 19
Auslautsverhärtung, see hardening in final position

Baden, 118–19
Baer-Baur, spelling system, 25
Barr, 124, 126–7, 134, 144, 158–9
Basle, 30–1, 119, 129
Bastian, Ferdinand, 117, 124–5, 132, 156–7
be-, prefix, 33, 43–4, 46, 49, 121, 128, 134, 164, 204, 212, 252, 263, 303, 310, 341, 348
Böhmer-Ascoli, phonetic script, 19
Borchling, C., spelling system, 24
Bühnenaussprache, 5, 201

-chen, suffix, 197, 253, 269–70, 293
Christian names, 61 fn. 2, 81, 220–1, 317
cht (lengthening effect), 121, 128, 164, 171, 252, 259, 261-2
circumflexion, 252, 260–2
clusters (consonantal), 49, 90, 121, 128, 131, 212, 216, 303, 322, 341, 349
comparative, 222, 253, 272
complementary distribution, 47, 124, 173, 214, 312
compounds, 43–4, 53, 128, 212, 261, 268, 377
conditional, analytical, 67, 101, 144, 186, 227, 254, 277
conditional, synthetic, 67, 186, 227, 276–7
consonants, length of, 27, 46, 48–9, 352, 355 (see also *Schwebelaute*)
consonants, syllabic, 204, 216, 310, 321, 348, 355
correption, 252, 257 fn. 1, 260, 262

dat/das isogloss, 162, 249
dative, 34, 57–8, 62, 97–9, 137, 140, 179, 260, 270, 317, 319, 335
dative, ethic, 336
dative plural, 33, 56, 205, 220, 270, 317, 319, 335
Deutscher Sprachatlas, 4, 11, 19, 119, 127, 251
diachronic, 3
dialect and language, delimitation of, 9

391